ACCA

PAPER P7

ADVANCED AUDIT AND ASSURANCE

(INTERNATIONAL)

STUDY TEXT

BPP Learning Media is an **ACCA Approved Content Provider**. This means we work closely with ACCA to ensure this Study Text contains the information you need to pass your exam.

In this Study Text, which has been reviewed by the **ACCA examination team,** we:

- Highlight the **most important elements** in the syllabus and the **key skills** you need

- **Signpost** how each chapter links to the syllabus and the Study Guide

- **Provide** lots of **exam focus points** demonstrating what is expected of you in the exam

- **Emphasise key points** in regular **fast forward** summaries

- Test your knowledge in **quick quizzes**

- Examine your understanding in our **practice question bank**

- Reference all the important topics in our **full index**

BPP's **Practice & Revision Kit** also supports this paper.

FOR EXAMS IN SEPTEMBER 2016, DECEMBER 2016, MARCH 2017 AND JUNE 2017

BPP
LEARNING MEDIA

First edition 2007

Ninth edition February 2016

ISBN 9781 4727 4434 0
(Previous ISBN 9781 4727 2685 8)

e-ISBN 9781 4727 4676 4

British Library Cataloguing-in-Publication Data

A catalogue record for this book
is available from the British Library

Published by

BPP Learning Media Ltd
BPP House, Aldine Place
London W12 8AA

www.bpp.com/learningmedia

Printed in the United Kingdom by

Polestar Wheatons
Hennock Road
Marsh Barton
Exeter
EX2 8RP

Your learning materials, published by BPP Learning Media Ltd,
are printed on paper obtained from traceable sustainable
sources.

Contents

BPP
LEARNING MEDIA

Helping you to pass

BPP Learning Media – ACCA Approved Content Provider

As an ACCA **Approved Content Provider**, BPP Learning Media gives you the **opportunity** to use study materials reviewed by the ACCA examination team. By incorporating the examination team's comments and suggestions regarding the depth and breadth of syllabus coverage, the BPP Learning Media Study Text provides excellent, **ACCA-approved** support for your studies.

The PER alert

Before you can qualify as an ACCA member, you not only have to pass all your exams but also fulfil a three year **practical experience requirement** (PER). To help you to recognise areas of the syllabus that you might be able to apply in the workplace to achieve different performance objectives, we have introduced the 'PER alert' feature. You will find this feature throughout the Study Text to remind you that what you are **learning to pass** your ACCA exams is **equally useful to the fulfilment of the PER requirement**.

Your achievement of the PER should now be recorded in your online *My Experience* record.

Tackling studying

Studying can be a daunting prospect, particularly when you have lots of other commitments. The **different features** of the Study Text, the **purposes** of which are explained fully on the **Chapter features** page, will help you while studying and improve your chances of **exam success**.

Developing exam awareness

Our Study Texts are completely **focused** on helping you pass your exam.

Our advice on **Studying P7** outlines the **content** of the paper, the **necessary skills** you are expected to be able to demonstrate and any **brought forward knowledge** you are expected to have.

Exam focus points are included within the chapters to highlight when and how specific topics have been examined, or how they might be examined in the future.

Using the Syllabus and Study Guide

You can find the syllabus and study guide on page xvi to xxvii of this Study Text.

Testing what you can do

Testing yourself helps you develop the skills you need to pass the exam and also confirms that you can recall what you have learnt.

We include **Questions** – lots of them – both within chapters and in the **Practice Question Bank**, as well as **Quick Quizzes** at the end of each chapter to test your knowledge of the chapter content.

BPP LEARNING MEDIA

Chapter features

Each chapter contains a number of helpful features to guide you through each topic.

Topic list

Topic list	Syllabus reference

Tells you what you will be studying in this chapter and the relevant section numbers, together with ACCA syllabus references.

Introduction

Puts the chapter content in the context of the syllabus as a whole.

Study guide

Links the chapter content with ACCA guidance.

Exam guide

Highlights how examinable the chapter content is likely to be and the ways in which it could be examined.

Knowledge brought forward from earlier studies

What you are assumed to know from previous studies/exams.

FAST FORWARD ▶▶

Summarises the content of main chapter headings, allowing you to preview and review each section easily.

Examples

Demonstrate how to apply key knowledge and techniques.

Key terms

Definitions of important concepts that can often earn you easy marks in exams.

Exam focus points

Tell you when and how specific topics have been examined, or how they may be examined in the future.

Formula to learn

Formulae that are not given in the exam but which have to be learnt.

PER alert

This is a new feature that gives you a useful indication of syllabus areas that closely relate to performance objectives in your Practical Experience Requirement (PER).

 Question

Essential practice of techniques covered in the chapter.

 Case Study

Real world examples of theories and techniques.

Chapter Roundup

A full list of the Fast Forwards included in the chapter, providing an easy source of review.

Quick Quiz

A quick test of your knowledge of the main topics in the chapter.

Practice Question Bank

Found at the back of the Study Text with more comprehensive chapter questions. Cross referenced for easy navigation.

Studying P7

As the name suggests, this paper examines advanced audit and assurance topics. Paper P7 is one of the professional level Options papers and as such candidates must consider carefully whether they have the required competencies.

The P7 examination team

The examination team expects you to demonstrate a highly **professional approach** to all questions – not just presenting information in a professional manner, but also **integrating knowledge and understanding** of topics from across the syllabus. The examination team is also very keen for students to demonstrate evidence of **wider reading** and to demonstrate an understanding of current issues as they affect audit and assurance. At the absolute minimum you should read *Student Accountant*. The examination team often examines topics that it has written about in *Student Accountant*.

Syllabus update

The P7 syllabus has been updated for the September 2016 sitting onwards. The full syllabus and Study Guide can be found in this Study Text on pages xvi to xxvii.

1 What P7 is about

The aim of the syllabus is to analyse, evaluate and conclude on the assurance engagement and other audit and assurance issues in the context of best practice and current developments.

The paper builds on the topics covered in Paper F8 *Audit and Assurance* but as an advanced paper it tests much more than just your knowledge of ISAs and your ability to list standard audit procedures. You must be able to apply your knowledge to more complex audit and assurance scenarios, identifying and formulating the work required to meet the objectives of audit and non-audit assignments and to evaluate the findings and results of work performed. Accounting knowledge examined in Paper P2 *Corporate Reporting* is also assumed. Therefore, candidates studying for P7 should refer to the Accounting Standards listed under P2.

The syllabus is divided into **seven** main sections:

(a) **Regulatory environment**

This section introduces the legal and regulatory environment including **corporate governance** issues. It also examines the topics of **money laundering** and the consideration of laws and regulations.

(b) **Professional and ethical considerations**

The details of the various **ethical codes** should be familiar to you from your earlier studies, however the importance of this topic should not be underestimated. The examination team has indicated that ethical and professional issues are likely to feature in every sitting. This section also covers **fraud and professional liability**, both of which are topical issues.

(c) **Practice management**

This part of the syllabus covers quality control, tendering and professional appointments. It also covers advertising, publicity, obtaining professional work and fees.

(d) **Audit of historical financial information**

This is the largest section of the syllabus looking in detail at the procedures involved in a range of audit and assurance assignments. The examination team has indicated that evidence gathering is a key part of the syllabus and is likely to feature at each sitting. Requirements are likely to focus on **specific assertions, balances or transactions**.

(e) **Other assignments**

This section also covers a range of **audit-related and assurance services**. The examination team has stressed the need for candidates to be able to tackle these types of scenario.

(f) **Reporting**

The detail of audit reports should be familiar to you from your earlier studies. At this level you will be expected to **apply this knowledge** to more complex scenarios. The examination team has also stressed the importance of the **relationship between financial reporting and auditing**. This will be particularly important when forming an appropriate audit opinion. This section of the syllabus also includes reports to management and other reports.

(g) **Current issues and developments**

Current issues and developments includes a wide range of topics including the IAASB clarity project, professional, ethical and corporate governance, information technology, going concern, transnational audits and social and environmental auditing. The examination team has indicated that this is likely to be examined at each sitting, and that candidates are expected to have read around the issues for themselves. You will need to be able to discuss current issues topics **in the context of a client scenario**.

2 Skills you have to demonstrate

2.1 Knowledge and application

Even with exams you've previously taken, you'll remember that passing didn't only mean reproducing knowledge. You also had to **apply** what you knew. At Professional level, the balance is tilted much more towards application. You will need a sound basis of technical knowledge. The exams will detect whether you have the necessary knowledge. However, you won't pass if you just spend your time acquiring knowledge. Developing application skills is vital.

2.2 Application skills

- A thorough understanding of the relevant audit, assurance and financial reporting regulations that fall within the syllabus
- The ability to apply knowledge to specific client scenarios
- The ability to have an independent opinion, backed by reasoned argument
- An appreciation of commercial factors which influence practice management
- An appreciation of fast-moving developments in audit and assurance practices

The P7 examination team made very similar comments in a number of recent examiner's reports which is so important that we will quote it here. These pitfalls tend not to change from year to year:

'Similar factors as detailed in previous examiner's reports continue to contribute to the unsatisfactory pass rate:

- Failing to answer the specific question requirements
- Not applying knowledge to question scenarios
- Not explaining or developing points in enough detail
- Lack of knowledge on certain syllabus areas
- Illegible handwriting'

'As seen in previous sittings, **what makes the difference between a pass and a fail script is usually the level of application skills which have been demonstrated. Candidates who answer the specific question requirement, and tailor their answers to the scenarios provided are likely to do well**.'

(Examiner's Report, June 2011)

BPP
LEARNING MEDIA

3 How to pass

3.1 Study the whole syllabus

Study the **entire** syllabus. Although Section B of the paper contains an optional element, the two questions in Section A are compulsory and could cover a range of topics from across the syllabus. Moreover, Section B questions may focus on several areas of the syllabus, so if you have not studied the whole syllabus then you could find yourself unable to answer any Section B question in full. Question spotting at this level is unwise and not recommended.

3.2 Focus on themes, not lists

There are quite a number of lists in the Texts. This is inevitable because technical guidance often comes in list form. Lists are also sometimes the clearest way of presenting information. However, the examination team has stressed that passing the exam is not a matter of learning and reproducing lists. Good answers will have to **focus on the details in the scenario** and **bring out the underlying themes** that relate to the scenario. The points in them will have more depth than a series of single-line bullet points.

3.3 Read around

Read the financial press and relevant websites for real life examples – the examination team is specifically looking for evidence of **wider reading**.

Read *Student Accountant* (the ACCA's student magazine) regularly – it often contains technical articles written either by or on the recommendation of the examination team which can be invaluable for future exams, not least because they tend to focus on examinable areas of the syllabus.

3.4 Lots of question practice

You can **develop application skills** by attempting questions in the Exam Question Bank and later on in the BPP Learning Media Practice & Revision Kit.

4 Answering questions

Practise as many questions as you can under **timed conditions** – this is the best way of developing good exam technique. Make use of the **Question Bank** at the back of this Text. **BPP's Practice & Revision Kit** contains numerous exam-standard questions (many of them taken from past exam papers) as well as three mock exams for you to try.

Section A questions will be the case study type of question – make sure you relate your answers to the scenario rather than being generic. Answers that are simply regurgitated from Texts are unlikely to score highly.

Present your answers in a **professional** manner – there are between four and six **professional marks** available for setting answers out properly and for coherent, well structured arguments and recommendations. You should be aiming to achieve all of these marks.

Consider the **question requirement** carefully so that you answer the actual question set.

Answer plans will help you to focus on the requirements of the question and enable you to manage your time effectively.

Answer the question that you are most comfortable with first – it will help to settle you down if you feel you have answered the first question well.

4.1 Analysing question requirements

It's particularly important to **consider the question requirements carefully** to make sure you understand exactly what the question is asking, and whether each question part has to be answered in the **context of the scenario** or is more general. You also need to be sure that you understand all the **tasks** that the question is asking you to perform.

Remember that every word will be important. If for example you are asked to 'Explain the importance of identifying all audit risks arising at the planning stage of the audit of Company X', then you would **not** identify all the audit risks at Company X. This would be a waste of your time and would gain no marks. You must focus your answer on the requirement that is set.

4.2 Understanding the question verbs

Verbs that are likely to be frequently used in this exam are listed below, together with their intellectual levels and guidance on their meaning.

Intellectual level		
1	**Define**	Give the meaning of
1	**Explain**	Make clear
1	**Identify**	Recognise or select
1	**Describe**	Give the key features
2	**Distinguish**	Define two different terms, viewpoints or concepts on the basis of the differences between them
2	**Compare and contrast**	Explain the similarities and differences between two different terms, viewpoints or concepts
2	**Contrast**	Explain the differences between two different terms, viewpoints or concepts
2	**Analyse**	Give reasons for the current situation or what has happened
3	**Assess**	Determine the strengths/weaknesses/importance/ significance/ability to contribute
3	**Examine**	Critically review in detail
3	**Discuss**	Examine by using arguments for and against
3	**Explore**	Examine or discuss in a wide-ranging manner
3	**Criticise**	Present the weaknesses of / problems with the actions taken or viewpoint expressed, supported by evidence
3	**Evaluate/critically evaluate**	Determine the value of in the light of the arguments for and against (critically evaluate means weighting the answer towards criticisms / arguments against)
3	**Construct the case**	Present the arguments in favour or against, supported by evidence
3	**Recommend**	Advise the appropriate actions to pursue in terms the recipient will understand

A lower level verb such as define will require a more **descriptive answer**. A higher level verb such as evaluate will require a more **applied, critical answer**. The examination team has stressed that **higher-level requirements and verbs** will be most significant in this paper, for example critically evaluating a statement and arguing for or against a given idea or position. The examination team is looking to set questions that provide evidence of student understanding.

Certain verbs have given students particular problems.

(a) **Identify and explain**

Although these verbs are both Level 1, the examination team sees them as requiring different things. You have to go into more depth if you are asked to **explain** than if you are asked to **identify**. An explanation means giving more detail about the problem or factor identified, normally meaning that you have to indicate **why** it's significant. If you were asked to:

(i) **Identify the main problem with the same person acting as chief executive and chairman** – you would briefly say excessive power is exercised by one person.

(ii) **Explain the main problem with the same person acting as chief executive and chairman** – you would say excessive power is exercised by one person and then go on to say it would mean that the same person was running the board and the company. As the board is meant to monitor the chief executive, it can't do this effectively if the chief executive is running the board. Also, you may be asked to explain or describe something complex, abstract or philosophical in nature.

(b) **Evaluate**

Evaluate is a verb that the examination team uses frequently. Its meaning may be different from the way that you have seen it used in other exams. The examination team expects to see arguments for **and** against, or pros **and** cons for what you are asked to evaluate.

Thus for example if a question asked you to:

'Evaluate the contribution made by non-executive directors to good corporate governance in companies'

You would not only have to write about the factors that help non-executive directors make a worthwhile contribution (independent viewpoint, experience of other industries). You would also have to discuss the factors that limit or undermine the contribution non-executive directors make (lack of time, putting pressure on board unity).

If the examination team asks you to critically evaluate, you will have to consider both viewpoints. However you will concentrate on the view that you are asked to critically evaluate, as the mark scheme will be weighted towards that view.

4.3 Content of answers

Well-judged, clear recommendations grounded in the scenario will always score well, as markers for this paper have a wide remit to reward good answers. You need to be **selective**. As we've said, lists of points memorised from Texts and reproduced without any thought won't score well.

Important!

The examination team identified lack of application skills as a serious weakness in many student answers. What constitutes good application will vary question by question but is likely to include:

- Only including technical knowledge that is **relevant** to the scenario. For example, although some mnemonics can be a useful memory aids, you shouldn't quote them in full just because the question requirements seem to point to them. Only discuss the parts of it that are relevant.

- **Only** including scenario details that **support the points** you are making, for example using words or phrases taken from the scenario to explain why you're making a particular recommendation – there are no marks available for repeating material from the scenario.

- **Tackling the problems** highlighted in the scenario and the question requirements

- Explaining **why** the factors you're discussing are significant

- Taking a **top-down strategic approach** – excessive detail about the minutiae of auditing is not important.

5 Gaining professional marks

As P7 is a Professional level paper, four **professional level marks** will be awarded in a Section A question. These are marks allocated not for the content of an answer, but for the degree of professionalism with which certain parts of the answer are presented.

The examination team has stated that some marks may be available for presenting your answer in the form of a letter, presentation, memo, report, briefing notes, management reporting, narrative or press statement. You may also be able to obtain marks for the layout, logical flow and presentation of your answer. You should also make sure that you provide the points required by the question.

Important!

> Whatever the form of communication requested, you will **not** gain professional marks if you fail to follow the basics of good communication. Keep an eye on your **spelling and grammar**. Also think carefully, am I saying things that are **appropriate in a business communication**?

6 Brought forward knowledge

The P7 syllabus assumes knowledge brought forward from F8 *Audit and Assurance*. It also assumes knowledge from Paper F7 *Financial Reporting* and Paper P2 *Corporate Reporting*. It is very important to be comfortable with your financial reporting studies because these are likely to be drawn upon by the scenario-based questions in Sections A and B of this paper.

> The P7 examination team has written a number of articles relevant to the P7 exam and it is highly recommended that you read them. A list of these articles can be found after Chapter 18 of this Study Text.

Analysis of past papers

The table **below** provides details of when each element of the syllabus has been examined and the question number and section in which each element appeared. Further details can be found in the Exam Focus Points in the relevant chapters.

With the introduction of the four exam sessions, ACCA will continue to publish the same number of exams, two per year, and at the same times, after the December and June exam sessions. These exams will be compiled from questions selected from the two preceding sessions. The first of this kind was published in December 2015, compiled from September 2015 and December 2015 exams, and this has been included in the analysis below.

Covered in Ch		D 15	J 15	D 14	J 14	D 13	J 13	D 12	J 12	D 11	J 11	D 10	J 10	D 09
	Regulatory environment													
1	International regulatory frameworks for audit and assurance services												2(d)	
1	Money laundering				2(b)				3(a)					2(c)
1	Laws and regulations		2(b)			3(b)								
	Professional and ethical considerations													
2	Codes of ethics for professional accountants	4	3(a), 4	1(d), 4(b)	4	1(c) 4	1(b), 2(a)	1(a), 3(b)	1(b), 3(b), 4	2(b)	3(a)	2(a), 4(b)	3(b), 4	4(b)
3	Fraud and error						4(a)						2(d)	
3	Professional liability						4(a)						5(b)	
	Practice Management													
4	Quality control	5(c)	4	5(a)	3(b)		2(a)	5(a)		1(b)				2(b)
5	Advertising, publicity, obtaining professional work and fees									1(b)		4(a)		4(b)
5	Tendering			4(a)					3(a)					
5	Professional appointments										3(a)	4(a)		
	Assignments													
6,7,8, 9,10	The audit of historical financial information including: (i) Planning, materiality and assessing the risk of misstatement (ii) Evidence (iii) Evaluation and review	1, 2(a)	1, 2(a), 3(b), 5(a)-(b)	1(a)–(c), 2, 3(a), 5(b)	1, 3, 4	1, 3, 5	1(a), 3, 4(b), 5(b), (c)	1, 2, 3(a)-(b), 5(a)	1(a), 2(b), 3(a)-(b), 5(a)	1(a), 2(a)-(b), 3(a)-(c), 5(a)-(b)	1, 2, 3(b)	1(a), 2(c), 3(a)-(c)	1, 3(b), 5(a)	1, 2(a)-(b), 5
11	Group audits	5(b)				1(b)	5(a)		1(a)		5(b)			

Covered in Ch		D 15	J 15	D 14	J 14	D 13	J 13	D 12	J 12	D 11	J 11	D 10	J 10	D 09
	Other assignments													
12	Audit-related services	3				2					4			
12	Assurance services											2(a), 2(b)		
13	Prospective financial information				2(a)				2(a)		2(a)			3
14	Forensic audits		3(c)				2(b)	3(c)		4(a)-(b)			2(c)	
15	Social and environmental auditing			3(b)					2(b)			2(a), 2(b)		
15	Public sector audit of performance information	2(b)												
16	Internal audit and outsourcing										4(a)		2(b), (b)	
	Reports													
17	Auditor's reports	5(a)–(b)	5		5	5(b)	5	5	5(b)	5(a)-(b)	5(a)	5(a)	5(a)	
17	Reports to management											5(b)		
17	Other reports													
	Current issues and developments													
1,2,3	Professional, ethical and corporate governance									4(c)		4(b)		
18	Other current issues				5(a)			4(a)					3(a)	4(a)

The exam paper

Format of the paper

		Number of marks
Section A:	Two compulsory questions:	
	Question one	35
	Question two	25
Section B:	Choice of two from three questions (20 marks each)	40
		100

Time allowed: 3 hours and 15 minutes

Guidance

Section A will consist of two compulsory 'case study' style questions. These will include detailed information including, for example, extracts from financial statements and audit working papers. The questions will include a range of requirements covering different syllabus areas.

Section B questions will tend to be more focused towards specific topic areas, such as ethical issues and auditor's reports. Short scenarios will be provided as a basis for these questions.

Syllabus and Study Guide

Syllabus

```
┌──────────┐        ┌──────────────┐
│ CR (P2)  │ ─ ─ ─▶ │  AAA (P7)    │
└──────────┘        └──────────────┘
                           ▲
                           │
                    ┌──────────────┐
                    │   AA (F8)    │
                    └──────────────┘
```

AIM

To analyse, evaluate and conclude on the assurance engagement and other audit and assurance issues in the context of best practice and current developments.

MAIN CAPABILITIES

On successful completion of this paper candidates should be able to:

A Recognise the legal and regulatory environment and its impact on audit and assurance practice

B Demonstrate the ability to work effectively on an assurance or other service engagement within a professional and ethical framework

C Assess and recommend appropriate quality control policies and procedures in practice management and recognise the auditor's position in relation to the acceptance and retention of professional appointments

D Identify and formulate the work required to meet the objectives of audit assignments and apply the International Standards on Auditing

E Identify and formulate the work required to meet the objectives of non-audit assignments

F Evaluate findings and the results of work performed and draft suitable reports on assignments

G Understand the current issues and developments relating to the provision of audit-related and assurance services

RELATIONAL DIAGRAM OF MAIN CAPABILITIES

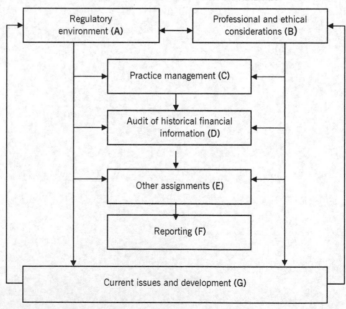

RATIONALE

The Advanced Audit and Assurance syllabus is essentially divided into seven areas.

The syllabus starts with the legal and regulatory environment including money laundering, and professional and ethical considerations, including the Code of Ethics and professional liability. This then leads into procedures in practice management, including quality control and the acceptance and retention of professional engagements.

The syllabus then covers the audit of financial statements, including planning, evidence and review. It then covers other assignments including prospective financial information, and other assurance assignments, as well as the reporting of these assignments.

The final section covers current issues and developments relating to the provision of audit-related and assurance services.

5

BPP
LEARNING MEDIA

DETAILED SYLLABUS

A   Regulatory Environment

1.   International regulatory frameworks for audit and assurance services

2.   Money laundering

3.   Laws and regulations

B   Professional and Ethical Considerations

1.   Code of Ethics for Professional Accountants

2.   Fraud and error

3.   Professional liability

C   Practice Management

1.   Quality control

2.   Advertising, publicity, obtaining professional work and fees

3.   Tendering

4.   Professional appointments

D   Audit of historical financial information

1.   Planning, materiality and assessing the risk of misstatement

2.   Evidence

3.   Evaluation and review

4.   Group audits

E   Other assignments

1.   Audit-related and assurance services

2.   Prospective financial information

3.   Forensic audits

4.   Internal audit

5.   Outsourcing

6.   The audit of performance information (pre-determined objectives) in public sector

F   Reporting

1.   Auditor's reports

2.   Reports to those charged with governance and management

3.   Other reports

G   Current Issues and Developments

1.   Professional and ethical developments

2.   Transnational audits

3.   The audit of social, environmental and integrated reporting

4.   Other current issues

6

APPROACH TO EXAMINING THE SYLLABUS

The examination is a three hour 15 minutes paper constructed in two sections. Questions in both sections will be largely discursive. However, candidates will be expected, for example, to be able to assess materiality and calculate relevant ratios where appropriate.

Section A questions will be based on 'case study' type questions. That is not to say that they will be particularly long, rather that they will provide a setting within a range of topics, issues and requirements can be addressed. Different types of question will be encountered in Section B and will tend to be more focussed on specific topics, for example 'auditor's reports', 'quality control' and topics of ISAs which are not examinable in Paper F8, *Audit and Assurance*. (This does not preclude these topics from appearing in Section A). Current issues will be examined across a number of questions.

Section A: 2 compulsory questions
Question 1   35 marks
Question 2   25 marks

Section B: Choice of 2 from 3   40 marks
questions- 20 marks each
                                 100

7

Study Guide

A REGULATORY ENVIRONMENT

1. International regulatory frameworks for audit and assurance services

a) Explain the need for laws, regulations, standards and other guidance relating to audit, assurance and related services.[2]

b) Outline and explain the need for the legal and professional framework including:[2]
   i) public oversight of audit and assurance practice
   ii) the role of audit committees and impact on audit and assurance practice.

2. Money laundering

a) Define 'money laundering'.[1]

b) Explain how international efforts seek to combat money laundering.[2]

c) Explain the scope of criminal offences of money laundering and how professional accountants may be protected from criminal and civil liability.[2]

d) Explain the need for ethical guidance in this area.[2]

e) Describe how accountants meet their obligations to help prevent and detect money laundering including record keeping and reporting of suspicion to the appropriate regulatory body.[2]

f) Explain the importance of customer due diligence (CDD).[2]

g) Recognise potentially suspicious transactions and assess their impact on reporting duties.[2]

h) Describe, with reasons, the basic elements of an anti-money laundering program.[2]

3. Laws and regulations

a) Compare and contrast the respective responsibilities of management and auditors concerning compliance with laws and regulations in an audit of financial statements.[2]

b) Describe the auditors' considerations of compliance with laws and regulations and plan audit procedures when possible non-compliance is discovered.[2]

c) Discuss how and to whom non-compliance should be reported.[2]

d) Recognise when withdrawal from an engagement is necessary.[2]

B PROFESSIONAL AND ETHICAL CONSIDERATIONS

1. Code of Ethics for Professional Accountants

a) Explain the fundamental principles and the conceptual framework approach.[1]

b) Identify, evaluate and respond to threats to compliance with the fundamental principles.[3]

c) Discuss and evaluate the effectiveness of available safeguards.[3]

d) Recognise and advise on conflicts in the application of fundamental principles.[3]

e) Discuss the importance of professional scepticism in planning and performing an audit.[2]

f) Assess whether an engagement has been planned and performed with an attitude of professional scepticism, and evaluate the implications.[3]

2. Fraud and error

a) Define and clearly distinguish between the terms 'error', 'irregularity', 'fraud' and 'misstatement'.[2]

b) Compare and contrast the respective responsibilities of management and auditors for fraud and error.[2]

c) Describe the matters to be considered and procedures to be carried out to investigate

actual and/or potential misstatements in a given situation.[2]

d) Explain how, why, when and to whom fraud and error should be reported and the circumstances in which an auditor should withdraw from an engagement.[2]

e) Discuss the current and possible future role of auditors in preventing, detecting and reporting error and fraud.[2]

3. Professional liability

a) Recognise circumstances in which professional accountants may have legal liability.[2]

b) Describe the factors to determine whether or not an auditor is negligent in given situations.[2]

c) Explain the other criteria for legal liability to be recognised (including 'due professional care' and 'proximity') and apply them to given situations.[2]

d) Compare and contrast liability to client with liability to third parties.[3]

e) Evaluate the practicability and effectiveness of ways in which liability may be restricted.[3]

f) Discuss liability limitation agreements.[2]

g) Discuss and appraise the principal causes of audit failure and other factors that contribute to the 'expectation gap' (e.g. responsibilities for fraud and error).[3]

h) Recommend ways in which the expectation gap might be bridged.[2]

C PRACTICE MANAGEMENT

1. Quality control

a) Explain the principles and purpose of quality control of audit and other assurance engagements.[1]

b) Describe the elements of a system of quality control relevant to a given firm.[2]

c) Select and justify quality control procedures that are applicable to a given audit engagement.[3]

d) Assess whether an engagement has been planned and performed in accordance with professional standards and whether reports issued are appropriate in the circumstances.[3]

2. Advertising, publicity, obtaining professional work and fees

a) Recognise situations in which specified advertisements are acceptable.[2]

b) Discuss the restrictions on practice descriptions, the use of the ACCA logo and the names of practising firms.[2]

c) Discuss the extent to which reference to fees may be made in promotional material.[2]

d) Outline the determinants of fee-setting and justify the bases on which fees and commissions may and may not be charged for services.[3]

e) Discuss the ethical and other professional problems, for example, lowballing, involved in establishing and negotiating fees for a specified assignment.[3]

3. Tendering

a) Discuss the reasons why entities change their auditors/professional accountants.[2]

b) Recognise and explain the matters to be considered when a firm is invited to submit a proposal or fee quote for an audit or other professional engagement.[2]

c) Identify the information to be included in a proposal.[2]

4. Professional appointments

a) Explain the matters to be considered and the procedures that an audit firm/professional accountant should carry out before accepting a specified new client/engagement including:[3]
   i)   client acceptance
   ii) engagement acceptance

iii) establish whether the preconditions for an audit are present

iv) agreeing the terms of engagement.

b) Recognise the key issues that underlie the agreement of the scope and terms of an engagement with a client.[2]

D AUDIT OF HISTORICAL FINANCIAL INFORMATION

1. Planning, materiality and assessing the risk of misstatement

a) Define materiality and performance materiality and demonstrate how it should be applied in financial reporting and auditing.[2]

b) Identify and explain business risks for a given assignment.[3]

c) Identify and explain audit risks for a given assignment.[3]

d) Identify and explain risks of material misstatement for a given assignment.[3]

e) Discuss and demonstrate the use of analytical procedures in the planning of an assignment.[3]

f) Explain how the result of planning procedures determines the relevant audit strategy.[2]

g) Explain the planning procedures specific to an initial audit engagement.[2]

h) Identify additional information that may be required to assist the auditor in obtaining an understanding of the entity.[2]

i) Recognise matters that are not relevant to the planning of an assignment.[2]

2. Evidence

a) Identify and describe audit procedures to obtain sufficient audit evidence from identified sources.[2]

b) Identify additional information that may be required to effectively carry out a planned assignment.[2]

c) Identify and evaluate the audit evidence expected to be available to

i) support the financial statement assertions and accounting treatments (including fair values)

ii) support disclosures made in the notes to the financial statements. [3]

d) Apply analytical procedures to financial and non-financial data.[2]

e) Explain the specific audit problems and procedures concerning related parties and related party transactions.[2]

f) Recognise circumstances that may indicate the existence of unidentified related parties and select appropriate audit procedures.[2]

g) Evaluate the use of written representations from management to support other audit evidence.[2]

h) Recognise when it is justifiable to place reliance on the work of an expert (e.g. a surveyor employed by the audit client).[2]

i) Assess the appropriateness and sufficiency of the work of internal auditors and the extent to which reliance can be placed on it. [2]

3. Evaluation and review

a) Evaluate the matters (e.g. materiality, risk, relevant accounting standards, audit evidence) relating to:[3]

i) inventory

ii) standard costing systems

iii) statement of cash flows

iv) changes in accounting policy

v) taxation (including deferred tax)

vi) segmental reporting

vii) non-current assets

viii) fair values

ix) leases

x) revenue from contracts with customers

xi) employee benefits

xii) government grants

xiii) related parties

xiv) earnings per share

xv) impairment

xvi) provisions, contingent liabilities and contingent assets

xvii) intangible assets
xviii) financial instruments
xix) investment properties
xx) share-based payment transactions
xxi) business combinations
xxii) assets held for sale and discontinued operations
xxiii) events after the end of the reporting period
xxiv) the effects of foreign exchange rates
xxv) borrowing costs.

b) Explain the use of analytical procedures in evaluation and review.[3]

c) Explain how the auditor's responsibilities for corresponding figures, comparative financial statements, and 'other information', are discharged.[3]

d) Apply the further considerations and audit procedures relevant to initial engagements.[2]

e) Discuss the courses of action available to an auditor if a material inconsistency or material misstatement exists in relation to other information such as contained in the integrated report.[2]

f) Specify audit procedures designed to identify subsequent events that may require adjustment to, or disclosure in, the financial statements of a given entity.[2]

g) Identify and explain indicators that the going concern basis may be in doubt and recognise mitigating factors.[2]

h) Recommend audit procedures, or evaluate the evidence that might be expected to be available and assess the appropriateness of the going concern basis in given situations.[3]

i) Assess the adequacy of disclosures in financial statements relating to going concern and explain the implications for the auditor's report with regard to the going concern basis.[3]

4. Group audits

a) Recognise the specific matters to be considered before accepting appointment as group auditor to a group in a given situation.[3]

b) Explain the responsibilities of the component auditor before accepting appointment, and the procedures to be performed in a group situation. .[2]

c) Identify and explain the matters specific to planning an audit of group financial statements including assessment of group and component materiality, the impact of non-coterminous year ends within a group, and changes in group structure.[2]

d) Justify the situations where a joint audit would be appropriate.[2]

e) Recognise the audit problems and describe audit procedures specific to a business combination, including goodwill, accounting policies, inter-company trading, the classification of investments, equity accounting for associates and joint ventures, changes in group structure, and accounting for a foreign subsidiary.[3]

f) Identify and explain the audit risks, and necessary audit procedures relevant to the consolidation process.[3]

g) Identify and describe the matters to be considered and the procedures to be performed at the planning stage, when a group auditor considers the use of the work of component auditors.[3]

h) Consider how the group auditor should evaluate the audit work performed by a component auditor.[2]

i) Explain the implications for the auditor's report on the financial statements of an entity where the opinion on a component is modified in a given situation.[2]

E OTHER ASSIGNMENTS

1. Audit-related and assurance services

a) Describe the nature of audit-related services, the circumstances in which they might be required and the comparative levels of assurance provided by professional accountants and distinguish between:[2]

11

i) audit-related services and an audit of historical financial statements
ii) an attestation engagement and a direct engagement.[2]

b) Plan review engagements, for example: [2]
i) a review of interim financial information
ii) a 'due diligence' assignment (when acquiring a company, business or other assets).

c) Explain the importance of enquiry and analytical procedures in review engagements and apply these procedures.[2]

d) Describe the main categories of assurance services that audit firms can provide and assess the benefits of providing these services to management and external users.[3]

e) Describe the level of assurance (reasonable, high, moderate, limited, negative) for an engagement depending on the subject matter evaluated, the criteria used, the procedures applied and the quality and quantity of evidence obtained.[3]

2. Prospective financial information

a) Define 'prospective financial information' (PFI) and distinguish between a 'forecast', a 'projection', a 'hypothetical illustration' and a 'target'.[1]

b) Explain the principles of useful PFI.[1]

c) Identify and describe the matters to be considered before accepting a specified engagement to report on PFI.[2]

d) Discuss the level of assurance that the auditor may provide and explain the other factors to be considered in determining the nature, timing and extent of examination procedures.[1]

e) Describe examination procedures to verify forecasts and projections.[2]

f) Compare the content of a report on an examination of PFI with reports made in providing audit-related services.[2]

3. Forensic audits

a) Define the terms 'forensic accounting', 'forensic investigation' and 'forensic audit'.[1]

b) Describe the major applications of forensic auditing (e.g. fraud, negligence, insurance claims) and analyse the role of the forensic auditor as an expert witness.[2]

c) Apply the fundamental ethical principles to professional accountants engaged in forensic audit assignments.[2]

d) Plan a forensic audit engagement.[2]

e) Select investigative procedures and evaluate evidence appropriate to determining the loss in a given situation.[3]

4. Internal audit

a) Evaluate the potential impact of an internal audit department on the planning and performance of the external audit.[2]

b) Explain the benefits and potential drawbacks of outsourcing internal audit.[2]

c) Consider the ethical implications of the external auditor providing an internal audit service to a client.[2]

5. Outsourcing

a) Explain the different approaches to 'outsourcing' and compare with 'insourcing'.[2]

b) Discuss and conclude on the advantages and disadvantages of outsourcing finance and accounting functions.[3]

c) Recognise and evaluate the impact of outsourced functions on the conduct of an audit.[3]

6 The audit of performance information (pre-determined objectives) in the public sector

a) Describe the audit of performance information (pre-determined objectives) and differentiate from performance auditing. [2]

b) Plan the audit of performance information (pre-determined objectives), and describe examination procedures to be used in the audit of this type of information. [3]

c) Discuss the audit criteria of reported performance information, namely compliance with reporting requirements, usefulness, measurability and reliability. [3]

d) Discuss the form and content of a report on the audit of performance information [2]

e) Discuss the content of an audit conclusion on an integrated report of performance against pre-determined objectives [3]

F   REPORTING

1   Auditor's reports

a) Determine the form and content of an unmodified audit report and assess the appropriateness of the contents of an unmodified audit report. [3]

b) Recognise and evaluate the factors to be taken into account when forming an audit opinion in a given situation and justify audit opinions that are consistent with the results of audit procedures. [3]

c) Critically appraise the form and content of an auditor's report in a given situation. [3]

d) Assess whether or not a proposed audit opinion is appropriate. [3]

e) Advise on the actions which may be taken by the auditor in the event that a modified audit report is issued. [3]

f) Recognise when the use of an emphasis of matter paragraph and other matter paragraph would be appropriate. [3]

2.   Reports to those charged with governance and management

a) Critically assess the quality of a report to those charged with governance and management. [3]

b) Advise on the content of reports to those charged with governance and management in a given situation. [3]

3.   Other reports

a) Analyse the form and content of the professional accountant's report for an assurance engagement as compared with an auditor's report. [2]

b) Discuss the content of a report for an examination of prospective financial information. [2]

c) Discuss the effectiveness of the 'negative assurance' form of reporting and evaluate situations in which it may be appropriate to modify a conclusion. [3]

G   CURRENT ISSUES AND DEVELOPMENTS

Discuss the relative merits and the consequences of different standpoints taken in current debates and express opinions supported by reasoned arguments.

1.   Professional and ethical developments

a) Discuss the relative advantages of an ethical framework and a rulebook. [2]

b) Identify and assess relevant emerging ethical issues and evaluate the safeguards available. [3]

c) Discuss IFAC developments. [2]

2.   Transnational audits

a) Define 'transnational audits' and explain the role of the Transnational Audit Committee (TAC) of IFAC. [1]

b) Discuss how transnational audits may differ from other audits of historical financial information (e.g. in terms of applicable financial reporting and auditing standards, listing requirements and corporate governance requirements). [2]

13

3. The audit of social, environmental and integrated reporting

a) Plan an engagement to provide assurance on integrated reporting (performance measures and sustainability indicators).[2]

b) Describe the difficulties in measuring and reporting on economic, environmental and social performance and give examples of performance measures and sustainability indicators.[2]

c) Explain the auditor's main considerations in respect of social and environmental matters and how they impact on entities and their financial statements (e.g. impairment of assets, provisions and contingent liabilities).[2]

d) Describe substantive procedures to detect potential misstatements in respect of socio-environmental matters.[2]

e) Discuss the form and content of an independent verification statement of an integrated report [2]

4. Other current issues

a) Explain current developments in auditing standards including the need for new and revised standards and evaluate their impact on the conduct of audits. [3]

b) Discuss other current legal, ethical, other professional and practical matters that affect accountants, auditors, their employers and the profession. [3]

14

SUMMARY OF CHANGES TO P7

ACCA periodically reviews its qualification syllabuses so that they fully meet the needs of stakeholders such as employers, students, regulatory and advisory bodies and learning providers. These syllabus changes are effective from September 2016 and will be updated with effect from 1st September each year, thereafter.

The changes are introduced to the syllabus to reflect the latest business and educational developments affecting this paper. These are summarised in the table below.

Section and subject area	Syllabus content
D1h) Amended to clarify the need for additional information to obtain an understanding of the entity	h) Identify additional information that may be required to assist the auditor in obtaining an understanding of the entity.[2]
D2b) New learning outcome specifically relating to additional information required for planning	b) Identify additional information that may be required to effectively carry out a planned assignment.[2]
D3e) Amended terminology to comply with changes to ISA 720 *The Auditor's Responsibilities Relating to Other Information*	e) Discuss the courses of action available to an auditor if a material inconsistency or material misstatement exists in relation to other information such as contained in the integrated report.[2]
F1a) New learning outcome to introduce the new requirements of reporting standards - ISA 700 and ISA 701	a) Determine the form and content of an unmodified audit report and assess the appropriateness of the contents of an unmodified audit report.[3]
G1 Amendment to heading to focus on developments	1. Professional and ethical developments

15

Regulatory environment

BPP
LEARNING MEDIA

International regulatory environments for audit and assurance services

Topic list	Syllabus reference
1 International regulatory frameworks for audit and assurance services	A1
2 Corporate governance and audit committees	A1
3 Internal control effectiveness	A1
4 Money laundering	A2
5 Laws and regulations	A3

Introduction

This chapter covers a wide range of regulations that affect the work of audit and assurance professionals. You need to be aware of the international nature of the audit and assurance market and the main issues driving the development of regulatory frameworks.

The detailed requirements relating to money laundering are then discussed. You should be prepared to explain the responsibilities of professional accountants in this area and to outline the procedures that audit firms should implement.

The final section looks at the auditor's responsibilities in respect of laws and regulations that apply to an audit client. This is a topic that could be built in to a practical case study question.

Study guide

		Intellectual level
A	**Regulatory environment**	
A1	**International regulatory frameworks for audit and assurance services**	
(a)	Explain the need for laws, regulations, standards and other guidance relating to audit, assurance and related services.	2
(b)	Outline and explain the legal and professional framework including: (i) Public oversight to an audit and assurance practice (ii) The role of audit committees and impact on audit and assurance practice	2
A2	**Money laundering**	
(a)	Define 'money laundering'.	1
(b)	Explain how international efforts seek to combat money laundering.	2
(c)	Explain the scope of criminal offences of money laundering and how professional accountants may be protected from criminal and civil liability.	2
(d)	Explain the need for ethical guidance in this area.	2
(e)	Describe how accountants meet their obligations to help prevent and detect money laundering including record keeping and reporting of suspicion to the appropriate regulatory body.	2
(f)	Explain the importance of customer due diligence (CDD).	2
(g)	Recognise potentially suspicious transactions and assess their impact on reporting duties.	2
(h)	Describe, with reasons, the basic elements of an anti money laundering programme.	2
A3	**Laws and regulations**	
(a)	Compare and contrast the respective responsibilities of management and auditors concerning compliance with laws and regulations in an audit of financial statements.	2
(b)	Describe the auditor's considerations of compliance with laws and regulations and plan audit procedures when possible non-compliance is discovered.	2
(c)	Discuss how and to whom non-compliance should be reported.	2
(d)	Recognise when withdrawal from an engagement is necessary.	2

Exam guide

The technical content of this part of the syllabus is mainly drawn from your earlier studies. Questions in this paper are unlikely to ask for simple repetition of this knowledge, but are more likely to require explanation or discussion of the reasons behind the regulations.

1 International regulatory frameworks for audit and assurance services

FAST FORWARD Major developments in international regulation of audit and assurance have recently concluded, with far-reaching effects on ISAs.

1.1 The need for laws, regulations, standards and other guidance

Corporate scandals, such as Enron and Worldcom in the US, Olympus in Japan and Autonomy in the UK, have brought the audit profession under close scrutiny from investors, businesses, regulators and others.

There is a trend towards businesses becoming more complex and global, and firms of accountants have expanded their range of services well beyond traditional assurance and tax advice. This has led to a great deal of re-examination of regulatory and standard-setting structures both nationally and internationally in recent years.

Laws are in many respects a last resort in the task of ensuring that audits are conducted properly and are of a high quality. As a generalisation, laws tend to be prescriptive and dissuasive. They are external to the auditor, requiring them to act within the letter (although not necessarily the spirit) of the law in order to avoid punishment. Law is a relatively blunt instrument for regulation.

At the other extreme would be a moral code that is purely internal to the auditor's self, which the individual would adhere to irrespective of external consequences. The audit profession does not attempt to set out such a code, this being the more proper area for broader social, moral or religious authority.

Audit regulations do take the presence of external laws and internal morality as their starting points, but sit somewhere in between these two extremes. International standards are principles-based, representing a common set of principles and practices which are more flexible than statutory laws, allowing for an element of ambiguity and judgement on the part of the auditor. At the same time, however, auditing standards are not simply general statements of morality: they contain specific suggestions for the auditor to consider in specific circumstances, which are not legally binding but which provide a starting point for the auditor in a given situation.

1.2 The legal and professional framework

One of the competencies you require to fulfil Performance Objective 18 of the PER is the ability to apply up to date auditing standards and applicable frameworks. You can apply the knowledge you obtain from this section of the Study Text to help you demonstrate this competency.

You have studied the regulatory framework in earlier papers. The following summaries will provide a quick reminder. Note that the UK regulatory framework is given in this International-stream Study Text as an example only.

1.2.1 Overview of the UK regulatory framework

The EU Eighth Directive on company law requires that persons carrying out statutory audits must be approved by the authorities of EU member states. The authority to give this approval in the UK is delegated to Recognised Supervisory Bodies (RSBs). An auditor must be a member of an RSB and be eligible under its own rules. The ACCA is an RSB.

The RSBs are required by the Companies Act to have rules to ensure that persons eligible for appointment as a company auditor are either:

- Individuals holding an appropriate qualification
- Firms controlled by qualified persons

The Financial Reporting Council

The Financial Reporting Council (FRC) is the UK's independent regulator for corporate reporting and governance. It has the following core structure and responsibilities under the overarching FRC Board.

- Codes and Standards Committee – responsible for actuarial policy, audit and assurance, corporate governance, and accounting and reporting policy

- Conduct Committee – responsible for audit quality review, corporate reporting review, professional discipline, professional oversight, and supervisory inquiries

- Executive Committee – providing day to day oversight of the work of the FRC

The main changes that concern P7 students are:

- Auditing standards (ISAs) are the direct responsibility of the FRC Board – but the Board is advised by the new 'Codes and Standards Committee', which is in turn advised by the new 'Audit and Assurance Council'. Auditing standards were formerly the responsibility of the APB.

- Accounting standards are the responsibility of the FRC Board, which is advised by the 'Codes and Standards Committee' and the 'Accounting Council' in turn. Accounting standards were formerly the responsibility of the ASB.

The revised role of the FRC Board is:

- To set high standards of corporate governance through the UK Corporate Governance Code
- To set standards for corporate reporting and actuarial practice
- To monitor and enforce accounting and auditing standards
- To oversee regulatory activities of the actuarial profession and professional accountancy bodies
- To operate independent disciplinary arrangements for public interest cases

The revised structure is shown by the following diagram.

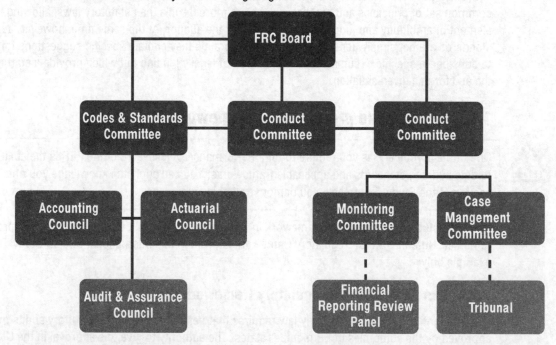

Point to note | Although this restructure took place some time ago, the FRC is still in the process of 'rebranding' documents and other publications issued by the former APB and other bodies under the old structure. You will therefore see references in the Text to APB pronouncements where these still exist and are in force.

1.2.2 International standard setting

International Standards on Auditing (ISAs) are produced by the International Auditing and Assurance Standards Board (IAASB), a technical standing committee of the International Federation of Accountants (IFAC). You should also be familiar with the International Ethics Standards Board for Accountants (IESBA), another body of IFAC and the producer of the *Code of Ethics* (see Chapter 2).

IFAC
(International Federation of Accountants)

IAASB
(International Auditing and Assurance Standards Board)
- ISAs (International Standards on Auditing)
- ISQCs (International Standards on Quality Control)
- ISREs (International Standards on Review Engagements)
- ISAEs (International Standards on Assurance Engagements)
- ISRSs (International Standards on Related Services)

IESBA
(International Ethics Standards Board for Accountants)

- *Code of Ethics for Professional Accountants*

The IAASB's *Preface to International Standards on Quality Control, Auditing, Assurance and Related Services Pronouncements* states that all the IAASB's 'engagement standards' above are 'authoritative material', which means that they must be followed in an audit that is conducted in accordance with ISAs.

The IAASB also publishes four kinds of 'non-authoritative material'.

- International Auditing Practice Notes (IAPNs). These do not impose additional requirements on auditors, but provide them with practical assistance.

- Practice Notes Relating to Other International Standards, eg in relation to ISREs, ISAEs or ISRSs

- Staff Publications, which are used to help raise awareness of new or emerging issues, and to direct attention to the relevant parts of IAASB pronouncements

- Consultation Papers, which seek to generate discussion with stakeholders

Within each country, local regulations govern, to a greater or lesser degree, the practices followed in the auditing of financial or other information. Such regulations may be either of a statutory nature, or in the form of statements issued by the regulatory or professional bodies in the countries concerned.

National standards on auditing and related services published in many countries differ in form and content. The IAASB takes account of such documents and differences and, in the light of such knowledge, issues ISAs which are intended for international acceptance.

The European Union, for example, has since 2014 required ISAs (as issued by the IAASB) to be adopted at EU level. Member states may impose additional requirements on auditors (such as the FRC, whose ISAs (UK and Ireland) are in some places more stringent than the IAASB's ISAs) but these must not contradict EU ISAs.

Point to note

The IAASB issued *A Framework for Audit Quality* in this area, which is covered in Chapter 18.

1.2.3 Current ISAs and other examinable documents

	Title	F8	P7
	International Standards on Auditing (ISAs)		
	Glossary of Terms	✓	✓
	International Framework for Assurance Assignments	✓	✓
	Preface to the International Standards on Quality Control, Auditing, Review, Other Assurance and Related Services	✓	✓
ISA 200	*Overall Objectives of the Independent Auditor and the Conduct of an Audit in Accordance with ISAs*	✓	✓
ISA 210	*Agreeing the Terms of Audit Engagements*	✓	✓
ISA 220	*Quality Control for an Audit of Financial Statements*		✓
ISA 230	*Audit Documentation*	✓	✓
ISA 240	*The Auditor's Responsibilities Relating to Fraud in an Audit of Financial Statements*	✓	✓
ISA 250	*Consideration of Laws and Regulations in an Audit of Financial Statements*	✓	✓
ISA 260	*Communication with Those Charged with Governance*	✓	✓
ISA 265	*Communicating Deficiencies in Internal Control to Those Charged with Governance and Management*	✓	✓
ISA 300	*Planning an Audit of Financial Statements*	✓	✓
ISA 315	*Identifying and Assessing the Risks of Material Misstatement through Understanding the Entity and Its Environment*	✓	✓
ISA 320	*Materiality in Planning and Performing an Audit*	✓	✓
ISA 330	*The Auditor's Responses to Assessed Risks*	✓	✓
ISA 402	*Audit Considerations Relating to an Entity Using a Service Organisation*	✓	✓
ISA 450	*Evaluation of Misstatements Identified During the Audit*	✓	✓
ISA 500	*Audit Evidence*	✓	✓
ISA 501	*Audit Evidence – Specific Considerations for Selected Items*	✓	✓
ISA 505	*External Confirmations*	✓	✓
ISA 510	*Initial Audit Engagements – Opening Balances*	✓	✓
ISA 520	*Analytical Procedures*	✓	✓
ISA 530	*Audit Sampling*	✓	✓
ISA 540	*Auditing Accounting Estimates, Including Fair Value Accounting Estimates and Related Disclosures*	✓	✓
ISA 550	*Related Parties*		✓
ISA 560	*Subsequent Events*	✓	✓
	International Standards on Auditing (ISAs)		
ISA 570	*Going Concern*	✓	✓
ISA 580	*Written Representations*	✓	✓

	Title	F8	P7
ISA 600	*Special Considerations - Audits of Group Financial Statements (Including the Work of Component Auditors)*		✓
ISA 610	*Using the Work of Internal Auditors*	✓	✓
ISA 620	*Using the Work of an Auditor's Expert*	✓	✓
ISA 700	*Forming an Opinion and Reporting on Financial Statements*	✓	✓
ISA 701	*Communicating Key Audit Matters in the Independent Auditor's Report*	✓	✓
ISA 705	*Modifications to the Opinion in the Independent Auditor's Report*	✓	✓
ISA 706	*Emphasis of Matter Paragraphs and Other Matter Paragraphs in the Independent Auditor's Report*	✓	✓
ISA 710	*Comparative Information – Corresponding Figures and Comparative Financial Statements*	✓	✓
ISA 720	*The Auditor's Responsibilities Relating to Other Information in Documents Containing Audited Financial Statements*	✓	✓
Amendments	Conforming amendments to other ISAs	✓	✓
Amendments	Addressing Disclosures in the Audit of Financial Statements – Revised ISAs and Related Conforming Amendments	✓	✓
International Standards on Assurance Engagements (ISAEs)			
ISAE 3000	*Assurance Engagements other than Audits or Reviews of Historical Financial Information*	✓	✓
ISAE 3400	*The Examination of Prospective Financial Information*		✓
ISAE 3402	*Assurance Reports on Controls at a Service Organisation*		✓
ISAE 3420	*Assurance Engagements to Report on the Compilation of Pro Forma Financial Information Included in a Prospectus*		✓
International Auditing Practice Notes (IAPNs)			
IAPN 1000	*Special considerations in auditing financial instruments*		✓
International Standards on Quality Control (ISQCs)			
ISQC 1	*Quality Controls for Firms that Perform Audits and Reviews of Financial Statements, and Other Assurance and Related Services Engagements*		✓
International Standards on Related Services (ISRSs)			
ISRS 4400	*Engagements to Perform Agreed-Upon Procedures Regarding Financial Information*		✓
ISRS 4410	*Compilation Engagements*		✓
International Standards on Review Engagements (ISREs)			
ISRE 2400	*Engagements to Review Financial Statements*	✓	✓
ISRE 2410	*Review of Interim Financial Information Performed by the Independent Auditor of the Entity*		✓

Title	F8	P7
Exposure Drafts (EDs)		
IAASB *Responding to Non-Compliance or Suspected Non-Compliance with Laws and Regulations*		✓
IESBA *Responding to Non-Compliance with Laws and Regulations*		✓
IESBA *Responding to a Suspected Illegal Act*		✓
Other Documents		
ACCA *Code of Ethics and Conduct*	✓	✓
IESBA *Code of Ethics for Professional Accountants* (Revised May 2015)		✓
ACCA *Technical Factsheet 145 – Anti Money-Laundering Guidance for the Accountancy Sector*		✓
The UK Corporate Governance Code as an example of a code of best practice (Revised September 2014)	✓	✓
FRC Guidance on Audit Committees (Revised September 2012) as an example of guidance on best practice in relation to audit committees		✓
IAASB Practice Alert Challenges in Auditing Fair Value Accounting Estimates in the Current Market Environment (October 2008)		✓
IAASB Practice Alert Audit Considerations in Respect of Going Concern in the Current Economic Environment (January 2009)		✓
IAASB Applying ISAs Proportionately with the Size and Complexity of an Entity (August 2009)		✓
IAASB XBRL : The Emerging Landscape (January 2010)		✓
IAASB Auditor Considerations Regarding Significant Unusual or Highly Complex Transactions (September 2010)		✓
IAASB Questions and Answers Professional Scepticism in an Audit of Financial Statements (February 2012)		✓
IESBA Staff Questions and Answers on Implementing the Code of Ethics		✓
IAASB Staff Questions & Answers - Applying ISQC1 Proportionately with the Nature and Size of a Firm (October 2012)		✓
IAASB A Framework for Audit Quality: Key Elements that Create an Environment for Audit Quality (February 2014)		✓

Note. Topics of exposure drafts are examinable to the extent that relevant articles about them are published in *Student Accountant*.

Exam focus point

International standards are quoted throughout this Text and you must understand how they are applied in practice. Make sure you refer to auditing standards when answering questions.

1.3 Public oversight

FAST FORWARD

Public oversight of the audit profession and of standard setting has been a trend in recent regulatory developments internationally.

1.3.1 Public oversight internationally

The **Public Interest Oversight Board (PIOB)** exists to exercise oversight for all of IFAC's 'public interest activities' including its standard-setting bodies such as the IAASB. Its work involves:

* Monitoring the standard-setting boards

- Overseeing the nomination process for membership of these boards
- Co-operation with national oversight authorities

The objective of the international PIOB is to increase the confidence of investors and others that the public interest activities of IFAC are properly responsive to the public interest. The PIOB is based in Madrid, Spain, where it operates as a non-profit Spanish foundation.

1.3.2 Other examples of public oversight

An example of public oversight is the Professional Oversight team of the UK's FRC (formerly the Professional Oversight Board, or POB), which has a number of statutory responsibilities. These include:

- Independent **oversight of the regulation of statutory** auditors by the RSBs (eg ACCA)

- Independent **supervision of Auditors General** in respect of the exercise of their function as statutory auditors

- The **receipt** of statutory **change of auditor notifications** from companies and statutory auditors in respect of 'major audits'

 Case Study

Among other significant scandals in America in recent history was the Enron scandal, when one of the country's biggest companies filed for bankruptcy. The scandal also resulted in the disappearance of Arthur Andersen, one of the then-Big Five accountancy firms who had audited Enron's financial statements. The main reasons why Enron collapsed were over-expansion in energy markets, too much reliance on derivatives trading which eventually went wrong, breaches of federal law, and misleading and dishonest behaviour. However, enquiries into the scandal exposed a number of deficiencies in the company's governance:

(a) A lack of transparency in the financial statements, especially in relation to certain investment vehicles that were kept off balance sheet.

(b) The non-executive directors were weak, and there were conflicts of interest.

(c) Inadequate scrutiny by the external auditors. Arthur Andersen failed to spot or failed to question dubious accounting treatments. Since Andersen's consultancy arm did a lot of work for Enron, there were allegations of conflicts of interest.

(d) Information asymmetry where the directors and managers knew more than the investors.

(e) Executive compensation methods were meant to align the interests of shareholders and directors, but seemed to encourage the overstatement of short-term profits. Particularly in the USA, where the tenure of Chief Executive Officers is fairly short, the temptation is strong to inflate profits in the hope that share options will have been cashed in by the time the problems are discovered.

In the US, the response to the breakdown of stock market trust caused by perceived inadequacies in corporate governance arrangements and the Enron scandal was the **Sarbanes-Oxley Act 2002.** The Act applies to all companies that are required to file periodic reports with the Securities and Exchange Commission (SEC).

The **Public Company Accounting Oversight Board (PCAOB)** is a private sector body in the USA created by Sarbanes-Oxley. Its aim is to oversee the auditors of public companies. Its stated purpose is to 'protect the interests of investors and further the public interest in the preparation of informative, fair and independent audit reports'. Its powers include setting auditing, quality control, ethics, independence and other standards relating to the preparation of audit reports by issuers. It also has the authority to regulate the non-audit services that audit firms can offer.

Sarbanes-Oxley has been criticised in some quarters for **not being strong enough** on certain issues, for example the selection of external auditors by the audit committee, and at the same time being over-rigid on others. Directors may be less likely to consult lawyers in the first place if they believe that legislation could override lawyer-client privilege.

In addition, it has been alleged that a Sarbanes-Oxley compliance industry has sprung up focusing companies' attention on complying with all aspects of the legislation, irrespective of how significant they may be. This has distracted companies from **improving information flows** to the market and then allowing the market to make well-informed decisions. The Act has also done little to address the temptation provided by generous stock options to inflate profits, other than requiring possible forfeiture if financial statements are subsequently restated.

Most significantly, perhaps, there is recent evidence of companies turning away from the US stock markets and towards other markets, such as London. An article in the *Financial Times* suggested that this was partly due to companies tiring of the **increased compliance costs** associated with Sarbanes-Oxley implementation. In addition, the nature of the **regulatory regime** may be an increasingly significant factor in listing decisions.

2 Corporate governance and audit committees

FAST FORWARD

Audit committees are made up of non-executive directors and are perceived to increase confidence in financial reports.

Point to note

The detail on corporate governance issues in this chapter is based on UK law and regulations. It is included as an example of how law and regulations affect the auditor in this area.

2.1 General requirements of codes of corporate governance

Point to note

Corporate governance was a part of Paper F8, and your knowledge of it continues to be relevant to Paper P7. What follows in this section (2.1) is a summary of that material, but if you are unsure of your knowledge then you should go back to your F8 notes to refresh your memory.

Knowledge brought forward from Paper F8

Corporate governance is the system by which companies are directed and controlled. Good corporate governance is important because the owners of a company and the people who manage the company are not always the same.

The **OECD Principles of Corporate Governance** set out the rights of shareholders, the importance of disclosure and transparency and the responsibilities of the board of directors.

2.1.1 UK Corporate Governance Code

The FRC's UK Corporate Governance Code sets out standards of good practice regarding board leadership and effectiveness, accountability (including audit), remuneration and relations with shareholders.

All companies with a Premium Listing of equity shares in the UK are required under the Listing Rules to report on how they have applied the Code in their annual report and accounts (regardless of whether the company is incorporated in the UK or elsewhere).

The Code contains **broad principles** and more **specific provisions**. Listed companies have to report how they have applied the principles, and either confirm that they have applied the provisions or provide an explanation if they have not. There is a separate section of the Code devoted to the application of this '**comply or explain**' concept. It sets out that choosing not to follow a provision may be justified by the board if good governance is achieved by other means. However, the reasons for not complying should be clearly and fully explained to the shareholders. Any explanation must include details as to how actual practices are consistent with the overall principle to which a provision relates.

The broad principles of the Code are as follows.

Principles of the UK Corporate Governance Code (for listed UK companies)

Leadership

- Every company should be headed by an effective board, which is collectively responsible for the long-term success of the company.

- There should be a clear division of responsibilities at the head of the company between the running of the board and the executive responsibility for the running of the company's business. No one individual should have unfettered powers of decision.

- The chairman is responsible for leadership of the board and ensuring its effectiveness on all aspects of its role.

- As part of their role as members of a unitary board, non-executive directors should constructively challenge and help develop proposals on strategy.

Effectiveness

- The board and its committees should have the appropriate balance of skills, experience, independence and knowledge of the company to enable them to discharge their respective duties and responsibilities effectively.

- There should be a formal, rigorous and transparent procedure for the appointment of new directors to the board.

- All directors should be able to allocate sufficient time to the company to discharge their responsibilities effectively.

- All directors should receive induction on joining the board and should regularly update and refresh their skills and knowledge.

- The board should be supplied in a timely manner with information in a form and of a quality appropriate to enable it to discharge its duties.

- The board should undertake a formal and rigorous annual evaluation of its own performance and that of its committees and individual directors.

- All directors should be submitted for re-election at regular intervals, subject to continued satisfactory performance.

Accountability

- The board should present a balanced and understandable assessment of the company's position and prospects.

- The board is responsible for determining the nature and extent of the principal risks it is willing to take in achieving its strategic objectives. The board should maintain sound risk management and internal control systems.

- The board should establish formal and transparent arrangements for considering how it should apply the corporate reporting and risk management and internal control principles and for maintaining an appropriate relationship with the company's auditor.

Remuneration

- Executive directors' remuneration should be designed to promote the long-term success of the company. Performance-related elements should be transparent, stretching and rigorously applied.

- There should be a formal and transparent procedure for developing policy on executive remuneration and for fixing the remuneration packages of individual directors. No director should be involved in deciding their own remuneration.

Relations with shareholders

- There should be a dialogue with shareholders based on the mutual understanding of objectives. The board as a whole has responsibility for ensuring that a satisfactory dialogue with shareholders takes place.

- The board should use the AGM to communicate with investors and to encourage their participation.

The UK Corporate Governance Code was revised in September 2012. The revisions stated that **FTSE 350 companies must put the external audit out to tender at least every ten years**. The change was designed to improve both competition in the audit market and the public perception of auditors' independence. In a market where, as a committee of the UK Parliament has pointed out, there is a 'dearth of competition', this was an important shift.

In September 2012, the FRC revised the *UK Corporate Governance Code*, *Stewardship Code* and *Guidance on Audit Committees* to introduce further guidance aimed at ensuring management, audit committees and auditors report material issues to investors completely and fairly.

Following a consultation in late 2013, the FRC published a revised *UK Corporate Governance Code* again in September 2014, this time targeting the going concern, executive remuneration, and risk management reporting. The changes, made in response to the Sharman Inquiry in 2012, are controversial with companies and investors. The changes around the assessment of going concern by companies, in particular, have been criticised for failing to address the investors' concerns, and placing a heavy risk management and reporting burden on the boards.

2.2 UK Corporate Governance Code provisions

The key requirement of the UK Corporate Governance Code is that the board **must establish** an audit committee of **at least three or, in the case of smaller companies, two independent non-executive directors**. The main role and responsibilities of the audit committee are listed below.

- To monitor the integrity of the financial statements of a company, and any formal announcements relating to the company's performance, reviewing significant financial reporting judgements contained in them

- To review the company's internal financial controls and, unless expressly addressed by a separate board risk committee composed of independent directors or by the board itself, to review the company's internal control and risk management systems

- To monitor and review the effectiveness of the company's internal audit function

- To make recommendations to the board, for it to put to shareholders for their approval in general meeting, in relation to the appointment, re-appointment and removal of the external auditor and to approve the remuneration and terms of engagement of the external auditor

- To review and monitor the external auditor's independence and objectivity and the effectiveness of the audit process, taking into consideration relevant UK professional and regulatory requirements

- To develop and implement policy on the engagement of the external auditor to supply non-audit services, taking into account relevant ethical guidance regarding the provision of non-audit services by the external audit firm, and to report to the board, identifying any matters in respect of which it considers that action and improvement is needed and making recommendations as to the steps to be taken

- To report to the Board how it has discharged its responsibilities, including:

  - How it has addressed significant issues arising in the financial statements
  - How it has assessed the effectiveness of the audit process
  - How auditor objectivity and independence is safeguarded, where the auditor provides non-audit services.

The Code also requires the **Annual Report** to contain **a separate section** describing the work of the committee. This deliberately puts the spotlight on the audit committee and gives it an authority that it might otherwise lack.

2.3 FRC Guidance on Audit Committees

The FRC issued its *Guidance on Audit Committees* in September 2012, which aims to help companies to implement the requirements of the *UK Corporate Governance Code*.

The particular arrangements for an audit committee should be **tailored to the circumstances** of the company. Audit committees need to be proportionate to the size, complexity and risk profile of the company.

The *Guidance* should not be taken as a simple list of rules. Rather, it notes that, in respect of the relationship between the audit committee and the board, 'the most important features of this relationship cannot be drafted as guidance or put into a code of practice'. The relationship should be frank and open, and it should be possible for **disagreement** between the audit committee and the board to be **robust** and based on **information made freely available** to the audit committee.

2.3.1 Establishment of the audit committee

As noted above, there should be three independent non-executive directors on the committee, two in the case of smaller companies. At least one member should have recent and relevant financial experience (and a professional accountancy qualification).

Appointments are recommended by the **nomination committee**, and are for a maximum of **three years**, but this may be extended by a further two three-year periods (nine years in total).

There should be a **minimum of three meetings per year**, but the precise number depends on the circumstances. No one who is not on the committee has a right to attend meetings (but they may be there if invited). The committee should **meet external auditors at least annually**.

The committee should have **sufficient resources** to undertake its duties, including **remuneration** for its members.

2.3.2 Relationship with the Board

The Board decides the role of the audit committee, and it is to the board that the audit committee reports. The audit committee should report to the board on how it has discharged its responsibilities.

The committee's terms of reference should be tailored to the circumstances, and should be reviewed at least annually.

If the committee disagrees with the Board then it should be able to report its point of view to shareholders.

2.3.3 Role and responsibilities

Financial reporting. The audit committee reviews **significant issues and judgements**. Management is responsible for preparing the financial statements – the audit committee then reviews them, taking into account the external auditor's point of view.

Narrative reporting. If the board requests it to, the audit committee will review the annual report and advise on whether it is fair, balanced and understandable.

Whistleblowing. The committee reviews arrangements by which staff can raise concerns about improper financial reporting.

Internal controls and risk management systems. These systems are **management's responsibility**, but the audit committee reviews them and approves statements made about them in the annual report.

Internal audit. The audit committee reviews the effectiveness of the internal audit function, including assessing whether one is needed (if it is not already present).

In its review of the work of the internal audit function, the audit committee should:

- Ensure that the internal auditor has direct access to the board chairman and to the audit committee, and is accountable to the audit committee
- Review and assess the annual internal audit work plan
- Receive a report on the results of the internal auditors' work on a periodic basis
- Review and monitor management's responsiveness to the internal auditor's findings and recommendations

- Meet with the head of internal audit at least once a year without the presence of management
- Monitor and assess the role and effectiveness of the internal audit function in the overall context of the company's risk management system

2.3.4 Role and responsibilities in relation to external auditor

The audit committee is the body responsible for overseeing the company's relations with the external auditor.

Role and responsibilities of audit committee towards external auditor	
Appointment and tendering	The audit committee **makes a recommendation on the appointment**, reappointment and removal of the external auditors.
	If this is not accepted then the **annual report** must contain a statement explaining the differing opinions of the audit committee and the board.
	The committee **assesses the auditor's qualifications, expertise, resources, and independence annually**.
	FTSE 350 companies put the audit out to **tender** at least every **ten years**.
Terms and remuneration	The audit committee **approves the terms of engagement and the remuneration** of the **external auditor**.
	The audit committee reviews: • The engagement letter (each year) • The scope of the audit
Annual audit cycle	At the start of each annual audit cycle, the audit committee ensures appropriate plans exist for the audit.
	Considers whether the **auditor's overall work** plan, including planned levels of **materiality**, and proposed **resources are appropriate**.
	Discuss with auditor: • Major issues found • Key judgements • Levels of errors, including uncorrected misstatements
	Review: • **Written representations** from management • Auditor's **management letter**
	Review the effectiveness of the audit process annually, and report to the board on its findings.
Independence	Annually **assess auditor's independence**
	Recommend and develop **company's policy on the provision of non-audit services** by the auditor.

2.3.5 Communication with shareholders

The audit committee **section of annual report** should include the following.

- A **summary of the role** of the audit committee

- The **names and qualifications of all members** of the audit committee during the period

- The **number** of audit committee **meetings**

- The **significant issues considered** in relation to the financial statements and how these issues were addressed

- An explanation of **how it has assessed the effectiveness of the external audit** process and the approach taken to the appointment or reappointment of the external auditor, and information on the

length of tenure of the current audit firm, when a tender was last conducted, and any contractual obligations that acted to restrict the audit committee's choice of external auditors

- If the external auditor provides **non-audit services**, how auditor objectivity and independence is safeguarded

2.4 Advantages and disadvantages of audit committees

The key advantage to an external auditor of having an audit committee is that such a committee of independent non-executive directors provides the auditor with an independent point of reference other than the executive directors of the company, in the event of disagreement arising.

Other **advantages** that are claimed to arise from the existence of an audit committee include:

(a)   It will lead to **increased confidence** in the credibility and objectivity of financial reports.

(b)   By specialising in the problems of financial reporting and thus, to some extent, fulfilling the directors' responsibility in this area, it will allow the **executive** directors to **devote their attention to management**.

(c)   In cases where the interests of the company, the executive directors and the employees conflict, the audit committee might provide an **impartial body** for the auditors to consult.

(d)   The internal auditors will be able to report to the audit committee.

Opponents of audit committees argue that the **disadvantages** are:

(a)   There may be **difficulty selecting** sufficient non-executive directors with the necessary competence in auditing matters for the committee to be really effective.

(b)   The establishment of such a **formalised reporting procedure** may **dissuade** the **auditors** from raising matters of judgement and limit them to reporting only on matters of fact.

(c)   **Costs** may be **increased**.

Question   Audit committees

Since 1978 all public companies in the US have been required to have an audit committee as a condition of listing on the New York Stock Exchange.

(a)   Explain what you understand by the term audit committee.

(b)   List and briefly describe the duties and responsibilities of audit committees.

(c)   Discuss the advantages and disadvantages of audit committees.

Answer

(a)   An **audit committee** reviews financial information and liaises between the auditors and the company. It normally consists of the non-executive directors of the company.

(b)   (i)   To monitor the integrity of the financial statements of the company, reviewing significant financial reporting issues and judgements contained in them

        (ii)   To review the company's internal financial control system and, unless expressly addressed by a separate risk committee or by the board itself, risk management systems

        (iii)   To monitor and review the effectiveness of the company's internal audit function

        (iv)   To make recommendations to the board in relation to the appointment of the external auditor and to approve the remuneration and terms of engagement of the external auditors

        (v)   To monitor and review the external auditor's independence, objectivity and effectiveness, taking into consideration relevant professional and regulatory requirements

(vi)   To develop and implement policy on the engagement of the external auditor to supply non-audit services, taking into account relevant ethical guidance regarding the provisions of non-audit services by the external audit firm

In addition to these responsibilities, any responsible audit committee is likely to want:

(i)   To **ensure that the review procedures** for interim statements, rights documents and similar information are **adequate**

(ii)   To **review both the management accounts** used internally and the **statutory financial statements** issued to shareholders for reasonableness

(iii)   To make **appropriate recommendations for improvements in management control**

(c)   There are a number of advantages and disadvantages.

Disadvantages

(i)   It is possible that the audit committee's **approach** may prove somewhat **pedestrian,** resolving little of consequence but acting as a drag on the drive and entrepreneurial flair of the company's senior executives.

(ii)   Unless the requirement for such a body were made compulsory, as in the US, it is likely that those **firms most in need** of an audit committee would nevertheless **choose not to have one**. (**Note.** The UK Corporate Governance Code requires listed companies to have an audit committee.)

Advantages

(i)   By its very existence, the audit committee should make the **executive directors more aware of their duties and responsibilities**.

(ii)   It could act as a **deterrent to the committing of illegal acts** by the executive directors and may discourage them from behaving in ways which could be prejudicial to the interests of the shareholders.

(iii)   Where **illegal or prejudicial acts** have been carried out by the executive directors, the **audit committee** provides an **independent body** to which the auditor can turn. In this way, the problem may be resolved without the auditor having to reveal the matter to the shareholders, either in their report or at a general meeting of shareholders.

3 Internal control effectiveness

FAST FORWARD

Internal control is a key part of good corporate governance. Directors are responsible for maintaining a system of control that will safeguard the company's assets.

3.1 Importance of internal control and risk management

The UK Corporate Governance Code states that directors 'should maintain sound risk management and internal control systems' (Section C2). Internal control systems help a company to manage the risks that it takes in trying to achieve its strategic objectives. Internal control also helps to prevent and detect fraud, and to safeguard the company's assets for the shareholders.

3.2 Directors' responsibilities

The **ultimate responsibility** for a company's system of internal controls lies with the board of directors. **The UK Corporate Governance Code requires directors to review the effectiveness of internal controls at least annually.**

Part of setting up an internal control system will involve **assessing the risks** facing the business, so that the **system** can be **designed** to ensure those **risks are avoided**. As you know from your earlier studies in auditing the system of internal control in a company will reflect the **control environment**, which includes the attitude of the directors towards risk, and their awareness of it.

Internal control systems will always have **inherent limitations**, the most important being that a system of internal control cannot eliminate the possibility of human error, or the chance that staff will collude in fraud.

Once the directors have set up a system of internal control, they are responsible for **reviewing** it regularly, to ensure that it **still meets its objectives**.

The board may decide that in order to carry out their review function properly they have to employ an **internal audit function** to undertake this task. The role of internal audit is discussed in more detail in Chapter 16, but this is potentially part of its function.

If the board does not see the need for an internal audit function, the UK Corporate Governance Code suggests that it revisits this decision on an annual basis, so that the **need for internal audit is regularly reviewed**.

The UK Corporate Governance Code requires the board of directors of listed companies to **report** on its review of internal controls as part of the **annual report**. The statement should be based on an annual assessment of internal control which should confirm that the board has considered **all significant aspects** of internal control. In particular the assessment should cover:

(a)   The **changes** since the last **assessment** in **risks** faced, and the company's **ability** to **respond** to **changes** in its business environment

(b)   The **scope** and **quality** of management's monitoring of risk and internal control, and of the work of internal audit, or consideration of the need for an internal audit function if the company does not have one

(c)   The **extent** and **frequency** of reports to the board

(d)   **Significant controls**, **failings** and **deficiencies** which have or might have material effects on the financial statements

(e)   The effectiveness of the public reporting processes

In addition, in September 2012, the Code was revised to require directors to include a statement in the annual report that they consider the annual report and accounts as a whole to be fair, balanced and understandable and provides the information necessary for shareholders to assess the entity's performance, business model and strategy.

The 2014 revision of the Code adds another specific requirement, this time about going concern. The directors are required to state in annual and half-yearly financial statements whether they considered it appropriate to adopt the going concern basis of accounting, and identify any material uncertainties in going concern over a period of at least twelve months from the date of approval of the financial statements.

3.3 Auditors' responsibilities

In the UK, the FRC's Bulletin 2006/5 *The combined code on corporate governance: requirements of auditors under the listing rules of the financial services authority and the Irish stock exchange* considers what auditors should do in response to a statement on internal controls by directors.

Auditors should **concentrate on the review carried out by the board**. The objective of the auditors' work is to assess whether the company's summary of the process that the board has adopted in reviewing the effectiveness of the system of internal control is supported by the documentation prepared by the directors and reflects that process.

The auditors should make appropriate enquiries and review the statement made by the board in the financial statements and the supporting documentation.

Auditors will have gained an understanding of controls as part of their audit (ISA 315). However, the requirements of ISAs are much narrower than the review performed by the directors. To avoid

misunderstanding of the scope of the auditors' role, the auditors are recommended to use the following wording in the auditor's report.

> 'We are not required to consider whether the board's statements on internal control cover all risks and controls, or form an opinion on the effectiveness of the company's corporate governance procedures or its risk and control procedures.'

This could be included as part of the 'Scope of the audit of financial statements' section of the report.

It is particularly important for auditors to communicate quickly to the directors any significant deficiencies they find, because of the requirements for the directors to make a statement on internal control.

The directors are required to consider the material internal control aspects of any significant problems disclosed in the financial statements. Auditors' work on this is the same as on other aspects of the statement; the auditors are not required to consider whether the internal control processes will remedy the problem.

The auditors may report by exception if problems arise, such as:

(a) The **board's summary** of the process of review of internal control effectiveness does **not reflect** the **auditors' understanding** of that process.

(b) The **processes** that **deal with** material internal control aspects of **significant problems** do **not reflect** the **auditors' understanding** of those processes.

(c) The board has **not made** an **appropriate disclosure** if it has **failed** to **conduct** an **annual review**, or the disclosure made is not consistent with the auditors' understanding.

The report should be included in a separate paragraph below the opinion paragraph. For example:

> **Other matter**
>
> We have reviewed the board's description of its process for reviewing the effectiveness of internal control set out on page x of the annual report. In our opinion the board's comments concerning ... do not appropriately reflect our understanding of the process undertaken by the board because ...

3.4 Assurance services

Accountants may also provide assurance services relating to internal control systems. This is discussed in Chapter 12.

4 Money laundering Pilot paper, 12/07, 12/09, 6/12, 6/14

> Money laundering law is an increasingly important issue for auditors to be aware of.

Point to note

> This section is based on UK law and regulation. It is included as an example of how law and regulation affects the auditor in this area.

Key term

> '**Money laundering** is the process by which criminals attempt to conceal the true origin and ownership of the proceeds of their criminal activity, allowing them to maintain control over the proceeds and, ultimately, providing a legitimate cover for their sources of income.'   (ACCA *Code of Ethics and Conduct*)

Money laundering is a particularly hot topic internationally. Clearly, auditors should consider it when assessing compliance risks at a client.

4.1 What is money laundering?

4.1.1 Background

Once they have gotten hold of money through crime, criminals face a difficulty when it comes to actually using it. For example, a group of organised criminals might generate huge amounts of money from dealing illegal drugs, but as soon as they try to spend it they end up drawing attention to the fact that they obtained the money from drug dealing. Usually the money to be laundered is in the form of **cash**.

Money laundering is the attempt to conceal the origin of this money by making it look legitimate or 'clean'. This is a big problem for the world economy: the International Monetary Fund (IMF) has stated that something like 2-5% of world GDP is likely to be related to money laundering.

4.1.2 How money is laundered

There are essentially three stages in laundering money.

1. **Placement**. This is the introduction or placement of the illegal funds into the financial system. Examples include (amongst many possibilities):

    *   Making **lots of small cash deposits** into numerous **bank accounts**

    *   Using a **cash-intensive business**, such as a betting shop or a used car dealership, to disguise 'dirty' money as legitimate revenue

2. **Layering**. This is passing the money through a large number of transactions or 'layers', so that it becomes very difficult to trace back it to its original source. Examples include:

    *   **Transferring** the money **through multiple bank accounts**, perhaps across several **different national jurisdictions**

    *   Making numerous purchases and sales of **investments**

    *   Making fake sales between controlled companies (this can often be extremely subtle, eg through the use of invoices that do involve a transfer of goods, but which exaggerate the price)

3. **Integration**. This is the final integration of funds back into the legitimate economy. The criminal now has 'clean' money which can be spent or invested.

Question	Money laundering

Required

(a) Explain the reasons why a criminal may want to launder money, even if this means that they may have to pay tax on it.

(b) Explain the reasons why it would be difficult for an external auditor to detect money laundering activity.

Answer

(a) Although money laundering does usually diminish the amount of money possessed by the criminal in absolute terms, it actually increases the amount of money they can actually use. There is little point in owning lots of cash if none of it can be spent without arousing suspicion – for instance, a criminal buying a new Porsche with $100,000 in cash would be at risk of being detected by the authorities. Money laundering enables criminals to enjoy at least some benefit from their activities.

The aim of money laundering is to 'clean' the 'dirty' money by passing it through an apparently legitimate business, so that it can then be accessed without fear of the authorities becoming aware of it.

It may therefore be preferable to have 'clean' money on which tax is paid, since, although the tax paid would be an expense, the alternative would be to have money that cannot be spent at all.

(b)   In common with fraud generally, money laundering is difficult to detect because those perpetrating it have an obvious incentive to cover their tracks very carefully. The nature of money laundering means that the owners or senior management of the business would likely be implicated. These people are likely to be able to manipulate a company's records, so that the auditor will struggle to detect any problems.

Money laundering would be more difficult to detect than a typical fraud because it involves **cash** flowing into the business, whereas fraud more typically involves attempts to conceal an outflow of assets. It would be difficult to design audit procedures to detect the recording of fictitious revenue that was backed up by cash in the bank.

As money laundering is associated with criminal activity, it is possible that those involved may be subject to intimidation to co-operate with the scheme, or to deny knowledge of it. This could even extend to members of the audit team. This makes it very difficult for auditors to detect money laundering.

4.2 International recommendations and UK law

An intergovernmental body, the Financial Action Task Force on Money Laundering (FATF) was established to set standards and develop policies to combat money laundering and terrorist financing. In 1990, FATF issued 49 recommendations for governments on how to combat these offences and these recommendations have now been endorsed by more than 130 countries.

Relevant legislation in the **UK** includes:

- The Terrorism Act 2000
- The Proceeds of Crime Act 2002
- Money Laundering Regulations 2007

This UK legislation applies to any professional work carried out in the UK, even if the accountant is based outside the UK.

Ireland has legislation which is broadly equivalent to that in the UK.

In **Singapore**, there are various pieces of legislation:

- Corruption, Drug Trafficking and Other Serious Crimes (Confiscation of Benefits) Act 1992
- United Nations Act 2001
- United Nations (Anti-Terrorism Measures) Regulations 2001
- Terrorism (Suppression of Financing) Act 2002

In **Australia**, the Anti-Money Laundering and Counter-Terrorism Financing Act 2006 is relevant.

In the **United States** there is a raft of relevant legislation, including:

- The Bank Secrecy Act

- The Money Laundering Control Act 1986

- The PATRIOT Act of 2001, which requires all financial institutions to establish anti-money laundering programmes.

US legislation affects entities based outside the US if they use US Dollars ($) or use US banks.

4.3 Ethical guidance

4.3.1 Need for ethical guidance

Ethical guidance on money laundering is needed because applying the law involves making difficult judgements, particularly if there are confidentiality issues.

The ACCA has issued *Technical Factsheet 145* on *Anti-money laundering for the accounting sector* as guidance for its members on their responsibilities under this legislation. The ACCA's *Code of Ethics and Conduct* also includes detailed guidance for members on money laundering. Its requirements are very similar to those in the Technical Factsheet, but less detailed. The Technical Factsheet gives guidance in the context of current UK law, whereas the ethical guidance emphasises the international nature of money laundering and the need for ACCA members to be aware of local legal frameworks and the basic procedures to be applied, irrespective of where in the world their work is taking place.

4.3.2 Confidentiality and ethical conflict

'Ethical conflict' means conflict between the auditor's duty to be ethical and the auditor's relationship with the client. This conflict may be particularly sharp where an auditor suspects the client of money laundering. In the UK, there is a **legal requirement to report** even a **suspicion** of money laundering (see Section 4.6 below), which would be likely to **conflict** with the auditor's **duty of confidentiality** to their client.

The situation is further complicated by the need to avoid 'tipping off' the client that the auditor suspects money laundering (see Section 4.6.3 below), which could make it very difficult for an auditor to decide whether they have a duty to report their suspicions, as it would be hard to gather evidence of money laundering without tipping the client off.

If such an ethical conflict cannot be resolved then the auditor may consider **obtaining professional advice** from the ACCA or from legal advisers. This can generally be done without breaching the fundamental principle of confidentiality if the matter is discussed anonymously with the ACCA, or under legal privilege with a legal adviser.

4.4 Accountants' obligations

Many countries have now made money laundering a criminal offence. In some countries, such as the UK, Australia, Singapore and the USA, the criminal offences include those directed at accountants. It is useful to look in detail at the obligations of UK accountants in relation to the law regarding money laundering as an example.

In the UK, the basic requirements are for accountants to keep records of clients' identity and to report suspicions of money laundering to the **National Crime Agency** (**NCA**, formerly SOCA). These obligations apply both to firms and to individuals. A firm must establish an anti-money laundering programme such as that set out below, which includes appointing a Money Laundering Reporting Officer (MLRO) who is responsible for reporting to the NCA. Individuals within the firm are then legally required to report any offences to the MLRO.

Elements of a money laundering programme:

Procedures	Explanations
• Appoint a Money Laundering Reporting Officer (MLRO) and implement internal reporting procedures	• The MLRO should have a suitable level of seniority and experience. • Individuals should make internal reports of money laundering to the MLRO. • The MLRO must consider whether to report to the NCA, and document the process.
• Train **individuals** to ensure that they are aware of the relevant legislation, know how to recognise and deal with potential **money laundering**, how to report suspicions to the **MLRO**, and how to identify **clients**	• Individuals should be trained in the firm's obligations under law, and their personal obligations. • They must be made aware of the firm's identification, record keeping and reporting procedures. • They must be aware that 'tipping off' is an offence, to reduce the risk of this happening inadvertently.

Procedures	Explanations

• Establish internal procedures appropriate to forestall and prevent **money laundering**, and make relevant **individuals** aware of the procedures	• Procedures should cover:
	  – Client acceptance
	  – Gathering 'know your client' (KYC) / 'Customer Due Diligence' (CDD) information (see Section 4.4.1 below)
	  – Controls over client money and transactions through the client account
	  – Advice and services to clients that could be of use to a money launderer
	  – Internal reporting lines
	  – The role of the MLRO

• Verify the identity of new and existing **clients** and maintain evidence of identification (ie customer due diligence measures)	• The firm must be able to establish that new clients are who they claim to be. • Typically, this will include taking copies of evidence, such as passports, driving licences and utility bills. • For a company this will include identities of directors and certificates of incorporation.
• Maintain records of **client** identification, and any transactions undertaken for or with the **client**	• Special care needs to be taken when handling clients' money to avoid participation in a transaction involving money laundering.
• **Report** suspicions of **money laundering** to the NCA	• The NCA has designed standard disclosure forms.

4.4.1 'Customer due diligence' information

The firm must gather 'know your client' information. This includes:

- Who the client is
- Who controls it
- The purpose and intended nature of the business relationship
- The nature of the client
- The client's source of funds
- The client's business and economic purpose

KYC enables the audit firm to understand its client's business well enough to spot any unusual business activity. This assists the firm in identifying suspicions of money laundering.

In the UK the Money Laundering Regulations 2007 extended the circumstances under which Customer due diligence (CDD) must be carried out from new to existing clients.

CDD is the term used in the Money Laundering Regulations for the steps that businesses must take to:

(a)   Identify the customer and verify their identity using documents, data or information obtained from a reliable and independent source.

(b)   Identify any beneficial owner who is not the customer. This is the individual (or individuals) behind the customer who ultimately owns or controls the customer or on whose behalf a transaction or activity is being conducted.

(c)   Where a business relationship is established, you will need to understand the purpose and intended nature of the relationship, for example details of the customer's business or the source of the funds.

Businesses must also conduct ongoing monitoring to identify large, unusual or suspicious transactions as part of CDD.

The requirement to confirm the identity of customers and other individuals clearly links to the concept of KYC described above.

4.5 Risk-based approach

On any assignment, the auditor should assess the risk of money laundering activities. Clearly, every circumstance is different, but the following diagram illustrates some key risk factors.

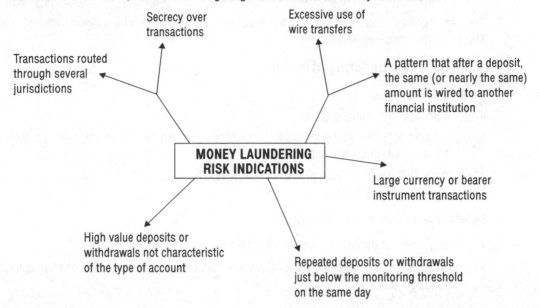

Money laundering II

You are the audit manager of Loft Co, a chain of nightclubs across the North-West of England. During the course of the audit Mr Roy, an employee of the company, informed you that a substantial cash deposit was paid into the company's bank account and a month later, the same amount was paid by direct transfer into a bank account in the name of Evissa, a company based overseas. The employee also informed you that Mr Fox, the managing director of Loft Co, had instructed him not to record the transaction in the accounting records as it had nothing to do with Loft Co's business.

Required

Comment on the situation outlined above.

Answer

The transaction described in the scenario raises suspicion of money laundering for several reasons.

(a)   It has been alleged by Mr Roy that the purpose of the transaction has nothing to do with the nightclub business. This could be a sign that Mr Fox is attempting to legitimise the proceeds of a crime through Loft Co by concealing the illegal source of the cash.

(b)   The amount of the transaction is substantial for Loft Co. An unusually large transaction should alert the auditor to the possibility of money laundering, especially as it does not seem to relate to the business of Loft Co.

(c)   The cash amount paid into Loft Co's bank account is the same as the amount paid to Evissa. This could be an attempt by Mr Fox to make the cash appear legitimate by moving it through several companies and jurisdictions.

(d)   Mr Roy was instructed not to record the transaction in the accounting records of Loft Co. Increased secrecy over transactions is another indicator of money laundering.

Loft Co's bank statement should be checked to confirm Mr Roy's assertion. The suspicious transaction should be reported to the firm's MLRO or the NCA as soon as possible and any 'tipping off' (see Section 4.5.3) must be avoided. It is a criminal offence to not report suspicions of money laundering.

4.6 The scope of criminal offences

The firm requires these procedures to avoid committing any of the wide range of offences under the UK's Money Laundering Regulations.

4.6.1 Money laundering offences

These include:

- Concealing criminal property
- 'Arranging' – becoming involved in an arrangement which is known or is suspected of facilitating the acquisition of criminal property
- Acquiring, using or possessing criminal property
- Tipping off (see below)

Defences against these offences include:

- Reporting to the NCA or the MLRO before the act took place
- Reporting to the NCA or the MLRO after the act took place if there was good reason for the failure to report earlier

4.6.2 Failure to report offences under the legislation

Key terms

> **Knowledge**
>
> - Actual knowledge
> - Shutting one's mind to the obvious
> - Deliberately deterring a person from making disclosures, the content of which one might not care to have knowledge of
> - Knowledge of circumstances which would indicate the facts to an honest and reasonable person
> - Knowledge of circumstances which would put an honest and reasonable person on inquiry and failing to make the reasonable inquiries which such a person would have made
>
> **Suspicion** is not defined in existing legislation. Case law and other sources indicate that suspicion is more than speculation but it falls short of proof or knowledge. Suspicion is personal and subjective but will generally be built on some objective foundation and so there should be some degree of consistency in how a **business's MLRO** treats possible causes of suspicion.

- Failure by an individual in the regulated sector to inform the NCA or the MLRO as soon as practicable of knowledge or suspicion of money laundering
- Failure by the MLRO to pass on a report to the NCA as soon as possible

The defences here for an individual would include that there was a reasonable excuse for not having made a report, or that the person did not know or suspect money laundering and their employer has not provided them with appropriate training.

The defence for the MLRO is that there is a reasonable excuse for not having made a report. The Court would consider whether relevant guidance, such as the ACCA Technical Factsheet, had been followed.

4.6.3 Tipping off and other offences

Tipping off is when the MLRO or any individual discloses something that might prejudice any investigation. If the auditor tells a client that they suspect money laundering has taken place, then this is an offence. It is a defence if the person did not know or suspect that it was likely to prejudice the investigation.

Other **offences** include:

- Falsifying, concealing, destroying or disposing of documents relevant to the investigation
- Consenting to a transaction which they know or suspect is money laundering, where consent has not been received from the NCA

This is an extremely difficult area for auditors and accountants, as it can be very easy to tip off a client inadvertently. For example, a client might ask an accountant to perform a transaction which the accountant suspects might involve criminal property. In this case, even just delay in carrying out the instruction might alert the criminal client to the fact that the accountant is suspicious: this would be tipping off. The way the legislation gets around this is by requiring the accountant to report suspicions as quickly as possible before undertaking such a transaction. Legal advice should also be obtained.

Exam focus point

The June 2012 exam featured nine marks on money laundering. In order to get them, however, you first had to spot that money laundering was happening in the scenario. The question itself did not mention 'money laundering' anywhere, which is like real life: money laundering is something that you need to be alert for, because criminals who launder money do not tell you that this is what they are doing!

The requirement itself was to discuss the implications of the circumstances in the scenario (six marks), and to explain the auditor's reporting responsibilities for money laundering.

The June 2014 paper had 11 marks on money laundering, with a requirement first to explain the stages of money laundering and to comment on why a client in a scenario might be high-risk, and then to recommend elements of an anti-money laundering programme.

4.6.4 Interaction of reporting duties

Auditors have several reporting duties which can interact with the duty to report under anti-money laundering legislation. The main problem is how to avoid tipping off. Other reporting duties include:

- Auditors' reports under ISAs
- Communications to those charged with governance (ISA 260)
- Reports to regulators
- The 'statement of circumstances' upon resignation as an auditor

In general, one cannot obtain consent to tip off. Instead, the firm which suspects money laundering should agree the wording of its reports with the relevant authority. If this cannot be done, then legal advice should be obtained.

If an auditor who suspects a client resigns and receives a professional clearance letter from a prospective auditor, then they should not respond to questions concerning the identity of the individual, or any suspicions regarding money laundering.

5 Laws and regulations   6/12, 12/13, 6/15

FAST FORWARD

Auditors must be aware of laws and regulations as part of their planning and must be aware of any statutory duty to report non-compliance by the company.

In addition to the laws and regulations which bind the audit firm, the audit client is itself subject to laws and regulations.

5.1 Legal requirements relating to the company

Companies are increasingly subject to laws and regulations with which they must comply. Some examples are given in the following diagram.

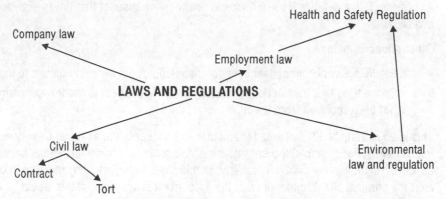

An auditor must be aware of the effect that non-compliance with the laws and regulations would have on the financial statements.

ISA 250 *Consideration of laws and regulations in an audit of financial statements* provides guidance on the auditor's responsibility to consider laws and regulations in an audit of financial statements.

5.2 Responsibility of management for compliance

It is the responsibility of management (with oversight from those charged with governance) to ensure that a client's operations are conducted in accordance with laws and regulations.

The following policies and procedures, among others, may be implemented to assist management in the prevention and detection of non-compliance with laws and regulations.

- **Monitor legal requirements** and ensure that operating procedures are designed to meet these requirements.
- **Institute and operate** appropriate systems of **internal control** including internal audit and an audit committee.
- **Develop, publicise and follow a code of conduct**.
- Ensure that **employees** are properly **trained** and **understand the code of conduct**.
- **Monitor compliance** with the code of conduct and act appropriately to **discipline** employees who fail to comply with it.
- **Engage legal advisers** to assist in monitoring legal requirements.
- **Maintain a register** of significant laws with which the entity has to comply within its particular industry, and a record of complaints.

'Non-compliance' refers to acts of omission or commission by the entity, either intentional or unintentional, which are contrary to the prevailing laws or regulations. Such acts include transactions entered into by the entity, or on its behalf by its management or employees. It does **not** include personal misconduct.

5.3 Responsibility of the auditor

As with fraud and error, the auditor is not, and cannot be held responsible for preventing non-compliance. There is an unavoidable risk that some material misstatements in the financial statements go undetected, even though the audit is properly planned and performed.

Certain factors will increase the risk of material misstatements due to non-compliance with laws and regulations not being detected by the auditor.

(a)   There are many laws and regulations, relating principally to the operating aspects of an entity, that typically do **not affect the financial statements** and are not captured by the entity's information systems relevant to financial reporting.

(b)   Non-compliance may involve conduct **designed to conceal** it, such as collusion, forgery, deliberate failure to record transactions, management override of controls or intentional misrepresentations being made to the auditor.

(c)   Whether an act constitutes non-compliance is ultimately a matter for legal determination by a court of law.

Laws and regulations governing a business entity can vary enormously (financial disclosure rules, health and safety, pollution, employment, etc). Whether an act constitutes non-compliance is a legal matter that may be beyond the auditor's professional competence, although the auditor may have a fair idea in many cases through his knowledge and training. Ultimately such matters can only be decided by a court of law.

The further removed non-compliance is from the events and transactions normally reflected in the financial statements, the less likely the auditor is to become aware of it or recognise non-compliance.

ISA 250.10

The objectives of the auditor are:

(a)   To obtain sufficient appropriate audit evidence regarding compliance with the provisions of those laws and regulations generally recognised to have a direct effect on the determination of material amounts and disclosures in the financial statements;

(b)   To perform specified audit procedures to help identify instances of non-compliance with other laws and regulations that may have a material effect on the financial statements; and

(c)   To respond appropriately to non-compliance or suspected non-compliance with laws and regulations identified during the audit.

5.4 The auditor's consideration of compliance

ISA 250.12

As part of obtaining an understanding of the entity and its environment in accordance with ISA 315, the auditor shall obtain a general understanding of:

(a)   The legal and regulatory framework applicable to the entity and the industry or sector in which the entity operates

(b)   How the entity is complying with that framework.

The auditor may obtain a general understanding of laws and regulations affecting the entity in the following ways.

- **Use the auditor's existing understanding** of the entity's industry, regulatory and other external factors
- **Update the understanding** of those laws and regulations that **directly** determine the reported amounts and disclosures in the financial statements
- **Enquire of management** as to other laws or regulations that may be expected to have a fundamental effect on the operations of the entity
- **Enquire of management** concerning the entity's **policies and procedures** regarding compliance with laws and regulations
- **Discuss with management** the **policies or procedures** adopted for identifying, evaluating and accounting for **litigation claims**

The auditor should obtain sufficient appropriate audit evidence of compliance with those **laws and regulations which have a direct effect on the determination of material amounts** and disclosures in the financial statements. These laws and regulations will be well-established, will be known both to the entity and within the entity's industry, and will be relevant to the entity's financial statements. They could relate to:

- The form and content of financial statements
- Industry-specific financial reporting issues
- Accounting for transactions under government contracts
- The accrual or recognition of expenses for income tax or pension costs

In obtaining this general understanding the auditor should obtain an understanding of the procedures followed by the entity to ensure compliance. The auditor should recognise that some laws and regulations may have a **fundamental effect** on the operations of the entity, ie they may cause the entity to cease operations or call into question the entity's continuance as a going concern. For example, non-compliance with the requirements of the entity's licence or other title to perform its operations could have such an impact (for example, for a bank, non-compliance with capital or investment requirements).

ISA 250.14

The auditor shall perform the following audit procedures to help identify instances of non-compliance with **other laws and regulations that may have a material effect** on the financial statements:

(a)   Inquiring of management and, where appropriate, those charged with governance, as to whether the entity is in compliance with such laws and regulations; and

(b)   Inspecting correspondence, if any, with the relevant licensing or regulatory authorities.

ISA 250.15

During the audit, the auditor shall remain alert to the possibility that other audit procedures applied may bring instances of non-compliance or suspected non-compliance with laws and regulations to the auditor's attention.

Examples include:

- Reading minutes

- Enquiring of the entity's management and in-house legal counsel or external legal counsel concerning litigation, claims and assessments

- Performing substantive tests of details of classes of transactions, account balances or disclosures

---

ISA 250.16

The auditor shall request management and, where appropriate, those charged with governance to provide written representations that all known instances of non-compliance or suspected non-compliance with laws and regulations whose effects should be considered when preparing financial statements have been disclosed to the auditor.

In the absence of identified or suspected non-compliance, the auditor is not required to perform audit procedures other than those detailed above.

5.4.1 Audit procedures when non-compliance is identified or suspected

---

ISA 250.18

If the auditor becomes aware of information concerning an instance of non-compliance or suspected non-compliance with laws and regulations, the auditor shall obtain:

(a)   An understanding of the nature of the act and the circumstances in which it has occurred; and

(b)   Further information to evaluate the possible effect on the financial statements.

The ISA sets out examples of the type of information that might come to the auditor's attention that may indicate non-compliance.

- **Investigation** by a **regulatory organisation** or **government department** or payment of fines or penalties

- **Payments** for **unspecified services** or loans to consultants, related parties, employees or government employees
- **Sales commissions** or agents' fees that appear excessive in relation to those normally paid by the entity or in its industry or to the services actually received
- **Purchasing** at **prices significantly above** or **below market price**
- **Unusual payments** in **cash**, purchases in the form of cashiers' cheques payable to bearer or transfers to numbered bank accounts
- **Unusual transactions** with companies registered in **tax havens**
- **Payments for goods or services made other than to the country from which** the goods or services **originated**
- **Payments without proper exchange control documentation**
- **Existence** of an **information system** that **fails**, whether by design or by accident, to **provide an adequate audit trail** or sufficient evidence
- **Unauthorised transactions** or improperly recorded transactions
- **Adverse media comment**

When evaluating the possible effect on the financial statements, the auditor should consider:

- The **potential financial consequences**, such as fines, penalties, damages, threat of expropriation of assets, enforced discontinuation of operations and litigation
- Whether the **potential financial consequences** require **disclosure**
- Whether the potential financial consequences are so serious as to call into question the **fair presentation** given by the financial statements, or otherwise make the financial statements misleading

> **ISA 250.19**
>
> If the auditor suspects there may be non-compliance, the auditor shall discuss the matter with management and, where appropriate, those charged with governance.

Such discussions are subject to the laws concerning 'tipping off' (see Section 4.5.3). If information provided by management is not sufficient, the auditor may find it appropriate to consult the entity's lawyer and, if necessary, their own lawyer on the application of the laws and regulations to the particular circumstances.

> **ISA 250.20/21**
>
> If sufficient information about suspected non-compliance cannot be obtained, the auditor shall evaluate the effect of the lack of sufficient appropriate audit evidence on the auditor's opinion.
>
> The auditor shall evaluate the implications of non-compliance in relation to other aspects of the audit, including the auditor's risk assessment and the reliability of written representations, and take appropriate action.

On this last point, as with fraud and error, the auditor must reassess the risk assessment and the validity of written representations. In exceptional cases, the auditor may consider whether withdrawal from the engagement is necessary. If withdrawal from the engagement is not possible under applicable law or regulation, the auditor may consider alternative actions including describing the non-compliance in an Other Matters paragraph in the auditor's report.

5.5 Reporting of identified or suspected non-compliance

5.5.1 To those charged with governance

> **ISA 250.22/23/24**
>
> [...] the auditor shall communicate with those charged with governance matters involving non-compliance with laws and regulations that come to the auditor's attention during the course of the audit, other than when the matters are clearly inconsequential.
>
> If, in the auditor's judgment, the non-compliance... is believed to be intentional and material, the auditor shall communicate the matter to those charged with governance as soon as practicable.
>
> If the auditor suspects that management or those charged with governance are involved in non-compliance, the auditor shall communicate the matter to the next higher level of authority at the entity, if it exists, such as an audit committee or supervisory board.

In relation to the last point, where no higher authority exists, or if the auditor believes that the communication may not be acted on or is unsure as to the person to whom to report, the auditor shall consider seeking legal advice.

5.5.2 To the users of the auditor's report

> **ISA 250.25/26/27**
>
> If the auditor concludes that the non-compliance has a material effect on the financial statements, and it has not been adequately reflected in the financial statements, the auditor shall ... express a qualified opinion or an adverse opinion on the financial statements.
>
> If the auditor is precluded by management or those charged with governance from obtaining sufficient appropriate audit evidence to evaluate whether non-compliance that may be material to the financial statements has, or is likely to have, occurred, the auditor shall express a qualified opinion or disclaim an opinion on the financial statements on the basis of a limitation on the scope of the audit [...].
>
> If the auditor is unable to determine whether non-compliance has occurred because of limitations imposed by the circumstances rather than by management or those charged with governance, the auditor shall evaluate the effect on the auditor's opinion [...].

5.5.3 To regulatory and enforcement authorities

Confidentiality is an issue again here, but it may be overridden by the law, statute or the courts of law. The auditor should obtain legal advice. If the auditor has a statutory duty to report, a report should be made without delay.

Alternatively, it may be necessary to make disclosures in the public interest. In practice it will often be extremely difficult for an auditor to decide whether making a disclosure in the public interest is warranted. As elsewhere, the auditor should obtain professional advice, either anonymously from the ACCA, or under legal privilege from a legal adviser.

5.6 Withdrawal from the engagement

As is the case for fraud or error, withdrawal may be the only option if the entity does not take the remedial action the auditor thinks is necessary, even for non-material matters.

5.7 Documentation

The auditor must document identified or suspected non-compliance with laws and regulations and the results of discussions with management and, where applicable, those charged with governance and other parties outside the entity.

5.8 Practical problems with ISA 250

5.8.1 Distinction between types of law

The most difficult distinction in practice is between:

- Laws which have a **direct effect** on the determination of material amounts in the financial statements; and

- Other laws and regulations.

In practice:

(a) For some businesses, certain laws and regulations have a direct effect on material amounts in the financial statements; for other businesses, the **same** laws and regulations will not.

(b) For some businesses, laws and regulations which did not have a direct or material effect last year may have this year (for example, where the maximum penalty for a first offence is a warning, but subsequent infringements may lead to closure of the business).

5.8.2 Procedures that should be performed

There is a distinction between checking systems of compliance and checking actual compliance. An example would be emissions from a chemical factory; auditors would review the company's systems for keeping these under control, and would also review correspondence with the environmental authority. However, the auditors would not be expected to check the actual emissions.

Chapter Roundup

- Major developments in international regulation of audit and assurance have recently concluded, with far-reaching effects on ISAs.

- Public oversight of the audit profession and of standard setting has been a trend in recent regulatory developments internationally.

- Audit committees are made up of non-executive directors and are perceived to increase confidence in financial reports.

- Internal control is a key part of good corporate governance. Directors are responsible for maintaining a system of control that will safeguard the company's assets.

- Money laundering law is an increasingly important issue for auditors to be aware of.

- Auditors must be aware of laws and regulations as part of their planning and must be aware of any statutory duty to report non-compliance by the company.

Quick Quiz

1   Fill in the blanks:

    ISAs are set by the ....
    .... This is a technical
    standing committee of the ....
    .... Oversight for all of IFAC's public interest activities is undertaken by the
    ....

2   List four potential duties of the audit committee.

    (1)   ....

    (2)   ....

    (3)   ....

    (4)   ....

3   Auditors are responsible for a company's system of internal controls.

    True   ☐

    False   ☐

4   List the main elements of an anti money laundering programme that should be followed by a firm of
    professional accountants.

    (1)   ....

    (2)   ....

    (3)   ....

    (4)   ....

    (5)   ....

    (6)   ....

5   Name four areas of law which might affect a company.

    (1)   ....

    (2)   ....

    (3)   ....

    (4)   ....

6   It is the responsibility of the auditor to ensure that a client's operations are conducted in accordance with
    laws and regulations.

    True   ☐

    False   ☐

Answers to Quick Quiz

1   International Auditing and Assurance Standards Board, International Federation of Accountants, Public
    Interest Oversight Board

2   (1)   Review of financial statements
    (2)   Liaison with external auditors
    (3)   Review of internal audit
    (4)   Review of internal controls

3   False – this is the directors' duty.

4   (1)   Appoint a Money Laundering Reporting Officer (MLRO) and set up internal reporting procedures
    (2)   Train individuals on the legal requirements and the firm's procedures
    (3)   Establish appropriate internal procedures
    (4)   Verify the identity of new clients / existing clients
    (5)   Maintain records of client identification
    (6)   Report suspicions of money laundering to the NCA (in the UK)

5   From:

    (1)   Company law
    (2)   Contract law
    (3)   Tort law
    (4)   Employment law
    (5)   Environmental law

6   False – it is the responsibility of management (with oversight from those charged with governance).

Now try the question below from the Practice Question Bank.

Number	Level	Marks	Time
Q1	Introductory	7	14 mins

Professional and ethical considerations

Code of ethics and conduct

Topic list	Syllabus reference
1 Fundamental principles and the conceptual framework approach	B1, G1
2 Specific guidance: independence	B1
3 Specific guidance: confidentiality	B1
4 Specific guidance: conflicts of interest	B1
5 Conflicts in application of the fundamental principles	B1

Introduction

You have already learnt about ethical rules for auditors in your earlier studies. We will examine the issues in more detail and consider some of the complex ethical issues that auditors may face.

We also refer to the ethical guidance of the International Federation of Accountants. This is similar to the ACCA's guidance. Both approach issues of ethics in a conceptual manner.

ISQC 1 *Quality control for firms that perform audits and reviews of financial statements and other assurance and related services engagements* is also relevant in providing the ethical aspects of quality control and review.

Some of this chapter is likely to be revision, but that does not mean you should ignore it. Ethics is a key syllabus area. Complex ethical issues are introduced in this chapter. You particularly need to work through the questions given so that you practise **applying** ethical guidelines in given scenarios, as this is how this topic will be tested in the exam.

Study guide

		Intellectual level
B1	**Code of ethics for professional accountants**	
(a)	Explain the fundamental principles and the conceptual framework approach.	1
(b)	Identify, evaluate and respond to threats to compliance with the fundamental principles.	3
(c)	Discuss and evaluate the effectiveness of available safeguards.	3
(d)	Recognise and advise on conflicts in the application of fundamental principles.	3
(e)	Discuss the importance of professional scepticism in planning and performing an audit.	2
(f)	Assess whether an engagement has been planned and performed with an attitude of professional scepticism, and evaluate the implications.	3
G1	**Professional and ethical developments**	
(a)	Discuss the relative advantages of an ethical framework and a rulebook.	2
(b)	Identify and assess relevant emerging ethical issues and evaluate the safeguards available.	3
(c)	Discuss IFAC developments.	2

Exam guide

Professional ethics are of vital importance to the audit and assurance profession and a major area of the syllabus, so this is likely to be a regular feature of the exam.

Questions are likely to be practical, giving scenarios where you are required to assess whether the situations are acceptable. Some of these can be answered by reference to specific guidance in the ACCA *Code of Ethics and Conduct* but others may require you to apply your understanding of the fundamental principles underlying the Code. Ethics may be examined alongside other areas within scenarios; commonly, practice management.

You may also have to suggest appropriate safeguards that the audit firm should implement.

1 Fundamental principles and the conceptual framework approach
Pilot paper, 12/07, 6/09

FAST FORWARD ⟫ Accountants require an ethical code because they hold positions of trust, and people rely on them.

1.1 The importance of ethics

The IESBA's *Code of Ethics for Professional Accountants* gives the key reason why accountancy bodies produce ethical guidance: **the public interest**.

'A distinguishing mark of the accountancy profession is its acceptance of the responsibility to act in the public interest. Therefore, a professional accountant's responsibility is not exclusively to satisfy the needs of an individual client or employer.'

The public interest is considered to be the collective wellbeing of the community of people and institutions the professional accountant serves, including clients, lenders, governments, employers, employees, investors, the business and financial community, and others who rely on the work of professional accountants.

The **key reason** why **accountants need** to have an **ethical code** is that **people rely on them and their expertise**.

Accountants deal with a range of issues on behalf of clients. They often have access to confidential and sensitive information. Auditors claim to give an independent view. It is therefore critical that accountants and particularly auditors are, and are seen to be, independent.

1.2 Sources of ethical guidance

As the auditor is required to be, and seen to be, ethical in their dealings with clients, ACCA publishes guidance for its members in its *Code of Ethics and Conduct*. This guidance is given in the form of fundamental principles, guidance and explanatory notes. (This guidance is contained within the ACCA *Rulebook*, which you can find on the ACCA website and which is of crucial importance for ACCA members.)

The IESBA (International Ethics Standards Board for Accountants), a body of IFAC, also lays down fundamental principles in its *Code of Ethics for Professional Accountants*. The fundamental principles of the two associations are extremely similar (much of the ACCA *Code* is drawn directly from the IESBA). IFAC also issues quality control standards and auditing standards (ISAs), which work together to promote auditor independence and audit quality.

One of the competences you require to fulfil Performance Objective 1 of the PER is the ability to act diligently and honestly, following codes of conduct, giving due regard to, and keeping up to date with, relevant legislation. You can apply the knowledge you have obtained from this chapter of the Text to help demonstrate this competence.

1.3 The fundamental principles

The IESBA and ACCA *Codes of ethics* are principles-based. These fundamental principles underpin the detailed guidance, which we expound in this chapter, and should be used by members to help interpret that guidance.

ACCA/IESBA *Codes of ethics*
Integrity. To **be straightforward and honest** in all professional and business relationships.
Objectivity. To **not allow bias, conflict of interest or undue influence of others** to override professional or business judgements.
Professional competence and due care. To maintain professional knowledge and skill at a level required to ensure that a client or employer receives competent professional services based on current developments in practice, legislation and techniques and act diligently and in accordance with applicable technical and professional standards when providing professional services.
Confidentiality. To **respect the confidentiality of information** acquired as a result of professional and business relationships and, therefore, **not disclose any such information to third parties without proper and specific** authority, unless there is a legal or professional **right or duty to disclose**, nor use the information for the personal advantage of the professional accountant or third parties.
Professional behaviour. To **comply** with relevant **laws and regulations** and **to avoid any action** that **discredits the profession**.

1.4 The conceptual framework

The ethical guidance discussed above is in the form of a conceptual framework. It contains some rules, for example, prohibiting making loans to clients, but in the main it is flexible guidance. It can be seen as a **framework rather than a set of rules**. There are a number of advantages of a framework over a system of ethical rules. These are outlined in the table below.

Advantages of an ethical framework over a rules-based system
A framework of guidance places the onus on the auditor to **actively consider** independence for every given situation, rather than just agreeing a checklist of forbidden items. It also requires them to **demonstrate** that a responsible conclusion has been reached about ethical issues.
The framework **prevents auditors interpreting rules-based requirements narrowly** to get around them. There is a sense in which lists of prohibitive rules engender deception, whereas principles encourage the formation of the positive practices which result in compliance.
A framework **allows for** the variations that are found in every **individual situation**. Each situation is likely to be different.
A framework can accommodate a **rapidly changing environment**, such as the one that auditors are constantly in.
However, a **framework can contain prohibitions** (as noted above) where these are necessary as safeguards are not feasible.

1.5 Threats to compliance with the fundamental principles

There are five general sources of threat.

- **Self-interest** threat (for example, having a financial interest in a client)
- **Self-review** threat (for example, auditing financial statements prepared by the firm)
- **Advocacy** threat (for example, promoting shares in a listed entity when that entity is a financial statement audit client)
- **Familiarity** threat (for example, an audit team member having family at the client)
- **Intimidation** threat (for example, threats of replacement due to disagreement)

1.6 Available safeguards

In order to counteract these threats to compliance, audits are subject to safeguards. There are two general categories of safeguard.

- Safeguards created by the profession, legislation or regulation, eg training requirements for entry into the profession, continuing professional development (CPD) requirements, professional standards, corporate governance regulations
- Safeguards in the work environment, which can be either firm-wide or engagement-specific

Examples of firm-wide safeguards in the work environment include:

Examples of firm-wide safeguards
Leadership of the firm that **stresses the importance of compliance** with the fundamental principles
Policies and procedures that will enable the **identification of interests** or relationships between the firm or staff and clients
Policies and procedures to monitor and, if necessary, manage the **reliance on revenue received from a single client** (this could create a self-interest and an intimidation threat)
Policies and procedures to **encourage and empower** staff to communicate any issue relating to compliance with the fundamental principles that concerns them

Specific threats and safeguards within these general areas will be considered in the next section. However, you may be able to use the following general list to help generate ideas in the exam.

Examples of engagement-specific safeguards
Having a professional accountant who was not involved with audit **review the work performed**, or provide advice
Consulting an independent third party, such as a committee of independent directors, a professional regulatory body or another professional accountant

Examples of engagement-specific safeguards
Discussing ethical issues **with those charged with governance** of the client
Disclosing to those charged with governance of the client the nature of services provided and extent of fees charged
Involving **another firm** to perform or **reperform** part of the engagement
Rotating senior assurance team **personnel**

1.7 Breach of a provision of the *Code of Ethics*

The IESBA *Code* states:

> **IESBA *Code of Ethics*, 290.40**
>
> When the firm concludes that a breach has occurred, the firm shall terminate, suspend or eliminate the interest or relationship that caused the breach and address the consequences of the breach.

When a breach occurs, the firm should consider whether any **legal or regulatory requirements** apply, and if necessary **report the breach** to a member body or regulator.

The breach should be **communicated** to the engagement partner (and other relevant personnel).

Evaluate the significance of the breach, based on:

- The **nature** and **duration** of the breach
- Any **previous breaches** re. the current audit engagement
- Whether a member of the audit team had knowledge of the interest or relationship that caused the breach
- Whether the individual who caused the breach is a **member of the audit team**
- If they were on the audit team, their **role**
- The **impact** of any relevant services **on the accounting records** or the amounts recorded in the financial statements
- The **extent of any threats** created by the breach

Examples of actions that the firm may consider include:

- **Removing the individual from the audit team**
- Conducting an additional **review of the affected audit work** (or reperforming it), using different personnel
- **Recommending that the audit client engage another firm** to review/reperform the affected audit work to the extent necessary
- Where the breach relates to a **non-assurance service** that affects the accounting records or an amount that is recorded in the financial statements, **engaging another firm** to evaluate the results of (or reperform) the non-assurance service

If necessary, terminate the audit engagement. If this is not necessary, **discuss with those charged with governance** and communicate the matter in writing.

1.8 ACCA Disciplinary procedures

If a member breaches regulations or fails to conduct themselves professionally, then they may be liable to disciplinary action. Breaches include the following.

- Being guilty of misconduct in the course of carrying out professional duties or otherwise
- Performing work erroneously, inadequately, inefficiently or incompetently to such an extent, or on such a number of occasions, as to amount to misconduct
- Breaching any ACCA Bye-law or Regulation

- Being disciplined by another professional body

- Becoming insolvent or entering into a voluntary arrangement or similar

- Failing to satisfy a judgment debt without reasonable excuse for two months

Anyone may bring a complaint. Complaints are considered first by an assessor, who decides whether to pass it onto the Disciplinary Committee. The Committee can impose the following penalties on members and students.

Members and Firms	Registered Students
Member excluded from membership	Student removed from student register
Member severely reprimanded, reprimanded or admonished	A specified period of the student's experience is not recognised as approved accountancy experience
Member's certificate(s), and/or ability to conduct specific activities, suspended or made subject to conditions	Student is declared ineligible to be admitted to membership for a specified period of time.
Member pays a fine of up to £50,000	Student is ineligible to sit ACCA exams for a period of time
Member pays compensation of up to £5,000	Student is disqualified from exams
Member waives/reduces fees charged to complainant	Student is severely reprimanded or admonished

2 Specific guidance: Independence 6/08, 12/08, 6/09, 6/10, 6/12, 12/12, 6/13, 12/13, 6/14, 12/14, 6/15

FAST FORWARD 〉〉 The ACCA's guidance complies with the requirements of the IESBA *Code*.

2.1 Objective of the guidance

You should be familiar with the concept of independence from your earlier studies. The IESBA *Code* discusses independence requirements for audit and review engagements in Section 290. The guidance states its purpose in a series of steps, which you should learn and understand. It aims to help firms and members:

Step 1 **Identify threats** to independence

Step 2 **Evaluate** the **significance** of the threats identified

Step 3 **Apply safeguards** when necessary to eliminate the threats or reduce them to an acceptable level.

It also recognises that there may be occasions **where no safeguard is available**. In such a situation, it is only appropriate to:

- **Eliminate the interest** or activities causing the threat; or
- **Decline the engagement**, or discontinue it.

Where the *Code* contains a prohibition (eg on providing a non-audit service in a particular situation), then this means that no safeguards could ever reduce the threat to an acceptable level.

Applying safeguards should not be a **mechanical process**. Where the *Code* contains a list of safeguards, these lists are generally not exhaustive – if you can think of further relevant safeguards, then these may also be applied. Further, applying the safeguards given by the *Code* does not automatically mean that the threat has been reduced to an acceptable level – this depends on your judgement in the situation.

Applying safeguards should not be a **mechanical process**. Where the *Code* contains a list of safeguards, these lists are generally not exhaustive – if you can think of further relevant safeguards, then these may also be applied. Further, applying the safeguards given by the *Code* does not automatically mean that the threat has been reduced to an acceptable level – this depends on your judgement in the situation. You should apply the three steps set out above when approaching questions of independence, and show the marker that you have done so in your answer. It is important for this exam that you do not simply learn the rules for each situation, but that you can apply the spirit of the guidance to a given situation. Finally, remember that if there appears to be no safeguard, then you must consider the fallback option of not continuing with the professional relationship.

2.1.1 Current issues in ethical guidance

This is currently a very topical area within the profession. Auditor independence has been under intense outside scrutiny since the financial crisis of 2007-8. Recent debate has focused on the provision of non-audit services alongside the external audit.

April 2015 saw some revisions to the IESBA *Code of Ethics* in relation to these non-assurance services. These are covered at the appropriate points in this chapter, and in Chapter 18.

In June 2014, the European Union brought into force legislation aimed at improving audit quality, which EU member states have until June 2016 to implement. The legislation introduces mandatory auditor rotation, prohibits some non-audit services, and introduces a cap on the level of fees received from non-audit services at 70% of the audit fee. These are not part of the core material examinable for P7, but you should be aware of this as an important current issue in the profession.

In March 2013, the Code was revised to address conflicts of interest, breaches of a requirement of the Code, and to amend the definition of the term 'engagement team' to include any internal auditors who provide direct assistance on an audit engagement.

In September 2012, the UK Corporate Governance Code was revised to require FTSE 350 companies in the UK to put the external audit out to tender at least every ten years.

The December 2011 paper contained a topical requirement offering six marks for evaluating the arguments for and against the outright prohibition on auditors providing **any** non-audit services at all. This was a very topical issue at the time, and you should be prepared for something comparably topical in your exam.

Professional skepticism (see Sections 2.2 and 2.4 below) is another topical area, with several bodies having issued publications recently. The IAASB itself issued a useful Q&A Paper in this area (see Chapter 18), and the FRC in the UK and the AASB in Canada have also issued their own publications. Professional skepticism is a crucial component of professional judgement, and therefore of the skillset of an auditor.

2.1.2 Public interest entities

The IESBA *Code* distinguishes between 'public interest entities' and other entities. The ethical requirements applicable to public interest entities are frequently stricter than for other entities.

Public interest entity is defined as follows.

Public interest entity

(a) Any listed entity; and

(b) Any entity defined by regulation or legislation as a public interest entity; or

(c) Any entity that is required by legislation or regulation to have an audit that is as independent as an audit of a listed entity would be; and

(d) Any other entity the firm determines to be a public interest entity, because it has a large number and wide range of stakeholders. Factors to be considered include:

    (i) The nature of the business, such as the holding of assets in a fiduciary capacity for a large number of stakeholders. Examples may include financial institutions, such as banks and insurance companies, and pension funds

    (ii) Size

    (iii) Number of employees

Exam focus point

At P7 level you must be able to do more than just recite this definition in your exam. You should be able to recognise a public interest entity in a question, and adapt your answer accordingly.

2.2 What is independence?   6/15

A provider of assurance services must be, and be seen to be, independent. What is required for this to be the case?

Key terms

Independence of mind. The state of mind that permits the provision of an opinion without being affected by influences that compromise professional judgement, allowing an individual to act with integrity, and exercise objectivity and professional scepticism.

Independence in appearance. The avoidance of facts and circumstances that are so significant that a reasonable and informed third party, having knowledge of all relevant information, including safeguards applied, would reasonably conclude that a firm's, or a member of the assurance team's, integrity, objectivity or professional scepticism had been compromised.

Professional scepticism. An attitude that includes a questioning mind, being alert to conditions which may indicate possible misstatement due to error or fraud, and a critical assessment of audit evidence.

The degree of independence required is less stringent for a firm providing a low-level assurance engagement to a non-audit client than for audit. This is summarised in the following table.

	Audit	Non-audit, general use	Non-audit, restricted use
Audit client	The assurance team, the firm and the network firm* must all be independent of the client.	The assurance team, the firm and the network firm must all be independent of the client.	The assurance team, the firm and the network firm must all be independent of the client.
Non-audit assurance client	N/A	The assurance team and the firm must be independent of the client.	The assurance team and the firm must have no material financial interest in the client.

*For an explanation of the term 'network firm', see Chapter 3.

2.2.1 When must the assurance provider be independent?

The team and the firm should be independent '**during the period of the engagement**'.

The period of the engagement is from the commencement of work until the signing of the final report being produced. For a **recurring audit**, independence may only cease on **termination of the contract** between the parties.

2.3 Management responsibilities

The Code's guidance on non-assurance services is given in the relation to each individual type of service below, but the Code does also include some general considerations. The main issue is management responsibilities, with the point being that:

IESBA *Code of Ethics*, 290.161 (extract)

A firm shall not assume a management responsibility for an audit client. The threats created would be so significant that no safeguards could reduce the threats to an acceptable level.

Management responsibilities are defined as follows.

Key term

Management responsibilities involve controlling, leading and directing an entity, including making decisions regarding the acquisition, deployment and control of human, financial, technological, physical and intangible resources.   IESBA *Code of Ethics*, 290.159

Avoiding taking on management responsibilities is one of the key problems for the auditor when providing many types of non-assurance service. But in general, an important **prerequisite** is that the firm is 'satisfied' that the client's management is actually taking on its responsibilities, ie so that none of these are left to the auditor.

2.4 A dilemma: independence vs effectiveness

Auditor independence is rarely a matter of clear questions with black and white answers. It is not just an issue of whether the 'rules' say that an audit engagement should be accepted or declined ('yes or no'), but rather of the auditor exercising proper judgement in the complex circumstances of an actual audit.

The basic dilemma is this. The auditor must be independent of the client in order to express their own opinion on whether the client's financial statements give a true and fair view. However, the auditor must also place some trust in the client if the audit is to be conducted effectively, as they will need to rely on anything from the accounting systems and controls to explanations provided by management.

It is between the two extremes of this dilemma that the concept of 'professional skepticism' attempts to place itself:

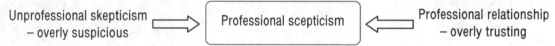

Unprofessional skepticism — overly suspicious ⟹ Professional scepticism ⟸ Professional relationship — overly trusting

If the auditor is **too** skeptical about everything the client does or says, then it will be impossible for them to conduct the audit effectively. At the extreme, this would mean checking every transaction in the financial statements, without accepting any internal records or documents at all as genuine. More practically, a breakdown in trust would mean that the audit would be conducted less efficiently: if the auditor must assume that management is not at all competent to prepare the financial statements, then much more audit work will need to be done than if management could be trusted. This would take more time and would make the audit more costly. Some degree of trust is therefore essential to the effective and professional running of the audit process.

On the other hand, if the auditor is not skeptical enough then the quality of the audit is likely to suffer. The auditor may easily be deceived in the case of fraud, or may mistakenly place too much trust in the validity of evidence and explanations provided by the client. ISA 200 *Overall objectives of the independent auditor and the conduct of an audit in accordance with international standards on auditing* lists the following examples of risks that may arise from a lack of professional scepticism.

> **ISA 200.A19**
>
> Maintaining professional scepticism is necessary to reduce the risks of:
>
> - Overlooking unusual circumstances.
> - Overgeneralising when drawing conclusions from audit observations.
> - Using inappropriate assumptions in determining the nature, timing and extent of the audit procedures and evaluating the results thereof.

In the UK, the FRC's Audit Quality Review team (formerly the Audit Inspection Unit) has found a lack of professional scepticism to be a significant problem in every year since at least 2010-11. The 2014-15 report stated that a common issue was:

> 'Insufficient scepticism in challenging the appropriateness of assumptions in key areas of audit judgment such as impairment testing and property valuations..'

> (FRC *Audit Quality Inspections, Annual Report 2014-15*, p6 s2.3)

This links with the question of independence generally, and the risk that the audit is not conducted with professional competence and due care as a result of a lack of scepticism. In the end, the auditor must balance being sceptical with being trusting, and the concept of 'professional scepticism' is an attempt to convey this. It has also been said elsewhere that the auditor should 'trust, but verify' what the client tells them.

2.5 Revision of threats to independence

The area of threats to independence should not be new to you. You should be aware of many of the threats to independence from your earlier studies in auditing. To refresh your memory about independence issues, try the following question.

| Question | Revision of audit independence |

From your knowledge brought forward from your previous studies, and any practical experience of auditing you may have, write down as many potential ethical risk areas as you can in the areas below. (Some issues may be relevant in more than one column.)

Personal interests	Review of your own work	Disputes	Intimidation

Personal interests	Review of your own work	Disputes	Intimidation
Undue dependence on an audit client due to fee levels	Auditor prepares the accounts	Actual litigation with a client	Any threat of litigation by the client
Overdue fees becoming similar to a loan	Auditor participates in management decisions	Threatened litigation with a client	Personal relationships with the client
An actual loan being made to a client	Provision of any other services to the client	Client refuses to pay fees and they become long overdue	Hospitality
Contingency fees being offered			Threat of other services provided to the client being put out to tender
Accepting commissions from clients			Threat of any services being put out to tender
Provision of lucrative other services to clients			
Relationships with persons in associated practices			
Relationships with the client			
Long association with clients			
Beneficial interest in shares or other investments			
Hospitality			

The ACCA and IESBA Codes give extensive lists of examples of threats to independence and applicable safeguards. In the rest of this section, these threats and some relevant factors and potential safeguards will be outlined. Definite rules are shown in bold. You should learn these.

2.6 Self-interest threat

The ACCA *Code of Ethics and Conduct* highlights a great number of areas in which a self-interest threat might arise.

2.6.1 Financial interests

Key term

A **financial interest** exists where an audit firm has a financial interest in a client's affairs, for example, the audit firm owns shares in the client, or is a trustee of a trust that holds shares in the client.

A financial interest in a client constitutes a substantial self-interest threat. According to both the ACCA and the IESBA, **the parties listed below are not allowed to own a direct financial interest or an indirect material financial interest in a client**.

- The assurance firm
- A member of the assurance team
- An immediate family member of a member of the assurance team

The following safeguards may therefore be relevant.

- Disposing of the interest
- Removing the individual from the team if required
- Keeping the client's audit committee informed of the situation
- Using an independent partner to review work carried out if necessary

Such matters will involve judgement on the part of the partners making decisions about such matters. For example, what constitutes a material interest? A small percentage stake in a company might be material to its owner. How does the firm judge the closeness of a relationship between staff and their families, in other words, what does immediate mean in this context?

Audit firms should have quality control procedures requiring staff to disclose relevant financial interests for themselves and close family members. They should also foster a culture of voluntary disclosure on an ongoing basis so that any potential problems are identified on a timely basis.

Question

Financial interests

You are the Ethics Partner at Stewart Brice & Co, a firm of Chartered Certified Accountants. The following situations exist.

Teresa is the audit manager assigned to the audit of Recreate, a large quoted company. The audit has been ongoing for one week. Yesterday, Teresa's husband inherited 1,000 shares in Recreate. Teresa's husband wants to hold on to the shares as an investment.

The Stewart Brice & Co pension scheme, which is administered by Friends Benevolent, an unconnected company, owns shares in Tadpole Group, a listed company with a number of subsidiaries. Stewart Brice & Co has recently been invited to tender for the audit of one of the subsidiary companies, Kermit Co.

Stewart Brice has been the auditor of Kripps Bros, a limited liability company, for a number of years. It is a requirement of Kripps Bros' constitution that the auditor owns a token $1 share in the company.

Required

Comment on the ethical and other professional issues raised by the above matters.

Answer

(a) Teresa is at present a member of the assurance team and a member of her immediate family owns a direct financial interest in the audit client. This is unacceptable.

In order to mitigate the risk to independence that this poses on the audit, Stewart Brice & Co needs to apply one of two safeguards.

- Ensure that the connected person divests the shares
- Remove Teresa from the engagement team

Teresa should be appraised that these are the options and removed from the team while a decision is taken regarding whether to divest the shares. Teresa's husband appears to want to keep the shares, in which case Teresa should be removed from the team immediately.

The firm should appraise the audit committee of Recreate of what has happened and the actions they have taken. The partners should consider whether it is necessary to bring in an independent

partner to review audit work. However, given that Teresa's involvement is subject to the review of the existing engagement partner and she was not connected with the shares while she was carrying out the work, a second partner review is likely to be unnecessary in this case.

(b) The audit firm has an indirect interest in the parent company of a company it has been invited to tender for by virtue of its pension scheme having invested in Tadpole Group.

This is no barrier to the audit firm tendering for the audit of Kermit Co.

Should the audit firm win the tender and become the auditors of Kermit Co it should consider whether it is necessary to apply safeguards to mitigate against the risk to independence on the audit as a result of the indirect financial interest.

The factors that the partners will need to consider are the materiality of the interest to either party and the degree of control that the firm actually has over the financial interest.

In this case, the audit firm has no control over the financial interest. An independent pension scheme administrator is in control of the financial interest. In addition, the interest is unlikely to be substantial and is therefore immaterial to both parties. Only if the threat is significant should the interest be divested.

It is likely that this risk is already sufficiently minimal so as not to require safeguards. However, if the audit firm felt that it was necessary to apply safeguards, it could consider the following.

- Notifying the audit committee of the interest
- Requiring Friends Benevolent to dispose of the shares in Tadpole Group.

(c) In this case, Stewart Brice & Co has a direct financial interest in the audit client, which is technically forbidden by ACCA guidance. However, it is a requirement of any firm auditing the company that the share be owned by the auditors.

The interest is not material. The audit firm should safeguard against the risk by not voting on its own re-election as auditor. The firm should also strongly recommend to the company that it removes this requirement from its constitution, as it is at odds with ethical requirements for auditors.

2.6.2 Close business relationships

Examples of when an audit firm and an audit client have an inappropriately close business relationship include:

- Having a material financial interest in a joint venture with the assurance client
- Arrangements to combine one or more services or products of the firm with one or more services or products of the assurance client and to market the package with reference to both parties
- Distribution or marketing arrangements under which the firm acts as distributor or marketer of the assurance client's products or services or *vice versa*

Again, it will be necessary for the partners to judge the materiality of the interest and therefore its significance. However, **unless the interest is clearly insignificant, an assurance provider should not participate in such a venture with an assurance client**. Appropriate safeguards are therefore to end the assurance provision or to terminate the (other) business relationship.

If an individual member of an audit team had such an interest, they should be removed from the audit team.

However, if the firm or a member (and immediate family of the member) of the audit team has an interest in an entity when the client or its officers also has an interest in that entity, the threat might not be so great.

Generally speaking, **purchasing goods and services from an assurance client on an arm's length basis does not constitute a threat to independence**. If there are a substantial number of such transactions, there may be a threat to independence and safeguards may be necessary.

2.6.3 Temporary staff assignments

Staff may be loaned to an audit client, but only **for a short period of time. Staff must not assume management responsibilities**, or undertake any assurance work that is prohibited elsewhere in the Code. The audit client must be responsible for directing and supervising the activities of the loaned staff.

Possible safeguards include:

- Conducting an additional review of the work performed by the loaned staff;
- Not giving the loaned staff audit responsibility for any function or activity on the audit, that they performed during the temporary staff assignment; or
- Not including the loaned staff in the audit team.

2.6.4 Partner on client board

A partner or employee of an assurance firm should not serve on the board of an assurance client.

It may be acceptable for a partner or an employee of an assurance firm to perform the role of company secretary for an assurance client, if the role is essentially administrative and if this practice is specifically permitted under local law and professional rules.

Although a partner or employee cannot serve on a client's board, it is possible for them to attend board meetings. This is common practice, and moreover may be necessary if there are issues that need to be raised with management.

2.6.5 Compensation and evaluation policies

There is a self-interest threat when a member of the audit team is evaluated on selling non-assurance services to the client. The significance of the threat depends on:

- The proportion of the individual's compensation or performance evaluation that is based on the sale of such services
- The role of the individual on the audit team
- Whether promotion decisions are influenced by the sale of such services

The firm should either revise the compensation plan or evaluation process, or put in place appropriate safeguards. Safeguards include:

- Removing the member from the audit team; or
- Having the team member's work reviewed by a professional accountant.

A key audit partner shall not be evaluated based on their success in selling non-assurance services to their audit client.

Point to note

In the UK, the Audit Quality Review Team's annual report for 2010-11 expressed concern over the selling of non-audit services to audited entities. The report stated that partners and staff were too often compromised by an inappropriate focus on this area, with the result that firms sometimes failed to identify the nature and extent of threats, and therefore failed to apply appropriate safeguards.

2.6.6 Gifts and hospitality

Unless the value of the gift/hospitality is clearly trivial and inconsequential, a firm or a member of an assurance team should not accept.

2.6.7 Loans and guarantees

The advice on loans and guarantees falls into two categories:

- The client is a bank or other similar institution
- Other situations

If a lending institution client lends an immaterial amount to an audit firm or member of the assurance team on normal commercial terms, there is no threat to independence. If the loan were material, it would be necessary to apply safeguards to bring the risk to an acceptable level. A suitable safeguard is likely to be an independent review (by a partner from another office in the firm).

Loans to members of the assurance team from a bank or other lending institution client are likely to be material to the individual but, provided that they are on normal commercial terms, these do not constitute a threat to independence.

An audit firm or individual on the assurance engagement should not enter into any loan or guarantee arrangement with a client that is not a bank or similar institution.

2.6.8 Overdue fees

In a situation where there are overdue fees, the auditor runs the risk of, in effect, making a loan to a client, whereupon the guidance above becomes relevant.

Audit firms should guard against fees building up and being significant by discussing the issues with those charged with governance, and, if necessary, the possibility of resigning if overdue fees are not paid.

2.6.9 Percentage or contingent fees

Key term

> **Contingent fee.** A fee calculated on a predetermined basis relating to the outcome of a transaction or the result of the services performed by the firm. A fee that is established by a court or other public authority is not a contingent fee.

A firm shall not enter into a contingent fee arrangement in respect of an assurance engagement. For both audit and assurance engagements, a contingent fee would carry a threat so great that no safeguards could reduce it to an acceptable level.

For non-assurance engagements (eg tax services), where the client is not also an audit client, the significance of the threat depends on:

- The range of possible fee amounts
- Whether an appropriate authority determines the outcome of the matter on which the contingent fee will be determined
- The nature of the service
- The effect of the event or transaction on the subject matter information.

Possible safeguards include:

- Having a **professional accountant review** the relevant assurance work or otherwise advise as necessary; or
- Using professionals who are not members of the assurance team to perform the non-assurance service.

2.6.10 High percentage of fees

When a firm receives a high proportion of its fee income from just one audit client, there is **a self-interest** or **intimidation threat**, as the firm will be concerned about losing the client. A high percentage fee income does not by itself create an insurmountable threat. This depends on the following.

- The **structure** of the **firm**
- Whether the **firm** is established or **new**
- The **significance of the client** to the firm

Exam focus point

> These caveats are important for all of the threats to independence in this chapter. You should know most of the rules from your previous studies, but at P7 level you will need to be able to apply them in detail.

Possible safeguards include:

- **Reducing** the **dependence** on the client;
- **External** quality control **reviews**; or
- **Consulting a third party**, such as a professional regulatory body or a professional accountant, **on key audit judgements**.

Point to note It is not just a matter of the audit firm actually **being** independent in terms of fees, but also of it being **seen to be independent by the public**. It is as much about public perception as reality.

The *Code* also states that a threat may be created where an individual partner or office's percentage fees from one client is high. The safeguards are as above, except that internal quality control reviews are also relevant.

For audit clients that are **public interest entities**, the Code states that where **total fees** from the client (for the audit and any non-audit services) represent **more than 15% of the firm's total fees for two consecutive years**, the firm shall:

- **Disclose** this to **those charged with governance**

- **Conduct a review**, either by an external professional accountant or by a regulatory body. This review can be either before the audit opinion on the second year's financial statements is issued (a 'pre-issuance review'), or after it is issued (a '**post-issuance review**').

If total fees **significantly exceed 15%,** then a post-issuance review may not be sufficient, and a **pre-issuance review** will be required.

Exam focus point Be careful when making points about fee dependence in the exam – as a rule, it is best not to make the point unless there is information in the question that specifically indicates that this is an issue. Your examination team does not like it when candidates routinely mention fee dependence in ethics questions, so marking schemes often do not include marks here.

2.6.11 Lowballing

When a firm quotes a significantly lower fee level for an assurance service than would have been charged by the predecessor firm, there is a significant self-interest threat. If the firm's tender is successful, the firm must apply safeguards such as:

- Maintaining records such that the firm is able to demonstrate that appropriate staff and time are spent on the engagement
- Complying with all applicable assurance standards, guidelines and quality control procedures

2.6.12 Recruitment

Recruiting senior management for an assurance client, particularly those able to affect the subject matter of an assurance engagement, creates a self-interest threat for the assurance firm.

Assurance providers must not make management decisions for the client. Their involvement could be limited to reviewing a shortlist of candidates, providing that the client has drawn up the criteria by which they are to be selected.

2.7 Self-review threat

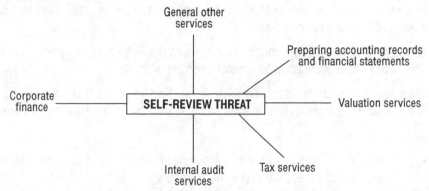

The key area in which there is likely to be a self-review threat is where an assurance firm provides services other than assurance services to an assurance client (providing multiple services). There is a great deal of guidance in the ACCA and IESBA *Codes* about various other services that accountancy firms might provide to their clients, and these are dealt with below.

Exam focus point

> In exam questions, bear in mind the nature of the entity being audited. Is it a small owner-managed business where the auditor is in effect an all-round business adviser and accountant, or is it a listed company where the above rule is relevant?

In the US, rules concerning auditor independence for **listed** companies state that an accountant is **not** independent if they provide certain non-audit services to an audit client. The relevant services are:

- Bookkeeping
- Financial information systems design and implementation
- Appraisal or valuation services or fairness opinions
- Actuarial services
- Internal audit services
- Management functions
- Human resources
- Broker-dealer services
- Legal services

The rules, found in the Sarbanes-Oxley Act, have an international impact because they apply not only to any company listed on the US Stock Exchange, but also **to all subsidiaries of US-listed companies no matter where they are based**. So, for example, a UK-based subsidiary of a multinational group that is listed in the US must comply with the Sarbanes-Oxley requirements.

2.7.1 General other services

For assurance clients, accountants are not allowed to:

- Authorise, execute or consummate a transaction
- Determine which recommendation of the company should be implemented
- Report in a management capacity to those charged with governance

Having custody of an assurance client's assets, supervising client employees in the performance of their normal duties, and preparing source documents on behalf of the client also pose significant self-review threats which should be addressed by safeguards. These could be:

- Ensuring non-assurance team staff are used for these roles
- Involving an independent professional accountant to advise
- Quality control policies on what staff are and are not allowed to do for clients
- Making appropriate disclosures to those charged with governance
- Resigning from the assurance engagement

2.7.2 Preparing accounting records and financial statements

There is clearly a significant risk of a self-review threat if a firm prepares accounting records and financial statements and then audits them.

On the other hand, auditors routinely assist management with the preparation of financial statements and give advice about accounting treatments and journal entries.

Therefore, assurance firms must analyse the risks arising and put safeguards in place to ensure that the risk is at an acceptable level. If this can be done, then **these services may be provided**.

Safeguards include:

- Using staff members other than assurance team members to carry out the work
- Obtaining client approval for work undertaken

The rules are more stringent when the client is listed or public interest. **Firms should not prepare accounts or financial statements for listed or public interest clients**. Note that there used to be an exception here for 'emergency situations', in which the auditor used to be allowed to prepare accounts, but this was removed in 2015.

For any client, assurance firms are also not allowed to:

- **Determine or change journal entries without client approval**
- **Authorise or approve transactions**

2.7.3 Valuation services

Key term

A **valuation** comprises the making of assumptions with regard to future developments, the application of certain methodologies and techniques, and the combination of both in order to compute a certain value, or range of values, for an asset, a liability or a business as a whole.

If an audit firm performs a valuation which will be included in financial statements audited by the firm, a self-review threat arises.

Audit firms should not carry out valuations on matters which will be material to the financial statements. If the valuation is for an immaterial matter, the audit firm should apply safeguards to ensure that the risk is reduced to an acceptable level. Matters to consider when applying safeguards are the extent of the audit client's knowledge of the relevant matters in making the valuation and the degree of judgement involved, how much use is made of established methodologies and the degree of uncertainty in the valuation. Safeguards include:

- Second partner review
- Confirming that the client understands the valuation and the assumptions used
- Ensuring the client acknowledges responsibility for the valuation
- Using separate personnel for the valuation and the audit

2.7.4 Taxation services

The *Code* divides taxation services into four categories.

(a) Tax return preparation
(b) Tax calculations for the purpose of preparing the accounting entries
(c) Tax planning and other tax advisory services
(d) Assistance in the resolution of tax disputes

Guidance in respect of each of these categories is:

(a) **Tax return preparation does not generally threaten independence**, as long as management takes responsibility for the returns.

(b) **Tax calculations for the purpose of preparing the accounting entries may not prepared for public interest entities**. There used to be an exception for 'emergency situations', but changes in 2015 meant that taxation services cannot provided in any circumstances at all.

For non-public interest entities, it is acceptable to do so provided that safeguards are applied.

(c) **Tax planning may be acceptable in certain circumstances**, eg where the advice is clearly supported by tax authority or other precedent. However, if the effectiveness of the tax advice depends on a particular accounting treatment or presentation in the financial statements, the audit team has reasonable doubt about the accounting treatment, and the consequences of the tax advice would be material, then the service should not be provided.

(d) **Assistance in the resolution of tax disputes may be provided**, depending on whether the firm itself provided the service which is the subject of the dispute, and whether the effect is material to the financial statements. Safeguards include using professionals who are not members of the audit team to perform the service, and obtaining advice on the service from an external tax professional.

2.7.5 Internal audit services

A firm may provide internal audit services to an audit client. However, it should ensure that the client acknowledges its responsibility for establishing, maintaining and monitoring the system of internal controls. It may be appropriate to use safeguards, such as ensuring that an employee of the client is designated as responsible for internal audit activities and that the client approves all the work that internal audit does.

If the client is a **public interest entity**, then internal audit services must not be provided if they relate to:

(a) A **significant** part of **the internal controls** over **financial reporting**;

(b) Financial accounting systems generating information which is significant to the financial statements; or

(c) Amounts or disclosures which are **material** to the financial statements.

2.7.6 Corporate finance

Certain aspects of corporate finance will create self-review threats that cannot be reduced to an acceptable level by safeguards. Therefore, **assurance firms are not allowed to promote, deal in or underwrite an assurance client's shares. They are also not allowed to commit an assurance client to the terms of a transaction or consummate a transaction on the client's behalf.**

Other corporate finance services, such as assisting a client in defining corporate strategies, assisting in identifying possible sources of capital and providing structuring advice, may be acceptable, providing that safeguards are put in place, such as using different teams of staff and ensuring no management decisions are taken on behalf of the client.

2.7.7 Other services

The audit firm might sell a variety of other services to audit clients, such as:

- IT services
- Litigation support
- Legal services

The assurance firm should consider whether there are any threats to independence, such as if the firm were asked to design internal control IT systems, which it would then review as part of its audit. The firm should consider whether the threat to independence could be reduced by appropriate safeguards.

2.8 Advocacy threat

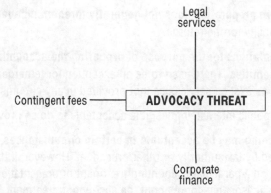

An advocacy threat arises in certain situations where the assurance firm is in a position of taking the client's part in a dispute or somehow acting as their advocate. The most obvious instances of this would be when a firm offered legal services to a client and, say, defended them in a legal case or provided evidence on their behalf as an expert witness. Advocacy threat might also arise if the firm carried out corporate finance work for the client, for example, if the audit firm was involved in advice on debt reconstruction and negotiated with the bank on the client's behalf.

Exam focus point

> The December 2013 exam featured a scenario in which the auditor was asked to attend a meeting with the client's bank in relation to a possible new loan. Although most students would have sensed that this was wrong, many would not have gotten the marks for saying specifically that it was an advocacy threat.

As with the other threats above, the firm has to appraise the risk and apply safeguards as necessary. Relevant safeguards might be using different departments in the firm to carry out the work and making disclosures to the audit committee. Remember, the ultimate option is always to withdraw from an engagement if the risk to independence is too high.

Question

Advocacy threat

Explain why contingent fees represent an advocacy threat.

Answer

If an accountant is paid fees on a contingency basis, then their interest becomes too closely aligned to that of the client. They will both want the same thing to occur (ie the thing the fee is contingent on) and the risk is that the accountant will act in the interests of the client to ensure it happens.

2.9 Familiarity threat

A familiarity threat arises where independence is jeopardised by the audit firm and its staff becoming over familiar with the client and its staff. There is a substantial risk of loss of professional scepticism in such circumstances.

We have already discussed some examples of when this risk arises, because very often a familiarity threat arises in conjunction with a self-interest threat.

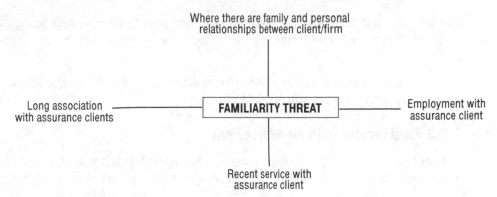

Where there are family and personal
relationships between client/firm

Long association
with assurance clients — **FAMILIARITY THREAT** — Employment with
assurance client

Recent service with
assurance client

2.9.1 Long association of senior personnel with audit clients

Having an audit client for a **long period of time may create a familiarity threat** to independence. The severity of the threat depends on such factors as how long the individual has been on the audit team; how senior the person is; whether the client's management has changed; and whether the client's accounting issues have changed in nature or complexity.

Possible **safeguards** include:

- **Rotating** the **senior personnel** off the **audit team**;

- Having a **professional accountant** who was not a member of the audit team **review** the work of the senior personnel; or

- **Regular** independent **internal or external quality reviews** of the engagement.

The rules for **public interest entities** are stricter. If an individual is a **key audit partner** for **seven years**, they must be rotated off the audit for **two years**. During this time they cannot be on the audit team, and cannot consult with the audit team or the client on any issues that may affect the engagement (including giving just general industry advice).

The *Codes* do allow some flexibility here: **if** key partner **continuity** is particularly beneficial to **audit quality**, and there is some **unforeseen circumstance** (such as the intended engagement partner becoming seriously ill), then the key audit partner **can remain on the audit for an additional year**, making eight years in total.

If a client that was not a public interest entity becomes one, then the seven year limit still applies, starting from the date when the key audit partner originally became the key partner for that audit client.

Finally, it is possible for an independent regulator to give permission for an audit partner to remain a key audit partner indefinitely, provided alternative safeguards are applied (eg external review).

Exam focus point

> The December 2010 exam contained four marks for evaluating the advantages and disadvantages of **compulsory firm rotation**. The candidates who score well on questions of this sort are those who don't just know the rules, but are also able to think through the issues underlying them. They are also those who have done a bit of reading around the syllabus.
>
> That being said, you don't need to be intimidated by questions like this: they are within reach of virtually every P7 candidate, provided that you can come up with some sensible points both for and against, and can then draw a reasonable conclusion from what you have written. These are skills that you have demonstrated in the earlier P-level papers; they just need to be applied to the subject matter of P7.

2.9.2 Recent service with an audit client

Individuals who have been a director or officer of the client (or an employee in a position to exert direct and significant influence over the subject matter information of the assurance engagement) in the period under review should not be assigned to the assurance team.

If an individual had been closely involved with the client prior to the time limits set out above, the assurance firm should consider the threat to independence arising and apply appropriate safeguards, such as:

- Obtaining a quality control review of the individual's work on the assignment
- Discussing the issue with the audit committee

2.9.3 Employment with an audit client

It is possible that staff might transfer between an assurance firm and a client, or that negotiations or interviews to facilitate such movement might take place. Both situations are a threat to independence:

- An audit staff member might be motivated by a desire to impress a future possible employer (objectivity is therefore affected – self-interest threat).

- A former partner turned finance director has too much knowledge of the audit firm's systems and procedures.

In general there may be **familiarity** and **intimidation threats** when a member of the audit team joins an audit client. If a **'significant connection'** still **remains** between the audit firm and the former employee/partner, **then no safeguards could reduce the threat to an acceptable level**. This would be the case where:

- The individual is entitled to benefits from the audit firm (unless fixed and predetermined, and not material to the firm)

- The individual continues to participate in the audit firm's business or professional activities

If there is no significant connection, then the threat depends on:

- The **position** the individual has taken at the client

- Any **involvement** the individual will have **with the audit team**

- The **length of time** since the individual was a member of the audit team or partner of the firm

- The **former position** of the individual **within the audit team or firm**; for example, whether the individual was responsible for maintaining regular contact with the client's management or those charged with governance

Safeguards could include:

- **Modifying** the **audit plan**;

- **Assigning individuals** to the audit team **who have sufficient experience** in relation to the individual who has joined the client; or

- Having an independent professional accountant **review** the work of the former member of the audit team.

If the **audit client** is a **public interest entity**, 'cooling off' periods are required. Both the ACCA and IESBA Codes state that **when a key audit partner joins such a client**, either as a director or as an employee with significant influence on the financial statements, the client must have issued audited financial statements covering at least 12 months before the employment can begin. The partner in question must also not have been a member of the audit team in relation to those audited financial statements.

In the case of a **senior or managing partner joining an audit client**, 12 months must have passed (ie there is no requirement for audited financial statements to have been issued).

The **key audit partner** is the:

- Engagement partner,
- Individual responsible for the engagement quality control review,
- Other audit partners on the engagement team,

who make key decisions or judgements on significant matters with respect to the audit of the financial statements on which the firm will express an opinion. Depending upon the circumstances and the role of the individuals on the audit, 'other audit partners' may include, for example, audit partners responsible for significant subsidiaries or divisions.

2.9.4 Family and personal relationships

Family or close personal relationships between assurance firm staff and client staff could seriously threaten independence. Each situation has to be evaluated individually. Factors to consider are:

- The individual's responsibilities on the assurance engagement
- The closeness of the relationship
- The role of the other party at the assurance client

When an immediate family member of a member of the assurance team is a director, an officer or an employee of the assurance client in a position to exert direct and significant influence over the subject matter information of the assurance engagement, the individual should be removed from the assurance team.

The audit firm should also consider whether there is any threat to independence if an employee who is not a member of the assurance team has a close family or personal relationship with a director, an officer or an employee of an assurance client.

A firm should have quality control policies and procedures under which staff should disclose if a close family member employed by the client is promoted within the client.

If a firm inadvertently violates the rules concerning family and personal relationships they should apply additional safeguards, such as undertaking a quality control review of the audit and discussing the matter with the audit committee of the client, if there is one.

2.10 Intimidation threat

An intimidation threat arises when members of the assurance team have reason to be intimidated by client staff.

These are also examples of self-interest threats, largely because intimidation may only arise significantly when the assurance firm has something to lose.

The following examples of intimidation threats are taken from the IESBA *Code*.

Examples of intimidation threats
A **threat of dismissal** from a client engagement, if it continues to disagree with the client/plans to modify the auditor's report
A **threat of not giving a firm a contract for non-assurance work**
A **threat of litigation** by the client (see below)
Pressure to reduce the amount of work done in order to reduce **fees**
Pressure to agree with the client because the client has **more experience** on the matter
A **partner** within the firm telling a member of the audit team that they will **not be promoted if they disagree with the client**

2.10.1 Actual and threatened litigation

There may be an intimidation threat when the client threatens to sue, or indeed sues, the assurance firm for work that has been done previously. The firm is then faced with the risk of losing the client, bad publicity and the possibility that they will be found to have been negligent, which will lead to further problems. This could lead to the firm being under pressure to produce an unmodified audit report when they have been modified in the past, for example.

Generally, assurance firms should seek to avoid such situations arising. If they do arise, factors to consider are:

- The materiality of the litigation
- The nature of the assurance engagement
- Whether the litigation relates to a prior assurance engagement

The following safeguards could be considered.

- Disclosing to the audit committee the nature and extent of the litigation
- Removing specific affected individuals from the engagement team
- Involving an additional professional accountant on the team to review work

However, if the litigation is at all serious, it may be necessary to resign from the engagement, as the threat to independence is so great.

2.10.2 Second opinions

Another way that auditors can suffer an intimidation threat is when the audit client is unhappy with a proposed audit opinion, and seeks a **second opinion** from a different firm of auditors.

In such a circumstance, the second audit firm **will not be able to give a formal audit opinion** on the financial statements – only an appointed auditor can do that. However, the problem is that if a different firm of auditors indicates to someone else's audit client that a different audit opinion might be acceptable, the appointed auditor may feel under pressure to change the audit opinion. In effect, a self-interest threat arises, as the existing auditor may feel that they will lose next year's audit if they does not change this year's opinion.

There is nothing to stop a company director talking to a second firm of auditors about treatments of matters in the financial statements. However, the firm being asked for a second opinion should **be very careful**, because it is possible that the opinion they form could be incorrect anyway if the director has not given them all the relevant information. For that reason, firms giving a second opinion should ensure that they seek permission to communicate with the existing auditor and they are appraised of all the facts. If permission is not given, the second auditors should decline to comment on the audit opinion.

Given that second opinions can cause independence issues for the existing auditors, audit firms should generally take great care if asked to provide one anyway.

Increasingly, new accounting standards do not give a choice of accounting treatments, meaning that second opinions might be less called for.

You are a partner in a firm of Chartered Certified Accountants. The following issues have emerged in relation to three of your clients.

(a) Easter is a major client. It is listed on a major Stock Exchange. The audit team consists of eight members, of whom Paul is the most junior. Paul has just invested in a personal pension plan that invests in all the listed companies on the exchange.

(b) You are at the head of a team carrying out due diligence work at Electra, a limited company which your client, Powerful, is considering taking over. Your second in command on the team, Peter, has confided in you that in the course of his work he has met the daughter of the managing director of Electra, and he is keen to invite her on a date.

(c) Your longest standing audit client is Teddies, which you have been involved in for ten years, four as engagement partner. You recently went on an extended cruise with the managing director on their yacht.

Required

Comment on the ethical and other professional issues raised by the above matters. Your answer should outline the threat arising, the significance of the threat, any factors you have taken into account and, if relevant, any safeguards you could apply to eliminate or mitigate the threat.

Answer

(a) In relation to Easter, there is a threat of self-interest arising, as a member of the audit team has an indirect financial interest in the client.

The **relevant factors** are:

(i) The interest is unlikely to be **material** to the client or Paul, as the investment is recent and Paul's interest is in a pool of general investments made by the pension scheme on his behalf.

(ii) Paul is the **audit junior** and **does not have a significant role** on the audit in terms of drawing audit conclusions or identifying audit risk areas.

The risk that arises to the independence of the audit here is **not significant**. It would be inappropriate to require Paul to divest his interest in the audit client. If I wanted to eliminate all elements of risk in this situation, I could simply change the junior assigned to my team, but such a step is not vital in this situation.

(b) In relation to Powerful, two issues arise. The first is that the firm appears to be providing multiple services to Powerful, which could raise a **self-interest threat**. The second is that the manager assigned to the due diligence assignment wants to engage in a personal relationship with a person connected to the subject of the assignment, which could create a **familiarity or intimidation threat**.

With regard to the issue of multiple services, **insufficient information** is given to draw a conclusion as to the significance of the threat. **Relevant factors** would be matters such as the nature of the services, the fee income and the team members assigned to each. **Safeguards** could include using different staff for the two assignments. The risk is likely to be significant only if one of the services provided is **audit**, which is not indicated in the question.

In relation to the second issue, the **relevant factors** are as follows.

- The assurance team member has a significant role on the team as second in command
- The other party is closely connected to a key staff member at the company being reviewed
- Timing

In this situation, the firm is carrying out a one-off review of the company, and **timing is a key issue**. Presently Peter does not have a personal relationship which would significantly threaten the

independence of the assignment. In this situation, the **safeguard is to request that Peter does not take any action in that direction until the assignment is completed**. If he refuses, then I may have to consider rotating my staff on this assignment, and removing him from the team.

(c) In relation to Teddies, there is a risk that my long association and personal relationship with the client will result in a **familiarity** threat. This is compounded by my acceptance of significant hospitality on a personal level.

The **relevant factors** are:

- I have been involved with the client for ten years and have a personal relationship with client staff.
- The company is not a listed or public interest company.
- It is an audit assignment.

The risk arising here is **significant** but, as the client is not listed, it is not insurmountable. However, it would be a good idea to implement some safeguards to mitigate against the risk. I could invite a second partner to provide a **hot review** of the audit of Teddies, or even consider requesting that I am **rotated** off the audit of Teddies for a period, so that the engagement partner is another partner in my firm. In addition, I must cease accepting hospitality from the directors of Teddies unless it is clearly insignificant.

Exam focus point

When answering exam questions, do not just identify the ethical threats in a given scenario. You must also be able to **explain why** the issue is an ethical threat. Ideally you should say what type of threat it is (self-interest, self-review, advocacy, familiarity or intimidation), as this will help to show the marker that you are applying specific knowledge of ethical codes to the scenario.

2.11 Quality control: independence

The quality control standard for firms, ISQC 1 *Quality control for firms that perform audits and reviews of financial statements, and other assurance and related services engagements*, which we shall look at in detail in Chapter 4, contains a section looking at the firm's procedures with regard to ethics and, in particular, independence.

ISQC 1.20

The firm shall establish policies and procedures designed to provide it with reasonable assurance that the firm and its personnel comply with relevant ethical requirements.

The policies and procedures should be in line with the fundamental principles, which should be reinforced by:

- The leadership of the firm
- Education and training
- Monitoring
- A process for dealing with non-compliance

ISQC 1.22

Such policies and procedures shall require:

(a) Engagement partners to provide the firm with relevant information about client engagements, including the scope of services, to enable the firm to evaluate the overall impact, if any, on independence requirements

(b) Personnel to promptly notify the firm of circumstances and relationships that create a threat to independence so that appropriate action can be taken

(c) The accumulation and communication of relevant information to appropriate personnel so that:

    (i) The firm and its personnel can readily determine whether they satisfy independence requirements

    (ii) The firm can maintain and update its records relating to independence

    (iii) The firm can take appropriate action regarding identified threats to independence that are not at an acceptable level

ISQC 1.23

The firm shall establish policies and procedures designed to provide it with reasonable assurance that it is notified of breaches of independence requirements, and to enable it to take appropriate actions to resolve such situations. The policies and procedures shall include requirements for:

(a) Personnel to promptly notify the firm of independence breaches of which they become aware

(b) The firm to promptly communicate identified breaches of these policies and procedures to:

    (i) The engagement partner who, with the firm, needs to address the breach

    (ii) Other relevant personnel in the firm and, where appropriate, the network, and those subject to the independence requirements who need to take appropriate action

(c) Prompt communication to the firm, if necessary, by the engagement partner and the other individuals referred to in subparagraph (b)(ii) of the actions taken to resolve the matter, so that the firm can determine whether it should take further action

ISQC 1.24

At least annually, the firm shall obtain written confirmation of compliance with its policies and procedures on independence from all firm personnel required to be independent by relevant ethical requirements.

2.11.1 Familiarity threat

Lastly, the ISQC sets out some specific guidance in relation to the threat of overfamiliarity with clients.

ISQC 1.25

The firm shall establish policies and procedures:

(a) Setting out criteria for determining the need for safeguards to reduce the familiarity threat to an acceptable level when using the same senior personnel on an assurance engagement over a long period of time; and

(b) Requiring, for audits of financial statements of listed entities, the rotation of the engagement partner and the individuals responsible for engagement quality control review and, where applicable, others subject to rotation requirements, after a specified period in compliance with relevant ethical requirements.

3 Specific guidance: confidentiality   12/13

FAST FORWARD

The ACCA and the IESBA *Codes* recognise a duty of confidence and several exceptions to it.

3.1 Duty of confidence

Confidentiality is a fundamental principle, defined in Section 1.3 above. Here is the definition again:

Key term

> **Confidentiality.** To **respect the confidentiality of information** acquired as a result of professional and business relationships and, therefore, **not disclose any such information to third parties without proper and specific** authority, unless there is a legal or professional **right or duty to disclose**, nor use the information for the personal advantage of the professional accountant or third parties.
>
> (IESBA and ACCA *Codes of Ethics*)

The key parts of this definition are:

- Do **not** disclose information **without proper authority**.
- Do **not** use information for **personal advantage**.
- Information **may be disclosed** if there is a **right or duty** to do so.

In exchange for this duty of confidence owed by the auditor to the client, the client must agree to disclose in full all information relevant to the engagement. The professional accountant must make the client aware of the duty of confidentiality, and of the fact that it can be overridden where there is a right or duty to disclose.

Maintaining confidentiality means avoiding **inadvertent disclosure** as much as intentional disclosure. For instance, information must not be disclosed unintentionally when socialising. The *Codes* also note that the **duty of confidentiality continues even after the end of the relationship with the client**.

3.2 Exceptions to the rule of confidentiality

Binding though the duty of confidence is, there are nevertheless exceptions to it. The *Codes* identify three general circumstances where disclosure may be appropriate.

- Disclosure is permitted by law **and authorised by the client**.

- Disclosure is **required by law** (eg for legal proceedings).

- There is a **professional duty or right** to disclose (eg to comply with a quality review by a professional body such as ACCA; to respond to an investigation by a regulatory body; to protect the professional accountant's interests in legal proceedings; to comply with ethics requirements).

Disclosure may be **obligatory** or merely **voluntary**, depending on the situation.

ACCA and IESBA *Codes of Ethics*

Obligatory disclosure. A professional accountant who believes that a **client has committed terrorist offences**, or has reasonable cause to believe that a client has committed treason, is bound to disclose that knowledge to the proper authorities immediately.   *(Code, B 1.22)*

Voluntary disclosure. In certain cases a professional accountant is free to disclose information, whatever its nature:

- When it is in the **public interest**
- In order to **protect a professional accountant's interests**
- Where it is **authorised by statute**
- To **non-governmental bodies**

                                                                        (Code, B 1.30)

In **deciding whether to disclose**, some general factors to consider include:

- Whether it would **harm the interests of all parties** (including third parties)
- Whether **all relevant information is known** and substantiated
- The **type of communication** that is expected
- Whether the **parties** to whom the **communication** is addressed are **appropriate** recipients

The following four subsections address the four kinds of voluntary disclosure.

3.2.1 Disclosure in the public interest

The courts have never given a definition of 'the public interest', which makes things difficult for the auditor as it is not certain exactly when they must disclose. But the *Codes* state that disclosure is probably only permitted to 'one who has a proper interest to receive that information', such as:

- The police;
- The government department for trade and industry; or
- A recognised stock exchange.

Whether disclosure is justified depends on the following factors (*Code* B1.32).

- The size of the amounts involved and the extent of likely financial damage
- Whether members of the public are likely to be affected
- The possibility or likelihood of repetition
- The reasons for the client's unwillingness to make disclosures to the proper authority
- The gravity of the matter
- Relevant legislation, accounting and auditing standards
- Any legal advice obtained

The *Codes* do state that this is a difficult area to decide on, and that **it will often be appropriate to take legal advice** (*Code* B1.33).

Under ISA 250, if auditors become aware of a suspected or actual instance of non-compliance with law and regulation which gives rise to a statutory right or duty to report, they should report it to the proper authority immediately. They should also seek legal advice.

Exam focus point

If you are required to make judgements about whether such a disclosure should be made in a given scenario, you should apply a checklist like the one above to the scenario to ensure you have shown evidence of your consideration of all the relevant factors.

3.2.2 Disclosure to protect a professional accountant's interests

Disclosure can be made to protect a professional accountant's interests to:

- Enable the professional accountant to **defend themselves against a criminal charge** or **suspicion**
- **Resist proceedings** in relation to a **taxation** offence
- **Resist legal action by a client** or a third party
- Enable the professional accountant **to defend themselves against disciplinary proceedings** by the ACCA or another body
- **Enable** the professional accountant **to sue for their fees**

3.2.3 Disclosure authorised by statute

There are two areas where legislation may require the auditor to break their duty of confidentiality:

- Where required to disclose by **anti money laundering legislation** (see Chapter 1)
- Where required to disclose by any **whistleblowing responsibilities**, eg for an auditor of certain financial institutions in the UK

3.2.4 Disclosure to non-governmental bodies

Disclosure **must** be made to a **recognised non-governmental body** where the body **has statutory powers requiring disclosure**, but where the body does not have these powers then the professional accountant must obtain the client's consent to disclose.

3.3 Responding to illegal acts/non-compliance with laws and regulations

3.3.1 2012 ED: *Responding to a suspected illegal act*

In August 2012 the IESBA issued an Exposure Draft (ED), *Responding to a Suspected Illegal Act*. The ED described the circumstances in which a professional accountant is required or expected to **override confidentiality** and disclose a suspected illegal act to an appropriate authority.

The ED proposed adding two new sections addressing illegal acts to the *Code of Ethics*, in order to clearly delineate the expected course of action for an accountant to take if those charged with governance do not respond to the issue appropriately.

If they **suspect** that an illegal act has taken place, accountants must take **reasonable steps to confirm** this (or dispel the suspicion). They must **discuss it with management**, and escalate it to higher levels of management if the response received is inadequate.

If an appropriate response is still not received, then the accountant's next action depends on whether they are dealing with an audit client or not:

- Audit client: **disclose to relevant authority**

- Non-audit client/'professional accountant in business': **disclose to the entity's external auditor** and, if possible, to a relevant authority

It may be necessary to **terminate the professional relationship** or, if the accountant is an employee, **resign from the organisation**.

3.3.2 2015 ED: *Responding to Non-Compliance with Laws and Regulations*

In May 2015 a further Exposure Draft was issued, *Responding to Non-Compliance with Laws and Regulations*, as a result of feedback from the 2012 ED on 'illegal acts'. A new framework was proposed which focused more on achieving outcomes that were in the public interest, ie trying to discourage professional accountants from 'turning a blind eye' to non-compliance.

We now have a new acronym: NOCLAR, or **N**on-**C**ompliance with **L**aws **A**nd **R**egulations.

The **objectives** of the framework are:

- To comply with the fundamental principles of integrity and professional behaviour

- By alerting management, to seek to:

    - Enable them to rectify, remediate or mitigate the consequences of the identified or suspected NOCLAR; or

    - Deter the commission of NOCLAR

- To take such further action as may be needed in the public interest.

The laws and regulations covered by the framework are those within the scope of the accountant's expertise, ie which are fundamental to the financial statements or to the client's business. Outside the scope are: matters which are clearly inconsequential; personal misconduct unrelated to a client's business, and; NOCLAR acts committed by someone other than the client.

Requirements of Auditors include:

- Raise the identified or suspected NOCLAR with management/TCWG.

- Fulfill professional responsibilities, eg comply with professional standards.

- Determine if further action (eg disclosure to relevant authority) is needed to achieve the objectives, depending on management's response.

- Document how the objectives have been met.

4 Specific guidance: conflicts of interest   6/09, 6/11

FAST FORWARD   Auditors should identify potential conflicts of interest, as they could result in the ethical codes being breached.

There are two kinds of conflict of interest:

- Conflicts between the interests of different clients
- Conflicts between members' and clients' interests

Audit firms should take reasonable steps to identify circumstances that could pose a conflict of interest.

Examples of conflicts of interest
Using **confidential information** obtained during an audit to help another client to acquire the audit client
Advising **two clients at the same time** who are competing to acquire the same company
Providing **services to both a vendor and a purchaser** in relation to the same transaction
Representing **two clients who are in a legal dispute** with each other (eg during divorce proceedings)
Advising a client to invest in a business in which, for example, the spouse of the professional accountant in public practice has a **financial interest**

The test of whether a threat is **significant** is whether a reasonable and informed third party, weighing all the specific facts and circumstances available to the professional accountant at the time, would be likely to conclude that compliance with the fundamental principles is not compromised.

The *Code* emphasises the importance of considering potential conflicts of interest **before accepting a new client**. An issue here is first **identifying that there is a conflict** – it may be that, for example, the engagement partner for a new client is not aware that there is a conflict because they do not know all of the firm's other clients. It is therefore necessary to have an **effective conflict identification process**.

As with all threats, **safeguards** should be applied if necessary. If safeguards would not be enough, then the engagement should be declined or discontinued.

Examples of safeguards
Disclosure of the nature of the conflict of interest (and related safeguards) to clients affected, to **obtain their consent** to the professional accountant performing the services
Mechanisms to **prevent unauthorised disclosure of confidential information**, such as: • Separate engagement teams • Creating separate areas of practice for specialty functions within the firm Establishing policies and procedures to limit access to client files
Review of safeguards by a senior individual not involved with the engagement(s)
External **review** by a professional accountant
Consulting with third parties, such as a professional body, legal counsel or another professional accountant

Disclosure is the key safeguard here. If the **client refuses** to give consent, then the engagement giving rise to the conflict should be discontinued.

5 Conflicts in application of the fundamental principles

FAST FORWARD

The *Codes* give some general guidance to members who encounter a conflict in the application of the fundamental principles.

5.1 The problem

Both the IESBA and ACCA *Codes* are principles-based. The application of the principles they contain requires a degree of **judgement** (much like the application of an ISA). As a result of this judgemental aspect, it is possible to have **more than one 'right answer' in a given situation** – more than one reasonable judgement of how the fundamental ethical principles should be applied.

Contrast this to the situation with a rules-based code of ethics. There, applying the rules strictly should result in only one possible outcome. It might not be an outcome that is ethical, eg because it is a result of a loophole, but it will be the only correct outcome (assuming that the rules themselves are not ambiguous). By contrast, a principles-based code may allow for several outcomes that are equally 'correct'.

What is at issue here is that there may be conflict between different ethical principles. The aim here must be to use judgement to resolve the conflict, or to try to balance the principles involved.

5.2 Matters to consider

The resolution process should include consideration of:

- Relevant facts – do I have all the relevant facts? Eg an organisation's policy and procedures

- Relevant parties – who is affected by the ethical issue? Eg shareholders, employees, employers, the public

- Ethical issues involved – what kinds of issues are these? Would they affect the profession's reputation? Eg professional ethical issues, personal ethical issues

- Fundamental principles related to the matter in question – what are the threats? Refer to ethical code

- Established internal procedures – are there procedures for dealing with this sort of situation? Eg discuss with your supervisor, or firm's legal department

- Alternative courses of action – have all the consequences been evaluated? Consider laws and regulations, long-term consequences, public consequences

5.2.1 Unresolved conflict

If the matter is unresolved, the member should consult with other appropriate persons within the firm. They may then wish to obtain advice from the ACCA or legal advisers. If after exhausting all relevant possibilities the ethical conflict remains unresolved, members should consider withdrawing from the engagement team, a specific assignment, or to resign altogether from the engagement.

5.3 Example

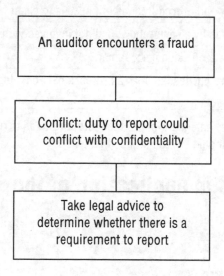

An auditor encounters a fraud

Conflict: duty to report could conflict with confidentiality

Take legal advice to determine whether there is a requirement to report

Chapter Roundup

- Accountants require an ethical code because they hold positions of trust, and people rely on them.

- The ACCA's guidance complies with the requirements of the IESBA *Code*.

- The ACCA and IESBA *Codes* give examples of a number of situations where independence might be threatened and suggest safeguards to independence.

- The ACCA and IESBA *Codes* recognise a duty of confidence and several exceptions to it.

- Auditors should identify potential conflicts of interest, as they could result in the ethical codes being breached.

- The *Codes* give some general guidance to members who encounter a conflict in the application of the fundamental principles.

Quick Quiz

1   Match the fundamental principle to the characteristic.

    (a)   Integrity

    (b)   Objectivity

        (i)   Members should be straightforward and honest in all professional and business relationships.

        (ii)   Members should not allow bias, conflict of interest or undue influence of others to override professional or business judgements.

2   Name five general threats to independence.

    (1)   ....

    (2)   ....

    (3)   ....

    (4)   ....

    (5)   ....

3   Name four relevant safeguards against a financial interest in a client.

    (1)   ....

    (2)   ....

    (3)   ....

    (4)   ....

4   Complete the definition:

.... are fees calculated on a predetermined basis relating to the outcome or result of a transaction or the result of the work performed.

5   Name four exceptions to the duty of confidentiality in which voluntary disclosure may be made.

1   (a)(i), (b)(ii)

2   (1)   Self-review
     (2)   Self-interest
     (3)   Familiarity
     (4)   Intimidation
     (5)   Advocacy

3   (1)   Disposing of the interest
     (2)   Removing the relevant individual from the assurance team
     (3)   Informing the audit committee of the situation
     (4)   Independent partner review of work undertaken

4   Contingent fees

5   In certain cases a professional accountant is free to disclose information, whatever its nature:

     •   When it is in the public interest
     •   In order to protect a professional accountant's interests
     •   Where it is authorised by statute
     •   To non-governmental bodies

Now try the questions below from the Practice Question Bank.

Number	Level	Marks	Time
Q2	Examination	15	29 mins
Q3	Examination	15	29 mins

Professional liability

Topic list	Syllabus reference
1 Legal liability	B3
2 Negligence	B3
3 Restricting liability	B3
4 Current issues in auditor liability	B3
5 Fraud and error	B2
6 The expectations gap	B3

Introduction

Auditors have responsibilities to several parties. This chapter explores the various **responsibilities** and the **liability that can arise** in respect of them. It also looks at ways of restricting liability, including professional indemnity insurance.

The auditors' responsibility to members and other readers of the accounts in tort and contract can give rise to **liability**, particularly in the event of **negligence**. Case law on this matter is complex and not wholly satisfactory. It results in auditors being liable to some readers and not others. However, **auditors' liability** is a dynamic issue in that it **evolves as cases are brought to court**.

There are some interesting issues for auditors with regard to liability, for example **limited liability partnerships**. This and other current issues pertaining to the topics covered in this chapter are discussed in Section 4.

Critically, and contrary to widespread public belief, **auditors do not have a responsibility to detect and prevent fraud**. The responsibilities that auditors do have with regard to fraud and error are outlined in Section 5. Auditors are required to follow the guidance of ISA 240 *The auditor's responsibilities relating to fraud in an audit of financial statements*.

Reasons for audit failure and other factors contributing to the 'expectation gap' are covered in Section 6.

Study guide

		Intellectual level
B2	**Fraud and error**	
(a)	Define and clearly distinguish between the terms 'error', 'irregularity', 'fraud' and 'misstatement'.	2
(b)	Compare and contrast the respective responsibilities of management and auditors for fraud and error.	2
(c)	Describe the matters to be considered and procedures to be carried out to investigate actual and/or potential misstatements in a given situation.	2
(d)	Explain how, why, when and to whom fraud and error should be reported and the circumstances in which an auditor should withdraw from an engagement.	2
(e)	Discuss the current and possible future role of auditors in preventing, detecting and reporting error and fraud.	2
B3	**Professional liability**	
(a)	Recognise circumstances in which professional accountants may have legal liability.	2
(b)	Describe the factors to determine whether or not an auditor is negligent in given situations.	2
(c)	Explain the other criteria for legal liability to be recognised (including 'due professional care' and 'proximity') and apply them to given situations.	2
(d)	Compare and contrast liability to client with liability to third parties.	3
(e)	Evaluate the practicability and effectiveness of ways in which liability may be restricted.	3
(f)	Discuss liability limitation agreements.	2
(g)	Discuss and appraise the principal causes of audit failure and other factors that contribute to the 'expectation gap' (eg responsibilities for fraud and error).	3
(h)	Recommend ways in which the expectation gap might be bridged.	2

Exam guide

Auditor liability is a key issue facing the profession globally, and is linked in with ongoing debate about the role of audit in the future. This area can be examined in topical discussion questions, or in practical scenarios considering whether an auditor may be held to have been negligent in specific circumstances.

The extent of the auditor's responsibilities in relation to fraud and error is a critical element of the public's perception of the auditor's role. The requirements of ISA 240 in this regard are core knowledge for this paper and may have to be applied in practical scenarios.

1 Legal liability

FAST FORWARD

> Professional accountants may have professional liability under statutory law.

The auditor has a contractual relationship with their client. If they breach the contract then they can be sued. In addition to this, auditors have a duty to carry out their work with reasonable skill and care.

Under certain legislation, notably **insolvency** legislation, auditors may be found to be officers of the company and could be charged with criminal offences or found liable for civil offences in connection with the winding up of the company.

Auditors may also be found guilty of financial market abuse offences, such as **insider dealing**, since they are privy to inside information and may use this information for their own gain.

Auditors could be found guilty of a criminal offence if they knew or suspected a person was laundering money and they failed to report their suspicions to the proper authority.

2 Negligence   6/10, 6/13

FAST FORWARD

Auditors may have professional liability in the tort of negligence.

Negligence is a common law concept. It seeks to provide compensation to a person who has suffered loss due to another person's wrongful neglect. To succeed in an action for negligence, an injured party must prove three things:

(a)   That a **duty of care** which is enforceable by law existed

(b)   This duty of care was **breached**

(c)   The breach caused the injured party **loss**. In the case of negligence in relation to financial advisers/auditors, this loss must be pecuniary (ie financial) loss.

2.1 Who might bring an action for negligence?

The parties likely to want to bring an action in negligence against the auditors, for example, if they have given the wrong audit opinion through lack of care, include:

- The company
- Shareholders
- The bank
- Other lenders
- Other interested third parties

A key difference between the various potential claimants is the extent of the **proximity** between the auditor and the potential claimant, and whether the relationship is sufficiently **proximal** for the auditor to owe them a **duty of care**.

2.2 The audit client

FAST FORWARD

The auditor owes a duty of care to the audit client automatically under law.

The audit client is the **company**. It is a basic maxim of company law that the company is **all of the shareholders acting as a body**. In other words, the 'company' cannot be represented by a single shareholder.

| COMPANY | = | SHAREHOLDERS AS A BODY |

| COMPANY | ≱ | SHAREHOLDER | + | SHAREHOLDER |

The **company** has a **contract** with the auditor. In the law of many countries, a contract for the supply of a service such as an audit contains a duty of reasonable care implied by statute.

In other words, whatever the express terms of any written contract between the company and the audit firm, the law always implies a duty of care into it. Therefore, if the company (all the shareholders acting as a body) wants to bring a case for negligence, the situation would be as follows.

Client	
Duty of care exists?	AUTOMATIC
Breached?	MUST BE PROVED
Loss arising?	MUST BE PROVED

In order to prove whether a duty of care had been breached, the court has to give further consideration to what the duty of 'reasonable' care means in practice.

2.2.1 The auditor's duty of care

The standard of work of auditors is generally as defined by legislation. A number of judgements made in law cases show how the auditor's duty of care has been gauged at various points in time because legislation often does not state clearly the manner in which the auditors should discharge their duty of care. It is also not likely that this would be clearly spelt out in any contract setting out the terms of an auditor's appointment.

Exam focus point

You are not expected to know all the precise details of the cases described in this section for your exam. At Paper P7 level, you will not just be tested on your knowledge in the exam but also on your ability to apply what you know – perhaps to specific scenarios. The cases here are useful illustrations of the issues surrounding the professional liability of auditors, and will help you get to know the main principles which you will then have to apply in your exam.

 Case Study

Re Kingston Cotton Mill 1896

When Lopes L J considered the degree of skill and care required of an auditor he declared:

'... it is the duty of an auditor to bring to bear on the work he has to perform that skill, care and caution which a reasonably competent, careful and cautious auditor would use. What is reasonable skill, care and caution, must depend on the particular circumstances of each case.'

Lopes was careful to point out that what constitutes reasonable care depends very much on the **facts** of a particular case. Another criteria by which the courts will determine the adequacy of the auditors' work is by assessing it in relation to the generally accepted auditing standards of the day.

 Case Study

The courts will be very much concerned with accepted advances in auditing techniques, demonstrated by Pennycuick J in *Re Thomas Gerrard & Son Ltd 1967* where he observed:

'... the real ground on which *Re Kingston Cotton Mill* ... is, I think, capable of being distinguished is that the standards of reasonable care and skill are, upon the expert evidence, more exacting today than those which prevailed in 1896.'

 Case Study

Lord Denning in the case of *Fomento (Sterling Area) Ltd v Selsdon Fountain Pen Co Ltd 1958* sought to define the auditor's proper approach to their work by saying:

'... they must come to it with an inquiring mind – not suspicious of dishonesty ... – but suspecting that someone may have made a mistake somewhere and that a check must be made to ensure that there has been none.'

The auditors have a responsibility to keep themselves abreast of professional developments. Auditing standards are likely to be taken into account when the adequacy of the work of auditors is being considered in a court of law or in other contested situations.

When the auditors are exercising judgement they must act both honestly and carefully. Obviously, if auditors are to be 'careful' in forming an opinion, they must give due consideration to all relevant matters. Provided they do this and can be seen to have done so, then their opinion should be above criticism.

However if the opinion reached by the auditors is one that no reasonably competent auditor would have been likely to reach, then they would still possibly be held negligent. This is because however carefully the auditors may appear to have approached their work, it clearly could not have been careful enough, if it enabled them to reach a conclusion which would be generally regarded as unacceptable.

If the auditors' suspicions are aroused, they must conduct further investigations until such suspicions are either confirmed or allayed. Over the years, there have been many occasions where the courts have had to consider cases in which it has been held, on the facts of those cases, that the auditors ought to have been put upon enquiry.

2.3 Third parties

FAST FORWARD

The auditor only owes a duty of care to parties other than the audit client if one has been established.

'Third parties' in this context means anyone other than the company (audit client) who wishes to make a claim for negligence. It therefore includes any individual shareholders in the company and any potential investors. It also includes, importantly, the bank, who is very often a key financier of the company.

The key difference between third parties and the company is that third parties have no contract with the audit firm, thus there is therefore no implied duty of care. The situation is therefore as follows.

Third parties	
Duty of care exists?	MUST BE PROVED
Breached?	MUST BE PROVED
Loss arising?	MUST BE PROVED

Traditionally the courts have been **averse** to **attributing a duty of care to third parties** to the auditor. We can see this by looking at some past cases that have gone to court.

A **very important case** is *Caparo Industries plc v Dickman and Others 1990*, which is described here.

 Case Study

The **facts as pleaded** were that in 1984 Caparo Industries purchased 100,000 Fidelity shares in the open market. On 12 June 1984, the date on which the financial statements (audited by Touche Ross) were published, they purchased a further 50,000 shares. Relying on information in the financial statements, further shares were acquired. On 4 September, Caparo made a bid for the remainder and by October had acquired control of Fidelity. Caparo alleged that the financial statements on which they had relied were misleading in that an apparent pre-tax profit of some £1.3 million should in fact have been shown as a loss of over £400,000. The plaintiffs argued that Touche owed a duty of care to investors and potential investors.

The conclusion of the **House of Lords** hearing of the case in February 1990 was that the auditors of a public company's financial statements owed **no duty of care** to members of the public at large who relied on the financial statements in deciding to buy shares in the company. And as a purchaser of further shares, while relying on the auditor's report, a shareholder stood in the same position as any other investing member of the public to whom the auditor owed no duty. The purpose of the audit was simply that of fulfilling the statutory requirements of the Companies Act. There was nothing in the statutory duties of company auditors to suggest that they were intended to protect the interests of investors in the market.

And in particular, there was no reason why any special relationship should be held to arise simply from the fact that the affairs of the company rendered it susceptible to a takeover bid.

In its report *The Financial Aspects of Corporate Governance*, the Cadbury Committee gave an opinion on the situation as reflected in the *Caparo* ruling. It felt that *Caparo* did not lessen auditors' duty to use skill and care because auditors are **still fully liable in negligence** to the companies they audit and their shareholders collectively. Given the number of different users of financial statements, it was impossible for the House of Lords to have broadened the boundaries of the auditor's legal duty of care.

The decision in *Caparo v Dickman* considerably **narrowed the auditor's potential liability to third parties**. The judgement appears to imply that members of various such user groups, which could include suppliers, potential investors or others, will not be able to sue the auditors for negligence by virtue of their placing reliance on audited annual financial statements, as their relationship with the auditor is **insufficiently proximate**.

 Case Study

In *James McNaughton Paper Group Ltd v Hicks Anderson & Co 1990,* Lord Justice Neill set out the following position in the light of *Caparo* and earlier cases.

(a)   'In England a restrictive approach was now adopted to any extension of the scope of the duty of care beyond the person directly intended by the maker of the statement to act upon it.

(b)   In deciding whether a duty of care existed in any particular case it was necessary to take all the circumstances into account.

(c)   Notwithstanding (b), it was possible to identify certain matters which were likely to be of importance in most cases in reaching a decision as to whether or not a duty existed.'

A more recent court case produced a **development** in the subject of audit liability. In December 1995, a High Court judge awarded electronic security group ADT £65m plus interest and costs (£40m) in damages for negligence against the former BDO Binder Hamlyn (BBH) partnership.

 Case Study

The firm had jointly audited the 1988/89 financial statements of Britannia Security Group (BSG), which ADT acquired in 1990 for £105m, but later found to be worth only £40m. Although, under *Caparo*, auditors do not owe a duty of care in general to third parties, the judge found that BBH audit partner Martyn Bishop, who confirmed that the firm stood by BSG's financial statements at a meeting with ADT in the run-up to the acquisition, had thereby **taken on a contractual relationship** with ADT. This development occurred, apparently, because (post-*Caparo*) solicitors and bankers were advising clients intent on acquisitions to get direct assurances from the target's auditors on the truth and fairness of the financial statements.

BBH appealed this decision; the liable partners, because of a shortfall in insurance cover, were left facing the prospect of coming up with £34m. An out of court settlement was reached with ADT.

A case in 1997 appeared to take a slightly different line, although this case related to some management accounts on which no written report had been issued.

 Case Study

In *Peach Publishing Ltd v Slater & Co 1997* the Court of Appeal ruled that accountants are not automatically liable if they give oral assurances on accounts to the purchaser of a business. The case involved management accounts, which the accountant stated were right subject to the qualification that

they had not been audited. The Court held that the purpose of giving the assurance was not to take on responsibility to the purchaser for the accuracy of the accounts. The purchaser's true objective in this case was to obtain a warranty from the accountant's client, the target. Therefore the accountant was not assuming responsibility to the purchaser by giving their client information on which it could decide whether or not to give the warranty. The Court of Appeal also observed that the purchaser should not have relied on the management accounts without having them checked by its advisers.

 ## Case Study

In a further case, the Court of Appeal gave guidance on the effect of a disclaimer which stated that the report had been prepared for the client only and no-one else should rely on it. In *Omega Trust Co Ltd v Wright Son & Pepper 1997* (which related to surveyors but the facts of which can be applied to accountants) the court held that the surveyor was entitled to know who their client was and to whom their duty was held. They were entitled to refuse liability to an unknown lender or any known lender with whom he had not agreed.

All this case law raised some **problems**. In spite of the judgement in *Caparo*, the commercial reality is that creditors and investors (especially institutional ones) do use audited financial statements. In the UK the Companies Act requires a company to file financial statements with the Registrar. Why is this a statutory requirement? It is surely because the public, including creditors and potential investors, have a need for a credible and independent view of the company's performance and position.

It would be unjust if auditors, who have **secondary responsibility** for financial statements being prepared negligently, bore the full responsibility for losses arising from such negligence just because they are insured. It would also be unjust if the auditors could be sued by all and sundry. While the profession has generally welcomed *Caparo*, two obvious problems are raised by the decision.

- Is a restricted view of the usefulness of audited financial statements in the profession's long-term interests?

- For private companies there will probably be an increase in the incidence of personal guarantees and warranties given by the directors to banks and suppliers.

Developments in the US in recent years appear to try to redress the **balance of liability** by highlighting the responsibilities of management with regard to published financial statements. The Sarbanes-Oxley Act requires chief executive officers and finance officers to certify that the financial statements of listed companies are not misleading and present the company's financial position and results fairly. In addition, they are required to confirm that they are responsible for internal controls and have reported significant control deficiencies to the auditors/audit committee.

The UK Companies Act 2006 requires the directors' report to contain a statement to the effect that, in the case of each director:

(a) So far as the director is aware, there is no relevant audit information of which the auditor is unaware

(b) They have taken all the steps that they ought to have taken as a director in order to make themselves aware of any relevant audit information and to establish that the auditor is aware of that information

If the statement in the directors' report is false, every director who knew it was false or who was reckless as to whether it was false, and failed to take reasonable steps to prevent the report from being approved, commits an offence.

In addition, Companies Act 2006 now makes it possible for auditors to limit their liability by agreement with a company. We will look at this issue in more detail in Section 4.

2.3.1 Banks and other major lenders

Banks and other major lenders have generally been **excluded** from the extent of negligent auditor's liability by the decision in *Caparo*.

Banks often include clauses in loan agreements referring to audited financial statements and requesting that they have access to audited financial statements on a regular basis or when reviewing the loan facility. In other words, banks may **document a 'relationship'** with the auditors to establish that there is sufficient proximity and that a duty of care exists.

The following Scottish case involved a situation similar to this.

 Case Study

In *Royal Bank of Scotland v Bannerman Johnstone Maclay and Others 2002* the bank, who provided an overdraft facility to the company being audited, claimed the company had misstated its position due to a fraud and that the auditors were negligent in not discovering the fraud. The auditors claimed that they had no duty of care to the bank. However, the judge determined that the auditors would have known that the bank required audited financial statements as part of the overdraft arrangement and could have issued a disclaimer to the bank. The fact that they had not issued a disclaimer was an important factor in deciding that the auditors did owe a duty of care to the bank.

2.3.2 Assurance services

The audit firm might be able and prepared to **offer assurances** to the bank in relation to financial statements, position, internal controls or other matters of interest to a primary lender. If this is the case, and the service is required by the bank, the **auditor should seek to create an engagement with the bank itself**.

You should bear in mind that providing assurance services to a lender could result in a **conflict of interest** arising, of course.

Exam focus point

It is vital that you use the right kind of **language** when answering questions in this area. Your correct use of such terms as **duty of care**, **liability**, **negligence**, **proximity** and **third party** can help to demonstrate to the marker that you are familiar with the subject matter and are simply **applying** it to the circumstances in the question.

2.4 Disclaimers   6/08

FAST FORWARD

Auditors may attempt to limit liability to clients. This may not always be effective in law.

The cases above suggest that a duty of care to a third party may arise when an accountant does not know that their work will be relied on by a third party, but only knows that it is work of a kind which is liable in the ordinary course of events to be relied on by a third party.

Conversely, an accountant may sometimes be informed or be aware, before they carry out certain work, that a third party will rely on the results. An example is a report on the business of a client which the accountant has been instructed to prepare for the purpose of being shown to a potential purchaser or potential creditor of that business. In such a case, an accountant should assume that they will be held to owe the same duty to the third party as to their client. The Bannermann case suggests this will also be necessary for **audit work**. Since the Bannermann case, many audit firms have included a disclaimer in their audit report.

When ACCA's Council considered the use of disclaimers, its view was:

'Standard disclaimers are not an appropriate or proportionate response to the Bannermann decision. Their incorporation as a standard feature of the audit report could have the effect of devaluing that report.'

BPP
LEARNING MEDIA

However, there are areas of professional work (for example when acting as an auditor under the Companies Act on behalf of shareholders and no liability limitation agreement is in place) where it is not possible for liability to be limited or excluded. There are other areas of professional work (for example when preparing reports on a business for the purpose of being submitted to a potential purchaser) where, although such a limitation or exclusion may be included, its effectiveness will depend on the view that a court may subsequently form of its reasonableness.

2.5 Litigation avoidance

The other aspect of how firms are trying to deal with litigation is what they are trying to do to avoid litigation. This strategy has various aspects.

- **Client acceptance procedures**. These are very important, particularly the screening of new clients and the use of engagement letters. This is covered in more detail in Chapter 5.

- **Performance of audit work**. Firms should make sure that all audits are carried out in accordance with professional standards and best practice.

- **Quality control**. This includes not just controls over individual audits but also stricter 'whole-firm' procedures. This is considered in more detail in Chapter 4.

- **Issue of appropriate disclaimers**. We discussed above the importance of these.

In ACCA's view the best way of restricting liability is for auditors to carry out their audit work in accordance with auditing standards. Where work is properly conducted the auditor should not need to subject it to blanket disclaimers.

Exam focus point

> Read the financial and accountancy press on a regular basis between now and your examination and note any new cases or developments in the question of auditor liability.

Question
Negligence claims

Although auditors can incur civil liability under various statutes, it is far more likely that they will incur liability for negligence under the common law, as the majority of cases against auditors have been in this area. Auditors must be fully aware of the extent of their responsibilities, together with the steps they must take to minimise the danger of professional negligence claims.

Required

(a) Discuss the extent of an auditor's responsibilities to shareholders and others during the course of their normal professional engagement.

(b) List six steps which auditors should take to minimise the danger of claims against them for negligent work.

Answer

(a) *Responsibility under statute*

An auditor of a limited company has a responsibility, imposed upon him by statute, to form and express a professional opinion on the financial statements presented by the directors to the shareholders. He must report upon the truth and fairness of such statements and the fact that they comply with the law. In so doing, the auditor owes a duty of care to the company imposed by statute. But such duty also arises under contract and may also arise under the common law (law of tort).

Responsibility under contract

In the UK the Companies Act does not state expressly the manner in which the auditor should discharge their duty of care; neither is it likely that this would be clearly spelt out in any contract setting out the terms of an auditor's appointment (eg the engagement letter). Although the articles of

a company may extend the auditor's responsibilities beyond those envisaged by the Companies Act, they cannot be used so as to restrict the auditor's statutory duties; neither may they place any restriction upon the auditor's statutory rights which are designed to assist them in the discharge of those duties.

The comments of Lopes L J when considering the degree of skill and care required of an auditor in *Re Kingston Cotton Mill 1896* are still relevant.

> '... It is the duty of an auditor to bring to bear on the work he has to perform the skill, care and caution which a reasonably competent, careful and cautious auditor would use. What is reasonable skill, care and caution must depend on the particular circumstances of each case.'

Clearly, with the advent of auditing standards, a measure of good practice is now available for the courts to take into account when considering the adequacy of the work of the auditor.

Responsibility in tort

The law of tort has established that a person owes a duty of care and skill to 'our neighbours' (common and well-known examples of this neighbour principle can be seen in the law of trespass, slander, libel and so on). In the context of the professional auditor the wider implications, however, concern the extent to which the auditor owes a duty of care and skill to third parties who rely on financial statements upon which they have reported but with whom he has no direct contractual or fiduciary relationship.

Liability to third parties

In *Caparo Industries plc v Dickman & Others 1990*, it was held that the auditors of a public company's financial statements owed no duty of care to members of the general public who relied upon the financial statements in deciding to buy shares in the company. Furthermore as a purchaser of more shares, a shareholder placing reliance on the auditor's report stood in the same position as any other investing member of the public to whom the auditor owed no duty. This decision appeared to radically reverse the tide of cases concerning the auditor's duty of care. The purpose of the audit was simply that of meeting the statutory requirements of the Companies Act. There was nothing in the statutory duties of a company auditor to suggest that they were intended to protect the interests of investors in the market. In particular, there was no reason why any special relationship should be held to arise simply from the fact that the affairs of the company rendered it susceptible to a takeover bid.

The case between BDO Binder Hamlyn and ADT seems to have moved the argument on. In this case, it was argued that proximity between a prospective investor and the auditor of a company could be created if the investor asked the auditor whether they stood by their last audit. An appeal is likely in this case, as the auditor involved face a large shortfall in the proceeds of an insurance claim. The Scottish Bannerman case suggests that judges may be more likely to impute a duty of care to the auditors if they were aware that the bank made use of audited financial statements and did not disclaim liability to them.

(b) In order to provide a means of protection for the auditor arising from the comments in (a) above, the following steps should be taken.

   (i) Agreements concerning the duties of the auditor should be:

      (1) Clear and precise

      (2) In writing

      (3) Confirmed by a letter of engagement, including matters specifically excluded

   (ii) Audit work should be:

      (1) Relevant to the system of internal control, which must be ascertained, evaluated and tested. Controls cannot be entirely ignored: for the auditor to have any confidence in an accounting system, there must be present and evident the existence of minimum controls to ensure completeness and accuracy of the records

      (2) Adequately planned before the audit commences

      (3) Reviewed by a senior member of the firm to ensure quality control of the audit and to enable a decision to be made on the form of audit report

(iii) Any queries arising during the audit should be:

    (1) Recorded on the current working papers

    (2) Cleared and filed

(iv) A management letter should be:

    (1) Submitted to the client or the board of directors in writing immediately following an audit

    (2) Seen to be acted on by the client

(v) All members of an auditing firm should be familiar with:

    (1) The standards expected throughout the firm

    (2) The standards of the profession as a whole by means of adequate training, which should cover the implementation of the firm's audit manual and the recommendations of the professional accountancy bodies

(vi) Insurance should be taken out to cover the firm against possible claims.

3 Restricting liability

FAST FORWARD

ACCA requires that auditors take out professional indemnity insurance.

Whether an auditor can restrict their liability to clients **depends on the jurisdiction** in question. Historically it has been rare for liability to be restricted, but there are now some important exceptions to this such as the UK (see section 4.1 below).

3.1 Professional indemnity insurance (PII)

Key terms

> **Professional indemnity insurance (PII)** is insurance against civil claims made by clients and third parties arising from work undertaken by the firm.
>
> **Fidelity guarantee insurance** is insurance against liability arising through any acts of fraud or dishonesty by any partner, director or employee in respect of money or goods held in trust by the firm.

These types of insurance do not actually restrict the auditor's liability, but rather provide compensation to the auditor for liabilities that are incurred.

It is important that auditors have insurance so that if negligence occurs:

- The audit firm does not find itself with a liability that is too big for it to pay; and

- The client can be **compensated** for the error. An insurance policy would enable this to happen even where the compensation is greater than the resources of the firm.

Remember that accountants usually trade as **partnerships**, so all the partners are jointly and severally liable to claims made against individual partners.

3.2 ACCA requirements

ACCA requires that all firms which hold practising and auditing certificates have PII with a reputable insurance company. If the firm has employees, it must also have fidelity guarantee insurance.

The insurance must cover 'all civil liability incurred in connection with the conduct of the firm's business by the partners, directors or employees'.

The cover must continue to exist for **six years** after a member ceases to engage in public practice.

3.3 Advantages and disadvantages

The key **advantage** of such insurance is that it provides funds for an innocent party to be compensated in the event of a wrong having been done to it.

An **advantage** to the auditor is that it provides some protection against bankruptcy in the event of successful litigation against the firm. This is particularly important for a partnership, as partners may be sued personally for the negligence of their fellow partners.

A key **disadvantage** is that the existence of insurance against the cost of negligence might encourage auditors to take less care than:

- Would otherwise be the case
- Their professional duty requires

Another problem associated with such insurances are that there are limits of cover (linked with the cost of buying the insurance) and any compensation arising from a claim could be higher than those limits. This could lead to partners being bankrupted despite having insurance. A simple disadvantage associated with the above is the regular cost of the insurance to the partnership.

3.4 Incorporation

The major accountancy firms have been interested in methods of reducing personal liability for partners in the event of negligence for some time. For example, some years ago KPMG (one of the Big Four accountancy firms) incorporated its UK audit practice. This was allowed under the UK's Companies Act 1989.

The new arrangement created 'a firm within a firm'. KPMG Audit plc is a limited company wholly owned by the partnership, KPMG. The reason behind this is to protect the partners from the crushing effects of litigation. The other side of incorporation means that KPMG Audit plc is subject to the statutory disclosure requirements of companies.

An alternative to incorporation as a company is incorporation as a limited liability partnership.

Limited liability partnership can be operated in some countries, for example some US states and the UK, which we will look at briefly below.

3.5 Limited liability partnerships

The Limited Liability Partnership Act 2000 enabled UK firms to establish limited liability partnerships as separate legal entities. These combine the flexibility and tax status of a partnership with limited liability for members.

The effect of this is that **the partnership, but not its members, will be liable to third parties**. However, the personal assets of **negligent** partners will still be at risk.

Limited liability partnerships could be formed from 6 April 2001. Several prominent professional partnerships have incorporated as LLPs.

Limited liability partnerships are set up by similar procedures to those for incorporating a company. An incorporation document is sent to the Registrar of Companies. The Registrar will issue a certificate of incorporation to confirm that all statutory requirements have been fulfilled.

In a similar way to traditional partnerships, relations between partners will be governed by internal partner agreements, or by future statutory regulations. Each member of the partnership will still be an agent of the partnership unless they have no authority to act and an outside party is aware of this lack of authority.

3.6 Advantages and disadvantages of different structures

	Advantages	Disadvantages
Partnership	• Less regulation than for companies • Financial statements not on public record	• Joint and several liability • Personal assets at risk
Incorporation	• Limited liability	• Public filing of audited financial statements • Management must comply with Companies Acts
LLP	• Protection of personal assets • Limited liability of members • Similar tax effect of partnership • Flexible management structures	• Public filing of audited financial statements

4 Current issues in auditor liability

FAST FORWARD ▶▶ | Auditor liability is an important practical issue.

Even with PII and other means of restricting liability there has been great concern throughout the audit profession globally about the remaining risks to firms' survival in the face of claims which might exceed their insurance cover.

The profession has lobbied for further protection in the form of **proportionate liability** or **capping liability**.

Key terms

Proportionate liability allows claims arising from successful negligence claims to be split between the auditors and the directors of the client company, the split being determined by a judge on the basis of where the fault was seen to lie. This would require the approval of shareholders.

Capping liability sets a maximum limit on the amount that the auditor would have to pay out under any claim.

4.1 UK Companies Act 2006

The Companies Act 2006 made it possible for auditors to limit their liability by agreement with a company. It does this by defining a **liability limitation agreement**, which is a contractual limitation of the auditor's liability to a company, requiring shareholder agreement by resolution and only effective if it is **fair and reasonable**.

The agreement can cover liability for negligence, default, breach of duty or breach of trust by the auditor in relation to the audit of financial statements for a particular year. For the agreement to be valid it cannot cover more than one financial year. The company can also withdraw its authorisation of the agreement by passing an ordinary resolution.

It is currently open to negotiation between auditors and their client companies as to what form the agreement will take, for example a liability cap (fixed or variable), or proportionate liability but the Act leaves it open for the Government to issue regulations in future as to the nature of these agreements.

Under current legislation, it is possible for auditors to suffer the entire liability for corporate collapse even if they are found to be only partly to blame. The Big Four firms lobbied the then Department of Business, Enterprise and Regulatory Reform (BERR) to get a limit on their exposure in the event of claims from investors and others in the event of a company failure. This was prompted by fears that a blockbuster lawsuit, if successful, could put one or more of them out of business, which in turn could trigger a collapse of the audit market and cause chaos for business.

The Big Four have been pushing for proportionate liability ever since the collapse of Arthur Andersen, then one of the world's five biggest accounting firms, over its involvement in the Enrol scandal in 2002.

4.2 Ongoing debate

There have been concerns that regulations such as the UK Companies Act 2006 may distort competition in the audit market. If the biggest firms set caps at very high levels, mid-tier firms could be disadvantaged. In the UK the Government has left a provision for the relevant government ministers to issue specific rules specifying what can and cannot be included in agreements in case competition problems arise.

There are also arguments that capping liability will reduce the value of the audit to investors and may put pressure on firms to reduce fees.

Overall, the profession has reacted positively to these rules. The reaction was less positive to the other major effect of the bill, introducing a criminal offence of 'knowingly or recklessly' including in the auditor's report any matter that is misleading, false or deceptive in a material particular. The Government saw this as being a necessary change in order to maintain audit quality.

4.3 Network firms

Several accountancy firms have moved towards network models over recent years. This is where member firms are part of a larger structure, often sharing a name (or using a similar name) and professional resources. As part of a global network, member firms have been able to sell services based on the value and reputation of their global brand name. However in recent liability cases, some network firms have claimed the network is not liable for negligence in an individual member firm even though they appear to be operating under the same brand.

 Case Study

BDO Seidman, a member firm of the global network BDO International, faced audit negligence claims to the sum of $500m over the audit of ES Bankest, a company owned by the Portuguese bank Banco Espirito Santo. Auditors from BDO Seidman had been accused of being grossly negligent in audits some seven years previously. BDO International had claimed that they should not be held liable as member firm audits are conducted independently.

It is possible that the network model may disappear or be modified in future years. The current situation where network firms advertise under one brand and then claim they are separate firms when things go wrong may not be sustainable given the outcome of current legal activity.

Point to note There is a useful article on auditor liability on the ACCA website, entitled 'Auditor liability: 'fair and reasonable' punishment?'

5 Fraud and error

6/09, 6/13

FAST FORWARD Misunderstanding of the auditor's responsibilities in respect of fraud is a major component of the 'expectations gap'.

The key difference between fraud and error is that fraud is intentional.

5.1 What is fraud?

Key term

Fraud is an **intentional** act by one or more individuals among management, those charged with governance (management fraud), employees (employee fraud) or third parties involving the use of deception to obtain an unjust or illegal advantage. Fraud may be perpetrated by an individual, or in collusion with people internal or external to the business.

Fraud is a wide legal concept, but the auditor's main concern is with fraud that causes a material misstatement in financial statements. Specifically, there are two types of fraud causing material misstatement in financial statements:

- Fraudulent financial reporting
- Misappropriation of assets

Fraud is distinguished from error, which is when a material misstatement is caused by mistake, for example in the application of an accounting policy. Other examples of errors are mistakes in gathering or processing financial data, and errors in making accounting estimates.

5.1.1 Fraudulent financial reporting

This may include:

- Manipulation, falsification or alteration of accounting records/supporting documents
- Misrepresentation (or omission) of events, transactions or other significant information in the financial statements
- Intentional misapplication of accounting principles

Such fraud may be carried out by overriding controls that would otherwise appear to be operating effectively, eg by recording fictitious journal entries or improperly adjusting assumptions or estimates used in financial reporting.

Aggressive earnings management is a topical issue and, at its most aggressive, may constitute fraudulent financial reporting. Auditors should consider such issues as unsuitable revenue recognition, accruals, liabilities, provisions and reserves accounting and large numbers of immaterial breaches of financial reporting requirements to see whether together, they constitute fraud.

Exam focus point

Revenue recognition is perhaps the single most common area of fraudulent financial reporting, and is an area that your examination team has highlighted as important. If a scenario in your exam features complex or material revenue recognition, immediately think 'risk of fraudulent financial reporting'.

5.1.2 Misappropriation of assets

This is the theft of the entity's assets (for example, cash, inventory). Employees may be involved in such fraud in small and immaterial amounts; however, it can also be carried out by management for larger items who may then conceal the misappropriation, for example by:

- Embezzling receipts (for example, diverting them to private bank accounts)
- Stealing physical assets or intellectual property (inventory, sales data)
- Causing an entity to pay for goods not received (payments to fictitious vendors)
- Using assets for personal use

From the auditor's point of view, the main problem with theft is while it is ongoing and undiscovered, it may result in the accounting records being misstated. For example, if inventory is stolen then the accounting records will show more items in inventory than there really are.

5.2 Responsibilities with regard to fraud

FAST FORWARD

Management and those charged with governance are primarily responsible for preventing and detecting fraud.

It is up to **management** to put a strong emphasis within the company on fraud prevention, putting in place **systems to prevent fraud**.

Management must also establish a **strong control environment**, with an emphasis on the principles of good corporate governance but also a **culture** of honesty and ethical behaviour. In relation to fraud in particular, this would mean eg putting policies in place to help ensure that employees are aware of their responsibilities regarding fraud, issuing guidance for employees on what they should do if they encounter or suspect a fraud.

Auditors are responsible for carrying out an audit in accordance with international auditing standards, one of which is ISA 240 *The auditor's responsibilities relating to fraud in an audit of financial statements*, which we shall look at now. The **auditor is not responsible for preventing fraud**; the auditor may be deemed responsible only if they have not conducted their audit properly.

5.3 The auditor's approach to the possibility of fraud

5.3.1 General

The key responsibility of an auditor is set out early in ISA 240: essentially the auditor is only concerned about fraud if it causes the financial statements to be misstated. The auditor's concern is with misstatements, whatever their cause. The main objective is to obtain reasonable assurance that there are no material misstatements, whether they are caused by fraud or by error.

Fraud and error are, however, different. If the auditor is to detect misstatements caused by fraud, then they must focus on the risks that are specific to fraud. ISA 240 therefore gives the following objectives, which are specific to fraud.

> **ISA 240.10**
>
> The objectives of the auditor are:
>
> (a)   To identify and assess the risks of material misstatement of the financial statements due to fraud;
>
> (b)   To obtain sufficient appropriate audit evidence regarding the assessed risks of material misstatement due to fraud, through designing and implementing appropriate responses; and
>
> (c)   To respond appropriately to fraud or suspected fraud identified during the audit.

Fraud may be harder to detect than error, because with a fraud the fraudster is actively trying to hide what they have done.

An overriding requirement of the ISA is that auditors are aware of the possibility of there being misstatements due to fraud. The mindset of **professional scepticism** is important here, with the auditor always being alert to the possibility that things are not as they seem, and that the management who have always appeared honest may not really be.

5.3.2 Discussion with the engagement team

ISA 240 requires there to be discussion by members of the engagement team of the susceptibility of the entity's financial statements to material misstatement due to fraud, including how fraud might occur.

The engagement partner must consider what matters discussed should be passed on to other members of the team not present at the discussion. The discussion itself usually includes consideration of:

- How fraud could be done
- Circumstances that might be indicative of aggressive earnings management
- Known factors that might give incentive to management to commit fraud
- Management's oversight of employees with access to cash/other assets
- Any unusual/unexplained changes in lifestyle of management/employees
- How to maintain professional scepticism throughout the audit
- The types of circumstance that might indicate fraud
- How unpredictability will be incorporated into the audit

- What audit procedures might be carried out to answer any suspicions of fraud
- Any allegations of fraud that have come to the auditors' attention
- The risk of management override of controls.

5.3.3 Risk assessment procedures

The auditor would undertake risk assessment procedures as set out in ISA 315 *Identifying and assessing the risks of material misstatement through understanding the entity and its environment* (see Chapter 6) which would include assessing the risk of fraud. These will include:

- Inquiries of management and those charged with governance
- Consideration of whether fraud risk factors are present
- Consideration of results of analytical procedures
- Consideration of any other relevant information

In identifying the risks of fraud, the auditor is required by the ISA to carry out some specific procedures.

The auditor must ask management about:

- Management's assessment of the risk of misstatement due to fraud
- How management identifies and responds to fraud risks, and details of any specific risks identified
- Whether they know of any actual or suspected fraud.

If the entity has an **internal audit function**, the auditor must ask it for its views on the risks of fraud, and whether fraud has taken place.

The size, complexity and ownership characteristics of the entity have a significant influence on the consideration of relevant fraud risk factors. For example in the case of a large entity there may be factors that generally constrain improper conduct by management including effective oversight by those charged with governance, an effective internal audit function and a written code of conduct. These considerations are less likely in the case of a small entity.

Examples of fraud risk factors

ISA 240 does not attempt to provide a definitive list of risk factors but, in an appendix, identifies and gives examples of two types of fraud that are relevant to auditors:

- Fraudulent financial reporting
- Misstatements arising from misappropriation of assets

For each of these, the risk factors are classified according to three conditions that are generally present when misstatements due to fraud occur:

- Incentives/pressures
- Opportunities
- Attitudes/rationalisations

Fraudulent financial reporting

Incentives/pressures
- Financial stability/profitability is threatened
- Pressure on management to meet the expectations of third parties
- Personal financial situation of management threatened by the entity's financial performance
- Excessive pressure on management or operating personnel to meet financial targets

Opportunities
- Significant related-party transactions
- Assets, liabilities, revenues or expenses based on significant estimates
- Domination of management by a single person or small group
- Complex or unstable organisational structure
- Internal control components are deficient

Attitudes/rationalisations
- Ineffective communication or enforcement of the entity's values or ethical standards by management
- Known history of violations of securities laws or other laws and regulations
- A practice by management of committing to achieve aggressive or unrealistic forecasts
- Low morale among senior management
- Relationship between management and the current or predecessor auditor is strained

Misappropriation of assets

Incentives/pressures
- Personal financial obligations
- Adverse relationships between the entity and employees with access to cash or other assets susceptible to theft

Opportunities
- Large amounts of cash on hand or processed
- Inventory items that are small in size, of high value, or in high demand
- Easily convertible assets, such as bearer bonds, diamonds, or computer chips
- Inadequate internal control over assets

Attitudes/rationalisations
- Overriding existing controls
- Failing to correct known internal control deficiencies
- Behaviour indicating displeasure or dissatisfaction with the entity
- Changes in behaviour or lifestyle

ISA 240.26

When identifying and assessing the risks of material misstatement due to fraud, the auditor shall, based on a presumption that there are risks of fraud in revenue recognition, evaluate which types of revenue, revenue transactions or assertions give rise to such risks.

ISA 240.27

The auditor shall treat those assessed risks of material misstatement due to fraud as significant risks and accordingly, to the extent not already done so, the auditor shall obtain an understanding of the entity's related controls, including control activities, relevant to such risks.

Generally, the auditor:

- Identifies fraud risks
- Relates this to what could go wrong at a financial statement level
- Considers the likely magnitude of potential misstatement

Question | **Fraud risk factors**

You are an audit manager for Elle and Emm, Chartered Certified Accountants. You are carrying out the planning of the audit of Sellfones Co, a listed company, and a high street retailer of mobile phones, for the year ending 30 September 20X7. The notes from your planning meeting with Pami Desai, the financial director, include the following.

(1)   One of Sellfones' main competitors ceased trading during the year due to the increasing pressure on margins in the industry and competition from online retailers.

(2)   A new management structure has been implemented, with 10 new divisional managers appointed during the year. The high street shops have been allocated to these managers, with approximately 20 branch managers reporting to each divisional manager. The divisional managers have been set challenging financial targets for their areas, with substantial bonuses offered to incentivise them to meet the targets. The board of directors have also decided to cut the amount that will be paid to shop staff as a Christmas bonus.

(3)   In response to recommendations in the prior year's Report to Management, a new inventory system has been implemented. There were some problems in its first months of operation but a report has been submitted to the board by Steven MacLennan, the chief accountant, confirming that the problems have all been resolved and that information produced by the system will be accurate. Pami commented that the chief accountant has had to work very long hours to deal with this new system, often working at weekends and even refusing to take any leave until the system was running properly.

(4)   The company is planning to raise new capital through a share issue after the year-end in order to finance expansion of the business into other countries in Europe. As a result, Pami has requested that the auditor's report is signed off by 15 December 20X7 (six weeks earlier than in previous years).

(5)   The latest board summary of results includes:

9 months to 30 June 20X7 (unaudited)		*Year to 30 September 20X6 (audited)*	
	$m		$m
Revenue	320	Revenue	280
Cost of sales	215	Cost of sales	199
Gross profit	105	Gross profit	81
Operating expenses	(89)	Operating expenses	(70)
Exceptional profit on sale of properties	30		–
Profit before tax	46		11

(6)   Several shop properties owned by the company were sold under sale and leaseback arrangements.

Required

Identify and explain any fraud risk factors that the audit team should consider when planning the audit of Sellphones Co.

Part B Professional and ethical considerations | **3: Professional liability**   93

Approaching the answer

Look for key words and ask questions of the information given to you. This is illustrated below.

 Question

> **Identify the stage of the audit**

You are an audit manager for Elle and Emm, Chartered Certified Accountants. You are carrying out the planning of the audit of Sellfones Co, a listed company, and a high street retailer of mobile phones, for the year ending 30 September 20X7. The notes from your planning meeting with Pami Desai, the financial director, include the following.

> **Indication of level of competition**

> **Nature of industry – very competitive**

(1) One of Sellfones' main competitors ceased trading during the year due to the increasing pressure on margins in the industry and competition from online retailers.

> **Is it effective? Do they have the expertise?**

> **Increased risk?**

> **Morale?**

(2) A new management structure has been implemented, with 10 new divisional managers appointed during the year. The high street shops have been allocated to these managers, with approximately 20 branch managers reporting to each divisional manager. The divisional managers have been set challenging financial targets for their areas, with substantial bonuses offered to incentivise them to meet the targets. The board of directors have also decided to cut the amount that will be paid to shop staff as a Christmas bonus.

> **Pressure on management to be successful**

(3) In response to recommendations in the prior year's Report to Management, a new inventory system has been implemented. There were some problems in its first months of operation but a report has been submitted to the board by Steven MacLennan, the chief accountant, confirming that the problems have all been resolved and that information produced by the system will be accurate. Pami commented that the chief accountant has had to work very long hours to deal with this new system, often working at weekends and even refusing to take any leave until the system was running properly.

> **Reliability?**

> **Under pressure?**

> **Suspicious?**

> **Pressure on results**

(4) The company is planning to raise new capital through a share issue after the year-end in order to finance expansion of the business into other countries in Europe. As a result, Pami has requested that the auditor's report is signed off by 15 December 20X7 (six weeks earlier than in previous years).

> **Increased audit risk?**

(5) The latest board summary of results includes:

9 months to 30 June 20X7 (unaudited)   *Year to 30 September 20X6 (audited)*

	$m		$m
Revenue	320	Revenue	280
Cost of sales	215	Cost of sales	199
Gross profit	105	Gross profit	81
Operating expenses	(89)	Operating expenses	(70)
Exceptional profit on sale of properties	30		–
Profit before tax	46		11

> **Changes in margin in line with expectations?**

(6) Several shop properties owned by the company were sold under sale and leaseback arrangements.

> **Substance**

Required

Identify and explain any fraud risk factors that the audit team should consider when planning the audit of Sellphones Co.

Answer plan

Not all the points you notice will necessarily be relevant and you may also find that you do not have time to mention all the points. You may also notice that certain issues are related and should be dealt with together. Prioritise your points in a more formal plan and then write out your answer.

Risk factors:

- Nature of industry and operating conditions
- Management structure and incentives
- New inventory system/chief accountant
- Results
- Exceptional gain
- Time pressure
- Theft of assets

Answer

In this scenario there are a large number of factors that should alert the auditors to the possibility of misstatements arising from fraudulent financial reporting, and others that could indicate a risk of misstatements arising from misappropriation of assets.

(1) **Operating conditions within the industry**

The failure of a competitor in a highly competitive business sector highlights the threat to the survival of a business such as Sellphones and this could place the directors under pressure to overstate the performance and position of the company in an attempt to maintain investor confidence, particularly given the intention to raise new share capital.

(2) **Management structure and incentives**

It is not clear in the scenario how much involvement the new divisional managers have in the financial reporting process but the auditors would need to examine any reports prepared or reviewed by them very carefully, as their personal interest may lead them to overstate results in order to earn their bonuses.

(3) **New inventory system/chief accountant**

The problems with the implementation of the new inventory system suggest that there may have been control deficiencies and errors in the recording of inventory figures. Misstatements, whether deliberate or not, may not have been identified. The amount of time spent by the chief accountant on the implementation of the new inventory system could be seen as merely underlining the severity of the problems, but the fact that they have not taken any leave should also be considered as suspicious and the auditors should be alert to any indication that they may have been involved in any deliberate misstatement of figures.

(4) **Results**

The year on year results look better than might be expected given the business environment. The gross profit margin has increased to 32.8% (20X6 25.3%) and the operating profit margin has increased to 5% (20X6 3.9%). This seems to conflict with what is known about the industry and should increase the auditor's professional scepticism in planning the audit.

(5) **Exceptional gain**

The sale and leaseback transaction may involve complex considerations relating to its commercial substance. It may not be appropriate to recognise a gain or the gain may have been miscalculated.

(6) **Time pressure on audit**

The auditors should be alert to the possibility that the tight deadline may have been set to reduce the amount of time the auditors have to gather evidence after the end of the reporting period, perhaps in the hope that certain deliberate misstatements will not be discovered.

(7) **Risk of misappropriation of assets**

The nature of the inventory held in the shops increases the risk that staff may steal goods. This risk is perhaps increased by the fact that the attitude of the staff towards their employer is likely to have been damaged by the cut in their Christmas bonus. The problems with the new inventory recording system increase the risk that any such discrepancies in inventory may not have been identified.

5.3.4 Responding to assessed risks

The auditor must then come up with responses to the assessed risks.

ISA 240.28

In accordance with ISA 330 the auditor shall determine overall responses to address the assessed risks of material misstatement due to fraud at the financial statement level.

In determining overall responses to address the risks of material misstatement due to fraud at the financial statement level the auditor should:

(a)   Consider the assignment and supervision of personnel

(b)   Consider the accounting policies used by the entity

(c)   Incorporate an element of unpredictability in the selection of the nature, timing and extent of audit procedures

---
ISA 240.30

In accordance with ISA 330, the auditor shall design and perform further audit procedures whose nature, timing and extent are responsive to the assessed risks of material misstatement due to fraud at the assertion level.

The auditor may have to **amend** the **nature, timing or extent** of planned audit procedures to address assessed risks. The auditor should also consider the following.

*   Audit procedures responsive to management override of controls
*   Journal entries and other adjustments
*   Accounting estimates
*   Business rationale for significant transactions

Examples: specific audit procedures

The auditor might to choose to attend previously unvisited branches to carry out inventory or cash checks.

The auditor might perform detailed analytical procedures using disaggregated data, for example, comparing sales and costs of sales by location.

The auditor might use an expert to assess management estimates in a subjective area.

5.4 Evaluation of audit evidence

The auditor evaluates the audit evidence obtained to ensure it is consistent and that it achieves its aim of answering the risks of fraud. This will include a consideration of results of analytical procedures and any misstatements found. The auditor must also consider the reliability of written representations.

The auditor must obtain written representation that management accepts its responsibility for the prevention and detection of fraud and has made all relevant disclosures to the auditors.

5.5 Documentation

The auditor must document:

*   The significant decisions reached as a result of the team's discussion of fraud
*   The identified and assessed risks of material misstatement due to fraud
*   The overall responses to assessed risks
*   Results of specific audit tests
*   Any communications with management
*   Reasons for concluding that the presumption that there is a risk of fraud related to revenue recognition is not applicable

5.6 Reporting

There are various reporting requirements in ISA 240.

> **ISA 240.40**
>
> If the auditor has identified a fraud or has obtained information that indicates a fraud may exist, the auditor shall communicate these matters on a timely basis to the appropriate level of management in order to inform those with primary responsibility for the prevention and detection of fraud of matters relevant to their responsibilities.
>
> **ISA 240.41**
>
> Unless all of those charged with governance are involved in managing the entity, if the auditor has identified or suspects fraud involving:
>
> (a) management;
> (b) employees who have significant roles in internal control; or
> (c) others, where the fraud results in a material misstatement in the financial statements,
>
> the auditor shall communicate these matters to **those charged with governance** on a timely basis. If the auditor suspects fraud involving management, the auditor shall communicate these suspicions to those charged with governance and discuss with them the nature, timing and extent of audit procedures necessary to complete the audit.

The auditor should also make relevant parties within the entity aware of significant deficiencies in the design or implementation of controls to prevent and detect fraud which has come to the auditor's attention, and consider whether there are any other relevant matters to bring to the attention of those charged with governance with regard to fraud.

The auditor may have a **statutory duty** to report fraudulent behaviour to **regulators** outside the entity. If no such legal duty arises, the auditor must consider whether to do so would breach their **professional duty of confidence**. In either event, the auditor should take **legal advice**.

5.7 Auditor unable to continue

The auditor should consider the need to withdraw from the engagement if they uncover exceptional circumstances with regard to fraud.

Exam focus point

> Remember the confidentiality issues from Chapter 2. When you are considering whether to make a public interest disclosure, you should always bear it in mind.

Question

Detection of fraud

Required

(a) Discuss what responsibility auditors have to detect fraud.
(b) Explain how the auditors might conduct their audit in response to an assessed risk of:
    (i) Misappropriation
    (ii) Fraudulent financial reporting

Answer

(a) The primary responsibility for the prevention and detection of fraud and irregularities rests with management and those charged with governance. This responsibility may be partly discharged by the institution of an adequate system of internal control including, for example, authorisation controls and controls covering segregation of duties.

The auditors should recognise the possibility of material irregularities or frauds which could, unless adequately disclosed, distort the results or state of affairs shown by the financial statements. ISA 240 states that the auditor is responsible for obtaining reasonable assurance that the financial statements taken as a whole are free from material misstatement whether caused by fraud or error. Auditors are required to carry out their audit with professional skepticism.

Auditors are required to carry out risk assessment procedures in respect of fraud. This will involve making enquiries of management, considering if any risk factors (such as the existence of pressure for management to meet certain targets) are present and considering the results of analytical procedures if any method or unexpected relationships have been identified.

If there is an assessed risk of fraud, the auditor must make suitable responses. Overall responses include considering the personnel for the assignment (for example, using more experienced personnel), considering the accounting policies used by the entity (have they changed? Are they reasonable?) and incorporating an element of unpredictability into the audit.

Specific responses to the risk of misstatement at the assertion level due to fraud will vary depending on the circumstances but could include:

(i)   Changing the nature of audit tests (for example, introducing computer-assisted audit techniques if more detail is required about a computerised system)

(ii)   Changing the timing of audit tests (for example, testing throughout an audit period, instead of extending audit conclusions from an interim audit)

(iii) Changing the extent of audit tests (for example, increasing sample sizes)

(b)   (i)   **Misappropriation**

Employee frauds such as misappropriation are likely to take place when controls are weak. If controls are weak, auditors may not test controls and therefore evidence of employee fraud might go undetected. However, if auditors have identified a risk of employee fraud, they might as a response test controls in the relevant area (such as purchases or sales) in order to identify any unexplained patterns in the company's procedures. For example, if a purchase fraud is suspected, auditors might scrutinise authorisation controls to see if a particular member of staff always authorises certain items/for certain people, where the system does not require that.

Many substantive procedures normally performed by the auditors may assist in isolating employee frauds, if they are occurring. For example, tests performed on the receivables ledger may be aimed at revealing overstatement or irrecoverable receivables, but the design of such tests also assists with cash understatement objectives and may reveal irregularities such as 'teeming and lading'.

(ii)   **Fraudulent financial reporting**

If the auditors conclude that there is a high risk of fraudulent financial reporting by management, they will concentrate on such techniques as analytical procedures, scrutiny of unusual transactions and all journal entries, review of events after the reporting period (including going concern evaluation), and review of the financial statements and accounting policies for any changes or material distortions.

6 The expectations gap

FAST FORWARD

The 'expectations gap' refers to the difference between the public's and auditors' expecations of the audit process.

The 'expectations gap' can be narrowed either by educating the users of audited financial statements, or by extending the auditor's role.

ISA 240 sets out the current position on the auditor's responsibility to consider fraud. There remains a debate as to whether this is sufficient, as the area of fraud is a key part of the expectations gap between what users of auditors' reports believe to be the purposes of the audit compared with the actual nature of the assurance reported to them by auditors.

The issue of the expectations gap is consistently in and out of the financial press. In recent years, there has been a focus on the role of auditors in evaluating whether a company is a going concern. In the USA, the collapse of Lehman Brothers brought with it accusations from some quarters that its auditor, Ernst & Young, had failed to discharge its responsibilities as auditor.

A recent example of such coverage relates to auditors Ernst & Young (EY) and its audit client, the Olympus Corporation. A scandal was precipitated when Olympus's recently-appointed chief executive was ousted from his position after having exposed what was described as a loss-hiding arrangement of fraudulent financial reporting. A succession of auditors had issued unmodified reports throughout this period. An internal Olympus inquiry into the fraud concluded that the scheme had been too well-concealed for the auditors to detect it:

> 'The masterminds of this case were hiding the illegal acts by artfully manipulating experts' opinions…'

> *Reuters report,* at www.webcitation.org/65x0p5rgR

High profile cases such as these have brought up the question of the extent to which auditors should be responsible for detecting fraud, and how this differs from the way that the responsibilities of the auditor are perceived.

6.1 Narrowing the expectations gap

Logically, the expectations gap could be narrowed in two ways.

(1) **Educating users** – The auditor's report as outlined in ISA 700 *Forming an opinion and reporting on financial statements* includes an explanation of the auditor's responsibilities, but also quite extensive discussions of the key matters arising from the audit.

(2) **Extending the auditor's responsibilities** – Research indicates that extra work by auditors with the inevitable extra costs is **likely to make little difference to the detection of fraud** because:

- Most material frauds involve management
- More than half of frauds involve misstated financial reporting but do not include diversion of funds from the company
- Management fraud is unlikely to be found in a financial statement audit
- Far more is spent on investigating and prosecuting fraud in a company than on its audit

Suggestions for expanding the auditor's role have included:

- Requiring auditors to report to boards and audit committees on the adequacy of controls to prevent and detect fraud
- Encouraging the use of targeted forensic fraud reviews (see Chapter 14)
- Increasing the requirement to report suspected frauds

Chapter Roundup

- Professional accountants may have professional liability under statutory law.

- Auditors may have professional liability in the tort of negligence.

- The auditor owes a duty of care to the audit client automatically under law.

- The auditor only owes a duty of care to parties other than the audit client if one has been established.

- Auditors may attempt to limit liability to clients. This may not always be effective in law.

- ACCA requires that auditors take out professional indemnity insurance.

- Auditor liability is an important practical issue.

- Misunderstanding of the auditor's responsibilities in respect of fraud is a major component of the 'expectations gap'.

  The key difference between fraud and error is that fraud is intentional.

- Management and those charged with governance are primarily responsible for preventing and detecting fraud.

- The 'expectations gap' refers to the difference between the public's and auditors' expectations of the audit process.

  The 'expectations gap' can be narrowed either by educating the users of audited financial statements, or by extending the auditor's role.

Quick Quiz

1 Define fraud.

2 Draw a table showing the reporting requirements of ISA 240 *The auditor's responsibilities relating to fraud in an audit of financial statements.*

3 Determine whether each of the following is an example of fraud or of error.

	Fraud or error?
Clerical mistake resulting in overstatement of profit before taxation	……..
Theft of cash from the company	……..
Failing to consolidate a loss-making subsidiary in order to improve group results	……..
Misinterpretation of facts resulting in incorrect accounting estimate	……..

4 What three matters must an injured party satisfy to the court in an action for negligence?

(1) …………………………………

(2) …………………………………

(3) …………………………………

5 Name four aspects of litigation avoidance.

(1) …………………………………

(2) …………………………………

(3) …………………………………

(4) …………………………………

6 Professional indemnity insurance is insurance against liability arising through any acts of fraud or dishonesty by partners in respect of money held in trust by the firm.

True ☐

False ☐

Answers to Quick Quiz

1   Fraud is the use of deception to obtain unjust or illegal financial advantage and intentional misrepresentation by management, employees or third parties.

2

Management	If the auditors suspect or detect any fraud (even if immaterial) they should tell management as soon as they can.
Those charged with governance	If the auditor has identified fraud involving management, employees with significant roles in internal control, or others, if it results in a material misstatement, they must report it to those charged with governance.
Third parties	Auditors may have a statutory duty to report to a regulator. Auditors are advised to take legal advice if reporting externally to the company.

3

Clerical mistake resulting in overstatement of profit before taxation	Error
Theft of cash from the company	Fraud
Failing to consolidate a loss-making subsidiary in order to improve group results	Fraud
Misinterpretation of facts resulting in incorrect accounting estimate	Error

4   (1)   A duty of care existed
     (2)   Negligence occurred
     (3)   The injured party suffered pecuniary loss as a result

5   (1)   Client acceptance procedures
     (2)   Performance of audit work in line with ISAs
     (3)   Quality control
     (4)   Disclaimers

6   False. That is fidelity guarantee insurance. Professional indemnity insurance is insurance against civil claims made by clients and third parties arising from work undertaken by the firm.

Now try the questions below from the Practice Question Bank.

Number	Level	Marks	Time
Q4	Examination	15	29 mins
Q5	Examination	20	39 mins

Practice management

Quality control

4

Topic list	Syllabus reference
1 Principles and purpose	C1
2 Quality control at a firm level	C1
3 Quality control on an individual audit	C1

Introduction

The role performed by auditors represents an activity of significant public interest. Quality independent audit is crucial, both to users and to the audit profession as a whole. Poor audit quality damages the reputation of the firm and may lead to loss of clients and thus fees, as well as an increased risk of litigation and concomitant professional insurance costs.

Although there are specific standards giving guidance on how auditors should perform their work with satisfactory quality, these can never cater for every situation. Two standards deal with quality at a general level. These are ISQC 1 *Quality control for firms that perform audits and reviews of financial statements, and other assurance and related services engagements*, and ISA 220 *Quality control for an audit of financial statements*.

Study guide

		Intellectual level
C1	**Quality control**	
(a)	Explain the principles and purpose of quality control of audit and other assurance engagements.	1
(b)	Describe the elements of a system of quality control relevant to a given firm.	2
(c)	Select and justify quality control procedures that are applicable to a given audit engagement.	3
(d)	Assess whether an engagement has been planned and performed in accordance with professional standards and whether reports issued are appropriate in the circumstances.	3

Exam guide

Issues relating to quality control can be linked with almost any area of the P7 syllabus, from ethics and auditor liability covered in Part B to any of the specific areas covered in Part D of this Study Text. You could be asked to suggest quality control procedures that a firm should implement in specific circumstances; to review a firm's procedures and assess their adequacy; or to assess procedures planned or performed, and evidence obtained, for a specific engagement.

1 Principles and purpose

> **FAST FORWARD**
>
> There is no simple definition of audit quality because there is no one 'correct' way to audit. It is often a matter of conducting an audit in line with the spirit as well as the letter of professional guidance.

Audit quality is not defined in law or through regulations, and neither do auditing standards provide a simple definition.

Although each stakeholder in the audit will give a different meaning to audit quality, at its heart it is about delivering an **appropriate** professional **opinion** supported by the necessary **evidence** and **judgements**.

Many principles contribute to audit quality, including good leadership, experienced judgement, technical competence, ethical values and appropriate client relationships, proper working practices and effective quality control and monitoring review processes.

The standards on audit quality provide guidance to firms on how to achieve these principles.

2 Quality control at a firm level   Pilot, 6/09, 12/11, 6/14

> **FAST FORWARD**
>
> The International Standard on Quality Control (ISQC 1) helps audit firms to establish quality standards for their business.

The fact that auditors follow international auditing standards provides a general quality control framework within which audits should be conducted. There are also specific quality control standards.

2.1 Purpose of ISQC 1

ISQC 1.11

The objective of the firm is to establish and maintain a system of quality control to provide it with reasonable assurance that:

(a) The firm and its personnel comply with professional standards and applicable legal and regulatory requirements; and

(b) Reports issued by the firm or engagement partners are appropriate in the circumstances.

All quality control policies and procedures should be **documented** and **communicated** to the firm's personnel.

We have already considered the sections of this standard relating to ethics in Chapter 2 and those relating to client acceptance will be covered in Chapter 5 of this Study Text. We shall now consider the requirements of the rest of the standard, which fall into the following areas.

- Firm and leadership responsibilities for quality within the firm
- Human resources
- Engagement performance (see also below, the requirements of ISA 220)
- Monitoring

2.2 Firm and leadership responsibilities for quality within the firm

ISQC 1.13

Personnel within the firm responsible for establishing and maintaining the firm's system of quality control shall have an understanding of the entire text of this ISQC, including its application and other explanatory material, to understand its objective and to apply its requirements properly.

Firms are required to ensure that the appropriate training is provided to ensure there is complete understanding of the objectives and procedures under ISQC 1. The standard stipulates further that some firms may need to apply additional procedures (beyond those of the standard) to ensure that the objectives are met.

The standard requires that the firm implements policies such that the **internal culture** of the firm is one where **quality** is considered to be **essential**. Such a culture must be inspired by the leaders of the firm, who must promote this culture by the example of their actions and messages. In other words, the entire business strategy of the audit firm should be driven by the need for quality in its operations.

The firm may appoint an individual or group of individuals to oversee quality in the firm. Such individuals must have:

- Sufficient and appropriate experience
- The ability to carry out the job
- The necessary authority to carry out the job

2.3 Human resources

The firm's overriding desire for quality will necessitate policies and procedures on ensuring excellence in its staff, to provide the firm with 'reasonable assurance that it has sufficient personnel with the **capabilities**, **competence**, and **commitment to ethical principles** necessary to perform its engagements in accordance with professional standards and regulatory and legal requirements, and to enable the firm or engagement partners to issue reports that are appropriate in the circumstances'.

These will cover the following issues.

- Recruitment
- Capabilities
- Career development
- Compensation

- Performance evaluation
- Competence
- Promotion
- The estimation of personnel needs

The firm is responsible for the ongoing excellence of its staff, through continuing professional development, education, work experience and coaching by more experienced staff.

2.3.1 Assignment of engagement teams

The assignment of engagement teams is an important matter in ensuring the quality of an individual assignment.

This responsibility is given to the audit engagement partner. The firm should have policies and procedures in place to ensure that:

- Key members of client staff and those charged with governance are aware of the identity of the audit engagement partner
- The engagement partner has appropriate capabilities, competence, authority and time to perform the role
- The engagement partner is aware of their responsibilities as engagement partner

The engagement partner should ensure that they assign staff with sufficient capabilities, competence and time to individual assignments so that they will be able to issue an appropriate report.

2.4 Engagement performance

The firm should take steps to ensure that engagements are performed correctly, that is, in accordance with standards and guidance. Firms often produce a **manual of standard engagement procedures** to give to all staff so that they know the standards they are working towards. These may be in an electronic format.

Ensuring good engagement performance involves a number of issues:

- Direction
- Supervision
- Review

- Consultation
- Resolution of disputes

Many of these issues will be discussed in the context of an individual audit assignment (see Section 3 below).

ISQC 1.34

The firm shall establish policies and procedures designed to provide it with reasonable assurance that:

(a) Appropriate consultation takes place on difficult or contentious matters

(b) Sufficient resources are available to enable appropriate consultation to take place

(c) The nature and scope of, and conclusions resulting from, such consultations are documented and are agreed by both the individual seeking consultation and the individual consulted

(d) Conclusions resulting from consultations are implemented

This may involve consulting externally, for example with other firms, or the related professional body (ACCA), particularly when the firm involved is small.

When there are differences of opinion on an engagement team, a report should not be issued until the dispute has been resolved. This may involve the intervention of the quality control reviewer.

A **peer review** is a review of an audit file carried out by another partner in the assurance firm.

A **hot review** (also known as a pre-issuance review) is a peer review carried out before the audit report is signed.

A **cold review** (also known as a post-issuance review) is a peer review carried out after the audit report is signed.

The firm should have policies and procedures to determine when a quality control reviewer will be necessary for an engagement. This will include all audits of financial statements for listed companies. When required, such a review must be completed before the report is signed.

The firm must also have standards as to what constitutes a suitable quality control review (the nature, timing and extent of such a review, the criteria for eligibility of reviewers and documentation requirements).

Quality control reviews	
Nature, timing and extent	It ordinarily includes discussion with the engagement partner, review of the financial statements/other subject matter information and the report, and consideration of whether the report is appropriate. It will also involve a selective review of working papers relating to significant judgements made.
Eligibility	The reviewer must have sufficient technical expertise and be objective towards the assignment.
Documentation	Documentation showing that the firm's requirements for a review have been met, that the review was completed before the report was issued and a conclusion that the reviewer is not aware of any unresolved issues.
Listed companies	The review should include: • The engagement team's evaluation of the firm's independence in relation to the specific engagement • Significant risks identified during the engagement and the responses to those risks • Judgements made, particularly with respect to materiality and significant risks • Whether appropriate consultation has taken place on matters involving differences of opinion or other difficult or contentious matters, and the conclusions arising from those consultations • The significance and disposition of corrected and uncorrected misstatements identified during the engagement • The matters to be communicated to management and those charged with governance and, where applicable, other parties such as regulatory bodies • Whether working papers selected for review reflect the work performed in relation to the significant judgements and support the conclusions reached • The appropriateness of the report to be issued

2.5 Monitoring

The standard states that firms must have policies in place to ensure that their quality control procedures are:

- **Relevant**
- **Adequate**
- **Operating effectively**
- **Complied with**

In other words, they must monitor their system of quality control. Monitoring activity should be reported to the management of the firm on an annual basis.

There are two types of monitoring activity, an ongoing evaluation of the system of quality control and periodic inspection of a selection of completed engagements. An ongoing evaluation might include such questions as, 'have we kept up to date with regulatory requirements?'

A periodic inspection cycle would usually fall over a period such as three years, in which time at least one engagement per engagement partner would be reviewed.

The people monitoring the system are required to evaluate the effect of any **deficiencies** found. These deficiencies might be one-offs. Monitors will be more concerned with **systematic or repetitive deficiencies that require corrective action**. When evidence is gathered that an inappropriate report might have been issued, the audit firm may want to take legal advice.

Corrective action

- Remedial action with an individual
- Communication of findings with the training department
- Changes in the quality control policies and procedures
- Disciplinary action, if necessary

<table>
<tr><td>

Exam focus point

</td><td>

Read the requirements of any quality control questions carefully. If you are asked to comment on the procedures relevant to the individual audit, firm-wide procedures will not be relevant. This point has been made in a number of recent Examiner's Reports.

</td></tr>
</table>

3 Quality control on an individual audit   12/07, 6/08, 6/09
6/11, 12/12, 6/13, 6/14, 12/14, 6/15

> **FAST FORWARD**

> ISA 220 requires firms to implement quality control procedures over individual audit engagements.

The requirements concerning quality control on individual audits are found in ISA 220 *Quality control for an audit of financial statements*. This international auditing standard (ISA) applies the general principles of the ISQC we looked at in the previous section to an individual audit.

> **ISA 220.6**
>
> The objective of the auditor is to implement quality control procedures at the engagement level that provide the auditor with reasonable assurance that:
>
> (a)   The audit complies with professional standards and applicable legal and regulatory requirements; and
>
> (b)   The auditor's report issued is appropriate in the circumstances.

The burden of this falls on the audit engagement partner, who is responsible for the audit and the ultimate conclusion.

3.1 Leadership responsibilities

The engagement partner is required to set an example with regard to the importance of quality.

> **ISA 220.8**
>
> The engagement partner shall take responsibility for the overall quality on each audit engagement to which that partner is assigned.

3.2 Ethical requirements

> **ISA 220.9**
>
> Throughout the audit engagement, the engagement partner shall remain alert, through observation and making inquiries as necessary, for evidence of non-compliance with relevant ethical requirements by members of the engagement team.

This includes the ACCA *Code of Ethics and Conduct*, with its fundamental principles and all the other detailed requirements. The ISA also contains some detailed guidance about independence in particular.

> **ISA 220.11**
>
> The engagement partner shall form a conclusion on compliance with independence requirements that apply to the audit engagement. In doing so, the engagement partner shall:
>
> (a) Obtain relevant information from the firm and, where applicable, network firms, to identify and evaluate circumstances and relationships that create threats to independence;
>
> (b) Evaluate information on identified breaches, if any, of the firm's independence policies and procedures to determine whether they create a threat to independence for the audit engagement; and
>
> (c) Take appropriate action to eliminate such threats or reduce them to an acceptable level by applying safeguards, or, if considered appropriate, to withdraw from the audit engagement, where withdrawal is possible under applicable law and regulation. The engagement partner shall promptly report to the firm any inability to resolve the matter for appropriate action.
>
> **ISA 220.24**
>
> The auditor shall include in the audit documentation ... conclusions on compliance with independence requirements that apply to the audit engagement, and any relevant discussions with the firm that support these conclusions.

3.3 Acceptance/continuance of client relationships and specific audit engagements

The partner is required to ensure that the requirements of ISQC 1 in respect of accepting and continuing with the audit are followed. If the engagement partner obtains information that would have caused them to decline the audit in the first place they should communicate that information to the firm so that swift action may be taken. They must document conclusions reached about accepting and continuing the audit.

3.4 Assignment of engagement teams

As discussed in the previous section, this is also the responsibility of the audit engagement partner. They must ensure that the team is appropriately qualified and experienced as a unit.

3.5 Engagement performance

Several factors are involved in engagement performance, as discussed above (Section 2.4).

3.5.1 Direction

The partner directs the audit. They are required by other auditing standards to hold a meeting with the audit team to discuss the audit, in particular the risks associated with the audit. This ISA suggests that direction includes 'informing members of the engagement team of:

(a) Their responsibilities (including objectivity of mind and professional scepticism)

(b) Responsibilities of respective partners where more than one partner is involved in the conduct of the audit engagement

(c) The objectives of the work to be performed

(d)   The nature of the entity's business

(e)   Risk-related issues

(f)   Problems that may arise

(g)   The detailed approach to the performance of the engagement'

3.5.2 Supervision

The audit is supervised overall by the engagement partner, but more practical supervision is given within the audit team by senior staff to more junior staff, as is also the case with review (see Section 3.5.3 below). It includes:

- Tracking the progress of the audit engagement
- Considering the capabilities and competence of individual members of the team, and whether they have sufficient time and understanding to carry out their work
- Addressing significant issues arising during the audit engagement and modifying the planned approach appropriately
- Identifying matters for consultation or consideration by more experienced engagement team members during the audit engagement

3.5.3 Review

Review includes consideration of whether:

- The work has been performed in accordance with professional standards and regulatory and legal requirements
- Significant matters have been raised for further consideration
- Appropriate consultations have taken place and the resulting conclusions have been documented and implemented
- There is a need to revise the nature, timing and extent of work performed
- The work performed supports the conclusions reached and is appropriately documented
- The evidence obtained is sufficient and appropriate to support the auditor's report
- The objectives of the engagement procedures have been achieved

Before the audit report is issued, the engagement partner must be sure that sufficient and appropriate audit evidence has been obtained to support the audit opinion. The audit engagement partner need not review all audit documentation, but may do so. They should review critical areas of judgement, significant risks and other important matters.

3.5.4 Consultation

The partner is also responsible for ensuring that if difficult or contentious matters arise the team takes appropriate consultation on the matter and that such matters and conclusions are properly recorded.

If differences of opinion arise between the engagement partner and the team, or between the engagement partner and the quality control reviewer, these differences should be resolved according to the firm's policy for such differences of opinion.

3.5.5 Quality control review

The audit engagement partner is responsible for **appointing** a reviewer, if one is required. They are then responsible for discussing significant matters that arise with the reviewer and for not issuing the audit report until the quality control review has been completed.

A quality control review should include:

- An evaluation of the **significant judgements** made by the engagement team
- An evaluation of the **conclusions** reached in formulating the auditor's report

> **ISA 220.25**
>
> The engagement quality control reviewer shall document, for the audit engagement reviewed, that:
>
> (a)   The procedures required by the firm's policies on engagement quality control review have been performed;
>
> (b)   The engagement quality control review has been completed on or before the date of the auditor's report; and
>
> (c)   The reviewer is not aware of any unresolved matters that would cause the reviewer to believe that the significant judgements the engagement team made and the conclusions it reached were not appropriate.

A quality control review for a listed entity will include a review of:

- Discussion of significant matters with the engagement partner
- Review of financial statements and the proposed report
- Review of selected audit documentation relating to significant audit judgements made by the audit team and the conclusions reached
- Evaluation of the conclusions reached in formulating the auditor's report and consideration of whether the auditor's report is appropriate
- The engagement team's evaluation of the firm's independence towards the audit
- Whether appropriate consultations have taken place on differences of opinion/contentious matters and the conclusions drawn
- Whether the audit documentation selected for review reflects the work performed in relation to significant judgements/supports the conclusions reached

Other matters relevant to evaluating significant judgements made by the audit team are likely to be:

- The significant risks identified during the engagement and the responses to those risks (including assessment of, and response to, fraud)
- Judgements made, particularly with respect to materiality and significant risks
- Significance of corrected and uncorrected misstatements identified during the audit
- Matters to be communicated with management / those charged with governance

Exam focus point

> Quality control is often examined as one part of a requirement that also covers professional and ethical matters. A typical requirement might be 'Comment on the quality control, ethical and professional issues raised [by the scenario]'. The scenario might then depict an audit that had problems in each of these areas.
>
> Alternatively, whole questions (or parts of questions) may be set on quality control alone.

3.6 Monitoring

The audit engagement partner is required to consider the results of monitoring of the firm's (or network firm's) quality control systems and consider whether they have any impact on the specific audit they are conducting.

You are an audit senior working for the firm Addystone Fish. You are currently carrying out the audit of Wicker Co, a manufacturer of waste paper bins. You are unhappy with Wicker's inventory valuation policy and have raised the issue several times with the audit manager. They have dealt with the client for a number of years and does not see what you are making a fuss about. They have refused to meet you on site to discuss these issues.

The former engagement partner to Wicker retired two months ago. As the audit manager had dealt with Wicker for so many years, the other partners have decided to leave the audit of Wicker in their capable hands.

Required

Comment on the situation outlined above.

Answer

Several quality control issues are raised in the above scenario:

Engagement partner

An engagement **partner** is usually appointed to each audit engagement undertaken by the firm, to take responsibility for the engagement on behalf of the firm. Assigning the audit to the experienced audit manager is not sufficient.

The lack of an audit engagement partner also means that several of the requirements of ISA 220 about ensuring that arrangements in relation to independence and directing, supervising and reviewing the audit are not in place.

Conflicting views

In this scenario the audit manager and senior have conflicting views about the valuation of inventory. This does not appear to have been handled well, with the manager refusing to discuss the issue with the senior.

ISA 220 requires that the audit engagement partner takes responsibility for settling disputes in accordance with the firm's policy in respect of resolution of disputes as required by ISQC 1. In this case, the lack of engagement partner may have contributed to this failure to resolve the disputes. In any event, at best, the failure to resolve the dispute is a breach of the firm's policy under ISQC 1. At worst, it indicates that the firm does not have a suitable policy concerning such disputes as required by ISQC 1.

Exam focus point

> The June 2013 exam contained a 13-mark requirement to evaluate the quality control, ethical and professional matters in relation to the performance of a particular audit. When answering questions in this area, many candidates are aware that there is something wrong with the scenario, but those who score well are able to state precisely **why** it is wrong too.

3.7 Applying ISQC 1 proportionately with the nature and size of a firm

The International Auditing and Assurance Standards Board has issued guidance for small firms in applying ISQC 1 in the form of a 'Questions & Answers' document. Small firms do have to apply ISQC 1 in full, but this should not result in 'standards overload' because ISQC 1 is drafted in such a way that it can be applied proportionately.

3.7.1 Only comply with relevant requirements

Importantly, firms only have to comply with requirements that are **relevant** to them and to the services they are providing.

> **ISQC 1.14**
>
> The firm shall comply with each requirement of this ISQC **unless**, in the circumstances of the firm, **the requirement is not relevant** to the services provided in respect of audits and reviews of financial statements, and other assurance and related services engagements.

So a small practitioner who does not provide audit services would clearly not be required to follow ISQC 1's requirements in relation to audit services.

3.7.2 Structure and formality is proportionate

Smaller firms may use less structured means and simpler processes to comply with ISQC 1. Communications may be more informal than in a larger firm.

Smaller firms still need to read ISQC 1, but they may legitimately use their **judgement** in **tailoring** it to their circumstances. For example, it would not be necessary for a sole practitioner to establish an explicit process for assigning personnel to engagement teams (because the 'process' in this case would be the nonsensical statement that there is no process because there are no teams).

3.7.3 Using external resources

In order to comply with ISQC 1's requirements, it may be necessary to make use of the services of another organisation, such as another firm or a professional or regulatory body. This may be particularly helpful where ISQC 1 requires an **engagement quality control review**, or where there is a need for **monitoring** processes which could be carried out by an external person or firm.

3.7.4 Documentation

ISQC 1 does require all firms to document the operation of its system of quality control. However, the form and content of this documentation is a matter of judgement and would depend on the size of the firm and complexity of its organisation. Smaller firms would therefore have less to document, and could make use of less formal methods of documentation such as manual notes and checklists.

Chapter Roundup

- There is no simple definition of audit quality because there is no one 'correct' way to audit. It is often a matter of conducting an audit in line with the spirit as well as the letter of professional guidance.

- The International Standard on Quality Control (ISQC 1) helps audit firms establish quality standards for their business.

- ISA 220 requires firms to implement quality control procedures over individual audit engagements.

Quick Quiz

1 The objective of a firm applying ISQC 1 is to:

'Establish and maintain a system of .... to provide it with .... assurance that

    (a)   The firm and its personnel comply with .... standards and .... and .... requirements and

    (b)   .... issued by the firm or engagement partners are .... in the circumstances.'

2 List five issues relating to good engagement performance that should be addressed in an audit firm's procedures manual.

    (1)

    (2)

    (3)

    (4)

    (5)

3 Who reviews audit work in an audit of financial statements?

4 Who is responsible for the overall quality of an individual audit assignment?

    (a)   Ethics partner

    (b)   Pre-issuance reviewer

    (c)   Engagement partner

    (d)   Managing partner

5 ISQC 1 sets out requirements about the nature of the firm's internal culture.

True ☐

False ☐

Answers to Quick Quiz

1 Quality control, reasonable, professional, regulatory, legal, reports, appropriate

2 (1) Direction
  (2) Supervision
  (3) Review
  (4) Consultation
  (5) Resolution of disputes

3 Audit work is generally reviewed by the staff member who is more senior on the team than the person who did the work. The partner must carry out a review to ensure there is sufficient and appropriate evidence to support the audit opinion. It might also be necessary under the firm's quality control policies to obtain a quality control review by a suitable person outside the audit team. This will be necessary if the audit is of a listed entity.

4 (c) Engagement partner

5 True. ISQC 1 requires the firm to establish policies and procedures to promote an internal culture that recognises that quality is essential in performing engagements.

Now try the question below from the Practice Question Bank.

Number	Level	Marks	Time
Q6	Examination	15	29 mins

Obtaining and accepting professional appointments

Topic list	Syllabus reference
1 Change in auditors	C3
2 Advertising and fees	C2
3 Tendering	C3
4 Acceptance	C4
5 Terms of the engagement	C4

Introduction

It is a commercial fact that companies change their auditors. The question that firms of auditors need to understand the answer to is: why do companies change their auditors? We shall examine some of the common reasons here.

Related to the fact that entities change their auditors is the fact that many auditing firms advertise their services. The ACCA has set out rules for professional accountants who advertise their services. We shall examine these rules and the reasons behind them in Section 2.

As we will discover in Section 1, the audit fee can be a very key item for an entity when it makes decisions about its auditors. Determining the price to offer to potential clients can be a difficult process, but it is just one part of the whole process that is tendering. Audits are often put out to tender by companies. We shall examine all the matters firms consider when tendering for an audit in Section 3.

Linked in with the tendering process is the process of determining whether to accept the audit engagement if it is offered. ISQC 1 *Quality control for firms that perform audits and reviews of financial statements, and other assurance and related services engagements* sets out some basic requirements for all audit firms accepting engagements. This is discussed in Section 4.

ISA 210 *Agreeing the terms of audit engagements* sets out the agreement necessary when an audit is accepted and this is covered in Section 5.

Study guide

		Intellectual level
C2	**Advertising, publicity, obtaining professional work and fees**	
(a)	Recognise situations in which specified advertisements are acceptable.	2
(b)	Discuss the restrictions on practice descriptions, the use of the ACCA logo and the names of practising firms.	2
(c)	Discuss the extent to which reference to fees may be made in promotional material.	2
(d)	Outline the determinants of fee-setting and justify the bases on which fees and commissions may and may not be charged for services.	3
(e)	Discuss the ethical and other professional problems, for example, lowballing, involved in establishing and negotiating fees for a specified assignment.	3
C3	**Tendering**	
(a)	Discuss the reasons why entities change their auditors/professional accountants.	2
(b)	Recognise and explain the matters to be considered when a firm is invited to submit a proposal or fee quote for an audit or other professional engagement.	2
(c)	Identify the information to be included in a proposal.	2
C4	**Professional appointments**	
(a)	Explain the matters to be considered and the procedures that an audit firm/ professional accountant should carry out before accepting a specified new client/engagement including: (i) Client acceptance (ii) Engagement acceptance (iii) Establish whether the preconditions for an audit are present (iv) Agreeing the terms of engagement	3
(b)	Recognise the key issues that underlie the agreement of the scope and terms of an engagement with a client.	2

Exam guide

Many of the issues in this chapter are ethical. You could be faced with a change in appointment scenario in the exam. The issues surrounding a change in auditor have often been examined in the past, with scenarios featuring tendering and practical issues around audit planning.

1 Change in auditors   6/09

FAST FORWARD

> Common reasons for companies changing their auditor include audit fee, auditor not seeking re-election and change in the size of company.

1.1 Why do companies change their auditor?

It is a fact of life that companies change their auditors sometimes. Not all new clients of a firm are new businesses, some have decided to change from their previous auditors. Obviously, it is often not in the interests of audit firms to lose clients. Therefore a key issue in practice management for auditors is to understand why companies change their auditors so that, as far as they are able, they can seek to prevent it.

Before you read the rest of this chapter, spend a minute thinking about the reasons why companies might change their auditors. You might want to close the Study Text and write them down and then compare them with the reasons that we give in the rest of this section.

Answer

Read through the rest of Section 1 and compare your answer with ours.

The following diagram shows some of the more common reasons that companies might change their auditors.

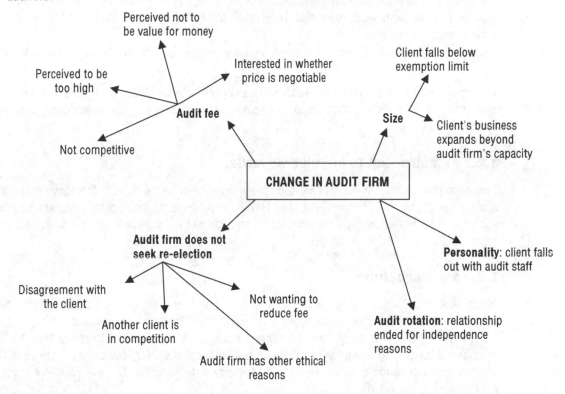

1.2 Audit fee

The audit fee can be a very **sensitive issue**. Audit is required by statute for many companies. Many people perceive that it has very little intrinsic value. Therefore, when setting audit fees, auditors must take account of the fact that clients may hold this opinion. Setting fees will be discussed later in the chapter. Here, we shall explore some of the fee-related reasons why companies change their auditors.

1.2.1 Perceived to be too high

This is a common reason for auditors being changed. It is strongly linked to people's perception that audit has no intrinsic value. If directors of a company believe that audit is a necessary evil, they will seek to obtain it for as little money as they can.

Much of the 'value', in cost terms, of an audit is carried out away from a client's premises. This is because the most expensive audit staff (managers and partners) often do not carry out their audit work on site. If the client does not understand this, the following sort of situation may arise.

Bob is the owner-manager of Fixings Co, a small business which manufactures metal fixings. It has a revenue of $4.5 million and the auditors come in for the second week of October every year. Every year a different senior is in charge and they ask similar questions to the ones asked the previous year, because the business rarely changes and the audit is low risk. The partner and manager rarely attend the audit itself because it is not considered cost-effective or necessary to do so.

Bob's audit fee was set at $4,500 five years ago when the business was incorporated for tax and inheritance reasons, and has gone up at 3% a year ever since. It now stands at $5,200. During that time, he has paid the same firm $1,200 a year to organise his tax return and deal with the tax authorities on his behalf. He considers this service far more valuable, as he has no understanding of tax issues and is exceedingly nervous of a taxation inspection.

Bob cannot understand how the audit fee is four times the size of the tax fee when the auditors attend for a week and do the same work every year. He is also irritated that it continues to steadily rise while the service does not change.

The example given above is a little exaggerated and generalisations have been made. However, there is some truth in it. An auditor understands the costs that go in to making up the audit fee. It is essential that the client does too.

1.2.2 Perceived not to be value for money

This often goes hand in hand with the audit fee being seen to be too high. In the above example of Bob and Fixings Co, this was certainly the case. However, it is possible that a company could be paying its audit firm a fee that it considers reasonable for an audit, but it just believes that another firm could give them a better audit for a similar fee.

1.2.3 Not competitive

Again, this issue can be linked with the value for money perception. It is true to say that in some cases, audit firms will offer audit services at low prices. This is on the grounds that they then sell other services to the same clients at profitable prices. It is through practices like this that the problem of lowballing can arise. You should remember the issue of lowballing from your earlier studies. In such conditions, a well-set audit fee may not be competitive even if it is a reasonable fee for the service provided.

1.2.4 Interest in whether price is negotiable

This reason may be linked to all the above fee-related issues, or it may just arise out of interest on the client's part. It costs the client very little except some time on their part to put their audit out to tender. They might even do this with every intention of keeping the present auditor.

Putting the audit out to tender would give them more insight into how competitive his audit fee is and keep their auditor 'honest', in that they will have to justify their fee and risk it being higher than competitors in the tender.

The by-product might be that they receive a competitive tender which offers them far more than they receive from their current auditor and they change their auditor anyway. It could also mean that, when forced to justify their position, the current auditor reassesses their service and comes up with a far more competitive deal.

1.3 The auditor does not seek re-election

Another key reason for the auditor changing is that the auditor chooses not to stand for election for another year. You should be familiar with many of the reasons behind this:

* There could be ethical reasons behind the auditor choosing not to stand
* The auditor might have to resign for reasons of competition between clients
* The auditor might disagree with the client over accounting policies
* The auditor might not want to reduce their audit fee.

Question

Ethical reasons

Name three ethical reasons why an auditor might not seek re-election or might resign, explaining the nature of the problem and the reasoning behind the resignation.

Answer

As you know from your earlier studies and from Chapter 2, there are countless ethical issues that could have arisen. Here are some common ones. Refer back to Chapter 2 if you have included any that do not appear here.

(a) **Fee level**

The audit fee which is necessary to carry out the audit at a profit may have reached a level which is inappropriate according to the ACCA's guidance on fee levels for a public interest entity. If the audit fee constituted more than 15% of the total practice income, this would be considered to be an independence problem. This is because the audit opinion might be influenced by a fear of losing the client. The auditor should consider the need for a pre-issuance or post-issuance review.

In such a situation, or if the practice had a large client below the limits but whose forecast suggested future growth, it might be necessary for the auditor to end the relationship to ensure that they did not become dependent on the client.

(b) **Integrity of management**

The auditor might feel that they have reason to doubt the integrity of management. There are many reasons why this could be the case. It could be as a result of a breakdown in the relationship, or an unproven suspected fraud.

If the auditor does not feel that the client is trustworthy they should not continue their relationship with them.

(c) **Other services**

The auditor may offer a number of services to the client. They may be offered some lucrative consultancy work by the client which they want to undertake, but they feel that the independence of the audit will be severely affected by the provision of the consultancy work because of the heavy involvement this would require in the client's business.

As the audit fee is substantially lower than the fees associated with the consultancy work and the auditor is trying to develop their business advice department, they may decide to resign from the audit to take on the consultancy.

1.4 Size of the company

This can be a major reason for a change in auditors. There are two key reasons, one of which has been touched on already:

* The client experiences rapid growth to the point where the audit is no longer practicable for the audit firm.
* The client retrenches or restructures in such a way that it no longer needs a statutory audit.

In the first instance, the auditor may no longer be able to provide the audit for several reasons:

- Insufficient resources
- Staff
- Time
- Fee level issue

In the second instance, the client may choose not to have an audit.

In either situation, there is little that the auditor can do to prevent losing the work.

1.5 Other reasons

These reasons may have been touched on in relation to the other reasons given above. We shall consider them briefly here.

1.5.1 Personality

For many small owner-managed companies, audit is almost a personal service. The relationship between such a client and its auditor may be strongly based on personality and, if relationships break down, it may be necessary for the audit relationship to discontinue.

Personality may not be such an issue for bigger entities and audit firms where the audit engagement partner could be transferred if required, while the audit stayed within the firm.

1.5.2 Audit rotation

Rotation of audit staff was discussed in Chapter 2 as a safeguard to audit independence. However, the partners in a firm may sometimes conclude that the firm as a whole has been associated with a client for too long, and therefore give up the audit.

1.5.3 UK Corporate Governance Code requirements

The UK Corporate Governance Code requires some companies to put the audit out to tender at least every ten years. This will not always result in a change in auditor – it is possible that the current auditor will win the tender. But it means that management will have to consider whether the audit meets its needs discussed above.

1.6 Statement of circumstances

Under the UK Companies Act 2006, for a quoted company an auditor must now always submit a statement of circumstances surrounding their leaving office, even where there are no matters which the auditor believes should be brought to the attention of members or creditors. (Previously the auditor was able to submit a negative statement, ie that there were no relevant circumstances.)

Exam focus point

From the nature of the issues raised above, it is clear that some of them will affect small firms and not larger ones and some will more predominantly affect larger ones. You should bear that in mind when approaching exam questions and, as usual, apply common sense.

Question | Control over reappointment

(a) Of the reasons for a change in auditors given above, which do you feel that an auditor may have control over and therefore guard against? Ignore the cases when the auditor does not seek re-election or resigns.

(b) What should the auditor do to guard against the issues you have identified in part (a)?

(a) **Issues auditor may have control over**

There are two key issues identified above that an auditor may have some control over:

(i) **Fees**

(1) Perception
(2) Competitiveness

(ii) **Personality**

(b) **Actions to guard against issues arising**

(i) With regard to fees, the auditor can ensure that the audit is conducted in such a way as to foster the perception that the audit is good value for the fee. This can be done by encouraging the attitude of audit staff and ensuring that a professional manner is always maintained. It also requires a constant awareness by staff of the need to add value, and to ensure that the audit provides more of a service than fulfilling a statutory requirement. This can be achieved by offering relevant advice to the client as a by-product of the audit, predominantly through the report to management, but also as an integral part of the culture of the audit.

Also with regard to fees, the auditor can ensure they are competitive in the first instance, by setting reasonable fees and in the second instance by conducting research into what their competitors charge. As companies have to file accounts and the audit fee must be disclosed, this is readily available information.

(ii) Personality is obviously not an issue that an auditor can guard against. However, part of an auditor's professionalism is to ensure that if personality problems arise, they are handled sensitively and they only arise due to issues on the side of the client.

If serious conflict arises, firms should have a procedure for rotating audits between audit partners.

2 Advertising and fees

12/09, 12/10

FAST FORWARD

ACCA's general rule on advertising is 'the medium shall not reflect adversely on the professional accountant, ACCA or the accountancy profession'.

2.1 ACCA guidance

Auditors are in business, and in business it is necessary to advertise. However, accountants are professional people and people rely on their work. It is important therefore that their advertisements do not project an image that is inconsistent with that fact.

ACCA gives guidance about advertising in the *Code of Ethics and Conduct*. This is one area in which ACCA ethical guidance is considerably more detailed than that provided by the IESBA *Code of Ethics* alone. **In general, ACCA allows professional accountants to advertise their work in any way they see fit**. In other words, it is a matter of judgement for the professional accountant. This is subject to the following general principle.

> **ACCA *Code of Ethics***
>
> 'The medium **shall not reflect adversely** on the professional accountant, ACCA or the accountancy profession.'
> *(Code of Ethics, para 250A)*

Advertisements and promotional material should **not**:

- Bring ACCA into disrepute or bring discredit to the professional accountant, firm or the accountancy profession
- Discredit the services offered by others whether by claiming superiority for the professional accountant's or firm's own services or otherwise
- Be misleading, either directly or by implication
- Fall short of any local regulatory or legislative requirements, such as the requirements of the United Kingdom Advertising Standard and Authority's Code of Advertising and Sales Promotion, notably as to legality, decency, clarity, honesty and truthfulness

(Code of Ethics, para 250.2A)

2.2 Fees

FAST FORWARD It is generally inappropriate to advertise fees.

Three issues arise with regard to fees:

- Referring to fees in promotional material
- Commissions
- Setting and negotiating fees

The last two issues are interrelated and are also closely connected with tendering, which is discussed in the next section.

2.2.1 Advertising fees

The fact that it is difficult to explain the service represented by a single fee in the context of an advertisement and that **confusion might arise as to what a potential client might expect to receive in return for that fee** means that it is **seldom appropriate** to include information about fees in short advertisements.

In longer advertisements, where reference is made to fees in promotional material, the **basis** on which those fees are calculated (hourly and other charging rates etc) **should be clearly stated**.

The key issue to remember with regard to advertising fees is that the **greatest care should be taken not to mislead potential clients**. It is appropriate to advertise free consultations to discuss fee issues. This free consultation will allow fees to be explained, thus avoiding the risk of confusion.

2.2.2 Setting and negotiating fees

As this is a key part of the tendering process, this is discussed in Section 3.

2.2.3 Commissions

FAST FORWARD Professional accountants may accept or pay referral fees if appropriate safeguards exist.

ACCA members may offer commission (and by implication receive commission) for introducing clients. However, they should only do so if there are appropriate safeguards, such as making full disclosure.

Commissions could be a threat to objectivity – refer back to Chapter 2 for more information on this.

2.3 Practice descriptions and the ACCA logo

Members of the ACCA may be either associates or fellows, in which case they are allowed to use the designatory letters ACCA or FCCA after their names.

A firm may describe itself as a firm of 'Chartered Certified Accountants' where:

- At least half the partners are ACCA members
- Those partners hold at least 51% of voting rights under the partnership agreement

Such a firm may use the ACCA logo on its stationery and website.

A firm in which all the partners are Chartered Certified Accountants may use the description 'Members of the Association of Chartered Certified Accountants'. A firm must not, however, use this term as part of its registered practice name.

A firm which holds a firm's auditing certificate from ACCA may describe itself as 'Registered Auditors'.

Question
Advertising and fees

Felicity Carr and Frank Harrison both qualified as Chartered Certified Accountants five years ago. They have now decided to set up in practice together. Their new firm holds an auditing certificate from ACCA and they intend to undertake small audits and some tax work. They will charge themselves out at $200 per hour initially. They will operate from Frank's home. They are a little rusty on the rules concerning advertising and obtaining professional work and so have asked you to advise them.

They have decided to call their practice Harrison Carr and to advertise in the local paper. As they are launching themselves, they have decided to take out a full page advertisement one week and then run a series of smaller adverts in the future. They have also decided to advertise in a local business newspaper.

Required

(a)   Explain the ACCA guidance on advertising, including advertising fees.

(b)   Advise Harrison Carr how they should proceed in relation to:

(i)   How they may describe the firm
(ii)   The adverts in the paper

Answer

(a)   **General guidance on advertising**

Generally professional accountants may not advertise in a manner that reflects adversely on themselves and their profession. This means that they should consider the quality of the paper they intend to advertise in. The local paper is appropriate. They should also ensure that they do not discredit the services offered by others in their advert.

Advertising fees

The key issue of importance when advertising fees is to ensure that the reference to fees is not misleading. Generally, it is seldom appropriate to mention fees in a small advert.

(b)   (i)   **Description of firm**

As both partners are Chartered Certified Accountants it is acceptable to advertise the firm as being a member of the ACCA. They may also describe themselves as registered auditors.

(ii)   **The proposed advertisements**

While they are planning a larger advert followed by several smaller ones, it may still not be appropriate to mention fees. This is because while they could refer to charge out rates, it would be impossible in the paper to describe how much each service would cost without estimating the time jobs would take. It is impossible to generalise such matters and the reference to fees could therefore be misleading.

It would be more appropriate to advertise that they will give free consultations to discuss fees. They may include all the details given above, their name, the membership of the ACCA and their registered auditor status.

3 Tendering

> **FAST FORWARD**
>
> When approaching a tender, it is important to consider both fees and practical issues.

3.1 Approach

A firm puts together a tender if:

- It has been approached by a prospective client
- The partners have decided that they are capable of doing the work for a reasonable fee

When approached to tender, the auditor has to consider whether they want to do the work. You should be aware of all the ethical considerations that would go into this decision. The auditor will also have to consider:

- Fees
- Practical issues

3.1.1 Fees

Determining whether the job can be done for a reasonable price will involve a substantial number of estimates. The key estimate will be how long the partner thinks it will take to do the work. This will involve meeting with the prospective client to discuss its business and systems and making the estimate from there.

The first stage of setting the fee is therefore to ascertain **what the job will involve**. The job should be broken down into its respective parts, for example, audit and tax, or if it is a complex and/or pure audit, what aspects of the job would be undertaken by what level of staff.

The second stage is therefore closely linked with the first. It involves **ascertaining which staff**, or which level of staff, **will be involved** and in what proportions they will be involved.

Once estimates have been made of how long the work will take and what level of expertise is needed in each area, **the firm's standard charge out rates can be applied** to that information, and a **fee estimated**.

Clearly, it is **commercially vital** that the estimates of time and costs are **reasonable**, or the audit firm will be seeking to undertake the work at a loss. However, it is also ethically important that the fee estimate is reasonable, or the result will be that the client is being misled about the sustainable fee level.

3.1.2 Lowballing

Problems can arise when auditing firms appear to be charging a fee level that is unsustainably low, or at least less than the 'market rate' for the audit. The practice of undercutting, usually at tender for the audit of large companies, has been called **lowballing**. In other cases, the audit fee has been reduced even though the auditors have remained the same. The problem here is that, if the audit is being performed for less than it is actually worth, then the auditors' independence is called into question.

This is always going to be a topical debate, but in terms of negotiating the audit fee the following factors need to be taken into account.

(a) The audit is perceived to have a fluctuating 'market price' as any other commodity or service. In a recession, prices would be expected to fall as companies aim to cut costs everywhere and as auditors chase less work (supply falls). Audit firms are also reducing staffing levels and their own overhead costs should be lower.

(b) Companies (especially groups of companies) can **reduce external audit costs** through various legitimate measures:

    (i) Extending the size and function of internal audit

    (ii) Reducing the number of different audit firms used worldwide

    (iii) Selling off subsidiary companies leaving a simplified group structure to audit

    (iv) The tender process itself simply makes auditors more competitive

    (v) Exchange rate fluctuations in audit fees

(c)   Auditing firms have increased productivity, partly through the use of more sophisticated information technology techniques in auditing.

The ACCA's guidance on quotations states that it is **not improper** to secure work by **quoting a lower fee** so long as the **client has not been misled** about the level of work that the fee represents.

In the event of investigations into allegations of unsatisfactory work, the level of fees would be considered with regard to a member's conduct with reference to the ethical guidelines.

3.1.3 Practical issues

The firm will have to consider the practical points arising from the approach. Common considerations include:

* Does the proposed timetable for the work fit with the current work plan?
* Does the firm have suitable personnel available?
* Where will the work be performed and is it accessible/cost effective?
* Are (non-accounting) specialist skills necessary?
* Will staff need further training to do the work?
* If so, what is the cost of that further training?

Certain information will be required to put together a proposal document. This has already been touched on briefly, when discussing the audit fee. It is likely that audit staff would have to have a meeting with the prospective client to discuss the following issues.

* What the client requires from the audit firm (for example, audit, number of visits, tax work)
* What the future plans of the entity are, for example:
    – Is it planning to float its shares on an exchange in the near future?
    – Is growth or diversification anticipated?
* Whether the entity is seeking its first auditors and needs an explanation of audit
* Whether the entity is seeking to change its auditors
* If the entity is changing its auditors, the reason behind this

Exam focus point	The December 2011 paper examined this area with a twist, asking candidates to comment on the practice management and quality control issues raised by a suggestion to guarantee to clients that all audits will be completed quicker than last year.

3.2 Content of an audit proposal (tender document)

An audit proposal, or tender, does not have a set format. The prospective client will indicate the format that they want the tender to take. This may be merely in document form, or could be a presentation by members of the audit firm.

Although each tender will be tailored to the individual circumstances, there are some matters which are likely to be covered in every one. These are set out below.

Matters to be included in audit proposal
• The fee, and how it has been calculated • An assessment of the needs of the prospective client • An outline of how the firm intends to meet those needs • The assumptions made to support that outline • The proposed approach to the engagement • A brief outline of the firm • An outline of the key staff involved

If the tender is being submitted to an **existing client**, some of those details will be unnecessary. However, if it is a competitive tender, the firm should ensure they submit a comparable tender, even if some of the details are already known to the client. This is because the tender must be **comparable** to competitors and must appear professional.

Exam focus point

In their review of this Study Text, your examination team commented specifically that students must apply the points above to the question scenario, and must not simply repeat them as pre-learned knowledge.

This area was examined in December 2014, with 8 marks available for 'explaining the specific matters to be included in the audit proposal (tender document)'. The candidates who did best used the information from this section **as a starting point** for their answers, picking up information from the scenario that was relevant to each of the bullet points in the previous box.

4 Acceptance   6/08, 6/09, 6/11

FAST FORWARD

ISQC 1 sets out what a firm must consider and document in relation to accepting or continuing an engagement, which is the integrity of the client, whether the firm is competent to do the work, and whether the firm meets the ethical requirements in relation to the work.

4.1 Ethical requirements

There are a number of ethical procedures associated with accepting engagements which you have studied previously.

Knowledge brought forward from earlier studies

From Paper F8 *Audit and Assurance* (or equivalent)

Procedures before accepting nomination

(a)   Ensure that there are **no ethical issues** which are a **barrier** to accepting nomination.

(b)   Ensure that the auditor is **professionally qualified** to act and that there are no legal or technical barriers.

(c)   Ensure that the existing **resources** are **adequate** in terms of staff, expertise and time.

(d)   Obtain **references for the directors** if they are not known personally to the audit firm.

(e)   **Consult the previous auditors** to ensure that there are no reasons behind the vacancy which the new auditors ought to know. This is also a courtesy to the previous auditors.

Procedures after accepting nomination

(a)   **Ensure** that the **outgoing auditors' removal** or **resignation** has been **properly conducted** in accordance with the law.

The new auditors should see a valid notice of the outgoing auditors' resignation, or confirm that the outgoing auditors were properly removed.

(b)   **Ensure** that the **new auditors' appointment is valid**. The new auditors should obtain a copy of the resolution passed at the general meeting appointing them as the company's auditors.

(c)   Set up and **submit a letter of engagement** to the directors of the company (see below).

4.2 Requirements of ISQC 1

We touched on the bulk of the requirements of ISQC 1 *Quality control for firms that perform audits and reviews of financial statements, and other assurance and related services engagements* in Chapter 4. However, it also sets out standards and guidance in connection with the acceptance and continuance of client relationships and specific engagements, which we shall consider here.

The firm should carry out the following steps.

Step 1   Obtain relevant information

Step 2   Identify relevant issues

Step 3   If resolvable issues exist, resolve them and document that resolution

4.2.1 Obtain information

The standard outlines three general sources of information:

- The communications auditors must make with the previous auditors according to the IESBA *Code*
- Other relevant communications, for example with other parties in the firm, bankers or legal counsel
- Searches on relevant databases

In deciding whether to continue an engagement with an existing client, or to accept a new engagement with an existing client, the firm should also consider significant matters that have arisen in the course of the previous/existing relationship, for example, expansion into a business area in which the audit firm has no experience.

4.2.2 Identify issues

The standard gives a list of matters that the auditors might consider in relation to the acceptance decision.

Matters to consider	
Integrity of a client	The identity and business reputation of the client's principal owners, key management, related parties and those charged with governance
	Nature of the client's operations, including its business practices
	Information concerning the attitude of the client's principal owners, key management, those charged with governance towards matters such as aggressive interpretation of accounting standards/internal control environment
	Whether the client is aggressively concerned with maintaining the firm's fees as low as possible
	Indications of an inappropriate limitation in the scope of work
	Indications that the client might be involved in money laundering or other criminal activities
	The reasons for the proposed appointment of the firm and non-reappointment of the previous firm

Matters to consider	
Competence of the firm	Do firm personnel have knowledge of relevant industries / subject matters?
	Do firm personnel have experience with relevant regulatory or reporting requirements, or the ability to gain the necessary skills and knowledge effectively?
	Does the firm have sufficient personnel with the necessary capabilities and competence?
	Are experts available, if needed?
	Are individuals meeting the criteria and eligibility requirements to perform the engagement quality control review available where applicable?
	Is the firm able to complete the engagement within the reporting deadline?

In addition, the firm needs to consider whether acceptance would create any conflicts of interest.

> **ISQC 1.28**
>
> The firm shall establish policies and procedures on continuing an engagement and the client relationship addressing the circumstances where the firm obtains information that would have caused it to decline the engagement had that information been available earlier. Such policies and procedures shall include consideration of:
>
> (a) The professional and legal responsibilities that apply to the circumstances, including whether there is a requirement for the firm to report to the person or persons who made the appointment or, in some cases, to regulatory authorities, and
>
> (b) The possibility of withdrawing from the engagement or from both the engagement and the client relationship.

Such procedures might include discussions with client management and those charged with governance and, if required, discussions with the appropriate regulatory authority.

Exam focus point

> The examination team wrote an article on this area entitled 'Acceptance decisions for audit and assurance engagements'. The article discussed the engagement acceptance process, but with a particular emphasis on the importance of establishing whether the preconditions for an audit are present.
>
> Preconditions for an audit (see Section 5.2 below) were then examined in the next exam sitting. So make sure you read *Student Accountant*, as it is likely to give a good indication of the topics that will be examined, and the areas that will be emphasised.

Question
Accepting nomination

You are a partner in Hamlyn, Jones and Co, a firm of Chartered Certified Accountants. You have just successfully tendered for the audit of Lunch Co, a chain of sandwich shops across West London. The tender opportunity was received cold, that is, the company and its officers are not known to the firm. The company has just been incorporated and has not previously had an audit. You are about ready to accept nomination.

(a) Explain the procedures you should carry out prior to accepting nomination.

In the course of your acceptance procedures you received a reference from a business contact of yours concerning one of the five directors of Lunch Co, Mr V Loud. It stated that your business contact had done some personal tax work for Mr Loud ten years previously, when he had found Mr Loud to be difficult to keep in contact with and slow to provide information and he had suspected Mr Loud of being less than entirely truthful when it came to his tax affairs. As a result of this distrust, he had ceased to carry out work for him.

(b) Comment on the effect this reference would have on accepting nomination.

Answer

(a)   The following procedures should be carried out.

   (i)   Ensure that my audit team and I are professionally qualified to act and consider whether there are ethical barriers to my accepting nomination.

   (ii)   Review the firm's overall work programme to ensure that there are sufficient resources to enable my firm to carry out the audit.

   (iii)   Obtain references about the directors, as they are not known personally by me or anyone else in my firm.

(b)   The auditor must use their professional judgement when considering the responses they get to references concerning new clients. The guidance cannot legislate for all situations so it does not attempt to do so. In the circumstance given above there is no correct answer, so in practice an auditor would have to make a justifiable decision which they would then document.

   Matters to be considered

   The reference raises three issues for the auditor considering accepting nomination:

   (i)   The issue that the director has been difficult to maintain a relationship with in the past
   (ii)   The issue that the director was slow to provide information in the past
   (iii)   The suspicion of a lack of integrity in relation to his tax affairs

   The auditor must **consider** these **in the light of several factors**:

   (i)   The length of time that has passed since the events
   (ii)   What references which refer to the interim time say
   (iii)   The difference between accepting a role of auditing a company and personal tax work
   (iv)   The director's role in the company and therefore the audit
   (v)   The amount of control exercised by the director
       (1)   Relationships with other directors
       (2)   Influence

   At this stage they **should not be considering** how highly they **value** the **opinion** of the referee. That should have been considered before they sent the reference. At this stage they should only be considering the implications of the reference for their current decision.

   Auditing a company is different from auditing personal affairs in terms of obtaining information and contacting personnel. In this case, the **key issue** is the question over the **integrity** of the director.

   As we do not have information about interim references and details of the business arrangements it is difficult to give a definite answer to this issue. However, Mr Loud is likely to only have **limited control over decisions** of the entity being one of five directors, which might lead to the auditor deciding that the reference was insufficient to prevent him accepting nomination. If Mr Loud were the **finance director**, the auditor would be more inclined not to take the nomination.

Exam focus point

> You can see from the answer above that there are no easy answers to ethical questions. You might be asked questions in the exam similar to the one above as part of a scenario highlighting several ethical issues. It is not enough just to state the rules at this level, you must **explain** what the practical issues are and try to **draw conclusions** based on the facts you know. Once qualified, you may face issues like this in your working life and will have to make judgements like this in practice. That is what the exam is trying to imitate.

4.3 Money laundering

As we discussed in Chapter 1, accountants are now required to carry out specific client identification procedures when accepting new clients.

'**Know your client**' (KYC) is an important part of being in a position to comply with the law on money laundering, because knowledge of the client is at the bottom of 'suspicion' in the context of making reports about money laundering.

It is important from the outset of a relationship with a new client to obtain KYC information, such as:

- Expected patterns of business
- The business model of the client
- The source of the client's funds

When the client's money is to be handled by the professional, there is a higher than normal risk to the professional, so even more detailed KYC procedures will be required.

4.4 Politically exposed persons (PEPs)

Being involved with PEPs may be particularly risky for firms, particularly in terms of reputation risks if things go wrong.

Key term

> **Politically exposed persons (PEPs)** are individuals who are, or have been, entrusted with prominent public functions in a foreign country (for example, heads of state or senior politicians and officials).

Firms and institutions should have risk management systems set up to determine whether an individual is a PEP when client identification procedures are being carried out. When a person has been identified as a PEP, a member of senior management should approve establishing a business relationship with that person.

The firm should then take reasonable measures to establish the source of that individual's wealth and funds and conduct enhanced ongoing monitoring of the firm's relationship with that individual.

4.5 Client screening

Many audit firms use a client acceptance checklist to assist them in making the decision and ensuring that ISQC 1 requirements are met.

5 Terms of the engagement   6/11

FAST FORWARD

> The auditor must agree terms of the audit engagement with relevant personnel at the client and must ensure that preconditions for an audit exist in order to agree to those terms.

5.1 Objective of ISA 210

ISA 210 *Agreeing the terms of audit engagements* sets out best practice concerning this issue.

> **ISA 210.3**
>
> The objective of the auditor is to accept or continue an audit engagement only when the basis on which it is to be performed has been agreed, through:
>
> (a)   Establishing whether the **preconditions for an audit** are present, and
>
> (b)   Confirming that there is a **common understanding** between the auditor and management and, where appropriate, those charged with governance of the terms of the audit engagement.

Key term

> The **preconditions for an audit** are the use by management (those charged with governance in the UK) of an acceptable financial reporting framework in the preparation of the financial statements and the agreement of management and, where appropriate, those charged with governance to the premise on which an audit is conducted.

5.2 Preconditions for an audit

The auditor needs to carry out tests to ensure that the preconditions for an audit outlined above are met.

> **ISA 210.6**
>
> In order to establish whether the preconditions for an audit are present, the auditor shall determine whether the financial reporting framework to be applied in the preparation of the financial statements is acceptable.

ISA 210 then goes on to require the auditor to ensure that management understands its responsibilities:

> **ISA 210.6**
>
> (i) For the preparation of the financial statements in accordance with the applicable financial reporting framework, including where relevant their fair presentation;
>
> (ii) For such internal control as management determines is necessary to enable the preparation of financial statements that are free from material misstatement, whether due to fraud or error;
>
> (iii) To provide the auditor with:
>
>   a. Access to all information of which management is aware that is relevant to the preparation of the financial statements;
>
>   b. Additional information that the auditor may request from management for the purpose of the audit; and
>
>   c. Unrestricted access to persons within the entity from whom the auditor determines it necessary to obtain audit evidence.

This will all be confirmed in the engagement letter.

If any of these conditions does not exist (eg the framework used is unacceptable or management does not acknowledge its responsibilities), the **auditor shall not accept the audit** unless legally required to so do.

In addition, the auditor should not accept the engagement if those charged with governance impose a limitation on the scope of the auditor's work likely to result in a disclaimer of opinion, again, unless the auditor is legally required to accept the audit.

5.3 Clarifying the agreement

It is important when entering into a contract to provide services to ensure that both parties fully understand their respective responsibilities and what the agreed services are. Misunderstanding could lead to a breakdown in the relationship, and eventually result in legal action being undertaken.

5.4 Engagement letter

An auditor will outline the basis for the audit agreement in their tender to provide services. However, once they have accepted nomination, It is vital that the basis of their relationship is discussed with the new client and laid out in contractual form. This is the role of the **engagement letter**, which you should be familiar with from your earlier studies.

Matters which SHALL be clarified in the engagement letter

- Objective and scope of the audit
- Auditor's responsibilities
- Management's responsibilities
- Identification of applicable financial reporting framework
- Expected form and contents of reports to be issued by the auditor and statement that there may be circumstances when a report may differ from this

Matters which MAY be clarified in the engagement letter

- More detail on the scope of the audit, including references to law, auditing and other standards the auditor follows
- Form of other audit communications
- Limitation of audit and internal controls and resulting risk that material misstatements may not be detected
- Composition of the audit team and other practical arrangements
- Expectation that the management will provide written representations
- Agreement of management to make draft financial statements and other documents available in good time
- Agreement of management to inform the auditors of facts that may affect the financial statements before the date of the audit report
- Basis on which fees are computed and billing arrangements
- A request for management to acknowledge receipt of audit engagement letter and agree to its terms
- Arrangements concerning the use of experts or other auditors
- Arrangements concerning the use of internal auditors and other entity staff
- Arrangements to be made with predecessor auditors (in the case of a new audit)
- Any restrictions of the auditor's liability
- References to any other agreements between parties
- Any obligations to provide working papers to other parties

An auditor shall not agree to a change in the terms of the engagement letter where there is no reasonable justification for the change. If the terms of the engagement **are** changed, this should be recorded. If the auditor is unable to agree to a change, they shall withdraw from the engagement and consider whether they have an obligation to report the circumstances to other parties.

In practice, the auditors and the new client will meet to negotiate the terms of the audit agreement which the auditor will later clarify in the engagement letter.

 Question   Engagement letter

ISA 210 *Agreeing the terms of audit engagements* lists a series of matters which shall be referred to in an engagement letter. What are they?

Answer

The International Auditing Standard (ISA) includes the following matters in paragraphs 10 and A22 to A24.

- The objective of the audit of financial statements
- Management's responsibility for the financial statements and auditor's responsibility
- The scope of the audit, including reference to applicable legislation, regulations, or pronouncements of professional bodies to which the auditor adheres
- The form of any reports or other communication of results of the engagement

- The fact that because of the test nature and other inherent limitations of an audit, together with the inherent limitations of internal control, there is an unavoidable risk that even some material misstatement may remain undiscovered
- Unrestricted access to whatever records, documentation and other information requested in connection with the audit
- The agreement of management to make available to the auditor draft financial statements and any accompanying other information in time to allow the auditor to complete the audit in accordance with the proposed timetable
- Arrangements regarding the planning and performance of the audit
- Expectation of receiving from management written confirmation concerning representations made in connection with the audit
- Request for the client to confirm the terms of engagement by acknowledging receipt of the engagement letter
- Description of any other letters or reports the auditor expects to issue to the client
- Basis on which fees are computed and any billing arrangements
- Arrangements concerning the involvement of other auditors and experts in some aspects of the audit
- Arrangements concerning the involvement of internal auditors and other client staff
- Arrangements to be made with the predecessor auditor, if any, in the case of an initial audit
- Any restriction of the auditor's liability when such possibility exists
- A reference to any further agreements between the auditor and the client

Exam focus point

The June 2011 exam contained a scenario with a potential new audit client which had not been audited before. To score well, **candidates needed to spot that a number of preconditions for an audit did not appear to be present**: management did not acknowledge its responsibility for preparing the financial statements (it did not want to prepare a statement of cash flows), and wanted to restrict access to the company's books and records (management did not want auditors to see board minutes).

To score well on this question you need to know your auditing standards well enough to spot when a standard is relevant, even though it has not been asked for specifically by the requirement.

5.4.1 Recurring audits

In a recurring audit, the auditor is not required to send a new letter for each audit, but must ensure that the client still understands the existing terms.

It may be necessary to revise the terms in the event of new circumstances arising, as you are aware from previous studies.

5.5 Other changes in agreement terms

ISA 210.14

The auditor shall not agree to a change in the terms of the audit engagement where there is no reasonable justification for doing so.

If there is reasonable justification for changing the terms, the new terms should be agreed on and recorded.

If the auditor is not able to agree to new terms, and management refuses to let the firm continue on the basis of the old ones, the auditors should:

- Withdraw, if legally entitled to
- Consider if it is necessary to report the circumstances to other parties such as the shareholders or regulators

Chapter Roundup

- Common reasons for companies changing their auditors include audit fee, auditor not seeking re-election and change in the size of company.

- ACCA's general rule on advertising is 'the medium shall not reflect adversely on the professional accountant, ACCA or the accountancy profession'.

- It is generally inappropriate to advertise fees.

- Professional accountants may accept or pay referral fees if appropriate safeguards exist.

- When approaching a tender, it is important to consider both fees and practical issues.

- ISQC 1 sets out what a firm must consider and document in relation to accepting or continuing an engagement which is the integrity of the client, whether the firm is competent to do the work, and whether the firm meets ethical requirements in relation to the work.

- The auditor must agree terms of the audit engagement with relevant personnel at the client and must ensure that preconditions for an audit exist in order to agree to those terms.

1   Name three reasons why an auditor might not seek re-election.

2   Fill in the blanks:

Advertising and promotional material should not:

– .... the service offered ....

– Be ...., either directly or by implication

– Fall short of the requirements of the ....
....

3   Why should accountants not usually advertise fees?

4   List six practical issues that an auditor should consider when approaching a tender.

5   Draw a diagram showing the key stages in a tender, explaining what happens at each stage.

6   List three sources of information about a new client given in ISQC 1.

7   According to ISQC 1, when considering whether to accept an engagement with a new or existing client, the auditors must consider whether a .... arises.

8   List five matters which may be referred to in an engagement letter.

Answers to Quick Quiz

1   (1)   Ethical reasons (eg fees)
        (2)   Another client in competition
        (3)   Disagreement over accounting policy

2   Discredit, by others, misleading, United Kingdom Advertising Standard Authority's Code of Advertising and Sales Promotion (or equivalent)

3   The advert is unlikely to be detailed, and facts given about fees could mislead potential clients.

4   (1)   Does the timetable fit with current work plan?
        (2)   Are suitable personnel available?
        (3)   Where will work be performed? Is it cost effective?
        (4)   Are specialist skills needed?
        (5)   Will staff need further training?
        (6)   If so, what is the cost?

5

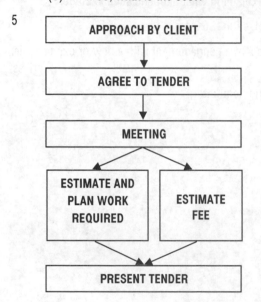

Auditor considers if it is possible to undertake work at a reasonable fee

Arrange meeting to obtain information prior to tender

Obtain knowledge of the business and the service required

Allocate potential staff to work plan and calculate fee by reference to standard charge out rates

This could be in the form of:

–   Letter
–   Report
–   Presentation

6   (1)   Communications with existing/previous auditors
        (2)   Communications with other third parties (eg bankers / legal counsel)
        (3)   Relevant databases

7   Conflict of interest

8   See the answer to the question in Section 5.4 in the body of the chapter.

Now try the question below from the Practice Question Bank.

Number	Level	Marks	Time
Q7	Examination	20	39 mins

P
A
R
T

D

Audit of historical financial information

Planning and risk assessment

Topic list	Syllabus reference
1 Revision: overview of audit planning	D1, D2
2 Audit methodologies	D1
3 Materiality	D1
4 Risk	B1, D1
5 Analytical procedures	D1
6 Planning an initial audit engagement	D1

Introduction

The issue of audit planning should not be new to you. You learnt how to plan an audit in your previous auditing studies. Why, then, is this chapter here? There are three key reasons:

- To provide you with a technical update

- To **revise** the details that should be included in an **audit plan** and the general considerations included in planning

- To **consider** some of the **finer points of planning** from the point of view of the engagement partner, specifically to consider the issue of the **risk associated with the assignment** (which is a personal risk to the partner in the event of litigation arising)

Risk is an important factor in the audit. It falls into two categories:

- Specific **assignment risk** (known as audit risk), which you have studied previously

- **Business risk** associated with the client, which may form a part of inherent risk and therefore impacts on the audit

Risk is a key issue in an audit, and the most common approach to audits incorporates a recognition of those risks in the approach taken. This and other audit methodologies are compared in Section 2.

Study guide

		Intellectual level
D	**Audit of historical financial information**	
D1	**Planning, materiality and assessing the risk of misstatement**	
(a)	Define materiality and performance materiality and demonstrate how it should be applied in financial reporting and auditing.	2
(b)	Identify and explain business risks for a given assignment.	3
(c)	Identify and explain audit risks for a given assignment.	3
(d)	Identify and explain risks of material misstatement for a given assignment.	3
(e)	Discuss and demonstrate the use of analytical procedures in the planning of an assignment.	3
(f)	Explain how the result of planning procedures determines the relevant audit strategy.	2
(g)	Explain the planning procedures specific to an initial audit engagement.	2
(h)	Identify additional information that may be required to assist the auditor in obtaining an understanding of the entity.	2
(i)	Recognise matters that are not relevant to the planning of an assignment.	2
D2	**Evidence**	
(b)	Identify additional information that may be required to effectively carry out a planned assignment.	2
B1	**Code of ethics for professional accountants**	
(e)	Discuss the importance of professional scepticism in planning and performing an audit.	2
(f)	Assess whether an engagement has been planned and performed with an attitude of professional scepticism, and evaluate the implications.	3

Exam guide

Exam case study questions are often set in the context of audit planning, identifying risk areas and considering the audit strategy to apply to the audit. This would usually come up in Section A of the exam.

1 Revision: overview of audit planning

 FAST FORWARD

Auditors must plan their work so that it is done effectively.

PER alert

One of the competences you require to fulfil Performance Objective 18 of the PER is the ability to determine the level of audit risk and risk areas, including considering any internal or external information that may have implications for the audit, and to use this to document the audit plan, designing audit programmes and planning audit tests for an internal or external audit. You can apply the knowledge you gain from this chapter of the Study Text to help demonstrate this competence.

1.1 ISA 200 *Overall objectives of the independent auditor and the conduct of an audit in accordance with international standards on auditing*

> **ISA 200.11**
>
> In conducting an audit of financial statements, the overall objectives of the auditor are:
>
> (a) To obtain reasonable assurance about whether the financial statements as a whole are free from material misstatement, whether due to fraud or error, thereby enabling the auditor to express an opinion on whether the financial statements are prepared, in all material respects, in accordance with an applicable financial reporting framework; and
>
> (b) To report on the financial statements, and communicate as required by the ISAs, in accordance with the auditor's findings.

ISA 200 states that the key requirements for the auditor to obtain reasonable assurance and to express an opinion are:

- **Ethics**: comply with relevant ethical requirements (ISA 200.14)

- **Professional scepticism**: plan and perform an audit with professional scepticism, recognising that circumstances may exist that cause the financial statements to be materially misstated (ISA 200.15)

- **Professional judgement**: exercise professional judgement in planning and performing an audit (ISA 200.16)

- **Sufficient appropriate audit evidence and audit risk**: obtain sufficient appropriate audit evidence to reduce audit risk to an acceptably low level (ISA 200.17)

The auditor then fulfils these requirements by conducting the audit in accordance with ISAs.

1.2 ISA 300 *Planning an audit of financial statements*

ISA 300 *Planning an audit of financial statements* states that the objective of the auditor is to plan the audit so that it will be performed in an effective manner.

The International Auditing Standard (ISA) refers to two documents, the **overall audit strategy** and the **audit plan**. The overall audit strategy sets out in general terms how the audit is to be carried out. Considerations in establishing the overall audit strategy include:

- Characteristics of the engagement
- Reporting objectives, timing of the audit and nature of communications
- Significant factors, preliminary engagement activities and knowledge gained on other engagements
- Nature, timing and extent of resources

The audit plan details specific procedures to be carried out to implement the strategy and complete the audit.

In the case of a smaller entity the strategy is likely to be a brief memorandum and the audit plan a series of tailored standard audit programmes.

ISA 300 tends to conceive of audit planning as a series of **activities** rather than as a single event: the planning is not just something written out at the start of the audit, which is then stuck to rigidly, but is an activity that goes on throughout the audit process. For example, audit procedures need to be performed with their planned objectives in mind, and it may be necessary to revise the audit plan during the course of the audit if significant new information or events come to light.

Amendments to ISA 200 and ISA 300 in 2015 emphasised that the financial statements include the disclosures, and that audit planning should include considering how to audit disclosures. This then carries advantages for the audit overall, helping the auditor to identify important issues such as changes in the entity's environment, changes in the financial reporting framework, or the need to involve an auditor's expert in relation to some disclosures.

1.3 ISA 315 *Identifying and assessing the risks of material misstatement through understanding the entity and its environment* 6/09, 6/12

The objective of ISA 315 (Revised) *Identifying and assessing the risks of material misstatement through understanding the entity and its environment* is as follows.

> **ISA 315.3**
>
> The objective of the auditor is to identify and assess the risks of material misstatement, whether due to fraud or error, at the financial statement and assertion levels, through understanding the entity and its environment, including the entity's internal control, thereby providing a basis for designing and implementing responses to the assessed risks of material misstatement.

The emphasis here is on **risk** and **understanding**. ISA 315 is all about getting away from the idea of the audit as 'checking' transactions, and emphasises instead the need to gain a real understanding of the entity first, and then to use this to work out where the greatest risks of material misstatement might be.

Exam focus point

ISA 315 is examined indirectly in virtually every P7 exam Question One, where you are often required to identify, explain or evaluate risks, be they audit risks, risks of material misstatement or simply business risks.

Understand the entity, in order to ...

| Identify and assess **risks of material misstatement** | Design and perform **audit procedures** | Provide a **frame of reference** for judgements |

1.3.1 *What* do we need to get an understanding of?

The ISA sets out a number of areas of the entity and its environment that the auditor should gain an understanding of.

Areas to gain an understanding of
Industry, regulatory and other external factors
Nature of the entity
Selection, application and reasons for changes of accounting policies
Objectives, strategies and related business risks
Measurement and review of the entity's financial performance
Internal control

ISA 315 was revised in March 2012 as part of the IAASB's project on using the work of internal auditors to require the external auditor to obtain an understanding of internal audit.

Amendments to ISA 315 (in 2015) point out that as well as understanding how information is obtained from within the general and subsidiary ledgers, auditors must gain an understanding of the system relating to information obtained outside of the ledgers.

Exam focus point	Paper P7 questions in this area are likely to give you a scenario, and then a requirement such as 'Identify and explain the risks of material misstatement' in the scenario. You can use this list – and the one below – to help you generate ideas when answering such a question. You can even show off to your marker by stating that applying ISA 315 would require you to gain an understanding of these areas.
	A word of warning, though: do not be tempted to simply recite these lists in the exam. Your answers need to be very specific about addressing the requirement and the scenario. If your answer looks like a pre-learned list then your marker is not likely to give you many marks – if any at all!

1.3.2 *How* do we get this understanding?

The ISA sets out **ways of getting this understanding**:

Methods of obtaining an understanding of the entity
Enquiries of management (and others within the entity)
Analytical procedures (on both financial and non-financial data)
Observation and inspection
Audit team discussion of the susceptibility of the financial statements to material misstatement
Prior period knowledge (but should check that it is still relevant)

The auditors must use a combination of the top three techniques, and must engage in the discussion for every audit. The auditor may use their prior period knowledge, but must carry out procedures to ensure that there have not been changes in the year meaning that it is no longer valid.

For each risk identified, ISA 315 requires the auditor to take the following steps.

Step 1   **Identify risks** throughout the process of obtaining an understanding of the entity

Step 2   **Assess** whether the identified risks relate more pervasively to the financial statements as a whole

Step 3   **Relate the risks** to what can go wrong at the **assertion level**, and assess the controls in place to address each risk

Step 4   Consider the likelihood of misstatement and whether the risks are of a **magnitude** that **could result in a material misstatement**

Throughout this process, the size of the entity being audited must be considered. For example, in a small entity there is likely to be limited segregation of duties. This may be compensated for by increased management oversight, however this in turn increases the risk of override of controls.

 Case Study

The audit team at Ockey Co has been carrying out procedures to obtain an understanding of the entity. In the course of making enquiries about the inventory system, they have discovered that Ockey Co designs and produces tableware to order for a number of high street stores. It also makes a number of standard lines of tableware, which it sells to a number of wholesalers. By the terms of its contracts with the high street stores, it is not entitled to sell uncalled inventory designed for them to wholesalers. Ockey Co regularly produces 10% more than the high street stores have ordered, in order to ensure that they meet requirements when the stores do their quality control check. Certain stores have more stringent control requirements than others and regularly reject some of the inventory.

The knowledge above suggests two risks, one that the company may have obsolescent inventory, and another that if their production quality standards are not sufficiently high then they risk losing custom.

We shall look at each of these risks in turn and relate them to the assertion level.

Inventory

If certain of the inventory is obsolescent due to the fact that it has been produced in excess of the customer's requirement and there is no other available market for it, then there is a risk that inventory as a whole in the financial statements will not be carried at the appropriate value. Given that inventory is likely

to be a material balance in the statement of financial position of a manufacturing company, and the value could be up to 10% of the total value, this has the capacity to be a material misstatement.

The factors that will contribute to the likelihood of these risks causing a misstatement are such matters as:

- Whether management regularly review inventory levels and scrap items that are obsolescent
- Whether such items are identified and scrapped at the inventory count
- Whether such items can be put back into production and changed so that they are saleable

Losing custom

The long-term risk of losing custom is that in the future the company will not be able to continue as a going concern (we shall revise going concern in Chapter 8). A further risk is of customer disputes leading to sales returns which may not be recognised, in which case sales and receivables could be overstated. However, it appears less likely that this would be a material problem in either area, as the issue is likely to be restricted to a few customers, and only a few sales to those customers.

Again, review of the company's controls over the recording of sales and the debt collection procedures of the company would indicate how likely these risks to the financial statements are to materialise.

Some risks identified may be **significant risks**.

<table>
<tr><td>**Key term**</td><td>**Significant risks** are those that require special audit consideration.</td></tr>
</table>

The following factors indicate that a risk might be significant.

- Risk of **fraud**
- The degree of **subjectivity** in the financial information
- **Unusual** transactions
- Significant transactions with a **related party**
- **Complexity** of the transactions

<table>
<tr><td>**Exam focus point**</td><td>Try to be on the lookout for these factors in exam questions/scenarios. If you spot one – and mentioning it is relevant to the requirement – then try to use the term 'significant risk'. This will signal to the marker that you are applying the ISA to the scenario.</td></tr>
</table>

Routine, non-complex transactions are less likely to give rise to significant risk than unusual transactions or matters of director judgement because the latter are likely to have more management intervention, complex accounting principles or calculations, greater manual intervention or there is less opportunity for control procedures to be followed.

When the auditor identifies a significant risk, if they haven't done so already, they should evaluate the design and implementation of the entity's controls in that area. If management has not implemented appropriate internal controls, then this may point to a significant deficiency in internal control.

Additional information

The auditor will often need to **obtain additional information** in order to gain the required understanding of the entity, and in order to perform planned procedures. Much of the time the auditor only has incomplete information about the entity being audited, and it is important to be able to recognise when more is needed.

This can be a bit like performing an audit procedure, because the auditor must go out and get the information in order to find something out about the entity. The difference is that at this stage, the auditor is obtaining preliminary information that it can then use to plan and perform the detailed audit procedures. For instance, a client might have made an investment during the year which it classifies as an associate. The auditor will need to obtain information about this purchase – eg the purchase agreement – in order to determine whether it really is an associate. The auditor must also ask management why the purchase was made, as part of understanding the entity's objectives and strategies. This must be all be done at the planning stage because it will then determine the auditor's assessment of risk and the audit procedures which must then be performed – these would be very different if the investment was actually a subsidiary, for example.

One approach to questions in this area (to identify further information needed) is to think about:

1. What **risks** might there be in relation to a particular issue (eg that an investment is classified incorrectly); then

2. What information would help us to plan our procedures (eg the purchase agreement).

P7 exams often contain a requirement to identify additional information needed, eg in relation to audit risks identified in a scenario. These are often easy marks, and to get them you need to:

*   **Be specific** about what information you need

*   State **why** you need the information.

For example, Question One of the June 2014 paper featured a company which had material investment properties. Further information was needed on whether there had been any additions or disposals during the year.

It is not necessary at this stage to speculate in too much detail about what might go wrong in each area. Questions will usually contain a little bit of information – eg that a company runs a bonus scheme for managers – but with clear gaps in it – eg how the bonuses are determined will not be stated. All you need to do is to point out this gap and say what information is needed to fill it.

Additional information does not have to be a document, but can be eg the reason why management has done something in the scenario.

1.4 ISA 330 *The auditor's responses to assessed risks*

ISA 330 *The auditor's responses to assessed risks* states that the objective of the auditor is to 'obtain sufficient, appropriate audit evidence regarding the assessed risks of material misstatement, through designing and implementing appropriate responses to these risks'.

Overall responses include emphasising to the audit team the need for professional scepticism, assigning additional/alternative staff to the audit, using experts, providing more supervision on the audit and incorporating more unpredictability into the audit.

The evaluation of the control environment that will have taken place as part of the assessment of the client's internal control systems will help the auditor determine whether they are going to take a **substantive approach** (focusing mainly on substantive procedures) or a **combined approach** (tests of control and substantive procedures).

In accordance with this approach, the auditor should then determine **further audit procedures** designed to address the assessed risks.

The auditor **must** carry out substantive procedures on material items. In addition, the auditor must carry out the following substantive procedures.

*   Agreeing the financial statements to the underlying accounting records
*   Examining material journal entries
*   Examining other adjustments made in preparing the financial statements

1.5 Documentation requirements

ISAs 315 and 330 contain a number of documentation requirements. The following matters should be documented.

*   The discussion among the audit team concerning the susceptibility of the financial statements to material misstatements, including any significant decisions reached
*   Key elements of the understanding gained of the entity including the elements of the entity and its control specified in the ISA as mandatory, the sources of the information gained and the risk assessment procedures carried out
*   The identified and assessed risks of material misstatement
*   Significant risks identified and related controls evaluated
*   The overall responses to address the risks of material misstatement

- Nature, extent and timing of further audit procedures linked to the assessed risks at the assertion level
- If the auditors have relied on evidence about the effectiveness of controls from previous audits, conclusions about how this is appropriate

Question

Revision of audit planning

You have been informed by the senior partner of your firm that you are to be in charge of the audit of a new client, Peppermint Chews, for the year ended 31 December 20X4. She tells you that the company is engaged in the manufacture and wholesaling of sweets and confectionery, with revenue of approximately $10,000,000 and a workforce of about 150. The company has one manufacturing location, sells mainly to the retail trade but also operates ten shops of its own. The senior partner asks you to draw up an outline audit plan for the assignment showing when you anticipate visits to the client will be made and what kind of work will be carried out during each visit. The deadline for your audit report is 28 February 20X5.

Required

Draw up an outline plan for the audit of Peppermint Chews for the year ended 31 December 20X4, including:

(a)   Approximate timing in the company's year of each stage of the audit of this new client. State why you have selected the approximate timing

(b)   The objective of each stage

(c)   The kind of work that will be carried out at each stage

Answer

Initial visit

(a)   Timing. As this is a new client, this visit should take place as soon as possible after the terms of engagement have been agreed with and accepted by the directors of Peppermint Chews.

(b)   Objective. To build up a background knowledge of the company to assist in the more detailed planning of audit work that will be required at a later stage.

(c)   Audit work. We shall need to obtain details of the following:

(i)   The history and development of the company
(ii)   The nature of the commercial environment within which the company operates
(iii)   The nature of the company's products and manufacturing processes
(iv)   The plan of organisation within the company
(v)   The accounting and internal control systems operating within the company
(vi)   The accounting and other records of the company and how they are maintained

The above will be obtained using such techniques as interview, observation, reviewing the client's systems documentation, and so on.

We shall not at this stage carry out detailed tests of controls on the company's systems, but we should carry out 'walk-through' tests to gain confirmation that the systems outlined to us in theory appear to operate that way in practice.

Interim visit(s)

(a)   Timing. As this is the first audit of Peppermint Chews, it may, in view of the extra work involved, be necessary to have more than one interim visit. If we decided that only one such visit would be needed, however, then ideally it should take place reasonably close to the year end, in, say, October 20X4. If it were decided that more than one visit were needed, then perhaps the first interim visit should take place in April/May 20X4.

(b)   Objective. The purpose of interim audits is to carry out detailed tests on a client's accounting and internal control systems to determine the reliance that may be placed thereon.

(c) Audit work. Following the initial visit to the client, we should have completed our documentation of the client's systems using narrative notes and flowcharts. We should also have assessed the strengths and deficiencies of the systems and determined the extent to which we wish to place reliance on them.

Given effective controls, we shall select and perform tests designed to establish compliance with the system. We shall therefore carry out an appropriate programme of tests of controls. The conclusion from the results may be either:

(i) That the controls are effective, in which case we shall only need to carry out restricted substantive procedures; or

(ii) That the controls are ineffective in practice, although they had appeared strong on paper, in which case we shall need to carry out more extensive substantive procedures.

After carrying out tests of controls, it is normal practice, as appropriate, to send management a letter identifying any deficiencies and making recommendations for improvements.

Final visit

(a) Timing. This may well be split into a pre-final visit in December 20X4 and a final audit early in 20X5, or it could be a continuous process.

(b) Objective. We should visit the client prior to the year end to assist in the planning of the final audit so as to agree with the client detailed timings such as year-end inventory count and trade receivables circularisation, preparation of client schedules, finalisation of accounts and so forth.

The object of the final audit is to carry out the necessary substantive procedures, these being concerned with substantiating the figures in the accounting records and, eventually, in the financial statements themselves. The completion of these tests, followed by an overall review of the financial statements, will enable us to decide whether we have obtained 'sufficient appropriate audit evidence to be able to draw reasonable conclusions' so that we are in a position to express an opinion on the company's financial statements, the expression of an opinion in their audit report being the primary objective of the audit.

(c) Audit work. The audit work to be carried out at this final stage would include:

- Consideration and discussion with management of known problem areas
- Attendance at inventory count
- Verification of assets and liabilities / income and expenditure
- Following up interim audit work
- Carrying out review of events after the reporting period
- Analytical procedures
- Obtaining representations from management
- Reviewing financial statements
- Drafting the audit report

2 Audit methodologies

The audit strategy document will describe the audit methodology to be used in gathering evidence. This section describes the main methodologies currently used by auditors.

Exam focus point

Exam questions in this area are as always likely to involve application to a scenario. There are unlikely to be many marks available for pre-learned knowledge about the various kinds of audit methodology. Instead, you will need to stick to the scenario to explain how the results of planning procedures determine the audit strategy. The audit methodologies discussed in this section may be a good starting point for doing this.

2.1 Risk-based audit

Risk-based auditing refers to the development of auditing techniques that are responsive to risk factors in an audit. As we set out in Section 4, the auditors apply judgement to determine what level of risk pertains to different areas of a client's system and devise appropriate audit tests.

This approach should ensure that the greatest audit effort is directed at the areas in which the financial statements are most likely to be misstated, so that the chance of detecting misstatements is improved and time is not spent on unnecessary testing of 'safe' areas.

The increased use of risk-based auditing reflects two factors.

(a) The growing complexity of the business environment increases the danger of fraud or misstatement. Factors such as the developing use of computerised systems and the growing internationalisation of business are relevant here.

(b) Pressures are increasingly exerted by audit clients for the auditors to keep fee levels down while an improved level of service is expected.

The risk approach is best illustrated by a small case study.

 Case Study

Audit risk approach

Your audit firm has as its client a small manufacturing company. This company owns the land and buildings in its statement of financial position, which it depreciates over 50 years (buildings only) and has always been valued at cost.

The other major item in the statement of financial position is inventory.

Looking at these two items from the point of view of the audit firm, the following conclusions can be drawn.

(1) There is only a small chance that the audit engagement partner will draw an inappropriate conclusion about land and buildings.

(2) In a manufacturing company, inventory is likely to be far more complex. There may be a significant number of lines to count and value, the quantity will change all the time, inventory may grow obsolete. The chance of the audit engagement partner drawing an inappropriate conclusion about inventory is higher than the risk in connection with land and buildings.

The auditors will have to do less work to render audit risk acceptable for land and buildings than on inventory. The audit risk approach will mean doing less work on land and buildings than on inventory.

2.2 'Top-down' approach

FAST FORWARD

> With a 'top-down' approach (also known as the business risk approach) controls testing is aimed at high level controls, and substantive testing is reduced.

ISA 315 requires that auditors consider the entity's process for assessing its own business risks, and the impact that this might have on the audit in terms of material misstatements. Auditors consider:

* What factors lead to the problems which may cause material misstatements?
* What can the audit contribute to the business pursuing its goals?

This 'business risk' approach was developed because it is sometimes the case that the auditors believe the risk of the financial statements being misstated arises predominantly from the business risks of the company.

The table below highlights some of the factors that exist.

Principal risk	Immediate financial statement implications
(1) Economic pressures causing reduced unit sales and eroding margins	Inventory values (IAS 2) Going concern
(2) Economic pressures resulting in demands for extended credit	Receivables recoverability
(3) Product quality issues related to inadequate control over supply chain and transportation damage	Inventory values – net realisable value and inventory returns
(4) Customer dissatisfaction related to inability to meet order requirements	Going concern
(5) Customer dissatisfaction related to invoicing errors and transportation damage	Receivables valuation
(6) Unacceptable service response call rate related to poor product quality	Going concern Litigation – provisions and contingencies Inventory – net realisable value
(7) Out of date IT systems affecting management's ability to make informed decisions	Anywhere

The business risk audit approach tries to mirror the risk management steps that have been taken by the directors. In this way, the auditor will **seek to establish that the financial statement objectives have been met**, through an investigation into whether all the other business objectives have been met by the directors.

This approach to the audit has been called a **'top-down' approach** because it starts at the business and its objectives and works back down to the financial statements, rather than working up from the financial statements which has historically been the approach to audit.

The other key element of a business risk approach is that as it is focused on the business more fully, rather than the financial statements, there is greater opportunity for the auditor to add value to the client's business and to assist in managing the risks that the business faces.

2.2.1 Advantages of business risk approach

There are a number of reasons why firms who use the business risk approach prefer it to historic approaches:

- Added value is given to clients, as the approach focuses on the business as a whole.
- Audit attention focused on high level controls with extensive use of analytical procedures, increases audit efficiency and therefore reduces cost.
- It does not focus on merely routine processes, which technological developments have rendered less prone to error than has historically been the case.
- It responds to the importance placed by regulators and the Government on corporate governance.
- Engagement risk (risk of auditor being sued) is lower as a result of broader understanding of the client's business and practices.

2.3 Other audit strategies

In addition to the 'top-down' or business risk approach, a variety of different audit strategies may be adopted. These have been covered in your previous studies, and will only be mentioned briefly here. They include:

- Systems audit
- Balance sheet approach
- Transaction cycle approach
- Directional testing

2.3.1 Systems audit

An auditor may predominantly test controls and systems, but substantive testing can never be eliminated entirely.

2.3.2 Balance sheet approach

This is the most common approach to the substantive part of the audit, after controls have been tested. It is named after the old name for the statement of financial position, the 'balance sheet'.

The statement of financial position gives a snapshot of the financial position of the business at a point in time. It follows that if it is not a misstatement, and the previous snapshot was fairly stated, then it is reasonable to undertake lower-level testing on the transactions which connect the two snapshots, for example, analytical procedures.

Under this approach, therefore, the auditors seek to concentrate efforts on substantiating the closing position in the year, shown in the statement of financial position, having determined that the closing position from the previous year (also substantiated) has been correctly transferred to the opening position in the current year.

In some cases, particularly small companies, the business risks may be strongly connected to the fact that management is concentrated on one person. Another feature of **small companies** may be that their **statement of financial position** is **uncomplicated** and contains one or two material items, for example, receivables or inventory. When this is the case, it is **often more cost effective** to undertake a **highly substantive statement of financial position audit** than to undertake a business risk assessment, as it is relatively simple to obtain the assurance required about the financial statements from taking that approach.

However, when not undertaken in conjunction with a risk-based approach or systems testing, the level of detailed testing can be high in a balance sheet approach, rendering it costly.

2.3.3 Transaction cycle approach

Cycles testing is in some ways closely linked to systems testing, because it is based on the same systems. However, here we are looking at them in terms of **substantive testing**.

When auditors take a cycles approach, they test the transactions which have occurred, resulting in the entries in the statement of profit or loss (for example, sales transactions, inventory purchases, wages payments, other expenses).

They would select a sample of transactions and test that each transaction was complete and processed correctly throughout the cycle. In other words, they substantiate the transactions which appear in the financial statements.

Point to note

> The auditors may assess the systems of a company as **ineffective**. In this case, they would carry out extensive substantive procedures. The substantive approach taken in this situation could be a transaction cycles approach. In fact, if systems have been adjudged to be ineffective, the auditor is more likely to take a transaction cycles approach than a balance sheet approach, as it will be essential that the auditor substantiates that the transactions have been recorded properly in spite of the poor systems.

2.3.4 Directional testing

Directional testing is a method of undertaking detailed substantive testing. Substantive testing seeks to discover misstatements and omissions, and the discovery of these will depend on the direction of the test.

Broadly speaking, substantive procedures can be said to fall into two categories:

(a) Tests to discover **misstatements** (resulting in over- or under-statement). These tests will **start with the accounting records** in which the transactions are recorded and check from the entries to supporting documents or other evidence. Such tests should detect any over-statement and also any under-statement through causes other than omission.

(b)   Tests to discover **omissions** (resulting in under-statement). These tests must **start from outside the accounting records** and then check back to those records. Understatements through omission will never be revealed by starting with the account itself, as there is clearly no chance of selecting items that have been omitted from the account.

The concept of directional testing derives from the principle of **double entry** bookkeeping, in that for every **debit** there is a **corresponding credit** (assuming that the double entry is complete and that the accounting records balance). Therefore, any **misstatement** of a **debit entry** will result in either a **corresponding misstatement** of a **credit entry** or a **misstatement** in the opposite direction, of **another** debit entry.

By designing audit tests carefully, the auditors are able to use this principle in drawing audit conclusions, not only about the debit or credit entries that they have directly tested but also about the corresponding credit or debit entries that are necessary to balance the books. Tests are therefore designed in the following way.

The matrix set out below demonstrates how directional testing is applied to give assurance on all account areas in the financial statements.

Type of account	Purpose of primary test	Primary test also gives comfort on			
		Assets	Liabilities	Income	Expenses
Assets	Overstatement (O)	U	O	O	U
Liabilities	Understatement (U)	U	O	O	U
Income	Understatement (U)	U	O	O	U
Expense	Overstatement (O)	U	O	O	U

A test for the overstatement of an asset simultaneously gives comfort on understatement of other assets, overstatement of liabilities, overstatement of income and understatement of expenses.

So, by performing the primary tests shown in the matrix, the auditors obtain audit assurance in other audit areas. Successful completion of the primary tests will therefore result in them having tested all account areas both for overstatement and understatement.

The major advantage of the directional audit approach is its cost effectiveness.

(a)   Assets and expenses are tested for overstatement only, and liabilities and income for understatement only, that is, items are not tested for both overstatement and understatement.

(b)   It audits directly the more likely types of transactional misstatement, ie unrecorded income and improper expense (arising intentionally or unintentionally).

Point to note

Directional testing is particularly useful when there is a high level of detailed testing to be carried out, for example, when the auditors have assessed the company's controls and accounting system as ineffective.

Question
Audit strategy

As audit senior, you have recently attended a meeting with the managing director of Go Shop Co (audit client) and the new audit partner assigned to the audit, Mike Kenton, who has recently joined your firm, Eastlake and Pond. The audit partner is familiarising himself with the client.

Go Shop Co is a large limited liability building company set up by John Yeams, who has been managing director since incorporation. It operates in the south of the country, purchasing land outside of major towns and building retail parks, which the company then manages. You are familiar with the client, as you have taken part in the audit for the last three years. The other key member of the board is Kathleen Hadley, who set up the business with John Yeams and is finance director. Kathleen is a qualified accountant, and the accounting systems and procedures at Go Shop Co have always appeared sound.

You took minutes of the meeting, which are given below.

> **Minutes of a meeting between Mike Kenton and John Yeams, 30 March 20X2**
>
> MK introduced himself to JY and asked for a brief history of the business, which was given. Currently, the majority of income is from the property management side, as the building market is becoming saturated. With interest rates set to rise, JY is less keen to borrow and build in the current climate.
>
> MK asked JY whether a recent spate of terrorist bomb attacks had had any effect on business. JY commented that he had been given the impression that retail was down and that customers were staying away from the retail centres – but he felt that some of that could be attributed to a rise in interest rates and was likely to be temporary. The first months of the year are always poor for retail ...
>
> MK asked whether there had been a rise in empty units in the retail centres. JY said there had been a small rise.
>
> MK asked JY about his views in relation to the current proposed legislation before the Government concerning quality standards in the building trade. JY commented that it seemed like a 'load of nonsense' to him, and expressed some dissatisfaction with the current political situation ... MK pressed the matter, enquiring as to JY's opinion on the likely effects on his business were more stringent standards to be required in the future. JY is of the firm belief that it would not be passed. MK expressed his fear that the legislation was more than likely to be passed, and would have far-reaching and expensive effects on most builders in the country. JY repeated some of his previous comments about politicians.
>
> MK enquired as to whether there were any anticipated developments in the business that he should know about. JY made reference to KH's plans to retire from full-time work in the business. MK asked how JY was going to replace her. JY commented that he was hoping to persuade her to stay on as she deals with all the financial side, and he'd be lost without her. MK tried to enquire how firm her retirement plans were, but JY was not forthcoming.

After the meeting, Mike Kenton asked you to ring Kathleen and discuss her plans. She confirmed that she does plan to retire. She informed you that she plans to emigrate to Australia, and is not keen to put back her plans. She asked about the possibility of Eastlake and Pond assisting in the recruitment process for her replacement, as she does not feel that John Yeams has the technical ability to recruit someone without her, and has not accepted her plans enough to recruit before her retirement. She said that she has even wondered about the possibility of someone being seconded to the company from Eastlake and Pond to cover her position after she has left and before her replacement is found.

Mike is keen to reappraise the audit strategy taken towards the audit of Go Shop, as he feels the audit could be conducted more efficiently than it has been in the past. Historically the audit has been highly substantive.

Required

(a)   Identify and explain the key business risks that exist at Go Shop.
(b)   Explain what is meant by the 'business risk approach' to an audit.
(c)   Propose and justify a strategy for the audit of Go Shop.
(d)   Discuss the ethical implications for the audit of the two suggestions made by Kathleen.

Approaching the answer

 | Question | | Audit strategy

As audit senior, you have recently attended a meeting with the managing director of Go Shop Co (audit client) and the new audit partner assigned to the audit, Mike Kenton, who has recently joined your firm, Eastlake and Pond. The audit partner is familiarising himself with the client.

> Cumulative knowledge and understanding

> Volatile industry

Go Shop Co is a large limited liability building company set up by John Yeams, who has been managing director since incorporation. It operates in the south of the country, purchasing land outside of major towns and building retail parks, which the company then manages. You are familiar with the client, as you

have taken part in the audit for the last three years. The other key member of the board is Kathleen Hadley, who set up the business with John Yeams and is finance director. Kathleen is a qualified accountant, and the accounting systems and procedures at Go Shop Co have always appeared sound.

Good control environment

You took minutes of the meeting, which are given below.

Minutes of a meeting between Mike Kenton and John Yeams, 30 March 20X2

Going concern

MK introduced himself to JY and asked for a brief history of the business, which was given. Currently, the majority of income is from the property management side, as the building market is becoming saturated. With interest rates set to rise, JY is less keen to borrow and build in the current climate.

Impact on any borrowing

MK asked JY whether a recent spate of terrorist bomb attacks had had any effect on business. JY commented that he had been given the impression that retail was down and that customers were staying away from the retail centres – but he felt that some of that could be attributed to a rise in interest rates and was likely to be temporary. The first months of the year are always poor for retail ...

Knock on going concern issues?

Pressure on major customers

MK asked whether there had been a rise in empty units in the retail centres. JY said there had been a small rise.

Compliance risk if legislation is passed – likely?
And going concern?

MK asked JY about his views in relation to the current proposed legislation before the Government concerning quality standards in the building trade. JY commented that it seemed like a 'load of nonsense' to him, and expressed some dissatisfaction with the current political situation … MK pressed the matter, enquiring as to JY's opinion on the likely effects on his business were more stringent standards to be required in the future. JY is of the firm belief that it would not be passed. MK expressed his fear that the legislation was more than likely to be passed, and would have far-reaching and expensive effects on most builders in the country. JY repeated some of his previous comments about politicians.

MK enquired as to whether there were any anticipated developments in the business, which he should know about. JY made reference to KH's plans to retire from full-time work in the business. MK asked how JY was going to replace her. JY commented that he was hoping to persuade her to stay on as she deals with all the financial side, and he'd be lost without her. MK tried to enquire how firm her retirement plans were, but JY was not forthcoming.

Operational risk – loss of key staff member, and implications for FS and control environment

After the meeting, Mike Kenton asked you to ring Kathleen and discuss her plans. She confirmed that she does plan to retire. She informed you that she plans to emigrate to Australia, and is not keen to put back her plans. She asked about the possibility of Eastlake and Pond assisting in the recruitment process for her replacement, as she does not feel that John Yeams has the technical ability to recruit someone without her, and has not accepted her plans enough to recruit before her retirement. She said that she has even wondered about the possibility of someone being seconded to the company from Eastlake and Pond to cover her position after she has left and before her replacement is found.

Independence issues

Mike is keen to reappraise the audit strategy taken towards the audit of Go Shop, as he feels the audit could be conducted more efficiently than it has in the past. Historically the audit has been highly substantive.

> Link with senior's cumulative knowledge and understanding – analytical review? Use of business risk approach. Control environment is sound …

Answer plan

(a) Business risks

Operational – industry

(i) Building industry volatile and apparently saturated

(ii) Retail management – retail industry volatile and affected by bomb threats / interest rates

Operational – personnel

About to lose key management on the financial side and no current plans to replace her. Could severely affect systems in the finance department – could have knock-on effects on sales and purchases relationships – suppliers/customers.

Finance

Likely that Go Shop has high borrowings against buildings built and managed – therefore increase in interest rates could be bad – particularly if they have borrowed lots while interest rates were low.

Compliance

Potential statute concerning quality standards:

(i) Far reaching
(ii) Expensive
(iii) Going concern?

(b) Business risk approach (BRA)

Define BRA – link to Audit Risk Approach, etc …

Indicator of going concern problem?

Receivables' recoverability

Tangible non-current assets impairment

Effect on financial statements (FS) themselves – more prone to error?

Also, impact on control environment?

Going concern

Interest rates

Going concern

(c) **Strategy**

BRA – have identified business risk

Key risks to financial statements as identified above – linked strongly … seems reasonable to extend audit risk approach in this way.

Control environment strong – therefore reasonable to do controls testing – but question if this will still be the case when KH leaves.

Also, senior has cumulative knowledge and understanding – therefore analytical procedures will be good. Explanations available for analytical review.

BRA is generally more efficient than highly substantive – due to top-down procedures.

(d) **Ethical implications**

Recruitment mustn't make management decisions.

Secondment – must ensure that there are 'Chinese walls' between staff on audit team and seconded staff – may represent too great a loss of objectivity due to familiarity.

Answer

(a) **Key business risks at Go Shop**

Operational – industry

The building industry is generally considered to be a volatile industry and sensitive to changes in economic climate. The managing director has identified that the particular market that the company operates in, retail parks, has become saturated. Go Shop's business is therefore likely to be volatile generally and the market for the services Go Shop provides is saturated. This is an operational risk – what will Go Shop do if it does not do what it has done historically?

The company is not only strongly connected with the building industry but also the retail industry. This is another industry that is volatile. It has recently been affected by higher interest rates and reduced consumer spending. It has also suffered due to the bomb threats made against retail parks, which have discouraged consumers from shopping.

Operational – personnel

The business is about to lose a key member of personnel on the financial side, and there appear to be no current plans to replace her. This could severely affect systems in the finance department, which could have a knock-on effect on crucial supplier and customer relations and therefore the operations of the wider business.

Finance

It is likely that Go Shop has a **high level of borrowings secured** on the buildings that they have built and now manage. If this is the case, the **increase in interest rates** will adversely affect their business directly in the form of **interest** on these loans. This may be particularly severe if they have overborrowed when interest rates were low.

Compliance

There is currently legislation before the Government that is likely to have far-reaching effects on the operations of Go Shop's building arm. The law relates to quality standards in the building industry and is likely to be costly to implement. It is possible that Go Shop will struggle to **afford to implement such standards**. An even more significant concern is that it appears that the director has taken **no steps to mitigate this risk** and has put **no action plans into place** to ensure that the law would be complied with, if passed. This could mean that the company could be liable to legal action and fines.

(b) **Business risk approach**

The business risk approach is an extension of the audit risk approach. When using an audit risk approach, the auditors focus their attention on matters that they feel are the most significantly risky to the financial statements so that they can provide a cost-effective audit.

The audit risk approach concentrates on three areas of risk; inherent risk, control risk and detection risk.

> In a business risk approach, the auditors determine that the risks that are most likely to adversely affect the financial statements are the business risks of the company, hence they direct their testing to the business risks apparent in the business.

This can be illustrated in the given scenario by looking at the significant links between the business risks identified and the financial statements.

Operational – industry	
Volatile industry	Significant issues relating to **going concern** arising, auditors should direct their audit work in this area.
Retail units affected by bomb threats	Potential issues relating to **receivables' recoverability**. Retail units may not be able to pay rent/honour leases if they are not receiving sufficient income from sales. The potential fall in income related to the retail units could affect the valuation **of tangible non-current assets** – is there a need for an impairment review?
Operational – personnel	
Loss of FD	This could have a significant impact on the **calculation and presentation of the financial statements** if they are now drafted by an inexperienced person. There is also a significant impact on the **control environment**, which will affect assessment of control risk.
Finance	
Interest rates	The issues relating to high interest rates will affect the **interest figure** in the statement of profit or loss. It may also affect the **going concern** assumption.
Compliance	
New law	Depending on the timing of the new legislation and the outcomes discussed above, this could affect **events after the reporting period**, contingencies or **provisions**. It could also potentially affect going concern.

(c)   **Audit strategy**

The audit strategy will depend on certain matters, such as the date when Kathleen Hadley leaves the business. Assuming that she leaves after the audit, a **business risk approach** would be appropriate.

This is because business risks have already been identified and, as outlined above, there are **significant links between the business risks and the financial statements**.

The **control environment has historically been strong**, so making use of controls testing would appear to be appropriate. This in particular is highly dependent on the presence of Kathleen Hadley at the audit date.

The **audit senior** has **experience** of the client and significant **knowledge** of the business therefore it seems appropriate that a high use be made of **analytical procedures**. It also appears that strong explanations will be available for movements on accounts over the period. Again, this is dependent on the presence of Kathleen Hadley.

Lastly, the business risk approach is considered an **efficient approach** as it uses 'top-down' procedures, so as strong evidence appears to be available, it is sensible to take the most efficient approach possible, while ensuring that a quality audit is conducted.

(d)   **Ethical implications**

(i)   *Recruitment*

It is very important that the audit firm does not take management decisions on behalf of the entity. Hence it would be appropriate for it to take an advisory role in the recruitment process, perhaps reviewing CVs and advising as to qualifications and factors to look for. However, it should not get heavily involved in the interviewing process, as this could lead it to, in effect, make management decisions on behalf of the directors.

(ii) *Secondment*

If a staff member of the audit firm is to be seconded to the audit client to work in this significant role, the firm would have to be very clear that there were boundaries in place between that staff member and the audit team. This may in practice be impossible.

However, provided that objectivity can be retained for the audit team and that there is not a problem of familiarity, a secondment might be appropriate.

A problem of familiarity could arise in either of the following scenarios.

(1) The person seconded had previously worked on the audit and the strategy and approach were not changed.

(2) The audit team were familiar with the person seconded and had a personal relationship with them that presented a significant risk to objectivity.

Exam focus point

Your approach to scenario questions should be to read the scenario as closely as you can, making notes of anything that will help you answer the requirement. However, although it is true that everything in the scenario has been put there on purpose by the examination team, not all of it will be relevant to the requirement. Some of it could have been put there as a distraction, so you will need to make a judgement about whether it is relevant or not.

A common example of this is where information on the business's operations is included in a scenario, but this is not relevant to the audit. You should bear in mind that **operations only affect the audit if they result in an audit risk**. Another example of irrelevant information would be matters that are clearly immaterial to the audit in question.

Finally, just as the scenario may include irrelevant information, it may also be missing out information that is relevant to you. A common requirement is to identify and explain any further information that will be required. It is important here that you think practically about the evidence you would need to address the audit risks you have found in the scenario.

Question

More information needed?

You are currently planning the audit of Howling Wolf Co, a logistics firm. One of Howling Wolf's trucks was involved in an unfortunate accident which resulted in the deaths of a number of sheep that belonged to a local farmer. The farmer is angry, and is threatening to take legal action against Wolf unless it agrees to compensate them for the damage done.

Howling Wolf's financial statements include a provision for the cost of replacing the sheep.

Required

Identify and explain the additional information that you would require to obtain audit evidence in respect of the provision.

Answer

Information required includes:

– The date of the incident with the sheep, which should already have happened. IAS 37 specifies that a provision can only be created in relation to a present obligation arising as a result of a past event.

– The probability that Wolf will be required to pay compensation to the farmer. If Wolf is likely to win in any legal action, then no provision should be set up.

– The number of sheep involved in the incident, along with an estimate of the cost of replacing them.

- An estimate of the amount most likely to be paid to the farmer as compensation (if payment is likely).

- An estimate of the date by when the farmer is likely to paid. The time value of money is unlikely to be material here, so the provision would be unlikely to be discounted.

- Whether Howling Wolf's truck suffered significant damage as a result of the accident, and if so what the costs of rectifying this damage are likely to be.

3 Materiality   12/10, 12/11, 6/13, 12/13, 6/14

FAST FORWARD

Materiality considerations are important in both planning and performing the audit. An item might be material due to its nature, value or impact on the users of the financial statements as a group.

3.1 ISA 320 *Materiality in planning and performing an audit*

Materiality issues are dealt with in two standards:

- ISA 320 *Materiality in planning and performing an audit*
- ISA 450 *Evaluation of misstatements identified during the audit*

Key terms

Materiality. Misstatements, including omissions, are considered to be material if they, individually or in the aggregate, could reasonably be expected to influence the economic decisions of users taken on the basis of the financial statements.

Performance materiality. The amount or amounts set by the auditor at less than materiality for the financial statements as a whole to reduce to an appropriately low level the probability that the aggregate of uncorrected and undetected misstatements exceeds materiality for the financial statements as a whole. If applicable, performance materiality also refers to the amount or amounts set by the auditor at less than the materiality level or levels for particular classes of transactions, account balances or disclosures.

(ISA 320)

ISA 320 requires auditors to **set materiality** (and **performance materiality**) **at the planning stage**. The assessment of materiality at this stage should be based on the most recent and reliable financial information and will help to determine an effective and efficient audit approach. Materiality assessment will help the auditors to decide:

- **How many** and **what items** to examine
- Whether to use **sampling techniques**
- What **level of misstatement** is likely to lead to a modified audit opinion

The resulting combination of audit procedures should help to reduce audit risk to an appropriately low level.

Materiality criteria	
An item might be material due to its:	
Nature	Given the definition of materiality as an item that would affect the readers of the financial statements, some **items** might **by their nature affect readers**. Examples include **transactions related to directors**, such as remuneration and contracts with the company.
Value	Some items will be significant in the financial statements by virtue of their **size**; for example, if the company had bought a piece of land with a value which comprised three-quarters of the asset value of the company, that would be material. That is why materiality is often expressed in terms of **percentages** (of assets, of profits).
Impact	Some **items may by chance have a significant impact** on financial statements; for example, a proposed journal which is not material in itself could convert a profit into a loss. The difference between a small profit and a small loss could be material to some readers.

3.1.1 Performance materiality

The concept of performance materiality allows an auditor to set different materiality levels for different areas of the financial statements, according to their judgement of the audit risk that is particular to that area. The idea is that overall materiality needs to be adjusted for the actual 'performance' of the audit in particular areas, and cannot just be applied blindly. A better word for the concept might have been '**applied materiality**', since it is mainly about how overall materiality is applied to particular areas.

The concept of performance materiality focuses in on the difference between the level of tolerable misstatement and the level of actual misstatements detected. For example, if a misstatement were detected that was just below overall materiality, then there is a difficulty for the auditor: the financial statements are not materially misstated, but there is a risk that there may be undetected misstatements which would push over the materiality threshold. The auditor should not just compare the amount of detected misstatements with materiality as a whole, but should take into account the fact that only some specific items have been tested (eg because sampling is used). Consideration of materiality needs to take into account the possible undetected misstatements which might be lurking. Thinking in terms of performance materiality means thinking of what the effect of individual misstatements might be on audit risk for the financial statements as a whole. This provides the auditor with a margin of safety in relation to any undetected misstatements, which are then less likely to exceed materiality as a whole.

Performance materiality therefore entails a prudent approach to materiality, and to determining the procedures that are needed to conclude on whether or not the financial statements are materially misstated. The higher the assessed risk, the lower the performance materiality must be set. This means that the auditor will perform more audit work than if the concept of performance materiality did not exist.

As with overall materiality, setting performance materiality involves the use of professional judgement. This judgement must take into account qualitative aspects, such as the level of risk attached to a particular balance in the financial statements.

Example

An auditor might judge an entity's non-current assets to be a high-risk area. If non-current assets were $20m and total assets $50m, then overall materiality might be set at 2% of total assets, ie $1m.

Performance materiality for non-current assets could then be set as a simple proportion of materiality, eg $400,000 (= $20m/$50m × $1m).

Taking into account the auditor's judgement that non-current assets are higher risk, this could thus be decreased to $300,000 in order to provide a greater margin of safety. Any misstatements above this level would be judged material.

3.2 Guidelines for materiality

It is clear from the points made about materiality criteria that materiality is judgemental, and an issue that auditors must be aware of when approaching all their audit work.

However, you will know from your previous studies that generally accepted rules about materiality exist. Examples are:

- Items relating to directors are normally always material.
- Percentage guidelines are often given for materiality.

While materiality **must always be a matter of judgement** for the auditor, it is **helpful to have some guidelines** to bear in mind. Reasons for this are:

- The guidelines give the auditor a **framework** within which to base their thoughts on materiality.
- The guidelines provide a **benchmark** against which to assess the quality of auditing, for example, in the event of litigation or disciplinary action.

The following figures are appropriate **starting points** for the consideration of materiality.

Value	%
Profit before tax	5
Gross profit	½–1
Revenue	½–1
Total assets	1–2
Net assets	2–5
Profit after tax	5–10

3.2.1 Qualitative materiality

Most of the discussion on materiality focuses on quantitative materiality, but materiality must also be applied to **qualitative disclosures** in the financial statements. ISA 320 and ISA 315 were revised in 2015 to include guidance here. Essentially the same concept of materiality applies, ie a misstatement must be viewed in terms of its effect on the economic decisions of users.

Examples of disclosures to which misstatements might be material include:

- Liquidity/debt covenants
- Events leading to recognition of impairment losses
- Changes in accounting policies, eg because of a new IFRS, where this has a significant impact
- Share-based payments
- Related parties (and transactions with related parties)

3.3 Problems with materiality

As discussed above, materiality is a matter of judgement for the auditor. Therefore, prescriptive rules will not always be helpful when assessing materiality. A **significant risk** of prescriptive rules is that a **significant matter**, which **falls outside the boundaries of the rules**, could be overlooked, leading to a **material misstatement in the financial statements**.

The percentage guidelines of assets and profits that are commonly used for materiality must be handled with care. The auditor must bear in mind the **focus** of the company being audited.

In some companies, **post-tax profit** is the key figure in the financial statements, as the level of dividend is the most important factor in the accounts.

In **owner managed businesses**, if owners are paid a salary and are indifferent to dividends, the key profit figure stands higher in the statement of profit or loss, say at **gross profit** level. Alternatively in this situation, the auditor should consider a figure that does not appear in the statement of profit or loss: **profit before directors' salaries and benefits**.

Some companies are **driven by assets** rather than the need for profits. In such examples, higher materiality might need to be applied to assets. In some companies, say charities, **costs** are the driving factor, and materiality might be considered in relation to these.

While rules or guidelines are helpful to auditors when assessing materiality, they must always keep in mind the **nature** of the business they are dealing with. Materiality must be **tailored to the business and the anticipated user** of financial statements, or it is not truly materiality. Refer back to the definition of materiality and consider **all the elements** of it.

Exam focus point

In earlier studies, you may have calculated materiality by taking a weighted average of the calculated percentages of revenue (½–1%), profit before tax (5%) and net assets (2–5%). This is appropriate when calculating preliminary (planning) materiality. In this paper, you will often be calculating materiality in relation to a specific item. You must only use the relevant comparator; for example, total assets if the matter relates to the statement of financial position, profit before tax if the matter impacts on profit, and both if it relates to the statement of financial position and impacts on profit; for example, a provision.

Question   **Materiality**

You are the manager responsible for the audit of Albreda Co. The draft consolidated financial statements for the year ended 31 March 20X2 show revenue of $42.2 million (20X1 $41.8 million), profit before taxation of $1.8 million (20X1 $2.2 million) and total assets of $30.7 million (20X1 $23.4 million). In March 20X2, the management board announced plans to cease offering 'home delivery' services from the end of the month. These sales amounted to $0.6 million for the year to 31 March 20X2 (20X1 $0.8 million). A provision of $0.2 million has been made at 31 March 20X2 for the compensation of redundant employees (mainly drivers).

Required

Comment on the materiality of these two issues.

Answer

Home delivery sales

The appropriate indicator of materiality with regard to the home delivery sales is revenue, as the home delivery sales form part of the total revenue of the company.

$0.6 million is 1.4% of the total revenue for 20X2 (see Working 1).

An item is generally considered to be material if it is in the region of ½-1% of revenue, so the home delivery services are material.

Provision

The appropriate indicators of materiality with regard to the provision are total assets and profit, as the provision affects both the statement of financial position (it is a liability) and the statement of profit or loss and other comprehensive income (it is a charge against profit).

$0.2 million is 0.65% of total assets in 20X2 (see Working 2). As an item is generally considered to be material if it is in the region of 1–2% of total assets, the provision is not material to the statement of profit or loss and other comprehensive income.

However, $0.2 million is 11% of profit before tax for 20X2 (see Working 3 below). An item is considered material to profit before tax if it is in the region of 5%. Therefore, the provision is material to the statement of financial position.

Working 1	Working 2	Working 3
$\dfrac{\$0.6 \text{ million}}{\$42.2 \text{ million}} \times 100\% = 1.4\%$	$\dfrac{\$0.2 \text{ million}}{\$30.7 \text{ million}} \times 100 = 0.65\%$	$\dfrac{\$0.2 \text{ million}}{\$1.8 \text{ million}} \times 100 = 11\%$

Exam focus point

In the exam it is not necessary to comment, as in the question above, on the relevant indicator of materiality. The bits that would have earned marks in the exam are shown in grey shade above. Note that this question is for practice only, and is not representative of the actual P7 exam.

As a general rule, if an exam question gives you the information to calculate materiality then you should calculate it. You should then think about whether there is anything else to think about in relation to materiality or performance materiality – perhaps there will be a hint in the question that an item is material by nature or impact? At P7 you will need to spot things, eg an immaterial misstatement that becomes material by turning a profit into a loss.

Materiality is unlikely to be tested on its own, so once you have considered it you will probably need to go on to consider other audit issues, eg further evidence or procedures required and the effect of a misstatement on the audit report.

3.3.1 Revision as audit progresses

The auditor will revise the materiality level during the audit if they become aware of information that would have caused a different materiality level to have been set in the first place.

Exam focus point

Your ability to answer a question in the P7 exam often depends on little points like this. The December 2011 exam, for example, contained a scenario in which the audit manager stated that they wanted to 'fix materiality at the planning stage for all audits'.

Most candidates could probably have guessed that this was wrong, but to score the two marks you needed to state **why** it was wrong.

3.4 Documentation

The auditor must document:

- Materiality for the financial statements as a whole
- Materiality for particular balances, classes of transactions or disclosures
- Performance materiality
- Any revisions to the above

3.5 Evaluating material misstatements

ISA 450 *Evaluation of misstatements identified during the audit* provides more specific guidance on the documentation and communication of misstatements identified.

> **ISA 450.5**
>
> The auditor shall accumulate misstatements identified during the audit, other than those that are clearly trivial.

All misstatements (other than those that are clearly trivial) must be **communicated on a timely basis to management** with a request that they are corrected. If management does not correct them, then the auditor is obliged to communicate the individual uncorrected misstatements to those charged with governance, together with the effect on the audit opinion. Finally, for those misstatements that remain uncorrected, management must provide written representations that they believe that the effects of the misstatements (individually and in aggregate) are immaterial.

ISA 450.15

The auditor shall include in the audit documentation:

(a)   The amount below which misstatements would be regarded as clearly trivial;

(b)   All misstatements accumulated during the audit and whether they have been corrected; and

(c)   The auditor's conclusion as to whether uncorrected misstatements are material, individually or in aggregate, and the basis for that conclusion.

One of the competences you require to fulfil Performance Objective 19 of the PER is the ability to evaluate evidence collected, demonstrating professional scepticism, investigating areas of concern and ensuring documentation is complete and all significant matters and areas of judgement are highlighted. You can apply the knowledge you gain from this chapter of the Text to help demonstrate this competence.

4 Risk   12/07, 6/08, 6/09, 12/10, 12/11,
                                            6/12, 12/12, 6/13, 12/13, 6/14, 12/14, 6/15

As you know from your earlier auditing studies, the auditor must be aware of two types of risk.

*   **Audit risk** (sometimes known as assignment or engagement risk)
*   **Business risk**

Exam focus point

Risk is examined in virtually every P7 exam paper, usually in the first question.

4.1 Audit risk

FAST FORWARD

Auditors must assess the risk of material misstatements arising in financial statements and carry out procedures in response to assessed risks.

ISA 200 *Overall objectives of the independent auditor and the conduct of an audit in accordance with international standards on auditing* states that 'the auditor shall obtain sufficient appropriate evidence to reduce audit risk to an acceptably low level'. As discussed in Section 1, the way they do this is by carrying out risk assessment procedures, and then further audit procedures to respond to the risk assessment. We shall look in detail at audit risk here.

ISA 200.5

... ISAs require the auditor to obtain reasonable assurance about whether the financial statements as a whole are free from material misstatement ... It is obtained when the auditor has obtained sufficient appropriate audit evidence to reduce audit risk to an acceptably low level.

Key terms

Audit risk is the risk that the auditor expresses an inappropriate audit opinion when the financial statements are materially misstated. Audit risk is a function of the **risk of material misstatement** and **detection risk**. Risk of material misstatement breaks down into inherent risk and control risk.

Inherent risk is the susceptibility of an assertion about a class of transaction, account balance or disclosure to a misstatement that could be material, either individually or when aggregated with other misstatements, before consideration of any related controls.

Control risk is the risk that a misstatement that could occur in an assertion about a class of transaction, account balance or disclosure and that could be material, either individually or when aggregated with other misstatements, will not be prevented, or detected and corrected, on a timely basis by the entity's internal control.

Detection risk is the risk that the procedures performed by the auditor to reduce audit risk to an acceptably low level will not detect a misstatement that exists and that could be material, either individually or when aggregated with other misstatements.

 Case Study

Consider an oil company which has abandoned one of its oil rigs. This abandonment increases the risk of material misstatement because the abandonment gives rise to an impairment in the value of the rig, which might not be reflected in the financial statements. In other words, there is a risk that the financial statements are misstated in respect of this oil rig.

Exam focus point

You must be able to distinguish between audit risk and business risk. While many business risks will have consequences for the audit by increasing audit risk, they are two separate issues. For example, the fact that a company is exposed to foreign exchange risk is not an audit risk in itself. The audit risk is the potential for material misstatement of the financial statements, especially in relation to IAS 21 *The effects of changes in foreign exchange rates*. This issue is discussed more fully in section 4.2.1 below.

4.1.1 Inherent risk

Exam focus point

Although this section divides risks into inherent, control and detection risk, for your exam you will generally only need to discuss the specific risks in the scenario in line with the requirement. For example, if the requirement asks for a discussion of the audit risks in a scenario, then you should not spend time trying to place risks into these categories (unless you are asked to do so). It is better focus instead on describing the risks themselves.

Inherent risk is the risk that items will be misstated due to characteristics of those items, such as the fact that they are estimates or that they are important items in the accounts. The auditors must use their professional judgement and the understanding of the entity they have gained to assess inherent risk. If no such information or knowledge is available then the inherent risk is assessed as **high**.

Factors affecting client as a whole	
Integrity and **attitude to risk** of directors and management	Domination by a single individual can cause problems
Management experience and **knowledge**	Changes in management and quality of financial management
Unusual pressures on management	Examples include tight reporting deadlines, or market or financing expectations
Nature of business	Potential problems include technological obsolescence or overdependence on single product
Industry factors	Competitive conditions, regulatory requirements, technology developments, changes in customer demand

Factors affecting client as a whole	
Information technology	Problems include lack of supporting documentation, concentration of expertise in a few people, potential for unauthorised access

Factors affecting individual account balances or transactions	
Financial statement **accounts prone to misstatement**	Accounts which require adjustment in previous period or require high degree of estimation
Complex accounts	Accounts which require expert valuations or are subjects of current professional discussion
Assets at risk of being **lost or stolen**	Cash, inventory, portable non-current assets (eg laptop computers)
Quality of **accounting systems**	Strength of individual departments (sales, purchases, cash etc)
High volume transactions	Accounting system may have problems coping
Unusual transactions	Transactions for large amounts, with unusual names, not settled promptly (particularly important if they occur at period end) Transactions that do not go through the system, that relate to specific clients or are processed by certain individuals
Staff	Staff changes or areas of low morale

4.1.2 Control risk

Control risk is the risk that client controls fail to detect material misstatements. A **preliminary assessment** of **control risk** at the planning stage of the audit is required to determine the level of controls and substantive testing to be carried out.

If the auditor judges that the internal control system is good then control risk will probably be low. The appendix to ISA 315 contains a summary of the components of a good system of internal controls. Here is a summary of the summary.

Control environment. This encompasses:

- Communication and enforcement of integrity and ethical values
- Commitment to competence
- Participation by those charged with governance
- Management's philosophy and operating style
- Organisational structure
- Assignment of authority and responsibility
- Human resource policies and practices

Entity's risk assessment process. The entity should have a process for identifying risks that may affect its financial reporting, assessing these risks and then responding to them. Examples of risks that might affect financial reporting include:

- Changes in operating environment. Changes in the regulatory or operating environment can result in changes in competitive pressures and significantly different risks.

- New personnel. New personnel may have a different focus on or understanding of internal control.

- New or revamped information systems. Significant and rapid changes in information systems can change the risk relating to internal control.

- Rapid growth. Significant and rapid expansion of operations can strain controls and increase the risk of a breakdown in controls.

Information system. The information system relevant to financial reporting objectives, which includes the financial reporting system, encompasses methods and records that:

- Identify and record all valid transactions
- Describe on a timely basis the transactions in sufficient detail to permit proper classification of transactions for financial reporting
- Measure the value of transactions in a manner that permits recording their proper monetary value in the financial statements
- Determine the time period in which transactions occurred to permit recording of transactions in the proper accounting period
- Present properly the transactions and related disclosures in the financial statements

Control activities. These include:

- Performance reviews. These control activities include reviews and analyses of actual performance versus budgets, forecasts and prior period performance
- Information processing
- Physical controls, encompassing eg the physical security of assets
- Segregation of duties

Monitoring of controls. In addition to putting controls in place, management must monitor that they are operating effectively, and that they continue to be appropriate when there are changes in circumstances.

4.1.3 Detection risk

Point to note

Detection risk is part of audit risk, but it is **not included in the risk of material misstatement**.

Detection risk is the risk that audit procedures will fail to detect material misstatements. Detection risk relates to the inability of the auditors to examine all evidence. Audit evidence is usually persuasive rather than conclusive so some detection risk is usually present, allowing the auditors to seek 'reasonable assurance'.

The auditors' **inherent and control risk assessments** influence the **nature, timing and extent of substantive procedures** required to reduce detection risk and thereby audit risk.

Exam focus point

The P7 examination team has commented again and again in examiner's reports that students often fail to get the marks in questions on risk by not being specific enough about the **audit** risk being discussed.

The examiner's report for the December 2013 sitting is instructive in this regard. It identifies the following **common weaknesses** in answers to a question asking for an evaluation of business risk in a scenario, and identification and explanation of risks of material misstatement.

- Writing too little for the marks available
- Identifying issues but not explaining, evaluating or assessing the issues as required
- Lack of any real analytical or discursive skills
- Illegible handwriting and inadequate presentation
- Lack of audit knowledge
- Lack of basic accounting knowledge

FAST FORWARD

Business risk is the risk arising to companies through being in operation.

> One of the competences you require to fulfil Performance Objective 3 of the PER is the ability to evaluate activities in your area and identify potential risks of fraud, error or other hazards assessing their probability and impact. You can apply the knowledge you have obtained from this chapter of the Study Text to help demonstrate this competence.

Key terms

Business risk is the risk inherent to the company in its operations. It is risks at all levels of the business. It is split into three components.

Financial risks are the risks arising from the financial activities or financial consequences of an operation, for example, cash flow issues or overtrading.

Operational risks are the risks arising with regard to operations, for example, the risk that a major supplier will be lost and the company will be unable to operate.

Compliance risk is the risk that arises from non-compliance with the laws and regulations that surround the business. The compliance risk attaching to environmental issues, for example, is discussed in Chapter 15.

The above components of business risk are the risks that the company should seek to mitigate and manage.

The **process of risk management** for the business is:

- Identify significant risks that could prevent the business achieving its objectives
- Provide a framework to ensure that the business can meet its objectives
- Review the objectives and framework regularly to ensure that objectives are met

A key part of the process is therefore to **identify the business risks**. There are various tools used to do this that you may have come across before. They are listed below.

- SWOT analysis
- The five forces model
- The PEST analysis
- Porter's value chain

Exam focus point

The Study Guide states that you should be able to identify business risks in a question. If you have previously used any of the above techniques they may be useful to you, but in the exam it will be better to **use common sense** as you work through any given question, bearing in mind the three components of business risk given above. You are unlikely to get many marks just for explicitly applying the above four models to a scenario in P7.

4.2.1 Relationship between business risk and audit risk

On the one hand, business risk and audit risk are completely **unrelated**.

- Business risk arises in the operations of a business.
- Audit risk is focused on the financial statements of the business.
- Audit risk exists only in relation to an opinion given by auditors.

In other ways, the two are strongly **connected**. At the most basic level, almost everything that a company does results in some sort of financial effect, and where there are financial transactions there is always the risk that these transactions are reported wrongly. For example, if a business makes a sale, then there is a risk that this sale will not be reported in accordance with IFRS 15 *Revenue from contracts with customers*.

The links between business risk and audit risk can be seen in the inherent and control aspects of audit risk. In audit risk these are limited to risks pertaining to the financial statements, but the same risks that are inherent audit risks can also be business risks. For example, a business with significant trade receivables may have the business risk that cash is not recovered from receivables, and the audit risk that trade receivables are overstated.

Likewise, control risk. In response to business risk, the directors put in place a system of controls. These will include controls to help mitigate the financial aspect of business risk. These are the controls that audit control risk incorporates.

Therefore, although audit risk is very financial statements focused, business risk does form part of the inherent risk associated with the financial statements, not least because if the risks materialise, **the going concern basis of the financial statements could be affected**.

<table>
<tr><td>

Exam focus point

</td><td>

Your examination team has stated that P7 students frequently confuse business risk with audit risk. If a question asks for audit risks, do **not** write about business risks. The main way business risks directly affect audit risk is through going concern, so if you are making a point about any other business risks in a question on audit risk, then you need to be very clear and precise about the audit risk that the business risk gives rise to.

It is important that you do not simply identify business risks if a question is to do with the risk of material misstatement. In an article in *Student Accountant*, your examination team warns that 'the business risk must be developed into a specific risk of material misstatement in the financial statements'.

</td></tr>
</table>

4.3 Business risks from current trends in IT

4.3.1 The increasing risk of cyber incidents

Increasing connectivity and the openness of computer networks in the global business environment exposes businesses to system and network failures and to cyber attack. The 2011 *Norton Cyber Crime* report found that the total cost of cyber crime over the 24 countries being reported on was over $388bn, with more than 1m people becoming victims of cyber crime every day. This figure is made up of £113bn in lost cash (including the cost of repairing IT systems), along with $274bn in lost time.

4.3.2 Audit considerations

Auditors must assess their clients' procedures for identifying and addressing these risks. Some main considerations are:

- Has management established an information and internet security policy?
- How does the entity identify critical information assets and the risk to these assets?
- Does the entity have cyber insurance (many general policies now exclude cyber events)?
- Is there a process for assuring security when linked to third-party systems (eg partners/contractors)?
- What controls are in place to ensure that employees only have access to files and applications that are required for their job?
- Are regular scans carried out to identify malicious activity?
- Are procedures in place to ensure that security is not compromised when the company's systems are accessed from home or on the road?
- What plans are in place for disaster recovery in case of an incident?

These issues will be built into the auditor's assessment of the control environment of the entity and in some cases may influence the auditor's view as to whether there are any uncertainties relating to the going concern status of the entity.

4.3.3 E-commerce

Where an entity undertakes e-commerce, risk identification is crucial. E-commerce has become increasingly important in recent years, and to a large extent early fears about security have proven to be unfounded. However, a number of recent high-profile security breaches in relation to e-commerce systems have underlined that this is an area that can carry significant operational risks, to which auditors must give specific consideration.

Specific business risks include:

- Loss of transaction integrity
- Pervasive e-commerce security risks
- Improper accounting policies
- Non-compliance with tax, legal and regulatory requirements (eg local laws in relation to protection of customers' data)
- Overreliance on e-commerce
- Systems and infrastructure failures
- Damage to reputation if website fails or security is breached

Audit procedures regarding the integrity of the information in the accounting system relating to e-commerce transactions will be concerned with evaluating the reliability of the system for capturing and processing transactions.

Therefore in contrast to audit procedures for traditional business activities which focus separately on control processes relating to each stage of transaction processing, audit procedures for sophisticated e-commerce often focus on automated controls.

 Case Study

Risk in an e-commerce environment

Tripper Co is a travel agency operating in three adjacent towns. The directors have recently taken the decision that they should cease their operations and convert into a dot.com. The new operation, Trippers.com, will benefit from enlarged markets and reduced overheads, as they will be able to operate from single, cheaper premises.

Such a business decision has opened Tripper Co up to significant new business risks.

Customers

Converting to a dot.com company in this way enforces a loss of 'personal touch' with customers. Tripper staff will no longer meet the customers face to face. In a business such as a travel agency, this could be a significant factor. Customers may have appreciated the service given in branches and may feel that this level of service has been lost if it is now redirected through computers and telephones. Trippers should be aware of the possibility of, and mitigate against, loss of customers due to perceived reduction in service.

Competition

By leaving the local area and entering a wider market, Tripper is opening itself up to much more substantial competition. Whereas previously Trippers competed with other local travel agents, it will now be competing theoretically with travel agents everywhere that have internet facilities.

Technology issues

As Tripper has moved into a market that necessitates high technological capabilities, a number of business risks are raised in relation to technological issues:

Viruses

There is a threat of business being severely interrupted by computer viruses, particularly if the staff of Trippers are not very computer literate or the system the company invests in is not up to the standard required.

Viruses could cause interrupted sales and loss of customer goodwill, which could have a significant impact on the going concern status of the company.

Loss of existing custom

Technology could be another reason for loss of existing customers. Their existing customers might not have internet access or the ability to use computers. We do not know what Tripper's demographic was prior to conversion.

However, if conversion means that Tripper loses its existing client base completely and has to rebuild sales, the potential cost in advertising could be excessive.

Cost of system upgrades

Technology is a fast moving area and it will be vital that Tripper's website is kept up to current standards. The cost of upgrade, both in terms of money and business interruption, could be substantial.

New supply chain factors

Tripper may keep existing links with holiday companies and operators. However, it will have new suppliers, such as internet service providers, to contend with.

Personnel

Due to the conversion, Trippers.com will require technical staff and experts. It may not currently have these staff. If this is the case, it could be at risk of severe business interruption and customer dissatisfaction.

If the directors are not computer literate, they may find that they are relying on staff who are far more expert than they are to ensure that their business runs efficiently.

Legislation

There are a number of issues to consider here. The first is data protection and the necessity to comply with the law when personal details are given over the computer. It is important that the website is secure.

E-commerce is also likely to be an area where there is fast moving legislation as the law seeks to keep up with developments. Tripper must also keep up with developments in the law.

Lastly, trading over the internet may create complications as to what domain Tripper are trading in for the purposes of law and tax.

Fraud exposure

The company may find that it is increasingly exposed to fraud in the following ways.

- Credit card fraud relating from transactions not being face to face
- Hacking and fraud relating from the website not being secure
- Overreliance on computer expert personnel could lead to those people committing fraud

Tripper's auditors will be regarding the conversion with interest. The conversion will also severely affect audit risk.

Impact on audit risk

Inherent risk

Many of the business risks identified above could have significant impacts on going concern.

Control risk

The new operations will require new systems, many of which may be specialised computer systems.

Detection risk

The conversion may have the following effects.

(a)   Create a 'paperless office' as all transactions are carried out online – this may make use of computer-assisted auditing techniques essential.

(b)   The auditors may have no experience in e-commerce which may increase detection risk.

(c)   There are likely to be significant impacts on analytical review, as results under the new operations are unlikely to be very comparable to the old.

(d)   There may be a significant need to use the work of experts to obtain sufficient, appropriate audit evidence.

Point to note

> When answering questions, try to let key phrases trigger your thoughts about particular issues, such as systems and going concern. Above all, think about the nature of the business in the scenario and the strengths and deficiencies likely to exist within it.

4.4 Risk of material misstatement   12/08, 12/09, 6/11

4.4.1 Definition

Key term

> **Risk of material misstatement** is risk that the financial statements are materially misstated prior to audit. This consists of two components: inherent risk and control risk.   *(ISA 200)*

The material misstatement could involve:

- Misstatements of the amounts recorded in the statement of profit or loss and other comprehensive income or statement of financial position
- Misstatements of, or omissions from, the disclosure notes

4.4.2 Link with business risk

Many, if not all, business risks will produce a risk of material misstatement.

Using the information in the previous case study to illustrate the link:

Business risk	Risk of material misstatement
The business may lose sales as a result of computer viruses, which could threaten the company's going concern status.	Uncertainties over going concern may not be fully disclosed.
Breaches of data protection law and other regulations could result in the company suffering financial penalties.	Provisions relating to breaches of regulations may be omitted or understated.
The business may suffer losses from credit card fraud.	Losses arising from frauds may not be recognised in the financial statements.

Note that the definition of 'risk of material misstatement' given in ISA 200 refers to a misstatement 'prior to audit'. What is being referred to here is the risk of material misstatement in the financial statements as prepared by the client, completely apart from anything the auditor does. In terms of the audit risk model, **this can result from either a control risk or an inherent risk**, but **not a detection risk**. Detection risks are not 'prior to the audit', and do not meet ISA 200's definition of a 'risk of material misstatement'.

Exam focus point

> Your examination team stated in its April 2012 *Student Accountant* article that:
>
> > 'Candidates are therefore advised that when answering a requirement based on the risk of material misstatement they should focus their answer on inherent risk and control risk factors only. Detection risk is not part of the risk of material misstatement.'
>
> In other words, when you are asked for risks of material misstatement, you are not being asked for anything about the audit itself (detection risk), but about the financial statements and the risk that they are materially misstated. This is then a question of inherent risk and control risk, so when you are answering questions in this area you should be looking for these types of risk.

Forsythia is a small limited liability company offering garden landscaping services. It is partly owned by three business associates, Mr Rose, Mr White and Mr Grass, who each hold 10% of the shares. The major shareholder is the parent company, Poppy Co. This company owns shares in 20 different companies, which operate in a variety of industries. One of them is a garden centre, and Forsythia regularly trades with it. Poppy Co is in turn owned by a parent, White Holdings Co.

The management structure at Forsythia is simple. Of the three non-corporate shareholders, only Mr Rose has any involvement in management. He runs the day to day operations of the company (marketing, sales, purchasing etc) although the company employs two landscape gardeners to actually carry out projects. The accounts department employs a purchase clerk and a sales clerk, who deal with all aspects of the function. The sales clerk is Mr Rose's daughter, Justine. Mr Rose authorises and produces the payroll. The company ledgers are kept on Mr Rose's personal computer. Two weeks after the year end, the sales ledger records were severely damaged by a virus. Justine has a single printout of the balances as at year end, which shows the total owed by each customer.

Forsythia owns the equipment which the gardeners use and they pay them a salary and a bonus based on performance. Mr Rose is remunerated entirely on a commission basis relating to sales and, as a shareholder he receives dividends annually, which are substantial.

Forsythia does not carry any inventory. When materials are required for a project, they are purchased on behalf of the client and charged directly to them. Most customers pay within the 60 day credit period, or take up the extended credit period which Forsythia offers. However, there are a number of accounts that appear to have been outstanding for a significant period.

Justine and her father do not appear to have a very good working relationship. She does not live at home and her salary is not significant. However, she appears to have recently purchased a sports car, which is not a company car.

The audit partner has recently accepted the audit of Forsythia. You have been assigned the task of planning the first audit.

Required

Identify and explain the audit and engagement risks arising from the above scenario.

Approaching the answer

 Question **Audit risk**

Receivables likely to be significant

Look for **key words** and **ask questions** of the information given to you. This is illustrated here:

Forsythia is a small limited company offering garden landscaping services. It is partly owned by three

business associates, Mr Rose, Mr White and Mr Grass, who each hold 10% of the shares. The major

Complicated corporate structure – why?

shareholder is the parent company, Poppy Co. This company owns shares in 20 different companies,

which operate in a variety of industries. One of them is a garden centre, and Forsythia regularly trades

with it. Poppy Co is in turn owned by a parent, White Holdings Co.

Controlling party?

The management structure at Forsythia is simple. Of the three non-corporate shareholders, only Mr Rose has any involvement in management. He runs the day-to-day operations of the company (marketing, sales, purchasing etc) although the company employs two landscape gardeners to actually carry out projects. The accounts department employs a purchase clerk and a sales clerk, who deal with all aspects of the function. The sales clerk is Mr Rose's daughter, Justine. Mr Rose authorises and produces the payroll. The company ledgers are kept on Mr Rose's personal computer. Two weeks after the year end, the sales ledger records were severely damaged by a virus. Justine has a single printout of the balances as at year end, which shows the total owed by each customer.

Forsythia owns the equipment which the gardeners use and they pay them a salary and a bonus based on performance. Mr Rose is remunerated entirely on a commission basis relating to sales and as a shareholder he receives dividends annually, which are substantial.

Forsythia does not carry any inventory. When materials are required for a project, they are purchased on behalf of the client and charged directly to them. Most customers pay within the 60 day credit period, or take up the extended credit period which Forsythia offers. However, there are a number of accounts that appear to have been outstanding for a significant period.

Justine and her father do not appear to have a very good working relationship. She does not live at home and her salary is not significant. However, she appears to have recently purchased a sports car, which is not a company car.

The audit partner has recently accepted the audit of Forsythia. You have been assigned the task of planning the first audit.

Annotations (handwritten boxes):

- Key man? Over reliance?
- Is it slightly odd that a landscape gardening business isn't owned by landscape gardeners?
- No segregation of duties
- Poor controls
- Limitation? And given below, a suspicion of fraud? Teeming and lading?
- Very profit related focused – management bias?
- How accounted for?
- Any laws and regulations relevant?
- Problem with receivables fraud?
- Fraud?
- Any group planning issues?
- Why not all the other group companies? Why do they have different auditors?
- Detection risk / Opening balances / Comparatives – audited or not?

Answer plan

Not all the points you notice will necessarily be **relevant** and you may also find that you do not have **time** to mention all the points in your answer. Now you should prioritise your points in a more formal answer plan and then write your answer.

Audit risks

Inherent

Related party transactions/group issues
Receivables
Fraud – possible indicators, professional scepticism
Profit driven management
Credit extended – accounting/law and regs

Control

Lack of segregation of duties
PC/virus
Suspicion of fraud?
Key man insurance

Detection

First audit
Opening bals and comparatives – audited?

Engagement risks

Some questions raised which makes business look odd

- Group (complex/different auditors/who controls?)
- Nature of business – yet landscape gardeners hired

Indicators of potential fraud

Possible indicators of money laundering (complex structure/cash business)

These may be overstated, but auditor must   (a) Consider them
  (b) Be prepared for consequences

Answer

The following matters are relevant to planning Forsythia's audit.

Audit risks – inherent

Related parties and group issues

Forsythia is part of a **complicated group structure**. This raises several issues for the audit.

- There is a risk of related party transactions existing and not being properly disclosed in the financial statements in accordance with IAS 24 *Related party disclosures*.
- Similarly, there is a risk that it will be difficult to ascertain the controlling party for disclosure.
- There is likely to be some group audit implications. My firm may be required to undertake procedures in line with the group auditors' requirements if Forsythia is to be consolidated.

Receivables

Forsythia is a **service provider**, and it **extends credit** to customers. This is likely to mean that **trade receivables** will be a significant audit balance. However, there is **limited audit evidence** concerning trade receivables due to the effects of a computer virus. There are also indicators of a **possible fraud**.

Fraud

There are various factors that may indicate a sales ledger fraud has taken/is taking place.

- Lack of segregation of duties
- Extensive credit offered
- The virus only destroyed sales ledger information – too specific?
- Poorly paid sales ledger clerk – with expensive lifestyle
- Sales ledger clerk is daughter of a well-paid shareholder and they do not have a good relationship

None of these **factors** necessarily point to a fraud individually, but **added together raise significant concerns**.

Profit driven management

Mr Rose is motivated for the financial statements to show a profit for two reasons:

- He receives a commission (presumably sales driven, which impacts on profit).
- He receives dividends as shareholder, which will depend on profits.

There is a risk that the **financial statements** will be **affected by management bias**.

Credit extended

We should ensure that the credit extended to customers is standard business credit. There are unlikely to be any **complications**, for example interest, but if there were, we should be aware of any **laws and regulations** which might become relevant, and any **accounting issues** which would be raised.

Audit risk – control

There are three significant control problems at Forsythia.

Segregation of duties

There appears to be a **complete lack of segregation of duties** on the three main ledgers. This may have led to a **fraud** on the sales ledger. The fact that there is no segregation on payroll is also a concern as this is an area where frauds are carried out.

Lack of segregation of duties can also lead to **significant errors** being made and not being detected by the system. This problem means that **control risk** will have to be assessed as **high** and **substantial substantive testing** will need to be undertaken.

Personal computer

A PC is used for the accounting system. This is likely to have **poor built-in controls** and further exacerbate the problems caused by the lack of segregation of duties.

The **security** over PCs is also often poor, as has been the case here, where a **virus** has destroyed evidence about the sales ledger.

Key man

The fact that Mr Rose is dominant in management may also be a control problem, particularly if he were ever to be absent.

Audit risk – detection

The key detection risk is that this is the **first audit**, so we will have no prior understanding of the entity to draw on. We have not audited the **opening balances** and **comparatives**. We should have contacted any previous auditors and therefore be aware of whether these have been audited. If there were no previous auditors, these are unaudited. We must ensure that our audit report is clear on this issue.

There is also significant detection risk in relation to **related parties**, as discussed above.

Engagement risk

There are several indicators that Forsythia may be an 'odd' company.

The first indicator is that it is part of a **complex and unexplained group**, and that the group is not audited by the same firm of auditors, although it is unclear how many firms of auditors are involved in the group audit. There may be good reasons for this audit policy, but we should **investigate those reasons**, in case any other issues arise.

Another indicator is that it seems slightly odd that a small company should exist to provide landscape gardening services, when it appears that the owners are not landscape gardeners, or at least, if they are, they do not work in the business. Again, there may be valid reasons for this, but we should **discover and document them**.

It is particularly important that these issues are cleared up. A complex group structure and a company dealing in cash transactions (Forsythia's potentially are) could indicate the possibility that the owners are trying to **launder money**. There are also indicators of **fraud**. If either of these issues exist, the auditor may have **significant responsibility** to report and co-operate with relevant authorities, and the **professional relationship of client and auditor could be compromised**. Therefore, the audit firm must ensure that it has suitable 'know your client' procedures in place and the appropriate systems for making reports should a suspicion arise. The partners must ensure that staff have appropriate training so that they are able to comply fully with legal requirements in relation to money laundering.

4.5 Professional scepticism

Auditors are required to exercise professional scepticism at all stages of the audit, including planning. What this means for your exam is that you should be sceptical about any assumptions being made in scenario questions, and questions on audit planning are a particularly good place for you to show that you are being 'sceptical'. Here are some general areas that you might want to be sceptical about:

- Fraud (eg do the entity's systems provide opportunities for fraud?)
- Accounting estimates (eg are assumptions reasonable?)
- Going concern (eg are management's plans really feasible?)
- Related party relationships and transactions (eg transactions outside the normal course of business – misappropriation of assets?)
- Laws and regulations (eg where non-compliance may call into question going concern)

Of course, it is important when answering questions that you are not **too** sceptical. You cannot just write the above points down irrespective of whether the are relevant to the scenario. Rather, you need to be aware that there **may** be problems in these areas.

Point to note	There is an IAASB staff Q&A paper on professional scepticism, which is discussed in Chapter 18 of this Study Text. The above points are taken from this paper.

The Study Guide for Paper P7 states that you must be able to 'assess whether an engagement has been planned and performed with an attitude of professional scepticism, and evaluate the implications' (B1(f)). In order to do this you will first need to compare the judgements the auditor **has** made in the scenario with the judgements that they **should have** made. This will usually be a question of being more suspicious about something than the auditor in the scenario has been. For example, questioning whether a new piece of evidence is consistent with representations management has made, or whether it actually contradicts and casts doubt over what management has said before. Another common example would be whether there is an opportunity for fraud.

The implication of a lack of professional scepticism will usually be insufficient audit evidence being obtained. As a result, the auditor is likely to place too much reliance on the evidence that they have, and potentially express an inappropriate audit opinion.

 Question   Professional scepticism

Explain the meaning of the term 'professional scepticism'

Answer

Professional scepticism means having a questioning mind, being alert to conditions which may indicate possible misstatement due to error or fraud, and critically assessing audit evidence.

If professional scepticism is not maintained then the auditor may fail to obtain sufficient appropriate audit evidence – either by not spotting unusual circumstances, using unsuitable audit procedures, or reaching inappropriate conclusions.

5 Analytical procedures   6/09, 12/11, 6/13

FAST FORWARD

Analytical procedures are important at all stages of the audit.

Knowledge brought forward from previous studies

Guidance on analytical procedures is given in ISA 520 *Analytical procedures*

Analytical procedures can be used at three stages of the audit.

- Planning
- Substantive procedures
- Overall review

Analytical procedures consist of comparing items, for example current year financial information with prior year financial information, and analysing predictable relationships, for example the relationship between receivables and credit sales.

5.1 Use of analytical procedures generally

There are a number of occasions and assignments when an auditor will look to take an analytical procedures approach. One has already been mentioned in this chapter. When auditors use the business risk approach they seek to use a high level of analytical procedures. Other examples include:

- Reviews (Chapter 12)
- Assurance engagements (Chapter 12)
- Prospective financial information (Chapter 13)

5.2 Use of analytical procedures on an audit

ISA 520.3

The objectives of the auditor are:

(a) To obtain relevant and reliable audit evidence when using substantive analytical procedures; and

(b) To design and perform analytical procedures near the end of the audit that assist the auditor when forming an overall conclusion as to whether the financial statements are consistent with the auditor's understanding of the entity.

Exam focus point

You should note that whether or not auditors choose an analytical procedure approach for an audit, the knowledge you already have of analytical procedures **still applies**. In any audit, analytical procedures are used at the three stages mentioned. If the analytical procedures approach is taken, the use of analytical review at the second stage is expanded.

There are a number of factors which the auditors should consider when deciding whether to use analytical procedures as substantive procedures.

Factors to consider	Example
The **plausibility and predictability** of the relationships identified for comparison and evaluation	The strong relationship between certain selling expenses and revenue in businesses where the sales force is paid by commission
The **objectives** of the analytical procedures and the extent to which their results are reliable	
The **detail** to which information can be **analysed**	Analytical procedures may be more effective when applied to financial information or individual sections of an operation, such as individual factories or shops.
The **availability of information**	Financial: budgets or forecasts Non-financial: eg the number of units produced or sold
The **relevance of the information** available	Whether the budgets are established as results to be expected rather than as tough targets (which may well not be achieved)
The **comparability of the information** available	Comparisons with average performance in an industry may be of little value if a large number of companies differ significantly from the average.
The **knowledge gained during previous audits**	The effectiveness of the accounting and internal controls The types of problems giving rise to accounting adjustments in prior periods

Factors which should also be considered when determining the reliance that the auditors should place on the results of substantive analytical procedures are:

Reliability factors	Example
Other audit procedures directed towards the same financial statements assertions	Other procedures auditors undertake in reviewing the collectability of receivables, such as the review of subsequent cash receipts, may confirm or dispel questions arising from the application of analytical procedures to a profile of customers' accounts which lists for how long monies have been owed.
The **accuracy** with which the expected results of analytical procedures can be predicted	Auditors normally expect greater consistency in comparing the relationship of gross profit to sales from one period to another than in comparing expenditure which may or may not be made within a period, such as research or advertising.
The **frequency** with which a relationship is observed	A pattern repeated monthly as opposed to annually

The peculiarity of analytical procedures is that they aim to find out whether or not there is a relationship between variables (eg between sales and expenses) that is plausible and reasonable. This is the opposite of other substantive procedures, where the aim is to discover misstatements, rather than reasonability.

5.3 Practical techniques

When carrying out analytical procedures, auditors should remember that every industry is different and each company within an industry differs in certain aspects.

Important accounting ratios	Gross profit margins, in total and by product, area and months/quarter (if possible)
	Receivables ratio (average collection period)
	Inventory turnover ratio (inventory divided into cost of sales)
	Current ratio (current assets to current liabilities)
	Quick or acid test ratio (liquid assets to current liabilities)
	Gearing ratio (debt capital to equity capital)
	Return on capital employed (profit before tax to total assets less current liabilities)
Related items	Payables and purchases
	Inventory and cost of sales
	Non-current assets and depreciation, repairs and maintenance expense
	Intangible assets and amortisation
	Loans and interest expense
	Investments and investment income
	Receivables and bad debt expense
	Receivables and sales

Ratios mean very little when used in isolation. They should be calculated for **previous periods** and for **comparable companies**. The permanent file should contain a section with summarised accounts and the chosen ratios for prior years.

In addition to looking at the more usual ratios, the auditors should consider examining **other ratios** that may be **relevant** to the particular **client's business**, such as revenue per passenger mile for an airline operator client, or fees per partner for a professional office.

Exam focus point

The June 2013 paper contained a very typical P7 requirement in this area: to perform analytical procedures, but also to identify and explain additional information needed and evaluate audit risks. There were 24 marks available in total, but marks for calculations capped at six so candidates who spent most of their time calculating ratios did not score well. In order to pass, it was necessary to analyse the ratios calculated and connect these to possible audit risks.

Other analytical techniques include:

(a) **Examining related accounts** in conjunction with each other. Often revenue and expense accounts are related to statement of financial position accounts and comparisons should be made to ensure relationships are reasonable.

(b) **Trend analysis**. Sophisticated statistical techniques can be used to compare this period with previous periods.

(c) **Reasonableness tests**. These involve calculating **expected value** of an item and comparing it with its actual value, for example, for straight-line depreciation.

(Cost + Additions – Disposals) × Depreciation % = Charge in statement of profit or loss and other comprehensive income

Question

Copthalls is a ladies fashion retailer operating a chain of shops from a small head office. Your firm has been the auditor of Copthalls for some years.

During the current year one shop was closed and the product range of the remaining eight shops was extended to include accessories and footwear.

The company has a computerised accounting system and the audit manager is keen to ensure that the audit is as efficient as possible.

As senior in charge of the audit you are currently planning the audit work for trade payables and you have obtained the following draft financial statements from the client.

	Draft 20X7	Actual 20X6
	$'000	$'000
Summary statement of profit or loss		
Revenue	8,173	5,650
Gross profit	1,717	1,352
Summary statement of financial position		
Non-current assets	2,799	2,616
Current assets	1,746	1,127
Trade payables	991	718
Other payables	514	460

Required

State what observations you can draw from the extracts from the draft financial statements and how they may affect your audit of trade payables.

Answer

Observations	Impact on audit of trade payables
Gross profit margin has fallen from 24% last year to 21% this year.	Business strategy and performance must be discussed with the directors.
	The lower margin could arise from genuine business factors, including some relating to payables such as new suppliers charging higher prices increases in the cost of raw materials used by suppliers.
	These factors would have to be confirmed during the audit of payables.

Observations	Impact on audit of trade payables
Cost of sales has increased by 50% whilst revenue has increased by 45%.	Where the decline in margin cannot be adequately explained by business factors, accounting errors must be considered. These could include – An inaccurate cut-off on goods received which misstates purchases and trade payables – Misclassification between purchases and other expenses Potential misstatements would increase the level of work required on payables.
Trade payables have increased by 38%, which is less than the increase in cost of sales.	The scope of circularisation and/or supplier statement reconciliation work may have to be extended if there are trade payables that have not been recorded.
The trade payables payment period has been reduced slightly from 61 days last year to 56 days this year.	Information on payment terms with new suppliers (eg for footwear) must be obtained to establish expectations. There is a risk of unrecorded liabilities (eg due to omission of goods received not invoiced or inaccurate cut-off in the purchase ledger). Review of subsequent cash payments to payables should cover the two months after the year end.
Other payables have risen by 12% – this does not seem consistent with a reduction in the number of shops.	Payables for purchases may be misclassified as other payables.

5.3.1 Trend analysis

Trend analysis is likely to be very important if an analytical procedure approach is taken. Information technology can be used in trend analysis, to enable auditors to see trends graphically with relative ease and speed.

Methods of trend analysis include:

- 'Scattergraphs'
- Bar graphs
- Pie charts
- Any other visual representations
- Time series analysis
- Statistical regression

Time series analysis involves techniques such as eliminating seasonal fluctuations from sets of figures, so that underlying trends can be analysed. This is illustrated below.

Example

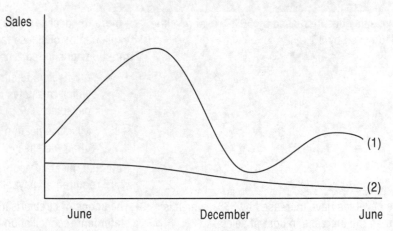

Line 1 in the diagram shows the actual sales made by a business. There is a clear seasonal fluctuation in the run-up to Christmas, in December. Line 2 shows a level of sales with 'expected seasonal fluctuations' having been stripped out. It shows that sales were lower than expected for December and continued to be low, despite December sales being higher than the other months.

In this analysis the seasonal fluctuations have been estimated. This analysis is useful however, because the estimate is likely to be based on past performance, so the conclusion from this is that there might be a problem:

- Sales are below the levels of previous years.
- Sales are below expectation.

5.4 Investigating results

If analytical procedures produce results that are inconsistent with other relevant information or expected values, the auditors should investigate this by making enquiries of management and performing other audit procedures as necessary.

Exam focus point

> A key point to remember when seeking to identify an appropriate strategy for a particular audit is that the approaches are linked and in some cases it may be best to use two or more together to achieve a good result. For example, directional testing would be used with a balance sheet approach because they are both substantive testing issues.
>
> Remember also to focus on details given in the question to determine what approach is relevant. For example, if the question relates to a business which has a low level of large transactions, a cycles based approach might be relevant. A business with substantial numbers of sales transactions resulting in a statement of financial position with substantial receivables in it might benefit from a balance sheet approach. It is likely that a risk approach would be taken in conjunction with these approaches. You should consider whether a business risk approach would be relevant.

6 Planning an initial audit engagement   6/13, 6/15

FAST FORWARD

> An initial audit engagement will often involve more work at the planning stage than a recurring audit engagement.

Auditors must make special considerations at the planning stage when they are auditing an entity for the first time, whether because the entity has never required an audit before, or because the entity has simply changed auditor.

New audits generally require a little **more work** than recurring engagements. But it is important to note that this is not because the auditor needs to do a first-time audit more thoroughly than other audits. Rather, it is because there are **specific risks** in relation to an auditor's relative **lack of knowledge** of new audit clients.

6.1 Audit strategy and audit plan

ISA 300.A20 states that the overall audit strategy and audit plan may include the following in an initial audit engagement.

- Arrangements to be made with the **predecessor auditor**, eg to review their working papers
- Any **major issues discussed** with management, eg relating to the application of IFRS, and how these issues affect the audit strategy and plan
- The audit procedures necessary in relation to **opening balances** (see Chapter 8)
- Any other procedures required by the firm for initial engagements, eg review of the audit strategy by another senior partner within the firm

It is likely that more audit work will need to be performed in order to lower detection risk (and thus audit risk) to the required level. This may result in a **higher audit fee** being charged for an initial engagement, since fees should relate to the amount of time spent on the engagement.

> The June 2015 exam featured six marks in Question 1 for discussing the matters specific to an initial audit engagement which should be considered when formulating the strategy. The examiner's report noted that 'the best answers focused on practical matters', while 'unfortunately the majority of candidates provided generic answers', or focused on 'general planning matters' which were not relevant.

6.2 Understanding the entity

ISA 315 requires the auditor to obtain an understanding of the entity and its environment in order to identify and assess the risks of material misstatement. In the case of an initial audit engagement this will tend to require more work, because the auditor will have less experience of the client.

The auditor must also understand the entity's **business risks** and how they are managed.

6.3 Other considerations

Detection risk may be higher for an initial audit engagement, as the auditor may not have the knowledge to design and perform procedures to obtain sufficient appropriate audit evidence.

Materiality is likely to be set at a lower level for initial engagements. The auditor will generally be less familiar with the entity's internal controls, which means that a comparatively small misstatement could be indicative of a pervasive failure of internal control.

The auditor will need to understand how the entity has chosen its **accounting policies**. They should be **appropriate for the business**, and in line with IFRSs.

> It is particularly important that you read exam questions in this area carefully, paying particular attention to what point has been reached in the audit process. Students often like to suggest pre-learned procedures in this area, but it is better to focus on the scenario.
>
> For example, you might spot that the client is new and then point out that the auditor needs to obtain professional clearance from the predecessor auditor. This is not wrong, but if the question is focussing on the planning stage then it is usually assumed that this has already been obtained – so you will get no (or very few) marks. You would be better served by focusing on the requirement and the scenario.

Chapter Roundup

- Auditors must plan their work so that it is done effectively.

- With a 'top down' approach (also known as the business risk approach) controls testing is aimed at high level controls, and substantive testing is reduced.

- Materiality considerations are important in both planning and performing the audit. An item might be material due to its nature, value or impact on the users of the financial statements as a group.

- Auditors must assess the risk of material misstatements arising in financial statements and carry out procedures in response to assessed risks.

- Business risk is the risk arising to companies through being in operation.

- Analytical procedures are important at all stages of the audit.

- An initial audit engagement will often involve more work at the planning stage than a recurring audit engagement.

Quick Quiz

1   What is the purpose of an audit strategy document?

2   What are the effects of a 'top-down' audit approach on:

    (a)   Tests of controls   (c)   Detailed testing
    (b)   Analytical procedures

3   Name four key control objectives for sales.

    (1) ....   (3) ....
    (2) ....   (4) ....

4   When undertaking a cycles approach to auditing, the auditor is ensuring that transactions are processed through the cycle.

    True ☐   False ☐

5   A balance sheet approach should never be combined with a business risk approach.

    True ☐   False ☐

6   Complete the matrix.

Type of account	Purpose of primary test	Primary test also gives comfort on			
		Assets	Liabilities	Income	Expenses
Assets		U	O	O	U
Liabilities		U	O	O	U
Income		U	O	O	U
Expense		U	O	O	U

7   Complete the definition.

    .... is an expression of the ....
    or .... of a particular matter in the context of financial statements.

8   Identify whether the following matters, which represent potential business risks to the company are financial, operational or compliance risks.

Item	Potential business risk
Going concern	
Physical disasters	
Breakdown of accounting systems	
Loss of key personnel	
Credit risk	
Breach of legislation	
Sales tax problems	
Currency risk	
Poor brand management	
Environmental issues	

1   The audit strategy document sets out in general terms how the audit is to be carried out.

2   (a)   Tests of control focused on high level controls
    (b)   Analytical procedures used more extensively
    (c)   Detailed testing consequently reduced

3   Any of:

    Ordering and granting of credit

    • **Goods** and **services** are **only supplied** to **customers** with **good credit ratings**.
    • **Customers** are encouraged to **pay promptly**.
    • **Orders** are **recorded correctly**.
    • **Orders** are **fulfilled**.

    Despatch and invoicing

    • All **despatches** of goods are **recorded**.
    • All **goods and services** sold are **correctly invoiced**.
    • All **invoices** raised **relate to goods and services** that have been **supplied** by the business.
    • **Credit notes** are only given for **valid reasons**.

    Recording, accounting and credit control

    • All sales that have been **invoiced** are **recorded** in the general and sales ledgers.
    • All **credit notes** that have been **issued** are **recorded** in the general and sales ledgers.
    • All **entries** in the sales ledger are **made** to the **correct** sales ledger **accounts**.
    • **Cut-off** is applied correctly to the sales ledger.
    • Potentially **doubtful debts** are **identified**.

4   True

5   False

6

Type of account	Purpose of primary test	Primary test also gives comfort on			
		Assets	Liabilities	Income	Expenses
Assets	Overstatement (O)	U	O	O	U
Liabilities	Understatement (U)	U	O	O	U
Income	Understatement (U)	U	O	O	U
Expense	Overstatement (O)	U	O	O	U

7   Materiality, relative significance, importance

8

Item	Potential business risk
Going concern	Financial
Physical disasters	Operational
Breakdown of accounting systems	Financial
Loss of key personnel	Operational
Credit risk	Financial
Breach of legislation	Compliance
Sales tax problems	Compliance
Currency risk	Financial
Poor brand management	Operational
Environmental issues	Compliance

Now try the questions below from the Practice Question Bank.

Number	Level	Marks	Time
Q8	Introductory	25	49 mins
Q9	Examination	35	68 mins

7

Evidence

Topic list	Syllabus reference
1 Audit evidence	D2
2 Related parties	D2
3 Written representations	D2
4 Reliance on the work of an auditor's expert	D2
5 Reliance on the work of internal audit	D2
6 Documentation	D2

Introduction

Audit evidence is a vital part of any audit. The basic issues relating to evidence
are that:

- Auditors must obtain evidence to support financial statement assertions
- This evidence must be sufficient and appropriate
- Audit evidence must be documented sufficiently

Related parties are a difficult area to obtain audit evidence on. The auditor must
bear in mind who the evidence is from and how extensive it is. Obtaining
evidence about related party transactions is considered in Section 2 of this
chapter.

Often the auditors will have to rely on written representations about related
parties and other issues. Written representations are subjective evidence, and the
auditor must proceed with caution when dealing with them. This is discussed in
Section 3.

Sometimes, the evidence the auditor requires is beyond the expertise of the
auditor, and they will need to rely on the work of an expert. The relevant
procedures that the auditor must undertake are outlined in Section 4. Similar
considerations arise if the external auditor intends to rely on the work of internal
audit.

The chapter concludes with the documentation of the audit evidence that has
been obtained.

Study guide

		Intellectual level
D2	**Evidence**	
(a)	Identify and describe audit procedures to obtain sufficient audit evidence from identified sources.	2
(c)	Identify and evaluate the audit evidence expected to be available to:	3
	(i) Support the financial statement assertions and accounting treatments (including fair values)	
	(ii) Support disclosures made in the notes to the financial statements	
(d)	Apply analytical procedures to financial and non-financial data.	2
(e)	Explain the specific audit problems and procedures concerning related parties and related party transactions.	2
(f)	Recognise circumstances that may indicate the existence of unidentified related parties and select appropriate audit procedures.	2
(g)	Evaluate the use of written management representations to support other audit evidence.	2
(h)	Recognise when it is justifiable to place reliance on the work of an expert (eg a surveyor employed by the audit client).	2
(i)	Assess the appropriateness and sufficiency of the work of internal auditors and the extent to which reliance can be placed on it.	2

Exam guide

Specific audit issues examined in this paper are likely to be at a higher level than in your previous auditing exams. Therefore, the more complex evidence issues of related parties, written representations and using the work of others are important. You should consider how they link in with specific accounting issues in Chapters 9 and 10.

1 Audit evidence

 FAST FORWARD

Auditors need to obtain sufficient, appropriate audit evidence.

1.1 Obtaining evidence

You should be aware of the key points of audit evidence from your previous auditing studies. We shall revise them briefly here. Substantive procedures are designed to obtain evidence about the financial statement assertions.

Exam focus point

It is essential that you tailor audit procedures to the specific scenario given in the question. After virtually every sitting, the examination team comments in its examiner's report that many students' suggested procedures are too vague and general.

Key term

Financial statement assertions are the representations by management that are embodied in the financial statements, as used by the auditor to consider the different types of potential misstatements that may occur. By approving the financial statements, the directors are making representations about the information therein. These representations or assertions may be described in general terms in a number of ways.

Guidance on assertions is found in ISA 315 *Identifying and assessing the risks of material misstatement through understanding the entity and its environment.*

ISA 315.25

The auditor shall identify and assess the risks of material misstatement at:

(a)   the financial statement level;
(b)   the assertion level for classes of transactions, account balances and disclosures;
(c)   to provide a basis for designing and performing further audit procedures.

It gives examples of assertions in these areas.

Assertions used by the auditor	
Assertions about **classes of transactions and events and related disclosures** for the period under audit	**Occurrence**: Transactions and events that have been recorded have occurred or disclosed have occurred, and such transactions and events pertain to the entity. **Completeness**: All transactions and events that should have been recorded have been recorded, and all related disclosures that should have been included in the financial statements have been included. **Accuracy**: Amounts and other data relating to recorded transactions and events have been recorded appropriately, and related disclosures have been appropriately measured and described. **Cut-off**: Transactions and events have been recorded in the correct accounting period. **Classification**: Transactions and events have been recorded in the proper accounts. **Presentation**: Transactions and events are appropriately aggregated or disaggregated and clearly described, and related disclosures are relevant and understandable in the context of the requirements of the applicable financial reporting framework.
Assertions about **account balances and related disclosures** at the period end	**Existence**: Assets, liabilities and equity interests exist. **Rights and obligations**: The entity holds or controls the rights to assets, and liabilities are the obligations of the entity. **Completeness**: All assets, liabilities and equity interests that should have been recorded have been recorded, and all related disclosures that should have been included in the financial statements have been included. **Accuracy, valuation and allocation**: Assets, liabilities and equity interests have been included in the financial statements at appropriate amounts and any resulting valuation or allocation adjustments are appropriately recorded, and related disclosures have been appropriately measured and described. **Classification**: Assets, liabilities and equity interests have been recorded in the proper accounts. **Presentation**: Assets, liabilities and equity interests are appropriately aggregated or disaggregated and clearly described, and related disclosures are relevant and understandable in the context of the requirements of the applicable financial reporting framework.

Examples of where disclosure is especially important would include: IFRS 5 on discontinued operations; IAS 37 on provisions and contingent liabilities; and IAS 24 on related parties.

ISA 500 *Audit evidence* outlines the objective of the auditor and procedures used by auditors to obtain evidence.

ISA 500.4

The objective of the auditor is to design and perform audit procedures in such a way as to enable the auditor to obtain sufficient appropriate audit evidence to be able to draw reasonable conclusions on which to base the auditor's opinion.

Procedures	
Inspection of assets	Inspection of assets that are recorded in the accounting records confirms **existence**, gives evidence of **valuation**, but does not confirm **rights and obligations**.
	Confirmation that assets seen are recorded in the accounting records gives evidence of **completeness**.
Inspection of documentation	Confirmation to documentation of items recorded in accounting records confirms that an asset **exists** or a transaction **occurred**. Confirmation that items recorded in supporting documentation are recorded in accounting records tests **completeness**.
	Cut-off can be verified by inspecting a reverse population, that is, checking transactions recorded **after** the end of the reporting period to supporting documentation to confirm that they occurred after the end of the reporting period.
	Inspection also provides evidence of **valuation/measurement**, **rights and obligations** and the nature of items **(presentation and disclosure)**. It can also be used to **compare** documents (and therefore test **consistency** of audit evidence) and confirm **authorisation**.
Observation	Observation involves watching a procedure being performed (for example, post opening).
	It is of **limited use**, as it only confirms the procedure took place when the auditor is watching.
Enquiries	Seeking information from **client staff** or **external sources**.
	Strength of evidence depends on knowledge and integrity of source of information.
Confirmation	Seeking **confirmation from another source** of details in client's accounting records, for example confirmation from the bank of bank balances.
Recalculations	**Checking arithmetic** of client's records, for example adding up ledger account.
Reperformance	Reperformance is the auditor's **independent** execution of procedures or controls originally performed as part of the entity's internal control, either manually or using computer-assisted auditing techniques (CAATs). CAATs are covered in Section 1.3.
Analytical procedures	Analytical procedures consist of **evaluations** of financial information made by a study of plausible relationships among both financial and non-financial data. Analytical procedures are covered in Section 1.4.

1.2 Sufficient and appropriate audit evidence

'Sufficiency' and 'appropriateness' are interrelated and apply to both tests of controls and substantive procedures.

- **Sufficiency** is the measure of the **quantity** of audit evidence.
- **Appropriateness** is the measure of the **quality** or **reliability** of the audit evidence.

Auditors are essentially looking for enough reliable audit evidence. Audit **evidence usually indicates what is probable** rather than what is definite (it is usually persuasive rather than conclusive) so different sources are examined by the auditors. However, auditors can only give **reasonable assurance** that the financial statements are free from misstatement, so **not all sources of evidence will be examined**.

When assessing the sufficiency and appropriateness of audit evidence, auditors must consider whether the evidence is consistent. Where **contradictory evidence** is discovered, for example, where one piece of evidence suggests that a specific liability has been settled prior to the year end while another piece of evidence throws doubt on this, the auditors must perform any other procedures necessary to resolve the inconsistency.

ISA 500.11

If:

(a)   audit evidence obtained from one source is inconsistent with that obtained from another; or

(b)   the auditor has doubts over the reliability of information to be used as audit evidence,

the auditor shall determine what modifications or additions to audit procedures are necessary to resolve the matter, and shall consider the effect, if any, on other aspects of the audit.

ISA 530 *Audit sampling* is based on the premise that auditors do not normally examine all the information available to them, as it would be impractical to do so and using audit sampling will produce valid conclusions.

Key terms

> **Audit sampling** involves the application of audit procedures to less than 100% of the items within a population of audit relevance such that all sampling units have an equal chance of selection in order to provide the auditor with a reasonable basis on which to draw conclusions about the entire population.
>
> **Statistical sampling** is any approach to sampling that involves random selection of a sample, and use of probability theory to evaluate sample results, including measurement of sampling risk.
>
> **Population** is the entire set of data from which a sample is selected and about which an auditor wishes to draw conclusions.
>
> **Sampling units** are the individual items constituting a population.
>
> **Stratification** is the process of dividing a population into sub-populations, each of which is a group of sampling units, which have similar characteristics (often monetary value).
>
> **Tolerable misstatement** is a monetary amount set by the auditor in respect of which the auditor seeks to obtain an appropriate level of assurance that the monetary amount set by the auditor is not exceeded by the actual misstatement in the population.
>
> **Tolerable rate of deviation** is a rate of deviation from prescribed internal control procedures set by the auditor in respect of which the auditor seeks to obtain an appropriate level of assurance that the rate of deviation set by the auditor is not exceeded by the actual rate of deviation in the population.
>
> **Anomaly** is a misstatement or deviation that is demonstrably not representative of misstatements or deviations in a population.
>
> **Sampling risk** arises from the possibility that the auditor's conclusion, based on a sample, may be different from the conclusion if the entire population were subjected to the same audit procedure.
>
> **Non-sampling risk** arises from factors that cause the auditor to reach an erroneous conclusion for any reason not related to the sampling risk. For example, most audit evidence is persuasive rather than conclusive, the auditor might use inappropriate procedures, or the auditor might misinterpret evidence and fail to recognise an error.

Some testing procedures do **not** involve sampling, such as:

- Testing 100% of items in a population
- Testing all items with a certain characteristic (for example, over a certain value) as the selection is not representative

The International Standard on Accounting (ISA) distinguishes between **statistically based sampling**, which involves the use of random selection techniques from which mathematically constructed conclusions about the population can be drawn, and **non-statistical methods**, from which auditors draw a judgemental opinion about the population. However the principles of the ISA apply to both methods. You should be aware of the major methods of statistical and non-statistical sampling.

The auditor's judgement as to what is sufficient appropriate audit evidence is influenced by a number of factors.

- **Risk assessment**
- The **nature** of the **accounting and internal control systems**
- The **materiality** of the item being examined
- The **experience gained during previous audits**
- The auditor's **knowledge of the business** and **industry**
- The **results of audit procedures**
- The **source** and **reliability of information** available

If they are unable to obtain sufficient, appropriate audit evidence, the auditors should **consider the implications for their report**.

1.2.1 External confirmations

The reliability of audit evidence is affected by its source. Audit evidence is more reliable when it is obtained from independent sources outside the entity.

Both ISA 330 *The auditor's responses to assessed risks* and ISA 505 *External confirmations* address the need for external confirmations in gathering sufficient and appropriate audit evidence.

> **ISA 330.19**
>
> The auditor shall consider whether external confirmation procedures are to be performed as substantive audit procedures.

ISA 330 identifies the following situations where external confirmations are appropriate.

- Bank balances and other information from bankers
- Accounts receivable balances
- Inventories held by third parties
- Property deeds held by lawyers
- Investments held for safekeeping by third parties or purchased from stockbrokers but not delivered at the end of the reporting period
- Loans from lenders
- Accounts payable balances

ISA 505.7 states that '**the auditor** shall maintain **control** over **external confirmation requests**'. So to take the example of a receivables circularisation, it is the auditor who should be in control of sending and receiving the requests and the responses from customers.

If management refuses to allow the auditor to send an external confirmation request, the auditor must consider whether this is reasonable and whether audit evidence can be obtained in another way. If evidence cannot be obtained from another source, the auditor should communicate this to those charged with governance, and consider the impact on the audit report (there is a possibility that the auditor's opinion will have to be modified (qualified) on the basis of an inability to obtain sufficient appropriate audit evidence, or that a disclaimer of opinion will be issued).

In November 2009 the IAASB issued a Practice Alert in this area, *Emerging Practice Issues Regarding the Use of External Confirmations in an Audit of Financial Statements*. In addition to re-emphasising the points contained in ISA 505, the alert made the following points.

It is important that consideration is given to whether the confirmation request **provides evidence** on the **specific assertion being tested**, as it may provide evidence for some assertions but not others.

All confirmation responses carry some **risk of interception, alteration or fraud**. Such risk exists regardless of whether a response is obtained in paper form, or through electronic or other medium. Accordingly, it is essential that the auditor maintains control over the confirmation process. It is also important that the auditor **maintains appropriate professional scepticism** throughout the confirmation process, particularly when evaluating the confirmation responses.

The ISAs do not preclude the use of electronic confirmations, as they can, if properly managed, provide appropriate audit evidence.

Disclaimers and other restrictions included in confirmation responses do not necessarily invalidate the reliability of the responses as audit evidence.

 Question   **Audit evidence**

'The objective of the auditor is to design and perform audit procedures in such a way as to enable the auditor to obtain sufficient appropriate audit evidence to be able to draw reasonable conclusions on which to base the auditor's opinion.'   (*ISA 500.4*)

Discuss the extent to which each of the following sources of audit evidence is sufficient and appropriate.

(a)   Oral representation by management in respect of the completeness of sales where the majority of transactions are conducted on a cash basis

(b)   Flowcharts of the accounting and control system prepared by a company's internal audit department

(c)   Year-end suppliers' statements

(d)   Physical inspection of a non-current asset by an auditor

(e)   Comparison of statement of profit or loss items for the current period with corresponding information for earlier periods

Answer

Appropriate – relevance

The relevance of audit evidence should be considered in relation to the overall audit objective of forming an opinion and reporting on the financial statements. The evidence should allow the auditor to conclude on:

- Statement of financial position items (existence, rights and obligations, completeness, valuation and allocation)

- Statement of profit or loss items (occurrence, completeness, accuracy, cut-off and classification)

(a)   The representation by management in respect of the completeness of sales is relevant when gathering evidence on statement of profit or loss items. Depending on the system operated by the client and the controls over cash sales there may be no other evidence as to the completeness of sales.

(b)   The flowcharts prepared by the internal audit department will not be directly relevant to the auditor's opinion on individual figures in the financial statements, but rather when the auditor is following the requirement in ISA 315 to ascertain the entity's system of recording and processing transactions. The auditor will wish to assess the adequacy of the system as a basis for the preparation of financial statements so the flowcharts will only be relevant if they are sufficiently detailed to allow the auditor to carry out this assessment. The auditor would also wish to make an initial assessment of internal controls at this stage so the flowcharts will be more relevant for control procedures that are specifically identified.

(c)   Year end suppliers' statements provide evidence relevant to the auditor's conclusions on:

(i)   The completeness of payables, as omissions from the purchase ledger listing would be identified by comparing statements received to that listing

(ii)   The existence of payables recorded in the purchase ledger

(iii)   The fact that the liabilities are properly those of the entity (for example, the statements are not addressed to, say, the managing director in their own name)

(iv)   The valuation of payables at the year end with respect to cut-off of invoices and credit notes, and discounts or allowances

(d)   The physical inspection of a non-current asset is clearly relevant to the auditor's opinion as to the existence of the asset and to some extent the completeness of recording of assets, that is, the auditor can check that all the assets inspected have been recorded. In certain circumstances, evidence relevant to valuation might be obtained, for example where a client has written down a building due to permanent diminution in value and the auditor sees it standing unused and derelict.

(e)   The comparison of statement of profit or loss items with prior periods will provide evidence as to:

(i)   Completeness of recording, as omissions can be identified and investigated

(ii)   Valuation, in cases where the auditor has appropriate information on which to base expectations, for example if the number of workers has doubled during the year and a set percentage wage increase had been effected in the year

(iii)   Disclosure, as the comparison should highlight any inconsistencies of classification and treatment from year to year

Appropriate – reliable

Reliability of audit evidence depends on the particular circumstances but the guideline offers three general presumptions:

- Documentary evidence is more reliable than oral evidence.

- Evidence obtained from independent sources outside the entity is more reliable than that secured solely from within the entity.

- Evidence originating with the auditor, eg by analysis or physical inspection, is more reliable than evidence originating with others.

(a)   The oral representations by management would be regarded as relatively unreliable using the criteria in the guidelines, as they are oral and internal. In the absence of any external or auditor-generated evidence, the auditor should ensure that these representations are included in the letter of representation so that there is at least some documentary evidence to support any conclusions.

(b)   The assessment of how reliable the flowcharts are would depend on the auditor's overall assessment of whether the work of the internal auditors is likely to be adequate for the purposes of the external audit. The factors to be considered would include its objectivity; the internal auditors' technical competence; whether the work is carried out with due professional care; and whether there is likely to be effective communication between the internal auditors and the external auditor. This assessment should be documented by the external auditor if they are to make use of the flowcharts in their audit planning and design of tests.

(c)   Suppliers' statements would generally be seen as reliable evidence, being documentary and from sources external to the entity. If the auditor had doubts as to the reliability of this evidence, it could be improved by the auditor originating similar evidence by means of a payables' circularisation rather than relying on suppliers' statements received by the client.

(d)   Physical inspection of a non-current asset is a clear example of auditor-originated evidence, so would usually be considered more reliable than that generated by others.

(e)   Analysis such as this comparison of statement of profit or loss items with the prior periods would again be termed auditor-generated evidence, and would be considered more reliable than evidence generated by others. Ultimately the reliability of such audit evidence depends on the reliability of the underlying data, which should be checked by compliance or substantive testing.

Sufficiency

The auditor needs to obtain sufficient relevant and reliable evidence to form a reasonable basis for his opinion on the financial statements. Their judgements will be influenced by such factors as:

- Their knowledge of the business and its environment
- The risk of misstatement
- The persuasiveness of the evidence

(a) To decide if the representations were sufficient with regard to concluding on the completeness of sales the auditor would consider:

    (i)   The nature of the business and the inherent risk of unrecorded cash sales

    (ii)   The materiality of the item; in this case it would appear that cash sales are material

    (iii)   Any possible management bias

    (iv)   The persuasiveness of the evidence in the light of other related audit work, for example, testing of cash receipts

If the auditor believes there is still a risk of material understatement of sales in the light of the above, they should seek further evidence.

(b) Client-prepared flowcharts are **not** sufficient as a basis for the auditor's evaluation of the system. To confirm that the system does operate in the manner described, the auditor should perform 'walk through' tests, tracing a small number of transactions through the system. There is, however, no need for the auditor to prepare their own flowcharts if they are satisfied that those produced by internal audit are accurate.

(c) The auditor's decision as to whether the suppliers' statements were sufficient evidence would depend on their assessment of materiality and the risk of misstatement. Its persuasiveness would be assessed in conjunction with the results of other audit work, for example substantive testing of purchases, returns and cash payments, and compliance testing of the purchases system.

(d) Inspection of a non-current asset would be sufficient evidence as to the existence of the asset (provided it was carried out at or close to the period end). Before concluding on the non-current asset figure in the accounts, the auditor would have to consider the results of their work on other aspects, such as the ownership and valuation of the asset.

(e) In addition to the general considerations such as risk and materiality, the results of a comparison alone would not give very persuasive evidence. It would have to be followed by a detailed investigation of variances (or lack of variances where they were expected). The results should be compared to the auditor's expectations based on their knowledge of the business, and explanations given by management should be verified. The persuasiveness of the evidence should be considered in the light of other relevant testing, for example compliance testing of payments systems, or substantive testing of expense invoices.

1.3 Computer-assisted audit techniques (CAATs)

1.3.1 Audit software

Audit software performs the sort of checks on data that auditors might otherwise have to perform by hand. Examples of uses of audit software are:

- Interrogation software, which accesses the client's data files
- Comparison programs, which compare versions of a program
- Interactive software for interrogation of online systems
- Resident code software to review transactions as they are processed

Although audit interrogation software may be used during many tests of controls and substantive procedures, its use is particularly appropriate during substantive testing of transactions and especially balances. By using audit software, the auditors may **scrutinise large volumes of data** and concentrate skilled manual resources on the investigation of results, rather than on the extraction of information and **selection** of **samples**.

Major considerations when deciding whether to use file interrogation software are as follows.

(a) As a minimum auditors will require a **basic understanding** of data processing and the entity's computer application, together with a detailed knowledge of the audit software and the computer files to be used.

(b)   Depending on the complexity of the application, the auditors may need to have a sound appreciation of **systems analysis**, operating systems and, where program code is used, experience of the programming language to be utilised.

(c)   Auditors will need to consider how easy it is to **transfer** the **client's data** onto the auditors' PC.

(d)   The client may **lack full knowledge** of the **computer system**, and therefore may not be able to explain fully all the information it produces.

1.3.2 Test data

An obvious way of seeing whether a system is **processing** data in the way that it should be is to input some valid test data and see what happens. The expected results can be calculated in advance and then compared with the results that actually arise. Test data can also be used to check the controls that prevent processing of **invalid data** by entering data with, say, a non-existent customer code or worth an unreasonable amount, or transactions which may if processed breach limits, such as customer credit limits.

A significant problem with test data is that any resulting corruption of the data files has to be corrected. This is difficult with modern real-time systems, which often have built in (and highly desirable) controls to ensure that data entered **cannot** easily be removed without leaving a mark.

Other problems with **test data** are that it only tests the operation of the system at a **single point of time**, and auditors are only testing controls in the programs being run and controls which they know about. The problems involved mean that test data is being used less as a CAAT.

1.3.3 Embedded audit facilities

The results of using test data would, in any case, be completely distorted if the programs used to process it were not the ones **normally** used for processing. For example, a fraudulent member of the IT department might substitute a version of the program that gave the correct results, purely for the duration of the test, and then replace it with a version that siphoned off the company's funds into their own bank account.

To allow a **continuous** review of the data recorded and the manner in which it is treated by the system, it may be possible to use CAATs referred to as 'embedded audit facilities'. An embedded facility consists of audit modules that are incorporated into the computer element of the entity's accounting system.

Two frequently encountered examples are Integrated Test Facility (ITF) and Systems Control and Review File (SCARF). Such systems allow auditors to give frequent and prompt audit reports on a wide variety of subject matters, key performance indicators and critical success factors.

The use of IT to produce such reports means additional risk to auditors. They need to ensure that the reports are filed properly (ie that no one relies on yesterday's report today) and are protected from interference (hacking). It also widens the amount of expertise needed from auditors, as they will need IT skills as well as expertise in a number of different areas being reported on.

1.4 Substantive analytical procedures

1.4.1 Considerations in using analytical procedures

Chapter 6 covered the use of analytical procedures at the planning stage of the audit, in assessing risk. Analytical procedures are also widely used as a substantive procedure and can be much more **cost-effective** than carrying out high volumes of tests of detail.

ISA 520 *Analytical procedures* notes that auditors should not rely on analytical procedures alone in respect of material balances but should combine them with tests of detail. Tests of detail are also required in areas where significant risks have been identified at the planning stage.

The auditor must:

(a)   **Determine the suitability** of particular substantive analytical procedures for given assertions, taking account of the **assessed risks of material misstatement** and tests of details performed

(b)   **Evaluate the reliability of data** from which the auditor's expectation of recorded amounts or ratios is developed, taking account of source, comparability, and nature and relevance of information available, and controls over preparation

(c) **Develop an expectation** of recorded amounts or ratios and evaluate whether the expectation is sufficiently precise to identify a misstatement that, individually or when aggregated with other misstatements, may cause the financial statements to be materially misstated

(d) **Determine the amount of any difference** of recorded amounts from expected values **that is acceptable** without further investigation

When used properly, analytical procedures can be extremely powerful and effective tests. This is because they can be tied in directly with the relevant financial statement assertion, and can cover all transactions during the period (for income/expenses) or the majority of a balance (for assets/liabilities).

1.4.2 Examples

Simple comparisons

A simple year on year comparison could provide very persuasive evidence that an expense such as rent is correctly stated, providing that the auditor has sufficient knowledge of the business, for example knowing that the same premises have been leased year on year and that there has been no rent review.

Comparisons with estimates prepared by the auditors

A common example of this is where a business may have a large number of items of plant and machinery that are depreciated at different rates. The auditor could perform a quick calculation:

$$\boxed{\text{Closing balance of plant and machinery (cost)}} \times \boxed{\text{Average depreciation rate}}$$

If this estimate was similar to the actual depreciation charge, it would go some way to allowing the auditor to conclude that the charge was materially correct.

Relationship between financial and non-financial information

In making an estimate of employee costs, probably for one specific department, such as manufacturing, the auditor might use information about the number of employees in the department, as well as rates of pay increases. The estimate might be:

$$\boxed{\text{Prior year wages expense}} \times \frac{\text{Average no. of employees current year}}{\text{Average no. of employees prior year}} \times \% \text{ pay increase}$$

If the actual expense does not make sense when compared with the estimate, explanations would need to be sought and corroborated. For example, management might explain that for several months of the year the factory ran double shifts, so a higher proportion of hours worked were paid at higher overtime rates.

Further examination of production records for those months would be required.

If no explanation is available, then more detailed substantive testing will be required, directed towards possible misstatements, such as mispostings, or frauds, such as payments to dummy employees.

2 Related parties   6/08, 6/11, 12/11

FAST FORWARD

It can be difficult to gain audit evidence about related party transactions.

2.1 Importance of related parties

Central to a number of government investigations in various countries have been companies trading with organisations or individuals **other than at arm's length**. Such transactions were made possible by a degree of control or influence exercised by directors over both parties to the transactions. ISA 550 *Related parties* covers this area.

Key terms

Related party is a party that is either:

(a) A related party as defined in the applicable financial reporting framework; or

(b) Where the applicable financial reporting framework establishes minimal or no related party requirements:

    (i) A person or other entity that has control or significant influence, directly or indirectly through one or more intermediaries, over the reporting entity;

    (ii) Another entity over which the reporting entity has control or significant influence, directly or indirectly through one or more intermediaries; or

    (iii) Another entity that is under common control with the reporting entity through having:

        • Common controlling ownership;

        • Owners who are close family members; or

        • Common key management.

(ISA 550)

Management is responsible for the identification of related party transactions. Such transactions should be properly approved as they are frequently not at arm's length. Management is also responsible for the **disclosure** of related party transactions.

It may not be self-evident to management whether a party is related. Furthermore, many accounting systems are not designed to either distinguish or summarise related party transactions, so management will have to carry out additional analysis of accounting information.

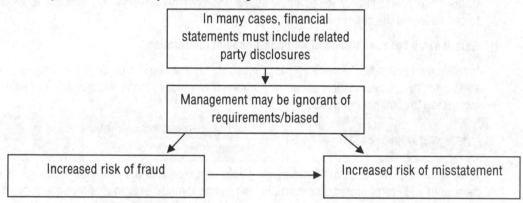

An audit cannot be expected to detect all material related party transactions. The risk that undisclosed related party transactions will not be detected by the auditors is especially high when:

• **Related party transactions** have **taken place without charge**

• **Related party transactions** are **not self-evident** to the auditors

• Transactions are with a party that the auditors could **not reasonably** be expected to **know** is a **related party**

• **Active steps** have been taken by **management** to **conceal** either the full terms of a transaction, or that a transaction is, in substance, with a related party

• The **corporate structure** is **complex**

ISA 550.9

The objectives of the auditor are:

(a) Irrespective of whether the applicable financial reporting framework establishes related party requirements, to obtain an understanding of related party relationships and transactions sufficient to be able:

    (i) To recognise fraud risk factors, if any, arising from related party relationships and transactions that are relevant to the identification and assessment of the risks of material misstatement due to fraud; and

---

> (ii) To conclude, based on the audit evidence obtained, whether the financial statements, insofar as they are affected by those relationships and transactions:
>
>   a. Achieve fair presentation (for fair presentation frameworks); or
>   b. Are not misleading (for compliance frameworks); and
>
> (b) In addition, where the applicable financial reporting framework establishes related party requirements, to obtain sufficient appropriate audit evidence about whether related party relationships and transactions have been appropriately identified, accounted for and disclosed in the financial statements in accordance with the framework.

2.2 Assessment and identification of risks

As part of the risk assessment procedures required by ISA 315, the auditor must carry out the following procedures to obtain information relevant to identifying risks associated with related parties.

- Audit team discussion of risk shall include specific consideration of susceptibility of financial statements to material misstatement through related parties and their transactions

- Auditor shall inquire of management:

    - The identity of related parties including changes from prior period
    - The nature of the relationships between the entity and its related parties
    - Whether any transactions occurred between the parties, and if so, what
    - What controls the entity has to identify, account for and disclose related party relationships and transactions
    - What controls the entity has to authorise and approve significant transactions and arrangements with related parties
    - What controls the entity has to authorise and approve significant transactions and arrangements outside the normal course of business

    (The auditor may have to perform risk assessment procedures in addition in respect of the latter three points.)

- Stay alert for evidence of related party transactions when obtaining other audit evidence, in particular when scrutinising bank and legal confirmations and minutes of meetings

- If significant transactions outside the normal course of business are discovered, inquire of management the nature of the transactions and whether related parties could be involved

- Share information obtained about related parties with the audit team

The following procedures may be helpful.

- **Enquire of management** and the directors as to whether transactions have taken place with related parties that are required to be disclosed by the disclosure requirements that are applicable to the entity
- **Review prior year working papers** for names of known related parties
- **Review minutes** of meetings of shareholders and directors and other relevant statutory records, such as the register of directors' interests
- **Review accounting records** for large or unusual transactions or balances, in particular transactions recognised at or near the end of the financial period
- **Review confirmations of loans receivable** and payable and confirmations from banks. Such a review may indicate the relationship, if any, of guarantors to the entity
- **Review investment transactions**, for example purchase or sale of an interest in a joint venture or other entity
- **Enquire** as to the **names** of all pension and other trusts established for the benefit of employees and the names of their management and trustees

- **Enquire** as to the **affiliation** of directors and officers with other entities
- **Review the register of interests in shares** to determine the names of principal shareholders
- **Enquire of other auditors** currently involved in the audit, or predecessor auditors, as to their knowledge of additional related parties
- **Review the entity's tax returns**, returns made under statute and other information supplied to regulatory agencies for evidence of the existence of related parties
- **Review invoices and correspondence** from lawyers for indications of the existence of related parties or related party transactions

If risks relating to related parties and their transactions are identified, they should be treated as **significant risks** in accordance with ISA 315. Also, due to the close connection between related parties and possible fraud, the auditor must consider the overlap with ISA 240 here as well.

2.3 Responses to the risks

ISA 550.20

As part of the ISA 330 requirement that the auditor respond to assessed risks, the auditor designs and performs further audit procedures to obtain sufficient appropriate audit evidence about the assessed risks of material misstatement associated with related party relationships and transactions[...].

The audit procedures discussed above must include the following.

Further audit procedures: risk of misstatement due to related parties	
Situation	**Actions by auditor**
Auditor suspects existence of related parties not disclosed by management.	Determine whether the information does confirm the existence of related parties.
Auditor identifies related parties not disclosed by management.	<ul><li>Tell the rest of the audit team</li><li>Request management to identify all transactions with identified related party</li><li>Inquire as to why company controls failed to identify related party</li><li>Perform substantive procedures relating to related party and its transactions with entity<ul><li>Making enquiries of third parties presumed to have knowledge, such as legal counsel</li><li>Conducting an analysis of accounting records for transactions with the related party (using a CAAT?)</li><li>Verifying terms and conditions of transactions by looking at the contract</li></ul></li><li>Reconsider the risk of further related parties existing and not being disclosed to the auditor</li><li>If non-disclosure appears intentional, and therefore indicative of fraud, evaluate implications for audit</li></ul>

Further audit procedures: risk of misstatement due to related parties	
Situation	**Actions by auditor**

Auditor identifies related party transactions outside normal course of business.	• Inspect contracts/agreements and evaluate whether:
	  – The business rationale (or lack thereof) suggests a fraudulent purpose (is it overly complex, does it have unusual terms of trade, does it lack a logical business purpose?)
	  – The terms of the transactions are consistent with management's explanations
	  – The transactions have been accounted for and disclosed properly

Management has asserted in the financial statements that related party transactions were conducted at arm's length.	• Obtain sufficient appropriate evidence that this is true by looking at the terms of the contract and assessing:
	  – Price
	  – Credit terms
	  – Contingencies
	  – Specific charges

2.4 Written representations

ISA 550.26

Where the applicable financial reporting framework establishes related party requirements, the auditor shall obtain written representations from management and, where relevant, those charged with governance, that:

(a)   they have disclosed to the auditor the identity of the entity's related parties and all the related party relationships and transactions of which they are aware; and

(b)   they have appropriately accounted for and disclosed such relationships and transactions in accordance with the requirements of the framework.

2.5 Audit conclusions and reporting

If the auditor is unable to obtain sufficient appropriate audit evidence concerning related parties and transactions with such parties or concludes that their disclosure in the financial statements is not adequate, the auditor should modify the audit report appropriately.

The auditor must communicate all significant matters arising during the audit in connection with the entity's related parties (unless all those charged with governance are involved in managing the entity).

Exam focus point

The June 2011 exam asked candidates to explain the inherent limitations to the identification of related parties and related party transactions (four marks), and to recommend audit procedures that are appropriate to the situation given in the question (four marks). To score well, students needed to show a specific awareness of the requirements of ISAs in this area – specifically ISA 500.

The June 2008 exam contained a very similar requirement, asking candidates to discuss why the identification of related parties and material related party transactions can be difficult for auditors. The examiner's report commented that few candidates mentioned the existence of ISA 550. Your response to this should not be to rote-learn the list of ISA names and numbers and then recite one for each answer you write. Instead, your marker would be pleased to see you writing something like, 'in this situation, ISAs would require the auditor to perform procedures to identify related parties not disclosed by management.'

Problems with applying ISA 550	
Identification of controlling party	Auditors may find it very difficult to identify the controlling party if the entity is part of a multinational group. If the controlling party is a trust, auditors may have problems determining who if anyone controls the trust. Alternatively the directors may state that they do not know the identity of the controlling party or that there is no controlling party. These statements may be difficult to disprove.
Materiality	This problem has two aspects: (a) Auditors may not be able to determine **whether transactions** are **material** to related parties who are individuals (directors, key management and their families). (b) Auditors may have particular problems **applying** the **definition** of **materiality** (an item is material if it affects the decisions of the users of the accounts). As materiality depends on circumstances as well as amounts, auditors have to decide whether the fact that certain transactions are on normal commercial terms influences whether they are disclosed.

2.6 Transactions with directors and management

Auditors may find it difficult to obtain sufficient assurance that they have identified all disclosable transactions because of:

(a) The **low value of certain transactions**, making them difficult to detect when using normal audit procedures

(b) Any **requirements** for **disclosure of transactions** between the company and the connected persons of a director, given that it may not always be easy for the auditors to identify such connected persons

(c) The fact that there may be little or no **documentary evidence** of **transactions** requiring disclosure

The complexity of the relevant legislation may give rise to difficulties of interpretation. For example, advances of expenses or remuneration on account may constitute a disclosable loan if the monies are outstanding for a long time.

2.6.1 Company procedures

Auditors should enquire as to the company's procedures for ensuring that all disclosable transactions are properly identified and recorded. Such procedures are likely to include the following.

- **Advise** all **directors** and **officers** that they have a **responsibility** to disclose transactions in which they have an interest, either directly or through connected persons. (Such disclosure should take place at a meeting of the directors.)

- **Record** all **transactions** notified in the minutes of directors' meetings

- **Maintain** a **register** in which details of all transactions requiring disclosure are recorded

- **Establish** some **method** of:

  - **Identifying proposed transactions** which will require the approval of the members in general meeting

  - **Ensuring** that the **company does not enter** into any **illegal transactions**

- **Monitor the system** by checking on a regular basis (as a minimum, once a year) that each director is in agreement with the company's record of their disclosable transactions and is satisfied that such records are both complete and accurate

- **Obtain** from **each director** at the end of each financial year a **formal statement** indicating the disclosures necessary for the purposes of the statutory accounts

With smaller organisations, auditors may well find that there may be no formalised procedures or that they are inadequate. Auditors should **advise each director** of their statutory responsibilities, and make a **written request** for **confirmation** of any disclosable transaction in which they have an interest.

2.6.2 Audit procedures

Further audit procedures to be adopted should include the following.

- **Inspect** the **board minutes** and other records of transactions with directors and connected persons to consider their adequacy and whether or not they appear to have been kept up to date

- **Examine** any **agreements** and **contracts** involving **directors and connected persons**, including tracing the details of such transactions to any source documentation available

- **Consider** whether **transactions** disclosed are on **commercial** terms

- **Assess** the **recoverability** of amounts due from directors or connected persons

- **Review** the **legality** of the disclosable transactions recorded by the company. Where auditors are of the opinion that a transaction is illegal, they should:

  - Immediately advise the directors of their view
  - Give careful consideration as to whether any reference to the matter will be required in the audit report

- **Advise** the **client** to **seek legal advice** in those cases where there are doubts as to the legality and/or disclosable nature of a transaction

- **Consider** the **possibility** that the **company's details** of **disclosable transactions** may be incomplete as regards those directors (and connected persons) who have not been in office throughout the year

- **Review subsequent events** in order to consider whether they might have any impact on the matters requiring disclosure

Finally, auditors should consider obtaining **written representations** from each director giving confirmation of any disclosable transaction which relates to themselves and any persons connected with them.

Question	Related party transactions

You are the senior in charge of the audit of AB Dryden Co for the year ended 31 May 20X1. Details of AB Dryden Co and certain other companies are given below.

AB Dryden Co

A building company formed by Arthur Dryden and his brother, Bertrand.

AB Dryden Co has issued share capital of 500 ordinary $1 shares, owned as shown below.

Arthur Dryden	210	42%	Founder and director
Bertrand Dryden	110	22%	Founder and director
Catherine Dryden (Bertrand's wife)	100	20%	Company secretary
Emma Hardy	20	4%	
Andrew Murray	60	12%	Director

Andrew Murray is a local businessman and a close friend of both Arthur and Bertrand Dryden. He gave the brothers advice when they set up the company and remains involved through his position on the board of directors. His own company, Murray Design Co, supplies AB Dryden Co with stationery and publicity materials.

Emma Hardy is Arthur Dryden's ex-wife. She was given her shares as part of the divorce settlement and has no active involvement in the management of the company. Arthur's girlfriend, Fiona Dyson, is the company's solicitor. She is responsible for drawing up and reviewing all key building and other contracts, and frequently attends board meetings so that she can explain the terms of a particular contract to the

directors. Her personal involvement with Arthur started in May 20X1 and, since that time, she has spent increasing amounts of time at the company's premises.

Cuts and Curls Co

A poodle parlour, of which 50% of the issued shares are owned by Emma Hardy and 50% by Gillian Dryden, who is Arthur and Emma's daughter.

Cuts and Curls operates from premises owned by AB Dryden Co for which it pays rent at the normal market rate.

Pope Dryden Roofing Co

A roofing company owned 60% by AB Dryden Co and 40% by Ian Pope, the managing director.

Pope Dryden Roofing Co carries out regular work for AB Dryden Co and also does roofing work for local customers. Arthur Dryden is a director of Pope Dryden Roofing Co and Catherine Dryden is the company secretary. All legal work is performed by Fiona Dyson.

Required

(a) Based on the information given above, identify the potential related party transactions you expect to encounter during the audit of AB Dryden Co and summarise, giving your reasons, what disclosure, if any, will be required in the full statutory accounts.

(b) Prepare notes for a training session for junior staff on how to identify related party transactions. Your notes should include:

    (i) A list of possible features which could lead you to investigate a particular transaction to determine whether it is in fact a related party transaction

    (ii) A summary of the general audit procedures you would perform to ensure that all material related party transactions have been identified

Answer

(a)

Person/entity	Related party	Why	Transaction
Arthur Dryden	✓	Director	No transactions mentioned
Bertrand Dryden	✓	Director	
Catherine Dryden	✓	Wife of director	
Andrew Murray	✓	Director	Purchases of stationery
Murray Designs	✓	Sub of director	
Emma Hardy	✗	No longer close family and ≥ 20%	
Fiona Dyson	✓	Presumed close family and shadow director	Contracts drawn
Cuts and Curls	?	(see below)	Rental agreement
Pope Dryden Roofing	✓	Sub of AB Dryden	Work done for AB (see below)
Ian Pope	✓/✗	Could be considered key management of group	

Cuts and Curls is not clear cut. For it to be a related party, Gillian Dryden would need to be in a position to control Cuts and Curls and then due to her relationship with Arthur Dryden her company would come under the related party umbrella. Gillian only holds 50% and therefore holds joint control with her mother.

Disclosure

Once a related party has been identified then IAS 24 *Related party disclosures* requires disclosure of the nature of the relationship, as well as information about the transactions and outstanding balances.

Transactions with subsidiaries, that is, Pope Dryden Roofing:

Disclosure is not required of transactions which are cancelled on consolidation. However, if group accounts are not prepared due to a small/medium group exemption then material transactions between the two companies would need to be disclosed.

Disclosure should include:

(i)   The amount of the transactions

(ii)   The amount of outstanding balances, including commitments:

    (1)   Their terms and conditions, including whether they are secured, and the nature of the consideration to be provided in settlement

    (2)   Details of any guarantees given or received

(iii)   Provisions for doubtful debts related to the amount of outstanding balances

(iv)   The expense recognised during the period in respect of bad or doubtful debts due from related parties

(b)   Notes for staff training sessions:

    (i)   A logical place to start the audit of related party transactions would be to identify all possible related parties. This would always include:

- Directors and shadow directors
- Group companies
- Pension funds of the company
- Associates

It is likely that the other related parties would include:

- Key management (perhaps identified by which staff have key man cover)
- Shareholder owning > 20% of the shares
- Close relatives, associates of any of the above

A related party transaction needs to be reported if it is material either to the reporting entity or to the other party to the transaction.

Related party transactions do not necessarily have to be detrimental to the reporting entity, but those which are will be easier to find. Features which may indicate this include:

- Unusually generous trade or settlement discounts
- Unusually generous payment terms
- Recorded in the general ledger code of any person previously identified as a related party (for example, director)
- Unusual size of transaction for customers (for example, if ABM were paying a suspiciously high legal bill for a building company)

    (ii)   Audit steps to find related party transactions may include:

- Identification of excessively generous credit terms by reference to aged trade accounts receivable analysis
- Identification of excessive discounts by reference to similar reports
- Scrutiny of cash book/cheque stubs for payments made to directors or officers of the company (probably more realistic for smaller entities)
- Review of board minutes for evidence of approval of related party transactions (directors are under a fiduciary duty not to make secret profits)

- Written representations from directors to give exhaustive list of all actual/potential related parties (that is, allow us to make the materiality assessment, not them)
- Review of accounting rewards for large transactions, especially near the year end and with non-established customers/suppliers
- Identification of any persons holding > 20% of the shares in the entity by reference to the shareholders' register

3 Written representations

FAST FORWARD

> Management is required to give written representations regarding the preparation and presentation of the financial statements, information provided to the auditor and management responsibilities. Other representations may also be sought, but it is important to remember they do not provide sufficient appropriate audit evidence on their own.

3.1 Representations

The auditors receive many representations during the audit, both unsolicited and in response to specific questions. Some of these representations may be critical to obtaining sufficient appropriate audit evidence. Representations are also required for general matters, eg full availability of accounting records. ISA 580 *Written representations* covers this area.

ISA 580.6

The objectives of the auditor are:

(a) To obtain appropriate representations from management and, where appropriate, those charged with governance that they believe that they have fulfilled their responsibility for the preparation of the financial statements and for the completeness of the information provided to the auditor;

(b) To support other audit evidence relevant to the financial statements or specific assertions in the financial statements by means of written representations if determined necessary by the auditor or required by other ISAs; and

(c) To respond appropriately to written representations provided by management and, where appropriate, those charged with governance, or if management or, where appropriate, those charged with governance do not provide the written representations requested by the auditor.

Written representations should be requested from management or directors with appropriate responsibilities for the financial statements and knowledge of the matters concerned.

3.2 Management from whom written representations are requested

---

ISA 580.9

The auditor shall request written representations from management with appropriate responsibilities for the financial statements and knowledge of the matters concerned.

ISA 580 requires the auditor to determine the appropriate individuals from whom to seek written representations. In most cases this is likely to be management, as they would be expected to have sufficient knowledge of the way in which the entity's financial statements have been prepared. However, the ISA goes on to point out that in circumstances where others are responsible for the financial statements, for example those charged with governance, then they should be requested to provide the representations.

The ISA emphasises the need for management to make **informed representations**. In some cases the auditor may request that management confirms that it has made appropriate enquiries to enable it to do so.

3.3 Written representations concerning management responsibilities

ISA 580.10

The auditor shall request management to provide a written representation that it has fulfilled its responsibility for the preparation of the financial statements in accordance with the applicable financial reporting framework, including, where relevant their fair presentation, as set out in the terms of the audit engagement.

ISA 580.11

The auditor shall request management to provide a written representation that:

(a)   It has provided the auditor with all the relevant information and access as agreed in the terms of the audit engagement; and

(b)   All transactions have been recorded and are reflected in the financial statements.

This can be done when the auditors receive a signed copy of the financial statements which incorporate a relevant statement of management responsibilities. Alternatively, the auditors may obtain such evidence in the form of a **written representation** from management, or a document written by the auditors and signed by the management.

The responsibilities of management should also be set out as they are in the terms of engagement.

3.4 Other written representations

In addition to written representations relating to responsibility for the financial statements, the auditors may wish to rely on written representations from management as audit evidence, and several other ISAs require them.

ISA 580.13

Other ISAs require the auditor to request written representations. If, in addition to such required representations, the auditor determines that it is necessary to obtain one or more written representations to support other audit evidence relevant to the financial statements or one or more specific assertions in the financial statements, the auditor shall request such other written representations.

As written representations do not form sufficient audit appropriate evidence on their own, when the auditors receive such representations they should:

- Seek **corroborative audit evidence** from sources inside or outside the entity

- **Evaluate** whether the **representations** made by management appear reasonable and are consistent with other audit evidence obtained, including other representations

- **Consider whether the individuals** making the representations can be expected to be **well informed** on the particular matters

The table below suggests areas where written representations may be required.

Other written representations	
Required by ISAs	The following ISAs require specific written representations: • ISA 240 • ISA 250 • ISA 450 • ISA 501 • ISA 540 • ISA 550 • ISA 560 • ISA 570 • ISA 710

Other management responsibility issues	• Whether the selection of accounting policies is appropriate
	• Whether the following matters have been recognised, measured, presented or disclosed correctly:
	  – Plans or intentions affecting values of assets
	  – Liabilities
	  – Title to or control over assets
	  – Aspects of laws and regulations that may affect the FS
	• Whether all deficiencies of internal controls have been communicated to the auditor

Concerning specific assertions	• Matters of director judgement and intention (corroborated to meeting minutes for example)

3.4.1 Doubt as to the reliability of written representations

The auditor will have to determine the effect of the following on the reliability of written representations (if one of the following arises).

- Concerns over the competence, integrity, ethical values or diligence of management
- Inconsistency of written representations with other evidence obtained

The auditor will seek to resolve the latter by performing audit procedures. However, if it remains unresolved, particularly in addition to the first point, the auditor will have to take appropriate actions, which may include modifying the audit report in accordance with ISA 705.

3.4.2 Requested written representations not provided

If requested representations are not provided, the auditor must:

- Discuss the matter with management

- Re-evaluate the integrity of management and the effect that this may have on other representations and audit evidence in general

- Take appropriate actions, including determining the possible effect on the auditor's report per ISA 705

3.5 Form, timing and documentation of representations by management

The auditors should include in audit working papers evidence of management's representations in the form of a summary of oral discussions with management or written representations from management.

A written representation shall take the form of a **representation letter** from management.

The date of the letter should be as near as practicable to the date the audit report is signed, **but not after it**.

You have seen an example of a written representation letter in your previous studies, so should be familiar with the form they should take.

Question

You are an audit manager reviewing the completed audit file of Leaf Oil Co.

(a) There have been no events subsequent to the period end requiring adjustment in the financial statements.

(b) The company has revalued two properties in the year. The directors believe that the property market is going to boom next year, so have decided to revalue the other two properties then.

(c) The directors confirm that the company owns 75% of the newly formed company, Subsidiary Co, at the year end.

(d) The directors confirmed that the 500 gallons of oil in Warehouse B belong to Flower Oil Co.

Required

Comment on whether you would expect to see these matters referred to in the written representation letter.

Answer

(a) I would expect to see this referred to in a representation letter. ISA 580 gives this as an example of a matter to be included in the letter, as management should inform auditors of relevant subsequent events.

(b) This should not appear on a representation letter, even though management opinion is involved. This indicates an incorrect accounting treatment which the auditors should be in disagreement with the directors over.

(c) This should not appear on a representation letter as there should be sufficient alternative evidence for this matter. The auditor should be able to obtain registered information about Subsidiary Co from the companies' registrar.

(d) This should not appear on a representation letter. The auditors should be able to obtain evidence from Flower Oil Co that the inventory belongs to them.

Exam focus point

A common requirement in the P7 exam is to identify and explain audit procedures in relation to some issue. Do not be tempted to pepper your answers with 'Obtain written representation' as a generic point, as your examinations team has stated that 'written representations' will only receive marks where they are specifically relevant, for example where the accounting treatment depends on management's intentions.

4 Reliance on the work of an auditor's expert   12/08

FAST FORWARD

Sometimes auditors may need to use the work of an auditor's expert to obtain sufficient, appropriate audit evidence.

4.1 Experts

Professional audit staff are highly trained and educated, but their experience and training is limited to accountancy and audit matters. In **certain situations** it will therefore be necessary to employ someone else with **different expert knowledge** to gain sufficient, appropriate audit evidence.

Key term

An **expert** is a person or firm possessing special skill, knowledge and experience in a particular field other than accounting and auditing.

Auditors have **sole responsibility** for their opinion, but may use the work of an expert in order to obtain **sufficient audit evidence** regarding certain financial statement assertions.

ISA 620 *Using the work of an auditor's expert* distinguishes between the 'auditor's expert' and 'management's expert'. The latter is used by the entity in the form of assistance in the preparation of financial statements.

<table>
<tr><td>**Key terms**</td><td>**Auditor's expert.** An individual or organisation possessing expertise in a field other than accounting or auditing, whose work in that field is used by the auditor to assist the auditor in obtaining sufficient appropriate audit evidence. An auditor's expert may be either an auditor's internal expert (who is a partner or staff, including temporary staff, of the auditor's firm or a network firm), or an auditor's external expert.

Management's expert. An individual or organisation possessing expertise in a field other than accounting or auditing, whose work in that field is used by the entity to assist the entity in preparing the financial statements.</td></tr>
</table>

4.2 Determining the need to use the work of an auditor's expert

ISA 620.3

...if the auditor using the work of an auditor's expert... concludes that the work of that expert is adequate for the auditor's purposes the auditor may accept that expert's findings or conclusions in the expert's field as appropriate audit evidence.

The following list of examples is given by the ISA of the audit evidence which might be obtained from the opinion, valuation etc of an expert.

- **Valuations of certain types of assets**, for example complex financial instruments, land and buildings, plant and machinery
- **Determination of quantities or physical condition of assets**
- **Determination of amounts** using specialised techniques, for example pensions accounting
- **The measurement of work completed** and **work in progress** on contracts
- **Legal opinions**

When considering whether to use the work of an expert, the auditors should review:

- The **importance** of the matter being considered in the context of the accounts
- The **risk of misstatement** based on the nature and complexity of the matter
- The **quantity** and **quality** of other available **relevant audit evidence**

ISA 620 requires that a written agreement exists covering instructions to the auditor's expert.

<table>
<tr><td>**Exam focus point**</td><td>Engaging an auditor's expert is a costly business and the client and auditors will only want to if there is a real need to do so, in other words, in circumstances where other relevant and reliable audit evidence is not available. When recommending audit procedures in the exam, only recommend using an auditor's expert if it is a relevant procedure. It is not a substitute for alternative procedures.</td></tr>
</table>

Once it is decided that an auditor's expert is required, the approach should be discussed with the management of the entity. Where the management is unwilling or unable to engage an expert, the auditors should consider engaging an expert themselves **unless sufficient alternative audit evidence can be obtained**.

ISA 620 distinguishes between 'internal' and 'external' auditor's experts.

- Auditor's internal experts – members of the engagement team
- Auditor's external experts – not members of the engagement team. They are **engaged** but not employed by the auditor.

4.3 Competence and objectivity of the auditor's expert

> **ISA 620.9**
>
> The auditor shall evaluate whether the auditor's expert has the necessary competence, capabilities and objectivity for the auditor's purposes. In the case of an auditor's external expert, the evaluation of objectivity shall include inquiry regarding interests and relationships that may create a threat to that expert's objectivity.

This will involve considering:

- The expert's **professional certification**, or licensing by, or membership of, an appropriate professional body
- The expert's **experience and reputation** in the field in which the auditors are seeking audit evidence

The risk that an expert's **objectivity is impaired** increases when the expert is:

- **Employed** by the entity
- **Related** in some other manner to the entity, for example, by being financially dependent upon, or having an investment in, the entity

If the auditors have **reservations** about the competence or objectivity of the expert they may need to carry out **other procedures**, or obtain **evidence from another expert**.

4.4 The scope of work of the auditor's expert

> **ISA 620.11**
>
> The auditor shall agree, in writing when appropriate, on ... the nature, scope and objectives of that expert's work.

Written instructions usually cover the auditor's expert's terms of reference and such instructions may cover such matters as follows.

- The **objectives** and **scope** of the expert's work
- A **general outline** as to the specific matters the expert's report is to cover
- The **intended use** of the expert's work
- The **extent** of the **expert's access** to appropriate records and files
- Clarification of the expert's relationship with the entity, if any
- Confidentiality of the entity's information
- Information regarding the **assumptions and methods intended** to be used by the expert and their consistency with those used in prior periods

4.5 Assessing the work of the auditor's expert

> **ISA 620.12**
>
> The auditor shall evaluate the adequacy of the auditor's expert's work for the auditor's purposes including ... the relevance and reasonableness of that expert's findings or conclusions.

Auditors should assess whether the substance of the auditor's expert's findings is properly reflected in the financial statements or supports the financial statement assertions. It will also require consideration of:

- The **source data used**
- The **assumptions and methods used**
- **When** the expert carried out the work
- The reasons for any **changes in assumptions and methods**

- The **results** of the expert's work in the light of the auditors' overall knowledge of the business and the results of other audit procedures

The auditors do **not** have the expertise to judge the assumptions and methods used; these are the responsibility of the expert. However, the auditors should seek to obtain an understanding of these assumptions, to consider their reasonableness based on other audit evidence, knowledge of the business and so on.

Relevant factors when evaluating the relevance and reasonableness of the findings or conclusions of the auditor's expert, whether in a report or other form, may include whether they are:

- Presented in a manner that is consistent with industry standards
- Clearly expressed, including reference to the objectives agreed and standards used
- Based on an appropriate period and take into account any subsequent events
- Subject to any reservation, limitation or restriction on use
- Based on appropriate consideration of errors or deviations encountered by the auditor's expert

---

ISA 620.13

If the auditor determines that the work of the auditor's expert is not adequate for the auditor's purposes, the auditor shall:

(a)   Agree with that expert on the nature and extent of further work to be performed by that expert; or
(b)   Perform additional audit procedures appropriate to the circumstances.

4.6 Reference to an auditor's expert in the audit report

ISA 620.14

The auditor shall not refer to the work of an auditor's expert in an auditor's report containing an unmodified opinion unless required by law or regulation to do so.

Such a reference may be misunderstood and interpreted as a modification of the audit opinion, or as a division of responsibility, neither of which is appropriate.

If the auditors issue a modified audit report, then they may refer to the work of the expert. In such cases, auditors may need to obtain permission in advance from the expert. If such permission is not given, then the auditors may have to seek legal advice.

 Question

Using an auditor's expert

The following situations are both extracted from an exam on the previous syllabus.

(a)   'The useful life of each oil platform is assessed annually on factors such as weather conditions and the period over which it is estimated that oil will be extracted.' You are auditing the useful lives of the oil platforms.

(b)   'Piles of copper and brass, that can be distinguished with a simple acid test, have been mixed up.' You are attending the inventory count.

Required

Explain whether it is necessary to use the work of an auditor's expert in these situations. Where relevant, you should describe alternative procedures.

Answer

(a) **Platforms**

It is not necessary to use an auditor's expert to audit the useful lives of the platforms as there are many other available sources of evidence. Relevant procedures include:

(i) Obtaining weather reports to see whether management's determination of useful lives is consistent with them

(ii) Comparing budgeted oil against actual oil extracted (if the budget was optimistic, so might the useful life be)

(iii) Reviewing published industry comparators (such as Shell and BP). If the useful lives of their platforms as published in financial statements are significantly different, discuss with management why that might be

(iv) Considering whether management's determination of useful lives in the past has been proved accurate

(b) It is not necessary to use an auditor's expert, as the question states that a 'simple' test is available. The auditors should confirm that the company will be making use of this test during the inventory count to separate the inventory. The auditor should reperform the test on a sample of 'brass' and 'copper' as counted to ensure it has been separated correctly.

Exam focus point

The exam question will often give a clear indicator of whether an auditor's expert is required or not. For instance in (a) above, information was given on what the useful lives were based on – which the auditor should be able to interpret themselves. In (b), the words '**simple** acid test' imply that an auditor's expert is not required.

5 Reliance on the work of internal audit
6/10, 12/13

FAST FORWARD

Internal audit's work can be relied upon, but only if it meets the needs of the external auditor.

ISA 610 (Revised) *Using the work of internal auditors* was issued in 2009, and revised in 2012 and 2014.

The basic issue here is the same as with using the work of any other expert: you cannot just rely on their work, but must decide whether it is actually suitable for the external audit. In the case of work done by internal audit, ISA 610 states that the external auditor must determine:

- Whether internal audit's work can be used at all

- If the work can be used, in which areas and to what extent? Is the work adequate for the purposes of the external audit?

Consideration should also be given to whether internal auditors will be used to provide direct assistance to the external audit team (Section 5.3 below).

Exam focus point

Using the work of internal audit was part of your studies for Paper F8. This section recaps some of that material, but if you are unsure then you will need to revisit it.

5.1 Assessing the internal audit function

Determining what work can be used involves considering three main things:

(a) Internal audit's **organisational status** and relevant policies and procedures. Are the internal auditors **objective**?

(b) The **level of competence** of the internal audit function

(c)   Whether the internal audit function applies a **systematic and disciplined approach**, including **quality control**

In assessing internal audit's **objectivity**, the external auditor should consider:

Assessing the objectivity of internal audit	
Organisational status	**High organisational status** may indicate greater objectivity. Does the internal audit function report to those charged with governance, or merely to management?
Conflicting responsibilities	Does internal audit have **other responsibilities** that affect its objectivity?
Employment decisions	Are employment **decisions overseen** by those charged with governance?
Constraints and restrictions	Is the internal audit function **restricted from communicating findings** to the external auditor?
Membership of a professional body	Are the internal auditors members of relevant **professional bodies**? Are they obliged to comply with relevant professional standards, including **continuing professional development requirements**?

In assessing internal audit's **competence**, the following factors should be considered.

Factors affecting the competence of internal audit
Level of resources relative to the size and nature of its operations
Established **policies** for hiring, training and assigning internal auditors to engagements
Whether internal auditors have **adequate technical training** and **proficiency** in auditing
Whether the internal auditors possess the required **financial reporting knowledge** and necessary skills
Whether the internal auditors are **members of relevant professional bodies**

The external auditor should also look for evidence of a **systematic and disciplined approach**. Internal audit should have documented internal audit procedures, including those covering such areas as risk assessment, work programmes, documentation and reporting. The external auditor will also consider whether appropriate **quality control** procedures are in place.

If internal audit lacks any of the above (ie objectivity, competence, or a systematic and disciplined approach), then **none of its work can be relied on**.

5.2 Determining the nature and extent of work that can be used

The key question is: is the work relevant to the overall audit strategy and audit plan?

ISA 610 envisages three ways of using the work of internal auditors:

(1)   To obtain information to be used when assessing the risk of material misstatement
(2)   To use internal auditors' work instead of performing procedures
(3)   To use internal auditors themselves to perform audit procedures (direct assistance)

The ISA lists the following as examples of internal audit work that can typically be used by the external auditor (instead of performing procedures).

Internal audit work that can typically be used
Testing of the **operating effectiveness of controls**
Substantive procedures involving limited judgement
Observations of **inventory counts**

Internal audit work that can typically be used
Tracing transactions through the financial reporting information system
Testing of **compliance with regulatory requirements**
In some circumstances, **audits** or reviews of the financial information **of subsidiaries** that are not significant components to the group

Any work that involves significant judgements cannot be used. Work in the following areas **cannot** be relied on.

- Assessing the risk of material misstatement
- Evaluating the sufficiency of tests performed
- Evaluating the appropriateness of management's use of the going concern assumption
- Evaluating significant accounting estimates; and
- Evaluating the adequacy of disclosures in the financial statements, and other matters affecting the auditor's report

5.3 Steps when relying on internal audit

If the external auditor plans to use the work of internal audit function, they must:

Step 1   **Discuss** the planned use of internal audit work **with the internal audit** function

Step 2   **Read the relevant internal audit reports** to understand the nature and extent of audit procedures performed and the findings

Step 3   **Carry out and document 'sufficient audit procedures'** on the internal audit work to be used to assess its adequacy for the purposes of the audit

Exam focus point

> The December 2013 paper featured a scenario in Q1 in which the audit client asked the auditor to make as much use as possible of a subsidiary's internal audit department in order to 'reduce the audit fee'. The requirement gave seven marks for a discussion of the impact of this suggestion on the audit plan.

5.4 Direct assistance

Key term

> **Direct assistance** refers to the use of internal auditors to perform audit procedures under the direction, supervision and review of the external auditor.

It is possible that members of the internal audit team will provide **direct assistance** to the external auditor, ie they will perform procedures on the auditor's behalf. This is permissible in line with ISA 610, unless the jurisdiction in which the audit is taking place prohibits this (such as the UK).

Previously, the ISAs have remained silent on the subject of whether, and how, external auditors should involve the entity's internal auditors in obtaining and evaluating audit evidence. While some jurisdictions categorically prohibit direct assistance, the IAASB notes that the use of direct assistance, where it is allowed, does not appear to compromise audit quality. Given appropriate planning, direction, supervision and review from the external audit team, the use of internal auditors could lead to savings both in terms of time and cost for the audit client.

However, it must be considered whether these internal auditors meet the **independence** requirements which apply to the external auditor. This is because the IESBA *Code of Ethics* (revised 2013) includes internal auditors used in this way within its definition of the 'engagement team'. In practice it appears unlikely that many internal auditors would meet these requirements.

5.4.1 Using direct assistance

Three key areas must be considered:

(1) The amount of **judgement** involved
(2) **Risk** of material misstatement
(3) The external auditor's evaluation of threats to the **objectivity** and the level of **competence** of the internal auditors

ISA 610 (Revised) **prohibits** the use of internal auditors to provide direct assistance to perform procedures that:

- Involve making **significant judgements**
- Relate to **higher assessed risks of material misstatement** where more than a limited degree of **judgement** is required
- Relate to work with which the **internal auditors have been involved**
- Relate to **decisions** the external auditor makes **regarding the internal audit function** and the use of its work or direct assistance.

Before using internal auditors to provide direct assistance, **written agreement must be obtained**:

- From an **authorised representative** of the entity
- From the **internal auditors**

It is especially important that the external auditor directs, supervises and reviews the work performed by the internal auditors, bearing in mind that the internal auditors are not independent of the entity. ISA 610 (Revised) requires the external auditor to check back to the underlying audit evidence for at least some of the work performed by the internal auditors.

Once the external auditors have evaluated the extent to which internal auditors can be used to provide direct assistance, they must **communicate the nature and extent of the planned use of direct assistance** to those charged with governance.

Question	Using the work of internal audit

You are an audit manager in Jobs & Co, and you are in the process of planning the upcoming audit of Work Co, a large private company.

In your initial conversation with Work Co's finance director, you discovered that there is a small internal audit team, under the supervision of Ruthie Rozario, a recently qualified accountant. Before heading up the internal audit department at Work Co, Ruthie worked for the business advisory department of a major firm of professional accountants.

The internal audit department has a manual of procedures that was created by Ruthie's predecessor. Internal audit work that is done each year includes observing the inventory count, as well as extensive testing of financial controls over the sales, purchases and wages systems.

Ruthie reports directly to Work Co's finance director, who has overall responsibility for the department. In the course of the year the finance director instructed the team to work on the implementation of cost-cutting measures being introduced across the company. This is in addition to the team's responsibilities for testing the existing financial and operational controls.

The internal audit team has three members, including Ruthie. The remaining team members are in the process of studying for professional accountancy qualifications. One team member left the company during the year, citing 'overwork' as their reason for leaving. As a result of financial pressures, Work Co is currently operating under a recruitment freeze and the team member has not been replaced. In addition, team members currently qualifying have been told that Work Co will no longer be able to offer them support in their professional studies.

Required

Identify and explain the matters that should be considered in respect of the extent to which reliance can be placed on the work of the internal audit function of Work Co.

ISA 610 requires the auditor to determine whether internal audit is objective, competent, and adopts a systematic and disciplined approach. If it fulfils all of these criteria then the external auditor may rely upon its work.

Competence of team

Ruthie only qualified recently, and may therefore have limited experience. However, she worked in a business advisory department, so it is possible that she has experience of internal audit. The precise nature of Ruthie's past experience should be ascertained as part of the evaluation of the competence of the department.

A further consideration is that remaining team members are still in the process of qualifying. They may not therefore have sufficient skill or experience in all of the areas that the internal audit team is responsible for.

Procedures

The internal audit function does have its own manual of procedures, which is a sign of a systematic and disciplined approach. If reliance is to be placed on internal audit, then this manual should be examined to discover whether any of the procedures are relevant to the external audit. At first glance, observation of the inventory count and testing of financial controls may be relevant, but this would depend on the audit strategy and plan adopted for the audit of Work Co.

However, this manual was, created by Ruthie's predecessor, and it is possible that it may not be adhered to anymore. Evidence would need to be obtained about the extent to which these procedures are actually followed by the team.

Size of department

Work Co is a large company but its internal audit team is small, with only three members. It is thus questionable whether the department has a level of resources that is adequate to fulfil its responsibilities. This throws doubt on the department's competence, and the precise nature of the department's responsibilities and resources should be ascertained.

Authority

The internal audit function is headed by a recently qualified accountant, which may result in it having comparatively little authority within Work Co as a whole. It is possible that any recommendations that it makes will not be listened to if this is the case.

Ruthie reports directly to the finance director. There is therefore no direct contact with those charged with governance, and Work Co does not appear to have an audit committee. This indicates a relatively low status within the organisation, and may contribute to a lack of objectivity in the department's work.

Work performed

The finance director instructed the team to focus on the implementation of cost cuts during the year. This operational focus may detract from the work the team does on financial controls, which casts further doubt on the competence with which that work was carried out.

Team member left

One team member left during the year as a result of work pressures, and has not been replaced. This raises very serious doubts over the competence of the department, and over its ability to carry out internal audit work of a quality that can be relied on by an external auditor. The fact that the team member has not been replaced will only make matters worse in this regard.

Remaining team

The remaining team members have been told that they will not be supported in their studies. This is likely to affect their motivation to work for Work Co, and raises further questions about the competence of the department.

Control environment

The matters above may have implications for the external auditor's assessment of the quality of the control environment at Work Co. The fact that the team member who left was not replaced may indicate a lack of value being placed on internal control by senior management. This will affect the auditor's understanding of the entity obtained under ISA 315.

6 Documentation

FAST FORWARD

All evidence obtained should be documented.

6.1 Document what?

One of the competencies you require to fulfil Performance Objective 19 of the PER is the ability to carry out and document compliance and substantive tests and other audit work in accordance with the audit programme. You can apply the knowledge you obtain in this chapter of the Text to help demonstrate this competence.

All audit work must be documented: the working papers are the **tangible evidence of all work done in support of the audit opinion**. ISA 230 *Audit documentation* provides guidance on documentation.

In the case of areas where the evidence is difficult to obtain, such as related parties, and may arise through discussions with management, it is vital that notes are made of conversations and that, as discussed earlier in this chapter, representations on material matters are confirmed in writing.

In your previous studies, you learned the practical issues surrounding how audit papers should be completed.

A key requirement of ISA 230 concerns what to include on a working paper:.

> **ISA 230.8**
>
> The auditor shall prepare audit documentation that is sufficient to enable an experienced auditor, having no previous connection with the audit, to understand:
>
> (a)   The nature, timing and extent of the audit procedures performed to comply with the ISAs and applicable legal and regulatory requirements;
>
> (b)   The results of the audit procedures performed, and the audit evidence obtained; and
>
> (c)   Significant matters arising during the audit, the conclusions reached thereon, and significant professional judgements made in reaching those conclusions.

The key reason for having audit papers therefore is that they provide evidence of work done. They may be required in the event of litigation arising over the audit work and opinion given.

The ISA sets out certain requirements about what should be recorded, such as the identifying characteristics of the specific items being tested.

It also sets out the points an auditor should record in relation to significant matters, such as the extent of professional judgement exercised in performing the work and evaluating the results.

If an auditor felt it necessary to depart from customary audit work required by audit standards, he should document why, and how the different test achieved audit objectives.

The ISA also contains details about how the audit file should be put together and actions in the event of audit work being added after the date of the audit report (for example, if subsequent events results in additional work being carried out).

Specific consideration is given to **smaller entities**. The ISA recognises that the documentation of a smaller entity will be less extensive, but emphasises the overriding requirement that it should be capable of being understood by an experienced auditor.

We shall briefly revise here the review of working papers. **Review** of working papers is important, as it allows a more senior auditor to **evaluate the evidence obtained** during the course of the audit for sufficiency and reliability, so that more evidence can be obtained to support the audit opinion, if required.

6.2 Review of audit working papers

Working papers should be reviewed by a more senior audit staff member before an audit conclusion is drawn.

Work performed by each assistant should be reviewed by personnel of appropriate experience to consider whether:

- The work has been performed in accordance with the audit programme
- The work performed and the results obtained have been adequately documented
- Any significant matters have been resolved or are reflected in audit conclusions
- The objectives of the audit procedures have been achieved
- The conclusions expressed are consistent with the results of the work performed and support the audit opinion

The following should be reviewed on a timely basis.

- The **overall audit strategy** and the **audit plan**
- The **assessments of inherent and control risks**
- The **results** of **control** and **substantive procedures** and the conclusions drawn including the results of consultations
- The **financial statements**, proposed audit adjustments and the proposed auditor's report

In some cases, particularly in large complex audits, personnel not involved in the audit may be asked to review some or all of the audit work, the auditor's report etc. This is sometimes called a **pre-issuance review**, a **peer review** or a **hot review**.

Chapter Roundup

- Auditors need to obtain sufficient, appropriate audit evidence.

- It can be difficult to gain audit evidence about related party transactions.

- Management is required to give written representations regarding the preparation and presentation of the financial statements, information provided to the auditor and management responsibilities. Other representations may also be sought, but it is important to remember they do not provide sufficient appropriate audit evidence on their own.

- Sometimes auditors may need to use the work of an auditor's expert to obtain sufficient appropriate audit evidence.

- Internal audit's work can be relied on, but only if it meets the needs of the external auditor.

- All evidence obtained should be documented.

- Working papers should be reviewed by a more senior audit staff member before an audit conclusion is drawn.

1   Give five examples of financial statement assertions.

    (1)   ....

    (2)   ....

    (3)   ....

    (4)   ....

    (5)   ....

2   Which of the following is not a procedure designed to obtain evidence?

    Documents

    Observation

    Inspection

    Assets

    Analytical procedures

    Computation

    Deduction

    Enquiries

    Management

    External sources

    Confirmation

3   Give five reasons why the nature of related party relationships and transactions may give rise to increased risk.

    (1)   ....

    (2)   ....

    (3)   ....

    (4)   ....

    (5)   ....

4   Written representations from management might take the form of a letter from the auditors acknowledged and signed by the director.

    True   ☐

    False   ☐

5   Complete the definition.

    An .... is a person or organisation possessing ....,

    in a field other than .... or ....

6   Give three examples of audit evidence which can be obtained from an auditor's expert.

    (1)   ....

    (2)   ....

    (3)   ....

7   What is a pre-issuance review?

Answers to Quick Quiz

1 From:

  (1) Existence
  (2) Rights and obligations
  (3) Occurrence
  (4) Completeness
  (5) Valuation
  (6) Cut-off
  (7) Classification
  (8) Accuracy
  (9) Allocation

2 Deduction

3 (1) Related parties may operate through a **wide** and **complex** range of relationships and structures.

  (2) **Management is unaware** of the existence of all related party relationships and transactions.

  (3) **Information systems may be ineffective** at identifying or summarising transactions and outstanding balances between an entity and its related parties.

  (4) Related party transactions may not be conducted under **normal market terms and conditions**.

  (5) Related party relationships provide a greater opportunity for **collusion, concealment or manipulation** by management.

4 True

5 Expert, expertise, accounting, auditing

6 (1) Valuations of assets
  (2) Determination of quantities of assets
  (3) Legal opinions

7 A pre-issuance review is when a member of staff who has not been involved in the audit is asked to review all the working papers before the audit report is signed.

Now try the question below from the Practice Question Bank.

Number	Level	Marks	Time
Q10	Examination	20	39 mins

Evaluation and review (I)

Topic list	Syllabus reference
1 Revision: review procedures and evaluation of findings	D3
2 Opening balances	D3
3 Revision: comparatives	D3
4 Revision: other information	D3
5 Revision: subsequent events	D3
6 Revision: going concern	D3

Introduction

Towards the end of an audit, a series of reviews and evaluations are carried out. You should be familiar with them from your previous auditing studies.

Section 1 outlines the **overall review** which is undertaken on the financial statements as a whole and the review of misstatements and potential misstatements.

In Sections 2 and 3, the issue of **opening balances and comparatives** is discussed. In the event of a recurring audit, both these items are audited as part of the review process. In special circumstances, notably the first audit, different considerations and procedures must be followed.

The auditor must review **other information** to establish whether it contradicts the financial statements. The detailed procedures and requirements are discussed in Section 4.

The auditor conducts reviews of the period between the period end and the signing of the audit report **(subsequent events)** and of the **going concern** presumption. There is guidance given on both these areas in ISAs, and they are dealt with in Sections 5 and 6 respectively.

Study guide

		Intellectual level
D3	**Evaluation and review**	
(b)	Explain the use of analytical procedures in evaluation and review.	3
(c)	Explain how the auditor's responsibilities for corresponding figures, comparative financial statements and 'other information' are discharged.	3
(d)	Apply the further considerations and audit procedures relevant to initial engagements.	2
(e)	Discuss the courses of action available to an auditor if a material inconsistency or misstatement exists in relation to other information such as contained in the integrated report.	2
(f)	Specify audit procedures designed to identify subsequent events that may require adjustment to, or disclosure in, the financial statements of a given entity.	2
(g)	Identify and explain indicators that the going concern basis may be in doubt and recognise mitigating factors.	2
(h)	Recommend audit procedures, or evaluate the evidence that might be expected to be available and assess the appropriateness of the going concern basis in given situations.	3
(i)	Assess the adequacy of disclosures in financial statements relating to going concern and explain the implications for the auditor's report with regard to the going concern basis.	3
(j)	Evaluate the matters (eg materiality, risk, relevant accounting standards, audit evidence) relating to: (xxiii) Events after the end of the reporting period	3

Exam guide

Going concern is a particularly important audit review which could be relevant in risks or evidence questions. Bear in mind the links with planning, knowledge of the business and analytical procedures. Subsequent events, corresponding figures and other information could also come up in an exam question in the context of auditor's reports.

1 Revision: review procedures and evaluation of findings

> **FAST FORWARD**
>
> The auditor must perform and document an overall review of the financial statements before they can reach an opinion.

Once the bulk of the substantive procedures have been carried out, the auditors will have a draft set of financial statements which should be supported by appropriate and sufficient audit evidence. This is known as the completion stage of the audit. It is a requirement of ISA 220 *Quality control for an audit of financial statements* that the auditor conducts an **overall review** of the audit evidence obtained in relation to the financial statements.

This review, in conjunction with the conclusions drawn from the other audit evidence obtained, gives the auditors a reasonable basis for their opinion on the financial statements. It should be carried out by a senior member of the audit team who has the appropriate skills and experience.

This area will often be examined by scenario questions asking for 'the matters to consider and the evidence you would expect to find'.

One of the competences you require to fulfil Performance Objective 20 of the PER is the ability to review the performance of an audit, ensuring the process has been undertaken effectively and that all work undertaken is accurate and complete and that sufficient evidence has been obtained. You can apply the knowledge you have obtained from this chapter of the Study Text to help demonstrate this competence.

1.1 Compliance with accounting regulations

The auditors should consider whether:

(a)   The information presented in the financial statements is in accordance with local/national statutory requirements

(b)   The accounting policies employed are in accordance with accounting standards, properly disclosed, consistently applied and appropriate to the entity

When examining the **accounting policies**, auditors should consider:

- Policies **commonly adopted in particular industries**
- Policies for which there is **substantial authoritative support**
- Whether any **departures from applicable accounting standards** are necessary for the financial statements to conform to the IASB *Conceptual framework*'s requirement of 'fair presentation'
- Whether the **financial statements reflect the substance** of the underlying transactions and not merely their form

When compliance with local/national statutory requirements and accounting standards is considered, the auditors may find it useful to use a **checklist**.

1.2 Review for consistency and reasonableness

The auditors should consider whether the financial statements are consistent with their knowledge of the entity's business and with the results of other audit procedures, and the manner of disclosure is fair. The principal considerations are:

(a)   Whether the financial statements adequately reflect the **information** and **explanations** previously obtained and conclusions previously reached during the course of the audit

(b)   Whether the review reveals any **new factors** which may affect the presentation of, or disclosure in, the financial statements

(c)   Whether analytical procedures applied when completing the audit, such as comparing the information in the financial statements with other pertinent information, **produce results** which assist in arriving at the overall conclusion as to whether the financial statements as a whole are consistent with their knowledge of the entity's business

(d)   Whether the **presentation** adopted in the financial statements may have been unduly influenced by the **directors' desire** to present matters in a favourable or unfavourable light

(e)   The potential impact on the financial statements of the **aggregate of uncorrected misstatements** (including those arising from bias in making accounting estimates) identified during the course of the audit and the preceding period's audit, if any

1.3 Analytical procedures

Your examining team has indicated that you may **sometimes** be required to perform **specific tasks** in relation to analytical procedures. Do not spend too much time rote-learning all the formulae given below. For one thing, using these formulae is unlikely to form a major part of a P7 exam. Furthermore, **it is far more important that you understand what the numbers in financial statements mean** than that you can calculate lots of ratios. You need to show that you can 'make the numbers talk'.

In Chapter 6 we discussed how analytical procedures are used as part of the overall review procedures at the end of an audit. The financial statements should be reviewed in line with the requirements of ISA 520 *Analytical procedures*. Remember the areas that the analytical procedures at the final stage must cover:

- Important accounting ratios
- Related items
- Changes in products and/or customers
- Price and mix changes
- Wages changes
- Variances
- Trends in production and sales
- Changes in material and labour content of production
- Other statement of profit or loss expenditure
- Variations caused by industry or economic factors

The analytical procedures performed at the completion stage are no different from those performed elsewhere in the audit process. The only difference is that by this time the auditor should know enough about the client to be able to point to evidence explaining the issues highlighted by the analytical review.

If the auditor finds a previously unrecognised risk of material misstatement at this stage, then it will have to revise its assessment of audit risk. This may affect materiality, for example, and may mean that further audit evidence is needed in certain areas.

You should be familiar with all of the following from your previous studies. You should read through the material here and make sure that you are comfortable calculating the ratios.

1.3.1 Revision of key ratios: profitability

ROCE $= \dfrac{\text{Profit before interest and taxation}}{\text{Total assets less current liabilities}} \times 100\%$

Capital employed $=$ Shareholders' equity plus non-current liabilities (**or** total assets less current liabilities)

What does ROCE mean? There are three main possibilities:

(a) The **change in ROCE from one year to the next** can be examined.

(b) The **ROCE being earned by other companies**, if this information is available, can be compared with the ROCE of this company.

(c) A comparison of the ROCE with **current market borrowing rates** may be made.

You also need to be familiar with **profit margin** and **asset turnover**, which both tie in nicely with the ROCE. The relationship between the three ratios can be shown mathematically:

Profit margin × Asset turnover = ROCE

$\therefore \quad \dfrac{\text{PBIT}}{\text{Sales}} \times \dfrac{\text{Sales}}{\text{Capital employed}} = \dfrac{\text{PBIT}}{\text{Capital employed}}$

It might be tempting to think that a high profit margin is good, and a low asset turnover means sluggish trading. In broad terms, this is so. But there is a trade-off between profit margin and asset turnover, and you cannot look at one without allowing for the other.

(a) A **high profit margin** means a high profit per $1 of sales, but if this also means that sales prices are high, there is a strong possibility that sales revenue will be depressed, and so asset turnover lower.

(b) A **high asset turnover** means that the company is generating a lot of sales, but to do this it might have to keep its prices down and so accept a low profit margin per $1 of sales.

1.3.2 Revision of key ratios: debt

> The **debt ratio** is the ratio of a company's total debts to its total assets.

There is no absolute guide to the maximum safe debt ratio but, as a very general guide, you might regard 50% as a safe limit to debt. In practice, many companies operate successfully with a higher debt ratio than this, but 50% is nonetheless a helpful benchmark. In addition, if the debt ratio is over 50% and getting worse, the company's debt position will be worth looking at more carefully.

$$\text{Gearing} = \frac{\text{Interest bearing debt}}{\text{Shareholders' equity} + \text{interest bearing debt}} \times 100\%$$

As with the debt ratio, there is **no absolute limit** to what a gearing ratio ought to be. A company with a gearing ratio of more than 50% is said to be high-geared (whereas low gearing means a gearing ratio of less than 50%). Many companies are high geared, but if a high geared company is becoming increasingly high geared, it is likely to have difficulty in the future when it wants to borrow even more, unless it can also boost its shareholders' capital, either with retained profits or by a new share issue.

$$\text{Interest cover} = \frac{\text{Profit before interest and tax}}{\text{Interest charges}}$$

An interest cover of two times or less would be low, and should really exceed three times before the company's interest costs are to be considered within acceptable limits.

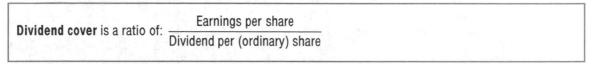

$$\text{Current ratio} = \frac{\text{Current assets}}{\text{Current liabilities}} \qquad \text{Quick ratio} = \frac{\text{Current assets less inventory}}{\text{Current liabilities}}$$

Both the current ratio and the quick ratio offer an indication of the company's liquidity position, but the absolute figures **should not be interpreted too literally**. It is often theorised that an acceptable current ratio is 1.5 and an acceptable quick ratio is 0.8, but these should only be used as a guide.

Finally, you should also be comfortable with the ratios of the cash operating cycle – receivables days, payables days, inventory holding period.

1.3.3 Revision of key ratios: shareholders' investment ratios

> **Dividend cover** is a ratio of: $\dfrac{\text{Earnings per share}}{\text{Dividend per (ordinary) share}}$

It shows the **proportion of profit for the year that is available for distribution to shareholders that has been paid (or proposed) and what proportion will be retained in the business to finance future growth**. A dividend cover of two times would indicate that the company had paid 50% of its distributable profits as dividends, and retained 50% in the business to help to finance future operations. Retained profits are an important source of funds for most companies, and so the dividend cover can in some cases be quite high.

> The **Price/Earnings (P/E) ratio** is the ratio of a company's current share price to the earnings per share.

A high P/E ratio indicates strong shareholder **confidence** in the company and its future, eg in profit growth, and a lower P/E ratio indicates lower confidence.

$$\text{Dividend yield} = \frac{\text{Dividend on the share for the year}}{\text{Current market value of the share (ex div)}} \times 100\%$$

(a) The dividend per share is taken as the dividend for the previous year.
(b) Ex-div means that the share price does **not** include the right to the most recent dividend.

Shareholders look for **both dividend yield and capital growth**. Obviously, dividend yield is therefore an important aspect of a share's performance.

1.4 Summarising misstatements

During the course of the audit, misstatements will be discovered which may be material or immaterial to the financial statements. It is very likely that the client will adjust the financial statements to take account of material and immaterial misstatements during the course of the audit. At the end of the audit, however, some misstatements may still be outstanding, and the auditors will summarise these **uncorrected misstatements**.

The summary of misstatements will not only list misstatements from the current year, but also those from the previous year(s). This will allow misstatements to be highlighted which are reversals of misstatements in the previous year, such as in the valuation of closing/opening inventory. Cumulative misstatements may also be shown, which have increased from year to year. It is normal to show both the statement of financial position and the statement of profit or loss and other comprehensive income effect, as in the example given here.

SCHEDULE OF UNCORRECTED MISSTATEMENTS

	20X2 Statement of profit or loss Dr $	20X2 Statement of profit or loss Cr $	20X2 Statement of financial position Dr $	20X2 Statement of financial position Cr $	20X1 Statement of profit or loss Dr $	20X1 Statement of profit or loss Cr $	20X1 Statement of financial position Dr $	20X1 Statement of financial position Cr $
(a) ABC Co receivable unprovided	10,470			10,470	4,523			4,523
(b) Opening/closing inventory undervalued*	21,540			21,540		21,540	21,540	
(c) Closing inventory undervalued		34,105	34,105					
(d) Opening unaccrued expenses								
Telephone*		453	453		453			453
Electricity*		905	905		905			905
(e) Closing unaccrued expenses								
Telephone	427			427				
Electricity	1,128			1,128				
(f) Obsolete inventory write off	2,528			2,528	3,211			3,211
Total	36,093	35,463	35,463	36,093	9,092	21,540	21,540	9,092
*Cancelling items	21,540			21,540				
		453	453					
		905	905					
	14,553	34,105	34,105	14,553				

234   **8: Evaluation and review (I)** | Part D Audit of historical financial information

BPP LEARNING MEDIA

1.4.1 Evaluating the effect of misstatements

FAST FORWARD As part of their completion procedures, auditors should consider whether the cumulative effect of uncorrected misstatements is material.

ISA 450.11

The auditor shall determine whether uncorrected misstatements are material, individually or in aggregate.

The aggregate of uncorrected misstatements comprises:

(a) **Specific misstatements** identified by the auditors, including the net effect of uncorrected misstatements identified during the audit of the previous period if they affect the current period's financial statements

(b) Their **best estimate** of **other misstatements** which cannot be quantified specifically (ie projected misstatements)

If the auditors consider that the aggregate of misstatements may be material, they must consider reducing audit risk by extending audit procedures or requesting management to adjust the financial statements (which management may wish to do anyway).

ISA 450.12

The auditor shall communicate with those charged with governance uncorrected misstatements and the effect that they, individually or in aggregate, may have on the opinion in the auditor's report[…].

If the aggregate of the uncorrected misstatements that the auditors have identified approaches the materiality level, the auditors should consider whether it is likely that undetected misstatements, when taken with aggregated uncorrected misstatements, could exceed the materiality level. Thus, as aggregate uncorrected misstatements approach the materiality level, the auditors should consider reducing the risk by:

- **Performing additional audit procedures**
- **Requesting management** to adjust the financial statements for identified misstatements

The schedule of uncorrected misstatements will be used by the audit manager and partner to decide whether the client should be requested to make adjustments to the financial statements to correct the misstatements.

1.4.2 Materiality of disclosures

Amendments to ISA 450 published in 2015 require auditors to consider misstatements in disclosures as well as those in transactions and balances.

Professional judgement is required in determining whether a misstatement in a qualitative disclosures is material. ISA 450 gives some examples of misstatements which may be material:

- The omission of information about the events which have led to an impairment loss (for example, in a mining company, this may be a significant long-term decline in the demand for a metal)

- The incorrect description of an accounting policy relating to a significant item in the statement of financial position, the statement of comprehensive income, the statement of changes in equity or the statement of cash flows

Depending on the circumstances, **misstatements in disclosures could also indicate fraud** – for example, where they result from management bias, or where the disclosures are intended to obscure a proper understanding of the financial statements. **Professional scepticism** is therefore required in considering misstatements in disclosures.

1.5 Completion checklists

Audit firms frequently use checklists, which must be signed off to ensure that all final procedures have been carried out, all material amounts are supported by sufficient appropriate evidence, etc.

1.6 Audit clearance meeting

At the end of the audit it is usual for a meeting to be held between the auditor and management (or those charged with governance). This is not a requirement of International Standards on Accounting (ISAs), but it is a good way of **ensuring that there are no misunderstandings** about the financial statements or the auditor's report to be issued. This will also be an opportunity for the auditor to discuss with management the adequacy of internal controls; proposed adjustments to the financial statements; any difficulties encountered during the audit; ethical matters to be clarified; and confirmation of management's written representations.

2 Opening balances   6/11

> **FAST FORWARD**
>
> Specific procedures must be applied to opening balances.

2.1 Audit procedures

Key term

> **Opening balances** are those account balances that exist at the beginning of the period. Opening balances are based on the closing balances of the prior period and reflect the effects of transactions and events of prior periods and accounting policies applied in the prior period.

ISA 510 *Initial audit engagements – opening balances* provides guidance on opening balances:

- When the financial statements for the prior period were not audited
- When the financial statements for the prior period were audited by a predecessor auditor

> **ISA 510.6**
>
> The auditor shall obtain sufficient appropriate audit evidence about whether the opening balances contain misstatements that materially affect the current period's financial statements by:
>
> (a) Determining whether the prior period's closing balances have been correctly brought forward to the current period or, when appropriate, have been restated;
>
> (b) Determining whether the opening balances reflect the application of appropriate accounting policies; and
>
> (c) Performing one or more of the following:
>
> > (i)   Where the prior year financial statements were audited, reviewing the predecessor auditor's working papers to obtain evidence regarding the opening balances;
> >
> > (ii) Evaluating whether audit procedures performed in the current period provide evidence relevant to the opening balances; or
> >
> > (iii) Performing specific audit procedures to obtain evidence regarding the opening balances.

The nature and extent of audit procedures necessary to obtain sufficient appropriate audit evidence on opening balances depends on matters such as:

- The **accounting policies** followed by the entity
- The **nature of the account balances, classes of transactions and disclosures** and the risks of material misstatement in the current period's financial statements
- The **significance** of the opening balances relative to the current period's financial statements
- Whether the **prior period's financial statements were audited** and, if so, whether the predecessor auditor's opinion was modified

If the auditor obtains audit evidence that the opening balances contain **misstatements** that could materially affect the current period's financial statements, the auditor shall perform such **additional audit procedures** as are appropriate in the circumstances to determine the effect on the current period's financial statements.

2.1.1 Specific audit procedures

For **current assets and liabilities** some audit evidence may be obtained as part of the current period's audit procedures. For example, the **collection** (or payment) of opening accounts **receivable** (or accounts payable) during the current period will provide some audit evidence of their existence, rights and obligations, completeness and valuation at the beginning of the period.

In the case of **inventories**, however, the current period's audit procedures on the closing inventory balance provide little audit evidence regarding inventory on hand at the beginning of the period. Therefore, additional procedures may be necessary, such as:

- **Observing a current physical inventory count** and reconciling it back to the opening inventory quantities
- **Performing audit procedures on the valuation** of the opening inventory items
- **Performing audit procedures on gross profit** and cut-off

A combination of these procedures may provide sufficient appropriate audit evidence.

For **non-current assets and liabilities**, some audit evidence may be obtained by examining the accounting records and other information underlying the opening balances. In certain cases, the auditor may be able to obtain some audit evidence regarding opening balances through confirmation with third parties, for example for long-term debt and investments. In other cases, the auditor may need to carry out additional audit procedures.

2.1.2 Consistency of accounting policies

The auditor shall obtain sufficient appropriate audit **evidence** about:

- Whether the **accounting policies** reflected in the opening balances have been **applied consistently** in the current period's financial statements
- Whether **changes** in the accounting policies have been accounted for properly and **adequately presented and disclosed** in accordance with the applicable financial reporting framework

2.1.3 Prior period balances audited by a predecessor auditor

When the prior period's financial statements were audited by a predecessor auditor, the current auditor must **read the most recent financial statements and predecessor auditor's report** for information relevant to opening balances. The current auditor may be able to obtain sufficient appropriate evidence regarding opening balances by performing this review depending on the professional competence and independence of the predecessor auditor. Relevant ethical and professional requirements guide the current auditor's communications with the predecessor auditor.

In all cases where there is a new auditor, the audit **report must contain an Other Matter paragraph** immediately below the Opinion paragraph. This applies whether or not the audit opinion being expressed is modified. ISA 510.A8 gives the following example of an Other Matter paragraph in this case.

Other Matter

The financial statements of ABC Company for the year ended 31 December 20X0 were audited by another auditor who expressed an unmodified opinion on those statements on 31 March 20X1.

If there was a **modification** to the opinion, the current auditor must evaluate the effect of the matter giving rise to the modification in assessing the risks of material misstatement in the current period's financial statements.

2.2 Audit conclusion and reporting

The effects on the audit report can be summarised as follows.

Problem	Materiality of issue	Effect on audit report (ISA 705)
Unable to obtain sufficient appropriate audit evidence on opening balances (ISA 510.10)	Material but not pervasive	Qualified opinion
	Material and pervasive	Disclaimer of opinion
Opening balances contain a misstatement **that materially affects the current period's FS** (ISA 510.11)	Material but not pervasive	Qualified opinion
	Material and pervasive	Adverse opinion
Accounting policies not applied consistently (ISA 510.12)	Material but not pervasive	Qualified opinion
	Material and pervasive	Adverse opinion
Predecessor auditor's opinion modified (ISA 510.13)	Consider whether the issue remains relevant and modify opinion accordingly. For example, if the prior year opinion was qualified on a material misstatement and the FS are still misstated this year, then qualify the opinion this year.	

3 Revision: comparatives

12/11

FAST FORWARD

The auditor's responsibilities for comparatives vary depending on whether they are corresponding figures or comparative financial statements.

3.1 Auditor objectives

ISA 710 *Comparative information – corresponding figures and comparative financial statements* provides guidance on the auditor's responsibilities regarding comparative information.

ISA 710.5

The objectives of the auditor are:

(a)   To obtain sufficient appropriate audit evidence about whether the comparative information included in the financial statements has been presented, in all material respects, in accordance with the requirements for comparative information in the applicable financial reporting framework

(b)   To report in accordance with the auditor's reporting responsibilities

Key term

Comparative information is the amounts and disclosures included in the financial statements in respect of one or more prior periods in accordance with the applicable financial reporting framework.

3.2 What type of comparative information?

ISA 710 distinguishes between two types of comparative information: corresponding figures and comparative financial statements.

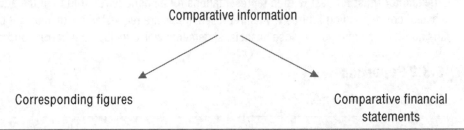

Comparative information

Corresponding figures   Comparative financial
                                    statements

Key terms

> **Corresponding figures** are amounts and other disclosures for the preceding period included as part of the current period financial statements, which are intended to be read in relation to the amounts and other disclosures relating to the current period (referred to as 'current period figures'). The level of detail presented in the corresponding amounts and disclosures is dictated primarily by its relevance to the current period figures.
>
> **Comparative financial statements** are amounts and other disclosures for the prior period included for comparison with the financial statements of the current period but, if audited, are referred to in the auditor's opinion. The level of information included in those comparative financial statements is comparable with that of the financial statements of the current period.

Here are some **examples** to help flesh out this distinction.

Corresponding figures: the set of prior-year figures that usually appear to the right of the current year figures in a set of financial statements.

Comparative financial statements: a full set of financial statements included within the current year's Annual Report for reference.

Comparatives are presented in compliance with the relevant financial reporting framework. The auditor's procedures are the same in respect of corresponding figures and comparative financial statements. The only difference is in the audit report:

(a)   For **corresponding figures**, the auditor's report only refers to the financial statements of the current period, because the corresponding figures are part of the current period's financial statements

(b)   For **comparative financial statements**, the auditor's report refers to each period that financial statements are presented.

3.3 Corresponding figures

3.3.1 The auditor's responsibilities

Audit procedures performed on the corresponding figures are usually limited to checking that the corresponding figures have been correctly reported and are appropriately classified. Auditors must assess whether:

(a)   **Accounting policies** used for the corresponding figures are **consistent** with those of the current period or whether appropriate adjustments and/or disclosures have been made

(b)   **Corresponding figures agree** with the **amounts** and other disclosures presented in the prior period or whether appropriate adjustments and/or disclosures have been made

When the financial statements of the prior period:

- Have been audited by other auditors,
- Were not audited,

the incoming auditor assesses whether the corresponding figures meet the conditions specified above and also follow the guidance in ISA 510.

If the auditor becomes aware of a possible material misstatement in the corresponding figures when performing the current period audit, then they must perform any necessary additional procedures.

The auditor must request written representations for all periods referred to in the auditor's opinion. In the case of corresponding figures written representations are requested for the current period only because the auditor's opinion is on those financial statements which include the corresponding figures.

3.3.2 Reporting

The basic principle is this:

> **ISA 710.10**
>
> When corresponding figures are presented, the auditor's opinion shall not refer to the corresponding figures.

The auditor's report will only make specific reference to corresponding figures when there is a problem in relation to them, in the circumstances described below. We will look at specific examples of the wording of the auditor's report in such circumstances.

Problem	Status in current period	Effect on audit report (current period)
Modified opinion in prior period (or disclaimer of opinion/adverse opinion)	Matter is **still unresolved**	**Modified opinion** as appropriate*
	Matter **has been resolved**	**No effect** on current year opinion
Unmodified opinion in prior period, but auditor becomes aware of a material misstatement in the prior period	Corresponding **figures not restated**	**Modified opinion** as appropriate (qualified or adverse) – see also Section 2.2 above on opening balances
	Corresponding figures **restated** with appropriate disclosures	**No effect** on current year opinion, but possible **Emphasis of Matter** referring to restatement and disclosures

* In the Basis for Modification paragraph in the auditor's report, either:

(a)   Refer to both the current period's figures and the corresponding figures in the description of the matter giving rise to the modification when the effects or possible effects of the matter on the current period's figures are material; or

(b)   In other cases, explain that the audit opinion has been modified because of the effects or possible effects of the unresolved matter on the comparability of the current period's figures and the corresponding figures.

ISA 710 requires that the auditor obtains written representations for all periods referred to in the audit opinion. This also applies where there is a current year restatement to correct a material misstatement in prior period financial statements that affects the comparative information.

3.3.3 Incoming auditors: additional requirements

When the prior period financial statements have been audited by other auditors, in some countries the incoming auditor can refer to the predecessor auditor's report on the corresponding figures in the incoming auditor's report for the current period.

> **ISA 710.13**
>
> If the financial statements of the prior period were audited by a predecessor auditor and the auditor is not prohibited by law or regulation from referring to the predecessor auditor's report on the corresponding figures and decides to do so, the auditor shall state in an Other Matter paragraph in the auditor's report:
>
> (a)   That the financial statements of the prior period were audited by the predecessor auditor

(b)	The type of opinion expressed by the predecessor auditor and, if the opinion was modified, the reasons therefore

(c)	The date of that report

The situation is slightly different if the prior period financial statements were **not audited**.

> **ISA 710.14**
>
> If the prior period financial statements were not audited, the auditor shall state in an Other Matter paragraph in the auditor's report that the corresponding figures are unaudited. Such a statement does not, however, relieve the auditor of the requirement to obtain sufficient appropriate audit evidence that the opening balances do not contain misstatements that materially affect the current period's financial statements.

3.4 Comparative financial statements

3.4.1 The auditor's responsibilities

This effectively involves the auditor following the same procedures on the prior period statements as noted above.

3.4.2 Reporting

> **ISA 710.15**
>
> When comparative financial statements are presented, the auditor's opinion shall refer to each period for which financial statements are presented and on which an audit opinion is expressed.

The auditor may therefore express a **modified opinion** or include an **emphasis of matter** paragraph with respect to one or more financial statements for one or more period, while issuing a different report on the other financial statements.

The auditor may become aware of circumstances or events that materially affect the financial statements of a prior period during the course of the audit for the current period.

> **ISA 710.16**
>
> When reporting on prior period financial statements in connection with the current period's audit, if the auditor's opinion on such prior period financial statements differs from the opinion the auditor previously expressed, the auditor shall disclose the substantive reasons for the different opinion in an Other Matter paragraph.

3.4.3 Incoming auditors: additional requirements

Again, there are additional considerations where the prior period financial statements have been audited by another auditor.

> **ISA 710.17**
>
> If the financial statements of the prior period were audited by a predecessor auditor, in addition to expressing an opinion on the current period's financial statements, the auditor shall state in an Other Matter paragraph:
>
> (a)	That the financial statements of the prior period were audited by a predecessor auditor,
>
> (b)	The type of opinion expressed by the predecessor auditor and, if the opinion was modified, the reasons therefore, and
>
> (c)	The date of that report,

unless the predecessor auditor's report on the prior period's financial statements is reissued with the financial statements.

In performing the audit on the current period financial statements, the incoming auditor may become aware of a material misstatement that affects the prior period financial statements on which the predecessor auditors had previously reported without modification.

ISA 710.18

... the auditor shall communicate the misstatement with the appropriate level of management and, unless all of those charged with governance are involved in managing the entity, those charged with governance and request that the predecessor auditor be informed. If the prior period financial statements are amended, and the predecessor auditor agrees to issue a new auditor's report on the amended financial statements of the prior period, the auditor shall report only on the current period.

In certain circumstances the prior period financial statements may not have been audited.

ISA 710.19

If the prior period financial statements were not audited, the auditor shall state in an Other Matter paragraph that the comparative financial statements are unaudited. Such a statement does not, however, relieve the auditor of the requirement to obtain sufficient appropriate audit evidence that the opening balances do not contain misstatements that materially affect the current period's financial statements.

Question
Opening balances and comparatives

Auditing standards have been issued on opening balances for initial engagements and comparatives, and one of the matters considered is where one firm of auditors takes over from another firm. You have recently been appointed auditor of Lowdham Castings, a limited liability company which has been trading for about 30 years, and are carrying out the audit for the year ended 30 September 20X0. The company's revenue is about $500,000 and its normal profit before tax is about $30,000. Comparatives are shown as corresponding figures only.

Required

Explain your responsibilities in relation to the comparatives included in the accounts for the year ended 30 September 20X0. You should also outline the information you would require from the retiring auditors.

Answer

Consideration of the financial statements of the preceding period is necessary in the audit of the current period's financial statements in relation to three main aspects:

(a) Opening position: obtaining satisfaction that those amounts which have a direct effect on the current period's results or closing position have been properly brought forward

(b) Accounting policies: determining whether the accounting policies adopted for the current period are consistent with those of the previous period

(c) Comparatives: determining that the comparatives are properly shown in the current period's financial statements

The auditors' main concern will therefore be to satisfy themselves that there were no material misstatements in the previous year's financial statements which may have a bearing on their work in the current year.

The new auditors do not have to 're-audit' the previous year's financial statements, but they will have to pay more attention to them than would normally be the case where they had themselves been the auditors in the earlier period. A useful source of audit evidence will clearly be the previous auditors and, with the client's permission, they should be contacted to see if they are prepared to co-operate. Certainly, any known areas of weakness should be discussed with the previous auditors and it is also possible that they might be prepared to provide copies of their working papers.

4 Revision: other information   12/10, 6/13

Auditors should always seek to resolve inconsistencies between financial statements and other information.

Point to note

The ISA in this area was revised recently. The main change is to the auditor's report, which must now include a section specifically on Other Information.

4.1 What other information?

ISA 720 *The auditor's responsibilities relating to other information in documents containing audited financial statements* sets out the requirements of the auditor with respect to other information, on which the **auditor has no obligation to report**, in documents containing financial statements. ISA 720 was revised in 2015 as part of the IAASB's project on audit reports.

Key terms

Other information is financial or non-financial information (other than financial statements and the auditor's report thereon) included in an entity's annual report.

A **misstatement of the other information** exists when the other information is incorrectly stated or otherwise misleading (including because it omits or obscures information necessary for a proper understanding of a matter disclosed in the other information.

Here are some examples of other information, ie information in the annual report:

- A report by management or the board of directors on operations
- Financial summaries or highlights
- Employment data
- Planned capital expenditure
- Financial ratios
- Names of officers and directors
- Selected quarterly data

Auditors have no responsibility to report that other information is properly stated because an audit is only an expression of opinion on the truth and fairness of the financial statements. However, they may be **engaged separately**, or **required by statute**, to report on elements of other information. In any case, the auditors should give consideration to other information as inconsistencies with the audited financial statements may undermine their opinion.

Some countries require the auditors to apply specific procedures to certain other information, for example, required supplementary data and interim financial information. If such other information is omitted or contains deficiencies, the auditors may be required to refer to the matter in their report.

When there is an obligation to report specifically on other information, the auditors' responsibilities are determined by the **nature of the engagement** and by **local legislation** and professional standards. When such responsibilities involve the review of other information, the auditors will need to follow the guidance on **review engagements** in the appropriate ISAs.

4.1.1 Integrated reports

The growth of integrated reporting is a topical area in the profession. The general idea is to integrate the various kinds of non-financial and financial reporting into a single coherent whole.

It is possible that integrated reports might qualify as 'other information' from the perspective of the auditor. This would only be if the integrated report also contains the audited financial statements. In this case the auditor would have a responsibility to read the integrated report just like any other information.

4.2 Access to other information

Timely access to other information will be required. The auditors therefore must make arrangements with the client to obtain such information prior to the date of their report.

If material inconsistencies are identified in the other information (and the audited financial statements need to be revised) once the audit report has already been signed, then ISA 560 *Subsequent events* applies (see Section 5 of this chapter).

4.3 Reading and considering the other information

The auditor must read the other information, looking for:

- Material inconsistencies between the other information and the financial statements
- Material inconsistencies between the other information and the auditor's knowledge obtained in the audit.

The auditor must then 'remain alert' for indications of material misstatements in the other information that is not related to the audit.

4.4 Material misstatements

> **ISA 720.16**
>
> If the auditor identifies that a material inconsistency appears to exist (or becomes aware that the other information appears to be materially misstated), the auditor shall discuss the matter with management and, if necessary, perform other procedures to conclude whether:
>
> (a)   A material misstatement of the other information exists;
> (b)   A material misstatement of the financial statements exists; or
> (c)   The auditor's understanding of the entity and its environment needs to be updated.

If a material misstatement is discovered, then the auditor's duties may be summarised as follows.

Material misstatement of other information	
Revision needed to	**Action**
Financial statements	Respond in line with other ISAs, ie further procedures if necessary.
	Consider effect on the auditor's report
Other information	Ask management to revise other information. If management refuses, ask those charged with governance.
	If still not corrected, then consider effect on audit report or withdraw from engagement.
Auditor's understanding	Respond in line with other ISAs (ISA 315)

4.4.1 Revision needed to financial statements

If it appears to be the financial statements which are misstated, then the auditor must obtain evidence about the misstatement by performing further procedures. This may involve obtaining a better understanding of the entity in line with ISA 315. The misstatement would then be evaluated in line with ISA 450 *Evaluation of Misstatements Identified during the Audit*.

If the financial statements are materially misstated then this is treated in the same way as any other material misstatement. If the financial statements are not amended, then the auditor's opinion would be modified as appropriate in line with ISA 700 *Forming an Opinion and Reporting on Financial Statements* (see Chapter 17).

The situation is slightly different if the material inconsistency is only identified after the auditor's report has already been issued. If the financial statements need to be revised, then the guidance given in ISA 560 *Subsequent events* applies (see Section 5.3).

4.4.2 Revision needed to other information

Some misstatements do not give rise to an inconsistency with the audited financial statements, or with evidence obtained by the auditor. There is no duty to look for these misstatements (the auditor 'remains alert' for them), but if the auditor does find one then the effect is the same as if there were an inconsistency with the financial statements, ie the table above applies.

Further explanation may be needed before a conclusion can be reached: it is possible that it really is a misstatement of fact, but it is also possible that the auditor will not be able to evaluate its validity, eg because the auditor does not have specialist knowledge of it. There could be a valid difference of opinion between the auditor and management on the matter. However the auditor should also consider whether management's rationale implies a lack of management integrity. The auditor may wish to obtain legal advice.

4.5 Auditor's report

The **auditor's report will always include a separate Other Information section** when the auditor has obtained some or all of the other information as of the date of the auditor's report. For listed entities, the section is also included if other information is expected to be received after the date of the audit report.

Where the other information is **not materially misstated**, the standard unmodified section is placed after the key audit matters (see Chapter 17), and looks like this. (The 'X report' means the annual report.)

Other Information

Management is responsible for the other information. The other information comprises the [information included in the X report, but does not include the financial statements and our auditor's report thereon.]

Our opinion on the financial statements does not cover the other information and we do not express any form of assurance conclusion thereon.

In connection with our audit of the financial statements, our responsibility is to read the other information and, in doing so, consider whether the other information is materially inconsistent with the financial statements or our knowledge obtained in the audit or otherwise appears to be materially misstated. If, based on the work we have performed, we conclude that there is a material misstatement of this other information, we are required to report that fact. We have nothing to report in this regard.

The auditor may only have obtained part of the other information, and ISA 720 covers various possible scenarios here. This is the effect on the auditor's report if **no other information has been received**:

Other Information

Management is responsible for the other information. The other information comprises the [information included in the X report, but does not include the financial statements and our auditor's report thereon]. The X report is expected to be made available to us after the date of this auditor's report.

Our opinion on the financial statements does not cover the other information and we will not express any form of assurance conclusion thereon.

In connection with our audit of the financial statements, our responsibility is to read the other information identified above when it becomes available and, in doing so, consider whether the other information is materially inconsistent with the financial statements or our knowledge obtained in the audit, or otherwise appears to be materially misstated.

The following example is for an unmodified opinion, but where there is a **material misstatement of the other information**. In this case, the other information section is placed immediately after the basis for opinion section, ie it moves up above the key audit matters:

Other Information

Management is responsible for the other information. The other information comprises the [information included in the X report, but does not include the financial statements and our auditor's report thereon.]

Our opinion on the financial statements does not cover the other information and we do not express any form of assurance conclusion thereon.

In connection with our audit of the financial statements, our responsibility is to read the other information and, in doing so, consider whether the other information is materially inconsistent with the financial statements or our knowledge obtained in the audit or otherwise appears to be materially misstated.

If, based on the work we have performed, we conclude that there is a material misstatement of this other information, we are required to report that fact. As described below, we have concluded that such a material misstatement of the other information exists.

[Description of material misstatement of the other information]

Example: Other information

The audit of Other Co is at the finalisation stage, with the auditor's report due to be issued in the next week. To be included with the financial statements is a lengthy statement by the company's chairman in which are to be found the following two statements.

- It is claimed that revenue is $102m. This was the figure in the draft financial statements, but the audited financial statements will show a figure of $90m.

- It is stated that it is likely that the company will win a case in which it is to be taken to court by a customer for damages resulting from some faulty products. The financial statements include a provision for these damages of $3m.

Required

For each of the above situations, explain the matters for the auditor to consider, any further actions and the effect on the auditor's report.

Revenue

This appears to be a misstatement of other information, and there is an inconsistency between the other information and the audited financial statements. The misstatement is likely to be considered material, at 13% of revenue.

The audit work performed on revenue should be reviewed to ensure that sufficient and appropriate evidence has been gained to support the figures in the financial statements.

The matter should be discussed with management, who should be asked to amend the disclosure in the chairman's statement. Management should be presented with the results of the audit work, to justify, if necessary, that the amendment needs to be made. The inclusion of the incorrect figure in the draft chairman's statement could be a genuine mistake, in which case management should be happy to make the change.

If management refuse to change the disclosure in the other information, then the Other Information section of the auditor's report should disclose the material misstatement of other information. This section should be presented immediately after the opinion section and should describe the inconsistency clearly.

The matter should also be communicated to those charged with governance.

Provision

In this case, either the other information or the financial statements could be misstated.

The audit work performed in this area should be reviewed to ensure that sufficient and appropriate evidence has been gained to support the figures in the financial statements. The work of any auditor's or management's experts in this area should be reviewed thoroughly.

It is possible that the auditor's understanding of situation has not been sufficient. Judgement may be required to determine the probability of a court case being won or lost, and the auditor may need to obtain a better understanding of the judgements underlying this assessment of probability.

The matter should be discussed with management, who should be asked why the chairman's statement differs from the financial statements.

If the chairman's statement is incorrect, ie the court case is not likely to be won and it is probable that a payment will be made, then management should be asked to amend this statement. If this is not done, then the Other Information section of the auditor's report should disclose the material misstatement of other information. This section should be presented immediately after the opinion section and should describe the inconsistency clearly.

If the financial statements are misstated, then the misstatement should be aggregated together with any other uncorrected misstatements identified. The auditor then considers whether the financial statements are materially misstated.

If the misstatements are not considered material, then they are still communicated to those charged with governance along with a request that they be corrected. However if the misstatements are material, then the auditor must consider the effect on the auditor's report. It is possible that the auditor will expressed a modified opinion in respect of this matter.

In both situations, the matter should also be communicated to those charged with governance.

5 Revision: subsequent events   Pilot, 12/09, 12/10, 6/13

FAST FORWARD Auditors should consider the effect of subsequent events (after the reporting period) on the financial statements.

5.1 Events after the reporting period

'Subsequent events' include:

- Events occurring between the period end and the date of the auditor's report
- Facts discovered after the date of the auditor's report

ISA 560 *Subsequent events* deals with this issue. It is also worth recalling basic requirements of the accounting standard in this area, IAS 10 *Events after the reporting period* identifies two types of event:

Type of event	Definition (IAS 10)	Example
Adjusting	Events that provide further evidence of conditions that existed at the end of the reporting period	Customer becomes insolvent after period end – trade receivable at period end is uncollectible. Settlement of a court case after period end – confirms entity's obligation at the period end.
Non-adjusting	Events that are indicative of conditions that arose after the reporting period	Inventory lost in fire after period end – non-adjusting because the inventory still existed at the period end (but needs to be disclosed, with possible EoM).

Between the end of the reporting period and the date the financial statements are authorised (ie for issue outside the organisation), events may occur which show that assets and liabilities at the end of the reporting period should be adjusted, or that disclosure of such events should be given.

In relation to **going concern**, ISA 560 states that, where operating results and the financial position have deteriorated after the reporting period, it may be necessary to reconsider whether the going concern assumption is appropriate in the preparation of the financial statements.

Note that, while they may be non-adjusting, some events after the reporting period will require disclosure.

5.2 Events occurring up to the date of the auditor's report

ISA 560.6

The auditor shall perform audit procedures designed to obtain sufficient appropriate audit evidence that all events occurring between the date of the financial statements and the date of the auditor's report that require adjustment of, or disclosure in, the financial statements have been identified.

These procedures should be applied to any matters examined during the audit which may be susceptible to change after the year end. They are in addition to tests on specific transactions after the period end, eg cut-off tests.

The ISA lists procedures to identify subsequent events which may require adjustment or disclosure. They should be performed as near as possible to the date of the auditor's report.

Procedures testing subsequent events	
Enquiries of management	New **commitments**, borrowings or guarantees
	Sales or **acquisitions of assets** occurred or planned
	Issues of **shares** or **debt instruments**, or an **agreement to merge** or **liquidate** made or planned
	Assets destroyed or appropriated by government
	Developments regarding **contingencies**
	Unusual accounting adjustments made or contemplated
	Events (eg going concern problems) bringing into question appropriateness of accounting policies
	Events relevant to measurement of **estimates** and **provisions**
	Events relevant to the **recoverability of assets**
Other procedures	**Consider procedures** of management for identifying subsequent events
	Read minutes of general board/committee meetings
	Review latest accounting records and financial information

ISA 560.8

[When] the auditor identifies events that require adjustment of, or disclosure in the financial statements, the auditor shall determine whether each such event is appropriately reflected in those financial statements in accordance with the applicable financial reporting framework.

Written representations will be sought that all events occurring subsequent to the date of the financial statements which require adjustment or disclosure have been adjusted or disclosed.

5.3 Facts discovered after the date of the auditor's report but before the financial statements are issued

The financial statements are management's responsibility. They should therefore inform the auditor of any material subsequent events between the date of the auditor's report and the date the financial statements are issued. The auditor does **not** have any obligation to perform procedures, or make enquiries regarding the financial statements **after** the date of their report.

> **ISA 560.10**
>
> The auditor has no obligation to perform any audit procedures regarding the financial statements after the date of the auditor's report. However, if after the date of the auditor's report but before the date the financial statements are issued, a fact becomes known to the auditor that, had it been known to the auditor at the date of the auditor's report, may have caused the auditor to amend the auditor's report, the auditor shall:
>
> (a)   Discuss the matter with management and, where appropriate, those charged with governance;
> (b)   Determine whether the financial statements need amendment and, if so,
> (c)   Inquire how management intends to address the matter in the financial statements.

When the financial statements are amended, the auditors should **extend the procedures** discussed above to the **date of their new report**, carry out any other appropriate procedures and issue a new audit report. The new report should not be dated earlier than the date of approval of the amended financial statements.

The situation may arise where the statements are not amended but the auditors feel that they should be.

If the auditor's report has already been issued to the entity then the auditor should notify those who are ultimately responsible for the entity (the management or possibly a holding company in a group), not to issue the financial statements or auditor's report to third parties. If management issues the financial statements despite the auditor's notification the auditor will take action to prevent reliance on the audit report. The action taken will depend on the auditor's legal rights and obligations and the advice of the auditor's lawyer.

5.4 Facts discovered after the financial statements have been issued

Auditors have no obligations to perform procedures or make enquiries regarding the financial statements after they have been issued.

However, when after the financial statements have been issued the auditor becomes aware of a fact that, had it been known to the auditor at the date of the auditor's report may have caused the auditor to amend the auditor's report, the auditor will carry out the following procedures:

(a)   Discuss the matter with management and, where appropriate, those charged with governance
(b)   Determine whether the financial statements need amendment and, if so
(c)   Enquire how management intends to address the matter in the financial statements.

The ISA gives the appropriate procedures which the auditors should undertake when management revises the financial statements:

(a)   **Carry out the audit procedures** necessary in the circumstances.
(b)   **Review the steps taken by management** to ensure that anyone in receipt of the previously issued financial statements together with the auditor's report thereon is informed of the situation.
(c)   **Extend the audit procedures** to the date of the new auditor's report.
(d)   **Issue a new report** on the revised financial statements.

ISA 560.16

The auditor shall include in the new or amended auditor's report an Emphasis of Matter paragraph or Other Matters paragraph referring to a note to the financial statements that more extensively discusses the reason for the amendment of the previously issued financial statements and to the earlier report provided by the auditor.

The following is an example of such a paragraph.

In our opinion, the revised financial statements give a true and fair view (or 'present fairly, in all material respects'), as at the date the original financial statements were approved, of the financial position of the company as of 31 December 20X1, and of the results of its operations and its cash flows for the year then ended in accordance with [relevant national legislation].

In our opinion the original financial statements for the year to 31 December 20X1 failed to comply with [relevant national standards or legislation].

Date   AUDITOR
Address

Where local regulations allow the auditor to restrict the audit procedures on the financial statements to the effects of the subsequent event which caused the revision, the new auditor's report should contain an emphasis of matter paragraph referring to a note in the financial statements which explains the situation fully.

Where management does **not** revise the financial statements but the auditors feel they should be revised, or if management does not intend to take steps to ensure anyone in receipt of the previously issued financial statements is informed of the situation, then the auditors should consider steps to take, on a timely basis, to prevent reliance on their report. The actions taken will depend on the auditors' legal rights and obligations (for example, to contact the shareholders directly) and legal advice received.

Exam focus point

Subsequent events have previously appeared in an audit reports question with five easy marks for outlining the auditors' responsibilities for subsequent events and then practical application in part (b).

 Question   **Subsequent events**

You are auditing the financial statements of Hope Engineering, a limited company, for the year ending 31 March 20X8. The partner in charge of the audit instructs you to carry out a review of the company's activities since the financial year end. Mr Smith, the managing director of Hope Engineering, overhears the conversation with the partner and is surprised that you are examining accounting information which relates to the next accounting period.

Mr Smith had been appointed on 1 March 20X8 as a result of which the contract of the previous managing director, Mr Jones, was terminated. Compensation of $500,000 had been paid to Mr Jones on 2 March 20X8.

As a result of your investigations you find that the company is going to bring an action against Mr Jones for the recovery of the compensation paid to him, as it had come to light that two months prior to his dismissal he had contractually agreed to join the board of directors of a rival company. The company's lawyer had informed Hope Engineering that Mr Jones's actions constituted a breach of his contract with them, and that an action could be brought against the former managing director for the recovery of the money paid to him.

Required

(a)   Explain the nature and purpose of a subsequent events review.

(b)   Describe the audit procedures which would be carried out in order to identify any material subsequent events.

(c)   Discuss the audit implications of the company's decision to sue Mr Jones for the recovery of the compensation paid to him.

(a)   The auditor's active responsibility extends to the date on which they sign their audit report. As this date is inevitably after the year end, it follows that in order to discharge his responsibilities, the auditor must extend the audit work to cover the period after the year end.

The objective of this review is to ascertain whether management has dealt correctly with any events, both favourable and unfavourable, which occurred after the end of the reporting period and which need to be reflected in the financial statements, if those statements are to show a true and fair view.

The general rule is that, in the preparation of year end financial statements, no account should be taken of subsequent events unless to do so is required by statute or to give effect to retrospective legislation, or to take into account an event which provides information about a condition existing at the end of the reporting period, for example realisable values of inventory, or indicates that the going concern concept is no longer applicable. Additionally, certain events may have such a material effect on the company's financial condition, for example a merger, that disclosure is essential to give a true and fair view.

(b)   (i)   Ask management if there have been any material subsequent events.

(ii)   Identify and evaluate procedures implemented by management to ensure that all events after the end of the reporting period have been identified, considered and properly evaluated as to their effect on the financial statements.

(iii)   Review relevant accounting records to identify subsequent cash received in relation to accounts receivable, to check items uncleared at the year end on the bank reconciliation, and to check net realisable value (NRV) of inventories from sales invoices.

(iv)   Review budgets, profit forecasts, cash flow projections and management accounts for the new period to assess the company's trading position.

(v)   Consider known 'risk' areas and contingencies, whether inherent in the nature of the business or revealed by previous audit experience or by lawyers' letters.

(vi)   Read minutes of shareholders' and management meetings, and correspondence and memoranda relating to items included in the minutes to identify any matters arising.

(vii)   Consider relevant information which has come to the auditors' attention from sources outside the entity, including public knowledge of competitors, suppliers and customers.

(viii) Obtain written representations concerning subsequent events from management.

(c)   The compensation paid to Mr Jones would be disclosed as part of directors' remuneration for the year ended 31 March 20X8. However, the question then arises as to whether or not the financial statements need to take any account of the possible recovery of the compensation payment.

The auditors should first ascertain from the board minutes that the directors intend to proceed with the lawsuit and should then attempt to assess the outcome by consulting the directors and the company's legal advisers. Only if it seems probable that the compensation will be recovered should a contingent gain be disclosed in the notes to the accounts, along with a summary of the facts of the case. A prudent estimate of legal costs should be deducted.

It could be argued that Mr Jones's breach of contract existed at the year end and that the compensation should therefore be treated as a current asset, net of recovery costs. However, this would not be prudent, given the uncertainties over the court case.

6 Revision: going concern

FAST FORWARD

> Auditors should consider whether the going concern assumption is appropriate, and whether disclosure of any going concern problems is sufficient.

Point to note

> This is now a **topical** area, and the relevant ISA has recently been revised.

6.1 The going concern assumption

Key term

> Under the '**going concern assumption**' an entity is viewed as continuing in business for the foreseeable future. General purpose financial statements are prepared on a going concern basis, unless management either intends to liquidate the entity or to cease operations, or has no realistic alternative but to do so. When the use of the going concern assumption is appropriate, assets and liabilities are recorded on the basis that the entity will be able to realise its assets and discharge its liabilities in the normal course of business.

ISA 570 *Going concern* states that the preparation of the financial statements requires **management** to **assess** the entity's ability to continue as a going concern, even if the financial reporting framework does not include an explicit requirement to do so.

When management are making their assessment, the following factors should be considered.

(a) The **degree of uncertainty** about the events or conditions being assessed increases significantly the further into the future the assessment is made.

(b) Judgements are affected by the **size** and **complexity** of the entity, the **nature** and **condition** of its business and the **degree** to which it is **affected** by **external factors.**

(c) Judgements are made on the basis of the **information available** at the time.

> **ISA 570.9**
>
> The objectives of the auditor are:
>
> (a) To obtain sufficient appropriate audit evidence regarding, and conclude on, the appropriateness of management's use of the going concern basis of accounting in the preparation of the financial statements;
>
> (b) To conclude, based on the audit evidence obtained, whether a material uncertainty exists related to events or conditions that may cast significant doubt on the entity's ability to continue as a going concern; and
>
> (c) To report in accordance with this ISA.

6.2 Examples of events causing doubts over going concern

The following are examples of events or conditions that may cast significant doubt about the going concern assumption.

(a) **Financial**

    (i) Net liabilities or net current liability position

    (ii) Fixed-term borrowings approaching maturity without realistic prospects of renewal or repayment, or excessive reliance on short-term borrowings to finance long-term assets

    (iii) Indications of withdrawal of financial support by lenders

    (iv) Negative operating cash flows indicated by historical or prospective financial statements

    (v) Adverse key financial ratios

    (vi) Substantial operating losses or significant deterioration in the value of assets used to generate cash flows

(vii)   Arrears or discontinuance of dividends

(viii)   Inability to pay creditors on due dates

(ix)   Inability to comply with the terms of loan agreements

(x)   Change from credit to cash-on-delivery transactions with suppliers

(xi)   Inability to obtain financing for essential new product development or other essential investments

(b)   **Operating**

(i)   Management intends to liquidate the entity or to cease operations
(ii)   Loss of key management without replacement
(iii)   Loss of a major market, key customer(s), franchise, licence or principal supplier(s)
(iv)   Labour difficulties or shortages of important supplies
(v)   Emergence of a highly successful competitor

(c)   **Other**

(i)   Non-compliance with capital or other statutory requirements

(ii)   Pending legal or regulatory proceedings against the entity that may, if successful, result in claims that the entity is unlikely to be able to satisfy

(iii)   Changes in law or regulation or government policy expected to adversely affect the entity

(iv)   Uninsured or underinsured catastrophes when they occur

The significance of such events and conditions often can be **mitigated** by other factors. For example, the loss of a key supplier may be mitigated by the availability of a suitable alternative source of supply. It is worth noting that the **size** of an entity may affect its ability to withstand adverse conditions. Small entities may be able to react quickly to exploit opportunities but may lack reserves to sustain operations.

Exam focus point

The June 2011 exam featured a 27-mark question which combined a requirement on going concern with prospective financial information (covered in Chapter 13). Candidates first had to review a draft statement of financial position and a draft cash flow forecast, identifying and explaining factors casting significant doubt over going concern. They then had to recommend procedures in relation to the cash flow forecast, before explaining the matters to consider in relation to the audit report if there are material uncertainties on going concern.

The December 2011 exam combined going concern with the auditor's report. Students had to make a judgement about the effect of a matter on going concern, and the knock-on effect on the auditor's report.

6.3 Evaluating management's assessment

ISA 570.10

When performing risk assessment procedures as required by ISA 315, the auditor shall consider whether there are events or conditions that may cast significant doubt on the entity's ability to continue as a going concern. In so doing, the auditor shall determine whether management has already performed a preliminary assessment of the entity's ability to continue as a going concern, and:

(a)   If such an assessment has been performed, the auditor shall discuss the assessment with management and determine whether management has identified events or conditions that, individually or collectively, may cast significant doubt on the entity's ability to continue as a going concern and, if so, management's plans to address them; or

(b)   If such an assessment has not yet been performed, the auditor shall discuss with management the basis for the intended use of the going concern assumption, and inquire of management whether events or conditions exist that, individually or collectively, may cast significant doubt on the entity's ability to continue as a going concern.

These procedures allow for more **timely discussions with management**, including a discussion of management's plans and resolution of any identified going concern issues.

The auditor shall remain **alert throughout the audit** for evidence of events or conditions that may cast significant doubt on the entity's ability to continue as a going concern. It may be necessary to revise the auditor's assessment of the risks of material misstatement if these are found.

ISA 570.12

The auditor shall evaluate management's assessment of the entity's ability to continue as a going concern.

The auditors may evaluate:

- The **process** management followed to make its assessment
- The **assumptions** on which management's assessment is based
- Management's **plans** for future action and whether these are feasible in the circumstances

Management do not need to make a detailed analysis, and auditors should not need to carry out detailed procedures, if the entity has a **history of profitable operations** and **ready access** to **financial resources.**

In evaluating management's assessment of the entity's ability to continue as a going concern, the auditor shall cover the **same period** as that used by management to make its assessment as required by the applicable financial reporting framework, or by law or regulation if it specifies a longer period.

If management's assessment covers a period of **less than 12 months** from the date of the financial statements, the auditor shall request management to extend its assessment period to at least 12 months from that date.

In evaluating management's assessment, the auditor shall consider whether management's assessment includes **all relevant information** of which the auditor is aware as a result of the audit.

ISA 570.15

The auditor shall inquire of management as to its knowledge of events or conditions beyond the period of management's assessment that may cast significant doubt on the entity's ability to continue as a going concern.

Because the time period is some way into the future, the indications of potential going concern problems would have to be significant. Auditors do not have to carry out specific procedures to identify potential problems which may occur after the period covered by management's assessment. However, they should be alert during the course of the audit for any **indications** of future problems.

6.3.1 Additional audit procedures

ISA 570.16

If events or conditions have been identified that may cast significant doubt on the entity's ability to continue as a going concern, the auditor shall obtain sufficient appropriate audit evidence to determine whether or not a material uncertainty exists related to events or conditions that may cast significant doubt on the entity's ability to continue as a going concern (hereinafter referred to as 'material uncertainty') through performing additional audit procedures, including consideration of mitigating factors. These procedures shall include:

(a) Where management has not yet performed an assessment of the entity's ability to continue as a going concern, requesting management to make its assessment

(b) Evaluating management's plans for future actions in relation to its going concern assessment, whether the outcome of these plans is likely to improve the situation and whether management's plans are feasible in the circumstances

---

(c) Where the entity has prepared a cash flow forecast, and analysis of the forecast is a significant factor in considering the future outcome of events or conditions in the evaluation of management's plans for future action:

    (i) Evaluating the reliability of the underlying data generated to prepare the forecast

    (ii) Determining whether there is adequate support for the assumptions underlying the forecast

(d) Considering whether any additional facts or information have become available since the date on which management made its assessment

(e) Requesting written representations from management and, where appropriate, those charged with governance, regarding their plans for future action and the feasibility of these plans.

When events or conditions are identified which cast doubt on the appropriateness of the going concern assumption, auditors may also have to carry out **additional procedures**. The ISA lists various procedures which the auditors may carry out in this context.

- **Analysing and discussing cash flow**, profit and other relevant forecasts with management
- **Analysing and discussing** the entity's latest available **interim financial statements**
- **Reading the terms of debentures and loan agreements** and determining whether any have been breached
- **Reading minutes** of the meetings of shareholders, those charged with governance and relevant committees for reference to financing difficulties
- **Enquiring** of the entity's legal counsel regarding **litigation and claims**
- **Confirming the existence, legality and enforceability** of arrangements to provide or maintain financial support with related and third parties and **assessing** the **financial ability** of such parties to **provide additional funds**
- Evaluating the entity's plans to deal with **unfilled customer orders**
- **Performing audit procedures regarding subsequent events** to identify those that either mitigate or otherwise affect the entity's ability to continue as a going concern
- Confirming the existence, terms and adequacy of **borrowing facilities**
- Obtaining and reviewing reports of **regulatory actions**
- Determining the adequacy of **support for any planned disposal of assets**

Evaluating management's **plans for future actions** may include enquiries of management regarding, for example its plans to liquidate assets, borrow money or restructure debt, reduce or delay expenditures, or increase capital.

Where management's assumptions include **continued support by third parties**, and such support is important to an entity's ability to continue as a going concern, the auditor may need to consider requesting written confirmation to obtain evidence of their ability to provide such support.

6.4 Audit conclusions and reporting

The following table summarises the various situations (there is an even briefer summary in Chapter 17, section 3.4). These are then explained in the sections that follow.

Is Going Concern assumption appropriate?	Are treatment and disclosures adequate?	Effect on auditor's report
Appropriate	Adequate	• Standard unmodified report, which describes both management's and the auditor's responsibilities in relation to going concern

Appropriate, but Material Uncertainty exists	Adequate	<ul><li>Unmodified opinion</li><li>Section headed 'Material Uncertainty Related to Going Concern'</li><li>Refer to FS disclosures</li><li>State that opinion is not modified</li></ul>
Appropriate, but Material Uncertainty exists	Inadequate	<ul><li>Qualified or adverse opinion</li><li>Statement in 'Basis for Qualified/Adverse Opinion' paragraph that disclosures are inadequate</li></ul>
Inappropriate	Inadequate FS inappropriately prepared using going concern assumption	<ul><li>Adverse opinion</li><li>Description of circumstances in 'Basis for Adverse Opinion' paragraph</li></ul>
Inappropriate	Adequate FS prepared on alternative basis, eg liquidation basis	<ul><li>Unmodified opinion</li><li>Consider using Emphasis of Matter paragraph to draw attention to alternative basis of preparation</li></ul>

6.4.1 Use of going concern appropriate but a material uncertainty exists

The auditor determines whether disclosures are adequate. Specifically, whether the financial statements adequately disclose the principal events or conditions that may cast significant doubt on the entity's ability to continue as a going concern, and management's plans to deal with these events or conditions.

The financial statements should clearly disclose that there is a material uncertainty and, therefore, that the entity may be unable to realise its assets and discharge its liabilities in the normal course of business.

If the **disclosures are adequate** then the auditor includes a **separate paragraph in the auditor's report**, headed '**Material uncertainty in relation to going concern**'. An example of this kind of paragraph is given in Chapter 17.

Point to note

> This is a **change** from previous versions of ISA 570, which required the auditor to include an Emphasis of Matter paragraph to refer to the disclosures already made in the financial statements. Emphasis of Matter paragraphs are now **not** included for going concern.

If **disclosures are not adequate** then the opinion will be either qualified or adverse:

ISA 570.23

If adequate disclosure is not made in the financial statements, the auditor shall:

(a)   Express a qualified opinion or adverse opinion, as appropriate, in accordance with ISA 705; and

(b)   In the Basis for Qualified (Adverse) Opinion section of the auditor's report, state that a material uncertainty exists that may cast significant doubt on the entity's ability to continue as a going concern and that the financial statements do not adequately disclose this matter.

6.4.2 Use of going concern assumption inappropriate

If the financial statements have been prepared on a going concern basis, but in the auditor's judgement this is inappropriate, the auditor must express an **adverse** opinion. This applies regardless of whether the financial statements include disclosure of the inappropriateness of management's use of the going concern assumption.

If the financial statements are prepared on an alternative basis, eg a liquidation basis, then the auditor's opinion is unmodified but it is sensible to include an Emphasis of Matter paragraph highlighting the use of an alternative basis.

6.4.3 Inadequate assessment by management

In certain circumstances, the auditor may believe it necessary to **request management to make or extend its assessment**. If management is unwilling to do so, a **qualified opinion** on the grounds of an inability to obtain sufficient appropriate audit evidence or a **disclaimer of opinion** in the auditor's report may be appropriate.

6.5 Communication with those charged with governance

Unless all those charged with governance are involved in managing the entity, the auditor shall communicate with those charged with governance events or conditions identified that may cast significant doubt on the entity's ability to continue as a going concern. This communication must include:

- Whether the events or conditions constitute a material uncertainty
- Whether the use of the going concern assumption is appropriate in the preparation and presentation of the financial statements
- The adequacy of related disclosures in the financial statements

6.6 Significant delay

When there is a significant delay in approving the accounts, auditors shall enquire as to the **reasons** for the delay. If the auditor believes that the delay could be related to events or conditions relating to the going concern assessment, the auditor shall **perform those additional audit procedures necessary**, as well as consider the **effect on the auditor's conclusion** regarding the existence of a material uncertainty.

6.7 Going concern statements

Some companies are required – eg by listing or industry-specific rules – to include a statement in their annual report that the business is a going concern.

In this case ISA 720 applies. The auditor must assess whether the statement is consistent with the audited financial statements and with the knowledge obtained from the audit.

6.8 Risk from economy overall

If there is a general economic recession then this may affect management's assessment of going concern. Increased uncertainty and difficult economic conditions could mean the going concern basis is not appropriate for many companies. Auditors should take extra care when reviewing management's assessment of going concern in such circumstances.

The ACCA has issued *Technical factsheet 143*, which contains a useful summary of the effect of recession on auditors:

> 'If there is **increased risk** of material misstatement **at the overall economy level**, such as that arising from the credit crunch, the auditor should **assess the specific risk** of misstatement **for each audited entity** and limit the detection risk by designing and performing appropriate audit procedures.'

Exam focus point

The P7 examination team wrote an article for *Student Accountant* entitled 'Going concern'. It focused on the IAASB's Practice Alert *Audit considerations in respect of going concern in the current economic environment*.

It might be tempting to think that this topic is no longer relevant, as several years have passed since the 'credit crunch'. The profession is still, however, working through its repercussions in relation to auditors and going concern.

The question that follows includes numerical information. In such a question it is vital that you attempt to use the figures in your answer.

 Question

Going concern

You are planning the audit of Crash Bang, whose principal activities are motorcycle courier services, and the repair and maintenance of commercial motorcycles. You have been provided with the draft accounts for the year ended 31 October 20X5.

	Draft 20X5 $'000	Actual 20X4 $'000
Summary statement of profit or loss		
Revenue	10,971	11,560
Cost of sales	(10,203)	(10,474)
Gross profit	768	1,086
Administrative expenses	(782)	(779)
Interest payable and similar charges	(235)	(185)
Net (loss) profit	(249)	122
Summary statement of financial position		
Non-current assets	5,178	4,670
Current assets		
Inventory (parts and consumables)	95	61
Receivables	2,975	2,369
	3,070	2,430
Current liabilities		
Bank loan	250	–
Overdraft	1,245	913
Trade payables	1,513	1,245
Lease obligations	207	–
Other payables	203	149
	3,418	2,307
Long-term liabilities		
Bank loan	750	1,000
Lease obligations	473	–
	1,223	1,000
Net assets	3,607	3,793

You have been informed by the managing director that the fall in revenue is due to:

(1)   The loss, in July, of a longstanding customer to a competitor
(2)   A decline in trade in the repair and maintenance of commercial motorcycles

Due to the reduction in the repairs business, the company has decided to close the workshop and sell the equipment and spares inventory. No entries resulting from this decision are reflected in the draft accounts.

During the year, the company replaced a number of vehicles, funding them by a combination of leasing and an increased overdraft facility. The facility is to be reviewed in January 20X6 after the audited accounts are available.

The draft accounts show a loss for 20X5 but the forecasts indicate a return to profitability in 20X6 as the managing director is optimistic about generating additional revenue from new contracts.

Required

(a) State the circumstances particular to Crash Bang which may indicate that the company is not a going concern. Explain why these circumstances give cause for concern.

(b) Describe the audit work to be performed in respect of going concern at Crash Bang.

Approaching the answer

Look for **key words** and **key balances**. Ask questions of the information given to you. This is illustrated here:

> Remember that the stage of the audit you are at will determine the kind of procedures you are concerned with.

You are planning the audit of Crash Bang, whose principal activities are motorcycle courier services, and the repair and maintenance of commercial motorcycles. You have been provided with the draft accounts for the year ended 31 October 20X5

> Reliability? Analysis of information? Key ratios?

	Draft 20X5 $'000	Actual 20X4 $'000
Summary statement of profit or loss		
Revenue	10,971	11,560
Cost of sales	(10,203)	(10,474)
Gross profit	768	1,086
Administrative expenses	(782)	(779)
Interest payable and similar charges	(235)	(185)
Net (loss) profit	(249)	122
Summary statement of financial position		
Non-current assets	5,178	4,670
Current assets		
Inventory (parts and consumables)	95	61
Receivables	2,975	2,369
	3,070	2,430
Current liabilities		
Bank loan	250	–
Overdraft	1,245	913
Trade payables	1,513	1,245
Lease obligations	207	–
Other payables	203	149
	3,418	2,307
Long-term liabilities		
Bank loan	750	1,000
Lease obligations	473	–
	1,223	1,000
Net assets	3,607	3,793

Annotations: Change in GPM? · Significant losses this year · Change in receivables ageing · Increase in short-term finance · Additional debt

> Is this information reliable?

You have been informed by the managing director that the fall in revenue is due to:

> Possible wider consequences?

(1) The loss, in July, of a longstanding customer to a competitor, and

(2) A decline in trade in the repair and maintenance of commercial vehicles.

> Need to remember this when analysing the financial information

> Further negative business trends

Due to the reduction in the repairs and maintenance business, the company has decided to close the workshop and sell the equipment and spares inventory. No entries resulting from this decision are reflected in the draft accounts.

| Shortage of cash | During the year, the company replaced a number of vehicles, funding them by a combination of leasing and an increased overdraft facility. The facility is to be reviewed in January 20X6 after the audited accounts are available. |

> **Pressure on management? Reliance by third parties**

| On what is this optimism based? | The draft accounts show a loss for 20X5 but the forecasts indicate a return to profitability in 20X6 as the managing director is optimistic about generating additional revenue from new contracts. |

Required

| Your answer must be tailored to the question. | (a) State the circumstances particular to Crash Bang which may indicate that the company is not a going concern. Explain why these circumstances give cause for concern. |

| What is the potential effect? | (b) Describe the audit work to be performed in respect of going concern at Crash Bang. |

> **Remember the key issue is likely to be assessing future events**

Answer plan

Not all the points you notice will necessarily be relevant and you may find that you do not have time to mention all the points in your answer. Now you should prioritise your points in a more formal answer plan and then write the answer.

(a)

Circumstances	Why cause for concern
(i) From review of financial information	
Fall in GP	Why? Calls into question future optimism. Lack of control over expenses and increased finance costs
Loss	Significant in relation to previous year. Impact on bank overdraft review
Increased receivables ageing	Cash flow problems Debt write-offs may be required
Increased short-term finance	Impact on continuing support from the bank
Liquidity ratio	Problems re commitments in future
Gearing	Finance cost Problems obtaining further finance
(ii) From other information	
Loss of major customer	Potential that others will follow?
Loss of commercial customers	Provided regular income source
Draft accounts	Impact of additional adjustments
Review of overdraft	Increased pressure/risk
Assessment of future by MD	Potentially too optimistic

(b) **Procedures**

(i) Analyse subsequent events
(ii) Review debt ageing
(iii) Discuss future plans with MD
(iv) Review bank records/correspondence particularly re overdraft facility
(v) Review sales orders/scrutinise new orders
(vi) Procedures on cash flow forecast
(vii) Written representations

Answer

(a)

Circumstances	Why cause for concern?
Fall in gross profit % achieved	While the fall in absolute revenue has been explained, the fall in gross profit margin is more serious. This will continue to be a problem, as expenses seem constant and interest costs are growing. This will make a future return to profitability difficult.
Losses $249,000	Such levels of losses by comparison to 20X4 profits will make negotiations with the bank difficult, especially with the loss of a major customer.
Increased receivables balance and increased ageing 20X4 74.8 days 20X5 96.7 days	Worsening debt collection is bad news when the company is making losses and has a deteriorating liquidity position. The increase in average debt collection period may be due to an irrecoverable receivable on the account of the major customer lost in the year. An irrecoverable receivable write-off would cause increased losses.
Worsening liquidity ratio 20X4 1.03 20X5 0.85	This is a significant fall which will worsen further if an allowance for irrecoverable receivables is required. The company has loan and lease commitments which possibly may not be met.
Increasing reliance on short-term finance	This does not secure the future. With the company going through so much change this may cause difficulties for the bank overdraft facility negotiations.
Gearing will have increased	This leads to an interest commitment which is a drain on future profits. This may also cause a problem in negotiating new finance arrangements.
Loss of major customer to competitor	Risk of unallowed-for irrecoverable receivables in the accounts. Other customers could follow suit, worsening the company's future prospects.
Loss of commercial customers	Commercial customers normally provide regular income which is important for a company with repayment commitments.
Draft accounts – final adjustments are outstanding	The company's net asset position could be worsened considerably if non-current assets are written down to their recoverable amount, and the repairs inventory is written down to net realisable value. As mentioned before further allowances for irrecoverable receivables may be necessary. The closure may necessitate redundancy provisions. All of these factors could increase losses considerably.
Overdraft facility to be reviewed three months after the year end	This time period is probably not long enough to see a real improvement in the company's fortunes. As auditors we will be reporting when faced with fundamental uncertainty. Trying to anticipate the bank's likely reaction to the financial statements would be a high risk.

Circumstances	Why cause for concern?
Future return to profits anticipated at a time when competitors are achieving success	The concern should be whether this is over optimistic. If so, too much reliance being placed upon written representations would be a high risk strategy.

Summary. If the company is not a going concern then the financial statements would be truer and fairer if prepared on a break-up basis. Material adjustments may then be required to the accounts.

(b) (i) Analyse sale proceeds for non-current assets, inventory and cash received from customers occurring after the end of the reporting period.

(ii) Review the debt ageing and cash recovery lists. Ask directors if outstanding amounts from lost customer are recoverable.

(iii) Discuss the optimistic view of likely future contracts with the MD. Orders received after the end of the reporting period should be reviewed to see if they substantiate their opinion.

(iv) Obtain their opinion about future contracts in a written representation letter.

(v) Review bank/loan records to assess the extent to which the company has met its loan and lease commitments in the period after the end of the reporting period.

(vi) Review sales orders/sales ledger for evidence of additional lost custom after the year end.

(vii) Obtain cashflow and profit forecasts:

- Discuss assumptions with the directors.

- Perform sensitivity analysis flexing the key assumptions ie interest rates, date of payment of payables and receipts from customers.

- Check all commitments have been cleared in accordance with legal agreements.

- Agree budgets to any actual results achieved after the year end.

- Assess reasonableness of assumptions in the light of the achievement of the company's budgets set for 20X5; discuss with the directors any targets not achieved.

- Reperform calculations.

- Ensure future budgeted profits are expected to meet likely interest charges

(viii) Review bank records to ensure that the company is operating within its overdraft facility after the end of the reporting period. Review bank certificate for terms and conditions of the facility. Review bank correspondence for any suggestion the bank is concerned about its current position.

(ix) Ask management whether the new motorcycle fleet is attracting new contracts as anticipated. Scrutinise any new contracts obtained and check improved gross profit margins will be achieved.

(x) Obtain written representations as to the likelihood of the company operating for 12 months from the date of approval of the financial statements.

Chapter Roundup

- The auditor must perform and document an overall review of the financial statements before they can reach an opinion.

- As part of their completion procedures, auditors should consider whether the cumulative effect of uncorrected misstatements is material.

- Specific procedures must be applied to opening balances.

- The auditor's responsibilities for comparatives vary depending on whether they are corresponding figures or comparative financial statements.

- Auditors should always seek to resolve inconsistencies between financial statements and other information.

- Auditors should consider the effect of subsequent events (after the reporting period) on the financial statements.

- Auditors should consider whether the going concern assumption is appropriate, and whether disclosure of going concern problems is sufficient.

1   Name eight items that analytical procedures at the final stage must cover.

(1) ....   (5) ....

(2) ....   (6) ....

(3) ....   (7) ....

(4) ....   (8) ....

2   The auditor will maintain a schedule of uncorrected misstatements. This will include:

• Specific misstatements identified by the auditors
• Best estimate of other misstatements

True   ☐

False ☐

3   Where prior period financial statements were unaudited, the auditor should make no reference to the comparatives in their report.

True   ☐

False ☐

4   Which of the items on the following list are not part of the 'other information' within the scope of ISA 720?

• Directors' report
• Financial ratios
• Statement of cash flows
• Employment data
• Auditor's report
• Financial summaries

5   Name two types of 'subsequent events'.

(1)...

(2)...

6   List five enquiries which may be made of management in testing subsequent events.

(1)...

(2)...

(3)...

(4)...

(5)...

7   Complete the definition:

Under the .... assumption an entity is viewed as continuing in business for the

....

8   The 'foreseeable future' is always a period of 12 months.

True   ☐

False ☐

Answers to Quick Quiz

1 From:

- Important accounting ratios
- Related items
- Changes in products; customers
- Price and mix changes
- Wages changes
- Variances
- Trends in production and sales
- Changes in material and labour content of production
- Other statement of profit or loss expenditure
- Variations caused by industry or economy factors

2 True

3 False

4 Statement of cash flows and auditor's report

5 (1) Events occurring between the period end and the date of the auditor's report
   (2) Facts discovered after the date of the auditor's report

6 From:

(1) Status of items involving subjective judgement
(2) Any new commitments
(3) Sales of assets
(4) Issues of shares or debentures
(5) Developments in risk areas
(6) Unusual accounting adjustments
(7) Other major events

7 Going concern, foreseeable future

8 False

> Now try the questions below from the Practice Question Bank.

Number	Level	Marks	Time
Q11	Examination	20	39 mins
Q12	Introductory	25	49 mins

BPP
LEARNING MEDIA

Evaluation and review (II) – matters relating to specific accounting issues

Topic list	Syllabus reference
1 Fair value	D3
2 Inventory	D3
3 Tangible non-current assets	D3
4 Intangible non-current assets	D3
5 Financial instruments	D3
6 Investment properties	D3
7 Foreign exchange rates	D3

Introduction

You must be able to consider four key matters in relation to items appearing in financial statements: risk, materiality, relevant accounting standards and audit evidence. In this chapter, we shall focus primarily on the last two of these, as the first two will depend more on the scenario presented in any given question.

You have previously studied the audit of a basic set of financial statements. At this level, the issues you are presented with will be more complex, but remember that key basic points apply. Bear in mind the relevant **assertions** for the financial statement items.

You need a strong knowledge of all the accounting standards you learnt up to P2 *Corporate Reporting* to apply in this paper.

Study guide

		Intellectual level
D3	**Evaluation and review**	
(j)	Evaluate the matters (eg materiality, risk, relevant accounting standards, audit evidence) relating to:	3
	(i) Inventory	
	(ii) Standard costing systems	
	(vii) Non-current assets	
	(viii) Fair value	
	(xv) Impairment	
	(xvii) Intangible assets	
	(xviii) Financial instruments	
	(xix) Investment properties	
	(xxii) Assets held for sale and discontinued operations	
	(xxiv) The effects of foreign exchange rates	

Exam guide

At this level it is assumed that you can audit all the items listed above and all items audited at the earlier auditing level. This is likely to be tested in a scenario-based long case study type question, typically in Section A, the compulsory part of the P7 paper.

1 Fair value

12/08

FAST FORWARD

> Key assertions relating to assets are existence, completeness, valuation and rights and obligations.

1.1 Accounting recap

Key term

> **Fair value** is the price that would be received to sell an asset or paid to transfer a liability in an orderly transaction between market participants at the measurement date.

Fair value accounting is increasingly important and affects the audit of valuation for both assets and liabilities. In May 2011 the International Accounting Standards Board (IASB) issued IFRS 13 *Fair value measurement*, as a result of a joint project with the US Financial Accounting Standards Board. Examples of accounting treatments where fair values are relevant include financial instruments, employee benefits and share-based payments.

IFRS 13 uses a 'fair value hierarchy', which categorises inputs into three levels:

- Level 1 inputs: quoted prices in active markets for identical assets or liabilities that the entity can access at the measurement date

- Level 2 inputs: inputs other than quoted market prices included within Level 1 that are observable for the asset or liability, either directly or indirectly

- Level 3 inputs: unobservable inputs for the asset or liability

1.2 Auditing fair values

Exam focus point

> Fair value is a very topical area at the moment, and is therefore likely to be tested, eg as part of a requirement to discuss the difficulties involved in auditing fair value estimates.

For auditors, the determination of fair value will generally be more difficult than determining historical cost. It will be more difficult to establish whether fair value is reasonable for complex assets and liabilities than for more straightforward assets or liabilities which have a market and therefore a market value. For example, for an apartment held as an investment property, a fair value might be relatively easy to estimate, as there may be a large and active market for similar properties that can be used as a guide to the value of the property in question. If, on the other hand, an entity has a large pension scheme, for which the fair value of the assets depends on actuarial assumptions about the future, then the fair value will be extremely difficult to measure, and the auditor will have to be very careful about the assumptions made in arriving at a valuation.

Generally speaking, balances held at fair value carry the following risks.

Component of audit risk	Risk
Inherent risk	**Estimates** are **inherently imprecise**, and involve judgements, eg about market conditions, timing of cash flows, or the intentions of the entity.
	Estimation **models are often complex**, eg discounted cash flows, or actuarial calculations. There is a risk of the model being misapplied.
	Assumptions often have to be made when estimating fair values, eg discount factors.
	However, obtaining a fair value for some assets will be **straightforward**, eg assets that are regularly traded on a stock exchange.
Control risk	Fair value assessment is likely to take place once a year, **outside of normal internal control systems**. Therefore, it may not be monitored as stringently as more routine transactions and balances. Alternatively, management may take extra care over a fair value assessment because it is a material amount, in which case control risk is low.
Detection risk	The auditor minimises **detection risk** through understanding the entity and its environment at the planning stage, determining whether and where fair values are present, and what the level of risk associated with them is.

Exam focus point

In the December 2008 exam, a question asked about the link between fair value and audit risk. Candidates who scored highly demonstrated commercial awareness in addition to strong technical knowledge.

1.3 Requirements of ISA 540

The relevant standard here is ISA 540 *Auditing accounting estimates, including fair value accounting estimates and related disclosures.*

Key term

Accounting estimate. An approximation of a monetary amount in the absence of a precise measurement. This term is used for an amount measured at fair value where there is estimation uncertainty as well as for other amounts that require estimation.

ISA 540's requirements are:

- The auditor shall obtain an understanding of the following as part of the process of understanding the business.
    - The requirements of the applicable financial reporting framework
    - The means by which the management identifies transactions, events and conditions that may give rise to the accounting estimate
    - How management makes the accounting estimate

    This means that the auditor must have a sound knowledge of the accounting requirements relevant to the entity and when fair value is allowed for example, IAS 16 allows fair value provided 'it can be measured reliably'.

- The auditor shall evaluate the degree of estimation uncertainty associated with the accounting estimate and assess whether this gives rise to significant risks.
- Based on the assessed risks the auditor will determine whether the financial reporting framework has been properly applied and whether methods for making estimates are appropriate and have been applied consistently.
- The auditor will also:
    - Determine whether events occurring up to the date of the audit report provide evidence regarding the accounting estimate
    - Test how management made the accounting estimate
    - Test the operating effectiveness of controls together with appropriate substantive procedures
    - Develop a point estimate or a range to evaluate the management's point estimate

<table>
<tr><td>Key term</td><td>**Management's point estimate** is the amount selected by management for recognition or disclosure in the financial statements as an accounting estimate.</td></tr>
</table>

- For accounting estimates which give rise to significant risks the auditor should also evaluate:
    - How management has considered alternative assumptions or outcomes
    - Whether the significant assumptions used are reasonable
    - Management intent to carry out specific courses of action and its ability to do so, where these affect the accounting estimate
    - Management's decision to recognise or to not recognise the accounting estimate
    - The selected measurement basis
- The possibility of management bias must be considered by the auditor.
- Written representations will be obtained from management as to whether management believes that significant assumptions used in making accounting estimates are reasonable.

1.4 Risk procedures: fair value

The auditor is required to assess the entity's process for determining accounting estimates, including fair value measurements and disclosures and the related control activities and to assess the arising risks of material misstatement.

Management's processes for determining fair values will vary considerably from organisation to organisation. Some companies will habitually value items at historical cost where possible, and may have very poor processes for determining fair value if required. Others may have complex systems for determining fair value if they have a large number of assets and liabilities which they account for at fair value, particularly where a high degree of estimation is involved in determining the fair value.

Once the auditors have assessed the risks associated with determining fair value, they should determine further procedures to address those risks.

1.5 Audit procedures: fair value

Audit procedures will depend heavily on the complexity of the fair value measurement. Where the fair value equates to market value, the auditor should be able to verify this with reference to the market, for example, published price quotations for marketable securities, or by using the work of an expert, such as an estate agent in the case of land and buildings.

However, in some cases, there may be a great deal of estimation and management assumption related to a fair value. Where this is the case, the auditor needs to consider matters such as the intent and ability of management to carry out certain actions stated in the assumptions. This includes:

- Considering management's past history of carrying out its stated intentions with respect to assets or liabilities
- Reviewing written plans and other documentation, including, where applicable, budgets, minutes etc

- Considering management's stated reasons for choosing a particular course of action
- Considering management's ability to carry out a particular course of action given the entity's economic circumstances, including the implications of its contractual commitments

If there are alternative allowable methods for measuring fair value, or a particular method is not prescribed by the relevant accounting standard, the auditor should consider whether the entity's method is consistent with other fair value measurements in the financial statements and whether it is applied consistently.

The auditor should consider the following when considering fair value measurements.

- The length of time any assumptions cover (the longer the time, the more subjective the value is)
- The number of assumptions made in relation to the item
- The degree of subjectivity in the process
- The degree of uncertainty associated with the outcome of events
- Any lack of objective data
- The timings of any valuations used
- The reliability of third party evidence
- The impact of subsequent events on the fair value measurement

Where a fair value measurement is based on assumptions reflecting management's intent and ability to carry out certain actions, then the auditor should obtain **written representations from management** that these assumptions are reasonable and achievable.

1.6 IAASB Practice Alert *Challenges in Auditing Fair Value Accounting Estimates in the Current Market Environment*

In October 2008 the International Auditing and Assurance Standards Board (IAASB) issued a Practice Alert, *Challenges in auditing fair value accounting estimates in the current market environment.* It discussed the following key points.

- Challenges faced in accounting on the basis of fair value

- Requirements and guidance in standards that are particularly relevant to fair values

- Other considerations in audits of fair value accounting estimates

- Initiatives of the IASB

- Recent revisions to extant standards on auditing accounting estimates and fair value measurements and disclosures which, while not yet effective, may be helpful to auditors

2 Inventory

2.1 Inventory   6/11, 12/11, 12/12

When standard costing is used, the auditor must assess whether the valuation is reasonable.

IAS 2 *Inventories*

Inventory should be measured at the lower of cost and net realisable value. Costs include costs of purchase, conversion and others incurred in bringing inventory to its present location and condition.

2.2 Inventory count

ISA 501 *Audit evidence – specific considerations for selected items* contains specific guidance on inventory. It says that **attending the inventory count is compulsory where inventory is material** (unless it is not practical to do so). The auditor must then perform procedures to determine whether inventory in the financial statements accurately reflects the inventory actually counted.

2.3 Standard costing

You studied the audit of inventory in detail in your studies for F8 *Audit and Assurance*. You should be able to design procedures to verify the existence and valuation of inventory. If you are in any doubt in this area, go back to your earlier study material and revise.

An additional thing to consider in the audit of inventory is what **evidence** to obtain about **cost**, when there is a **standard costing system** in operation. Remember that IAS 2 allows standard costs to be used when prices are fluctuating.

Where standard costing is being used the auditor will have **two objectives**:

- Ensure that standard costing is an **appropriate basis** for valuing inventory
- Ensure that the **calculation** of the standard cost is **reasonable**

In evaluating whether standard costs are an appropriate basis, the auditor must:

- **Establish whether prices have fluctuated**. This can be done by reviewing purchase invoices, consulting a price index and enquiry of management.
- **Consider if the use of standard costing is the best accounting policy to use**. This should be discussed with the directors.
- If the accounting policy has changed from the previous year, **consider the comparability of the accounts**.
- Ensure that the financial statements make adequate disclosure of any changes in accounting policies.

In ensuring that the calculation of the standard cost is reasonable, the auditor must:

- Obtain a copy of the calculation of standard cost
- Check the additions and calculations
- Consider whether the calculation is reasonable (for example, based on averages of costs over the year)
- Verify elements of the calculation to appropriate documentation, for example:
  - Purchase prices to invoices
  - Wages and salaries to personnel records
  - Overheads to expenses in the financial statements where possible
- Perform analytical procedures, eg wages should be approximately equal to the total wage cost (in the statement of profit or loss) divided by the production total for the year

Exam focus point

The June 2011 exam examined the audit of inventory not in isolation, but in relation to ISA 510 *Initial audit engagements – opening balances*. Candidates had to explain the audit procedures on inventory in the context of an entity whose prior year financial statements had not been audited, for seven marks. To score well, candidates needed to combine their knowledge of the two areas (ISA 510 and inventory) to come up with relevant procedures in the context of the scenario.

3 Tangible non-current assets   6/09, 12/09, 6/11, 6/12, 6/13

FAST FORWARD

Auditors should ensure that both tangible and intangible assets have been subjected to an annual impairment review.

You covered all the key aspects relating to tangible non-current assets in your earlier studies. If you are in any doubt in this area, go back to your previous material and revise. The issue of fair value discussed in Section 1 is likely to affect the audit of non-current assets.

3.1 Recognition of non-current assets

The key risk in relation to initial recognition is of costs being incorrectly recognised as assets, when they should in fact have been expensed to the statement of profit or loss.

IAS 16 *Property, plant and equipment* lists the following as components of cost:

- Purchase price, less any trade discount or rebate
- Import duties and non-refundable purchase taxes
- Directly attributable costs of bringing the asset to working condition for its intended use, eg:
  - The cost of site preparation
  - Initial delivery and handling costs
  - Installation costs
  - Testing
  - Professional fees (architects, engineers)
- Initial estimate of the unavoidable cost of dismantling and removing the asset and restoring the site on which it is located

However, the following should **not be included** in the cost of the **asset, and should be recognised as an expense**.

- Administration and other general overhead costs
- Start-up and similar pre-production costs
- Initial operating losses before the asset reaches planned performance
- Any incidental costs

3.2 Valuation of non-current assets

Non-current assets will be carried at cost or valuation (if an item has been revalued). **Cost is straightforward to audit**, as it can be verified to original purchase documentation. **Valuation** may be straightforward to audit – **it can be verified to the valuation certificate**. The carrying value of non-current assets is therefore depreciated cost, or depreciated valuation.

Once a company has revalued assets, it is required to continue revaluing them regularly so that the valuation is not materially different from the fair value at period end. The auditors should therefore check that valuation is comparable to market value. They would do this by comparing the existing valuation to current market values (for example, in an estate agent's window).

Assets are depreciated, so their carrying value will not be original cost or valuation. **Depreciation** can be verified by reperforming the depreciation calculations. Often a '**proof in total**' check will be sufficient, where auditors calculate the relevant depreciation percentage on the whole class of assets to see if it is comparable to the depreciation charged for that class of assets in the year.

The depreciation rate is determined by reference to the useful life of the asset. This is determined by management based on expectations of how long the asset is expected to be in use in the business. The auditors will audit this by scrutinising those expectations and verifying them where possible – for example, to the minutes of the meeting where management decided to buy the asset, to capital replacement budgets, to past practice in the business.

Exam focus point

In a real exam paper, the examination team asked candidates for principal audit procedures to obtain evidence about the useful lives of oil platforms. A significant amount of information about what management based their expectations on was given in the question and the examining team expected candidates to use that information. For example, management considered weather conditions that the rigs were subject to. Therefore, to audit the useful life, auditors should obtain weather reports to see if they corroborated the useful life. A platform severely affected by wind and storms will have a shorter useful life than one in calmer conditions.

Question   **Non-current assets**

You are reviewing the file on the audit, which is nearing completion, of a listed company, Apollo Co. Apollo produces two products, the X and the W. Apollo Co purchased two new pieces of plant in the year. Plant is valued at cost. The X103 was bought to replace the X102, which was scrapped at the start of the year. The W103 was bought to replace the W102. The W102 will no longer be used in producing the W, but will be used to test new products, particularly the V, which Apollo is hoping to be able to market and sell in the next two years.

Required

Describe matters you would consider and the audit evidence you would expect to see on file in respect of the valuation of these pieces of plant.

Answer

Matters to consider

The main matter to consider here is the valuation of the W102. Now it will no longer be used in production, it may be impaired. The asset should be valued in the financial statements at the lower of carrying amount or recoverable amount. Recoverable amount will be fair value, as the W102 no longer has a value in use because it will not generate cash inflows until the V is marketed. Whether the W102 has a market (fair) value will depend on how specialised a machine it is. The fact that it can be transferred to use on a different product from the W suggests that it is not highly specialised and that there may be a secondhand market from which a valuation can be taken.

Evidence that should be contained on the audit file

- Indication that the value of the X103 and W103 has been agreed to purchase invoices
- Recalculation of profit/loss on scrapping of X102
- Note of physical inspection to ensure that X102 is no longer on premises
- Minutes of directors' meeting approving the scrapping of the X102 and change in use of the W102 reviewed
- Copy of management's impairment review with regard to the W102
- Fair value of W102 verified by reference to price lists of suppliers of such secondhand machines
- Note of observation of operation of machines to ensure W102 no longer used in production

3.3 Impairment of non-current assets

An asset is impaired when its carrying amount (depreciated cost or depreciated valuation) exceeds its recoverable amount. You should be familiar with the following key terms from your accounting studies.

Key terms

> The **recoverable amount** of an asset or cash-generating unit is the higher of its fair value less costs to sell and its value in use.
>
> A **cash-generating unit** is the smallest identifiable group of assets that generates cash inflows which are largely independent of the cash inflows from other assets or groups of assets.
>
> **Value in use** is the present value of the future cash flows expected to be derived from an asset or cash-generating unit.

Management are required to determine if there is any indication that the assets are impaired. IAS 36 *Impairment of assets* specifies the following indicators of possible impairment.

External sources of information regarding possible impairment:

- Market value declines significantly
- Negative changes in technology, markets, economy or legal environment
- Increases in market interest rates that are likely to affect the discount rate using to calculate value in use
- Company stock price is below book value

Internal sources of information regarding possible impairment:

- Obsolescence or physical damage
- Significant changes with an adverse effect on use, eg asset will become idle, is part of a restructuring, or is held for disposal
- Internal evidence shows worse economic performance of the asset than was expected

The auditors will consider whether there are any **indicators of impairment** when carrying out risk assessment procedures. They will use the same impairment criteria laid out in IAS 36 as management do. If the auditors believe that impairment is indicated, **they should request that management show them the impairment review that has been carried out. If no impairment review has been carried out**, then the auditors should discuss the need for one with management and, if management refuse to carry out an impairment review, **qualify their opinion** on grounds of a material misstatement in respect of IAS 36 as a result of management not carrying out an impairment review.

If an impairment review has been carried out, then the auditors should audit that impairment review. Management will have estimated whether the recoverable amount of the asset/cash generating unit is lower than the carrying amount.

For auditors, the key risk is that the **recoverable amount requires estimation**, which involves **management** using their **judgement**. Auditors will need to consider whether the judgement made by management is reasonable in accordance with IAS 36.

Management have to determine if recoverable amount is higher than carrying amount. It may not have been necessary for them to estimate both fair value and value in use because, if one is higher than carrying amount, then the asset is not impaired. If it is not possible to make a reliable estimate of net realisable value, then it is necessary to calculate value in use.

Net realisable value is only calculable if there is an active market for the asset, and would therefore be audited in the same way as fair value which was set out in Section 1. Costs to sell, such as taxes, can be recalculated by applying the appropriate tax rate to the fair value itself. Delivery costs can be verified by comparing costs with published rates by delivery companies, for example on the internet.

If management have calculated the value in use of an asset or cash-generating unit, then the auditors will have to audit that calculation. The following procedures will be relevant.

Value in use

- Obtain management's calculation of value in use
- Reperform calculation to ensure that it is mathematically correct
- Compare the cash flow projections to recent budgets and projections approved by the board to ensure that they are realistic
- Calculate/obtain from analysts the long-term average growth rate for the products and ensure that the growth rates assumed in the calculation of value in use do not exceed it
- Refer to competitors' published information to compare how similar assets are valued by companies trading in similar conditions
- Compare with previous calculations of value in use to ensure that all relevant costs of maintaining the asset have been included
- Ensure that the cost/income from disposal of the asset at the end of its life has been included
- Review calculation to ensure cash flows from financing activities and income tax have been excluded
- Compare discount rate used with published market rates to ensure that it correctly reflects the return expected by the market

---

If the asset is impaired and has been written down to recoverable amount, the auditors should review the financial statements to ensure that the write-down has been carried out correctly and that the IAS 36 disclosures have been made correctly.

Although this section has been focused on impairment of tangible non-current assets, these considerations apply equally to intangibles, which can be impaired too – eg goodwill, which must be tested annually for impairment.

3.4 Held for sale non-current assets

IFRS 5 *Non-current assets held for sale and discontinued operations* applies to **non-current assets and disposal groups**. A disposal group is a group of assets and associated liabilities that are to be disposed of in a single transaction.

IFRS 5 requires that non-current assets and disposals groups that are 'held for sale' should be presented separately in the statement of financial position. 'Held for sale' here means that the non-current asset/disposal group's carrying amount will be recovered principally through a sale rather than through continuing use. A number of detailed **criteria** must be met:

(a)   The asset must be available for immediate sale in its present condition.
(b)   The sale must be highly probable.

For sale to be highly probable the following must apply.

(a)   Management must be committed to a plan to sell the asset.
(b)   There must be an active plan to locate a buyer.
(c)   The asset must be marketed at a price that is reasonable in relation to its current fair value.
(d)   The sale should be expected to take place within one year from the date of classification.
(e)   It is unlikely that significant changes to the plan will be made or that the plan will be withdrawn.

A non-current asset held for sale should be measured at the lower of its carrying amount and fair value less costs to sell. An impairment loss should be recognised where fair value less costs to sell is lower than the carrying amount.

Non-current assets held for sale should not be depreciated even if they are still being used by the entity.

The following audit procedures will therefore be relevant.

Confirm that the asset meets the definition of an asset held for sale:

- Discuss with management the availability of asset for sale
- Assess management commitment, eg minuted in board minutes
- Evaluate and assess practical steps being taken to sell the asset eg appropriate real estate agents appointed
- Determine when the sale is expected to take place by assessing progress to date
- Determine and assess the basis on which the sale price has been set
- Discuss with management any significant changes to the plans

Confirm that the asset has been valued as held for sale in accordance with IFRS 5 and assess how fair value has been determined.

Check that the asset has not been depreciated from the date of reclassification.

Confirm separate disclosure in accordance with IFRS 5.

3.5 Agriculture

IAS 41 *Agriculture* deals with **biological assets** (living animals or plants except for 'bearer plants' – see next section) and **agricultural produce** at the point of harvest, along with the process of **transformation** as assets grow, degenerate, produce and procreate in the course of their lifecycle.

The benchmark treatment in IAS 41 is to measure biological assets at **fair value less costs to sell**. Changes in carrying amount during the period arise from either **changes in fair value**, or the **physical change** of the biological asset. The financial statements must disclose these amounts, so there is an audit risk that adequate **disclosures** are not made.

Determining the **fair value** of assets must be done in line with IFRS 13 *Fair value measurement*. This involves an element of judgement, so the auditor must understand the basis for the valuation. Costs to sell must include fees, commissions and any other levies or taxes, and must be complete.

In practice, market values for most assets should be readily available, so depending on the scenario this is unlikely to represent a significant audit risk. However, the auditor may have **insufficient expertise** to determine what type of asset a plant or animal is – auditors are unlikely to be able to distinguish a Cotswold sheep from a Herdwick, for example, and thus assess the animal's market value. It may therefore be necessary to rely on an expert – either management's or the auditor's – which adds a degree of risk and cost to the audit.

3.5.1 Interactions with other accounting standards

IAS 41 was amended in 2014 as part of amendments which changed the financial reporting of **bearer plants**. Bearer plants are living plants which 'bear' other agricultural produce and which are not harvested themselves – they therefore survive for more than one reporting period. These plants are to be accounted for in the same way as property, plant and equipment in IAS 16 *Property, plant and equipment*. However, their agricultural produce (produce growing on bearer plants) continues to be accounted for under IAS 41.

Note that livestock is excluded from the definition of 'bearer plants', so all livestock (including milk cows and sheep farmed for wool) and their agricultural produce should also continue to be accounted for under IAS 41.

IAS 41 deals with assets up to the point when agricultural produce is harvested from the asset. After the point of harvest, IAS 2 *Inventories* applies. Examples might include a cow (biological asset) from which milk or meat is 'harvested' (agricultural produce). Once the produce has been harvested and **processing** has begun, IAS 2 applies. The following are examples of biological assets (IAS 41), agricultural produce (IAS 41), and products that are the result of processing (IAS 2).

Biological assets (IAS 41)	Agricultural produce (IAS 41)	Products that are the result of processing after harvest (IAS 2)
Sheep	Wool	Yarn, carpet
Trees in a timber plantation	Felled trees	Logs, lumber
Pigs	Carcass	Sausages, cured hams
Fruit trees	Picked fruit	Processed fruit
Sugarcane	Harvested cane	Sugar

Some assets may be physically attached to **land** – eg trees in a plantation forest – in which case IAS 41 is applied to the biological assets, but IAS 16 or IAS 40 is applied to the land. Care must therefore be taken to **split** the land from the biological asset in the financial statements, and there is a risk that this will not be done correctly.

Finally, IAS 41 contains its own criteria in relation to **government grants** and assistance, which differ from those in IAS 20 *Accounting for government grants and disclosure of government assistance*. IAS 41 requires grants to be recognised only when the grant becomes receivable, whereas IAS 20 allows recognition when there is 'reasonable assurance' that it will be received. There is thus a risk of improper recognition in the financial statements, eg overstating assets if the IAS 20 criteria are mistakenly applied.

Exam focus point

Exam questions in this area could be quite eventful and could include various accounting areas – imagine if animals on a farm were killed by an infectious disease. This would result in impairment of the assets involved, together with impairment reviews of other assets, but could also result in the entity being liable to others affected by any outbreak.

4 Intangible non-current assets

12/07, 6/09, 12/10
12/11, 6/13

FAST FORWARD

Accounting guidance for intangibles is given in IAS 38 *Intangible assets* and IFRS 3 *Business combinations*.

The types of asset we are likely to encounter under this heading include patents, licences, trademarks, development costs and goodwill. All intangibles should be subject to an annual impairment review.

IAS 38 *Intangible assets*

An **intangible asset** is an identifiable non-monetary asset without physical substance. It may be held for use in the production and supply of goods or services, or for rental to others, or for administrative purposes. The asset must be:

- Controlled by the entity as a result of events in the past
- Something from which the entity expects future economic benefits to flow

Examples of items that might be considered as intangible assets include computer software, patents, copyrights, motion picture film rights, customer lists, franchises and fishing rights. An item should not be recognised as an intangible asset, however, unless it **fully meets the definition** in the standard. The guidelines go into great detail on this matter.

Internally generated goodwill may **not** be recognised as an **asset**.

The auditor should carry out the following procedures.

Completeness

Prepare analysis of movements on cost and amortisation accounts

Rights and obligations

- **Obtain confirmation** of all **patents** and **trademarks** held by a patent agent
- **Verify payment** of **annual renewal fees**

Valuation

- **Review specialist valuations** of intangible assets, considering:
  - Qualifications of valuer
  - Scope of work
  - Assumptions and methods used
- **Confirm carried down balances** represent **continuing value**, which are proper charges to future operations

Additions (rights and obligations, valuation and completeness)

- **Inspect purchase agreements, assignments** and **supporting documentation** for intangible assets acquired in period
- **Confirm purchases** have been **authorised**
- **Verify amounts capitalised** of patents developed by the company with supporting costing records

Amortisation

- **Review amortisation**
  - Check computation
  - Confirm that rates used are reasonable

Income from intangibles

- **Review sales returns** and **statistics** to verify the reasonableness of income derived from patents, trademarks, licences etc
- **Examine audited accounts** of third party sales covered by a patent, licence or trademark owned by the company

---

278   **9: Evaluation and review (II) – matters relating to specific accounting issues** | Part D Audit of historical financial information   **BPP**
LEARNING MEDIA

4.1 Goodwill

Key tests are:

- **Agree consideration** to a **sales agreement**
- **Confirm valuation** of assets acquired is reasonable
- **Check purchased goodwill** is **calculated correctly**
- **Check goodwill** does **not include non-purchased goodwill**
- **Ensure valuation of goodwill is reasonable** by reviewing prior year's accounts and discussion with the directors
- Ensure impairment review has been carried out at least annually
- Review impairment review for reasonableness

Goodwill is covered in more detail in the context of the audit of groups in Chapter 11.

4.2 Development costs

IAS 38 *Intangible assets*

- Development costs may be included in the statement of financial position (that is to say, capitalised) only in 'special circumstances' laid out in IAS 38 *Intangible assets.*
- IAS 38 defines research and development as follows.

  - **Research** is original and planned investigation undertaken with the prospect of gaining new scientific or technical knowledge and understanding.
  - **Development** is the application of research findings or other knowledge to a plan or design for the production of new or substantially improved materials, devices, products, processes, systems or services prior to the commencement of commercial production or use.

- Expenditure on **research** is required to be recognised in profit or loss in the year of expenditure.
- IAS 38 states that the **development costs** of a project should be recognised as an asset only when all of the following criteria are met.

  - Completion of the asset will be technically feasible.
  - The business intends to complete the asset and use or sell it.
  - The business will be able to use or sell the asset.
  - The business can demonstrate how future economic benefits will be generated, either by demonstrating a market exists or the internal usefulness of the asset.
  - Adequate technical, financial and other resources will be available to complete the development and use or sell the intangible asset.
  - Expenditure attributable to the development of the asset can be measured reliably. General overhead expenditure, costs of inefficiencies and operating losses, and expenditure on training staff to operate the asset should not be capitalised.

  The development costs of a project recognised as an asset should not exceed the amount that is likely to be recovered from related future economic benefits, after deducting further development costs, related production costs, and selling and administrative costs directly incurred in marketing the product.

- In all other circumstances development costs should be recognised in profit or loss in the year of expenditure.

The key audit tests largely reflect the criteria laid down in IAS 38.

- **Check accounting records** to confirm that:
    - **Project** is **clearly defined** (separate cost centre or general ledger codes)
    - **Related expenditure** can be **separately identified**, and certified to invoices, timesheets
- **Confirm feasibility and viability**:
    - Examine market research reports, feasibility studies, budgets and forecasts
    - Consult client's technical experts
- **Review budgeted revenues** and **costs** by examining results to date, production forecasts, advance orders and discussion with directors
- **Review calculations** of **future cash flows** to ensure resources exist to complete the project
- **Review previously deferred expenditure** to ensure IAS 38 criteria are still justified
- **Check amortisation:**
    - Commences with production
    - Charged on a systematic basis

The good news for the auditors in this audit area is that many companies adopt a prudent approach and write-off research and development expenditure in the year it is incurred. The auditors' concern in these circumstances is whether the statement of profit or loss charge for research and development is complete, accurate and valid.

4.3 Brands

The key accounting issue with regard to brands is whether the asset is **internally generated** or not. Remember, IAS 38 forbids the capitalisation of internally generated brands.

If a brand has been purchased separately then auditors should test the value of the brand according to the sales documentation.

5 Financial instruments   6/09, 12/11, 6/13

FAST FORWARD

> When auditing financial instruments, the auditors will have to ensure that recognition and valuation is in accordance with IFRS 9 *Financial instruments*.

5.1 Background

If you read the financial press you will probably be aware of rapid international expansion in the use of financial instruments over the last 15 years or so. These vary from straightforward, traditional instruments, such as loans and deposits, through to various and exotic forms of derivative instruments, structured products and commodity contracts. Some of the more complex instruments played a role in the financial crisis of 2007–8.

This is a particularly risky area for auditors, as accounting for these instruments involves an unavoidable element of complexity, often requiring the use of management's own judgements. The amounts involved can be highly material, which adds not only audit risk but business risk too.

The guidance in this section is based on ISA 540 *Auditing accounting estimates, including fair value accounting estimates, and related disclosures* and IAPN 1000 *Special considerations in auditing financial instruments*.

Key terms | **Financial instrument**. Any contract that gives rise to both a financial asset of one entity and a financial liability or equity instrument of another entity.

Fair value. The price that would be received to sell an asset or paid to transfer a liability in an orderly transaction between market participants at the measurement date.

Derivative. A financial instrument or other contract with all three of the following characteristics.

(a)   Its value changes in response to the change in a specified interest rate, financial instrument price, commodity price, foreign exchange rate, index of prices or rates, credit rating or credit index, or other variable (sometimes called the 'underlying').

(b)   It requires no initial net investment or an initial net investment that is smaller than would be required for other types of contracts that would be expected to have a similar response to changes in market factors.

(c)   It is settled at a future date.

(IAS 32, IFRS 9 and IFRS 13)

Examples of financial assets include:

- Trade receivables
- Options
- Shares (when used as an investment)

Examples of financial liabilities include:

- Trade payables
- Debenture loans payable
- Redeemable preference (non-equity) shares
- Forward contracts standing at a loss

Financial instruments include:

(a)   Primary instruments, eg receivables, payables and equity securities
(b)   Derivative instruments, eg options, futures and forwards, interest rate swaps and currency swaps

The accounting requirements for financial assets are found in four standards:

(a)   IAS 32 *Financial instruments: presentation*, which deals with:

(i)   The classification of financial instruments between liabilities and equity
(ii)   Presentation of certain compound instruments

(b)   IFRS 7 *Financial instruments: disclosures*, which revised, simplified and incorporated disclosure requirements previously in IAS 32.

(c)   IFRS 9 *Financial instruments* was published in stages: new classification and measurement models (2009 and 2010) and a new hedge accounting model (2013). The version of IFRS 9 issued in 2014 supersedes all previous versions and completes the IASB's project to replace IAS 39. It covers recognition and measurement, impairment, derecognition and general hedge accounting. It does not cover portfolio fair value hedge accounting for interest rate risk ('macro hedge accounting'), which is a separate IASB project, currently at the discussion paper stage.

Point to note

The financial reporting standards in relation to financial instruments have recently changed, with the parts of IFRS 9 relating to impairment and hedge accounting having only recently been issued. It is therefore important that you are familiar with the current requirements, as things may have changed since you sat Paper P2.

Financial instruments should be recognised in the statement of financial position when the entity becomes a party to the **contractual provisions of the instrument**.

Point to note

An important consequence of this is that all derivatives should be in the statement of financial position.

Notice that this is **different** from the recognition criteria in the *Conceptual framework* and in most other standards. Items are normally recognised when there is a probable inflow or outflow of resources and the item has a cost or value that can be measured reliably.

5.1.1 Financial assets

IFRS 9 replaced the rule-based, complex classification rules in IAS 39 with a principles-based classification based on business model and nature of cash flows.

Initial recognition of a financial asset is at the fair value of the consideration. Subsequent to this initial recognition, IFRS 9 requires that **financial assets** are classified as measured at either:

- **Amortised cost**, or
- **Fair value**.

The IFRS 9 classification is made on the basis of both of the following.

(a) The **entity's business model** for managing the financial assets.
(b) The **contractual cash flow** characteristics of the financial asset.

An application of these rules means that **equity investments may not be classified as measured at amortised cost** and must be measured at fair value. This is because contractual cash flows on specified dates are not a characteristic of equity instruments. In addition, **all derivatives are measured at fair value**.

5.1.2 Financial liabilities

As with financial assets, a financial liability is initially measured at the fair value of the consideration received. Subsequent to this, IFRS 9 requires that financial assets are **classified as measured** at either:

(a) **Fair value through profit or loss**, or
(b) **Amortised cost** under the effective interest rate method.

A financial liability is classified at **fair value through profit or loss if**:

(a) It is **held for trading**; or
(b) Upon initial recognition it is designated at fair value through **profit or loss**.

IFRS 9 requires financial liabilities which are **designated as measured at fair value through profit or loss to be treated differently**. In this case the gain or loss in a period must be classified into:

- Gain or loss **resulting from credit risk**
- **Other** gain or loss

Derivatives are always measured at fair value through profit or loss.

5.1.3 Hedge accounting

IFRS 9's guidance on hedge accounting is significantly changed from IAS 39. IFRS 9 seeks to align accounting more closely with **risk management**, and to require improved disclosures. Overall IFRS 9 is a more principles-based standard than IAS 39 was.

The main types of hedging relationship are fair value hedges, cash flow hedges and foreign operation net investment hedges.

Hedge accounting can be begun or discontinued on the basis of the following.

- In relation to a **qualitative** assessment of hedge effectiveness (rather than IAS 39's quantitative threshold of 80–125%)
- Hedging relationships may be rebalanced without ending hedge accounting
- The entity **cannot voluntarily discontinue** hedge accounting once it has begun

The definition of **hedged items** has been **expanded to include non-financial items**, net positions of items, and equity investments held at fair value through OCI.

Extensive disclosures are now required in relation to the entity's **risk management** and hedging activities.

BPP
LEARNING MEDIA

5.1.4 Impairment

IFRS 9 introduced a new 'expected loss' model of impairment, as opposed to IAS 39's old 'incurred loss' model. The context here was that during the financial crisis of 2007-8, the delayed recognition of credit losses on loans (and other financial instruments) was identified as a weakness of then existing accounting standards. The 'expected loss' model requires more timely recognition of expected credit losses. It does this by:

- Requiring entities to account for expected credit losses from when financial instruments are first recognised
- Lowering the threshold for recognition of full lifetime expected losses.

On **initial recognition**, the entity creates a 'credit loss allowance' equal to 12 months' expected credit losses. This is calculated as an expected value: the probability of a default within 12 months is multiplied by the total lifetime losses that would result from such a default.

In **subsequent years**, if the credit risk increases significantly since initial recognition this amount will be replaced by lifetime expected credit losses. If the credit quality subsequently improves and the lifetime expected credit losses criterion is no longer met, the 12-month expected credit loss basis is reinstated.

Although IFRS 9 provides substantial guidance, estimating expected credit losses is always going to be judgemental (eg how are the probabilities for the expected values calculation decided?) and therefore risky for auditors – the chief risk being that losses which should have been foreseen at the date of the financial statements might not have been taken into account.

5.1.5 IFRS 7 *Financial instruments: disclosure*

IFRS 7 requires entities to make extensive disclosures in relation to financial instruments, which we will recap briefly here. The standard requires qualitative and quantitative disclosures about exposure to risks arising from financial instruments and specifies minimum disclosures about credit risk, liquidity risk and market risk.

Two types of disclosure need to be made: about the **significance** of the financial instruments, and about the **nature and extent of risks arising** from the financial instruments.

5.1.6 IAS 32 *Financial instruments: presentation*

One key requirement of IAS 32 relates to **compound financial instruments**. Convertible debt is a commonly examined example here, where IAS 32 requires the debt and equity elements of the instrument to be presented separately in the financial statements. Accounting in this area requires a level of **judgement**, which can be **risky** from an auditor's point of view. For example, judgement is required when calculating the present value of debt repayments (eg in selecting an appropriate discount rate).

5.2 Business risk

Financial instruments may help to reduce business risk if used well, but their inherent complexity may increase business risk. This is particularly likely where management:

- **Does not fully understand the risks** of using financial instruments and has insufficient skills and experience to manage those risks;
- **Does not have the expertise to value them** appropriately in accordance with IFRS;
- Does not have **sufficient controls** in place over financial instrument activities; or
- Inappropriately hedges risks or speculates.

5.3 Auditing financial instruments

5.3.1 Audit risk

Audit risk will probably be increased by the presence of complex financial instruments because:

- It may be **difficult to understand** the nature of financial instruments and what they are used for, and the risks to which the entity is exposed

- Market sentiment and liquidity can **change quickly**, placing pressure on management to manage their exposures effectively

- **Evidence** supporting valuation may be **difficult to obtain**

- There may be large individual payments, which may increase the **risk of misappropriation of assets**

- The **amounts** in the financial statements may not be proportionate to the **level of risk** involved

- There may be undue reliance on a few key employees, who may exert significant influence on the entity's financial instruments transactions, and whose compensation may be linked to the performance of these instruments. This may be a risk of **fraudulent financial reporting**

IAPN 1000 notes that 'the need for **professional scepticism** increases with the complexity of financial instruments' (IAPN 1000.72).

It is important to realise, however, that financial instruments do not always result in high audit risk. If the entity is making use of simple financial instruments, eg loans or bonds, then these can be audited without any particular difficulties. The International Auditing Practice Note (IAPN) lists the following factors as affecting the risk of material misstatement.

- The **volume** of financial instruments to which the entity is exposed

- The terms of the financial instrument, including **whether the financial instrument itself includes other financial instruments**

- The **nature** of the financial instruments

5.3.2 Audit planning

Where financial instruments are present, the auditor should focus on the following matters.

Financial instruments – matters to focus on in audit planning
Understanding the **accounting** and **disclosure** requirements (ie Section 5.2 above)
Understanding the financial instruments to which the entity is exposed, and their purpose and risks
Determining whether **specialised skills** and knowledge are **needed** in the audit
Understanding and evaluating the system of **internal control** in light of the entity's financial instrument transactions and the information systems that fall within the scope of the audit
Understanding the nature, role and activities of the **internal audit** function
Understanding **management's process for valuing** financial instruments, including whether management has used an expert or a service organisation
Assessing and responding to the **risk of material misstatement**

The auditor must decide to what extent **internal controls** can be relied upon. The IAPN points out that entities with a high volume of trading are more likely to have sophisticated controls (which might be relied on), whereas entities with a low volume of trading will probably have to be audited substantively in this area.

5.4 Audit procedures

5.4.1 General procedures

Analytical procedures are unlikely to be used as substantive procedures here (they are high-level, and may fail to pick up on risks arising from the complexity of the financial instruments).

IAPN 1000 suggests the following procedures for testing completeness, accuracy and existence.

Procedures on completeness, accuracy and existence
External confirmation of bank accounts, trades and custodian statements – eg direct confirmation with the counterparty
Reviewing reconciliations of statements or data feeds from custodians (eg investment funds) with the entity's own records
Reviewing journal entries and the controls over the recording of such entries
Reading individual contracts and reviewing supporting documentation of the entity's financial instrument transactions, including accounting records
Testing controls, eg by reperforming controls
Reviewing the entity's **complaints management systems**
Reviewing master netting arrangements to identify unrecorded instruments

Exam focus point

Exam questions in this area are often not as scary as they might appear to be. The June 2015 exam, for example, featured four marks in Question 1 for audit procedures on a portfolio of short-term investments. There was a half mark for writing 'confirm cost of investment to cash book and bank statements'. Make sure you get this mark! There were other easy marks available for procedures to confirm that disclosures are in line with IFRS 9, and to confirm that the fair value of the shares agreed with stock market share prices.

5.4.2 Procedures relating to valuation

Where financial instruments are held at fair value (in accordance with Sections 5.2.1-2 above), they must be valued. This is one of the riskiest aspects of auditing them. In developing a valuation, management may do any of three things:

(a)   Utilise information from **third-party** pricing sources, eg a broker
(b)   Gather data to **develop their own estimate** using various techniques including models
(c)   **Engage an expert** to develop an estimate

The following procedures apply generally.

Procedures on valuations of financial instruments
Test how management made the accounting estimate and the data used. Check that fair value is arrived at in accordance with IFRS 13, using the 'fair value hierarchy'.
Test the operating effectiveness of the **controls** over how management made the accounting estimate, together with **appropriate substantive procedures**.
Develop a point estimate or a range to evaluate management's point estimate, eg the auditor can make their own estimate of the fair value.
Determine whether events occurring up to the date of the auditor's report **provide audit evidence** regarding the accounting estimate, eg are there any indicators of impairment?

Where management has taken option (a) above (use information from a third party), the following considerations apply.

- The **type of third-party** pricing source – how much information is available about the valuation?

- The **nature of inputs used** and the **complexity** of the valuation technique – eg are inputs Level 1 or Level 3 inputs, per IFRS 13?

- The **reputation and experience** of the third-party pricing source – does their experience include this specific type of financial instrument?

- The **entity's controls** over the use of third-party pricing sources – has the entity assessed whether the third party is reliable?

- The third-party pricing source's controls

When management uses its own model ((b), above), there are two basic audit approaches. Either test management's model, or develop your own model.

Finally, management may use a **management's expert** ((c), above). In this case ISA 500 applies, and procedures may include:

- Evaluating the competence, capabilities and objectivity of management's expert
- Obtaining an understanding of the work of the management's expert
- Evaluating the appropriateness of that expert's work as audit evidence

5.4.3 Disclosures

IFRSs require extensive disclosures about financial instruments, and there is a risk that these have not been made. Check that disclosures comply with IFRS 7 and IFRS 9. This includes eg qualitative disclosures about exposure to risk and risk management, and quantitative disclosures of summary data about exposures.

Question
Financial instruments

On 1 January 20X8 Daniel Co issued a $20 million debenture at par, with a nominal rate of interest of 4%. The debenture is redeemable in five years' time, at which point the holder will have the option to convert the debenture to 12 million $1 ordinary shares in Daniel Co. The debenture has been recorded in the financial statements as a long-term liability at the net proceeds of issue. The first payment of interest on 31 December 20X8 has also been recorded.

Required

(a) Identify the audit issues.
(b) List the audit procedures you would perform.

Answer

(a) Audit issues

(i) The treatment of the debenture does not comply with IFRS 9.

(ii) It should be treated as a hybrid instrument, split into its equity and liability components.

(iii) The liability component should be calculated as the discounted present value of the cash flows of the debenture.

(iv) The remainder of the proceeds should be reclassified as equity.

(b) Audit procedures

(i) Check the nominal interest rate and conversion terms to the debenture deed.

(ii) Agree amount of initial proceeds and interest payment to cash book and bank statement.

(iii) Obtain schedule calculating the fair value of the liability at the date of issue and confirm that an appropriate discount rate has been used (assuming revised treatment adopted).

(iv) Confirm whether disclosures are adequate and in accordance with IFRS 9 and IFRS 7.

6 Investment properties

A key factor to consider when auditing investment properties is whether one **exists** according to the **criteria** of IAS 40 *Investment property*.

Investment property is property (land or a building – or part of a building – or both) held (by the owner or by the lessee under a finance lease) to earn rentals or for capital appreciation or both, rather than for:

- Use in the production or supply of goods or services or for administrative purposes; or
- Sale in the ordinary course of business.

Type of non-investment property	Applicable IAS
Property held for sale in the ordinary course of business	IAS 2 *Inventories*
Property being constructed or developed on behalf of third parties	IAS 11 *Construction contracts*
Owner-occupied property	IAS 16 *Property, plant and equipment*

Substantive tests

- Confirm that property meets the IAS 40 definition of investment property
- Verify **rental agreements**, ensuring that occupier is not a connected company and that the rent has been negotiated at arm's length

The second important assertion in relation to investment properties is **valuation**. IAS 40 requires that investment properties either be held at **cost** or at fair value. This approximates to open market value. Fair value should be determined in accordance with IFRS 13 *Fair value measurement*.

The last key issue with regard to investment properties is **disclosure**. The auditor should review the disclosures made in the financial statements in relation to investment properties to ensure that they have been made appropriately, in accordance with IAS 40.

While exam questions will require you to use your knowledge of corporate reporting it is important that the accounting knowledge is applied (see the answer above). Few marks will be awarded for listing facts from accounting standards without adequate application and audit focus.

7 Foreign exchange rates

The presence of **foreign exchange** is likely to **increase audit risk**, so the auditor must perform procedures to reduce this risk.

You will have studied the accounting rules in relation to foreign exchange in depth at Paper P2. At P7 level you will need to revise this material, and then think about the area from the perspective of the external auditor. The key issue here is that the introduction of foreign exchange into a scenario increases the level of audit risk. This is most likely to be examined in the context of a **group** that includes an **overseas subsidiary**.

This area is relatively new to the P7 syllabus, so it is likely that the examining team will seek to test it. You are advised to revise it thoroughly.

7.1 Individual company

Perhaps the most immediate audit risk here is that the entity fails to comply with the accounting requirements of IAS 21 *The effects of changes in foreign exchange rates*. For an individual company conducting trade in foreign currencies, there are two separate accounting issues: conversion and translation.

Conversion is uncontroversial, and relates to an entity conducting transactions in a foreign currency, and which incurs exchange gains/losses in relation to these transactions. The rule is simple: the gain or loss on conversion is recognised directly in profit or loss in the period in which it occurs. The principal risk here is of the wrong exchange rate being used, resulting in misstatement of the gain/loss in the financial statements.

Translation is more complex. Translation is required at the end of an accounting period when a company still holds assets or liabilities in its statement of financial position which were obtained or incurred in a foreign currency. IAS 21 distinguishes between **monetary items** and **non-monetary items**. The basic rule is that monetary items (eg cash, receivables) should be retranslated using the rate ruling at the end of each accounting period. Non-monetary items are left at the amount recognised at the date of the transaction.

Audit procedures here would therefore include:

- Check that foreign currency transactions are recorded at the historical rate on initial recognition (and in the statement of profit or loss)
- Check that monetary items included in the statement of financial position at the year end are translated at the closing rate of exchange
- Check that non-monetary items are translated at the historical rate of exchange

7.2 Groups

It is also possible that a parent company may have overseas subsidiaries. It must translate the financial statements of those operations into its own reporting currency before they can be consolidated into group accounts. There are two methods of achieving this. The method used depends on whether the foreign operation has the same functional currency as the parent.

<table>
<tr><td>**Exam focus point**</td><td>In a question on the audit of groups, one of the issues you may need to consider is whether the correct treatment has been adopted for the translation of a foreign entity.</td></tr>
</table>

7.2.1 Same functional currency as the reporting entity

In this situation the foreign operation normally carries on its business as though it were an extension of the reporting entity's operations.

We can summarise the treatment as follows.

Statement of profit or loss	Translate using actual rates. An average for a period may be used but not where there is a significant fluctuation and the average is therefore unreliable.
Non-monetary items	Translate using an historical rate at the date of purchase (or revaluation to fair value, or reduction to realisable/recoverable amount). This includes inventories and long-term assets (and their depreciation).
Monetary items	Translate at the closing rate
Exchange differences	Report as part of profit for the year

7.2.2 Different functional currency from the reporting entity

In this situation, although the reporting entity may be able to exercise control, the foreign operation normally operates in a semi-autonomous way. It accumulates cash and other monetary items, generates income and incurs expenses, and may also arrange borrowings, all in its own local currency.

We can summarise the treatment as follows.

Assets and liabilities	Translate at the closing rate at the period end. (The balancing figure on the translated statement of financial position represents the reporting entity's net investment in the foreign operation.)
Statement of profit or loss	Translate items at the rate ruling at the date of the transaction (an average rate will usually be used for practical purposes)
Exchange differences	Taken to equity

7.3 Other issues

The table below outlines some of the other audit risks that may be present with an overseas subsidiary, along with some possible audit procedures to mitigate those risks.

Audit risk	Procedures
Potential misstatement due to the effects of **high inflation**. IAS 29 requires financial statements to be **restated** in terms of measuring units current at the **end of the reporting period**, and a **gain or loss** on the net monetary position included within net income	<ul><li>Confirm that financial statements have been correctly restated</li><li>Check that disclosures have been made in line with IAS 29</li></ul>
Subsidiary may have been audited by **component auditors**	Need to consider the extent to which their work can be relied on, as per ISA 600
Different **accounting framework** may have been used by subsidiary	Confirm the accounting framework used, and that accounting policies are consistent with the rest of the group
Possible **difficulty** in the parent being able to **exercise control**, eg due to political instability, or laws and regulations	Need to consider whether there is still **control**, and whether it is correct to produce group accounts per IFRS 3
Currency **restrictions** limiting **payment of profits** to the parent	<ul><li>Need to consider whether there is still control</li><li>Need to consider impact on parent's status as a **going concern**</li></ul>

Chapter Roundup

- Key assertions relating to assets are existence, completeness, valuation and rights and obligations.

- When standard costing is used, the auditor must assess whether the valuation is reasonable.

- Auditors should ensure that both tangible and intangible assets have been subjected to an annual impairment review.

- Accounting guidance for intangibles is given in IAS 38 *Intangible assets* and IFRS 3 *Business combinations*.

- When auditing financial instruments the auditors will have to ensure that recognition and valuation is in accordance with IFRS 9 *Financial instruments*.

- The presence of **foreign exchange** is likely to **increase audit risk**, so the auditor must perform procedures to reduce this risk.

290   9: Evaluation and review (II) – matters relating to specific accounting issues | Part D Audit of historical financial information

BPP
LEARNING MEDIA

Quick Quiz

1   Match the accounting item with the relevant accounting standard(s).

(a)   Investment properties   (i)   IFRS 3
(b)   Intangible non-current assets (ii)   IAS 16
(c)   Tangible non-current assets   (iii)   IAS 40
                                      (iv)   IAS 38

2   IAS 41 applies once agricultural produce has been harvested.

True   ☐

False   ☐

3   Brands may never be capitalised.

True   ☐

False   ☐

4   Financial assets are recognised initially at their fair value.

True   ☐

False   ☐

5   Complete the definition:

.... is property held to earn.......................... or
for .... or both, rather than for use in the
.... or .... of goods or services or for administrative
purposes, or .... in the ordinary course of business.

Answers to Quick Quiz

1   (a) (iii)
     (b) (iv)
     (c) (ii)

2   False. IAS 41 applies until the point of harvest. After harvest, IAS 2 applies.

3   False. Internally generated brands may not be capitalised. Purchased brands with a separately identifiable value may be capitalised.

4   True. Subsequent measurement rules depend on the type of financial instrument being measured.

5   Investment property, rentals, capital appreciation, production, supply, sale

Now try the questions below from the Practice Question Bank.

Number	Level	Marks	Time
Q13	Examination	25	49 mins
Q14	Examination	20	39 mins

Evaluation and review (III) – matters relating to specific accounting issues

Topic list	Syllabus reference
1 Income	D3
2 Liabilities	D3
3 Expenses	D3
4 Disclosure	D3

Introduction

This chapter deals with further accounting issues that could appear in questions where you are required to consider materiality, risk, relevant accounting standards and audit evidence. As in Chapter 9, the content relates to the final two aspects on that list of matters.

Study guide

		Intellectual level
D3	**Evaluation and review**	
(j)	Evaluate the matters (eg materiality, risk, relevant accounting standards, audit evidence) relating to:	3
	(iii) Statements of cash flows	
	(iv) Changes in accounting policy	
	(v) Taxation (including deferred tax)	
	(vi) Segmental reporting	
	(ix) Leases	
	(x) Revenue from contracts with customers	
	(xi) Employee benefits	
	(xii) Government grants	
	(xiii) Related parties*	
	(xiv) Earnings per share	
	(xvi) Provisions, contingent liabilities and contingent assets	
	(xx) Share-based payment transactions	
	(xxi) Business combinations	
	(xxii) Assets held for sale and discontinued operations	
	(xxiv) The effects of foreign exchange rates	
	(xxv) Borrowing costs	

* Issues relevant to related parties were covered in Chapter 7, those relevant to business combinations will be covered in Chapter 11, and those relevant to events after the reporting period were covered in Chapter 8.

Exam guide

Scenario questions are likely to appear requiring you to apply your corporate reporting knowledge, to assess whether errors may have been made, determine materiality and identify appropriate evidence. These can feature any of the financial reporting topics you have studied in your ACCA exams.

1 Income

FAST FORWARD

Revenue recognition is an extremely important issue, with both the completeness and occurrence assertions being important.

1.1 Revenue from contracts with customers

12/12

Point to note

The accounting standard in this area is relatively new, and you may not have covered it when you sat Paper P2. You should therefore study this area carefully.

IFRS 15 *Revenue from contracts with customers* was issued in May 2014, and superseded **both** IAS 18 *Revenue recognition* and IAS 11 *Construction contracts*. IFRS 15 unifies accounting for these areas with a single five-step model for all contracts with customers. The standard was a result of co-operation between the IASB and the FASB, and is a step towards the harmonisation of accounting standards.

IFRS 15 conceives of a contract as a series of 'performance obligations' which are then transferred to the customer (whether goods or services). The transfer of goods and services is then understood in terms of the transfer of **control**, rather than of risks and rewards as in IAS 18. **Control of an asset** is described in the standard as the ability to direct the use of, and obtain substantially all the remaining benefits from, the asset.

For straightforward retail transactions IFRS 15 will have little, if any, effect on the amount and timing of revenue recognition. For contracts such as long-term service contracts and multi-element arrangements it could result in changes either to the amount or to the timing of revenue recognised.

The main requirements of IFRS 15 are as follows.

1.1.1 Definitions

Key terms

Contract. An agreement between two or more parties that creates enforceable rights and obligations.

Customer. A party that has contracted with an entity to obtain goods or services that are an output of the entity's ordinary activities in exchange for consideration.

Income. Increases in economic benefits during the accounting period in the form of inflows or enhancements of assets or decreases of liabilities that result in an increase in equity, other than those relating to contributions from equity participants.

Performance obligation. A promise in a contract with a customer to transfer to the customer either:

- A good or service (or a bundle of goods or services) that is distinct; or
- A series of distinct goods or services that are substantially the same and that have the same pattern of transfer to the customer.

Revenue. Income arising in the course of an entity's ordinary activities.

Transaction price. The amount of consideration to which an entity expects to be entitled in exchange for transferring promised goods or services to a customer, excluding amounts collected on behalf of third parties.

1.1.2 Steps in recognising revenue

Step 1   Identify the contract(s) with a customer

A contract with a customer is within the **scope** of IFRS 15 only when:

(a)   The parties have approved the contract and are committed to carrying it out

(b)   Each party's rights regarding the goods and services to be transferred can be identified

(c)   The payment terms for the goods and services can be identified

(d)   The contract has commercial substance

(e)   It is probable that the entity will collect the consideration to which it will be entitled

The contract can be written, verbal or implied.

Contracts should be combined when the following criteria are met.

(a)   The contracts are negotiated as a package with a single commercial objective.

(b)   The amount of consideration to be paid in one contract depends on the price or performance of the other contract.

(c)   The goods or services promised in the contracts are a single performance obligation.

Step 2   Identify the performance obligations in the contract

The key point is distinct goods or services. A contract includes promises to provide goods or services to a customer. Those promises are called performance obligations. A company would account for a performance obligation separately only if the promised good or service is distinct.

A good or service is distinct if:

- The customer can benefit from the good or services on its own or in conjunction with other readily available resources

- The entity's promise to transfer the good or service to the customer is separately identifiable from other promises in the contract

Step 3   Determine the transaction price

The transaction price is the amount of consideration a company expects to be entitled to from the customer, in exchange for transferring goods or services. The transaction price would reflect the company's probability-weighted estimate of variable consideration (including reasonable estimates of contingent amounts) in addition to the effects of the customer's credit risk and the time value of money (if material). Variable contingent amounts are only included where it is highly probable that there will not be a reversal of revenue when any uncertainty associated with the variable consideration is resolved.

Step 4   Allocate the transaction price to the performance obligations in the contract

Where a contract contains more than one distinct performance obligation a company allocates the transaction price to all separate performance obligations in proportion to the standalone selling price of the good or service underlying each performance obligation. If the good or service is not sold separately, the company would estimate its standalone selling price.

So, if any entity sells a bundle of goods and/or services which it also supplies unbundled, the separate performance obligations in the contract should be priced in the same proportion as the unbundled prices. This would apply to mobile phone contracts where the handset is supplied 'free'. The entity must look at the standalone price of such a handset and some of the consideration for the contract should be allocated to the handset.

Step 5   Recognise revenue when (or as) the entity satisfies a performance obligation

The entity satisfies a performance obligation by transferring control of a promised good or service to the customer. A performance obligation can be satisfied at a point in time, such as when goods are delivered to the customer, or over time. An obligation satisfied over time will meet one of the following criteria.

- The customer simultaneously receives and consumes the benefits as the performance takes place.

- The entity's performance creates or enhances an asset that the customer controls as the asset is created or enhanced.

- The entity's performance does not create an asset with an alternative use to the entity and the entity has an enforceable right to payment for performance completed to date.

The amount of revenue recognised is the amount allocated to that performance obligation in Step 4.

An entity must be able to reasonably measure the outcome of a performance obligation before the related revenue can be recognised. In some circumstances, such as in the early stages of a contract, it may not be possible to reasonably measure the outcome of a performance obligation, but the entity expects to recover the costs incurred. In these circumstances, revenue is recognised only to the extent of costs incurred.

1.1.3 Contract costs

The incremental costs of obtaining a contract (such as sales commission) are recognised as an asset if the entity expects to recover those costs, and if the contract would not have been obtained without incurring the costs.

1.1.4 Satisfaction of performance obligations

Revenue is recognised when the performance obligation is satisfied. This is when the promised good or service is transferred and the customer has control.

Performance obligations satisfied at a point in time (the subject of the old IAS 18) are recognised when control is transferred:

(a)   The entity has a present right to payment for the asset.
(b)   The customer has legal title to the asset.
(c)   The entity has transferred physical possession of the asset.
(d)   The significant risks and rewards of ownership have been transferred to the customer.
(e)   The customer has accepted the asset.

Alternatively, performance obligations may be satisfied over time ('construction contracts' under the old IAS 11). These are accounted for at an amount that approximates the selling price of the goods or services transferred to date. The entity must choose an appropriate method for estimating the amount of performance completed to date. Methods include output methods and input methods:

Output methods recognise revenue on the basis of the value to the customer of the goods or services transferred. They include surveys of performance completed, appraisal of units produced or delivered etc.

Input methods recognise revenue on the basis of the entity's inputs, such as labour hours, resources consumed and costs incurred. If using a cost-based method, the costs incurred must contribute to the entity's progress in satisfying the performance obligation.

1.1.5 Special situations

Sale with a right of return

If there is a right of return then the goods which are expected to be returned are not recognised in revenue. This may be calculated using expected values.

Warranties

If a customer has the option to purchase a warranty separately from the product to which it relates, it constitutes a distinct service and is accounted for as a separate performance obligation.

Principal versus agent

If the entity acts as the principal (ie controls the goods or services before they are transferred to the customer) then revenue is recognised as normal.

The entity acts as an agent if its performance obligation is to arrange for the provision of goods or services by another party. Satisfaction of this performance obligation will give rise to the recognition of revenue in the amount of any fee or commission to which it expects to be entitled in exchange for arranging for the other party to provide its goods or services.

Repurchase agreements

Repurchase agreements generally come in three forms:

(a)   An entity has an obligation to repurchase the asset (a forward contract).
(b)   An entity has the right to repurchase the asset (a call option).
(c)   An entity must repurchase the asset if requested to do so by the customer (a put option).

In the case of a forward or a call option the customer does not obtain control of the asset, even if it has physical possession. The entity will account for the contract as either of the following.

(a)   A lease in accordance with IAS 17, if the repurchase price is below the original selling price.

(b)   A financing arrangement if the repurchase price is equal to or greater than the original selling price. In this case the entity will recognise both the asset and a corresponding liability.

If the entity is obliged to repurchase at the request of the customer (a put option), it must consider whether or not the customer is likely to exercise that option.

Consignment arrangements

When a product is delivered to a customer under a consignment arrangement, the customer (dealer) does not obtain control of the product at that point in time, so no revenue is recognised upon delivery.

1.1.6 Presentation

Contracts with customers will be presented in an entity's statement of financial position as a **contract liability**, a **contract asset** or a **receivable**, depending on the relationship between the entity's performance and the customer's payment.

A contract liability is recognised in the statement of financial position where a customer has paid an amount of consideration prior to the entity performing by transferring control of the related good or service to the customer.

When the entity has performed but the customer has not yet paid the related consideration, this will give rise to either a contract asset or a receivable. A contract asset is recognised when the entity's right to consideration is conditional on something other than the passage of time, for instance future performance. A receivable is recognised when the entity's right to consideration is unconditional except for the passage of time.

In practice, this aligns with the previous IAS 11 treatment. Where revenue has been invoiced, a receivable is recognised. Where revenue has been earned but not invoiced, it is recognised as a contract asset.

1.1.7 Audit of revenue

Revenue is commonly audited using **analytical procedures**. This is because revenue should be predictable, and because there are good grounds on which to base analytical procedures, such as:

- Plenty of information, for example, last year's accounts, budgets, monthly analyses (companies tend to keep a lot of information about sales)
- Logical relationships with items such as inventory and receivables

Analytical procedures may be less reliable where controls testing indicates that revenue controls are deficient. In this case the auditor may place more reliance on tests of detail.

Unless complex transactions arise where revenue is not as clear cut as a product being supplied and invoiced for, revenue recognition is generally not an issue. However, it should not be thought that revenue recognition is generally a low-risk area to audit. Far from it: **revenue recognition is one of the commonest areas of fraudulent financial reporting**. Indeed, ISA 240 *The auditor's responsibilities relating to fraud in an audit of financial statements* states that the auditor should presume that there is a risk of fraud in relation to revenue recognition (ISA 240.26), and should obtain an understanding of the controls related to these risks (ISA 240.27). This presumption is 'rebuttable' (Para A30) if the auditor concludes that there is no risk of material misstatement due to fraud, but unless this is the case, the auditor must presume that there is a possibility of revenue recognition fraud, and that the entity should have put in place controls to mitigate this risk.

A recent example of difficulties in this area was Tesco in 2014, when a serious misstatement was discovered in relation to revenue in the interim financial statements. Rebates from suppliers were recognised too early, which resulted in profit being overstated by £250m.

Where performance obligations are satisfied over time, there may also be assets/liabilities in the statement of financial position. In industries dealing primarily in long-term contracts, revenue recognition can be a **material** issue. Examples of industries where this might be true are the:

- Building industry
- Engineering industry

The following audit procedures may provide a starting point for exam questions in this area.

<table>
<tr><td>**Exam focus point**</td><td>The P7 exam is very unlikely to require you to list out specific procedures such as those below. It will be far more important that you apply your knowledge to the information given in the question. You can use the procedures here to help generate ideas for your answer, but simply writing them out as they stand will be unlikely to impress the marker!</td></tr>
</table>

Audit procedures

Performance obligations satisfied at a point in time:

- Substantive procedures, eg agree revenue recognised to relevant documents (for example, work certificates or contracts)

- Analytical procedures, such as comparison with:

    - Prior year and with budgets

    - Related figures such as inventory and receivables

    - Similar industry information, eg comparison of the receivables days with industry averages or with other entities of comparable size in the same industry

- Analytical procedures based on operational factors, eg the prediction of total rental income on a building divided into apartments, taking the rental rates, the number of apartments and vacancy rates into consideration

Performance obligations satisfied over time:

- Obtain a copy of the calculation of revenue recognised in the period and recalculate, including any assets/liabilities recognised.

- Assess whether the basis of calculation is comparable with prior years.

- Confirm that the method for measuring progress for performance obligations is appropriate and reasonable in line with IFRS 15.

- Verify the figures in the calculation, such as:

    - Total contract price to original contract

    - Revenue to amount of performance completed to date

    - Performance completed to date to input methods, such as certification of work completed, cost of work completed (eg to invoices also payroll/clock cards/wage rates)

    - Receivables to sales invoices

    - Payments on account to remittance advices

From the auditor's point of view, the **performance completed to date** and the **assessment of the overall profitability of the contract** are **particularly risky areas** to audit, as they involve management exercising its **judgement**. Where this is the case, procedures would include discussion with management to obtain an understanding of (and to evaluate) any underlying assumptions used; review of subsequent events; use of an auditor's expert; and obtaining written representations.

Question

You are an audit senior on the audit of Laxman Co, a wholesale seller of stationery and office products.

Recognised within revenue are a series of credit sales of inventory totalling $200,000 that took place close to the year end. Laxman Co continues to hold the legal title to this inventory.

Laxman Co holds a bank loan whose covenants impose on it a number of conditions, one of which is that its financial statements show an acid test ratio of more than one.

The following amounts are shown in Laxman Co's draft financial statements.

	$
Revenue	1,200,000
Current assets	1,000,000
Inventory	100,000
Current liabilities	800,000

Required

Identify and explain the principal matters to consider when auditing the revenue of Laxman Co.

Answer

The two principal matters to consider here are interrelated: whether IAS 18 has been properly applied to Laxman Co's inventory, and whether Laxman Co is in breach of the conditions of its bank loan.

Inventory

IFRS 15 states that revenue is recognised when the entity has transferred control of the goods to the buyer.

In this case, the transfer of title would appear to indicate that this has not happened, and that these items should not be recognised within revenue.

However, as auditors it will be necessary to obtain further information regarding the sale, as in accordance with IFRS 15 the transfer of legal title is not sufficient evidence that control has been transferred. It is possible, for instance, that legal title has been retained in order to protect Laxman Co against the possibility of non-payment by the receivable, even though in substance a sale has in fact occurred.

Further audit evidence must be obtained in order to form a judgement over whether IFRS 15 has in fact been breached.

Loan condition

Laxman Co appears to be within the criteria laid down by the bank: it has an acid test ratio of 1.125 (= ($1,000,000 − $100,000) ÷ $800,000).

However, if the revenue recognised in respect of the inventory above has not been recognised in accordance with IFRS 15, the financial statements may need to be amended. The amendment could be by as much as £200,000 (decreasing receivables and increasing inventory), which would change the acid test ratio to 0.625 (= ($800,000 − $300,000) ÷ $800,000).

If the conditions set by the bank have been broken then it is likely that some negative consequence would result from this. This could range from a fine or penalty that would need to be recognised in the financial statements, to the possibility of Laxman Co having to repay the loan. If this were the case, it would be necessary to consider very carefully whether significant doubts exist over Laxman Co's ability to continue as a going concern.

300 10: Evaluation and review (III) – matters relating to specific accounting issues | Part D Audit of historical financial information

Possibility of fraud

The auditor needs to consider the possibility that management has engaged in fraudulent financial reporting in respect of revenue recognition in order not to breach the conditions set by the trade organisation. If this were the case, the auditor will need to re-examine any representations it has already received from management.

| Case Study | Revenue recognition in an e-commerce environment |

Companies that engage in e-commerce may have particular revenue recognition issues.

The entity may act as a **principal** or as an **agent**. They must determine whether to disclose their gross revenue, or merely their commission. For example, Lastminute.com discloses a figure 'TTV', which does not represent statutory revenue, but the price at which goods and services have been sold across the group's platforms. Revenue itself is largely made up of commission on selling those goods and services.

The company may engage in **reciprocal arrangements** with other companies whereby they both advertise on each other's website. Whether such an arrangement results in 'revenue' must be considered. It must then be accounted for appropriately.

The company may deal in unusual **discounts** or voucher systems to encourage customers to buy. These must also be reflected.

Lastly, the company must determine a policy for **cut-off**. This may be complex if the company acts as an agent. When is the sale made? When the customer clicks 'accept', when the company emails acknowledgement, when the sale is made known to the principal, when the goods are despatched, when the customer receives the goods, when the customer has taken advantage of the services…? The company must determine a reasonable policy for when the sale has been made.

Satyam Computer Services Ltd, a major Indian provider of IT services, was the subject of a major accounting scandal that has sometimes been referred to as 'India's Enron'.

Satyam manipulated its financial statements over a period of about seven years, when the public announcement was made that the accounts had been falsified. A number of methods were used to do this, including producing false invoices, which inflated reported revenue and led to the creation of significant fictitious assets in the statement of financial position.

Satyam's auditors failed to detect this fraud, which had an ongoing and highly material impact on the financial statements. As a result of their failure to conduct the audit properly, and of the broader failure of quality control of which this was symptomatic, five Indian affiliates of PricewaterhouseCoopers were given a record fine of $7.5m by the Securities and Exchange Commission in the US. The firms were also required to set up employee training programmes, to reform audit policies, and to appoint an independent monitor.

It is important to note that this is not a question of auditors being held **liable** for audit failings, but rather of auditors being fined by a regulatory body for failing to conduct audits in accordance with the required standards.

| Question | Revenue recognition and other matters |

The senior partner of JLPN, a firm of auditors, has issued an 'Audit Risk Alert' letter to all partners dealing with key areas of concern which should be given due consideration by their firm when auditing public companies. The letter outlines certain trends in audit reporting that, if not scrutinised by the auditors, could lead to a loss of reliability and transparency in the financial statements. The following three key concerns were outlined in the letter.

(a) Audit committees play a very important role together with the financial director and auditor in achieving high quality financial control and auditing. Recently the efforts of certain audit committees have been questioned in the press.

(b) The Stock Exchange had reported cases of inappropriate revenue recognition practices, including:

    (i) Accelerating revenue prior to the delivery of the product to the customer's site, or prior to the completion of the terms of the sales arrangement

    (ii) Recognition of revenue when customers have unilateral cancellation or termination provisions, other than the normal customary product return provisions

(c) It has been reported that the management of companies had intentionally violated International Financial Reporting Standards (IFRS). The reason for this has been the sensitivity of reported earnings per share (EPS) in a marketplace where missing the market's expectation of EPS by a small amount could have significant consequences.

Required

(a) Explain the importance of the role of an 'Audit Risk Alert' letter to a firm of auditors.

(b) Discuss the way in which the auditor should deal with each of the key concerns outlined in the letter in order to ensure that audit risk is kept to an acceptable level.

Answer

(a) The '**Audit Risk Alert**' **letter** is a memorandum used by the reporting partner to notify fellow partners of concerns emerging from dealings with clients, regulatory authorities or stock exchanges. It ensures that:

    (i) Key audit risk areas are reviewed

    (ii) Significant trends and irregularities are identified

    (iii) Quality is maintained

    (iv) Litigation risk is reduced

    (v) Investor confidence is maintained as it reduces manipulation

(b) (i) **Audit committees** are held to secure good standards of **internal control** and financial reporting in listed companies. If the auditor has doubts about the effectiveness of an audit committee then they should **review its structure, independence and membership** to ensure it meets its objectives. Any shortcomings should be reported to the board and/or the members.

    (ii) **Revenue acceleration** is a **creative accounting device**. Revenue should **not** be **recognised until earned and realised** (realisable), so the practices described are not acceptable. Only if the risks of ownership have fully transferred to the buyer and the seller has not retained any specific performance obligation should revenue be recognised earlier.

    Extended audit tests concerning revenue recognition and 'cut-off' tests may be appropriate if the auditor suspects anomalies.

    (iii) Where **IFRS violations** have occurred, **materiality judgement** may be affected. The auditor must ensure the audit team is aware that violations of IFRS **can affect EPS** for certain clients, and that staff are sufficiently experienced and trained in order to detect such violations. It may be that the errors are individually immaterial, but the **aggregate effect** must be considered. Furthermore, the practice of intentional misstatements may indicate that the **management** of the company **lacks integrity** and the auditor should consider whether the client should be retained.

1.2 Government grants and assistance

Government grants and assistance are accounted for under IAS 20 *Accounting for government grants and disclosure of government assistance*. They may be either revenue or capital grants relating to the assets or income.

> **IAS 20 *Accounting for government grants and disclosure of government assistance***
>
> - Only recognise grants when **reasonable assurance** that:
>
>   - Entity will **comply** with any conditions attached
>   - Entity will actually **receive** the grant
>
> - **Capital approach** (credit grant directly to shareholders' interests) **or**
>
>   **Income approach** (credit grant to P/L over one or more periods)
>
> - IAS 20 states **income approach must be used**
>
> - Grants related to assets:
>
>   - Set up grant as deferred income **or**
>   - Deduct grant in arriving at carrying amount of asset
>
> - Disclosures:
>
>   - Accounting policy adopted
>   - Nature and extent of government grants recognised
>   - Unfulfilled conditions and other contingencies

Grants where related costs have already been incurred offer no difficulties to account for or to audit. To audit them, the auditor should:

- Obtain documentation relating to the grant and confirm that it should be classified as revenue
- Agree the value to documentation (eg a letter outlining the details of the grant, or a copy of an application form sent by the client)
- Agree receipt of the grant to bank statements

Capitalised grants can be more difficult to audit, particularly if a non-monetary government grant is being accounted for at fair value.

Audit procedures:

- Consider whether the basis of accounting is comparable to the previous year.
- Discuss the basis of accounting with the directors to ensure that the method used is the best method.
- Ensure that any changes in accounting method are disclosed.

2 Liabilities 12/07, 6/09, 12/11, 6/13

> **FAST FORWARD**
>
> The relevant financial statement assertions for liabilities are completeness, rights and obligations and existence. Liabilities must be tested for understatement.

Fair value is a key issue when considering certain liabilities. This should be borne in mind when auditing liabilities.

2.1 Leases 12/11, 6/13, 6/15

> **FAST FORWARD**
>
> The classification of a lease can have a material effect on the financial statements.

The relevant accounting standard for leases is IAS 17 *Leases*.

IAS 17 *Leases*

- **Lease**. An agreement whereby the lessor conveys to the lessee in return for a payment or series of payments the right to use an asset for an agreed period of time.

The key principle is: substance over legal form.

- **Finance lease**. A lease that transfers substantially all the risks and rewards incident to ownership of an asset. Title may or may not eventually be transferred.
- **Operating lease**. A lease other than a finance lease.

Finance lease

- Capitalise asset on statement of financial position (SOFP) (at lower of fair value and present value of minimum lease payments)
- Set up finance lease liability on SOFP (current and non-current)
- Split payments between finance charge and capital
- Charge depreciation (over shorter of lease term and useful life)

Operating lease

- Charge rentals on a systematic basis over lease term
- Accruals or prepayments for rental in SOFP
- Rental expense in P/L

Disclosures: finance leases

- Net carrying amount at year end for each class of asset
- Reconciliation between total of minimum lease payments at year-end and their present value
- Total of minimum lease payments at year end and their present value (< 1 year, 1-5 years, > 5 years)

Disclosures: operating leases

- Total of future minimum lease payments under non-cancellable operating leases (< 1 year, 1-5 years, > 5 years)

Sale and leaseback transactions

- An asset is sold and then leased back. The resulting lease may be an operating lease or a finance lease.
- Finance lease: profit on disposal is deferred and then amortised over the period of the lease.
- Operating lease: any profit or loss on disposal is recognised immediately.

You can see that the **classification** of the lease is **likely to have a material effect on the financial statements**. If the lease is a finance lease, the statement of financial position will show substantial assets and liabilities. The net effect will be minimal, but the face of the statement of financial position will be materially different from what it would be if it was an operating lease.

It is important that the auditor ensures that the **classification** (which would fall under the assertion existence) is correct. Other important assertions are valuation, and rights and obligations.

The auditor needs to be alert to the possibility of **sale and leaseback** transactions. If there is a sale and leaseback, then you need to check that the profit on disposal of the asset is treated in line with IAS 17.

The following audit procedures are relevant.

Classification and rights and obligations

- Obtain a copy of the lease agreement
- Review the lease agreement to ensure that the lease has been correctly classified according to IAS 17

Valuation (finance leases)

- Obtain a copy of the client's workings in relation to finance leases
- Check the additions and calculations of the workings

> - Ensure that the interest has been accounted for in accordance with IAS 17
> - Recalculate the interest
> - Agree the opening position
> - Agree any new assets to lease agreements
> - Verify lease payments in the year to the bank statements
>
> **Valuation** (operating leases)
>
> - Agree payments to the bank statements (if material)
>
> **Disclosure**
>
> - Ensure the finance leases have been properly disclosed in the financial statements

Question

Audit of leases

You are the manager responsible for the audit of Makepeace Co for the year ended 31 December 20X2. Makepeace Co has leased an asset from 1 January 20X2. The terms of the lease are:

- A non-refundable deposit of $5,800 on inception
- Six annual instalments of $16,000 payable in arrears

The fair value of the asset (equivalent to the present value of the minimum lease payments) on 1 January 20X2 is $80,000 and the asset has a useful life to the company of five years.

As part of the lease agreement the company guaranteed to the lessor that the asset could be sold for $8,000 at the end of the lease term. It also incurred $2,000 of costs in setting up the lease agreement.

The lease has been classified as a finance lease in the books of Makepeace Co. The asset has been capitalised in the statement of financial position and is being depreciated straight-line over the life of the lease.

The interest rate implicit in the lease has been calculated at 10%.

The company has total assets of $1,600,000.

Required

List the audit issues you would consider in this situation.

Answer

Audit issues

The key risk is that the lease has been inappropriately classified as a finance lease. The fact that the present value of the minimum lease payments is equivalent to the fair value of the asset and that the residual value is guaranteed by the lessee would indicate that the treatment of the lease as a finance lease is correct. Further inspection of the lease agreement should be performed, however, to determine which party bears the risks and rewards of ownership.

Materiality needs to be considered. As the asset was capitalised as a finance lease, the statement of financial position should include a non-current asset stated at $67,200

$$\left[(80,000+2,000)-\big((80,000+2,000-8,000)\div5\big)\right].$$

There should also be a financial lease liability of $65,620 in total (see Working). If the lease is an operating lease these balances would be removed. At 4.2% and 4.1% of total assets respectively these balances are material to the statement of financial position.

Profit figures are required to determine the potential materiality of interest and depreciation charges.

The period over which the asset is being depreciated needs to be considered. The depreciation period is normally the shorter of the useful life and the lease term. In this case the asset is being depreciated over the lease term (six years) when it will only be of use to the company for five years.

The treatment of the costs incurred in setting up the lease need to be considered. These can be capitalised as part of the non-current asset and depreciated.

There is a need to check whether the rate implicit in the lease has been calculated correctly. In accordance with IAS 17 this is the rate that gives a constant rate on the outstanding liability. This can be checked by using a market value for the asset to calculate the internal rate of return.

Disclosures must comply with the requirements of IAS 17. In particular the liability must be analysed to show the present value of the minimum lease payments in the categories < one year, two to five years, > five years. In this case the liability would be split as follows.

		$
< one year (65,620 – 56,182)(W)		9,438
Two to five years (W)		56,182

Working

		$
Year ended 31 December 20X2		
1 January 20X2	Asset at fair value (FV)	80,000
1 January 20X2	Non-refundable deposit	(5,800)
		74,200
1 January 20X2 to 31 December 20X2	Interest at 10%	7,420
31 December 20X2	Instalment 1	(16,000)
Balance at 31 December 20X2		65,620
Year ended 31 December 20X3		
1 January 20X3 to 31 December 20X3	Interest at 10%	6,562
31 December 20X3	Instalment 2	(16,000)
Balance at 31 December 20X3		56,182

2.2 Deferred taxation   12/08

FAST FORWARD

> The auditor needs to audit the movement on the deferred tax liability.

Deferred tax is accounted for under IAS 12 *Income taxes*. This is revised briefly below.

IAS 12 *Income taxes*

- Deferred tax is the tax attributable to temporary differences, which are differences between the carrying amount of an asset or liability in the statement of financial position and its tax base.

- **Deferred tax liabilities** are the amounts of income taxes payable in future periods in respect of taxable temporary differences. All taxable temporary differences give rise to a deferred tax liability.

- **Deferred tax assets** are the amounts of income taxes recoverable in future periods in respect of:
  - Deductible temporary differences (eg provisions, unrealised profits on intra-group trading)
  - The carry forward of unused tax losses
  - The carry forward of unused tax credits

  All deductible temporary differences give rise to a deferred tax asset.

- **Temporary differences** are differences between the carrying amount of an asset or liability in the statement of financial position and its tax base. Temporary differences may be either:
  - **Taxable temporary differences**, which are temporary differences that will result in taxable amounts in determining taxable profit (or tax loss) of future periods when the carrying amount of the asset or liability is recovered or settled; or

  - **Deductible temporary differences**, which are temporary differences that will result in amounts that are deductible in determining taxable profit (or tax loss) of future periods when the carrying amount of the asset or liability is recovered or settled.

- The **tax base** of an asset or liability is the amount attributed to that asset or liability for tax purposes.

Deferred tax is the **tax attributable to timing differences**. For example, where a company 'saves tax' in the current period by having accelerated capital allowances, a **provision for the tax charge** is **made in the statement of financial position**.

The provision is made because over the course of the asset's life, the tax allowances will reduce until the depreciation charged in the accounts is higher than the allowances. This will result in taxable profit being higher than reported profit and the company will be 'suffering higher tax' in this period.

2.2.1 Types of taxable temporary difference

Accelerated capital allowances

The temporary difference is the difference between the carrying value of the asset in the statement of financial position at the end of the reporting period and its tax depreciated value.

Interest revenue (where interest is included in profit or loss on an accruals basis but taxed when received)

The temporary difference is equivalent to the income accrual in the statement of financial position at the end of the reporting period, as the tax base of the interest receivable is nil.

Development costs (where development costs are capitalised for accounting purposes but deducted from taxable profit in the period incurred)

The temporary difference is equivalent to the amount capitalised in the statement of financial position at the end of the reporting period. The tax base is nil since they have already been deducted from taxable profits.

Revaluation to fair value (in jurisdictions where the tax base of the asset is not adjusted)

The temporary difference is the difference between the asset's carrying value and tax base. A deferred liability is created even if the entity does not intend to dispose of the asset.

Fair value adjustments on consolidation

A temporary difference arises as for the revaluation above but the deferred tax effect is a consolidation adjustment in the same way as the revaluation itself.

Question	Revision: taxable temporary differences

Shelley Co purchased an asset costing $3,000. At the end of 20X1 the carrying amount is $2,000. The cumulative depreciation for tax purposes is $1,800 and the current tax rate is 30%.

Required

Calculate the deferred tax liability for the asset.

Answer

Tax base of the asset is $3,000 − $1,800 = $1,200

Deferred tax liability = $800 (2,000 − 1,200) × 30% = $240

2.2.2 Types of deductible temporary differences

Provisions

The provision is recognised for accounting purposes when there is a present obligation, but may not be deductible for tax purposes until the expenditure is incurred.

Losses

Current losses that can be carried forward to be offset against future taxable profits result in a deferred tax asset.

Fair value adjustments

For example, liabilities recognised on business combinations where the expenditure is not deductible for tax purposes until a later period.

Unrealised profits on intra-group trading

The profit is not realised from the group point of view until the items transferred are sold outside the group but, where the tax base is based on the cost to the individual receiving company and no equivalent adjustment for unrealised profit is made for tax purposes, a temporary difference arises.

Question

Revision: deductible temporary differences

Ontario Co recognises a liability of $20,000 for accrued product warranty costs on 31 December 20X1. These product warranty costs will not be deductible for tax purposes until the entity pays the claims. The tax rate is 30%.

Required

Calculate the deferred tax asset.

Answer

Tax base = Nil (carrying amount of $20,000 less the amount that will be deductible for tax purposes in respect of the liability in future periods)

Deferred tax asset = $20,000 (carrying amount) – Nil (tax base) = 20,000 × 25% = $6,000

This should be recognised in accordance with IAS 12 (see Section 2.2.3 below).

2.2.3 Measurement of deferred tax

The key points to remember are:

- IAS 12 adopts the **full provision** method of providing for deferred tax. This recognises that each timing difference at the period end has an effect on future tax payments.

- Deferred tax assets and liabilities are measured at the tax rates expected to apply to the period when the asset is realised or liability settled, based on the tax rates (and tax laws) that have been **enacted** (or substantively enacted) by the end of the reporting period.

- Deferred assets and liabilities **cannot be discounted**.

- Deferred tax assets are only recognised to the extent that it is **probable** that taxable profit will be available against which the deductible temporary difference can be utilised.

Point to note

In practice it is rare for a deferred tax asset to be recognised, as the asset only exists insofar as the entity's tax liability can be reduced in the future, which in turn depends on the entity being profitable enough to **have** a tax liability and therefore to be able to 'use' any tax losses.

From the auditor's perspective deferred tax assets are risky because a significant degree of judgement must be exercised in determining whether tax losses will in fact result in reduced tax liabilities in the future. This is an illustration of the importance of the auditor approaching the audit with professional scepticism. If you come across a deferred tax asset in an exam question, you should look to be skeptical about it (although it is of course always possible that the deferred tax asset could be stated correctly).

2.2.4 Audit issues and procedures

As part of the **planning process**, if the client receives tax services from the firm, the auditor should consult the tax department as to the company's future tax plans, to ascertain whether they expect a deferred tax liability to arise. This will assist any analytical procedures they carry out on the deferred tax provision.

Remember that **manipulating the deferred tax figure will not affect the actual tax position**. However, a **deferred tax charge** (the other part of the double entry for the statement of financial position provision) **is recognised in profit or loss before dividends**, even if it is not actually paid to the taxation authorities.

The following procedures will be relevant.

- Obtain a copy of the deferred tax workings and the corporation tax computation
- Check the arithmetical **accuracy** of the deferred tax working
- Agree the **figures used** to calculate timing differences to those on the **tax computation** and the **financial statements**
- Consider the assumptions made in the light of your knowledge of the business and any other evidence gathered during the course of the audit to ensure reasonableness
- Agree the opening position on the deferred tax account to the prior year financial statements
- Review the basis of the provision to ensure:
  - It is line with accounting practice under IAS 12
  - It is suitably comparable to practice in previous years
  - Any changes in accounting policy have been disclosed

Question
Audit of deferred tax

Guido Co, a company producing domestic appliances for the retail market, began trading on 1 January 20X1. Its draft accounts for the year ended 31 December 20X2 show profit before tax of $1,000,000, total assets of $5,200,000 and a deferred tax balance of $958,000.

You are the manager responsible for the audit of Guido Co and the following information relating to deferred tax has been provided by the client:

(1)   The deferred tax balance in the financial statements is the brought forward balance from previous years. No deferred tax adjustment has been made for the current period.

(2)   At the period end Guido Co has plant and equipment with a carrying amount of $5,200,000 and a tax base at that date of $2,400,000.

(3)   The tax rate to be applied is 30%.

Required

(a)   Identify the audit issues.

(b)   List the procedures you would perform in respect of the amounts relating to deferred tax in the financial statements of Guido Co.

Answer

(a)   **Audit issues**

(i)   The deferred tax balance has not been adjusted to reflect current period balances.

(ii)   Adjustment of deferred tax would result in the following balances.

Deferred tax liability $840,000 (W)
Credit in the statement of profit or loss $118,000 (W)

(iii) With the change in liability representing approximately 12% of profit before tax and 2% of total assets the adjustment is material to both the statement of profit or loss and the statement of financial position.

(iv)   Whether the tax rate of 30% is the correct rate to apply.

(v)   Whether the net book values and tax written down values provided are correct.

(vi)   Whether there are any additional taxable temporary differences or deductible temporary differences that should be taken account of.

(vii) Whether adequate disclosure is provided in accordance with IAS 12.

(b)   **Audit procedures**

(i)   Discuss with management why they have not adjusted the deferred tax liability for the period and request that they do so.

(ii)   Agree the brought forward balance for deferred tax to the previous year's financial statements.

(iii) Obtain a schedule of the temporary differences relating to the plant and equipment and agree these to tax computations and asset registers.

(iv)   Check that the rate of 30% applied is in accordance with IAS 12, ie the 'substantially enacted' rate of tax.

(v)   Enquire of management and review tax computation to establish whether there are any further differences that need to be adjusted for.

(vi)   Review disclosure notes to ensure that they comply with IAS 12, including disclosure of the components of the deferred tax liability, the change in the liability and the major components of the income tax expense.

Working

	$'000
Tax base of asset	2,400
Carrying amount	5,200
$2,800 \times 30\% =$	840
Brought forward liability	958
Decrease in liability	118

2.3 Provisions and contingencies   6/09, 12/09, 12/10, 12/11, 6/12
                                                            6/13, 12/13

FAST FORWARD

> A provision is accounted for as a liability, contingencies are disclosed, so auditors must ensure they have been classified correctly according to IAS 37.

Provisions are accounted for under IAS 37 *Provisions, contingent liabilities and contingent assets.*

IAS 37 *Provisions, contingent liabilities and contingent assets*

A **provision** is a liability of **uncertain timing or amount**.

A **liability** is a present obligation of the entity arising from past events, the settlement of which is expected to result in an outflow from the entity of resources embodying **economic benefits**.

Under IAS 37, an entity should not recognise a **contingent asset** or a **contingent liability** (ie a possible asset or liability). Contingent liabilities and contingent assets should only be disclosed, not recognised.

However, if the following conditions are met then a provision should be recognised in relation to a contingent liability.

- There is a present obligation as a result of a past event.
- There will be a probable outflow of resources (< 50% likely).
- A reliable estimate can be made.

Common examples include warranties, legal claims against an entity, onerous contracts and restructuring costs.

IAS 37 also gives guidance regarding a number of specific provisions. These include:

Provisions for restructuring

A restructuring is a programme that is planned and controlled by management and materially changes either:

- The scope of the business undertaken by an entity; or
- The manner in which that business is conducted.

The International Accounting Standard (IAS) gives the following examples of events that would fall under this definition.

- The **sale or termination** of a line of business
- The **closure of business locations** in a country or region or the **relocation** of business activities from one country or region to another
- **Changes in management structure**
- **Fundamental reorganisations** that have a material effect on the **nature and focus** of the entity's operations

In order to make a provision, an obligation (legal or constructive) must exist at the period end. In this context, a constructive obligation exists only in the following circumstances.

- An entity must have a **detailed formal plan** for the restructuring.
- It must have raised a **valid expectation** in those affected that it will carry out the restructuring by starting to implement that plan or announcing its main features to those affected by it.

A management or board decision alone would not normally be sufficient.

The IAS states that a restructuring provision should include only the **direct expenditures** arising from the restructuring.

Onerous contracts

An **onerous contract** is a contract in which the unavoidable costs of meeting the obligations under the contract exceed the economic benefits expected to be received under it. An example might be a vacant leasehold property.

If an entity has a contract that is onerous, a provision must be made for the **net loss**.

Decommissioning provisions

A provision is only recognised from the date on which the **obligating event** occurs.

For example, when an oil company initially purchases an oil field it is put under a legal obligation to decommission the site at the end of its life. The legal obligation exists therefore on the initial expenditure on the field and therefore the liability exists immediately. The IAS also takes the view that the decommissioning costs may be capitalised as an asset representing future access to oil reserves (ie an asset and a provision are recognised).

Contingent assets

Contingent assets should not be recognised, as IAS 37 requires an entity to be virtually certain that it will receive an inflow of economic benefits. The asset is only recognised when it is virtually certain that there is an asset (unlike contingent liabilities, which although not recognised may nevertheless be provided for). The recognition of contingent assets in financial statements therefore represents a **risk** for auditors, and should be investigated thoroughly.

2.3.1 Audit procedures

The audit tests that should be carried out on provisions and contingent assets and liabilities are as follows.

- **Obtain details** of all **provisions** which have been included in the **accounts** and all **contingencies** that have been disclosed
- **Obtain** a **detailed analysis** of all **provisions** showing opening balances, movements and closing balances
- **Determine** for each material provision **whether** the **company** has a **present obligation** as a result of past events by:
  - **Reviewing** of **correspondence** relating to the item
  - **Discussion** with the **directors**. Have they created a valid expectation in other parties that they will discharge the obligation?
- **Determine** for each material provision **whether** it is **probable** that a **transfer of economic benefits** will be required to settle the obligation by:
  - **Checking** whether any **payments** have been **made** after the year end in respect of the item
  - **Reviewing of correspondence** with solicitors, banks, customers, the insurance company and suppliers both pre and post year end
  - **Sending** a **letter** to the **solicitors** to obtain their views (where relevant)
  - **Discussing** the **position** of similar **past provisions** with the directors. Were these provisions eventually settled?
  - **Considering** the **likelihood** of **reimbursement**
- **Recalculate** all **provisions** made
- **Compare** the **amount provided** with any post year end payments and with any amount paid in the past for similar items
- In the event that it is not possible to estimate the amount of the **provision**, check that a **contingent liability** is **disclosed** in the accounts
- **Consider** the **nature** of the **client's business**. Would you expect to see any other provisions, for example warranties?
- **Consider** whether disclosures of **provisions, contingent liabilities and contingent assets** are correct and sufficient

2.3.2 Obtaining audit evidence of contingencies

Part of ISA 501 *Audit evidence – specific considerations for selected items* covers contingencies relating to litigation and legal claims, which will represent the major part of audit work on contingencies. Litigation and claims involving the entity may have a material effect on the financial statements, and so will require adjustment to/disclosure in those financial statements.

> **ISA 501.9**
>
> The auditor shall design and perform audit procedures in order to identify litigation and claims involving the entity which may give rise to a risk of material misstatement.

Such procedures would include:

- **Making appropriate inquiries of management** including obtaining representations
- **Reviewing board minutes** and correspondence with the entity's lawyers
- **Examining legal expense** account
- **Using any information** obtained regarding the entity's business, including information obtained from discussions with any in-house legal department

> **ISA 501.10**
>
> If the auditor assesses a risk of material misstatement regarding litigation or claims that have been identified, or when audit procedures performed indicate that other material litigation or claims may exist, the auditor shall … seek direct communication with the entity's external legal counsel.

This will help to obtain sufficient appropriate audit evidence as to whether potential material litigation and claims are known and management's estimates of the financial implications, including costs, are reliable.

The International Standard on Auditing (ISA) discusses the form that the letter to the entity's external legal counsel should take.

> **ISA 501.10 (cont'd)**
>
> The auditor shall do so through a letter of inquiry, prepared by management and sent by the auditor, requesting the entity's external legal counsel to communicate directly with the auditor.

If it is thought unlikely that the external legal counsel will respond to a general enquiry, the letter should specify:

(a) A list of **litigation and claims**

(b) **Management's assessment** of the outcome of the litigation or claim and its estimate of the financial implications, including costs involved

(c) A request that the **external legal counsel confirm the reasonableness** of management's assessments and provide the auditor with further information if the list is considered by the lawyer to be incomplete or incorrect

The auditors must consider these matters up to the date of their report and so a further, updating letter may be necessary. Written representations must be provided that all actual or possible litigations and claims have been disclosed to the auditor.

A meeting between the auditors and the external legal counsel may be required, for example where a complex matter arises, or where there is a disagreement between management and the external legal counsel. Such meetings should take place only with the permission of management, and preferably with a management representative present.

> **ISA 501.11**
>
> If:
>
> (a) management refuses to give the auditor permission to communicate or meet with the entity's external legal counsel, or the entity's external legal counsel refuses to respond appropriately to the letter of inquiry, or is prohibited from responding; and
>
> (b) the auditor is unable to obtain sufficient appropriate audit evidence by performing alternative audit procedures,
>
> the auditor shall modify the opinion in the auditor's report in accordance with ISA 705.

Question
Provisions

In February 20X0 the directors of Newthorpe Engineering Co, a listed company, suspended the managing director. At a disciplinary hearing held by the company on 17 March 20X0 the managing director was dismissed for gross misconduct, and it was decided the managing director's salary should stop from that date and no redundancy or compensation payments should be made.

The managing director has claimed unfair dismissal and is taking legal action against the company to obtain compensation for loss of their employment. The managing director says they have a service contract with the company which would entitle them to two years' salary at the date of dismissal.

The financial statements for the year ended 30 April 20X0 record the resignation of the director. However, they do not mention their dismissal and no provision for any damages has been included in the financial statements.

Required

(a)   State how contingent liabilities should be disclosed in financial statements according to IAS 37 *Provisions, contingent liabilities and contingent assets.*

(b)   Describe the audit work you will carry out to determine whether the company will have to pay damages to the director for unfair dismissal, and the amount of damages and costs which should be included in the financial statements.

Note. Assume the amounts you are auditing are material.

Answer

(a)   IAS 37 states that a provision should be recognised in the accounts if:

(i)   An entity has a **present obligation** (legal or constructive) as a result of a past event
(ii)   A **transfer** of **economic benefits** will **probably** be **required** to settle the obligation
(iii) A **reliable estimate** can be **made** of the amount of the obligation

Under IAS 37 contingent liabilities should not be recognised. However, they should be disclosed unless the prospect of settlement is remote. The entity should disclose the following.

(i)   The **nature** of the liability
(ii)   An estimate of its **financial effect**
(iii) The **uncertainties** relating to any possible payments
(iv)   The likelihood of any **reimbursement**

(b)   The following tests should be carried out to determine whether the company will have to pay damages and the amount to be included in the financial statements.

(i)   **Review** the director's **service contract** and **ascertain** the **maximum amount** to which they would be entitled and the **provisions** in the service contract that would **prevent** them from making a **claim**, in particular those relating to grounds for justifiable dismissal.

(ii)   **Review** the results of the **disciplinary hearing. Consider** whether the company has acted in accordance with **employment legislation** and its **internal rules**, the **evidence** presented by the **company** and the defence made by the **director**.

(iii) **Review correspondence** relating to the case and **determine** whether the **company** has **acknowledged** any **liability** to the director that would mean that an amount for compensation should be accrued in accordance with IAS 37.

(iv)   **Review correspondence** with the company's **solicitors** and **obtain legal advice**, either from the company's solicitors or another firm, about the likelihood of the claim succeeding.

(v)   **Review** correspondence and contact the company's solicitors about the likely **costs** of the case.

(vi)   **Consider** the **likelihood** of **costs** and **compensation** being **reimbursed** by **reviewing** the company's **insurance arrangements** and contacting the insurance company.

(vii) **Consider** the **amounts** that should be **accrued** and the **disclosures** that should be made in the accounts. Legal costs should be accrued, but compensation payments should only be accrued if the company has admitted liability or legal advice indicates that the company's chances of success are very poor. However, the claim should be disclosed unless legal advice indicates that the director's chance of success appears to be remote.

(viii) Obtain **written representations** that all details relating to actual cases and other possible litigations have been disclosed to the auditor.

3 Expenses

> Borrowing costs must be capitalised as part of the cost of an asset if they are directly attributable to acquisition/construction/production. Other borrowing costs must be expensed.

3.1 Borrowing costs

IAS 23 *Borrowing costs* gives guidance on how to account for borrowing costs.

IAS 23 *Borrowing costs*

IAS 23 deals with the treatment of borrowing costs, often associated with the construction of **self-constructed assets**, but which may also be applied to an asset purchased that takes time to get ready for use/sale.

Definitions

- **Borrowing costs**. Interest and other costs incurred by an entity in connection with the borrowing of funds.
- **Qualifying asset**. An asset that necessarily takes a substantial period of time to get ready for its intended use or sale.

Accounting treatment

- Borrowing costs are interest and other costs incurred by an entity in connection with the borrowing of funds.
- **All eligible borrowing costs must be capitalised**.

Examples of borrowing costs include:

- Interest on bank overdrafts, short- and long-term borrowings
- Amortisation of discounts or premiums related to borrowings
- Amortisation of ancillary costs incurred with arrangement of borrowings
- Finance charges for finance leases
- Exchange differences as far as they are an adjustment to interest costs

---

The **cost of borrowing is interest**, which is disclosed in the statement of profit or loss and other comprehensive income.

Interest can often be audited by **analytical procedures**, as it has a predictable relationship with loans (for example, bank loans or debentures).

Alternatively, it can be **verified to payment records** (bank statements) **and loan agreement** documents.

However, if borrowing costs are capitalised in accordance with IAS 23, the auditor should carry out the following procedures.

- Agree figures in respect of interest payments made to statements from lender and/or bank statements
- Ensure interest is directly attributable to construction

3.2 IAS 19 *Employee benefits*

IAS 19 *Employee benefits* covers the accounting for post-employment benefits, and was revised in 2011. Pension schemes are the most obvious example, but an employer might provide post-employment death benefits to the dependants of former employees, or post-employment medical care.

Post-employment benefit schemes are often referred to as 'plans'. The 'plan' receives regular contributions from the employer (and sometimes from current employees as well) and the money is invested in assets, such as stocks and shares and other investments. The post-employment benefits are paid out of the income from the plan assets (dividends, interest) or from money from the sale of some plan assets.

There are two types or categories of post-employment benefit plan: defined contribution plans and defined benefit plans.

3.2.1 IAS 19 recap

Accounting for payments into defined contribution plans is straightforward.

(a) The obligation is determined by the amount paid into the plan in each period.

(b) There are no actuarial assumptions to make.

(c) If the obligation is settled in the current period (or at least no later than 12 months after the end of the current period), there is no requirement for discounting.

IAS 19 requires:

(a) Contributions to a defined contribution plan should be recognised as an expense in the period they are payable (except to the extent that labour costs may be included within the cost of assets).

(b) Any liability for unpaid contributions that are due as at the end of the period should be recognised as a liability (accrued expense).

(c) Any excess contributions paid should be recognised as an asset (prepaid expense), but only to the extent that the prepayment will lead to eg a reduction in future payments or a cash refund.

(d) Disclosure is required of a description of the plan and the amount recognised as an expense in the period.

Accounting for defined benefit plans is more complex, although the 2011 revisions to IAS 19 have meant that this area is no longer as complicated as it once was.

(a) The future benefits (arising from employee service in the current or previous years) cannot be estimated exactly but, whatever they are, the employer will have to pay them, and the liability should therefore be recognised now. To estimate these future obligations, it is necessary to use actuarial assumptions.

(b) The obligations payable in future years should be valued, by discounting, on a present value basis. This is because the obligations may be settled in many years' time.

(c) If actuarial assumptions change, the amount of required contributions to the fund will change, and there may be actuarial gains or losses. A contribution into a fund in any period is not necessarily the total for that period, due to actuarial gains or losses.

An outline of the method used for an employer to account for the expenses and obligation of a defined benefit plan is given below.

Step 1 **Determine the deficit or surplus**:

(a) An **actuarial technique** (the **Projected Unit Credit Method**) should be used to make a reliable estimate of the amount of future benefits employees have earned from service in relation to the current and previous years. The entity must determine how much benefit should be attributed to service performed by employees in the current period, and in previous periods. Assumptions include those about employee turnover, mortality rates and future increases in salaries (if these will affect the eventual size of future benefits, such as pension payments).

(b) The benefit should be **discounted** to arrive at the present value of the defined benefit obligation and the current service cost.

(c) The **fair value** of any **plan assets** should be deducted from the present value of the defined benefit obligation.

Step 2 The surplus or deficit determined in Step 1 may have to be adjusted if a net benefit asset has to be restricted by the **asset ceiling**.

Step 3 Determine the amounts to be recognised in **profit or loss**:

(a) **Current service cost**

(b) Any **past service cost** and **gain or loss on settlement**

(c) **Net interest** on the **net defined benefit (asset)**

Step 4 Determine the **remeasurements** of the **net defined benefit (asset)**, to be recognised in **other comprehensive income**:

(a) **Actuarial gains and losses**

(b) **Return on plan assets** (excluding amounts included in net interest on the net defined benefit liability (asset)

(c) Any change in the effect of the **asset ceiling** (excluding amounts included in net interest on the net defined benefit liability (asset)

In the statement of financial position, the amount recognised as a **defined benefit liability** (which may be a negative amount, ie an asset) should be:

(a) The **present value of the defined obligation** at the year end; **minus**

(b) The **fair value of the assets of the plan** as at the year end (if there are any) out of which the future obligations to current and past employees will be directly settled.

Plan assets are:

(a) Assets such as stocks and shares, held by a fund that is legally separate from the reporting entity, which exists solely to pay employee benefits

(b) Insurance policies, issued by an insurer that is not a related party, the proceeds of which can only be used to pay employee benefits

Investments which may be used for purposes other than to pay employee benefits are not plan assets.

The standard requires that the plan assets are measured at fair value, as 'the price that would be received to sell an asset in an orderly transaction between market participants at the measurement date'.

IAS 19 includes the following specific requirements.

(a) The plan assets should exclude any contributions due from the employer but not yet paid.

(b) Plan assets are reduced by any liabilities of the fund that do not relate to employee benefits, such as trade and other payables.

All the gains and losses that affect the plan obligation and plan asset must be recognised. The **components of defined benefit cost must be recognised as follows** in the statement of profit or loss and other comprehensive income.

Component	Recognised in
(a) **Service cost**	Profit or loss
(b) **Net interest on the net defined benefit liability**	Profit or loss
(c) **Remeasurements of the net defined benefit liability**	Other comprehensive income

3.2.2 Audit evidence

Area	Procedures
Scheme assets (including quoted and unquoted securities, debt instruments, properties)	• Ask directors to reconcile the scheme assets valuation at the scheme year-end date with the assets valuation at the reporting entity's date being used for IAS 19 purposes • Obtain direct confirmation of the scheme assets from the investment custodian • Consider requiring scheme auditors to perform procedures

Scheme liabilities	• Auditors must follow the principles of ISA 620 *Using the work of an auditor's expert* to assess whether it is appropriate to rely on the actuary's work
	
	• Specific matters would include:
	   – The source data used
	   – The assumptions and methods used
	   – The results of actuaries' work in the light of auditors' knowledge of the business and results of other audit procedures

	Actuarial source data is likely to include: • Scheme member data (for example, classes of member and contribution details) • Scheme asset information (for example, values and income and expenditure items)
Actuarial assumptions (for example, mortality rates, termination rates, retirement age, changes in salary and benefit levels)	Auditors will not have the same expertise as actuaries and are unlikely to be able to challenge the appropriateness and reasonableness of the assumptions. Auditors can, however, through discussion with directors and actuaries: • Obtain a general understanding of the assumptions and review the process used to develop them • Compare the assumptions with those which directors have used in previous years • Consider whether, based on their knowledge of the reporting entity and the scheme, and on the results of other audit procedures, the assumptions appear to be reasonable and compatible with those used elsewhere in the preparation of the entity's financial statements • Obtain written representations from directors confirming that the assumptions are consistent with their knowledge of the business
Items charged to operating profit (current service cost, past service cost, gains and losses on settlements and curtailments, interest)	• Discuss with directors and actuaries the factors affecting current service cost (for example, a scheme closed to new entrants may see an increase year on year as a percentage of pay with the average age of the workforce increasing)

Where the results of actuaries' work is inconsistent with the directors', additional procedures, such as requesting directors to obtain evidence from another actuary, may assist in resolving the inconsistency.

3.3 Share-based payment   12/08, 12/11

IFRS 2 *Share-based payment* sets out rules for the measurement of expenses relating to share-based payment schemes. These arise most commonly in relation to payments for employee services and professional services.

3.3.1 IFRS 2 Recap

IFRS 2 requires entities to recognise the goods or services received as a result of share-based payment transactions.

There are three types of share-based payment transactions.

(a) **Equity-settled share-based payment transactions**, in which the entity receives goods or services in exchange for equity instruments of the entity

(b) **Cash-settled share-based payment transactions**, in which the entity receives goods or services in exchange for amounts of cash that are based on the price (or value) of the entity's shares or other equity instruments of the entity

(c) Transactions, in which the entity receives or acquires goods or services and either the entity or the supplier has a **choice** as to whether the entity settles the transaction in cash (or other assets) or by issuing equity instruments

An entity should recognise goods or services received or acquired in a share-based payment transaction when it obtains the goods or as the services are received. They should be recognised as expenses unless they qualify for recognition as assets. Transactions are measured at fair value.

- Equity-settled transactions:

    DEBIT   Assets/expense
    CREDIT   Equity

- Cash-settled transactions:

    DEBIT   Asset/expense
    CREDIT   Liability

3.3.2 Audit risks and evidence

The general audit risk here is that the requirements of IFRS 2 are not adhered to. This is a complex area of financial reporting, particularly in practice, and is therefore risky to audit. The risk is that the share-based payment is not measured correctly in relation to any conditions attached to the scheme.

The auditor will require evidence in respect of all the estimates feeding into the IFRS 2 calculation, in addition to reperforming the calculation itself for the expense for the current year.

Issue	Evidence
Number of employees in scheme/**number of instruments per employee/length of vesting period**	Revenue scheme details set out in a contractual documentation
Number of employees estimated to benefit	<ul><li>Enquire of directors</li><li>Compare to staffing numbers per forecasts and prediction</li></ul>
Fair value of instruments	<ul><li>For equity-settled schemes check that fair value is estimated at **measurement date**</li><li>For cash-settled schemes check that the fair value is recalculated at the **year end** and at the **date of settlement**</li><li>Check that the model used to estimate fair value is in line with IFRS 2</li></ul>
General	Obtain written representations from management confirming their view that: <ul><li>The assumptions used in measuring the expense are reasonable</li><li>There are no share-based payment schemes in existence that have not been disclosed to the auditors</li></ul>

> A question in the December 2008 exam asked for a description of audit procedures in relation to share-based payments. A similar requirement appeared in the December 2011 paper.

4 Disclosure

FAST FORWARD ››

The auditor must ensure disclosures in the financial statements are fairly stated.

4.1 Segment reporting

The disclosure of segmental information is governed by IFRS 8 *Operating segments*.

IFRS 8 *Operating segments*

An **operating segment** is a component of an entity:

- That engages in business activities from which it may earn revenues and incur expenses (including revenues and expenses relating to transactions with other components of the same entity)
- Whose operating results are reviewed regularly by the entity's chief operating decision maker to make decisions about resources to be allocated to the segment and assess its performance
- For which discrete financial information is available

IFRS 8 requires an entity to report financial and descriptive information about its reportable segments. **Reportable segments** are operating segments or aggregations of operating segments that meet specified criteria:

- Reported revenue, from both external customers and intersegment sales or transfers, is 10% or more of the combined revenue, internal and external, of all operating segments; or
- The absolute measure of reported profit or loss is 10% or more of the greater, in absolute amount, of (i) the combined reported profit of all operating segments that did not report a loss and (ii) the combined reported loss of all operating segments that reported a loss; or
- Assets are 10% or more of the combined assets of all operating segments.

If the total external revenue reported by operating segments constitutes less than 75% of the entity's revenue, additional operating segments must be identified as reportable segments (even if they do not meet the quantitative thresholds set out above) until at least 75% of the entity's revenue is included in reportable segments.

ISA 501 *Audit evidence – specific considerations for selected items* contains specific guidance on segment reporting.

ISA 501.13

The auditor shall obtain sufficient appropriate audit evidence regarding the presentation and disclosure of segment information in accordance with the applicable financial reporting framework by:

(a) Obtaining an understanding of the methods used by management in determining segment information, and:

    (i) Evaluating whether such methods are likely to result in disclosure in accordance with the applicable financial reporting framework; and

    (ii) Where appropriate, testing the application of such methods; and

(b) Performing analytical procedures or other audit procedures appropriate in the circumstances

---

The following procedures are relevant.

- Obtain a client schedule of revenue workings
- Discuss with management the basis for the segmentation and ensure that the basis for segmentation mirrors that used for internal reporting purposes (IFRS 8)
- Verify a sample of items to backing documentation (invoices) to ensure disclosure is correct

A key risk for auditors here is **management bias** in disclosure. This risk is particularly pronounced because IFRS 8 takes a **management approach** to reportable segments, which opens up the possibility of management adjusting its approach in order to change the way segment information is disclosed. For example, there is a risk that loss-making segments could effectively go unreported or be hidden within other segments.

4.2 Earnings per share   6/09, 6/15

Accounting for EPS is governed by IAS 33 *Earnings per share*. It requires that companies of a certain size disclose their EPS for the year.

Basic EPS should be calculated by dividing the net profit or loss for the period attributable to ordinary equity holders by the weighted average number of ordinary shares outstanding during the period as follows.

$$\frac{\text{Net profit /(loss) attributable to ordinary shareholders}}{\text{Weighted average number of ordinary shares outstanding during the period}}$$

Question   Revision: basic EPS

Fontmell Co has profit of $1.5 million for the year ended 31 December 20X8. On 1 January 20X8 the company had 500,000 shares in issue. During 20X8 the company announced a rights issue as follows.

Rights: One new share for every five outstanding (100,000 new shares in total)

Exercise price: $5.00

Last date to exercise rights: 1 March 20X8

Market (fair) value of one share in Fontmell immediately prior to exercise on 1 March 20X8: $11.00

The EPS for 20X7 as originally stated was $2.20.

Answer

Computation of theoretical ex-rights price

$$\frac{\begin{array}{c}\text{Fair value of all outstanding shares +}\\ \text{total received from exercise of rights}\end{array}}{\begin{array}{c}\text{Number of shares outstanding prior to exercise +}\\ \text{number of shares issued in exercise}\end{array}} = \frac{(\$11.00 \times 500,000) + (\$5.00 \times 100,000)}{500,000 + 100,000} = \$10.00$$

20X8 EPS

$$\frac{\$1,500,000}{(500,000 \times {}^{2}\!/_{12} \times {}^{11}\!/_{10}) + (600,000 \times {}^{10}\!/_{12})} = \$2.54$$

20X7 EPS (restated)

$2.20 \times {}^{10}\!/_{11} = \$2.00$

Diluted EPS is calculated by adjusting the net profit attributable to ordinary shareholders and the weighted average number of shares outstanding for the effects of all dilutive potential ordinary shares.

These include:

- A **separate class of equity shares**, which at present is not entitled to any dividend, but will be entitled in future
- **Convertible loan** stock or **convertible preferred shares**
- **Options** or **warrants**

The calculation would be:

$$\frac{\text{Diluted earnings}}{\text{Diluted weighted average number of shares}}$$

	$
Diluted earnings = Basic earnings	X
Interest saved on convertible debt (net of tax saving)	X
	X
Diluted shares = Basic weighted average	X
Convertible debt: additional shares on conversion	X
Share options: potential shares less shares purchasable at FV	X
	X

Finally, if an entity reports a **discontinued operation** under IFRS 5 (see below), then it must **disclose the basic and diluted EPS** for the discontinued operation.

4.2.1 Audit issues

The size of the figure is unlikely to be material in itself, but it is a key investor figure. As it will be of **interest to all the investors** who read it, it is **material by its nature**.

When considering earnings per share, the auditor must consider **two issues**:

- Whether it has been disclosed on a comparable basis to the prior year, and whether any changes in accounting policy have been disclosed
- Whether it has been calculated correctly

A key audit risk is that the entity fails to meet IAS 33's disclosure requirements. These are:

(a) The amounts used as the **numerators** in calculating basic and diluted EPS, and a **reconciliation** of those amounts to the net profit or loss for the period

(b) The weighted average number of ordinary shares used as the **denominator** in calculating basic and diluted EPS, and a **reconciliation** of these denominators to each other

The audit procedures are:

- Obtain a copy of the client's workings for earnings per share. (If a simple calculation has been used, this can be checked by redoing the fraction on the face of the statement of profit or loss and other comprehensive income.)
- Compare the calculation with the prior year calculation to ensure that the basis is comparable.
- Discuss the basis with the directors if it has changed to ascertain if it is the best basis for the accounts this year and whether the change has been adequately disclosed.
- Recalculate to ensure that it is correct.

4.3 Discontinued operations

Discontinued operations are accounted for under IFRS 5 *Non-current assets held for sale and discontinued operations*. The IFRS requires that certain disclosures are made for discontinued operations in the statement of profit or loss and other comprehensive income or in the notes. This may well be material for the following reasons.

- Potentially material through **size**
- May be **inherently material** if the change in operations is a sign of management policy or a major change in focus of operations

Essentially, the fact that some operations have been discontinued is of interest to shareholders, which is why the IFRS 5 disclosures came about.

IFRS 5 requires that assets which meet the criteria 'held for sale' are shown at the lower of carrying amount and fair value less costs to sell, and that held for sale assets are classified separately in the statement of financial position and the results of discontinued operations are presented separately in the statement of profit or loss and other comprehensive income. Held for sale assets are discussed in Chapter 9.

To require separate classification in the statement of profit or loss and other comprehensive income, discontinued operations must be:

- A component (ie separately identifiable)
- Which represents a separate major line of business/geographical area
- Part of a single co-ordinated plan to dispose of a separate major line of business/geographical area
- Or is a subsidiary acquired exclusively with a view to resale

An entity should **present and disclose information** that enables users of the financial statements to evaluate the financial effects of **discontinued operations** and disposals of non-current assets or disposal groups.

This allows users to distinguish between operations which will continue in the future and those which will not and makes it more possible to predict future results.

An entity should disclose a **single amount** in the statement of profit or loss and other comprehensive income comprising the total of:

(a)   The **post-tax profit or loss** of discontinued operations; and

(b)   The post-tax gain or loss recognised on the **measurement to fair value less costs to sell** or on the disposal of the assets or disposal group(s) constituting the discontinued operation.

An entity should also disclose an **analysis** of this single amount into:

(a)   The revenue, expenses and pre-tax profit or loss of discontinued operations

(b)   The related income tax expense

(c)   The gain or loss recognised on the measurement to fair value less costs to sell or on the disposal of the assets of the discontinued operation

(d)   The related income tax expense

This may be presented either in the statement of profit or loss and other comprehensive income or in the notes. If it is presented in the statement of profit or loss and other comprehensive income it should be presented in a section identified as relating to discontinued operations, ie separately from continuing operations. This analysis is not required where the discontinued operation is a newly acquired subsidiary that has been classified as held for sale.

An entity should disclose the **net cash flows** attributable to the operating, investing and financing activities of discontinued operations. These disclosures may be presented either on the face of the statement of cash flows or in the notes.

Relevant audit procedures include:

- Obtaining accounting records for the component to ensure it is separately identifiable
- Review company documentation (such as annual report) to ensure it is separately identifiable
- Review minutes of meetings/make enquiries of management Audit to ascertain management's intentions

To audit whether the disclosures have been made correctly, the auditor should undertake the following procedures.

- Obtain a copy of the client's workings to disclose the discontinued operations
- Review the workings to ensure that the figures are reasonable and agree to the financial statements
- Trace a sample of items disclosed as discontinuing items to backing documentation (invoices) to ensure that they do relate to discontinued operations

4.4 Statements of cash flows

Statements of cash flows are accounted for under the provisions of IAS 7 *Statement of cash flows*. The statement of cash flows is essentially a reconciliation exercise between items in the statement of profit or loss and other comprehensive income (operating profit) and the statement of financial position (cash).

As such, the statement of cash flows is often audited **by the auditor reproducing it from the audited figures in the other financial statements**. This can be done quickly and easily using computer programmes.

However, if the auditor wished to audit it another way, they could check and recalculate each reconciliation with the financial statements. This would involve checking each line of the statement by working through the client's workings and agreeing items to the accounting records and backing documentation (for example, tax paid to the bank statements) and the other financial statements.

Question   Statement of cash flows

Why is the statement of cash flows relevant to the auditors?

Answer

Report on the statement of cash flows

The statement of cash flows is specified in the auditor's report as a statement the auditors are reporting on. Financial reports are obliged to include a statement of cash flows under IAS 7 in order to show a true and fair view. The auditors must therefore assess the truth and fairness of the statement of cash flows as required by IAS 7.

Analytical procedures

The information in the statement of cash flows will be used by the auditors as part of their analytical procedures, for example, by adding further information on liquidity. This will be particularly helpful when comparing the statement to previous periods.

Going concern

The statement of cash flows may indicate going concern problems due to liquidity failings, overtrading and overgearing. However, the statement is an historical document, prepared well after the year-end, and is therefore unlikely to be the first indicator of such difficulties.

Audit evidence

The auditors will obtain very little direct audit evidence from the statement of cash flows. It has been prepared by the company (not the auditors or an independent third party) from records which are under scrutiny by the auditors in any case. Thus the auditors will already have most of this information, albeit in a different format.

However, the statement of cash flows should provide additional evidence for figures in the accounts, for example, the purchase or sale of tangible non-current assets. Consistency of evidence will be important and complementary evidence is always welcome.

 | Question | Accounting issues and audit evidence

You work for Pitmans, a firm of Chartered Certified Accountants. Tinga Co is a longstanding client of your firm, but this is the first year that Pitmans has carried out the audit. The firm also provides a number of other services to Tinga, including a range of tax planning services and business advisory services. Recently, the firm undertook a review of some forecast financial statements, which Tinga was required to present to the bank.

You have been asked to plan the forthcoming audit of the financial statements for the period ending 31 March 20X8. You have been given the following draft statement of financial position.

	20X8		20X7	
	$'000	$'000	$'000	$'000
Assets				
Non-current assets				
Tangible non-current assets		10,101		12,378
Investments		10,000		2,000
Current assets				
Inventory	196		191	
Receivables	1,012		678	
Bank	–		149	
Prepayments	4		5	
		1,212		1,023
		21,313		15,401
Equity and liabilities				
Equity				
Share capital		100		100
Share premium		1,000		1,000
Revaluation reserve		2,000		–
Retained earnings		(5,217)		(8,601)
		(2,117)		(7,501)
Long-term liabilities				
Bank loan		12,325		17,002
Deferred tax		5,000		5,000
Current liabilities				
Trade payables	938		900	
Bank overdraft	1,168		–	
Bank loan	3,999		–	
		6,105		900
		21,313		15,401

Required

Comment on any points arising for your planning of the audit for the year end 31 March 20X8. Your comments should include issues relating to risk and materiality, accounting issues and audit evidence issues and any limitations of the review you have undertaken to date. You should also highlight any further information that you intend to seek.

You work for Pitmans, a firm of Chartered Certified Accountants. Tinga Co is a longstanding client of your firm, but this is the first year that Pitmans has carried out the audit. The firm also provides a number of other services to Tinga, including a range of tax planning services and business advisory services. Recently, the firm undertook a review of some forecast financial statements, which Tinga was required to present to the bank.

You have been asked to plan the forthcoming audit of the financial statements for the period ending 31 March 20X8. You have been given the following draft statement of financial position.

	20X8		20X7	
	$'000	$'000	$'000	$'000
Assets				
Non-current assets				
Tangible non-current assets		10,101		12,378
Investments		10,000		2,000
Current assets				
Inventory	196		191	
Receivables	1,012		678	
Bank	–		149	
Prepayments	4		5	
		1,212		1,023
		21,313		15,401
Equity and liabilities				
Equity				
Share capital		100		100
Share premium		1,000		1,000
Revaluation reserve		2,000		–
Retained earnings		(5,217)		(8,601)
		2,117		7,501
Long-term liabilities				
Bank loan		12,325		17,002
Deferred tax		5,000		5,000
Current liabilities				
Trade payables	938		900	
Bank overdraft	1,168		–	
Bank loan	3,999		–	
		6,105		900
		21,313		15,401

Required

Comment on any points arising for your planning of the audit for the year end 31 March 20X8. Your comments should include issues relating to risk and materiality, accounting issues and audit evidence issues and any limitations of the review you have undertaken to date. You should also highlight any further information that you intend to seek.

Answer

Matters arising from preliminary review

Going concern

The statements of financial position show a worsening cash position over the year. There are some classic indicators of going concern problems.

- Substantial liabilities
- Excess of current liabilities over current assets
- Bank overdraft
- Substantial increase in receivables
- Bank requiring future profit forecasts, which have been verified by our firm

A profit has been made in the year, but it does not appear that sales are readily being converted into cash.

Sources of audit evidence

- Profit forecasts
- Correspondence with bank
- Any business plans in existence (consult with business advisory department)

Further information required

- We need to confirm for the audit file why the bank required profit forecasts.
- We need to review for audit purposes the results of our work on those forecasts.
- For the purposes of our audit we must satisfy ourselves that Tinga is a going concern.

Three items on the accounts stand out as being particularly interesting at the planning stage. These are:

- Deferred tax
- Increase in investments
- Revaluation in the year

Deferred tax

We will need to confirm what the deferred tax relates to, particularly as the non-current assets in the statement of financial position do not seem particularly high. The deferred tax balance does not appear to have moved, despite the movements on non-current assets. We will have to check that deferred tax has been accounted for correctly in accordance with IAS 12.

Increase in investments

Investments are usually a straightforward area to audit, with good audit evidence existing in terms of share certificates and valuation certificates.

However, as investments have increased, we must ensure that they have been accounted for correctly. We must also ensure that the increase does not represent a holding in another company that would require the results being consolidated into group results.

Revaluation

There appears to have been a revaluation in the year, although non-current assets have in fact decreased. We must discover what the revaluation reserve relates to, and ensure that it has been accounted for correctly.

Materiality

All the accounting issues discussed above are potentially material to the statement of financial position. Non-current assets is the key balance which does not show a liability. As the statement of financial position shows high liabilities, any as yet unrecorded impairment in either tangible non-current assets or investments could make the position of the company significantly worse. Conversely, if the liability shown in deferred tax was overstated, this would have the reverse effect.

Limitations of current review

The current review has only taken account of the statement of financial position, so is an incomplete picture. At present, we can only guess at factors in the statement of profit or loss and other comprehensive income which have had implications for the statement of financial position.

As this is a first year audit, and the audit department is not familiar with this client, we have little knowledge of the business to apply to this review.

It is important as part of the planning process that the audit partner and/or manager enter into discussions with the various departments which have dealings with Tinga to increase their knowledge of the business and to obtain audit evidence on such issues as going concern.

However, it is also important for the audit team to bear in mind that, as auditors, they must maintain their independence towards the audit. There is a danger to the audit firm of loss of objectivity in respect of this audit due to the other services offered to the client, which must not be forgotten.

4.5 Changes in accounting policy and errors   12/11, 6/14

FAST FORWARD

Changes in accounting policy and errors must be accounted for retrospectively, according to IAS 8.

4.5.1 Accounting policies and estimates

Where accounting standards allow alternative treatment of items in the accounts, then the accounting policy note should declare which policy has been chosen. It should then be applied consistently.

The effect of a change in accounting policy is treated as a retrospective adjustment to the opening balance of each affected component of equity as if the accounting policy had always applied.

IAS 8 *Accounting policies, changes in accounting estimates and errors* states that changes in accounting policies are rare, and only allowed if required by statute or if the change results in more reliable and relevant information.

Take care not to confuse a change in **accounting policy** with a **change in accounting estimate**. A change in policy is rare and per IAS 8 should be **accounted for retrospectively**, but a change in estimate (such as the method for calculating depreciation) is accounted for going forward (prospectively). In real life, clients may not want to make a change in accounting policy because of the work involved in retrospectively restating the financial statements (in reality, restating opening retained earnings and the comparatives), and because of the extensive disclosures that are required by IAS 8.

Exam focus point

This distinction was examined in the December 2011 paper, which contained a scenario in which a client wanted to account retrospectively for a change in accounting estimate (which is wrong).

An example of a change in **accounting estimate** is a change to an entity's **depreciation policy**. In this case, the entity's accounting **policy** is **to depreciate non-current assets**, and the 'depreciation policy' (which would include eg reducing balance or straight line depreciation, estimates of useful lives, etc) is merely the policy chosen by management in order to estimate how much depreciation should be charged.

Changes in accounting policy will be rare and should be made only if :

(a)   The change is required by an IFRS; or

(b)   The change will result in a **more appropriate presentation** of events or transactions in the financial statements of the entity, providing more reliable and relevant information.

The standard highlights two types of event which do **not** constitute changes in accounting policy:

(a)   Adopting an accounting policy for a **new type of transaction** or event not dealt with previously by the entity

(b)   Adopting a **new accounting policy** for a transaction or event which has not occurred in the past or which was not material

4.5.2 Prior period errors

By 'error', IAS 8 means mathematical mistakes, mistakes in applying accounting policies, oversights or misinterpretations of facts, and fraud.

If an error is discovered in the prior period financial statements, then IAS 8 states that it must be **corrected retrospectively** (like a change in accounting policy). This means restating opening retained earnings and comparatives, and does not affect, for example, profit in the current period.

BPP
LEARNING MEDIA

Part D Audit of historical financial information │ **10: Evaluation and review (III) – matters relating to specific accounting issues**

329

Chapter Roundup

- Revenue recognition is an extremely important issue, with both the completeness and occurrence assertions being important.

- The relevant financial statement assertions for liabilities are completeness, rights and obligations and existence. Liabilities must be tested for understatement.

- The classification of a lease can have a material effect on the financial statements.

- The auditor needs to audit the movement on the deferred tax liability.

- A provision is accounted for as a liability; contingencies are disclosed, so auditors must ensure they have been classified correctly according to IAS 37.

- Borrowing costs must be capitalised as part of the cost of an asset if they are directly attributable to acquisition/construction/production. Other borrowing costs must be expensed.

- The auditor must ensure that disclosures in the financial statements are fairly stated.

- Changes in accounting policy and errors must be accounted for retrospectively, according to IAS 8.

1   Complete the definition:

A .... lease is one that transfers substantially all the .... and .... incident to ownership of an asset.

2   Sort the following valuation tests into those relevant for finance leases and those relevant to operating leases.

- Obtain client's workings
- Ensure interest calculated in accordance with IAS 17
- Agree the opening position
- Agree new assets to lease agreements
- Verify payments to bank statements

3   Name three types of contingency often disclosed by companies.

(1)   ....

(2)   ....

(3)   ....

4   The auditor may request information directly from the client's solicitors.

True   ☐   False   ☐

5   Link the disclosure issue with the accounting guidance.

(a)	Segmental information	(i)	IFRS 15
(b)	EPS	(ii)	IFRS 8
(c)	Discontinued operations	(iii)	IFRS 5
(d)	Revenue recognition	(iv)	IAS 33

6   Why is EPS disclosure likely to be material?

7   Which of the following is not a reason why revenue is often audited by analytical procedures?

(1)   Availability of good, comparable evidence

(2)   Statement of profit or loss and other comprehensive income is not as important as statement of financial position

(3)   It is quicker than detailed substantive testing

(4)   Revenue has logical relationships with other items in the financial statements

8   Which of the following audit procedures relate to capitalised grants, and which relate to grants put straight to income?

- Obtain relating documentation and ensure classification is correct

- Agree value receipt of grant to:
  - Documentation (above)
  - Bank statements

- Consider reasonableness of transfers to revenue

- Ensure capitalisation method is comparable

9   Auditors do not report on the statement of cash flows (only the statement of financial position and statement of profit or loss and other comprehensive income as recorded in the opinion section of the report).

True   ☐   False   ☐

Answers to Quick Quiz

1   Finance, risks, rewards

2
- Obtain client's workings   F
- Ensure interest calculated in accordance with IAS 17   F
- Agree the opening position   F
- Agree new assets to lease agreements   F
- Verify payments to bank statements   F and O

3   From:

     (1)   Guarantees
     (2)   Discounted bills of exchange
     (3)   Uncalled liabilities on shares
     (4)   Lawsuits/claims pending
     (5)   Options to purchase assets

4   True. However the letter should be written by management and sent by the auditor.

5   (a)(ii), (b)(iv), (c)(iii), (d)(i)

6   It is of interest to the key users of financial statements – the shareholders.

7   (2) The statement of profit or loss and other comprehensive income **is just as important**. However, (3) **is true**, because it is cost effective to use analytical procedures where good evidence is available.

8
- Obtain relating documentation and ensure classification is correct.   C/I

- Agree value receipt of grant to: C/I

      –   Documentation (above)
      –   Bank statements

- Consider reasonableness of transfers to revenue   C

- Ensure capitalisation method is comparable   C

9   False

Now try the questions below from the Practice Question Bank.

Number	Level	Marks	Time
Q15	Examination	15	29 mins
Q16	Examination	20	39 mins
Q17	Examination	20	39 mins

11

Group audits and transnational audits

Topic list	Syllabus reference
1 Group accounting recap	D4
2 Associates and joint ventures recap	D4
3 Audit of groups	D4
4 The consolidation: problems and procedures	D4
5 Joint audits	D4
6 Transnational audits	G2

Introduction

This is a new auditing topic for you, one which is concerned with practical difficulties of communication between auditors and the issues of geography.

In auditing group accounts, as in so many other areas, the auditors require detailed accounting knowledge in order to fulfil their responsibilities.

Group audits fall into two categories:

(1) Where the same firm of auditors audits the whole group

(2) Where one firm of auditors has responsibility for the opinion on the consolidated accounts and a different firm audits part of the group

Even where the audit of each individual company in the group is carried out by the same firm, there may be administrative complications where some audits are carried out by different branches, perhaps overseas, with different practices and procedures.

Study guide

		Intellectual level
D4	**Group audits**	
(a)	Recognise the specific matters to be considered before accepting appointment as group auditor to a group in a given situation.	3
(b)	Explain the responsibilities of the component auditor before accepting appointment, and the procedures to be performed in a group situation.	2
(c)	Identify and explain the matters specific to planning an audit or group financial statements including assessment of group and component materiality, the impact of non-coterminous year ends within a group, and changes in group structure.	2
(d)	Justify the situations where a joint audit would be appropriate.	2
(e)	Recognise the audit problems and describe audit procedures specific to a business combination, including goodwill, accounting policies, inter-company trading, the classification of investments, equity accounting for associates, changes in group structure and accounting for a foreign subsidiary.	3
(f)	Identify and explain the audit risks, and necessary audit procedures relevant to the consolidation process.	3
(g)	Identify and describe the matters to be considered and the procedures to be performed at the planning stage when a group auditor considers the use of the work of component auditors.	3
(h)	Consider how the group auditor should evaluate the audit work performed by a component auditor.	2
(i)	Explain the implications for the auditor's report on the financial statements of an entity where the opinion on a component is qualified or otherwise modified in a given situation.	2
G2	**Transnational audits**	
(a)	Define 'transnational audits' and explain the role of the Transnational Audit Committee (TAC) of IFAC.	1
(b)	Discuss how transnational audits may differ from other audits of historical financial information (eg in terms of applicable financial reporting and auditing standards, listing requirements and corporate governance requirements).	2

Exam guide

Group audits are likely to be tested in case study type questions. Exam questions may focus on the audit of group financial statements, or on the requirements of the group auditor to report to management on matters all around the group.

1 Group accounting recap

FAST FORWARD

> A group of companies is required to prepare consolidated group financial statements. This entails the audit risk that the IFRS in this area are not complied with.

You will have covered IFRS 3 *Business combinations* in your studies for Papers F7 and P2. The other accounting standards relating to groups are:

- IAS 27 (Revised) *Separate financial statements*
- IFRS 10 *Consolidated financial statements*
- IFRS 11 *Joint arrangements*
- IFRS 12 *Disclosure of interests in other entities*
- IAS 28 *Investments in associates*

The key points that you should be aware of are summarised below. You can work through this section fairly quickly, as most of the material should already be familiar to you.

1.1 Content of group accounts

Consolidated (or group) accounts combine the information contained in the separate financial statements of a holding company and its subsidiaries as if they were the financial statements of a single entity.

Key terms

> **Control.** The power to govern the financial and operating policies of an entity so as to obtain benefits from its activities. *(IFRS 3 (revised), IFRS 10)*
>
> **Associate.** An entity, including an unincorporated entity such as a partnership, in which an investor has significant influence and which is neither a subsidiary nor an interest in a joint venture. *(IAS 28)*
>
> **Significant influence** is the power to participate in the financial and operating policy decisions of the investee but is not control or joint control over those policies. *(IAS 28)*
>
> **Joint arrangement.** An arrangement of which two or more parties have **joint control**. *(IAS 28)*
>
> **Joint control.** The **contractually agreed sharing of control** of an arrangement, which exists only when decisions about the relevant activities require the unanimous consent of the parties sharing control. *(IAS 28)*
>
> **Joint venture.** A joint arrangement whereby the parties that have joint control (the joint venturers) of the arrangement have **rights to the net assets** of the arrangement. *(IAS 28, IFRS 11)*
>
> **Contingent consideration.** Usually, an obligation of the **acquirer** to transfer additional assets or **equity** (IFRS 3 (Revised)) **interests** to the former owners of an **acquiree** as part of the exchange for **control** of the **acquiree** if specified future events occur or conditions are met. *(IFRS 3 (Revised))*
>
> **Fair value.** The price that would be received to sell an asset or paid to transfer a liability in an orderly transaction between market at the measurement date. *(IFRS 13)*

Before discussing IFRS 3 in detail, we can summarise the different types of investment **and** the required accounting for them as follows.

Investment	Criteria	Required treatment in group accounts
Subsidiary	Control	Full consolidation
Associate	Significant influence	Equity accounting
Joint venture	Contractual arrangement	Equity accounting
Investment which is none of the above	Asset held for accretion of wealth	As for single company accounts per IFRS 9

1.2 Identifying a business combination

IFRS 3 requires entities to determine whether a transaction or other event is a business combination by applying the definition in the International Financial Reporting Standard (IFRS).

1.3 The acquisition method

Entities must account for each business combination by applying the **acquisition method**. This requires:

(a) **Identifying the acquirer**. This is generally the party that obtains control.

(b) **Determining the acquisition date**. This is generally the date the consideration is legally transferred, but it may be another date if control is obtained on that date.

(c) Recognising and measuring the **identifiable assets acquired, the liabilities assumed** and any non-controlling interest in the acquiree (see below).

(d) Recognising and measuring goodwill or a gain from a bargain purchase.

1.4 Acquisition-related costs

Under IFRS 3 **costs relating to the acquisition must be recognised as an expense** at the time of the acquisition. They are not regarded as an asset. (Costs of issuing debt or equity are to be accounted for under the rules of IFRS 9.)

1.5 Contingent consideration

IFRS 3 (Revised) **requires recognition of contingent consideration, measured at fair value, at the acquisition date**.

IFRS 3 (Revised) defines contingent consideration as:

> 'Usually, an obligation of the acquirer to transfer additional assets or equity interests to the former owners of an acquiree as part of the exchange for control of the acquiree if specified future events occur or conditions are met. However, contingent consideration also may give the acquirer the right to the return of previously transferred consideration if specified conditions are met.'

1.5.1 IFRS 3

IFRS 3 recognises that, by entering into an acquisition, the acquirer becomes obliged to make additional payments. Not recognising that obligation means that the consideration recognised at the acquisition date is not fairly stated.

IFRS 3 **requires recognition of contingent consideration, measured at fair value, at the acquisition date**. This is arguably consistent with how other forms of consideration are fair valued.

The acquirer may be required to pay contingent consideration in the form of equity or of a debt instrument or cash. Debt instruments are presented in accordance with IAS 32. Contingent consideration may occasionally be an asset, for example if the consideration has already been transferred and the acquirer has the right to the return of part of it, an asset may occasionally be recognised in respect of that right.

1.5.2 Post-acquisition changes in the fair value of the contingent consideration

The treatment depends on the circumstances:

(a) If the change in fair value is due to additional information obtained that affects the position at the acquisition date, goodwill should be remeasured.

(b) If the change is due to events which took place after the acquisition date; for example, meeting earnings targets:

    (i) Account for under IFRS 9 if the consideration is in the form of a financial instrument, for example loan notes

(ii)   Account for under IAS 37 if the consideration is in the form of cash

(iii)   An equity instrument is not remeasured

1.6 Goodwill and the non-controlling interest

1.6.1 IFRS 3 methods – an introduction

The revised IFRS 3 views the group as an economic entity. This means that it treats all providers of equity – including non-controlling interests – as shareholders in the group, even if they are not shareholders of the parent. Thus goodwill will arise on the non-controlling interest. We now need to consider how IFRS 3 (revised) sets out the calculation for goodwill.

1.6.2 IFRS 3 goodwill calculation

In words, IFRS 3 states:

'Consideration paid by parent + fair value of non-controlling interest – fair value of the subsidiary's net identifiable assets = consolidated goodwill'

1.6.3 BPP proforma goodwill calculation

The proforma goodwill calculation should be set out like this.

	$	$
Consideration transferred		X
Non-controlling interests		X
Net assets acquired as represented by:		
Ordinary share capital	X	
Share premium	X	
Retained earnings on acquisition	X	
		(X)
Goodwill		X

1.6.4 Valuing non-controlling interest at acquisition

The non-controlling interest may be valued **either at fair value or at the non-controlling interest's proportionate share of the acquiree's identifiable net assets**.

The non-controlling interest now forms part of the calculation of goodwill. The question now arises as to how it should be valued.

The 'economic entity' principle suggests that the non-controlling interest should be valued at fair value. In fact, IFRS 3 gives a **choice**.

'For each business combination, the acquirer shall measure any non-controlling interest in the acquiree **either at fair value or at the non-controlling interest's proportionate share of the acquiree's identifiable net assets**.' *(IFRS 3)*

IFRS 3 suggests that the closest approximation to fair value will be the market price of the shares held by the non-controlling shareholders just before the acquisition by the parent.

Non-controlling interest at fair value will be different from non-controlling interest at proportionate share of the acquiree's net assets. The difference is goodwill attributable to non-controlling interest, which may be, but often is not, proportionate to goodwill attributable to the parent.

1.7 Investment in subsidiaries

The important point here is **control**. In most cases, this will involve the parent company owning a majority of the ordinary shares in the subsidiary (to which normal voting rights are attached). There are

circumstances, however, when the parent may own only a minority of the voting power in the subsidiary, **but** the parent still has control.

IFRS 10 *Consolidated financial statements* retains **control** as the key concept underlying the parent/subsidiary relationship but it has broadened the definition and clarified its application.

IFRS 10 states that an investor **controls** an investee if and only if it has all of the following.

(a)   **Power** over the investee
(b)   Exposure or rights, to **variable returns** from its involvement with the investee
(c)   The **ability to use its power** over the investee to affect the amount of the investor's returns

Accounting treatment in group financial statements

IFRS 10 requires a parent to present consolidated financial statements, in which the financial statements of the parent and subsidiary (or subsidiaries) are combined and presented **as a single entity**.

1.8 Consolidation process

The following summaries provide revision of the basic consolidation technique.

Summary of technique: consolidated statement of financial position

Step 1   Read the question and draw up the group structure (W1), highlighting useful information:

– The percentage owned
– Acquisition date
– Pre-acquisition reserves

Step 2   Draw up a proforma taking into account the group structure identified:

– Leave out cost of investment
– Put in a line for goodwill
– Put in a line for investment in associate
– Remember to include non-controlling interests
– Leave lines in case of any additions

Step 3   Work methodically down the statement of financial position, transferring:

– Figures to proforma or workings

– 100% of all assets/liabilities controlled at the year end aggregated in brackets on face of proforma, ready for adjustments

– Cost of subsidiary/associate and reserves to group workings, setting them up as you work down the statement of financial position

– Share capital and share premium (parent only) to face of proforma answer

– Open up a (blank) working for non-controlling interests

Step 4   Read through the additional notes and attempt the adjustments showing workings for all calculations.

Do the double entry for the adjustments onto your proforma answer and onto your group workings (where the group workings are affected by one side of the double entry).

Examples:

Cancel any intra-group items eg current account balances, loans

Adjust for unrealised profits:

Unrealised profit on intra-group sales	X	
% held in inventories at year end	%	
= Provision for unrealised profit (PUP)	X	DR Retained earnings
(adjust in company **selling** goods)		CR Group inventories

Make fair value adjustments:

	Acq'n date	Movement	Year end
Inventories	X	(X)	X
Depreciable non-current assets	X	(X)	X
Non-depreciable non-current assets	X	(X)	X
Other fair value adjustments	X/(X)	(X)/X	X/(X)
	X	(X)	X
	This total appears in the goodwill working	This total is used to adjust the subsidiary's reserves in the reserves working.	The individual figures here are used to adjust the relevant balances on the consolidated statement of financial position.

Step 5

Complete goodwill calculation:

Consideration transferred	X
Non-controlling interests (at % fair value (FV) of net assets or at 'full' FV)	X
Less net fair value of identifiable assets acquired and liabilities assumed:	

Share capital	X	
Share premium	X	
Retained earnings at acquisition	X	
Other reserves at acquisition	X	
Fair value adjustments at acquisition	X	
		(X)
		X
Less impairment losses on goodwill to date		(X)
		X

Step 6

Complete the consolidated retained earnings calculation:

	Parent	Subsidiary	Assoc
Per question	X	X	X
Adjustments	X/(X)	X/(X)	X/(X)
Fair value adjustments movement		X/(X)	X/(X)
Pre-acquisition retained earnings		(X)	(X)
Group share of post acq'n ret'd earnings:		Y	Z
Subsidiary (Y × %)	X		
Associate (Z × %)	X		
Less group share of impairment losses to date	(X)		
	X		

Note. Other reserves are treated in a similar way.

Step 7 Complete 'Investment in associate' calculation:

Cost of associate	X
Share of post-acquisition retained reserves (from reserves working Z × %)	X
Less group impairment losses on associate to date	(X)
	X

Complete the non-controlling interests (NCI) calculation:

NCI at acquisition (from goodwill working)	X
NCI share of post acq'n reserves (from reserves working Y × NCI %)	X
Less: NCI share of impairment losses (only if NCI at 'full' FV at acq'n)	(X)
	X

Summary of technique: consolidated statement of profit or loss and other comprehensive income

Overview

The statement of profit or loss and other comprehensive income shows a true and fair view of the group's activities since acquisition of any subsidiaries.

(a) The top part of the statement of profit or loss and other comprehensive income shows the income, expenses, profit and other comprehensive income controlled by the group.

(b) The reconciliation at the bottom of the statement of profit or loss and other comprehensive income shows the ownership of those profits and total comprehensive income.

Method

Step 1 Read the question and draw up the group structure and where subsidiaries/associates are acquired in the year identify the proportion to consolidate. A timeline may be useful.

Step 2 Draw up a proforma:

- Remember the non-controlling interests reconciliation at the foot of the statement

Step 3 Work methodically down the statement of profit or loss and other comprehensive income, transferring figures to proforma or workings:

- 100% of all income/expenses (time apportioned $\times\ ^{x}/_{12}$ if appropriate) in brackets on face of proforma, ready for adjustments

- Exclude dividends receivable from subsidiary

- Subsidiary's profit for the year (PFY) and total comprehensive income (TCI) (for NCI) to face of proforma in brackets (or to a working if many adjustments)

- Associate's PFY and other comprehensive income (OCI) to face of proforma in brackets

Step 4 Go through question, calculating the necessary adjustments showing workings for all calculations, transfer the numbers to your proforma and make the adjustments in the non-controlling interests working where the subsidiary's profit is affected.

Step 5 Calculate 'Share of profit of associate' and 'Share of other comprehensive income of associate' (where appropriate):

A's Profit for the year (PFY) × Group %	X
Any group impairment loss recognised on the associate during the period	(X)
	X

Shown before group profit before tax.

A's Other comprehensive income (OCI) × Group %   X

Both the associate's profit or loss and OCI are calculated based on after tax figures.

Step 6   Complete NCI in subsidiary's PFY and TCI calculation:

	PFY	TCI (if req'd)
PFY/TCI per question (time-apportioned × $^x/_{12}$ if appropriate)	X	X
Adjustments, eg PUP on sales made by S	(X)/X	(X)/X
Impairment losses (if NCI held at FV)	(X)	(X)
	X	X
× NCI%	X	X

2 Associates and joint ventures recap   6/15

Much of this will be revision from your earlier studies, but there are some significant changes to concepts and definitions introduced by IFRSs 10 and 11 and the revised IAS 28.

2.1 Investments in associates

This type of investment is something less than a subsidiary, but more than a simple investment (nor is it a joint venture). The key criterion here is **significant influence**. This is defined as the 'power to participate', but **not** to 'control' (which would make the investment a subsidiary).

Significant influence can be determined by the holding of voting rights (usually attached to shares) in the entity. IAS 28 states that if an investor holds **20% or more** of the voting power of the investee, it can be presumed that the investor has significant influence over the investee, **unless** it can be clearly shown that this is not the case.

Significant influence can be presumed **not** to exist if the investor holds **less than 20%** of the voting power of the investee, unless it can be demonstrated otherwise.

The **existence of significant influence** is evidenced in one or more of the following ways.

(a)   Representation on the **board of directors** (or equivalent) of the investee
(b)   Participation in the **policy making process**
(c)   **Material transactions** between investor and investee
(d)   Interchange of **management personnel**
(e)   Provision of **essential technical information**

Exam focus point

This area was tested in the June 2015 paper with a scenario in which management claimed that an investment was an associate, but held 52% of its equity shares. Its reason was that the entity's activities were not integrated with those of the group. Students sitting this exam would have needed to fall back on their knowledge from this section, discussing whether there was significant influence or whether the 52% shareholding indicated control.

Accounting treatment in group financial statements

IAS 28 requires the use of the **equity method** of accounting for investments in associates.

Financial statement	Treatment	
Statement of profit or loss and other comprehensive income	Profit before tax	Parent and subsidiary = group share of associate's profit after tax
	Other comprehensive income	Group share of associate's other comprehensive income
Statement of financial position	Interest in associated companies should be stated at:	$ Cost X Share of total comprehensive income for the year X — X — Also disclose group's share of post-acquisition reserves of associated companies and movements therein

2.2 Accounting for investments in joint arrangements

IFRS 11 classes joint arrangements as either **joint operations** or **joint ventures**. The classification of a joint arrangement as a joint operation or a joint venture depends on the rights and obligations of the parties to the arrangement.

Joint arrangements (joint ventures and joint operations) are dealt with by IFRS 11 *Joint arrangements*.

Key terms

> **Joint arrangement.** An arrangement of which two or more parties have **joint control**. *(IAS 28)*
>
> **Joint control.** The **contractually agreed sharing of control** of an arrangement, which exists only when decisions about the relevant activities require the unanimous consent of the parties sharing control. *(IAS 28)*
>
> **Joint venture.** A joint arrangement whereby the parties that have joint control (the joint venturers) of the arrangement have **rights to the net assets** of the arrangement. *(IAS 28, IFRS 11)*

Joint arrangements can be:

Type of joint arrangement	Explanation
Not structured through a separate vehicle	Joint ventures
Structured through a separate vehicle	Joint venture **or** joint operation, depending on: • Legal form of the separate vehicle • Terms of contract • Other facts and circumstances

Accounting treatment in group financial statements

Prior to the new group accounting standards issued in 2011, the old standard on joint ventures (IAS 31) permitted either equity accounting or proportionate consolidation to be used for joint ventures. **The choice has now been removed, and the equity method must be used**. (Proportionate consolidation meant including the investor's share of the assets, liabilities, income and expenses of the joint venture, line by line.)

IFRS 11 requires that a joint operator recognises line by line the following in relation to its interest in a **joint operation**:

(a)   Its assets, including its share of any jointly held assets
(b)   Its liabilities, including its share of any jointly incurred liabilities
(c)   Its revenue from the sale of its share of the output arising from the joint operation
(d)   Its share of the revenue from the sale of the output by the joint operation
(e)   Its expenses, including its share of any expenses incurred jointly

This treatment is applicable in both the separate and consolidated financial statements of the joint operator.

In its consolidated financial statements, IFRS 11 requires that a joint venturer recognises its interest in a **joint venture** as an investment and accounts for that investment using the equity method in accordance with IAS 28 *Investments in associates and joint ventures* unless the entity is exempted from applying the equity method.

In its separate financial statements, a joint venturer should account for its interest in a joint venture in accordance with IAS 27 (2011) *Separate financial statements*, namely:

(a)   At cost; or
(b)   In accordance with IFRS 9 *Financial instruments*.

2.3 Other investments

Investments which do not meet the definitions of any of the above should be accounted for according to IFRS 9 *Financial instruments*.

3 Audit of groups   6/12, 6/13, 12/13, 6/14

FAST FORWARD

> The group engagement partner is responsible for the direction, supervision and performance of the group audit.

Point to note

> Your examining team wrote an article in *Student Accountant* entitled 'Group audit issues', which you should make sure you read.

The standard here is ISA 600 *Special considerations – audits of group financial statements (including the work of component auditors)*.

ISA 600 states that the **objectives** of the auditor are:

ISA 600.8

The objectives of the auditor are:

(a)   Determine whether to act as the auditor of the group financial statements; and

(b)   If acting as the auditor of the group financial statements:

   (i)   To communicate clearly with component auditors about the scope and timing of their work on financial information related to components and their findings; and

   (ii)   To obtain sufficient appropriate audit evidence about the financial information of the components and the consolidation process to express an opinion on whether the group financial statements are prepared, in all material respects, in accordance with the applicable financial reporting framework.

The group auditor should gain an understanding of the group as a whole and assess risks for the group as a whole and for individually significant components. The group auditor has to ensure other auditors are professionally qualified, meet quality control and ethical requirements and will allow the group auditor access to working papers or components themselves.

3.1 Definitions

Component. An entity or business activity for which the group or component management prepares financial information that should be included in the group financial statements.

Component auditor. An auditor who, at the request of the group engagement team, performs work on financial information related to a component for the group audit.

Component materiality. The materiality level for a component determined by the group engagement team.

Group. All the components whose financial information is included in the group financial statements. A group always has more than one component.

Group audit. The audit of the group financial statements.

3.2 Responsibilities

Group financial statements may include amounts derived from financial statements which have not been audited by the group auditors, but by a different firm altogether: the **component auditor**. Components of group financial statements can include subsidiaries, associates, joint ventures and branches.

3.2.1 Audit opinion

FAST FORWARD

The group auditor takes sole responsibility for the group audit opinion.

ISA 600.11

The group engagement partner is responsible for the direction, supervision and performance of the group audit engagement in compliance with professional standards and applicable legal and regulatory requirements, and whether the auditor's report that is issued is appropriate in the circumstances.

Hence the auditor's report on the group financial statements **shall not refer to a component auditor**. If a reference to a component auditor is required (eg by local laws or regulations), the report shall indicate that this reference does not diminish the group auditor's responsibility for the group audit opinion. The component auditor therefore has no responsibility for the **group** auditor's opinion, although they are of course responsible for their own auditor's opinion in relation to the entity (component) that they have audited.

If the opinion on a component is qualified, the group audit opinion is only affected if the matter is material to the group. **Only a matter which is material in a group context will affect the group audit opinion**.

Example: group audit opinion

Aristotle & Co is the group auditor of the Plato Group. At the planning stage of the audit, group materiality is determined at $250,000.

Plato Co is the parent company of the group, and has a subsidiary called Socrates Co. The group auditor considers Socrates to be a significant component for the purposes of the group audit. Socrates Co is audited by a component auditor.

The component auditor's report on Socrates Co is qualified as a result of a material misstatement. The amount of the misstatement is $120,000.

Required

What is the effect on the audit report given on the Plato Group?

Solution

The group audit report is not modified, as the amount of the misstatement is not material to the group.

3.2.2 Parent company financial statements

Balances contained within only the parent company financial statements (but not the group accounts) will also have an effect on the group financial statements. For example, the parent's statement of financial position will include investments in subsidiaries as non-current assets, and the parent's statement of profit or loss will include dividend receipts from subsidiaries. The group auditor must obtain sufficient appropriate evidence in respect of these, in order to express an opinion on the financial statements of the parent as well as on the group.

3.3 Objectives

In practical terms, in order to achieve the group audit objectives the auditor needs to obtain evidence in relation to the:

(a) **Individual components** of the group – this is covered in the remainder of Section 3.
(a) **Consolidation process** – this is covered in Section 4.

3.4 Acceptance and continuance

FAST FORWARD

> The group auditor must consider whether it will be possible to obtain sufficient appropriate audit evidence about components.

ISA 600 places special emphasis on the need for the group auditor to determine whether or not to accept the appointment. This is particularly important here because it is possible for it to be straightforward to audit the parent company, but impossible to obtain sufficient appropriate evidence about the rest of the group.

If the group engagement partner concludes that it will **not be possible to obtain sufficient appropriate audit evidence on the group** and that this is serious enough to result in a disclaimer of opinion, then **the engagement should not be accepted** (or withdrawn from, if already accepted – ISA 600.13). For this purpose the group engagement partner **must obtain an understanding of the group before acceptance** (ISA 600.12).

The **component auditor** should consider whether there might be any **restrictions** on them providing the group auditor with access to information, such as laws relating to **confidentiality** or data privacy. It should be borne in mind that in general the component auditor is **not normally obliged to co-operate** with the group auditor (unless they are operating in a jurisdiction which requires them to do so). In practice this means that the same audit firm will often be appointed as auditor of the group and its significant components.

3.4.1 Obtaining an understanding of the group, its components and their environments

Possible sources of information include:

* Information provided by group management
* Communication with group management
* Communication with the previous group engagement team, component manager, or component auditors

Other matters to consider will include:

* The **group structure**
* **Components' business activities** including the industry and regulatory, economic and political environments in which those activities take place
* The use of **service organisations**
* A description of **group-wide controls**
* The **complexity of the consolidation** process

- **Whether component auditors** that are not from the group engagement partner's firm **will perform work** on the financial information of any of the components
- **Whether the group engagement team will have unrestricted access** to those charged with governance of the group, those charged with governance of the component, component management, component information and the component auditors (including relevant audit documentation sought by the group engagement team)

In the case of **continuing engagements** the group engagement team's ability to obtain sufficient appropriate audit evidence may be affected by **significant changes**, eg changes in group structure, changes in business activities and concerns regarding the integrity and competence of group or component management.

Exam focus point

> In addition to these points the group engagement team should also consider the general points relating to acceptance of appointment discussed earlier in this Study Text.

3.5 Planning and risk assessment

The planning and risk assessment process will need to take into account the fact that all elements of the group financial statements are not audited by the group auditor directly. **The group auditor will not be able to simply rely on the conclusions of the component auditor**. ISA 600 requires the group auditor to evaluate the reliability of the component auditor and the work performed. This will then determine the extent of further procedures.

3.5.1 Significant components

The ISA distinguishes between **significant components** and other components which are not individually significant to the group financial statements.

Key term

> **Significant component.** A component identified by the group engagement team: (a) that is of individual significance to the group, or (b) that, due to its specific nature or circumstances, is likely to include significant risks of material misstatement of the group financial statements.

ISA 600.A5 states that a significant component can be identified by using a **benchmark**. If component assets, liabilities, cash flows, profit or turnover (whichever is the most appropriate benchmark) **exceed 15% of the related group figure**, then the auditor may judge that the component is a **significant component**.

If a component is financially significant to the group financial statements then the group engagement team or a component auditor will perform a full audit based on the component materiality level.

The group auditor should be involved in the assessment of risk in relation to significant components. If the component is otherwise significant due to its nature or circumstances, the group auditors will require one of the following.

- A full audit using component materiality
- An audit of specified account balances related to identified significant risks
- Specified audit procedures relating to identified significant risks

Components that are not 'significant components' will be subject to analytical procedures at a group level – a full audit is not required.

3.5.2 Understanding the component auditor

ISA 600 requires the group engagement team to obtain an understanding of the component auditor. This involves an assessment of the following.

(a) Whether the component auditor is **independent** and understands and will comply with the ethical requirements that are relevant to the group audit
(b) The component auditor's **professional competence**

(c) Whether the group engagement team will be **involved in the work of the component auditor** to the extent that it is necessary to obtain sufficient appropriate audit evidence

(d) Whether the component auditor operates in a **regulatory environment** that actively oversees auditors

The group engagement team may obtain this understanding in a number of ways. In the first year, for example, the component auditor may be visited to discuss these issues. Alternatively, the component auditor may be asked to confirm these matters in writing or to complete a questionnaire. Confirmations from professional bodies may also be sought and the reputation of the firm will be taken into account.

3.5.3 Materiality

The group auditor is responsible for setting the materiality level for the group financial statements as a whole. Materiality levels should also be set for components which are individually significant. These should be set at a lower level than the materiality level of the group as a whole.

3.5.4 Involvement in the work of a component auditor

The extent of involvement by the group auditor at the planning stage will depend on the:

- Significance of the component
- Risks of material misstatement of the group financial statements
- Extent of the group auditor's understanding of the component auditor

The basic rule is that **where the component is significant, the group auditor must be involved in the component auditor's work**.

The group auditor may perform the following procedures.

- **Meeting** with the **component management or the component auditors** to obtain an understanding of the component and its environment.
- **Reviewing** the component auditor's overall **audit strategy and audit plan**.
- **Performing risk assessment** procedures to identify and assess risks of material **misstatement at the component level**. These may be performed with the component auditor or by the group auditor.

Where the component is a **significant component**, the nature, timing and extent of the group auditor's involvement is affected by their understanding of the component auditor but at a minimum should include the following procedures.

- Discussion with the component auditor or component management of the component's business activities that are significant to the group.
- Discussing with the component auditor the susceptibility of the component to material misstatement of the financial information due to fraud or error.
- Reviewing the component auditor's documentation of identified significant risks of material misstatements. This may be in the form of a memorandum including the conclusions drawn by the component auditors.

Example: component audit

Plato Group has recently established a new subsidiary, Plotinus Co. The group auditor does not consider Plotinus Co to be a significant component in accordance with ISA 600. The auditor of Plotinus Co has not communicated any of the findings of its audit to the group auditor. Aristotle & Co, the group auditor, has performed analytical procedures on the final financial statements of Plotinus Co, and is satisfied that there are unlikely to be any misstatements therein that are material to the group.

Required

What is the effect on the auditor's report issued in relation to the Plato Group?

LEARNING MEDIA

Solution

The group auditor's report is not modified, and the auditor's opinion is unmodified. ISA 600.29 specifies that where a component is not a significant component, then analytical procedures performed at a group level are sufficient.

3.6 Access to information about components

The group auditor may not be able to access all the information it needs about components or component auditors, eg because of laws relating to confidentiality or data privacy. The effect on the group audit opinion depends on the **significance of the component**.

If the **component is not significant**, then it may be sufficient just to have a complete set of financial statements, the component auditor's report, and information kept by group management.

If the **component is significant** then it is possible that there will be an **inability to obtain sufficient appropriate audit evidence** about the component, in which case the audit opinion is either **qualified** or a **disclaimer of opinion** is issued. In this case it would also be impossible to comply with ISA 600's requirement to be involved with the work of the component auditor (for significant components), which would also lead to an inability to obtain sufficient appropriate audit evidence.

3.7 Evaluating the work of the component auditor

For all companies in the group the group auditor is required to perform a review of the work done by the component auditor. This is normally achieved by reviewing a report or questionnaire completed by the component auditor which highlights the key issues which have been identified during the course of the audit. The effect of any uncorrected misstatements and any instances where there has been an inability to obtain sufficient appropriate audit evidence should also be evaluated. On the basis of this review the group auditor then needs to determine whether any additional procedures are necessary. These may include:

- Designing and performing further audit procedures. These may be designed and performed with the component auditors, or by the group auditor.
- Participating in the closing and other key meetings between the component auditors and component management
- Reviewing other relevant parts of the component auditors' documentation

Point to note

In co-operating with the group auditor the component auditor would be expected to provide access to audit documentation unless prohibited from doing so by law.

3.8 Communication with the component auditor

ISA 600 prescribes the types of information that must be sent by the group auditor to the component auditor and *vice versa*.

> **ISA 600.40**
>
> The group engagement team shall communicate its requirements to the component auditor on a timely basis. This communication shall set out the work to be performed, the use to be made of that work and the form and content of the component auditor's communication with the group engagement team.

These communications include:

(a)   A request that the component auditor confirms their co-operation with the group engagement team

(b)   The ethical requirements that are relevant to the group audit and in particular independence requirements

(c)   In the case of an audit or review of the financial information of the component, component materiality and the threshold above which misstatements cannot be regarded as clearly trivial to the group financial statements

(d)   Identified significant risks of material misstatement of the group financial statements, due to fraud or error that are relevant to the work of the component auditor; the group engagement team requests the component auditor to communicate any other identified significant risks of material misstatement and the component auditor's responses to such risks

(e)   A list of related parties prepared by group management and any other related parties of which the group engagement team is aware; component auditors are requested to communicate any other related parties not previously identified

> **ISA 600.41**
>
> The group engagement team shall request the component auditor to communicate matters relevant to the group engagement team's conclusion with regard to the group audit.

These communications include:

(a)   Whether the component auditor has complied with ethical requirements that are relevant to the group audit, including independence and professional acceptance

(b)   Whether the component auditor has complied with the group engagement team's requirements

(c)   Identification of the financial information of the component on which the component auditor is reporting

(d)   Information on instances of non-compliance with laws and regulations that could give rise to material misstatement of the group financial statements

(e)   A list of uncorrected misstatements of the financial information of the component (the list need not include items that are below the threshold for clearly trivial misstatements)

(f)   Indicators of possible management bias

(g)   Description of any material deficiencies identified in internal control over financial reporting at the component level

(h)   Other significant matters that the component auditor communicated or expects to communicate to those charged with governance of the component, including fraud or suspected fraud involving component management, employees who have significant roles in internal control at the component level or others where the fraud resulted in a material misstatement of the financial information of the component

(i)   Any other matters that may be relevant to the group audit or that the component auditor wishes to draw to the attention of the group engagement team, including exceptions noted in the written representations that the component auditor requested from component management

(j)   The component auditor's overall finding, conclusions or opinion

This communication often takes the form of a memorandum or report of work performed.

3.9 Communicating with group management and those charged with governance

ISA 600 identifies the following as matters which should be communicated to group management.

- Material deficiencies in the design or operating effectiveness of group-wide controls
- Material deficiencies that the group engagement team has identified in internal controls at components that are judged to be significant to the group
- Material deficiencies that component auditors have identified in internal controls at components that are judged to be significant to the group
- Fraud identified by the group engagement team or component auditors or information indicating that a fraud may exist

Where a component auditor is required to express an audit opinion on the financial statements of a component, the group engagement team will request group management to inform component management of any matters that they, the group engagement team, have become aware of that may be significant to the financial statements of the component. If group management refuses to pass on the communication the group engagement team will discuss the matter with those charged with governance of the group. If the matter is still unresolved, the group engagement team shall consider whether to advise the component auditor not to issue the audit report on the component financial statements until the matter is resolved.

3.10 Communication with those charged with governance of the group

The following matters should be communicated to those charged with governance of the group.

- An overview of the type of work to be performed on the financial statements of the component
- An overview of the nature of the group engagement team's planned involvement in the work to be performed by the component auditors on significant components
- Instances where the group engagement team's evaluation of the work of a component auditor gave rise to a concern about the quality of that auditor's work
- Any limitations on the group audit, for example, where the group engagement team's access to information may have been restricted
- Fraud or suspected fraud involving group management, component management, employees who have significant roles in group-wide controls or others where fraud resulted in a material misstatement of the group financial statements

3.11 Other aspects of the audit requiring consideration in a group context

6/12

3.11.1 Co-terminous year ends

It is possible that all the entities within a group will not have **coterminous reporting periods**. In this case, ISA 600.37 requires the group auditor to evaluate whether appropriate adjustments have been made to the financial statements that are not coterminous, in accordance with the relevant financial reporting framework. In the case of IFRSs, IFRS 10 requires that the difference between period-end dates of the parent and a subsidiary is **no more than three months**. Adjustments must be made for any significant events which occur between the date of the subsidiary's and the parent's financial statements.

3.11.2 Changes in group structure

The group structure may have changed in the course of the period being audited. For instance, there may have been acquisitions, disposals, reorganisations, or changes in how the group financial reporting system is organised (ISA 600.A12). The auditor must obtain an understanding of any such changes, and must consider their impact on the auditor's understanding of the group.

For example, it is possible that a new subsidiary has been acquired, in which case the auditor needs to consider whether or not it is a 'significant component' in accordance with ISA 600, in order to determine the extent of audit work that will be required on the subsidiary. It may then also be necessary to obtain evidence regarding the application of IFRS 3, including the assessment of fair values in accordance with IFRS 13 *Fair value measurement*, which will carry audit risk because it may involve the exercise of judgement on the part of the audited entity.

There may be **'hidden' changes in the group structure**. For instance, it may be that there has been a **part-disposal** of a subsidiary, in which case the auditor will need to obtain evidence regarding the extent to which control is present, in addition to the evidence it will need in relation to the actual transactions involved.

A further possibility is that an already existing subsidiary, which the auditor had not considered to be 'significant' in previous periods in accordance with ISA 600, might suddenly become so in the current

period. In this case the auditor would need to assess carefully the audit evidence they will need to obtain in relation to the subsidiary.

3.11.3 Support (comfort) letters

It sometimes happens that a component, when considered in isolation, does not appear to be a going concern, even though the group as a whole is a going concern. In such a case, the auditor may request a 'letter of support' (or 'comfort letter') from the management of the parent company. This letter states that the intention of the parent is to continue to support the subsidiary, which makes it a going concern.

From the auditor's perspective, if the letter of support is crucial to the assessment of the going concern of the subsidiary, then it will usually be necessary to obtain **some** further evidence on going concern. This would usually include obtaining evidence about whether the parent company (and the group as a whole) is indeed able to provide the support that the subsidiary will need.

3.11.4 Overseas subsidiaries in developing countries

Consolidating a subsidiary from a developing country may be a problem, as the **basis of preparation** of the subsidiary's financial statements may be so **different from IFRS** that the group auditor will not be able to conclude that the financial statements show a true and fair view.

This is only a problem **if** the financial statements, or the differences caused by the basis of preparation, are **material to the group**. The problem can be averted by asking the directors to restate the financial statements under IFRS. The group auditors might require that this restatement process is audited to ensure it is accurate.

Increased internationalisation of accounting practice is **reducing the risk** of this problem arising.

Other problems with audits involving entities in developing countries include:

- **Language problems** if eg English is not the business language.
- **External confirmations** may be harder to get (eg bank letters), depending on the country's infrastructure.
- **Lack of qualified personnel**. This includes accounting staff but also local experts, eg lawyers or valuers.
- **Corruption** is a problem in some countries, and although the developed world is certainly not immune to the problem, auditors should take it into account. This may pose the auditor with legal problems in the developed world, eg if they are to comply with the UK's Bribery Act.

3.11.5 Control environment and systems

ISA 600 requires the auditor to enhance their understanding of the group, its components and their environments including group-wide controls, obtained during the acceptance or continuance stage.

Key term

> **Group-wide controls.** Controls designed, implemented and maintained by group management over group financial statements.

Group-wide controls may include a combination of:

- Regular meetings between group and component management to discuss business developments and to review performance
- Monitoring of components' operations and financial results
- Group management's risk assessment process
- Monitoring, controlling, reconciling and eliminating intra-group transactions, unrealised profits and intra-group balances
- A process for monitoring the timeliness and assessing the accuracy and completeness of financial information received from components
- Monitoring of controls including internal audit

Assessment of the control environment and systems will include assessment of the overall group control environment. Factors to consider include:

- Organisational structure of the group
- Level of involvement of the parent company in components
- Degree of autonomy of management of components
- Supervision of components' management by parent company
- Information systems, and information received centrally on a regular basis

Question

Component auditors

You are the main auditor of Mouldings Holdings, a listed company, which has subsidiaries in the UK and overseas, many of which are audited by other firms. All subsidiaries are involved in the manufacture or distribution of plastic goods and have accounting periods coterminous with those of the holding company.

Required

(a) State why you would wish to review the work of the auditors of the subsidiaries not audited by you.
(b) Describe the principal audit procedures you would carry out in performing such a review.

Answer

(a) **Reasons for reviewing the work of other auditors**

The main consideration which concerns the audit of all group accounts is that the holding company's auditors are responsible to the members of that company for the audit opinion on the whole of the group accounts.

It may be stated (in the notes to the financial statements) that the financial statements of certain subsidiaries have been audited by other firms, but this does not absolve the group auditors from any of their responsibilities.

The auditors of a holding company have to report to its members on the truth and fairness of the view given by the financial statements of the company and its subsidiaries dealt with in the group accounts. The group engagement team should have powers to obtain such information and explanations as they reasonably require from the subsidiary companies and their auditors, or from the parent company in the case of overseas subsidiaries, in order to discharge their responsibilities as holding company auditors.

The auditing standard ISA 600 *Special considerations – audit of group financial statements (including the work of component auditors)* clarifies how the group auditors can carry out a review of the audits of components in order to satisfy themselves that, with the inclusion of figures not audited by themselves, the group accounts give a true and fair view.

The scope, standard and independence of the work carried out by the auditors of subsidiary companies (the 'component' auditors) are the most important matters which need to be examined by the group auditors before relying on financial statements audited by them. The group auditors need to be satisfied that sufficient appropriate audit evidence has been obtained and that all material areas of the financial statements of subsidiaries have been audited satisfactorily and in a manner compatible with that of the group auditors themselves.

(b) **Work to be carried out by group auditors in reviewing the component auditors' work**

(i) Send a questionnaire to all other auditors requesting detailed information on their work, including:

(1) An explanation of their general approach (in order to make an assessment of the standards of their work)

(2) Details of the accounting policies of major subsidiaries (to ensure that these are compatible within the group)

(3) The component auditors' opinion of the subsidiaries' overall level of internal control, and the reliability of their accounting records

(4) Any limitations placed on the scope of the auditors' work

(5) Any modifications, and the reasons for them, made or likely to be made to their audit reports

(ii) Carry out a detailed review of the component auditors' working papers on each subsidiary whose results materially affect the view given by the group financial statements. This review will enable the group auditors to ascertain whether:

(1) An up to date permanent file exists with details of the nature of the subsidiary's business, its staff organisation, its accounting records, the previous year's financial statements and copies of important legal documents

(2) The systems examination has been properly completed, documented and reported on to management after discussion

(3) Tests of controls and substantive procedures have been properly and appropriately carried out, and audit programmes properly completed and signed

(4) All other working papers are comprehensive and explicit

(5) The overall review of the financial statements has been adequately carried out, and adequate use of analytical procedures has been undertaken throughout the audit

(6) The financial statements agree in all respects with the accounting records and comply with all relevant legal requirements and accounting standards

(7) Minutes of board and general meetings have been scrutinised and important matters noted

(8) The audit work has been carried out in accordance with approved auditing standards

(9) The audit work has been properly reviewed within the firm of auditors and any laid-down quality control procedures adhered to

(10) Any points requiring discussion with the holding company's management have been noted and brought to the group auditor's attention (including any matters which might warrant a modification of the audit report on the subsidiary company's financial statements)

(11) Adequate audit evidence has been obtained to form a basis for the audit opinion on both the subsidiaries' financial statements and those of the group

If the group engagement partner is not satisfied as a result of the above review, they should arrange for further audit work to be carried out either by the component auditors on their behalf, or jointly with them. The component auditors are fully responsible for their own work; any additional tests are those required for the purpose of the audit of the group financial statements.

4 The consolidation: problems and procedures

Pilot paper, 6/08, 6/11

FAST FORWARD

Consolidation procedures include checking consolidation adjustments have been correctly made, checking treatment of additions and disposals have been accounted for correctly and arithmetical checks.

4.1 Audit procedures

ISA 600 requires the auditor to identify and assess the risks of material misstatement through obtaining an understanding of the entity and its environment. Part of that process involves **obtaining an understanding of the consolidation process**, including instructions issued by group management to components.

To achieve uniformity and comparability of financial information the group management will normally issue instructions to components. The instructions ordinarily cover:

- The accounting policies to be applied
- Statutory and other disclosure requirements including:
    - The identification and reporting of segments
    - Related party relationships and reporting of segments
    - Intra-group transactions and unrealised profits
    - Intra-group account balances
- A reporting timetable

The group engagement team will consider:

- The clarity and practicality of the instructions for completing the reporting package
- Whether the instructions:
    - Adequately describe the applicable financial reporting framework
    - Provide for adequate disclosures
    - Adequately provide for the identification of consolidation adjustments
    - Provide for the approval of the financial information by component management

The group auditor is also responsible for the audit of the consolidation process itself.

After receiving and reviewing all the subsidiaries' (and associates') financial statements, the group auditors will be in a position to audit the consolidated financial statements. An important part of the work on the consolidation will be checking the consolidation adjustments. Consolidation adjustments generally fall into two categories:

- **Permanent consolidation adjustments**
- **Consolidation adjustments** for the **current year**

The audit steps involved in the consolidation process may be summarised as follows.

Step 1	Compare the audited financial statements of each subsidiary/associate with the consolidation schedules to ensure that figures have been transposed correctly and that all components have been included.
Step 2	Review the adjustments made on consolidation to ensure that they are appropriate and comparable with the previous year. This will involve: – **Recording** the **dates** and **costs** of **acquisitions** of subsidiaries and the assets acquired – **Calculating goodwill** and **pre-acquisition reserves** arising on consolidation – **Preparing** an overall **reconciliation** of movements on reserves and non-controlling interests – **Reconciling** any inter-company balances, and eliminating intra-group items from profit or loss – **Verifying** that, where relevant, subsidiary balances have been included in the group accounts at **FV**, eg properties, which may be carried at depreciated cost in the subsidiary, must be at FV in the group accounts – **Verifying** that the **deferred tax** consequences of consolidation and FV adjustments have been accounted for correctly
Step 3	For business combinations determine: – Whether the combination has been **appropriately** treated as an acquisition – The **appropriateness** of the **date** used as the date of combination – The **treatment** of the **results** of **investments** acquired during the year – If acquisition accounting has been used, that the **FV** of acquired **assets** and **liabilities** is reasonable (to ascertainable market value by use of an expert)

<table>
<tr><td></td><td>– Goodwill has been calculated correctly and reviewed annually for indicators of impairment</td></tr>
<tr><td>Step 4</td><td>For disposals:</td></tr>
<tr><td></td><td>– Agree the date used as the date for disposal to sales documentation</td></tr>
<tr><td></td><td>– Review management accounts to ascertain whether the results of the investment have been included up to the date of disposal, and whether figures used are reasonable</td></tr>
<tr><td>Step 5</td><td>Consider whether previous treatment of existing subsidiaries or associates is still correct (consider level of influence, degree of support), and that there has not been, for example. a part-disposal during the period.</td></tr>
<tr><td>Step 6</td><td>Verify the arithmetical accuracy of the consolidation workings by recalculating them.</td></tr>
<tr><td>Step 7</td><td>Review the consolidated financial statements for compliance with the legislation, accounting standards and other relevant regulations. Care will need to be taken where:</td></tr>
<tr><td></td><td>– Group companies do not have coterminous accounting periods</td></tr>
<tr><td></td><td>– Accounting policies of group members differ because foreign subsidiaries operate under different rules</td></tr>
<tr><td></td><td>Other important areas include:</td></tr>
<tr><td></td><td>– Treatment of participating interests and associates
– Treatment of goodwill and intangible assets
– Taxation
– Foreign currency translation
– Treatment of loss-making subsidiaries
– Treatment of restrictions on distribution of profits of a subsidiary</td></tr>
<tr><td>Step 8</td><td>Review the consolidated financial statements to confirm that they give a true and fair view in the circumstances.</td></tr>
</table>

The audit of related party transactions was considered earlier in this Study Text. Remember that when auditing a consolidation, the relevant related parties are those related to the **consolidated group**. Transactions with consolidated subsidiaries need **not** be disclosed, as they are incorporated in the financial statements.

The group auditors are often requested to carry out the consolidation work even where the financial statements of the subsidiaries have been prepared by the client. In these circumstances the auditors are of course acting as accountants **and** auditors, and care must be taken to ensure that the **audit** function is carried out and documented.

IFRS 3 requires goodwill to be reviewed annually for impairment, in accordance with IAS 36. This is the responsibility of management, and the auditor's role is to obtain audit evidence regarding the impairment review that management has already conducted. Impairment reviews were covered in Chapter 9 of this Study Text.

<table>
<tr><td>Exam focus point</td><td>The June 2011 exam contained eight marks for explaining the principal audit procedures that are performed on the consolidation process. These were relatively easy marks, and you should make sure you are well prepared for a question like this. The June 2012 exam devoted about 30 marks to group audits, of which five easy marks were for recommending the principal audit procedures on goodwill on acquisition.</td></tr>
</table>

Question

Your firm is the auditor of Beeston Industries, a limited liability company, which has a number of subsidiaries in your country (and no overseas subsidiaries), some of which are audited by other firms of professional accountants. You have been asked to consider the work which should be carried out to ensure that inter-company transactions and balances are correctly treated in the group accounts.

Required

(a)   Describe the audit work you would perform to check that intra-group balances agree, state why intra-group balances should agree, and the consequences of them not agreeing.

(b)   Describe the audit work you would perform to verify that intra-group profit in inventory has been correctly accounted for in the group accounts.

Answer

(a)   Intra-group balances should agree because, in the preparation of consolidated financial statements, it is necessary to cancel them out. If they do not cancel out then the group accounts will be displaying an item which has no value outside of the group and profits may be correspondingly under- or overstated. The audit work required to check that intra-group balances agree would be as follows.

    (i)   Obtain and review a copy of the holding company's instructions to all group members relating to the procedures for reconciliation and agreement of year-end intra-group balances. Particular attention should be paid to the treatment of 'in-transit' items to ensure that there is a proper cut-off.

    (ii)   Obtain a schedule of intra-group balances from all group companies and check the details therein to the summary prepared by the parent company. The details on these schedules should also be independently confirmed in writing by the other auditors involved.

    (iii)   Nil balances should be confirmed by both the group companies concerned and their respective auditors.

    (iv)   The details on the schedules in (iii) above should also be agreed to the details in the financial statements of the individual group companies which are submitted to the parent company for consolidation purposes.

(b)   Where one company in a group supplies goods to another company at cost plus a percentage, and such goods remain in inventory at the year end, then the group inventory will contain an element of unrealised profit. In the preparation of the group accounts, best accounting practice requires that a provision should be made for this unrealised profit.

In order to verify that intra-group profit in inventory has been correctly accounted for in the group accounts, the audit work required would be as follows.

    (i)   Confirm the group's procedures for identification of such inventory and their notification to the parent company who will be responsible for making the required provision.

    (ii)   Obtain and review schedules of intra-group inventory from group companies and confirm that the same categories of inventory have been included as in previous years.

    (iii)   Select a sample of invoices for goods purchased from group companies and check to see that, where necessary, these have been included in year-end intra-group inventory. Obtain confirmation from other auditors that they have satisfactorily completed a similar exercise.

    (iv)   Check the calculation of the provision for unrealised profit and confirm that this has been arrived at on a consistent basis with that used in earlier years, after making due allowance for any known changes in the profit margins operated by various group companies.

    (v)   Check the schedules of intra-group inventory against the various inventory sheets and consider whether the level of intra-group inventory appears to be reasonable in comparison with previous years, ensuring that satisfactory explanations are obtained for any material differences.

5 Joint audits

FAST FORWARD

> In joint audits, more than one auditor is responsible for the audit opinion and it is made jointly.

The relationship between group and component auditors discussed in the previous sections is **not** the same as that between the auditors involved in a joint audit.

Key term

> A **joint audit** is one 'where two or more auditors are responsible for an audit engagement and jointly produce an audit report to the client'.

5.1 Reasons for joint audits

Two or more firms of accountants could act as joint auditors for a number of reasons.

(a) **Takeover.** The parent company may insist that its auditors act jointly with those of the new subsidiary.

(b) **Locational problems.** A company operating from widely dispersed locations may find it convenient to have joint auditors.

(c) **Political problems.** Overseas subsidiaries may need to employ local auditors to satisfy the laws of the country in which they operate. It is sometimes found that these local auditors act jointly with those of the holding company.

(d) Companies may prefer to use **local accountants**, while at the same time enjoying the wider range of services provided by a large international firm.

5.2 Accepting a joint audit

There are several practical points that must be borne in mind before accepting a joint audit. In particular it will be necessary to assess the **experience** and **standards** of the other firm by looking at the audit techniques used, by scrutinising its working papers and establishing whether it has had experience in similar jobs.

Where there are joint auditors, the audit engagement should be explained in similar terms by each set of auditors. The auditors should agree whether joint or separate letters should be sent to the client. Separate letters would normally need to be sent where other services are provided.

Once a joint position has been accepted, the **programme** to be adopted and the **split** of the **detailed work** will have to be discussed.

5.3 Problems with joint audits

One of the major criticisms of joint audits is that they may be expensive. This is probably true, but if the two firms have organised the work between them properly the difference should be minimal. Furthermore, an increase in the fees may be justified by improved services, not least because the two firms of accountants are likely to work as efficiently as possible from a sense of professional pride.

Both firms must sign the audit report and both are responsible for the whole audit whether or not they carried out a particular area of the audit programme. It follows that both firms will be **jointly liable** in the event of litigation.

Point to note

> This has been a topical area in recent years, with the European Union having considered requiring some entities to have **joint audits**. This requirement was not eventually put into legislation.

6 Transnational audits

FAST FORWARD

> Transnational audits are audits of financial statements which may be relied on outside an entity's home jurisdiction.

6.1 The Transnational Auditors Committee

The IAASB has set up the **Transnational Auditors Committee** (TAC) to provide guidance to the members of the FoF.

The TAC has issued the following definition of transnational audit.

Key term

> **Transnational audit** means an audit of financial statements which are or may be relied on outside the audited entity's home jurisdiction for purposes of significant lending, investment or regulatory decisions; this will include audits of all financial statements of companies with listed equity or debt and other public interest entities which attract particular public attention because of their size, products or services provided.

Guidance

Other public interest entities shall include those entities in either the public or the private sectors which **have significant transactions across national borders**, whether or not having either listed equity or debt. These would include, for example, large charitable organisations or trusts, major monopolies or duopolies, providers of financial or other borrowing facilities to commercial or private customers, deposit-taking organisations and those holding funds belonging to third parties in connection with investment or savings activities.

Significant transactions across national borders shall include transactions such that there is a reasonable expectation that the financial statements of the entity may be relied on by a user outside the entity's home jurisdiction for purposes of significant lending, investment or regulatory decisions. Significant in this context does not include use of financial statements to establish normal trade terms with vendors or to open accounts with financial institutions (ie accounts for purposes of collecting customer receipts or making vendor payments). For the avoidance of doubt, an office required solely for the purpose of legal formation and continuing legal existence in a particular jurisdiction does not constitute a significant transaction across national borders.

In principle, the definition of transnational audit should be applied to the consolidated entity as a whole, including the individual entities comprising the consolidated entity.

Examples to illustrate the definition:

Example	Explanation
Private company in US raising debt finance in Canada	This would qualify as a transnational audit, as it is reasonable to expect that the financial statements of the company would be used across national borders in obtaining the debt financing.
Private Savings and Loans operating entirely in the US (ie only US depositors and US investments)	Although it could be considered a public interest entity, this would not qualify as a transnational audit assuming it can be demonstrated that there are no transnational users.

In applying the definition of transnational audit, there should be a rebuttable presumption that all banks and financial institutions are included, unless it can be clearly demonstrated that there is no transnational element from the perspective of a financial statement user and that there are no operations across national borders. Potential transnational users would include investors, lenders, governments, customers, regulators, etc. |

Example	Explanation
International charity taking donations through various national branches and making grants around the world	This entity can clearly be considered a public interest entity and operating across borders. Further, the international structure would create a reasonable expectation that the financial statements could be used across national borders by donors in other countries if not by others for purposes of significant lending, investment or regulatory decisions.
Private internet betting company registered in BVI, which operates from Costa Rica and takes wagers by credit card on a worldwide basis via internet	Assuming there is no restriction on gamblers then it would be public interest and operate across borders and therefore classified as a transnational audit.

6.2 Features of transnational audits

In the globalised business and financial environment, many audits are clearly transnational, and this produces a number of specific problems which can limit the reliability of the audited financial statements:

- Regulation and oversight of auditors differs from country to country
- Differences in auditing standards from country to country
- Variability in audit quality in different countries

6.3 Role of the international audit firm networks

The Big Four and other international networks of firms can be seen as being ahead of governments and institutions in terms of their global influence. They are in a position to establish consistent practices worldwide in such areas as:

- Training and education
- Audit procedures
- Quality control procedures.

These firms may as a result be in a better position than national regulators to ensure consistent implementation of high quality auditing standards.

International networks do open up a **litigation risk** to some member firms, however. If a member firm is sued for eg negligence, then this can sometimes affect the network of firms as well as the individual audit firm involved. The issue hinges on **control**: if the network controls the member firm, then a principal/agent relationship exists and it may be possible to sue. This is complex and can be difficult to establish in reality. The key point here is that if an audit firm gets too close to its international network members – to the point of controlling them – then the benefits of this should be set against the risk of litigation.

6.3.1 Forum of Firms

In response to the trend towards globalisation an international grouping, the Forum of Firms (FoF) , was founded by the following networks: BDO, Deloitte, Ernst & Young, Grant Thornton, KPMG and PricewaterhouseCoopers.

Membership is open to firms and networks that have transnational audit appointments or are interested in accepting such appointments.

These firms have a voluntary agreement to meet certain requirements that are set out in their constitution. These relate mainly to:

- Promoting the use of high quality audit practices worldwide, including the use of ISAs and compliance with the IESBA *Code of Ethics*
- Maintaining quality control standards in accordance with International Standards on Quality Control issued by the IAASB, and conducting globally co-ordinated internal quality assurance reviews
- The need for firms to be subject to a programme of quality assurance.

Membership of the Forum of Firms imposes commitments and responsibilities, namely:

- To perform transnational audits in accordance with ISAs
- To comply with the IESBA *Code of Ethics for Professional Accountants*
- To be subject to a programme of quality assurance

6.4 International education standards

The IAESB (International Accounting Education Standards Board) is a body of IFAC in much the same way as the IAASB and the IESBA are. Its aim is to serve the public interest by establishing standards in the area of professional accounting education that prescribe technical competence and professional skills, values, ethics, and attitudes.

The general thrust of the IAESB's work is to improve levels of auditors' **education and training** worldwide, which should in turn help **improve audit quality**. In its own words:

> To meet the continual challenges facing the global economy, the accountancy profession needs to ensure that individuals who become professional accountants achieve an agreed level of competence

IAESB *Fact Sheet 2014*

This done by issuing International Education Standards (IESs), which give IFAC member bodies a common benchmark for education. Global education standards are hoped to reduce international differences – eg between the developed and developing worlds – and so improve the reliability of the accountancy profession globally, serving the public interest.

6.5 Current debate: dominance of the global accounting firms

6.5.1 Competition and choice

The preceding paragraphs have emphasised the strengths of the global accounting firms.

Questions have been raised recently as to whether the concentration in the audit market, with the Big Four firms supplying audit services to most large companies, creates any risks.

The study 'Competition and choice in the UK audit market' commissioned by the Financial Reporting Council (FRC) and the then Department of Trade and Industry (DTI) in the UK identifies these potential problems:

- If one or more firms are ineligible due to independence rules, a company may have no effective choice of auditor in the short term.
- If one of the Big Four left the market, a few large companies would be unable to find an auditor.
- Restricted choice may represent a risk to high quality and competitive prices.

6.5.2 Barriers to entry

The situation is unlikely to change in the short term as there are significant barriers to entry to the market for auditors of large companies. It may not be economical for other firms to break into this market given the need to demonstrate:

- A credible reputation with large companies, their investors and other stakeholders
- Appropriate resources and expertise in place to carry out large company audits, including relevant sector-specific skills
- An effective capability to secure timely and reliable audit opinions on overseas subsidiaries for audits of companies with significant international operations

Chapter Roundup

- A group of companies is required to prepare consolidated group financial statements. This entails the audit risk that the IFRS in this area are not complied with.

- The group engagement partner is responsible for the direction, supervision and performance of the group audit.

- The group auditor takes sole responsibility for the group audit opinion.

- The group auditor must consider whether it will be possible to obtain sufficient appropriate audit evidence about components.

- Consolidation procedures include checking consolidation adjustments have been correctly made, checking treatment of additions and disposals have been accounted for correctly and arithmetical checks.

- In joint audits, more than one auditor is responsible for the audit opinion and it is made jointly.

- Transnational audits are audits of financial statements which may be relied on outside an entity's home jurisdiction.

Quick Quiz

1   Define the term 'component auditor'.

2   Outline the responsibilities of the component auditor regarding co-operation with the group auditor.

3   If a component is significant due to its nature or circumstances one of three procedures will be required. List these three procedures.

    (1)   ....

    (2)   ....

    (3)   ....

4   List five matters which the component auditor should communicate to the group auditor.

    (1)   ....

    (2)   ....

    (3)   ....

    (4)   ....

    (5)   ....

5   What is a support letter?

6   List the eight steps involved in auditing a consolidation.

7   If two firms undertake a joint audit, they shall be jointly liable in the event of litigation.

    True   ☐

    False ☐

1   An auditor who, at the request of the group engagement team, performs work on financial information related to a component for the group audit

2   ISA 600 gives a professional responsibility to the component auditor to co-operate unless there are legal restrictions on their ability to do so. In some jurisdictions, for example the UK, component auditors may have a legal responsibility to co-operate in certain circumstances.

3   (1)   A full audit using component materiality

    (2)   An audit of specified account balances related to identified significant risks

    (3)   Specified audit procedures related to identified significant risks

4   Any five from:

- Compliance with ethical requirements
- Compliance with group engagement team's requirements
- Identification of component financial information
- Material non-compliance with laws and regulations
- Uncorrected misstatements
- Indicators of management bias
- Material deficiencies of internal control
- Other matters including fraud or suspected fraud
- Overall findings, conclusions or opinion

5   A letter to the auditors from the parent company of a subsidiary which individually does not appear to be a going concern, stating that it intends to continue to support the subsidiary, rendering it a going concern.

6

Step 1   Check the transposition from individual audited financial statements to the consolidation workings.

Step 2   Check consolidation adjustments are correct and comparable with previous years.

Step 3   Check for, and audit, business combinations.

Step 4   Check for, and audit, disposals.

Step 5   Consider whether previous treatment of subsidiaries and associates is still correct.

Step 6   Verify the arithmetical accuracy of the workings.

Step 7   Review the consolidated financial statements for compliance with laws and standards.

Step 8   Review the consolidated financial statements to ensure they give a true and fair view.

7   True

Now try the questions below from the Practice Question Bank.

Number	Level	Marks	Time
Q18	Introductory	20	39 mins
Q19	Examination	15	29 mins
Q20	Examination	25	49 mins
Q21	Examination	15	29 mins

PART

E

Other assignments

Audit-related services and other assurance services

Topic list	Syllabus reference
1 Audit-related services	E1, F3
2 Assurance engagements	E1, F3
3 Risk assessments	E1

Introduction

In this chapter we look at audit-related services and other assurance services.

Audit-related services include review engagements, such as interim financial information reviews and due diligence reviews. We consider the differences between the external audit and audit-related services.

Assurance services are also considered in this chapter and we examine the different levels of assurance that can be provided on such engagements. In particular we look at risk assessments, performance measurement and value for money audits. Finally in this chapter we look at the ways in which companies are using IT in their organisations and how this affects business risks.

Study guide

		Intellectual level
E	**Other assignments**	
E1	**Audit-related services**	
(a)	Describe the nature of audit-related services, the circumstances in which they might be required and the comparative levels of assurance provided by professional accountants and distinguish between: (i) Audit-related services and an audit of historical financial statements (ii) An attestation engagement and a direct reporting engagement	2
(b)	Plan review engagements, for example: (i) A review of interim financial information (ii) A 'due diligence' assignment (when acquiring a company, business or other assets)	2
(c)	Explain the importance of enquiry and analytical procedures in review engagements and apply these procedures.	2
(d)	Describe the main categories of assurance services that audit firms can provide and assess the benefits of providing these services to management and external users.	
(e)	Describe a level of assurance (reasonable, high, moderate, limited, negative) for an engagement depending on the subject matter evaluated, the criteria used, the procedures applied and the quality and quantity of evidence obtained.	3
F3	**Other reports**	
(a)	Analyse the form and content of the professional accountant's report for an assurance engagement as compared with an auditor's report.	2
(c)	Discuss the effectiveness of the 'negative assurance' form of reporting and evaluate situations in which it might be appropriate to express a reservation or deny a conclusion.	3

Exam guide

Assurance and audit-related services are very important areas for auditors in practice. Most of these topics have featured in practical questions in the past and are likely to continue to do so.

1 Audit-related services   12/07, 6/08, 6/11

FAST FORWARD ❯❯

> Audit-related services may be assurance engagements or non-assurance engagements.

A client would generally engage an auditor to undertake an audit-related engagement either because the client needs to make use of expertise that the auditor possesses but the client itself does not, or because it needs a relatively independent third party to provide assurance regarding some specific matter. For example, the client may lack the expertise to carry out a financial due diligence assignment on a potential acquisition, and may therefore engage the auditor to do this for it. Or it may be that the client needs to obtain new finance in the form of a bank loan, and engages the auditor to provide assurance over its prospective financial information because this will help strengthen its case with the bank.

There are many different types of audit-related services, which are summarised by the following diagram. The types of standard which apply to each type of engagement are given in brackets.

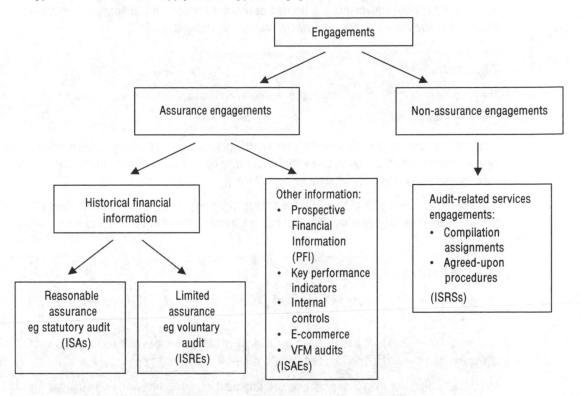

One important kind of engagement not included in this diagram is **due diligence**, as it could be placed within several of the above categories. It is covered later in this chapter.

This section focuses on reviews of historical financial information, which are limited assurance engagements. This includes several types of engagement:

* Review of financial statements (ISRE 2400)
* Review of interim financial information by the entity's auditor (ISRE 2410)

These are both types of review engagement:

Review engagements. The objective of a review engagement is to enable an auditor to state whether, on the basis of procedures which do not provide all the evidence that would be required in an audit, anything has come to the auditor's attention that causes the auditor to believe that the financial statements are not prepared, in all material respects, in accordance with an applicable financial reporting framework.

This is an exercise similar to an audit, except that in a review engagement the practitioner will rely more heavily on procedures such as **enquiry and analytical review** than on detailed substantive testing. The reasons for this are:

* He is seeking a **lower level of assurance than for an audit**, so these forms of evidence are sufficient due to risk being lower.
* Such techniques provide **indicators** that direct work to risk areas and from which to draw conclusions, and they are **quick** and, therefore, **cost-effective**.

You may be interested to note that International Standards on Review Engagements (ISREs) and International Standards on Assurance Engagements (ISAEs) use the term 'the practitioner', as opposed to 'the professional accountant' (used in the *Code of Ethics*) and of course 'the auditor' (ISAs). A 'practitioner' is defined as 'a professional accountant in public practice'.

Adopting the appropriate terminology in your exam answer can be a helpful signal to your marker that you know what you are talking about.

1.1 Review of financial statements

A review of financial statements is a **limited assurance** engagement. Guidance is contained in ISRE 2400 *Engagements to review historical financial statements* (revised in 2013).

> **ISRE 2400.7**
>
> The practitioner performs primarily **inquiry and analytical procedures** to obtain sufficient appropriate evidence [...]

Although inquiry and analytical procedures are the main sources of evidence, if the practitioner becomes aware of something that makes them think there may be a material misstatement, then further procedures may be necessary (such as substantive procedures).

Many of the requirements of the ISRE are similar to the requirements of an audit. Only **relevant** requirements must be complied with, but if a requirement is relevant then it must be complied with (ISRE 2400.19).

> **ISRE 2400.21-23**
>
> The practitioner shall **comply with relevant ethical requirements**, including those pertaining to independence.
>
> The practitioner shall plan and perform the engagement with **professional** recognizing that circumstances may exist that cause the financial statements to be materially misstated.
>
> The practitioner shall **exercise professional judgment** in conducting a review engagement.

1.1.1 Quality control

The ISRE contains requirements on quality control, in addition to the strictures of ISQC 1:

- The engagement partner is **competent** in assurance and financial reporting.

- The engagement partner is **responsible** for the engagement overall.

- The engagement partner must remain alert for **ethical issues** during the course of the engagement.

- A **monitoring** process must be in place to ensure that quality controls are sufficient and are working effectively.

1.1.2 Acceptance/continuation

The practitioner must **not** accept an engagement if:

- There is not a **rational purpose** for the engagement, or a review is not appropriate to the circumstances

- **Ethical requirements** will not be satisfied

- Information is likely to be **unavailable** or **unreliable**

- There is cause to doubt **management's integrity**

- The scope of the review has been limited such that a **disclaimer of opinion will be issued**

Preconditions must be present, including:

- An **acceptable financial reporting framework**

- Management **acknowledges its responsibilities** for internal control, for the financial statements and for providing access to information

1.1.3 Agreeing terms

> **ISRE 2400.36**
>
> The practitioner shall agree the terms of the engagement with management or those charged with governance, as appropriate, prior to performing the engagement.

This should be done in an **engagement letter** or other written form.

On recurring engagements, the practitioner assesses whether the terms need to change, or whether the engaging party needs to be reminded of the terms.

Sometimes, the nature of an assignment being carried out by a practitioner might change, and the responsible party might request that the practitioner provides less or no assurance on an engagement. In this case, the terms should be changed unless there is reasonable justification for not doing so.

1.1.4 Communication

ISRE 2400 includes a **requirement** to **communicate** with those charged with governance all matters that are important enough to merit their attention.

1.1.5 Performing the engagement

> **ISRE 2400.43**
>
> The practitioner shall determine **materiality** for the financial statements as a whole, and apply this materiality in designing the procedures and in evaluating the results obtained from those procedures.

Materiality must also be **revised** as the engagement progresses (like an audit).

> **ISRE 2400.45**
>
> The practitioner shall **obtain an understanding** of the entity and its environment, and the applicable financial reporting framework [...]

Procedures are then designed to address all material items and to focus on areas where material misstatements are more likely. The main procedures are **enquiry** and **analytical procedures**.

Procedures should be performed to address any specific issues, such as:

- **Related parties** (remain alert and if they are identified, inquire about them)
- **Fraud** and **non-compliance** with laws or regulations (if found, communicate and consider effect on conclusion)
- **Going concern**
- Use of **work performed by others** (take steps to ensure it is adequate for the purposes of the review)

It is a requirement to obtain evidence that the **financial statements agree to accounting records**.

If a material misstatement is discovered then **additional procedures** are performed to enable a conclusion to be formed.

Responsibilities in relation to **subsequent events** are similar to those on an audit.

1.1.6 Written representations

Various written representations are required:

- To confirm that management has fulfilled its responsibilities as set out in the engagement letter
- To confirm that management has disclosed various matters to the practitioner, eg the identity of any related parties, facts relating to any frauds

If these are not provided, then **discuss** the matter with management or those charged with governance, and **re-evaluate management's integrity**. If management lacks integrity, then the practitioner must **disclaim a conclusion**.

1.1.7 Reporting

There are some important differences between a review report and an auditor's report:

Review report	Auditor's report
Conclusion	Opinion
Limited assurance	Reasonable assurance
Negative form of words	Positive form of words

An **unmodified conclusion** uses a negative form of words, such as:

> 'Based on our review, nothing has come to our attention that causes us to believe that the financial statements do not present fairly, in all material respects (or do not give a true and fair view), … in accordance with the applicable financial reporting framework.'

Point to note

> The term 'negative assurance' does not exist in the current ISRE. The correct term is 'limited assurance', which is logical: this is still positive assurance, but there is just less of it than when 'reasonable assurance' is provided. The only thing that **is** negative is the way the conclusion is worded.

Modified conclusions are expressed in the same terms as the auditor's report (the terminology used for assurance conclusions and reports is now aligned with the International Standards on Auditing (ISAs)). And just like the auditor's report, a modified conclusion paragraph must be preceded by a 'Basis for' modified conclusion paragraph.

The type of modified conclusion given will depend on two things: the materiality of the issue, and the availability of evidence.

Nature of matter giving rise to the modification	Practitioner's judgement about the pervasiveness of the effects or possible effects on the subject matter information	
	Material but not pervasive	**Material and pervasive**
Subject matter information is materially misstated	Qualified conclusion	Adverse conclusion
Inability to obtain sufficient appropriate audit evidence	Qualified conclusion	Disclaimer of conclusion

It is also possible to modify the assurance report without modifying the actual conclusion, by including an Emphasis of Matter or an Other Matter paragraph. These are defined as follows.

> **ISRE 2400.87, 90**
>
> [An **Emphasis of Matter** paragraph will] draw intended users' attention to a matter presented or disclosed in the financial statements that, in the practitioner's judgment, is of such importance that it is fundamental to users' understanding of the financial statements.
>
> [An **Other Matter** paragraph will] communicate a matter other than those that are presented or disclosed in the financial statements that, in the practitioner's judgment, is relevant to users' understanding of the review, the practitioner's responsibilities or the practitioner's report and this is not prohibited by law or regulation.

The key difference here is:

Emphasis of Matter	Other Matter
Matter **is** already presented or disclosed in the subject matter information.	Matter **is not** already presented or disclosed in the subject matter information.

ISRE 2400 includes a sample unmodified report in its Appendix:

Form of Unqualified Review Report

INDEPENDENT PRACTITIONER'S REVIEW REPORT

[Appropriate Addressee]

Report on the Financial Statements

We have reviewed the accompanying financial statements of ABC Company, which comprise the statement of financial position as at 31 December 20X1, and the statement of comprehensive income, statement of changes in equity and statement of cash flows for the year then ended, and a summary of significant accounting policies and other explanatory information.

Management's Responsibility for the Financial Statements

Management is responsible for the preparation and fair presentation of these financial statements in accordance with the International Financial Reporting Standard for Small and Medium-sized Entities, and for such internal control as management determines is necessary to enable the preparation of financial statements that are free from material misstatement, whether due to fraud or error. Based on our review, nothing has come to our attention that causes us to believe that the accompanying financial statements do not give a true and fair view (or 'are not presented fairly, in all material respects,') in accordance with International Accounting Standards.

Practitioner's Responsibility

Our responsibility is to express a conclusion on the accompanying financial statements. We conducted our review in accordance with International Standard on Review Engagements (ISRE) 2400 (Revised), *Engagements to Review Historical Financial Statements*. ISRE 2400 (Revised) requires us to conclude whether anything has come to our attention that causes us to believe that the financial statements, taken as a whole, are not prepared in all material respects in accordance with the applicable financial reporting framework. This Standard also requires us to comply with relevant ethical requirements.

A review of financial statements in accordance with ISRE 2400 (Revised) is a limited assurance engagement. The practitioner performs procedures, primarily consisting of making inquiries of management and others within the entity, as appropriate, and applying analytical procedures, and evaluates the evidence obtained.

The procedures performed in a review are substantially less than those performed in an audit conducted in accordance with International Standards on Auditing. Accordingly, we do not express an audit opinion on these financial statements.

Conclusion

Based on our review, nothing has come to our attention that causes us to believe that these financial statements do not present fairly, in all material respects, (or do not give a true and fair view of) the financial position of ABC Company as at 31 December 20X1, and (of) its financial performance and cash flows for the year then ended, in accordance with the International Financial Reporting Standard for Small and Medium-sized Entities.

Report on Other Legal and Regulatory Requirements

[Form and content of this section of the practitioner's report will vary depending on the nature of the practitioner's other reporting responsibilities.]

[Practitioner's signature]

[Date of the practitioner's report]

[Practitioner's address]

A report with a **modified conclusion** would replace the 'Conclusion' paragraph above with the following.

Basis for Qualified Conclusion

The company's inventories are carried in the statement of financial position at xxx. Management has not stated the inventories at the lower of cost and net realisable value but has stated them solely at cost, which constitutes a departure from the requirements of the Financial Reporting Framework (XYZ Law) of Jurisdiction X. The company's records indicate that, had management stated the inventories at the lower of cost and net realisable value, an amount of xxx would have been required to write the inventories down to their net realisable value. Accordingly, cost of sales would have been increased by xxx, and income tax, net income and shareholders' equity would have been reduced by xxx, xxx and xxx respectively.

Qualified Conclusion

Based on our review, except for the effects of the matter described in the Basis for Qualified Conclusion paragraph, nothing has come to our attention that causes us to believe that the financial statements of ABC Company are not prepared, in all material respects, in accordance with the Financial Reporting Framework (XYZ Law) of Jurisdiction X.

1.2 Review of interim financial information performed by the independent auditor of the entity   12/12

This subject is covered by ISRE 2410 *Review of interim financial information performed by the independent auditor of the entity*.

1.2.1 General principles

The auditor should comply with **ethical principles** relevant to the audit when carrying out an interim review and should apply **quality control procedures** applicable to the individual engagement. In addition, the auditor should plan and perform the engagement with an attitude of **professional scepticism**. The auditor should agree the terms of the engagement with the client (these will not be the same terms as for the audit, as the review will result in a lower level of assurance than the annual audit), with a view to providing negative assurance.

1.2.2 Procedures

The procedures outlined below follow the same pattern as an audit, but, because this is a review not an audit, they are not as detailed as audit procedures.

The auditor should possess sufficient understanding of the entity and its environment to understand the types of misstatement that might arise in interim financial information and to plan the relevant procedures (mainly enquiry and analytical review) to enable them to ensure that the financial information is prepared in accordance with the applicable financial reporting framework. This will usually include:

- Reading last year's audit and previous review files
- Considering any significant risks that were identified in the prior year audit
- Reading the most recent and comparable interim financial information
- Considering materiality
- Considering the nature of any corrected or uncorrected misstatements in last year's financial statements
- Considering significant financial accounting and reporting matters of ongoing importance
- Considering the results of any interim audit work for this year's audit
- Considering the work of internal audit
- Asking management what their assessment is of the risk that the interim financial statements might be affected by fraud
- Asking management whether there have been any significant changes in business activity, and if so, what effect they have had

- Asking management about any significant changes in internal controls and the potential effect on preparing the interim financial information
- Asking how the interim financial information has been prepared and the reliability of the underlying accounting records

A recently appointed auditor should obtain an understanding of the entity and its environment, as it relates to both the interim review and final audit.

The key elements of the review will be:

- **Enquiries** of accounting and finance staff
- **Analytical procedures**

Ordinarily procedures would include:

- Reading the minutes of meetings of shareholders, those charged with governance and other appropriate committees
- Considering the effect of matters giving rise to a modification of the audit or review report, accounting adjustments or unadjusted misstatements from previous audits
- If relevant, communicating with other auditors auditing different components of the business
- Analytical procedures designed to identify relationships and unusual items that may reflect a material misstatement
- Reading the interim financial information and considering whether anything has come to the auditors' attention indicating that it is not prepared in accordance with the applicable financial reporting framework
- Agreeing the interim financial information to the underlying accounting records

The auditor should make enquiries of members of management responsible for financial and accounting matters about:

- Whether the interim financial information has been prepared and presented in accordance with the applicable financial reporting framework
- Whether there have been changes in accounting policies
- Whether new transactions have required changes in accounting policies
- Whether there are any known uncorrected misstatements
- Whether there have been unusual or complex transactions, eg disposal of a business segment
- Significant assumptions relevant to fair values
- Whether related party transactions have been accounted for and disclosed correctly
- Significant changes in commitments and contractual obligations
- Significant changes in contingent liabilities including litigation or claims
- Compliance with debt covenants
- Matters about which questions have arisen in the course of applying the review procedures
- Significant transactions occurring in the last days of the interim period or the first days of the next
- Knowledge or suspicion of any fraud
- Knowledge of any allegations of fraud
- Knowledge of any actual or possible non-compliance with laws and regulations that could have a material effect on the interim financial information
- Whether all events up to the date of the review report that might result in adjustment in the interim financial information have been identified
- Whether management has changed its assessment of the entity being a going concern

The auditor should evaluate discovered misstatements individually and in aggregate to see if they are material.

The auditor should obtain **written representations** from management that it acknowledges its responsibility for the design and implementation of internal control, that the interim financial information is prepared and presented in accordance with the applicable financial reporting framework and that the

effect of uncorrected misstatements are immaterial (a summary of these should be attached to the representations). The auditor should also obtain representations that all **significant facts** relating to **frauds or non-compliance with law and regulations**, and all **significant subsequent events**, have been disclosed to the auditor.

The auditor should read the other information accompanying the interim financial information to ensure that it is not inconsistent with it.

If the auditors believe a matter should be adjusted in the financial information, they should **inform management** as soon as possible. If management does not respond within a reasonable time, then the auditors should inform those charged with governance. If they do not respond, then the auditor should consider whether to modify the report or to withdraw from the engagement and the final audit if necessary. If the auditors uncover fraud or non-compliance with laws and regulations, they should communicate that promptly with the **appropriate level of management**. The auditors should communicate matters of interest arising to those charged with governance.

1.2.3 Reporting

The ISRE gives the following example standard report.

Note. ISRE 2410 has not yet been updated for the changes in terminology introduced by the revision of IAS 1 *Presentation of Financial Statements*.

Report on Review of Interim Financial Information

(Appropriate addressee)

Introduction

We have reviewed the accompanying balance sheet of ABC Entity as of 31 March 20X1 and the related statements of income, changes in equity and cash flows for the three-month period then ended, and a summary of significant accounting policies and other explanatory notes. Management is responsible for the preparation and fair presentation of this interim financial information in accordance with (indicate applicable financial reporting framework). Our responsibility is to express a conclusion on this interim financial information based on our review.

Scope of Review

We conducted our review in accordance with International Standard on Review Engagements 2410, 'Review of Interim Financial Information Performed by the Independent Auditor of the Entity'. A review of interim financial information consists of making inquiries, primarily of persons responsible for financial and accounting matters, and applying analytical and other review procedures. A review is substantially less in scope than an audit conducted in accordance with International Standards on Auditing and consequently does not enable us to obtain assurance that we would become aware of all significant matters that might be identified in an audit. Accordingly, we do not express an audit opinion.

Conclusion

Based on our review, nothing has come to our attention that causes us to believe that the accompanying interim financial information does not give a true and fair view of (or 'does not present fairly, in all material respects,') the financial position of the entity as at 31 March 20X1, and of its financial performance and its cash flows for the three-month period then ended in accordance with (applicable financial reporting framework, including a reference to the jurisdiction or country of origin of the financial reporting framework when the financial reporting framework used is not International Financial Reporting Standards).

AUDITOR

Date

Address

It also gives examples of modified reports:

Review report: Departure from the applicable financial reporting framework

Previous paragraphs as per standard report.

Basis for Qualified Conclusion

Based on information provided to us by management, ABC Entity has excluded from property and long-term debt certain lease obligations that we believe should be capitalised to conform with (indicate applicable financial reporting framework). This information indicates that if these lease obligations were capitalised at 31 March 20X1, property would be increased by $ _____, long-term debt by $ _____, and net income and earnings per share would be increased (decreased) by ($ _____, $ _____), $ _____, and $ _____ respectively for the three-month period then ended.

Qualified Conclusion

Based on our review, with the exception of the matter described in the preceding paragraph, nothing has come to our attention that caused us to believe that the accompanying interim financial information does not give a true and fair view of (or 'does not present fairly, in all material respects,') the financial position of the entity as at 31 March 20X1, and of its financial performance and its cash flows for the three-month period then ended in accordance with (indicate applicable financial reporting framework, including the reference to the jurisdiction or country of origin of the financial reporting framework when the financial reporting framework used is not International Financial Reporting Standards).

AUDITOR

Date

Address

Review report: Limitation on scope not imposed by management

Introduction paragraph – as per standard report

Scope paragraph

Except as explained in the following paragraph .... – as per standard report.

Basis for Qualified Conclusion

As a result of a fire in a branch office on (date) that destroyed its accounts receivable records, we were unable to complete our review of accounts receivable totalling $ _____ included in the interim financial information. The entity is in the process of reconstructing these records and is uncertain as to whether these records will support the amount shown above the related allowance for uncollectible accounts. Had we been able to complete our review of accounts receivable, matters might have come to our attention indicating that adjustments might be necessary to the interim financial information.

Qualified Conclusion

Except for the adjustments to the interim financial information that we might have become aware of had it not been for the situation described above, based on our review, nothing has come to our attention that causes us to believe that the accompanying interim financial information does not give a true and fair view of (or 'does not present fairly, in all material respects,') the financial position of the entity as at 31 March 20X1, and of its financial performance and its cash flows for the three-month period then ended in accordance with (indicate applicable financial reporting framework, including a reference to the jurisdiction or country of origin of the financial reporting framework when the financial reporting framework used is not International Financial Reporting Standards).

AUDITOR

Date

Address

1.3 Due diligence

12/13

Due diligence is a kind of review engagement, but in practice its definition is flexible and can mean a variety of different things.

A typical due diligence engagement is where an adviser (often an audit firm) is engaged by one company planning to take over another to perform an assessment of the material risks associated with the transaction (including validating the assumptions underlying the purchase), to ensure that the acquirer has all the necessary facts and that the perceived business opportunities are in fact real. This is important when determining purchase price. Similarly, due diligence can also be requested by sellers.

Due diligence may include some or all of the following aspects.

- Financial due diligence (a review of the financial position and obligations of a target to identify such matters as covenants and contingent obligations)
- Operational and IT due diligence (extent of operational and IT risks, including quality of systems, associated with a target business)
- People due diligence (key staff positions under the new structure, contract termination costs and costs of integration)
- Regulatory due diligence (review of the target's level of compliance with relevant regulation)
- Environmental due diligence (environmental, health and safety and social issues in a target)

A typical due diligence review could include enquiries into:

- Structure, including how the target is owned and constituted and what changes will be necessary
- Financial health, based on a detailed examination of past financial statements and an analysis of the existing asset base
- Credibility of the owners, directors and senior managers, including validation of the career histories of all the main players in the business
- Future potential, reflected in the strengths of its products or services and the probability of earnings growth over the medium to long term
- Assessment of the risk to the acquiring business, in terms of their markets, strategy and likely future events
- The business plan, in terms of how realistic it is, how solid the assumptions used are and how well it conveys the potential

When it comes to placing it in an engagement category, due diligence is something of a wildcard. It can be performed as any of the following.

- As a review of historical financial information (limited assurance)
- As an assurance engagement (limited assurance)
- As agreed-upon procedures (no assurance)

There is no international standard on due diligence engagements, so in practice the engagement would be conducted in accordance with whichever standard best fits the particular engagement being conducted – perhaps ISRE 2400, ISAE 3000 or ISRS 4400.

Exam focus point	Your P7 exam tends to focus on due diligence as a review engagement providing **limited assurance**, although it is possible that it may be examined in any of its forms. You may still be given credit for answering on the basis of it being agreed-upon procedures (unless the question specifically states otherwise). With exam questions in this area, it is crucial that the starting point for your answer is the **scenario**. Scenarios in P7 tend to contain so many potential marks that it is just not necessary to recite pre-learned material.

The following question is taken from an actual exam question. Even though you may not yet feel confident in your technical knowledge, you should still be able to score well if you answer the requirements specifically, and base your answer as much as possible on the scenario.

376   12: Audit-related services and other assurance services | Part E Other assignments

Your audit client, Prescott Co, is a national hotel group with substantial cash resources. Its accounting functions are well managed and the group accounting policies are rigorously applied. The company's financial year end is 30 June.

Prescott has been seeking to acquire a construction company for some time in order to bring in-house the building and refurbishment of hotels and related leisure facilities (eg swimming pools, squash courts and restaurants). Prescott's management has recently identified Robson Construction Co as a potential target and has urgently requested that you undertake a limited due diligence review lasting two days next week.

Further to its preliminary talks with Robson's management, Prescott has provided you with the following brief on Robson Construction Co.

- The chief executive, managing director and finance director are all family members and major shareholders. The company name has an established reputation for quality constructions.

- Due to a recession in the building trade the company has been operating at its overdraft limit for the last 18 months and has been close to breaching debt covenants on several occasions.

- Robson's accounting policies are generally less prudent than those of Prescott (eg assets are depreciated over longer estimated useful lives).

- Contract revenue is recognised on the percentage of completion method, measured by reference to costs incurred to date. Provisions are made for loss-making contracts.

- The company's management team includes a qualified and experienced quantity surveyor. Their main responsibilities include:

    - Supervising quarterly physical counts at major construction sites
    - Comparing costs to date against quarterly rolling budgets
    - Determining profits and losses by contract at each financial year end

- Although much of the labour is provided under subcontracts all construction work is supervised by full-time site managers.

In February 20X2 Robson received a claim that a site on which it built a housing development in 20W4 was not properly drained and is now subsiding. Residents are demanding rectification and claiming damages. Robson has referred the matter to its legal counsel and denied all liability, as the site preparation was subcontracted to Sarwar Services Co. No provisions have been made in respect of the claims, nor has any disclosure been made.

The auditor's report on Robson's financial statements for the year to 31 December 20X1 was signed, without modification, in September 20X2.

Required

(a) Explain the meaning of the term 'due diligence' and identify some practical examples of this type of assignment.

(b) Identify and explain the specific matters to be clarified in the terms of engagement for this due diligence review of Robson Construction Co.

(c) Recommend the principal additional information that should be made available for your review of Robson Construction Co, and explain the need for the information.

Answer

(a) **Due diligence** reviews are a specific type of review engagement. A typical due diligence engagement is where an adviser (often an audit firm) is engaged by one company planning to take over another to perform an assessment of the material risks associated with the transaction (including validating the assumptions underlying the purchase), to ensure that the acquirer has all the necessary facts. This is important when determining purchase price. Similarly, due diligence can also be requested by sellers.

Practical examples include:

- **Financial due diligence** (a review of the financial position and obligations of a target to identify such matters as covenants and contingent obligations)
- **Operational and IT due diligence** (extent of operational and IT risks, including quality of systems, associated with a target business)
- **People due diligence** (key staff positions under the new structure, contract termination costs and cost of integration)
- **Regulatory due diligence** (review of the target's level of compliance with relevant regulation)
- **Environmental due diligence** (environmental, health and safety and social issues in a target)

(b) **Matters to be clarified in engagement letter**

(i) The nature of the opinion must be agreed. On this assignment it is likely to be expressed as negative assurance, saying 'nothing has come to our attention to indicate that the information is not free from material misstatement'. This is a normal form of words used to express a moderate level of assurance.

(ii) The timescale of the review should be set out. Prescott has requested a limited review over two days. The deadline for reporting should also be set.

(iii) A liability disclaimer should be included to confirm that the engagement should not be relied on to disclose errors or other irregularities.

(iv) The terms of reference of the review should be set out, ie its aims and objectives. It should also state that the investigation will be mainly in the form of inquiry and analytical procedures.

(v) The letter should state that any decision made on whether to go ahead with the acquisition will be the responsibility of Prescott's management.

(vi) The engagement letter should contain the fee for the engagement and details of the team undertaking the review.

(c) **Additional information**

(i) Previous years' financial statements should be obtained for details of the accounting policies used by Robson, any provisions/contingent liabilities made in the accounts, and the assumptions made in estimating completion of construction contracts.

(ii) Recent management accounts and cash flow forecasts are required to assess the quality of management information. Robson has been operating at its overdraft limit for the last 18 months so the accuracy of this information will be critical to decision making.

(iii) The loan agreement with the bank and other lenders should be obtained so that details of the overdraft limit and other debt covenants are understood. The terms should be reviewed closely to determine whether any penalties or similar would be triggered by a takeover of Robson.

(iv) Any legal correspondence regarding the claim on the site on which Robson built a housing development in 20W4 should be obtained, together with any other claims or disputes that the company is involved with.

(v) The quantity surveyor's working papers for the last count they supervised and the latest quarterly rolling budgets should be obtained. Their assessment of profits/losses/degree of completion of recent contracts will need to be reviewed.

(vi) Information on the types of building work that Robson does is important. Prescott wants to acquire the company to undertake the building of hotels and other leisure facilities, such as swimming pools.

(vii) Details of current contract agreements with customers are required to get information on any guarantees, penalties etc that may be incurred.

1.4 Agreed-upon procedures

Agreed-upon procedures assignment. In an engagement to perform agreed-upon procedures, an auditor is engaged to carry out those procedures of an audit nature to which the auditor and the entity and any appropriate third parties have agreed and to report on factual findings. The recipients of the report must form their own conclusions from the report by the auditor. The report is restricted to those parties that have agreed to the procedures to be performed since others, unaware of the reasons for the procedures, may misinterpret the results.

Agreed-upon procedures assignments are discussed in ISRS 4400 *Engagements to perform agreed-upon procedures regarding financial information*.

1.4.1 Accepting appointment

ISRS 4400.9

The auditor should ensure with representatives of the entity, and ordinarily, other specified parties who will receive copies of the report of factual findings, that there is a clear understanding regarding the agreed procedures and the conditions of the engagement.

1.4.2 Carrying out procedures and reporting

The auditor should plan the assignment. They should carry out the agreed-upon procedures, documenting their process and findings.

ISRS 4400.18

The report of factual findings should contain:

(a)   Title

(b)   Addressee (ordinarily the client who engaged the auditor to perform the agreed-upon procedures)

(c)   Identification of specific financial or non-financial information to which the agreed-upon procedures have been applied

(d)   A statement that the procedures performed were those agreed upon with the recipient

(e)   A statement that the engagement was performed in accordance with the International Standard on Related Services applicable to agreed-upon procedure engagements, or with relevant national standards or practices

(f)   When relevant, a statement that the auditor is not independent of the entity

(g)   Identification of the purpose for which the agreed-upon procedures were performed

(h)   A listing of the specific procedures performed

(i)   A description of the auditor's factual findings including sufficient details of errors and exceptions found

(j)   Statement that the procedures performed do not constitute either an audit or a review and, as such, no assurance is expressed

(k)   A statement that had the auditor performed additional procedures, an audit or a review, other matters might have come to light that would have been reported

(l)   A statement that the report is restricted to those parties that have agreed to the procedures to be performed

(m)   A statement (when applicable) that the report relates only to the elements, accounts, items or financial and non-financial information specified and that it does not extend to the entity's financial statements taken as a whole

(n)   Date of the report

(o)   Auditor's address

(p)   Auditor's signature

2 Assurance engagements

FAST FORWARD

> Assurance services improve the quality of decision making for users of information.

Guidance here is found in ISAE 3000 *Assurance engagements other than audits or reviews of historical financial information*, which was revised in December 2013.

As the title of the ISAE indicates, we are **not** discussing assurance engagements on 'historical financial information', such as reviews of financial statements. Examples of engagements that may fall within the scope of ISAE 3000 are:

- Environmental, social and sustainability reports
- Information systems, internal control, and corporate governance processes
- Compliance with grant conditions, contracts and regulations

2.1 Elements of an assurance engagement

ISAE 3000 defines an assurance engagement as follows.

Key term

> **Assurance engagement.** An engagement in which a practitioner aims to obtain sufficient appropriate evidence in order to express a conclusion designed to enhance the degree of confidence of the intended users other than the responsible party about the subject matter information (that is, the outcome of the measurement or evaluation of an underlying subject matter against criteria). *(ISAE 3000.12)*

Assurance engagements are classified in terms of their basic type, and the **level of assurance** provided.

2.2 Engagement type

FAST FORWARD

> Assurance engagements may be attestation engagements or direct engagements.

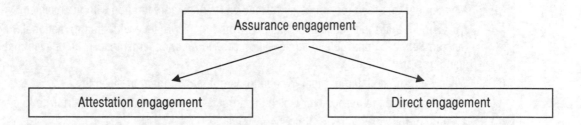

ISAE 3000's rather complex definitions of these terms are summarised below.

Key terms

> **Attestation engagement.** An assurance engagement in which a party other than the practitioner measures or evaluates the underlying subject matter against the criteria. A party other than the practitioner also often presents the resulting subject matter information in a report or statement. In some cases, however, the subject matter information may be presented by the practitioner in the assurance report. In an attestation engagement, the practitioner's conclusion addresses whether the subject matter information is free from material misstatement.
>
> **Direct engagement.** An assurance engagement in which the practitioner measures or evaluates the underlying subject matter against the applicable criteria and the practitioner presents the resulting subject matter information as part of, or accompanying, the assurance report. In a direct engagement, the practitioner's conclusion addresses the reported outcome of the measurement or evaluation of the underlying subject matter against the criteria.
>
> *(ISAE 3000.12)*

Broadly speaking, an **attestation engagement** is one in which the client prepares the information and the practitioner gives assurance on it. The auditor's report on the financial statements would be an example of this, except that auditor's reports are not within the scope of the ISAE.

A **direct engagement** is one in which the practitioner prepares the information and at the same time gives assurance on it.

Example

A professional accountant is engaged to provide assurance on the sales figures of Ocean Gift Shop Co, for its overseas owners. The company prepares the sales report itself, measuring its sales in line with the owners' criteria, and the professional accountant provides a limited assurance report which is appended to the sales report. This is an **attestation engagement**.

2.3 Assurance provided

FAST FORWARD
> Assurance engagements may give reasonable assurance or limited assurance.

The level of assurance may be **reasonable** or **limited**.

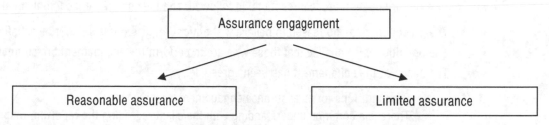

These levels of assurance were discussed in your earlier studies. Remember that absolute assurance can **never** be given on an assurance engagement due to the **inherent limitations** of such engagements.

The ISAE 3000 definitions are as follows. They are worth reading, but not memorising.

Key terms

> **Reasonable assurance engagement.** An assurance engagement in which the practitioner reduces engagement **risk** to an acceptably low level in the circumstances of the engagement as the basis for the practitioner's conclusion. The practitioner's conclusion is expressed in a form that conveys the practitioner's opinion on the outcome of the measurement or evaluation of the underlying subject matter against criteria.
>
> **Limited assurance engagement.** An assurance engagement in which the practitioner reduces engagement risk to a level that is acceptable in the circumstances of the engagement but where that risk is greater than for a reasonable assurance engagement as the basis for expressing a conclusion in a form that conveys whether, based on the procedures performed and evidence obtained, a matter(s) has come to the practitioner's attention to cause the practitioner to believe the subject matter information is materially misstated.
>
> The nature, timing and extent of procedures performed in a limited assurance engagement is limited compared with that necessary in a reasonable assurance engagement but is planned to obtain a level of assurance that is, in the practitioner's professional judgement, meaningful. To be meaningful, the level of assurance obtained by the practitioner is likely to enhance the intended users' confidence about the subject matter information to a degree that is clearly more than inconsequential.
>
> *(ISAE 3000.12)*

Some of the salient points here may be summarised as follows:

Assurance	Level of risk	Conclusion	Procedures
Reasonable	Low	Positive expression – opinion expressed	High
Limited	Acceptable in the circumstances	Negative expression – whether matters have come to attention indicating material misstatement	Limited, but still provides a meaningful level of assurance

2.4 Accepting and continuing appointment

FAST FORWARD
> Assurance engagements should only be accepted if the firm meets the requirements of the IESBA *Code of Ethics for Professional Accountants* and ISQC 1.

The standard requires that practitioners ensure they comply with the IESBA *Code of Ethics* (ISAE 3000.20).

Acceptance or continuation procedures must be followed, and the engagement can only be undertaken if:

- The practitioner has no reason to believe that **ethical requirements** will not be satisfied.
- The practitioner is satisfied that those who are to perform the engagement are **competent.**
- The basis for the engagement has been agreed, ie:
  - **Preconditions** for an assurance engagement are present
  - There is a common understanding with the client regarding the reporting **responsibilities**

2.4.1 Preconditions for an assurance engagement

FAST FORWARD
> The practitioner must ensure that the preconditions for an assurance engagement are present.

Preconditions include:

- The roles and responsibilities of the parties are suitable
- The engagement has the following characteristics:
  - **Subject matter** is **appropriate**.
  - **Criteria** to be applied are **suitable** – ie they are relevant, complete, reliable, neutral and understandable.
  - **Criteria** to be applied will be **available to users**.
  - **Evidence** should be **obtainable** (to support the conclusion).
  - Conclusion will be contained in a written report.
  - Engagement has a **rational purpose**, and a meaningful level of assurance may be obtained.

If the preconditions are not present then decline the engagement. If the engagement is a legal requirement, then it may be performed but without referring to ISAEs in the report.

If there is a limitation on the scope of the work such that the practitioner will disclaim a conclusion, then the engagement should not be accepted.

2.4.2 Agreeing terms

ISAE 3000.27

The practitioner shall agree on the terms of the engagement with the engaging party.

This should be done in an **engagement letter** or other written form.

On recurring engagements, the practitioner assesses whether the terms need to change, or whether the engaging party needs to be reminded of the terms.

Sometimes, the nature of an assignment being carried out by a practitioner might change, and the responsible party might request that the practitioner provides less or no assurance on an engagement. In this case, the terms should be changed unless there is reasonable justification for doing so, and the practitioner must not disregard evidence obtained prior to the change.

2.4.3 Report prescribed by law or regulation

If the **layout** or **wording** of the report are prescribed by law or regulation, then:

ISAE 3000.30

[...] the practitioner shall evaluate:

(a)   Whether intended **users might misunderstand** the assurance conclusion; and

(b)   If so, whether **additional explanation** in the assurance report can **mitigate possible misunderstanding**.

2.5 Quality control

FAST FORWARD

> Quality control requirements must be met in relation both to the engagement and to the firm.

The **engagement partner** must be a member of a firm which applies ISQC 1 (or another equivalent set of requirements), and must be **competent** both in **assurance skills** and in the **underlying subject matter**.

Further, the **team** must have the competence and capabilities to provide the required assurance.

If an expert is to be used (or another practitioner from outside the engagement team), then the partner must be able to be involved in their work to the extent that is necessary for the partner to accept responsibility for the conclusion expressed.

The **engagement partner** is responsible for the overall quality of the engagement, including responsibility for:

- **Client acceptance** procedures
- **Compliance** with professional standards, and legal and regulatory requirements
- **Reviews** being performed in line with the firm's procedures
- **Documentation** being maintained
- Appropriate **consultation** being taken on difficult or contentious matters

The engagement partner must be alert for evidence of the team not complying with ethical requirements. Moreover, they must consider the results of the firm's monitoring process and whether any deficiencies noted may affect the engagement.

If an engagement quality control reviewer is required by law or regulation, then the engagement partner must take responsibility for discussing significant matters with the reviewer.

2.6 Professional scepticism, judgement, skills and techniques

In common with many other recent standards, ISAE 3000 emphasises professional scepticism and the exercise of professional judgement. It adds into the mix the necessity of applying assurance skills and techniques.

ISAE 3000.37-39

The practitioner shall plan and perform an engagement with professional skepticism, recognizing that circumstances may exist that cause the subject matter information to be materiality misstated [sic].

The practitioner shall exercise professional judgment in planning and performing an assurance engagement, including determining the nature, timing and extent of procedures.

The practitioner shall apply assurance skills and techniques as part of an iterative, systematic engagement process.

2.7 Planning and performing the engagement

ISAE 3000.40

The practitioner shall plan the engagement so that it will be performed in an effective manner[...].

This involves:

- Setting the scope, timing and direction of the engagement
- Determining the nature, timing and extent of procedures
- Considering whether the criteria are suitable

Once the engagement has been accepted, if it is then discovered that preconditions are not present, the practitioner must discuss the matter with the appropriate parties and determine whether the issue can be resolved, and whether the engagement can be continued with. The practitioner should consider withdrawing from the engagement, or if this is not possible then what the effect might be on the conclusion expressed.

The practitioner must consider **materiality** in planning the engagement, and must **accumulate uncorrected misstatements** (other than those that are 'clearly trivial'). This is just like an audit engagement. Interestingly (or not), the ISAE says the following about 'clearly trivial': 'When there is any uncertainty about whether one or more items are clearly trivial, the matter is considered not to be clearly trivial' (A119).

2.8 Understanding the underlying subject matter

Some terminology:

Key terms

Underlying subject matter. The phenomenon that is measured or evaluated by applying criteria.

Subject matter information. The outcome of the measurement or evaluation of the underlying subject matter against the criteria, ie the information that results from applying the criteria to the underlying subject matter.

(ISAE 3000.12)

An example here might be the entity's actual environmental performance (underlying subject matter), and a set of KPIs that are calculated thereon (subject matter information).

The extent of the understanding required depends on the level of assurance being provided.

Limited assurance	Reasonable assurance
Understanding must:	Understanding must:
– Enable practitioner to **identify areas** where a material misstatement is likely	– Enable practitioner to **identify and assess the risks** of material misstatement
– Provide a basis for designing procedures to address these **areas**	– Provide a basis for designing procedures to respond to assessed **risks**
Practitioner must consider the process used to prepare the subject matter information.	Practitioner must obtain understanding of **internal control** over the preparation of subject matter information.
	This includes evaluating the design of controls and performing procedures to test their implementation.

Limited assurance	Reasonable assurance
If practitioner becomes aware that there may be a material misstatement, they must **perform procedures** to determine whether or not there is a material misstatement.	If practitioner becomes aware that there may be a material misstatement, they must **revise the risk assessment done at the planning stage** and perform additional procedures where necessary (ie rather than just addressing the misstatement itself, consider the impact on the whole of the subject matter information).

2.9 Using the work of an expert

The term 'practitioner's expert' appears in ISAE 3000 as the equivalent of 'auditor's expert' in ISA 620. There is no exact equivalent of 'management's expert' – it is either 'responsible party's expert', 'measurer's expert' or 'evaluator's expert'.

> **ISAE 3000.52**
>
> When the work of a **practitioner's expert** is to be used, the practitioner shall also:
>
> (a) Evaluate whether the practitioner's expert has the necessary **competence**, **capabilities** and **objectivity** for the practitioner's purposes […]
>
> (b) **Obtain a sufficient understanding** of the field of expertise of the practitioner's expert;
>
> (c) Agree with the practitioner's expert on the **nature**, **scope** and **objectives** of that expert's work; and
>
> (d) **Evaluate the adequacy** of the practitioner's expert's work for the practitioner's purposes.

The issues with a responsible party's expert are similar to these, except that clearly the practitioner does not need to agree the scope of the work to be done with the expert ((c) above), and the work must be evaluated as evidence, rather than for the practitioner's purposes ((d) above).

2.9.1 Using the work of internal audit

If planning to use the work of internal audit (IA), evaluate:

- IA's **organisational status** and relevant **policies and procedures**
- IA's **competence**
- Whether IA applies a **systematic and disciplined approach**
- Whether IA's **work is adequate** for the **purposes** of the engagement

2.10 Written representations

Some written representations must be requested in all engagements:

- That all relevant information of which the 'appropriate party' (ie management) are aware has been provided

- Confirmation of the measurement of subject matter information (ie what the amounts are), and that this information is complete

Written representations can be requested where necessary, but they must be evaluated for **reasonableness** and for the **competence** of the person making them.

If there are **doubts about reliability**, then discuss the matter with the appropriate party, re-evaluate any other representations received and take any 'appropriate actions'.

2.11 Subsequent events

The responsibilities here are similar to an audit:

- Consider events up to the date of the report.
- Respond appropriately to facts that 'become known' after the date of the report.
- There is no responsibility to perform procedures after the date of the report.

2.12 Other information

The practitioner **must read other information** in documents containing the assurance report. The action is the same for both material inconsistencies and material misstatements of fact that are identified: **discuss the matter with the appropriate party and take further action as appropriate**.

2.13 Concluding and reporting

2.13.1 Drawing a conclusion

Whereas an auditor's report gives an 'opinion', an assurance report gives a 'conclusion'.

The ISAE makes the following observations about reporting.

> **ISAE 3000.64/67**
>
> The practitioner shall evaluate the sufficiency and appropriateness of the evidence obtained in the context of the engagement and, if necessary in the circumstances, attempt to obtain further evidence.
>
> The assurance report shall be in writing and shall contain a clear expression of the practitioner's conclusion about the subject matter information.

2.13.2 Unmodified conclusions

A **reasonable assurance** engagement will result in a conclusion expressed in a **positive form of words**, giving a higher level of assurance. For example, the conclusion of a reasonable assurance report on forecast financial information might say:

> 'In our opinion, the forecast of the entity's financial performance is properly prepared, in all material respects, based on XYZ criteria.'

A **limited assurance** engagement will result in a conclusion expressed in a **negative form of words**, giving a lower level of assurance. For example, the conclusion of a limited assurance report on a company's compliance with some specified piece of law might say:

> 'Based on the procedures performed and evidence obtained, nothing has come to our attention that causes us to believe that [the entity] has not complied, in all material respects, with XYZ law.'

2.13.3 Modified conclusions

Although the level of assurance differs between a reasonable and a limited assurance engagement, the reasons for modifying the conclusion given are the same for both. The practitioner has several different types of modified conclusion to pick from. These are similar to those available for an auditor's report, and the same as those in ISRE 2400, covered earlier in this chapter.

The type of modified conclusion given will depend on two things: the materiality of the issue, and the availability of evidence.

Nature of matter giving rise to the modification	Practitioner's judgement about the pervasiveness of the effects or possible effects on the subject matter information	
	Material but not pervasive	Material and pervasive
Subject matter information is materially misstated	Qualified conclusion	Adverse conclusion
Inability to obtain sufficient, appropriate audit evidence	Qualified conclusion	Disclaimer of conclusion

It is also possible to modify the assurance report without modifying the actual conclusion, by including an Emphasis of Matter or an Other Matter paragraph.

[The following report is an example of an independent verification statement for a social and environmental audit. It is prepared in line with a superseded version of ISAE 3000, and combines a limited assurance report on a company's sustainability report, with a reasonable assurance report on some specific pieces of performance information. The report gives unmodified conclusions for both aspects.]

Independent assurance report

To the board of directors of Statoil ASA

We were engaged by the corporate executive committee of Statoil ASA ('Statoil') to provide assurance on the Sustainability Report 2012 ('the Report'), as presented in the section 'Sustainable performance' in the Statoil Annual and Sustainability Report 2012. The corporate executive committee is responsible for the preparation of the Report, including the identification of material issues and the determination of the GRI Application Level. Our responsibility is to issue an assurance report based on the engagement outlined below.

Scope

Our assurance engagement was designed to provide: limited assurance on whether the Report is presented fairly, in all material respects, in accordance with the reporting criteria; reasonable assurance on whether for the indicators in the table below the data and related explanatory notes are presented, in all material respects, in accordance with the reporting criteria.

- *Safety and security indicators*: Total Recordable Injury Frequency (TRIF), Total recordable injury frequency per country, Lost-time injury frequency, Serious Incident Frequency (SIF), Oil spills, Other spills;

- *Environmental indicators*: CO2 emissions, CH4 emissions, NOx emissions, nmVOC emissions, SOX emissions, Energy consumption, Non-hazardous waste recovery rate, Hazardous waste recovery rate, Regular discharges of oil to water, Fresh water consumption;

- *Health indicator*: Sickness absence; In addition we were asked to check whether Statoil's GRI Application Level, as disclosed in the section 'GRI and UN Global Compact index', is consistent with the GRI criteria for the disclosed Application Level.

We do not provide any assurance on the achievability of the objectives, targets and expectations of Statoil.

Procedures performed to obtain a limited level of assurance are aimed at determining the plausibility of information and are less extensive than those for a reasonable level of assurance.

Reporting criteria and assurance standard

Statoil applies the Sustainability Reporting Guidelines (G3.1), including the Oil and Gas Sector Supplement, of the Global Reporting Initiative supported by internally developed guidelines as described in the section 'About the report'. It is important to view the performance data in the context of these criteria.

We conducted our engagement in accordance with the International Standard for Assurance Engagements (ISAE 3000): Assurance Engagements other than Audits or Reviews of Historical Financial Information, issued by the International Auditing and Assurance Standards Board. This standard requires, among others, that the assurance team possesses the specific knowledge, skills and professional competencies needed to provide assurance on sustainability information, and that they comply with the requirements of the Code of Ethics for Professional Accountants of the International Federation of Accountants to ensure their independence.

Work undertaken

Our procedures for limited assurance on the Report involved:

- A media search to identify relevant sustainability, environmental, safety and social issues for Statoil in the reporting period;

- Evaluating the design and implementation of systems and processes for the collection, processing and control of the information in the Report, including the consolidation of data for the Report;

- Conducting interviews at corporate level with management responsible for the sustainability policies, communication and reporting and with relevant staff responsible for providing the information in the Report;

- Evaluating internal and external documentation, on a test basis, to determine whether the information in the Report is supported by sufficient evidence.

Our additional procedures for reasonable assurance on the indicators as outlined under Scope involved:

- Testing the application of the reporting criteria, including conversion factors, used in the preparation of the reported information and accompanying notes;

- Evaluating the design and existence, and testing the operating effectiveness, of systems and processes for collecting and processing the HSE information;

- Visiting six sites to test the source data to evaluate the design and implementation, and test the operating effectiveness, of controls at local level.

With respect to our work on the disclosed GRI Application Level, our procedures were limited to checking whether the GRI Content Index is consistent with the criteria for the disclosed Application Level and that the relevant information is publicly reported.

During the assurance process we discussed the necessary changes in the Report and reviewed the final version of the Report to ensure that it reflects our findings.

Conclusion in respect of the Report

Based on our procedures for limited assurance, nothing has come to our attention to indicate that the Report is not fairly presented, in all material respects, in accordance with the reporting criteria.

Opinion in respect of HSE performance information

In our opinion the data and related explanatory notes for the indicators as outlined under Scope above are presented, in all material respects, in accordance with the reporting criteria.

Report on GRI application level

Based on the procedures performed we conclude that the Application Level A+, as disclosed in the section 'GRI and UN Global Compact index' and based on the GRI Content Index available in the Download centre, is consistent with the GRI criteria for this Application Level.

Stavanger, 19 March, 2013

KPMG AS

Arne Frogner

State Authorized Public Accountant (Norway)   Egbert Eeftink

2.14 Documentation

ISAE 3000 requires practitioners to prepare engagement documentation that should 'enable an experienced practitioner' to understand the procedures performed (and their results), together with significant matters arising.

The important point here is that documentation should include more than just the results of testing: it should extend to professional judgements made.

Finally, once the engagement file has been completed, the practitioner must not delete any information from it!

2.15 References for a client

Sometimes a professional accountant will be asked for a reference concerning a client, particularly in relation to their ability to **service a loan**. Where **no additional work is required** to provide a reference, the following matters should be considered:

- Inherent uncertainty of future income and expenditure
- The difficulty of reporting on present solvency (given that the audit is a historic exercise. Such information might be available if a **separate engagement** was made)
- The possibility of a **duty of care** arising
- That clarification might be required (there has been no engagement and no fees, and that liability might have to be expressly disclaimed)

However, the professional accountant might be able to provide certain information without difficulty:

- The length of time they have acted for the client
- The results declared to the taxation authorities over past years
- A statement of a level of negative assurance given past performance

Where it is necessary to create a separate engagement in order to provide the relevant information, the professional accountant should consider the guidance in ISAE 3000, discussed above.

In the following sections we shall start to consider some examples of areas where the professional accountant can provide assurance services.

2.16 Assurance reports on compiled pro forma information

ISAE 3420 *Assurance engagements to report on the compilation of pro forma financial information included in a prospectus* does not deal with compilation engagements, but assurance engagements on financial information that has been compiled. This is different from other assurance engagements because its scope is limited to compiled pro forma information.

ISAE 3420 was developed in the context of the increasing globalisation of **capital markets**. Its main points are:

- **Pro forma financial information** is information that has been adjusted to show the impact of a future event or transaction. The 'pro forma adjustments' might be for eg an investment being made or sold.

- The professional accountant does not compile the information – this is done by eg the client (the 'responsible party'). The accountant then reports on whether the information has been compiled in line with 'applicable criteria'.

- The professional accountant must assess whether the **applicable criteria** are **suitable** (ie not misleading or in conflict with laws and regulations). The accountant then assesses whether the information has actually been compiled in line with these criteria.

- This involves (i) determining whether information has been extracted appropriately from its source; (II) obtaining an understanding of the events or transactions being adjusted for; and (iii) evaluating whether the adjustments made are appropriate and in line with the engagement criteria.

- ISAE 3420 allows two alternative forms of wording for the **opinion**:

  - The pro forma financial information has been compiled, in all material respects, on the basis of the (applicable criteria).
  - The pro forma financial information has been properly compiled on the basis stated.

2.17 Assurance reports on service organisations

ISAE 3000 covers assurance engagements in general, and ISAE 3402 *Assurance reports on controls at a service organization* deals with how ISAE 3000 is to be applied to reasonable assurance engagements on a service organisation's controls. ISAE 3402 only covers reports on service organisations relevant to an

entity's financial reporting. Examples of these might include payroll services, actuaries, or mortgage services.

ISAE 3402 requires the service auditor to carry out the following procedures.

- Consider **acceptance** and continuance issues
- Assess the **suitability of the criteria** used by the service organisation
- Consider **materiality**
- **Obtain an understanding** of the service organisation's system
- Obtain evidence about:
    - The service organisation's **description of its system**
    - **Whether controls implemented** to achieve the control objectives are **suitably designed**
    - The **operating effectiveness** of controls (when providing a type 2 report)
- Determine whether, and to what extent, to use the work of the **internal auditors** (where there is an internal audit function)

'Type 1 report' and 'Type 2 report' are terms from ISAE 3000. A type 1 report only provides assurance on the description and design of controls, whereas a type 2 report includes their operating effectiveness as well.

The form of opinion expressed in the report should be **positive**, providing reasonable assurance. ISAE 3402 gives the following example of an **unmodified opinion** in a type 2 report.

Opinion

Our opinion has been formed on the basis of the matters outlined in this report. The criteria we used in forming our opinion are those described at page [aa]. In our opinion, in all material respects:

(a)   The description fairly presents the [the type or name of] system as designed and implemented throughout the period from [date] to [date]

(b)   The controls related to the control objectives stated in the description were suitably designed throughout the period from [date] to [date]

(c)   The controls tested, which were those necessary to provide reasonable assurance that the control objectives stated in the description were achieved, operated effectively throughout the period from [date] to [date]

2.18 Compilation engagements

Compilation engagements as such are **not** on the P7 syllabus, and they are **not assurance engagements** (in spite of their inclusion at this point in your Study Text). However, ISRS 4410 *Compilation engagements* is an examinable document for P7, so you need to be aware of its contents.

The ISRS states that the practitioner must comply with **ethical requirements** (ie at a minimum, the ACCA and IESBA *Codes of Ethics*), and that the engagement partner must take responsibility for **engagement level quality control**.

Before **accepting or continuing** an engagement, the practitioner must **agree the terms of the engagement**. This will include: the **intended use** and distribution of the information (eg is it going to be made public?); applicable **FR framework** (IFRS or local GAAP?); the objective and scope of the engagement; the **practitioner's responsibilities**; **management's responsibilities**; and the expected **form and content of the report**.

The practitioner must **obtain an understanding of the entity** – its business, and the applicable FR framework. The information must then be compiled using records provided by management, but the practitioner must:

- Discuss any **significant judgements** made
- Bring it to management's attention **if information is incomplete**, inaccurate or unsatisfactory. The practitioner must **request additional or corrected information.**

- **Withdraw** from the engagement if management **fails to provide information**, or if management does not make any proposed changes to the financial information
- Read the financial information in light of the **understanding of the business** obtained

No opinion is provided, because no assurance is provided. There is neither reasonable assurance nor negative assurance, because no procedures have been performed to verify the information. Therefore the compilation report includes a sentence that states simply that:

'These financial statements and the accuracy and completeness of the information used to compile them are your responsibility.'

3 Risk assessments

FAST FORWARD

Risk assessment is important to investors and managers and therefore is an important area for assurance services.

We discussed business risk earlier in this Study Text. It has three elements; financial, operational and compliance. There are a number of specific risks within these elements, some of which are shown in the diagram below.

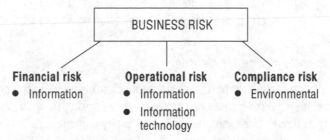

3.1 Need for assurance

Why is there a need for assurance in relation to risk assessment? For what reason would people want an independent opinion that gives them assurance? What criteria should this assurance be in relation to?

The key answer to the first question is that **the risk that the company enters into has a direct impact on the risk of the investment** that anyone purchasing shares in a company or loaning money to a company is making.

Interested stakeholders, **particularly investors**, need assurance that the risk taken by the company, in effect with their investment, is acceptable to them and that the returns that they receive are in accordance with that level of risk.

It is this need for assurance about the risks the company enters into that has led to the **importance of the issue of corporate governance and internal control effectiveness** that we looked at earlier and will continue to look at in Chapter 16 in the context of internal audit.

Other stakeholders will also be interested in the effectiveness of risk management in a company. Examples are lenders and employees. This is because the **ultimate risk is that a business might fail**.

3.2 Possible assurance criteria

The criteria by which risk assessment is evaluated will depend on the specific needs of the company and the user. However, some possibilities are:

- The requirements of the UK Corporate Governance Code
- Management's policy on risk management

There are no universally recognised criteria suitable for evaluating the **effectiveness** of an entity's risk evaluation. Assurance is likely to be limited to whether evaluation is carried out, rather than the quality of the evaluation.

3.3 Responsibility for risk assessment

There are three sets of people who can be involved in risk assessment in a company:

- Directors/management
- Internal audit
- External audit

We shall discuss the role of internal audit in Chapter 16. The responsibility of the directors was discussed earlier, and the role of the external auditor in risk assessment has been discussed in Chapter 6.

It is vital that you distinguish between the risk assessment carried out by the auditors and the directors. The directors are responsible for assessing and then managing the risks arising to the business; that is, the business risks.

As part of their audit, the auditors assess audit risk. Audit risk is the risk that the auditors make an inappropriate opinion on the financial statements. The auditors may consider business risk as part of their audit risk assessment. However, the **auditors are not responsible for risk management of their clients**.

3.4 Assessing risk

Methods of identifying risk were outlined in Chapter 6. You should be familiar with methods such as SWOT or PEST analysis. In practice, risk identification is likely to be done in all the various departments of a business.

These risks could include, for example:

- Contractual risks (important customers not agreeing to given contractual terms)
- Operational risks (scarce raw materials, risks arising through storage and use)
- Physical risks (for example, health and safety compliance)
- Product distribution (logistics, networks, outlets)
- Regulation (different jurisdictions, internet trading)
- Reputation (brands and staff profile)

The directors of a company need to determine guidelines for assessing risk. Risk might be assessed in terms of:

- Significance
- Likelihood
- Capacity to be managed

Mathematical methods could be used to assess risk, for instance using probability factors. Risks can be analysed using a grid, such as the example given:

Low likelihood Low impact	Low likelihood High impact
High likelihood Low impact	High likelihood High impact

3.5 Responses to risk

There are several responses that management take to risk:

- **Accept** risk (particularly if it is low likelihood, low impact)
- **Reduce** risk (by setting up a system of internal control to prevent the risk arising)
- **Avoid** risk (by not entering that market or not accepting certain contracts)
- **Transfer** risk (by taking out insurance)

If management choose to accept risk, they must set **risk thresholds**; that is, determine levels of risk where they will stop accepting risk and choose one of the other strategies. These thresholds are important because if directors or management are reckless with regard to risk they may be breaching their fiduciary duties.

3.6 Assurance

As stated above, assurance services may be provided. These may relate to the reliability of systems of internal control, which is important both for the financial statements and for the general running of the business. Assurance services could also relate to performance management.

Chapter Roundup

- Audit-related services may be assurance engagements or non-assurance engagements.

- Assurance services improve the quality of decision making for users of information.

- Assurance engagements may be attestation engagements or direct engagements.

- Assurance engagements may give reasonable assurance or limited assurance.

- Assurance engagements should only be accepted if the firm meets the requirements of the IESBA *Code of Ethics for Professional Accountants* and ISQC 1.

- The practitioner must ensure that the preconditions for an assurance engagement are present.

- Quality control requirements must be met in relation both to the engagement and to the firm.

- Risk assessment is important to investors and managers and therefore is an important area for assurance services.

Quick Quiz

1   Name the three types of engagement which comprise audit-related services.

(1)   ....

(2)   ....

(3)   ....

2   Link the review assignment with its description.

Review assignment:

(a)   Attestation engagement

(b)   Direct engagement

Descriptions:

(i)   The accountant is required to confirm whether:

(1)   Accounting policies are consistent with those in prior year financial statements
(2)   Any material modifications to the presented information are required

(ii)   The accountant is required to conduct a review and report on issues arising.

3   In an assurance engagement, the responsible party can also be an intended user.

A   Never
B   If there is more than one intended user
C   If there are more than ten intended users
D   In exceptional circumstances

4   When carrying out an assurance engagement the practitioner must assess the appropriateness of the subject matter and the criteria.

True   ☐

False   ☐

5   The assurance report should be in writing.

True   ☐

False   ☐

Answers to Quick Quiz

1   Review assignments, agreed-upon procedures assignments and compilation assignments

2   (a)(i)
    (b)(ii)

3   B

4   True

5   True

Now try the questions below from the Practice Question Bank.

Number	Level	Marks	Time
Q22	Examination	20	39 mins
Q23	Examination	15	29 mins

13

Prospective financial information (PFI)

Topic list	Syllabus reference
1 Reporting on prospective financial information (PFI)	E2
2 Accepting an engagement	E2
3 Procedures	E2
4 Expressing an opinion	E2, F3

Introduction

Reporting on prospective financial information (PFI) is covered by ISAE 3400 *The examination of prospective financial information.*

Forecasts are of significant interest to users. Some would say that PFI is of more interest to users of accounts than historical financial information (HFI) which, of course, auditors report on in the statutory financial audit.

This is an area in which the auditors can therefore provide an alternative service to audit, in the form of a review or assurance engagement. This chapter looks at the factors that the auditor should think about when taking on such an engagement. The basis for this chapter has been laid in Chapter 12 but, in this chapter, we consider issues specific to PFI.

Study guide

		Intellectual level
E2	**Prospective financial information**	
(a)	Define 'prospective financial information' (PFI) and distinguish between a 'forecast', a 'projection', a 'hypothetical illustration' and a 'target'.	1
(b)	Explain the principles of useful PFI.	1
(c)	Identify and describe the matters to be considered before accepting a specified engagement to report on PFI.	2
(d)	Discuss the level of assurance that the auditor may provide and explain the other factors to be considered in determining the nature, timing and extent of examination procedures.	1
(e)	Describe examination procedures to verify forecasts and projections.	2
(f)	Compare the content of a report on an examination of PFI with reports made in providing audit-related services.	2
F3	**Other reports**	
(b)	Discuss the content of a report on examination of prospective financial information.	2

Exam guide

The difficulties of reporting on PFI could be examined in an exam question. Case studies can easily be set in the context of a PFI assignment.

1 Reporting on prospective financial information (PFI)

FAST FORWARD

> Prospective financial information is difficult to give assurance about because it is highly subjective.

Key term

> **Prospective financial information (PFI)** is information based on assumptions about events that may occur in the future and possible actions by an entity.

From the definition given above, you can see that PFI is highly subjective. This makes it a difficult area to examine and report on. Guidance on reporting on PFI is given in ISAE 3400 *The examination of prospective financial information*.

The key issues that projections relate to are:

- Capital expenditure
- Profits
- Cash flows

These are the key areas which we will focus on in the procedure part of this chapter.

1.1 Principles of PFI

Increasingly, company directors are producing PFI, either voluntarily or because it is required by regulators, for example in the case of a public offering of shares.

Markets and investors need PFI that is understandable, relevant, reliable and comparable. Some specific issues arise in applying these principles to PFI.

Principle	Issue arising
Understandable	Disclosure is required of sources of uncertainty, assumptions made, determining factors that will affect whether the assumptions will be borne out, and alternative outcomes.
Relevant	No PFI-specific issues arise other than the need for the information to be relevant to the decision-making of investors or other users of the information.
Reliable	The reliability of PFI cannot be confirmed by evidence of past transactions or events. Its reliability depends on it being supported by analysis of the entity's business, strategies and plans.
Comparable	The PFI should be capable of comparison with eventual outcomes in the form of historical financial information (HFI). The accounting policies used in its preparation should also be disclosed.

1.2 Types of prospective financial information

PFI can be of two types (or a combination of both):

Key terms

Forecast. PFI based on assumptions as to future events which management expects to take place and the actions management expects to take (best-estimate assumptions).

Projection. PFI based on hypothetical assumptions about future events and management actions which are not necessarily expected to take place, such as when some entities are in a start-up phase or are considering a major change in the nature of operations, or a mixture of best-estimate and hypothetical assumptions. Such information illustrates the possible consequences as of the date the information is prepared if the events and actions were to occur (a 'what-if' scenario). (*ISAE 3400*)

Point to note

An exam question will not necessarily state that 'prospective financial information' is being examined, so you may have to spot it. It is possible, for example, that an integrated report (a topical area) could include forecast financial information.

2 Accepting an engagement   6/12, 6/14

FAST FORWARD

The auditor should agree the terms of the engagement with the directors, and should withdraw from the engagement if the assumptions made to put together the PFI are unrealistic.

2.1 General considerations

The International Standard on Assurance Engagements (ISAE) gives the following guidance about accepting an engagement to examine PFI.

ISAE 3400.11

The auditor should not accept, or should withdraw from, an engagement when the assumptions are clearly unrealistic or when the auditor believes that the prospective financial information will be inappropriate for its intended use.

ISAE 3400.12

The auditor and the client should agree on the terms of the engagement.

The ISAE also lists the following **factors** which the auditor should consider:

- The **intended use** of the information
- Whether the information will be for general or limited **distribution**

- The **nature of the assumptions**; that is, whether they are best estimate or hypothetical assumptions (hypothetical assumptions are based on events that may not take place, eg 'if the entity does *x*, then *y* may follow')
- The **elements** to be **included** in the information
- The **period covered** by the information

It also states that the auditor should have sufficient knowledge of the business to be able to evaluate the significant assumptions made.

A firm must also consider practical matters, such as the time available to them, their experience of the staff member compiling the information, any limitations on their work, and the degree of secrecy required beyond the normal duty of confidentiality.

3 Procedures   12/09, 6/11, 6/12, 6/14

Procedures could include:

- Analytical review (against similar historical projects)
- Verification of projected expenditure to quotes or estimates

3.1 General matters

In carrying out their review, the general matters to which attention should be directed are:

- The nature and background of the company's business
- The accounting policies normally followed by the company
- The assumptions on which the forecast is based
- The procedures followed by the company in preparing the forecast

3.1.1 The nature and background of the company's business

The accountant will review the company's character and recent history, with reference to such matters as the nature of its activities and its main products, markets, customers, suppliers, divisions, locations and trend of results.

3.1.2 The accounting policies normally followed by the company

The accountant will wish to establish the accounting principles normally followed by the company and ensure that they have been consistently applied in the preparation of forecasts.

3.1.3 The procedures followed by the company in preparing the forecast

In carrying out their review of the accounting bases and calculations for forecasts, and the procedures followed by the company for preparing them, the main points which the reporting accountant will wish to consider include:

(a)   Whether the forecast under review is based on forecasts regularly prepared for the purpose of management, or whether it has been separately and specially prepared for the specific purpose

(b)   Where forecasts are regularly prepared for management purposes, the degree of accuracy and reliability previously achieved, and the frequency and thoroughness with which estimates are revised

(c)   Whether the forecast under review represents the management's best estimate of results which they reasonably believe can and will be achieved rather than targets which the management have set as desirable

(d)   The extent to which forecast results for expired periods are supported by reliable interim accounts

(e)   The details of the procedures followed to generate the forecast and the extent to which it is built up from detailed forecasts of activity and cash flow

(f)   The extent to which profits are derived from activities having a proven and consistent trend and those of a more irregular, volatile or unproven nature

(g)   How the forecast takes account of any material extraordinary items and prior year adjustments, their nature, and how they are presented

(h)   Whether adequate provision is made for foreseeable losses and contingencies and how the forecast takes account of factors which may cause it to be subject to a high degree of risk, or which may invalidate the assumptions

(i)   Whether working capital appears adequate for requirements (normally this would require the availability of properly prepared cash flow forecasts) and, where short-term or long-term finance is to be relied on, whether the necessary arrangements have been made and confirmed

(j)   The arithmetical accuracy of the forecast and the supporting information and whether forecast statements of financial position and statements of cash flows have been prepared (as these help to highlight arithmetical inaccuracies and inconsistent assumptions)

ISAE 3400.17

When determining the nature, timing and extent of examination procedures, the auditor's considerations should include:

(a)   The likelihood of material misstatement;

(b)   The knowledge obtained during any previous engagement;

(c)   Management's competence regarding the preparation of prospective financial information;

(d)   The extent to which the prospective financial information is affected by the management's judgement; and

(e)   The adequacy and the reliability of the underlying data.

The ISAE goes on to say that the auditor should **seek appropriate evidence** on those areas that are **particularly sensitive to variation** and have a **material effect** on the information.

3.2 Specific matters

The following list of procedures may also be relevant when assessing prospective financial information. The auditor should undertake the review procedures discussed above in addition to these.

Profit forecasts

- Verify projected **income** figures to suitable evidence. This may involve:
    - Comparison of the basis of projected income to similar existing projects in the firm
    - Review of current market prices for that product or service
- Verify projected **expenditure** figures to suitable evidence. There is likely to be more evidence available about expenditure in the form of:
    - Quotations or estimates provided to the firm
    - Current bills for things such as services which can be used to reliably estimate
    - Market rate prices, for example, for advertising
    - Interest rate assumptions can be compared with the bank's current rates
    - Costs such as depreciation should correspond with relevant capital expenditure projections

Capital expenditure

The auditor should check the capital expenditure for **reasonableness**. For example, if the projection relates to buying land and developing it, it should include a sum for land.

- Projected costs should be **verified to estimates and quotations** where possible.
- The projections can be reviewed for **reasonableness**, including a comparison with prevailing **market rates** where such information is available (such as for property).

Cash forecasts

- The auditor should review cash forecasts to ensure the **timings involved** are **reasonable**.
- The auditor should check the cash forecast for **consistency with any profit forecasts** (income/expenditure should be the same, just at different times).
- If there is no comparable profit forecast, the income and expenditure items should be verified as they would have been on a profit forecast.

Working capital

- **Confirm sources** of short-term and long-term finance to evidence from external finance providers.
- Compare the reasonableness of **available** finance to cash flow forecasts.
- Assess the reasonableness of **projected working capital ratios** such as trade receivables days and the assumptions made in calculating these.
- Compare working capital projections to **historical trends** to assess reasonableness.

4 Expressing an opinion   12/09

4.1 Level of assurance

It is clear that as PFI is subjective information, it is **impossible** for an auditor **to give the same level of assurance** regarding it, as he would on **historical financial information**.

The ISAE suggests that the auditor express an opinion including:

- A statement of **negative assurance** as to whether the **assumptions** provide a reasonable basis for the prospective financial information
- An opinion as to whether the PFI is **properly prepared** on the basis of the assumptions and the relevant reporting framework
- Appropriate **caveats as to the achievability** of the forecasts

4.2 Reports under ISAE 3400

ISAE 3400.27

The report by an auditor on an examination of prospective financial information should contain:

(a)   Title;

(b)   Addressee;

(c)   Identification of the prospective financial information;

(d)   A reference to the ISAE or relevant national standards or practices applicable to the examination of prospective financial information;

(e)   A statement that management is responsible for the prospective financial information including the assumptions on which it is based;

(f)   When applicable, a reference to the purpose and/or restricted distribution of the prospective financial information;

(g)   A statement of negative assurance as to whether the assumptions provide a reasonable basis for the prospective financial information;

(h)   An opinion as to whether the prospective financial information is properly prepared on the basis of the assumptions and is presented in accordance with the relevant financial reporting framework;

(i)   Appropriate caveats concerning the achievability of the results indicated by the prospective financial information;

(j)   Date of the report which should be the date procedures have been completed;

(k)   Auditor's address; and

(l)   Signature.

ISAE 3400.30

When the auditor believes that the presentation and disclosure of the prospective financial information is not adequate, the auditor should express a qualified or adverse opinion in the report on the prospective financial information, or withdraw from the engagement as appropriate.

ISAE 3400.31

When the auditor believes that one or more significant assumptions do not provide a reasonable basis for the prospective financial information prepared on the basis of best-estimate assumptions or that one or more significant assumptions do not provide a reasonable basis for the prospective financial information given the hypothetical assumptions, the auditor should either express an adverse opinion in the report on the prospective financial information or withdraw from the engagement.

 Question — Prospective financial information

A new client of your practice, Peter Lawrence, has recently been made redundant. He is considering setting up a residential home for elderly people, as he is aware that there is an increasing need for this service with an ageing population (more people are living to an older age). He has seen a large house, which he plans to convert into an old people's home. Each resident will have a bedroom, there will be a communal sitting room and all meals will be provided in a dining room. No long-term nursing care will be provided, as people requiring this service will either be in hospital or in another type of accommodation for the elderly.

The large house is in a poor state of repair, and will require considerable structural alterations (building work), and repairs to make it suitable for an old people's home. The following will also be required.

*   New furnishings (carpets, beds, wardrobes and so on for the resident's rooms; carpets and furniture for the sitting room and dining room)

*   Decoration of the whole house (painting the woodwork and covering the walls with wallpaper)

*   Equipment (for the kitchen and for helping disabled residents)

Mr Lawrence and his wife propose to work full time in the business, which he expects to be available for residents six months after the purchase of the house. Mr Lawrence has already obtained some estimates of the conversion costs, and information on the income and expected running costs of the home.

Mr Lawrence has received about $30,000 from his redundancy. He expects to receive about $30,000 from the sale of his house (after repaying his house loan). The owners of the house he proposes to buy are asking $50,000 for it, and Mr Lawrence expects to spend $50,000 on conversion of the house (building work, furnishing, decorations and equipment).

Mr Lawrence has prepared a draft capital expenditure forecast, a profit forecast and a cash flow forecast which he has asked you to check before he submits them to the bank, in order to obtain finance for the old people's home.

Required

Describe the procedures you would carry out on:

(a)   The capital expenditure forecast
(b)   The profit forecast
(c)   The cash flow forecast

Answer

All three of the forecasts to be reviewed should be prepared on a monthly basis and the following work would be required in order to consider their reasonableness.

(a)   **Capital expenditure forecast**

(i)   Read estate agent's details and solicitors' correspondence and compare to the capital expenditure forecast to ensure that all expenditure (including sale price, surveyors' fees, legal costs, taxes on purchase) is included.

(ii)   Confirm the estimated cost of new furnishings by agreeing them to supplier price lists or quotations.

(iii)   Verify any discounts assumed in the forecast are correct by asking the suppliers if they will apply them to this transaction.

(iv)   Confirm projected building and decoration costs to the relevant suppliers' quotation.

(v)   Confirm the projected cost of specialist equipment (and relevant bulk discounts) to suppliers' price lists or websites.

(vi)   In the light of experience of other such ventures, consider whether the forecast includes all relevant costs.

(b)   **Profit forecast**

As a first step it will be necessary to recognise that the residential home will not be able to generate any income until the bulk of the capital expenditure has been incurred in order to make the home 'habitable'. However, while no income can be anticipated, the business will have started to incur expenditure in the form of loan interest, rates and insurance.

The only income from the new building will be rent receivable from residents. The rentals which Mr Lawrence is proposing to charge should be assessed for reasonableness in the light of rental charged to similar homes in the same area. In projecting income it would be necessary to anticipate that it is likely to take some time before the home is fully occupied and it would be prudent to allow for some periods where vacancies arise because of the 'loss' of some of the established residents.

The expenditure of the business is likely to include:

(i)   **Wages and salaries.** Although Mr and Mrs Lawrence intend to work full time in the business, they will undoubtedly need to employ additional staff to care for residents, cook, clean and tend to the gardens. The numbers of staff and the rates of pay should be compared with those of similar local businesses of which the firm has knowledge.

(ii)   **Rates and water rates.** The estimate of the likely cost of these can be confirmed by asking the local council and/or the estate agents dealing with the sale of property.

(iii) **Food.** The estimate of the expenditure for food should be based on the projected levels of staff and residents, with some provision for wastage.

(iv)   **Heat and light.** The estimates for heat, light and cooking facilities should be compared to similar clients' actual bills.

(v)   **Insurance.** This cost should be verified to quotes from the insurance broker.

(vi)   **Advertising.** The costs of newspaper and brochure advertising costs should be checked against quotes obtained by Mr Lawrence.

(vii) **Repairs and renewals.** Adequate provision should be made for replacement of linen, crockery and such like and maintenance of the property.

(viii) **Depreciation.** The depreciation charge should be recalculated with reference to the capital costs involved being charged to the capital expenditure forecast.

(ix)   **Loan interest and bank charges.** These should be checked against the bank's current rates and the amount of the principal agreed to the cash forecast.

(c)   **Cash flow forecast**

(i)   Check that the timing of the capital expenditure on the cash flow forecast is consistent with that shown on the capital expenditure forecast.

(ii)   Compare the cash flow forecast to the details within the profit forecast to ensure they tie up, for example:

–   Income from residents would normally be receivable weekly/monthly in advance.

–   The majority of expenditure for wages etc would be payable in the month in which it is incurred.

–   Payments to the major utilities (gas, electricity, telephone) will normally be payable quarterly, as will the bank charges.

–   Rates and taxes are normally paid half-yearly.

–   Insurance premiums will normally be paid annually in advance.

(iii) Redo the additions on the cash forecast and check that figures that appear on other forecasts are carried over correctly.

Question | More prospective financial information

Gunthorpe Plumbing Supplies ('Gunthorpe') is a wholly owned subsidiary of Lucknow Builders Merchants ('Lucknow') and has been trading at a loss for a number of years. The recent bleak economic climate has led the directors of Lucknow to decide to put Gunthorpe into liquidation and make all the employees redundant, including its three directors.

The three directors of Gunthorpe have decided to form a new company, Gunthorpe Plumbing Supplies (2008) ('Gunthorpe (2008)'), and use their redundancy pay and personal savings to purchase all the shares in the company.

The board of directors of Lucknow have agreed to sell the following assets and liabilities of Gunthorpe to the new company:

(a)   All the non-current assets except for one warehouse (see below)
(b)   Trading inventory
(c)   Trade receivables and payables

The price for the non-current assets has been agreed and the value of the trading inventory, receivables and payables will be confirmed at the date of transfer by an independent valuer.

The directors of Gunthorpe (2008) propose to obtain additional finance in the form of a long-term loan from a merchant bank and working capital will be financed by a bank overdraft from their existing bankers.

The directors have asked you to assist them in preparing a profit forecast and cash flow forecast for submission to the two banks. They have provided you with copies of the detailed accounts of Gunthorpe for the past five years, and they point out the following changes which, in their opinion, will enable the new company to trade at a profit.

(a)   The substantial management charge imposed by Lucknow will disappear. However, additional costs will have to be incurred for services which were provided by the parent company, such as maintaining the accounting records and servicing the company's vehicles.

(b)   Initially fewer staff will be employed.

(c)   Only one of the company's two premises is being taken over – the premises which are not being taken over will be sold by Lucknow on the open market.

The directors have provided you with the following brief details of Gunthorpe's trade. It currently has a revenue of about $1 million and is a wholesaler of plumbing equipment (copper pipes, pipe connections, water taps etc) which are sold mainly on credit to plumbers and builders. Trade discount is given to larger customers. There are some cash sales to smaller customers, but these represent no more than 10% of total sales.

Required

Describe the work you would perform to:

(a)   Verify that the value of items included in the profit forecast is reasonable.
(b)   Verify that the value of items included in the cash flow forecast is reasonable.

Answer

(a)   **Verification of items in the profit forecast**

The main items appearing in the profit forecast and the required work in relation to them would be as follows.

(i)   The budgeted sales income should be considered against that which has actually been achieved in recent years. If the new management are forecasting any increase in the level of sales, the justification for this must be carefully reviewed. Tests should be made to ensure that all expenditure directly related to income is properly accounted for. Confirmation should be sought that the projected income takes proper account of the trade discounts that it is assumed will have to be granted.

(ii)   The major form of expenditure is likely to be the purchase of goods for resale. Enquiry should be made as to whether suppliers will continue to grant the new company the same level of trade discounts as the old company and also whether the volume of purchases is such that a similar mark-up will be attained. Management explanations should be sought for any material differences in the anticipated gross profit rate, such explanations being fully investigated as to their plausibility.

(iii) The wages and salaries payable by the new company should be checked by asking management how many people they intend to employ and at what rates. The reasonableness of the projected charge for wages and salaries should be assessed by comparison with the figure for wages and salaries most recently paid by the old company.

(iv)   All other major items of expenditure included in the profit forecast (ie selling expenses, finance expenses and administration expenses) should be considered by comparison with the figures of the old company in previous years, ensuring that a reasonable allowance is made for the effects of inflation.

(v)   The charges for items previously covered by the management charge should be checked for their completeness and reasonableness.

(vi)   An overall review of the projected profits should be undertaken to ensure that it appears to be a realistic forecast and not merely an idealistic target figure.

(b) **Verification of items in the cash flow forecast**

As well as generally checking to ensure that the cash flow forecast appears to be consistent with the profit forecast, specific checks should be made as follows.

(i) The timing of payments due to the parent company.

(ii) The period of credit granted to customers by the old company, as it is unlikely that the new company will be in a position to insist on prompter payment by customers.

(iii) The period of credit taken from suppliers should be dealt with in a similar way, although enquiry should be made as to whether creditors are prepared to trade with the new company on the same terms as the old.

(iv) The timing of payment for overhead expenditure should be checked to see that it is reasonable and consistent with established practice.

(v) Although in the early months one would not expect there to be any major purchase or sale of non-current assets, the position here should be confirmed by discussion with management of their long-term plans.

Chapter Roundup

- Prospective financial information is difficult to give assurance about because it is highly subjective.

- The auditor should agree the terms of the engagement with the directors, and should withdraw from the engagement if the assumptions made to put together the PFI are unrealistic.

- Procedures could include:
  - Analytical review (against similar historical projects)
  - Verification of projected expenditure to quotes or estimates

- It is impossible to give the same level of assurance about PFI as it is on historical financial information but negative assurance may be given.

Quick Quiz

1   Complete the definition:

A .... means PFI prepared on the basis of .... as to .... events which management expects to take place and .... management expects to take as of the .... the .... is ....

2   Complete the matters an auditor should consider when undertaking a PFI engagement.

- The intended .... of the information
- Whether the information will be general or limited ....
- The nature of the ....
- The .... to be included in the information
- The .... to be covered by the information

3   Identify whether the following procedures are relevant to profit forecasts, capital expenditure forecasts or cash forecasts.

- Ensure the timings are reasonable
- Projected costs should be verified to estimates and quotations
- Analytical review on income (based on comparable projects)
- Review for reasonableness
- Review for consistency with profit forecast

4   Complete the definition:

.... is assurance of something in the .... of any evidence arising to the ....

5   Reporting accountants are responsible for the PFI they are giving an opinion on.

True   ☐

False   ☐

Answers to Quick Quiz

1   Forecast, assumptions, future, actions, date, information, prepared

2   Use, distribution, assumptions, elements, period

3   •   Ensure the timings are reasonable   Cash
     •   Projected costs should be verified to estimates and quotations   P/CapEx
     •   Analytical review on income (based on comparable projects)   P
     •   Review for reasonableness   P/CapEx/Cash
     •   Review for consistency with profit forecast   CapEx/Cash

4   Negative assurance, absence, contrary

5   False

Now try the question below from the Practice Question Bank.

Number	Level	Marks	Time
Q24	Examination	20	39 mins

14

Forensic audits

Introduction

In the current globalised business world there is an increasing demand for forensic services. Audit and assurance professionals are well-placed to provide these.

This chapter introduces forensic accounting and auditing and discusses its applications in practice. It also considers the ethical issues applicable to forensic accountants.

The chapter concludes with a look at investigative procedures and evidence.

Study guide

		Intellectual level
E3	**Forensic audits**	
(a)	Define the terms 'forensic accounting', 'forensic investigation' and 'forensic audit'.	1
(b)	Describe the major applications of forensic auditing (eg fraud, negligence, insurance claims) and analyse the role of the forensic auditor as an expert witness.	2
(c)	Apply the fundamental ethical principles to professional accountants engaged in forensic audit assignments.	2
(d)	Plan a forensic audit engagement.	2
(e)	Select investigative procedures and evaluate evidence appropriate to determining the loss in a given situation.	3

Exam guide

This topic is often examined in a very practical way. It is important to have an understanding of the framework but case study questions will involve the application of very similar procedures to those used in traditional audits of financial statements. Some specific knowledge is required of basic definitions, but otherwise the application of audit-style procedures is used.

1 Definitions   Pilot paper, 12/07, 12/08, 12/11

Key terms

> **Forensic auditing.** The process of gathering, analysing and reporting on data, in a pre-defined context, for the purpose of finding facts and/or evidence in the context of financial/legal disputes and/or irregularities and giving preventive advice in this area.
>
> **Forensic investigation.** Carried out for civil or criminal cases. These can involve fraud, money laundering or bribery.
>
> **Forensic accounting.** Undertaking a financial investigation in response to a particular event, where the findings of the investigation may be used as evidence in court or to otherwise help resolve disputes.

1.1 More general definitions

The range of assignments in this area is vast so to give specific definitions for each is not always practicable. In a publication by the Institute of Chartered Accountants of Canada *Standard practices for investigative and forensic accounting engagements* (November 2006) the following definition is established.

> **Investigative and forensic accounting engagements** are those that:
>
> (a) Require the application of professional accounting skills, investigative skills, and an investigative mindset
>
> (b) Involve disputes or anticipated disputes, or where there are risks, concerns or allegations of fraud or other illegal or unethical conduct

Forensic audit and accounting is a rapidly growing area. The major accountancy firms all offer forensic services, as do a number of specialist companies. The demand for these services arises partly from the increased expectation of corporate governance codes for:

- Company directors to take seriously their responsibilities for the prevention and detection of fraud, and also from
- Governments concerned about risks arising from criminal funding of terrorist groups.

The next section outlines a number of the main applications of forensic auditing.

2 Applications of forensic auditing

FAST FORWARD

Forensic auditing can be applied to a number of situations, including fraud and negligence investigations.

2.1 Fraud

Forensic accountants can be engaged to investigate fraud. This could involve:

- Quantifying losses from theft of cash or goods
- Identifying payments or receipts of bribes
- Identifying intentional misstatements in financial information, such as overstatement of revenue and earnings and understatement of costs and expenses
- Investigating intentional misrepresentations made to auditors

Forensic accountants may also be engaged to act in an advisory capacity to assist directors in developing more effective controls to reduce the risks from fraud.

2.2 Negligence

When an auditor or accountant is being sued for negligence, either or both parties to the case may employ forensic accountants to investigate the work done to provide evidence as to whether it did in fact meet the standards required. They may also be involved in establishing the amount of loss suffered by the plaintiff.

2.3 Insurance claims

Insurance companies often employ forensic accountants to report on the validity of the amounts of losses being claimed, as a means of resolving the disputes between the company and the claimant.

This could involve computing losses following an insured event such as a fire, flood or robbery. If a criminal action arises over an allegation that an insured event was deliberately contrived to defraud the insurance company, the forensic accountant may be called on as an expert witness (see Section 2.6).

Case Study

The following example illustrates that investigating fraud is sometimes a matter of applying common sense.

A forensic accountant was asked by an insurance company to quantify the value of loss to a firm following a robbery of gold bars. From the security tapes it was known that two men, of average height and build, only made one visit to the safe. The accountant compared the amount claimed with a calculation of the weight of gold bars the two men could have physically carried and found that the claim was vastly inflated!

2.4 Other disputes

Forensic accountants can be involved in the investigation of many other types of dispute, such as:

- Shareholder disputes
- Partnership disputes
- Contract disputes
- Business sales and purchase disputes
- Matrimonial disputes, including:
    - Valuing the family business
    - Gathering financial evidence
    - Identifying 'hidden' assets
    - Advising in settlement negotiations

2.5 Terrorist financing

In Chapter 1 we saw the legal requirements imposed on professional accountants in this area. In addition, governments are increasingly turning to forensic accountants as part of their counter-terrorism strategy.

The following quote is taken from a speech made by Gordon Brown, when he was the UK Chancellor of the Exchequer, in October 2006:

> '… forensic accounting of transaction trails across continents has been vital in identifying threats, uncovering accomplices, piecing together company structures, and ultimately providing evidence for prosecution. Most recently, forensic accounting techniques have tracked an alleged terrorist bomb maker, using multiple identities, multiple bank accounts and third parties and third world countries to purchase bomb making equipment and tracked him to and uncovered an overseas bomb factory.'

2.6 The forensic accountant as an expert witness

The preceding sections have identified a number of circumstances where the forensic accountant may be involved as an expert witness in civil or criminal cases. For civil cases in England and Wales the duties of expert witnesses are set out in the **Civil Procedure Rules (CPR)**.

2.6.1 Duties of experts

Experts always owe a duty to exercise reasonable skill and care to those instructing them, and to comply with any relevant professional code of ethics. However, when they are instructed to give or prepare evidence for the purpose of civil proceedings in England and Wales they have an overriding duty to help the court on matters within their expertise. This duty overrides any obligation to the person instructing or paying them. Experts must not serve the exclusive interest of those who retain them.

Experts should be aware of the overriding objective that courts deal with cases justly. This includes dealing with cases proportionately, expeditiously and fairly. Experts are under an obligation to assist the court so as to enable them to deal with cases in accordance with the overriding objective. However, the overriding objective does not impose on experts any duty to act as mediators between the parties or require them to trespass on the role of the court in deciding facts.

Experts should provide opinions which are independent, regardless of the pressures of litigation. In this context, a useful test of 'independence' is that the expert would express the same opinion if given the same instructions by an opposing party. Experts should not take it upon themselves to promote the point of view of the party instructing them or engage in the role of advocates.

Experts should confine their opinions to matters which are material to the disputes between the parties and provide opinions only in relation to matters which lie within their expertise. Experts should indicate without delay where particular questions or issues fall outside their expertise.

Experts should take into account all material facts before them at the time that they give their opinion. Their reports should set out those facts and any literature or any other material on which they have relied upon in forming their opinions. They should indicate if an opinion is provisional or qualified, or where they consider that further information is required or if, for any other reason, they are not satisfied that an opinion can be expressed finally and without qualification.

Experts should inform those instructing them without delay of any change in their opinions on any material matter and the reason for it.

Experts should be aware that any failure by them to comply with the CPR or court orders or any excessive delay for which they are responsible may result in the parties who instructed them being penalised in costs and even, in extreme cases, being debarred from placing the experts' evidence before the court.

2.6.2 Expert witness reports

The UK's Expert Witness Institute has produced a model form of expert's report to help expert witnesses, of whatever profession, to meet their legal duties. The main contents are outlined below.

Index/list of contents	Optional, but desirable
Brief curriculum vitae	Including expert's name, qualifications (eg ACCA) and relevant experience
Summary of conclusions	Brief list of main facts from the evidence and the conclusions/opinions arrived at
Instructions	Must give the substance of all instructions received by the expert, whether written or oral
Issues	The issues to be addressed and the questions to be answered must be clearly set out
Documentation	Full list of all documents and material on which the report is based
Chronology	This must deal only with **factual** evidence, not any matter of opinion
Technical background	Where technical aspects of the issues are outside the general knowledge or experience of those who will have to deal with the report, an explanation of the technical issues in this section may be necessary. For example, in a case involving fraudulent accounting, the requirements of specific accounting standards may have to be explained
Opinion	This should be presented clearly and unambiguously. The reasons for the opinions given should be explicit
References	A numbered list of all items of technical literature relied on. For example in a negligence case this may comprise a list of relevant accounting standards and auditing standards
Declaration	The expert must sign a declaration confirming his understanding of his legal duties, and including the following 'Statement of Truth':
	'I confirm that insofar as the facts stated in my report are within my own knowledge I have made clear which they are and I believe them to be true, and the opinions I have expressed represent my true and complete professional opinion.'

Exam focus point

The current P7 examination team wrote an article entitled 'Forensic auditing' in *Student Accountant*. This article can also be accessed via the ACCA website and covers some of the key issues relevant to forensic investigations.

3 Ethical principles

12/08

FAST FORWARD

The fundamental principles of the *Code of Ethics and Conduct* apply to ACCA members in all professional assignments.

Example

The following table contains a recap of the fundamental principles. Take a few minutes to think and note down any special relevance you see in them in relation to forensic assignments.

Question	Ethical principles
Integrity	
Objectivity	
Professional competence and due care	
Confidentiality	
Professional behaviour	

Answer

Integrity	Forensic accountants are often, by definition, working in an environment and dealing with individuals who are dishonest and lack integrity. If there is any risk that their own integrity may be compromised they should decline or withdraw from the assignment.
Objectivity	The previous section on the role of the expert witness emphasised the need for independence and objectivity. Any perceived threats to objectivity will undermine the credibility of the accountant's opinion.
Professional competence and due care	Forensic assignments may require very specialised skills, for example, where evidence gathering requires specific IT skills. A firm should consider very carefully whether it has adequate skills and resources before accepting the assignment.
Confidentiality	Forensic accountants will often be working for one party to a dispute, and have access to very sensitive information. Subject, of course, to legal rules of disclosure in court cases, it is clearly essential to maintain the strictest confidentiality.
Professional behaviour	Fraud cases and other situations such as takeover disputes can be very much in the public eye. Any lapse in the professionalism of, say, an expert witness could do serious damage to the reputation of the profession as a whole.

4 Planning, procedures and evidence

> **FAST FORWARD**
>
> Many of the techniques used in a forensic investigation will be similar to those used in the audit of financial statements, but the different objectives and risks of the assignment require some differences in approach.

4.1 Planning

The broad process of conducting a forensic audit bears some similarity to an audit of financial statements, in that it will include a planning stage, a period when evidence is gathered, a review process, and a report to the client. However, forensic investigations are not all of the same sort, and it is essential that the investigation team considers carefully exactly what it is that they have been asked to achieve in this particular investigation, and that they plan their work accordingly. Professional judgement will be required to:

- Identify the objectives of the engagement
- Obtain sufficient understanding of the circumstances and events surrounding the engagement
- Obtain sufficient understanding of the context within which the engagement is to be conducted (eg any relevant laws or regulations)
- Identify any limitation on the scope of the engagement (eg where information is not available)
- Evaluate the resources necessary to complete the work, and identifying a suitable engagement team

In order to meet these requirements, the engagement plan should include:

- Develop hypotheses to address the circumstances and context of the engagement
- Decide on the best approach to meet the engagement objectives within constraints such as cost and time
- Identify the financial (and other) information needed, and develop a strategy to acquire it
- Determine the impact of the nature and timing of any reporting requirements

One key difference in emphasis from an audit of financial statements is that the forensic accountant is stepping into an arena that is defined by conflict. It is therefore essential that the investigator obtains an understanding of the background and context to the engagement as well as of any limitations on its scope, as these will affect the extent of the conclusions that can be drawn. In the case of a matrimonial dispute, for example, the investigator would need to take a sceptical attitude towards all the information they are provided with, as it may be biased, false or incomplete.

Many forensic investigations involve investigating potential frauds. The objectives of a fraud investigation would include:

- Identifying the type of fraud that has been operating, how long it has been operating for, and how the fraud has been concealed
- Identifying the fraudster(s) involved
- Quantifying the financial loss suffered by the client
- Gathering evidence to be used in court proceedings
- Providing advice to prevent the recurrence of the fraud

The investigators should then consider the best way to gather evidence in the light of these objectives.

4.2 Audit procedures

The specific procedures which would be performed as part of a forensic audit will depend on the specific nature of the investigation. However, using a fraud investigation as an example, the following would normally apply.

- Develop a profile of the entity under investigation including its personnel
- Identify weaknesses in internal control procedures and basic recordkeeping, eg bank reconciliations not performed
- Perform trend analysis and analytical procedures to identify significant transactions and significant variations from the norm
- Identify changes in patterns of purchases/sales, particularly where a limited number of suppliers/customers are involved
- Identify significant variations in consumption of raw materials and consumables, particularly where consumption appears excessive
- Identify unusual accounts and account balances, eg closing credit balances on debit accounts and *vice versa*
- Review accounting records for unusual transactions and entries, eg large numbers of accounting entries between accounts, transactions not executed at normal commercial rates
- Review transaction documentation (eg invoices) for discrepancies and inconsistencies
- Once identified trace the individual responsible for fraudulent transactions
- Obtain information regarding all responsibilities of the individual involved
- Inspect and review all other transactions of a similar nature conducted by the individual
- Consider all other aspects of the business which the individual is involved with and perform further analytical procedures targeting these areas to identify any additional discrepancies

Exam focus point

> The December 2011 exam featured a very typical question in this area. After a short scenario, there were six marks for assessing the ethical issues raised by a request to investigate a fraud, and six marks for explaining matters in relation to planning the investigation. You can only really prepare for this sort of question by practising similar questions and, as always with P7, applying yourself to the specific scenario.

 Question   **Forensic audit**

You are a manager in the forensic investigation department of an audit firm. You have been approached by the financial director of Arnold Co to investigate a fraud. The finance director has identified a number of discrepancies between inventory records and the quarterly physical inventory counts which are performed. Their suspicions have been increased by the fact that the discrepancy always relates to the same product line and approximately the same number of items appear to be missing each time.

Required

Explain the procedures you would perform to determine whether a fraud has taken place and to quantify the loss suffered by the company.

Answer

> **Tutorial note.** In this case the approach taken is likely to involve elimination of legitimate reasons why the discrepancies may have arisen.

Procedures would involve the following.

To establish whether a fraud has taken place:

- Obtain an understanding of the business and in particular the roles and responsibilities of those involved in processing inventory transactions and those in the warehouse.

- Discuss with management the method adopted for conducting the quarterly inventory count and review the detail of the count instructions. Any weaknesses in the controls should be identified and considered as a possible explanation for the discrepancies, eg double counting of this particular line of inventory.
- Obtain confirmation of whether inventory is held at more than one location. If so confirm that this has been included in the physical inventory counts.
- Review procedures for the identification of obsolete and damaged items and in particular the disposal of such items. Determine who is responsible for making the decision and the procedures for updating records for these adjustments. If items have been disposed of but records not maintained, this could explain the discrepancy.
- Obtain an understanding of the system for the processing and recording of despatches and in particular consider the effectiveness of controls regarding completeness of despatches. Trace transactions from order to despatch in respect of the inventory line in question to confirm that all goods out have been recorded.
- Obtain an understanding of the system for the processing and recording of goods received for this inventory line. Controls over the initial booking in of inventory should be reviewed. If inventory is double counted at this stage, this could account for the discrepancy.
- Review the system for subsequent processing of goods received, in particular the controls and procedures regarding the accuracy of input. If goods in are processed more than once, this would give rise to a discrepancy between the book records and actual inventory.
- Assess the existence of general controls affecting access to the warehouse and inventory.

To quantify the loss

The evidence obtained above should enable the auditor to determine the accuracy of the book records and the accuracy of the physical inventory records. A reconciliation of the two figures should provide the number of units missing. The cost of each unit should be agreed to recent purchase invoices.

4.3 Differences in approach

While many of the techniques used in a forensic investigation will be similar to those used in an audit, the different objectives and risks involved will require some differences in approach.

Materiality	In many investigations there will be no materiality threshold.
Timing	Clearly less predictable than audit.
	Timing of procedures needs to be unpredictable.
Documentation	Needs to be reviewed more critically than on an audit.
	The example in this section shows what an experienced fraud investigator might identify in a fraudulent invoice.
Interviews	It may be appropriate to interview a suspected fraudster in the hope of obtaining an admission but this entails some problems:
	• Challenging and requires a high skill level
	• Legal issues including the risk of being sued for defamation
Computer-aided techniques	Data mining is a key part of many investigation processes. It allows the accountant to access and analyse thousands or millions of transactions that have passed through an accounting system and identify, say, unusual trends far more quickly than by traditional documentary analysis.
	100% of an entity's transactions can be checked for characteristics such as date, time, amount, approval, payee etc.
	If possible, data should be gathered prior to the initial field visit to reduce the risk of the data being compromised.

Example

Porridge Associates   **Invoice**

Suite 214
The Castle
Lancaster
LA1 1YL   **INVOICE NO: 000796**
                                               DATE: 5 February 20X7
                                    Registered Sales Tax Number 394/8126/07

To: **Attn: Peter Kenworthy**
      Silverfin Enterprises Limited   Our Reference:
      Century House
      Brook Street   **For the period: 1.3.X7 to 31.3.X7**
      London NW3 9HE

CONSULTANT	DESCRIPTION		AMOUNT
JFB	Fees in relation to testing of electronic payment systems		
	Total fees		£8,000.00
	Expenses	£500.00	£500.00
		SUBTOTAL	£8,500.00
		SALES TAX	1,487.50
		TOTAL DUE	£9,987.50

If you have any questions concerning this invoice, call: **0778 279 1789**
or write to **Porridge Associates, UK Head Office, 127 Elm Avenue, Nottingham, N12 7PY**
                    THANK YOU FOR YOUR BUSINESS!

Remittance Advice   Invoice Number: **LIA 000796**

To: Porridge Associates
      Bank of Wealth (Jersey) Ltd
      St Helier
      Jersey   Enclosed please find our cheque for
      Account number   87620549   **£9,987.50**
      Sort Code   16-58-79

                                               in settlement of your account
              Registered in Jersey: company Registration No. 02470290

'Porridge Associates'

There are 15 potential 'Red Flags of Fraud' which, taken together, should prevent an invoice such as
Porridge's from being paid. However, for the most part these indicators are not correctly recognised for
what they really are. As a result, fraudulent invoices get paid all the time.

(1)   The Castle is in fact 'HM Prison, The Castle, Lancaster'. Fraud investigators routinely check to see
       whether invoices are generated from prisons. A second indicator in this address is the use of a
       'Suite', which suggests temporary accommodation or the use of a business centre.

(2)   This is a mobile telephone number. This again suggests a temporary operation or one which does
       not have a permanent address.

(3)   A low invoice number suggests that the company may have begun trading only recently. A
       comparison against other invoices from the same company may reveal sequential invoice
       numbering which can indicate that an organisation is the only organisation being invoiced. This
       may indicate that the organisation is being specifically targeted for fraudulent purposes.

(4)   The date of the invoice predates that of the service provided. This may be part of the contract but it is worth checking for clarification.

(5)   The sales tax number contains a check digit. In this case the number is valid but it does not belong to Porridge Associates. The sales tax number, therefore, has been stolen to make this invoice appear legitimate.

(6)   All round value payments should be treated with caution. They should be reviewed in detail as they may be staged payments or commissions. They could also be completely false.

(7)   Round value expense items may indicate a percentage charge and should be checked carefully.

(8)   The address is that of a residential property and appears out of place for a company's UK Headquarters building. Invoices which contain 'The Close', 'The Crescent', 'The Avenue' or other such locations may all indicate a home address. Fraudsters make mistakes and, with care, these can be identified.

(9)   Offshore banking facilities may indicate that the supplier is trying to minimise its tax liability but it may also be the first leg of transferring fraudulently obtained funds beyond UK legal jurisdiction. The sort code in this case refers to a bank in Gibraltar and not Jersey and this kind of manipulation may suggest a sophisticated money laundering operation.

(10)   Company registration numbers follow specific formats and this number is not valid for Jersey.

(11)   The absence of a Purchase Order number may indicate a bogus invoice of the type used by certain infamous telex directories. Bogus invoices are routinely sent out by mailshot to hundreds of companies. The fraudsters work on the basis that many low value invoices get paid without being checked.

(12)   Vague descriptions of products, services and a lack of backup for expenses should always prompt further enquiries.

(13)   There are also different address details which should be looked into further.

(14)   Tear-off section at bottom is the only place that shows bank account details.

As a general point, any invoices which contain correction fluid or the use of sticky labels to change an address should be investigated further.

Chapter Roundup

- Forensic auditing can be applied to a number of situations, including fraud and negligence investigations.

- The fundamental principles of the *Code of Ethics and Conduct* apply to ACCA members in all professional assignments.

- Many of the techniques used in a forensic investigation will be similar to those used in the audit of financial statements, but the different objectives and risks of the assignment require some differences in approach.

Quick Quiz

1 Define the terms forensic auditing, forensic investigation and forensic accounting.

2 State three applications of the use of forensic auditing.

3 State five items that should ideally be included in an expert's report.

Answers to Quick Quiz

1 Forensic auditing is the process of gathering, analysing and reporting on data, in a pre-defined context, for the purpose of finding facts and/or evidence in the context of financial/legal disputes and/or irregularities and giving preventive advice in this area.

Forensic investigations are carried out for civil or criminal cases, which can involve fraud or money laundering.

Forensic accounting is undertaking a financial investigation in response to a particular event, where the findings of the investigation may be used as evidence in court or to otherwise help resolve disputes.

2 Any three of:
- Fraud
- Negligence
- Insurance claims
- Terrorist financing

3 Any five of:

- Index/list of contents
- Brief curriculum vitae
- Summary of conclusions
- Instructions
- Issues
- Documentation
- Chronology
- Technical background
- Opinion
- References
- Declaration

Now try the question below from the Practice Question Bank.

Number	Level	Marks	Time
Q25	Examination	15	29 mins

Social, environmental and public sector auditing

15

Topic list	Syllabus reference
1 Importance for the company	G3
2 Measuring social and environmental performance	G3
3 Implications for the statutory audit	G3
4 Implications for assurance services	G3
5 Audit of performance information in the public sector	E6
6 Integrated reporting	G3

Introduction

In this chapter we investigate the impact of social and environmental issues on the auditor. This takes two distinct forms:

- Impact on the statutory audit
- Impact on the provision of assurance services by the auditor

Increasing importance is placed on social and environmental issues in business. Recent years have seen a substantial weight of environmental legislation passed which puts a significant burden of compliance on companies. The danger of non-compliance (fines, bad publicity, impact on going concern) is an aspect of the environmental risk which companies face.

We also examine the work of the auditor in the context of public sector organisations. Auditors may take on varied roles here, and we focus on the audit of performance information.

Study guide

		Intellectual level
G3	**The audit of social, environmental and integrated reporting**	
(a)	Plan an engagement to provide assurance on integrated reporting (performance measures and sustainability indicators).	2
(b)	Describe the difficulties in measuring and reporting on economic, environmental and social performance and give examples of performance measures and sustainability indicators.	2
(c)	Explain the auditor's main considerations in respect of social and environmental matters and how they impact on entities and their financial statements (eg impairment of assets, provisions and contingent liabilities).	2
(d)	Describe substantive procedures to detect potential misstatements in respect of socio-environmental matters.	2
(e)	Discuss the form and content of an independent verification statement of an integrated report.	2
E6	**The audit of performance information (predetermined objectives) in the public sector**	
(a)	Describe the audit of performance information (predetermined objectives) and differentiate from performance auditing.	2
(b)	Plan the audit of performance information (predetermined objectives), and describe examination procedures to be used in the audit of performance information.	3
(c)	Discuss the audit criteria of reported performance information, namely compliance with reporting requirements, usefulness, measurability and reliability.	3
(d)	Discuss the form and content of a report on the audit of performance information.	2
(e)	Discuss the content of an audit conclusion on an integrated report of performance against predetermined objectives.	3

Exam guide

This topic could be the subject of a current issues discussion question. Measuring social and environmental performance can also be examined as part of a Section A case study question.

1 Importance for the company

FAST FORWARD

A company's stakeholders include employees, society and the environment.

Social and environmental audits have become increasingly important over the last decade or so, principally as a result of increasing recognition that what businesses do can affect their whole social and natural environment, in addition to just their shareholders.

 Case Study

Coal industry

Consider the coal industry. A coalmining company's financial statements will include the costs of employee wages, plant and machinery used, licences and future dismantling costs.

But the costs of the coal industry to the social and natural environment may be much more widespread than this. The environmental impact of the coal industry as a whole includes the following factors, not part of financial statements.

- Land use. Mining radically changes the landscape, eg by eliminating vegetation, changing soil profiles and stopping current land uses.
- Waste management. Burning coal (eg to make electricity) creates ash, much of which must be stored in the ground, which both uses up land and creates a potential hazard to communities.
- Wildlife. Mining damages wildlife principally by changing or destroying habitats, which can result in the depletion or total extinction of species from affected areas.
- Air pollution. Coal is the largest contributor to the man-made increase of carbon dioxide (CO_2) in the atmosphere, which is associated with climate change.

It is important to note, however, that the coal industry is usually seen as bringing economic benefits to society, through providing energy to consumers and employment for workers.

It is increasingly the case that investors want to know about a business's social and environmental impact, and a social or environmental audit enables them to do this. Since the 1980s there have been 'ethical' investment funds, but in general terms there is a widespread belief that environmental issues in particular are a source of risk to a company, eg through unforeseen liabilities, or reputational damage.

1.1 Stakeholders

A company can be seen from the perspectives of various **stakeholders**. Traditionally auditors are concerned with one set, the shareholders, to whom they report on the financial statements. The diagram below shows various other stakeholders that a company might have.

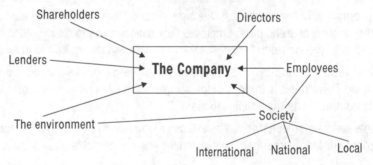

In this chapter we are concerned with the needs of three of the above categories: employees, the environment and society. These have knock-on effects on the shareholders, directors and the company itself.

The diagram links the first three together because in this context they are inextricably linked.

Company stakeholders	
Environment	The environment is directly impacted by many of our corporate activities today. This may be PRIMARY ⟶ The impact of processes SECONDARY ⟶ The impact of products
	The primary impact is regulated by environmental legislation, which has been prolific in recent years. The secondary impact is governed partly by legislation and partly by consumer opinion.

Company stakeholders	
Society	Society, from the point of view of the company, is made up of consumers or potential consumers. As recognised above, consumers increasingly have opinions about 'green', environmentally friendly products and will direct their purchasing accordingly.
	Society will also, through lobby groups, often speak out on behalf of the environment as it cannot speak out itself.
Employees	Employees have a relationship with the company in their own right, in terms of their livelihood and also their personal safety when they are at work.
	However, from the company's perspective, they are also a small portion of society at large, as they may purchase the products of the company or influence others to do so.

In some ways it is easier to see why the company is important to these stakeholders than why they are important to the company.

Company stakeholders	
Environment	The company can cause harm to natural resources in various ways, including: • Exhausting natural resources such as coal and gas • Emitting harmful toxins which destroy the atmosphere
Society	… is concerned with the harm to the natural resources as they and their children have to live on the planet and may suffer direct or indirect effects of pollution or waste.
Employees	… have all the concerns that society do and, more immediately, depend on the company for their livelihood and safety when at work.

For a company, however, there is one simple need. Companies desire above all else to keep providing returns for their shareholders. Employees are needed to keep making the product, as are natural resources, and consumers' (that is, society's) goodwill is required to keep selling it.

Obviously, loss of employees and consumers is going to make it impossible for companies to stay in business. Therefore it is important for companies to have policies in order to appease these stakeholders and to communicate the policies to them.

Companies are also constrained by extensive legislation regulating their behaviour towards the environment. Many countries have produced environmental legislation in recent years.

1.2 Implications for management: risk management

FAST FORWARD

> Social and environmental issues may present a risk to the company and, by implication, the shareholders' investment, which directors are required to manage as part of their corporate governance responsibilities.

The UK's Turnbull Guidelines state that management is responsible for internal controls which must comprise a sound system to manage risks to the business. Management may seek to discharge this responsibility by using some kind of risk audit. This is not a mandatory requirement, although some form of ongoing risk assessment and audit may be compulsory in some industry sectors (eg banking, financial services). Risk audit can be done internally or externally.

Social and environmental audit is a type of risk audit which management may decide to undertake, either as part of its overall risk management process or in order to address the concerns of stakeholders.

 Question   **Environmental and social risks**

(a) Describe the key environmental and social risks that a business might face.
(b) Explain why they might result in the failure of the business.

(a)   The mindmap below shows the risks that the business faces.

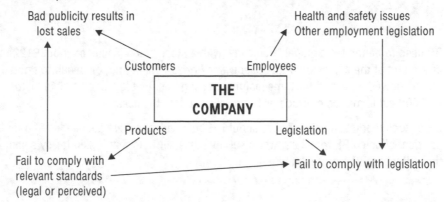

(b)   Any of these issues could be at a level serious enough to cause significant business interruption or even business failure, for the reasons given below.

    (i)   **Bad publicity.** This could lead to customers choosing other products, boycotts or loss of market share significant enough to prevent the business from continuing in operation.

    (ii)   **Legislation.** The company could be found not to be complying with legislation (through whistleblowing by employees or auditors, or investigation by a regulatory body). This could have the following effects.

        (1)   **Fines/compensation**. These could be significant enough to prevent the continuance of the business.

        (2)   **Disqualification of directors**. If the staff involved are key members of the organisation, this could threaten the ability of the company to continue.

        (3)   **Bad publicity**. See points made above.

1.3 Management controls

Key term

> An **environmental management system (EMS)** is a system for managing an organisation's overall risk associated with its environment, encompassing the organisational elements, the planning and the resources involved in developing, implementing and maintaining the organisation's policy in this area.

The specific controls that management put in place in line with their duties under the corporate governance codes will vary according to the needs of the business.

They are likely to involve specific measures designed to ensure that environmental legislation is complied with; for example they may relate to protective clothing, disposal of waste etc. The human resources department is likely to design policies to ensure that employment legislation is complied with.

The directors may also seek to **incorporate social and environmental values into the corporate culture** of the company, so that all employees are aware of the risks arising in these areas, and are focused on avoiding them. This can be achieved by implementing a corporate code, or by **setting targets** of social and environmental performance.

One such target might be to obtain the British Standards Institute's (BSI's) ISO 14001, relating to Environmental Management Systems. This will involve having an assessment by the BSI, and may involve updating management systems to comply with the standard (ISO 14001).

ISO 14001 is often a formal condition for entry into supply chains and certain markets. It does not require the company to produce an environmental report; however, the European equivalent, the Eco-Management and Audit Scheme (EMAS), does. This was introduced by a European Council regulation requiring implementation in all EU member states. The scheme provides recognition for all those companies who have established a programme of environmental action designed to protect and continuously improve their environmental performance.

 Case Study | **BP oil spill**

BP used to be the UK's biggest company, with a stock market value of about £122bn. However, in 2010, as a result of the explosion of the *Deepwater Horizon* drilling rig, oil began to flood into the Gulf of Mexico. The oil flowed unabated for three months, making this the biggest oil spill in history with approximately 800,000 cubic metres of crude oil being released into the ocean.

BP's stock market valuation fell by about £49bn, dividends were suspended and its CEO stood down. The accident affected BP for years, which set up a disaster fund that it paid for by selling a number of oil fields, thus affecting BP's profitability.

2 Measuring social and environmental performance
12/08, 12/10, 6/12, 12/14

FAST FORWARD ❯❯ Measuring social and environmental performance can be a difficult area. Auditors can provide assurance services in this area, giving opinions as to whether directors' assertions about performance are fair.

2.1 The problem of measurement – what? and for whom?

A key part of risk management is monitoring and evaluating results. Social and environmental performance is not as easy a thing to measure as financial performance. Financial performance can be measured fairly easily, eg by performing analytical procedures on the financial statements. But these methods will not work with social and environmental performance, because quantitative information on the firm's social and environmental impact is not usually available.

The first step in deciding what to measure is to **identify** who the key **stakeholders** are. With financial performance the main stakeholders are clear: the users of the financial statements, as defined by accounting standards. When it comes to social and environment performance, the business will need to think about its own specific stakeholders. Once these have been identified, the business must **identify** their **needs** and the **performance measures** that best relate to those needs.

2.1.1 Identifying and engaging stakeholders

Stakeholders can be grouped according to various criteria, eg internal/external, corporate/operational. You should be familiar with these from your earlier studies. Examples of stakeholders include:

- Internal: employees
- External: financial institutions, pressure groups, local communities, regulatory bodies, customers

A good way to do this in practice might be to map out the business's value chain, and to think of stakeholders at each point on the value chain.

The next step is to **engage stakeholders**, which means finding out their views on how they are affected by the business. This must be an active process, as it is possible that stakeholders will know more about the impact of the business than management do. The aim of this process is to prioritise the main issues that concern stakeholders, with a view to measuring the business's impact in these areas.

2.1.2 Generating performance measures

The next step is to translate the main stakeholder issues into performance measures. This could take the form of **Key Performance Indicators (KPIs)**, which you should be familiar with from your earlier studies.

A simple example of this could be:

Stakeholder	Issue	KPI
Local community	Noise	Number of noise complaints each year
Employee groups	Work-related injuries	Number of injuries sustained at work each year
Environmental groups	Pollution	Quantity of CO_2 emitted each year

In practice it is often **difficult** to generate appropriate KPIs. One key reason for this is that social and environmental effects may be **impossible to quantify**. For example, the issue for employees may be job satisfaction, but this can be difficult to measure. It is possible to gather statistical information on this, but whether or not this information is useful or reliable is open to question.

A **further difficulty** is that systems for gathering information on these KPIs may not be established well enough to allow accurate measurement.

Exam focus point

The December 2014 exam featured 4 marks for a discussion of 'the difficulties in measuring and reporting on social and environmental performance', and then a further 6 marks for recommending procedures in relation to some KPIs give in the question.

2.2 Targets and indicators

One way to measure social performance is to set targets and sustainability indicators and then appraise whether the targets have been met and the indicators exist.

These targets will vary from business to business, depending on what the issues are. To illustrate the point, a case study based on Shell is given below.

 Case Study

Shell

Shell is a large multinational group of companies that deals in oil, gas and chemicals. There are various issues which make social and environmental issues important to this company.

- It deals in the earth's natural resources.
- Its business is heavily environmentally legislated.
- It employs a significant number of people.
- Some employees work in risky environments.
- It operates in areas of the world where human rights issues are not given sufficient priority.

Targets

In response to the social and environmental issues raised above, Shell has set targets of social and environmental performance which it evaluates and reports on to shareholders on an annual basis.

The following are examples of targets which the company has set.

Environmental

- Reduce emissions of carbon dioxide from refinery activity
- Continue to develop cleaner fuels
- Reduce emissions of nitrogen oxides from burning fuel in operations
- Reduce spills of crude oil and chemicals

Social

- Zero employee fatalities in work-related incidents
- Not exploit children in any country where child labour exists, by
  - Not employing children under the legal age of employment
  - Dealing with other companies who employ children illegally
- Pursue equal opportunities for men and women in all countries where this is legally possible

Sustainability principles

The company has also set general sustainability principles which all staff should apply in daily business.

- Respect and safeguard people
- Engage and work with stakeholders
- Minimise impact on the environment
- Use resources efficiently
- Maximise benefits to the community

Reporting

The company reports on all these issues to its shareholders and, wherever possible, the facts included within this report are checked by independent verifiers.

The case study shows a number of targets and sustainability indicators. Some can be measured in mathematical terms, for example:

- Emissions
- Spills
- Elimination of work-related fatalities
- Employment of children

However, some of the targets are not specific enough to be able to measure in that way. For example, it is more difficult to identify where the company is in relation to achieving a target of developing cleaner fuels until the cleaner fuel appears. Such a development target cannot have a prescribed timescale.

Equally, it is difficult to measure the effect of the general principles which the company has included within the culture of the company.

 Case Study

The annual report of the Minerals and Metals Group (MMG) devotes four pages to Sustainability. A key area for the group is safety and health, in relation to which a KPI is the 'Total recordable injury frequency rate', which measures the rate of injuries sustained at work. The annual report contained a narrative account of the events during the year, along with figures which showed a fall from 6.3 injuries per million hours worked at the start of the year to 4.7 at the end of the year.

Source: MMG Annual Report 2010

2.3 Social audits

The process of checking whether a company has achieved set targets may fall within the scope of a social audit that a company carries out.

Social audits involve:

- Establishing whether the firm has a rationale for engaging in socially responsible activity
- Identifying that all current environmental programmes are congruent with the mission of the company
- Assessing objectives and priorities related to these programmes
- Evaluating company involvement in such programmes past, present and future

Whether or not a social audit is used depends on the degree to which social responsibility is part of the **corporate philosophy**. A cultural awareness must be achieved within an organisation in order to implement environmental policy, which requires Board and staff support.

In the US, social audits on environmental issues have increased since the Exxon Valdez catastrophe in 1989, when millions of gallons of crude oil were released into Alaskan waters.

The Valdez principles were drafted by the Coalition for Environmentally Responsible Economics to focus attention on environmental concerns and corporate responsibility:

- Eliminate pollutants and hazardous waste
- Conserve non-renewable resources
- Market environmentally safe products and services
- Prepare for accidents and restore damaged environments
- Provide protection for employees who report environmental hazards
- Appoint an environmentalist to the board of directors, name an executive for environmental affairs, and develop an environmental audit of global operations, which is to be made publicly available

2.4 Environmental audits

Key term

> **Environmental audits** seek to assess how well the organisation performs in safeguarding the environment in which it operates, and whether the company complies with its environmental policies.

Environmental auditing is exactly what is says: auditing a business to assess its impact on the environment or, as the UK's CBI expressed it, 'the systematic examination of the interactions between any business operation and its surroundings'.

The audit will cover a range of areas and will involve the performance of different types of testing. The scope of the audit must be determined and this will depend on each individual organisation. There are, however, some aspects of the approach to environmental auditing which are worth mentioning.

(a) **Environmental Impact Assessments (EIAs)**. These are required, under European Commission (EC) directive, for all major projects which require planning permission and have a material effect on the environment. The EIA process can be incorporated into any environmental auditing strategy.

(b) **Environmental surveys**. These are a good way of starting the audit process, by looking at the organisation as a whole in environmental terms. This helps to identify areas for further development, problems, potential hazards and so forth.

(c) **Environmental SWOT analysis**. A 'strengths, weaknesses, opportunities, threats' analysis is useful as the environmental audit strategy is being developed. This can only be done later in the process, when the organisation has been examined in much more detail.

(d) **Environmental Quality Management (EQM)**. This is seen as part of TQM (Total Quality Management) and it should be built in to an environmental management system. Such a strategy has been adopted by companies such as IBM, Dow Chemicals and by the Rhone-Poulenc Environmental Index which has indices for levels of water, air and other waste products.

(e) **Eco-audit**. The EC has adopted a proposal for a regulation for a voluntary community environmental auditing scheme, known as the eco-audit scheme. The scheme aims to promote improvements in company environmental performance and to provide the public with information about these improvements. Once registered, a company will have to comply with certain ongoing obligations involving disclosure and audit.

(f) **Eco-labelling**. Developed in Germany, this voluntary scheme will indicate those EC products which meet the highest environmental standards, probably as the result of an EQM system. It is suggested that eco-audit **must** come before an eco-label can be given.

(g) **BS 7750 Environmental Management Systems**. BS 7750 also ties in with eco-audits and eco-labelling and with the quality BSI standard BS 5750. Achieving BS 7750 is likely to be a first step in the eco-audit process.

(h) **Supplier audits**. These ensure that goods and services bought in by an organisation meet the standards applied by that organisation.

In general, an environmental audit encompasses three processes.

(a) Agreeing metrics: determining in what areas targets should be set, and at what level they should be set. This might be influenced by, for instance, the need to meet legal requirements (so that the metrics would be set in areas that are relevant to those requirements). Examples of metrics include:

- Emissions (pollution, greenhouse gases, waste)
- Consumption (water, gas, electricity, non-renewable feedstocks)

(b) Performance measurement: the measurement of actual performance in terms of the agreed metrics

(c) Reporting compliance: reporting on the implications of the results for compliance with the targets specified in (a)

In order to do this, the environmental auditor will carry out the following steps.

- Obtain a copy of the company's environmental policy
- Assess whether the policy is likely to achieve objectives:
  - Meet legal requirements
  - Meet British Standards
  - Satisfy key customers'/suppliers' criteria
- Test implementation and adherence to the policy by:
  - Discussion
  - Observation
  - 'Walk-though tests' where possible

Exam focus point

An article in *Student Accountant* entitled 'Risk and environmental auditing' looks at what social and environmental audits are and why they are important. Make sure you have looked at this useful background reading.

3 Implications for the statutory audit

Social and environmental issues can affect the statutory audit at the planning stage (risk), while undertaking substantive procedures (impairment/provisions) and during audit reviews (going concern).

3.1 Why important?

We now turn from the importance of social and environmental issues to the company and look at why they are important to the auditor in the context of the statutory audit.

The key reason that the issues are important to the statutory audit is that they are important to the company and therefore **can potentially affect the financial statements**.

The impact of the issues on an audit can be divided into three specific areas:

- Planning the audit
- Undertaking substantive procedures
- Audit reviews

Another important point to note is the duties of the auditor arising under ISA 250 *Consideration of laws and regulations in an audit of financial statements*. We shall also consider this below.

3.2 Planning the audit

Social and environmental issues can affect the audit in two main ways:

- Knowledge of the business (ISA 315)
- Inherent risk assessment (ISAs 315 and 330)

You should be aware of the principles involved in these two issues, so there is no need to go into a lot of further detail at this stage.

As part of their knowledge of the business, the auditor should have an awareness of any environmental regulations the business is subject to, and any key social issues arising in the course of the business.

The auditor may be able to obtain knowledge of this aspect of the business by reading the firm's procedures or reviewing any quality control documentation it has relating to standards. The auditor may be able to review the results of any environmental audits undertaken by the company.

This will then form part of the assessment of inherent risk.

3.3 Substantive procedures

Social and environmental issues, particularly environmental issues, may impact on the financial statements in a number of ways.

Examples of the impact of social and environmental matters on financial statements

- Provisions (for example, for site restoration, fines/compensation payments)
- Contingent liabilities (for example, in relation to pending legal action)
- Asset values (issues may impact on impairment or purchased goodwill/products)
- Capital/revenue expenditure (costs of clean-up or meeting legal standards)
- Development costs (new products)
- Going concern issues (considered later in this chapter, under reviews)

Exam focus point

When approaching a question about auditing specific items in financial statements, or issuing an audit opinion in respect of them, you should bear in mind whether there is an environmental/social issue which will impact on valuation or disclosure. Use your common sense; however do not make up such issues where no obvious indicators are given in the question.

The auditor will have to bear in mind the effects of social or environmental issues on the financial statements when designing audit procedures. We will now look at some potential audit procedures that would be relevant in three of the key areas above.

3.3.1 Substantive procedures: asset valuation

The key risk that arises with regard to valuation is that assets might be **impaired**. IAS 36 *Impairment of assets* requires an impairment review to be undertaken with regard to non-current assets if certain indicators of impairment exist. We have discussed the audit of impairments in Chapter 9, but shall consider the points specific to environmental and social issues here.

Knowledge brought forward from *Financial Reporting*

IAS 36 gives a list of indicators that an impairment review is required. The indicator relevant here is a significant change in the technological market, legal or economic environment of the business in which the assets are employed.

The auditor should be aware of the regulatory environment of the client as part of their knowledge of the business (as discussed above), but the following **general procedures** could be undertaken as part of the non-current asset testing to **establish whether an impairment review is required**.

- Review the board minutes for indications that the environmental regulatory environment has changed.
- Review relevant trade magazines or newspapers to assess whether any significant adverse change has taken place.
- Discuss the issue with management, particularly those nominated to have responsibility for environmental issues, if such a position exists.

If a significant adverse change has taken place, the directors may or may not have conducted an impairment review. If the directors have not, the auditors should discuss the matter with them. If the directors refuse to conduct an impairment review, the auditors should consider the result of that on their audit report.

If an impairment review has been undertaken, and the valuation of the asset has been adjusted accordingly, the auditor should **audit the impairment review**.

3.3.2 Substantive procedures: provisions

Guidance on accounting for provisions is given in IAS 37 *Provisions, contingent liabilities and contingent assets*. The audit of provisions has been discussed previously in Chapter 10. We shall consider the points specific to environmental and social issues here.

Knowledge brought forward from *Financial Reporting*

IAS 37 defines a **provision as a liability of uncertain timing or amount**. A liability is a present obligation of the entity arising from past events, the settlement of which is expected to result in an outflow from the entity of resources embodying economic benefits. A provision should be recognised when:

- An entity has a **present obligation** (legal or constructive) as a result of a past event
- It is probable that an outflow of resources embodying economic benefits will be required to settle the obligation
- A **reliable estimate** can be made of the obligation

The International Accounting Standard (IAS) provides some helpful examples of environmental issues that result in provisions being required. If a company has an environment policy such that the parties would expect the company to clean up contamination, or if the company has broken current environmental legislation, then a provision for environmental damage must be made.

The auditor needs to be aware of any circumstances that might give rise to a provision being required, and then apply the recognition criteria to it.

The **general substantive procedures** for **establishing if a provision is required** are the **same as** they were for identifying whether an **impairment review** was required.

If the directors have included provisions in the financial statements relating to environmental issues, the **audit procedures** will be the same as were discussed earlier. Specifically, the auditor may be able to **review correspondence** from any regulatory watchdog, or obtain a copy of the **relevant legislation** to review its requirements.

3.3.3 Substantive procedures: contingent liabilities

Accounting for contingent liabilities is also governed by IAS 37.

Knowledge brought forward from *Financial Reporting*

IAS 37 defines a contingent liability as either:

(a) A possible obligation that arises from past events and whose existence will be confirmed only by the occurrence or non-occurrence of one or more uncertain future events not wholly within the entity's control, or

(b) A present obligation that arises from past events but is not recognised because it is not probable that an outflow of resources embodying economic benefits will be required to settle the obligation or because the amount of the obligation cannot be measured with sufficient reliability.

Social and environmental issues may also impact here. In fact, a contingent liability is likely to arise through items being identified in a provision review, when the items highlighted do not meet the recognition criteria for a provision.

This was discussed earlier. Given their relationship with provisions, the **general audit procedures to establish if contingent liabilities exist** are the **same as** the ones for **provisions**, given above.

If the directors have made **disclosures relating to contingent liabilities** in respect of environmental and social issues, the **procedures** to test them were set out earlier. **Specific evidence** would be on similar lines as for provisions in respect of social and environmental issues: **correspondence with a regulator or relevant legislation**.

3.4 Going concern

Environmental and social issues can impact on the ability of the company to continue as a going concern.

The auditor will need to be aware of such issues when undertaking the going concern review. The procedures involved in going concern reviews were discussed earlier in Chapter 8.

3.5 Auditor responsibility in the event of non-compliance with laws and regulations

FAST FORWARD

> The auditor must bear in mind the requirements of ISA 250 *Consideration of laws and regulations in an audit of financial statements*.

The auditor's responsibility with regard to laws and regulations is set out in ISA 250 *Consideration of laws and regulations in an audit of financial statements*. This was discussed in Chapter 1, so you should refer back to this to remind yourself of the actions the auditor should take in the event of discovering non-compliance.

Environmental obligations would be core in some businesses (for example, our oil and chemical company given in the case study above), in others they would not. ISA 250 talks of 'other laws and regulations' where compliance may be fundamental to the operating aspects of the business, to an entity's ability to continue its business or to avoid material penalties.

Clearly, in the case of a company which stands to lose its operating licence to carry on business in the event of non-compliance, environmental legislation is fundamental to the business.

In the case of social legislation, this will be a matter of judgement for the auditor. It might involve matters of employment legislation, health and safety regulation, human rights law and such matters which may not seem fundamental to the objectives of the company, but which permeate the business due to the needs of employees.

The auditor is not expected to be a specialist in environmental law. However, as part of their professional duty, they must ensure that they have enough knowledge to undertake the assignment, or that they engage the use of an auditor's expert if necessary.

4 Implications for assurance services

FAST FORWARD

Many different assurance services could be offered within the broad context of social and environmental issues.

4.1 Types of service

Auditors can provide a variety of services in respect of environmental and social issues. Most of these services are familiar to us, so there is no need to revisit these in detail. Remember that most of the services we have discussed could be applied in an environmental and social context:

- Internal audit services (reviewing controls)
- Review of internal controls and procedures
- Management letter concerning controls as a by-product of statutory audit
- Assurance services (see below)

Management increasingly reports to members on social and environmental issues, and there is a growing public perception that this is an important area. This means that it is an issue that can give rise to **assurance services**.

Remember!

> An **assurance engagement** is one where a practitioner expresses a conclusion designed to enhance the degree of confidence of the intended users other than the responsible party about the outcome of the evaluation or measurement of a subject matter against criteria.

Assurance engagements give rise to assurance reports, which we outlined in Chapter 12. We shall consider the issue of specific verification reports in relation to social and environmental issues here.

If the directors issue an environmental and social report, it may contain figures and statements that are verifiable. Using the example of Shell (above), the directors could make the following assertions.

- Carbon dioxide emissions were x million tonnes in 2001, which represents a 2% decrease from 2000.
- We have implemented a strategy aimed at ensuring that in five years' time, no one we deal with will have an involvement in child labour.

These assertions can be reviewed and assurance given about them. For instance, in the first case, the level of emission could be traced to records of emission from the refineries, and the percentage calculation could be checked.

In the second instance, the accountant could obtain details of the strategy and ascertain how fully it has been implemented by making enquiries of the staff who should be implementing the strategy. They could also appraise the strategy and give an opinion of the chances of it achieving the objective within the given time frame.

4.2 Contents of an assurance report on environmental issues

There is no guidance in issue as to the contents of such a report. The box below shows some items that should be included as a minimum.

- Note of the objectives of the review
- Opinions
- Basis on which those opinions have been reached
- Work performed
- Limitations to the work performed
- Limitations to the opinion given

Question
Social and environmental audit

Your audit client, Naturascope Co, is a health food and homeopathic remedies retailer, with a strong marketing emphasis on the 'natural' elements of the products and the fact that they do not contain artificial preservatives.

The directors have decided that it would benefit the company's public image to produce a social and environmental report as part of their annual report. There are three key assertions which they wish to make as part of this report:

- Goods/ingredients of products for sale in Naturascope have not been tested on animals
- None of Naturascope's overseas suppliers use child labour (regardless of local laws)
- All Naturascope's packaging uses recycled materials.

The directors have asked the audit engagement partner whether the firm would be able to produce a verification report in relation to the social and environmental report.

Required

(a) Identify and explain the matters the audit engagement partner should consider in relation to whether the firm can accept the engagement to report on the social and environmental report.

(b) Comment on the matters to consider and the evidence to seek in relation to the three assertions.

Answer

(a) **Acceptance considerations**

There are four key things that the audit engagement partner should consider:

(i) **Impact of the new engagement on the audit**

The audit engagement partner needs to ensure that the **objectivity of the audit is not adversely affected** by accepting any other engagements from an audit client. This is of primary importance.

Factors that they will consider include the impact that any fees from the engagement will have on total fees from the client and what staff will be involved in carrying out the new engagement (ie will they be audit staff, or could the engagement be carried out by a different department?).

In favour of the engagement, they would consider that such an engagement should increase their knowledge of the business and its suppliers and systems, and might enhance the audit firm's understanding of the inherent audit risk attached to the business.

(ii) **Competence of the audit firm to carry out the assignment**

The audit engagement partner needs to consider whether the firm has the **necessary competence** to carry out the engagement in a quality manner, so as to minimise the risk of being sued for negligence.

This will depend on the nature of the engagement and assurance required (see below) and on whether the auditor felt it would be cost-effective to use the work of an auditor's expert, if required.

(iii) **Potential liability of the firm for the report**

As the engagement is not an audit engagement, the partner should consider to whom they would be **accepting liability** in relation to this engagement, and whether the risk that that entails is worth it, in relation to the potential fees and other benefits of doing the work (such as keeping an audit client happy, and not exposing an audit client to the work of an alternative audit firm).

Unless otherwise stated, liability is unlikely to be restricted to the shareholders for an engagement such as this; indeed, it is likely to extend to all the users of the annual report. This could include:

- The bank
- Future investors making ethical investing decisions
- Customers and future customers making ethical buying decisions

The partner should also consider whether it might be possible to limit the liability for the engagement, and **disclaim liability** to certain parties.

(iv) **Nature of the engagement/criteria/assurance being given**

Before the partner accepts any such engagement on behalf of the firm, they should **clarify** with the directors the **exact nature** of the engagement, the degree of assurance required and the criteria by which the directors expect the firm to assess the assertions.

As the engagement is not an audit engagement, the audit rules of 'truth and fairness' and 'materiality' do not necessarily apply. The partner should determine whether the directors want the firm to verify that the assertions are '**absolutely correct**' or 'correct in x% of cases' and also what **quality of evidence** would be sufficient to support the conclusions drawn – for example, confirmations from suppliers, legal statements, or whether the auditors would have to visit suppliers and make personal verifications.

This engagement might be less complex for the audit firm if it could conduct it as an 'agreed-upon procedures' engagement, rather than an assurance engagement.

(b) **Assertions**

(i) **Animal testing**

The assertion is **complex** because it does not merely state that products sold have not been tested on animals, but that ingredients in the products have not been tested on animals.

This may mean a **series of links** have to be checked, because Naturascope's supplier who is the manufacturer of one of their products may not have tested that product on animals, but may source ingredients from several other suppliers, who may in turn source ingredients from several other suppliers, etc.

The audit firm may also find that it is a **subjective issue**, and that the assertion 'not tested on animals' is not as clear cut as one would like to suppose. For example, the dictionary defines animal as either 'any living organism characterised by voluntary movement ...' or 'any mammal, especially man'. This could suggest that the directors could make the assertion if they didn't test products on mammals, and it might still to an extent be 'true', or that products could be tested on 'animals' that, due to prior testing, were paralysed. However, neither of these practices are likely to be thought ethical by animal lovers who are trying to invest or buy ethically.

Potential sources of evidence include: assertions from suppliers, site visits at suppliers' premises and a review of any licences or other legal documents in relation to testing held by suppliers.

(ii) **Child labour**

This assertion is less complex than the previous assertion because it is restricted to Naturascope's direct overseas suppliers.

It does, however, contain complexities of its own, particularly in relation to the definition of 'child labour'. It is not certain, for example, whether labour means 'any work', 'a certain type of work', or even 'work over a set period of time'. Further, the definition of a child is not given, when other countries do not have the same legal systems and practical requirements of schooling, marriage, voting etc.

There may also be a practical difficulty of verifying how old employees actually are in certain countries, where birth records may not be maintained.

Possible sources of evidence include assertions by the supplier and inspection by auditors.

(iii) **Recycled materials**

This may be the simplest assertion to verify, given that it is the least specific. All the packaging must have an element of recycled materials. This might mean that the assertion is restricted to one or a few suppliers. The definition of packaging may be wide; for example, if all goods are boxed and then shrink-wrapped, it is possible that those two elements together are termed 'packaging' and so only the cardboard element need contain recycled materials.

The sources of evidence are the same as previously – assertions from suppliers, inspections by the auditors or review of suppliers' suppliers to see what their methods and intentions are.

5 Audit of performance information in the public sector

FAST FORWARD

Auditing public sector performance information helps to make governments accountable to the public.

Exactly which organisations are in the public sector varies from country to country, but it commonly includes government itself, the armed forces, the police, education and healthcare.

Public sector organisations in many countries are subject to audit regimes which may involve the audit of performance information, in addition to the audit of public sector entities' financial statements. Performance measurement is an integral part of many modern government policies, and the audit of this information is a key component of the accountability of many public sector bodies.

Key term

Performance information is information published by public sector organisations regarding their objectives and their performance in relation to those objectives.

The main focus of an audit of performance information will be operational performance. This will usually be examined in terms of specific quantitative measures, such as KPIs, but is not limited to quantitative measures alone.

Point to note

There is a good article on this topic in *Student accountant*, entitled 'Performance information in the public sector' and available online at:

http://www.accaglobal.com/uk/en/student/exam-support-resources/professional-exams-study-resources/p7/technical-articles/performance-information.html

The following gives an illustration of performance information reported on by a real public sector body. This is an extract of the overall framework used by the Scottish Police. The full document is available at:

http://www.spa.police.uk/assets/128635/performanceindicators

'Scottish Police Authority Performance Framework 2013/14

'In overall terms, the Authority is responsible for maintaining policing, promoting the policing principles outlined in the Act, delivering continuous improvement in policing and holding the Chief Constable to account.

'Performance Framework

'To fulfil these duties, the SPA has developed a Performance Framework which enables it to monitor and evaluate the performance of the police and to assess the extent to which the aims and benefits resulting from a single police force in Scotland are being realised.

'The Framework is underpinned by the four Strategic Policing Priorities set out by Scottish Ministers and the seven SPA Strategic Objectives within the SPA's Strategic Plan which was published in March 2013. As such, it supports reporting against the Priorities and the underlying Strategic Objectives.

'The SPA will analyse, monitor and report on the information gathered through this Framework on a regular basis, using information primarily, but not exclusively, provided to them by the Police Service of Scotland.

Strategic Policing Priority 1: Make communities safer and reduce harm by tackling and investigating crime and demonstrating pioneering approaches to prevention and collabaratiob at a national and local level.

Strategic objectives:
- *Work in Partnership to improve safety for the citizens of Scotland and reduce crime.*
- *Ensure that all communities, includeing the most vulnerable, have access to the police service and are given the support they need to fell safe.*

NUMBER OF RECORDED CRIMES
Total number of recorded crimes in Scotland (Groups 1 to 5).

DETECTION RATE
Detection rates fro recorded crime.

ROAD CASUALTY REDUCTION
The number of people killed / seriously injured (KSI).
The number of children aged under 16 killed / seriously injured (KSI).

YOUTH CRIME
The number of young people who offend.
The number of young people who offend that are referred to EEL Co-ordinator.

PUBLIC PROTECTION.
Domestic Abuse – recorded incidents, crimes and detection rates.
The number of children referred to partner agencies.
The number of Adults at Risk referrals made to partner agencies.
The number of offenders managed under MAPPA

REQUIREMENT FOR SPECIALIST POLICE SUPPORT FUNCTIONS
The number of formal requests for specialist services.
the number and percentage of formal requests granted;

The audit of performance information must be distinguished from the related term 'performance audit', which refers to the audit of value for money, ie whether an organisation has achieved the '3 Es' of economy, efficiency and effectiveness. Performance information is **not** value for money information, although in practice the terms are often used loosely, and an audit of performance information may be conducted alongside a value for money audit.

The audit of performance information is usually against pre-determined objectives. The auditor's role is to focus on the credibility, usefulness and accuracy of the reported performance in relation to those objectives.

The body conducting the audit of performance information may differ from country to country, but it is commonly done by the State's supreme audit institution. Examples include the National Audit Office in the UK, the Government Accountability Office in the USA, and the Comptroller and Auditor General of India. Alternatively, it is possible for audits of this nature to be conducted by private sector audit firms.

5.1 Problems with measurement

FAST FORWARD

Performance measurement in the public sector is beset by problems, including the inherent difficulty of measuring non-financial performance, and the problem of reporting relevant information.

The overall performance of public sector entities is **harder to measure than financial performance**. In common with social and environmental performance, one comes up against the basic stumbling block of devising simple quantitative metrics with which to measure performance that is by nature complex and multifarious. The project is worthwhile because it enables public sector entities to be held to account for the work they do on behalf of government (and ultimately the public) but it is by no means straightforward.

This difficulty is partially resolved by the form of report that is issued. By producing an **integrated report**, it is possible to combine **quantitative** measures (such as KPIs) with **qualitative** verbal explanations of the entity's performance. This enables more information to be communicated to users than would be possible using quantitative measures alone.

5.1.1 Generating relevant quantitative measures

A key part of the process is generating relevant KPIs. This is a process with which you should already be familiar in the context of private sector organisations.

One approach to measuring performance might be to generate as much quantitative information as possible about an entity's operations. The problem with this approach is that not all of the information generated will be **relevant** to the needs of users. Before collecting data it is therefore necessary to consider the objectives of the organisation, and how it might be possible to measure performance in relation to those objectives.

Performance measures might be designed based on the objectives of the public sector entity itself. Just as in the private sector, public sector KPIs may be derived from stakeholder analysis. For the purposes of the P7 exam, the objectives will always be predetermined.

Using the example of the provision of health services, the following stakeholders and perspectives could be envisaged, from which KPIs might then be generated.

Stakeholder	Perspective
Patients	Waiting times for treatment; measures of effectiveness of treatment
Groups of patients with specific needs	Availability of multilingual services; availability of services to help people with disabilities; availability of 24 hour services for specific conditions
Managers	Measures of cost per treatment; number of people treated

A central problem in designing performance measures is that of the **validity** of the measure. Put simply, does the performance indicator measure what one intends to measure?

A key problem faced by social scientists conducting research (and in this context, auditors) is: how to measure the effect of one variable on another, when no independent variable can be isolated? This is the problem of the **complexity** of the social world. One might, for instance, decide to measure the performance of a school in terms of the examination performances of its students. The immediate difficulty is that a student's performance is not simply the result of one variable (the school) but results from a large number of different factors, such as the student's level of education on entering the school, the educational environment in the student's home life and the amount of time available to the student for study rather than paid work (the list goes on).

It is therefore necessary to take great care when designing performance measures to take into account the effect of other factors on the reported metric. In practice, the auditor will often **adjust** figures to take into account the effect of other variables.

Question

Audit of performance information

Two hospitals, North Hospital and South Hospital, are required to report information in relation to the mortality of patients undergoing cardiothoracic (heart) surgery. The following information was reported.

Hospital	Number of patients	Number of planned procedures	Number of deaths
North	763	610	23
South	549	494	19

Of the deaths experienced in North Hospital, 12 were patients who died during planned procedures (the rest were emergency procedures). At South Hospital 7 patients died during planned procedures.

Required

Analyse the performance of the two hospitals and identify the best performing hospital.

Answer

At first glance, North Hospital may appear to have the worst mortality rate, with 23 deaths compared with 19 at South Hospital. These absolute figures may be misleading, however, so it is necessary to calculate the **relative** mortality rates for each hospital:

North Hospital = 23/763 = 3.0%

South Hospital = 19/549 = 3.5%

On this basis, North appears to be the better performing hospital. On further investigation, however, the picture becomes more complex.

Adjusting for emergency patients

It is likely that emergency procedures carry a higher risk of death than planned procedures. An uneven distribution of emergency procedures between the two hospitals would indicate different risk profiles in each hospital's underlying patient population for the period, which would be expected to affect the mortality rate for each hospital.

At North Hospital, 12 patients died during planned procedures, which gives a mortality rate of 2.0% (12/610) for planned procedures.

At South Hospital, 7 patients died during planned procedures, which gives a mortality rate of 1.4% (7/494) for planned procedures.

After adjusting for emergency procedures, it would appear that South Hospital has the lower (better) mortality rate. This appears to indicate that South Hospital is performing better for ordinary planned procedures.

It should be noted, however, that South Hospital has a higher mortality rate for emergency procedures:

North Hospital: (23 – 12) / (763 – 610) = 11/153 = 7%

South Hospital: (19 – 7) / (549 – 494) = 12/55 = 22%

This could be indicative of problems at South Hospital in relation to emergency procedures. It may also be a sign of differences in the underlying populations. Further information on the types of patients operated on in each hospital would be needed in order to determine which performed better in emergency situations.

5.1.2 Incentives and manipulation

An important difficulty in the use of performance information is that of **manipulation** of the reported figures (indeed, this is part of the reason for this information being subject to audit in the first place). This could take the form of straightforwardly doctoring the report figures, but perhaps more damaging is the risk that those being measured change their **behaviour** in order to improve the reported figures, without actually improving performance. This is the problem of **perverse incentives**.

A simple example of a perverse incentive is a measure of the speed in answering letters, which is not balanced by a measure of the quality of responses. This might encourage people to answer letters quickly, but badly. Extending the theme, a publishing company might set deadlines for books going to print or for drafts being completed, irrespective of their quality.

 Case Study   **Healthcare targets**

A public sector healthcare provider was set a target for the maximum length of time a patient would have to wait in emergency departments before being seen by a doctor. The target was for patients to be seen within four hours of being admitted.

The response in some departments was simply to leave non-urgent patients to wait outside in ambulances. Patients still in the ambulance were not yet technically 'admitted' to the department, so the time in the ambulance did not count towards the four hour target even though it was clearly detrimental to patient care.

5.1.3 Existence of information

It is possible that the entity being reported on may not generate all (or any) of the performance information needed. In this case, it will be necessary for the auditor to consider whether sufficient information will be available for them to conduct an audit – whether the preconditions exist for an audit of performance information. A common situation is one where a lot of data exists in a raw form, which must then be analysed by the auditor in order to measure performance against the specified objectives.

5.2 Planning and conducting the audit of performance information

The first step is to **identify** the **objectives** against which the performance of the organisation is to be evaluated. The question the auditor seeks to answer is simply: is the organisation achieving its objectives?

Objectives will usually already have been determined by the organisation itself (or by a higher level of government). The organisation itself may already have determined its own specific numerical measures (KPIs). It may then be determined whether a targeted (aimed for) or standard (minimum acceptable) level of performance has been achieved on the basis of these measures. Alternatively, objectives can take the form of general verbal statements, such as 'to improve performance against quality indicators', from which numerical measures may then be derived by the auditor.

Having identified the objectives, the auditor plans **procedures** to test whether they have been achieved. The procedures used may include audit-type procedures, but may also involve an element of social-scientific research in the form of both quantitative and qualitative research methods. ISAE 3000 *Assurance engagements other than audits or review of historical financial information* is a potential source of guidance here.

Procedures may include:

- Tests of controls on the systems used to generate performance information
- Performing analytical review to evaluate trends and gauge the consistency of quantitative data
- Analysis of service-user activity data
- Review of service-user experience surveys
- Surveys of key management and staff
- Interviews with key management and staff
- Review of minutes of meetings where performance information has been discussed
- Confirmation of performance information to source documentation; this may be performed on a sample basis
- Conducting case studies
- Review of existing literature
- Review of results of internal and external challenges

The auditor must keep **documentation** of the planning process and of the audit evidence obtained.

Question   Procedures

The Department of Transport of Proculsia is currently undertaking a large infrastructure project to build a new underground metro system in the country's second largest city, Pravus. The supreme auditor of Proculsia has been tasked with conducting a study of the Department's role in developing the project and funding it.

Considerable local media attention has been directed at the progress of the project, focusing on the report of a whistleblower who claimed that delays mean that it will not be completed on time. In response, the Department has stated that the project will be completed within its budget of $14bn, and by a deadline in five years' time.

Required

Identify procedures that should be performed in order to assess:

(a)   The Department's management of its financial exposure on the project
(b)   The Department's confidence that it will meet the prescribed project schedule

Answer

Procedures include:

(a) • Review overall project expenditure and compare with budgeted expenditure

     • Interview relevant management and staff to determine reasons for any variations from budget

     • Interview key management and staff to identify their expectations of whether the project will be completed within budget

     • Analyse the Department's business case for the project to determine whether the planned expenditures will meet the overall aims of the project

(b) • Review project timetable and compare progress with planned schedule

     • In relation to the whistleblower's claim, identify the delays referred to and ascertain the impact these are likely to have on the timetable

     • Interview key management and staff to identify their expectations of whether the project will be completed on time, and in particular what the effect may be of any delays already experienced

- Ascertain any knock-on effects that the delays may have, and enquire of management what actions they have taken to mitigate these effects
- Review of results of any internal challenges to management in relation to the delays, ie how management responded

5.3 Concluding and reporting

The auditor expresses a conclusion on the entity's achievement of its objectives. There is no specific form of words that must be used.

Generally the auditor gives a conclusion on whether the public sector body has met its objectives. This can be either reasonable assurance (positive wording) or limited assurance (negative wording). The type of conclusion given will have been agreed in advance with the public sector organisation and its regulatory body.

The report may take the form of an **integrated report** of performance against the entity's objectives. Such a report would present the auditor's conclusion alongside the performance information itself. The conclusions of other audit processes may also be presented within the report, such as an audit conclusion on value for money.

If the auditors do not themselves produce the integrated report then it will be necessary for them to ensure that the performance information included in the report is consistent with the information on which they have given a conclusion.

 Case Study

In 2013 the National Audit Office (NAO) issued a report on maternity services in England. The report was an integrated report which presented audited Key Facts on maternity services, such as:

694,241	£2.6bn	1 in 133 babies is stillborn or
live births in England in 2012	cost of National Health Service (NHS) maternity care in 2012-13	dies within 7 days of birth

The report gave an overview of maternity services, the organisations involved in delivering the services, and the government department's objectives for maternity care. As the government department had few of its own quantified measures of performance (there was a problem with the existence of information), the NAO developed its own measures.

Key Findings were presented for the performance of maternity services (performance information) and the management of maternity services. A conclusion was given on value for money, and recommendations were made for the relevant department.

The report contained details of the methodology used for the audit, the evidence base on which conclusions were based, and progress made by the department against recommendations made in the past.

The following paragraph was included within Key Findings, and is illustrative of the matters which auditors consider in reports such as this.

> 'Outcomes in maternity care are good for the vast majority of women and babies but, when things go wrong, the consequences can be very serious. In 2011, 1 in 133 babies were stillborn or died within seven days of birth. This mortality rate has fallen, but comparisons with the other UK nations suggest there may be scope for further improvement. There are wide unexplained variations in the performance of individual trusts [regional healthcare organisations] in relation to complication rates and medical intervention rates, even after adjusting for maternal characteristics and clinical risk factors. This variation may be partly due to differences in aspects of women's underlying health not included in the data and inconsistencies in the coding of the data.'

(Source: *Maternity services in England*, © National Audit Office 2013, p8, §14)

The overall **conclusion** expressed is worth reading. It begins with a general conclusion (first paragraph below), and then outlines some difficulties found. It is noteworthy that one of the difficulties was that of measuring performance in this area.

> *'For most women, NHS maternity services provide good outcomes and positive experiences. Since 2007 there have been improvements in maternity care, with more midwifery-led units, greater consultant presence, and progress against the government's commitment to increase midwife numbers.*
>
> *'However, the Department's implementation of maternity services has not matched its ambition: the strategy's objectives are expressed in broad terms which leaves them open to interpretation and makes performance difficult to measure. The Department has not monitored progress against the strategy and has limited assurance about value for money. When we investigated outcomes across the NHS, we found significant and unexplained local variation in performance against indicators of quality and safety, cost, and efficiency. Together these factors show there is substantial scope for improvement and, on this basis, we conclude that the Department has not achieved value for money for its spending on maternity services.'*

(Source: *Maternity services in England*, © National Audit Office 2013, p40)

6 Integrated reporting

FAST FORWARD

Integrated reporting draws together the many different types of capital which an organisation has, and aims to paint a broad picture of an organisation's ability to create value into the medium to long term.

6.1 Growth of integrated reporting

Integrated reporting is topical, and is in line with the recent focus across the profession on non-financial forms of reporting. The idea is to produce a single report that integrates the various strands of information reported into a coherent whole – ie financial, management commentary, governance and remuneration, and sustainability reporting.

By reporting on more than just financial capital, users are to be provided with information on how an organisations creates **value over time**. This entails a more **forward-looking focus** than historical financial statements, which is more meaningful to determining business value. It is hoped that the integrated report will help prepare the foundation for the next generation of annual reports.

The International Integrated Reporting Council (IIRC) issued its '**International IR Framework**' in 2013, which aims to encourage the adoption of integrated reporting across the world. The IIRC has its headquarters at ACCA, and ACCA appears keen to incorporate integrated reporting into its qualifications. The *Framework* is **aimed primarily at private sector companies**, but it could also be adapted for public sector or not for profit organisations.

The *Framework* is **principles-based**, acting as a platform to explain what creates value in a business. It is envisaged that reports will draw on material that is already available to management from a variety of different sources.

The *Framework* refers to an organisation's resources as 'capitals'. Capitals are used to assess value creation. Increases or decreases in these capitals indicate the level of value created or lost over a period. Capitals cover various types of resources found in a standard organisation. These may include financial capitals, such as the entity's financial reserves through to its intellectual capital which is concerned with intellectual property and staff knowledge.

6.2 Key elements

The key elements of an integrated report are as follows.

- **Overview** of organisation and its environment
- **Governance structure** and how this supports value
- **Business model**
- **Risks and opportunities**
- **Strategy** and resource allocation
- **Performance** and **achievement of objectives**
- **Future outlook** and challenges
- **Basis of preparation and presentation** for the integrated report

6.3 Capital types

The integrated reporting framework classifies the capitals as:

Capital	Comment
Financial	The pool of funds that is: - Available for use in the production of goods/the provision of services - Obtained through financing, or generated through operations/investments
Manufactured	Manufactured physical objects, including: - Buildings - Equipment - Infrastructure (eg roads, ports, bridges and waste and water treatment plants) Manufactured capital is often created by other organisations, but includes assets manufactured by the reporting organisation for sale or when they are retained for its own use.
Intellectual	Organisational knowledge-based intangibles, including: - Intellectual property, eg patents, copyrights, software, rights and licences - 'Organisational capital' eg tacit knowledge, systems, procedures and protocols
Human	People's competencies, capabilities and experience, and their motivations to innovate, including their: - Alignment with and support for an organisation's governance framework, risk management approach and ethical values - Ability to understand, develop and implement an organisation's strategy - Loyalties and motivations for improving processes, goods and services, including their ability to lead, manage and collaborate
Natural	All environmental resources and processes that support the prosperity of an organisation, including: - Water, land, minerals and forests - Biodiversity and ecosystem health

Capital	Comment
Social and relationship	The institutions and the relationships within and between communities, groups of stakeholders and other networks, and the ability to share information to enhance individual and collective wellbeing.

Social and relationship capital includes:
- Shared norms and common values and behaviours
- Key stakeholder relationships and the trust and willingness to engage that an organisation has developed and strives to build and protect with external stakeholders
- Intangibles associated with the brand and reputation that an organisation has developed
- An organisation's social licence to operate |

Source: *The International Integrated Reporting Framework*, www.theiirc.org

6.4 Interaction of capitals

Capitals continually interact with one another, and an increase in one may result in a decrease in another. For example, a decision to purchase a new IT system would improve an entity's 'manufactured' capital while decreasing its financial capital in the form of its cash reserves.

At present, adopting integrated reporting is voluntary, and as a result organisations are free to report only on those 'capitals' felt to be most relevant in communicating performance.

6.5 Short term vs long term

Integrated reporting forces management to balance the organisation's short-term objectives against its longer-term plans. Business decisions which are solely dedicated to the pursuit of increasing profit (financial capital) at the expense of building good relations with key stakeholders such as customers (social capital) are likely to hinder value creation in the longer term. It is thought that by producing a holistic view of organisational performance that this will lead to improved management decision making, ensuring that decisions are not taken in isolation.

6.6 Monetary values

Integrated reporting is **not aimed at attaching a monetary value** to every aspect of the organisation's operations. It is fundamentally concerned with evaluating value creation through the communication of qualitative and quantitative performance measures. KPIs are effective in communicating performance. Fundamentally, the *Framework* takes the view that **assessments of value should be left to users**, with most of the information in the report being **qualitative** in nature.

For example, when providing detail on customer satisfaction this can be communicated as the number of customers retained compared with the previous year. Best practice in integrated reporting requires organisations to report on both positive and negative movements in 'capital' to avoid only providing half the story.

6.7 Materiality

When preparing an integrated report, management should disclose matters which are likely to impact on an organisations ability to create value. Both internal and external risks, opportunities and outcomes regarded as being materially important are evaluated and quantified.

Importantly, while the financial reporting model determines financial reporting entities based on concepts of control or significant influence, the integrated reporting standard encourages organisations to look further – to evaluate what might be the source of the main risks, opportunities and outcomes affecting the organisation. For example, if an organisation considers that its ability to create value is dependent upon its

suppliers' labour practices (ie ensuring that its suppliers do not engage in illegal child labour), then it will decide to disclose information about this in its integrated report.

6.8 Implications of introducing integrated reporting

Implications	Comment
IT costs	The introduction of integrated reporting will most likely require significant upgrades to be made to the organisation's IT and information system infrastructure. Such developments will be needed to capture KPI data. Due to the broad range of business activities reported on using integrated reporting (customer, supplier relations, finance and human resources) it is highly likely the costs of improving the infrastructure will be significant.
Time/staff costs	The process of gathering and collating the data for inclusion in the report is likely to require a significant amount of staff time. This may affect staff morale if they are expected to undertake this work in addition to existing duties. Additional staff may need to be employed.
Consultancy costs	Organisations producing their first integrated report may seek external guidance from an organisation which provides specialist consultancy on integrated reporting. Consultancy fees are likely to be significant.
Disclosure	There is a danger that organisations may volunteer more information about their operational performance than intended. Disclosure of planned strategies and key performance measures are likely to be picked up by competitors.

6.9 Auditing integrated reports

Auditors may be engaged to produce an independent verification statement on an integrated report. This is an assurance report and would therefore need to performed in line with the guidance contained in ISAE 3000 *Assurance engagements other than audits or reviews of historical financial information* (covered in detail in Chapter 12 of this Study Text).

This could be either a direct or an attestation engagement, with the practitioner presenting the integrated report themselves (direct), or providing a report on information presented by the entity.

Practitioners in this area face many of the difficulties outlined above in relation to the audit of public sector performance information. The measurement of financial or even physical capital is relatively unproblematic because these areas may be readily subject to quantification. But intellectual, human and social capital are much more difficult to present objectively; their measurement involves a good deal of judgement. It is therefore difficult to see how an assurance engagement on an integrated report could offer much more than **limited assurance**, sticking as much as possible to the factual assertions made by the report and wording its conclusion negatively.

Chapter Roundup

- A company's stakeholders include employees, society and the environment.

- Social and environmental issues may present a risk to the company and, by implication, the shareholders' investment, which the directors are required to manage as part of their corporate governance responsibilities.

- Measuring social and environmental performance can be a difficult area. Auditors can provide assurance services in this area, giving opinions as to whether directors' assertions about performance are fair.

- Social and environmental issues can affect the statutory audit at the planning stage (risk), while undertaking substantive procedures (impairment/provisions), and during audit reviews (going concern).

- The auditor must bear in mind the requirements of ISA 250 *Consideration of laws and regulations in an audit of financial statements*.

- Many different assurance services could be offered within the broad context of social and environmental issues.

- Auditing public sector performance information helps to make governments accountable to the public.

- Performance measurement in the public sector is beset by problems, including the inherent difficulty of measuring non-financial performance, and the problem of reporting relevant information.

- Integrated reporting draws together the many different types of capital which an organisation has, and aims to paint a broad picture of an organisation's ability to create value in the medium to long term.

Quick Quiz

1   Draw a mindmap showing the major stakeholders in a company.

2   Management have a duty to monitor risks arising from social and environmental issues as part of their corporate governance.

    True   ☐
    False   ☐

3   Name three areas of a statutory audit where social and environmental issues are relevant.

    (1)   ....
    (2)   ....
    (3)   ....

4   Give an example of why social and environmental issues might affect all of the following financial statement areas.

    •   Provisions
    •   Contingent liabilities
    •   Asset values
    •   Capital/revenue expenditure
    •   Development costs
    •   Going concern

5   List six items which should be covered in an assurance report relating to environmental issues.

    (1)   ....   (4)   ....
    (2)   ....   (5)   ....
    (3)   ....   (6)   ....

6   What are the six types of capital detailed in the IIRC's International IR Framework?

1

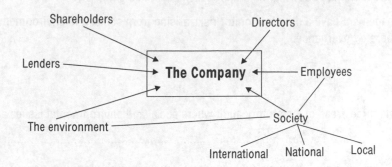

2   True

3   (1)   Planning (risks)
     (2)   Substantive testing (accounting issues arising)
     (3)   Reviews (going concern)

4   •   Provisions   (site restoration or fines/compensation payments)
     •   Contingent liabilities   (pending legal action)
     •   Asset values   (impairment due to new environmental legislation)
     •   Capital/revenue expenditure   (cost of clean-up or meeting legal standards)
     •   Development costs   (new, environmentally friendly products)
     •   Going concern   (operational existence threatened by new/proposed
                                        environmental laws)

5   (1)   Objectives   (4)   Work performed
     (2)   Opinions   (5)   Limitations on work
     (3)   Basis of opinions   (6)   Limitations on opinion

6   Financial, manufactured, intellectual, human, natural, social and relationship.

> **Now try the question below from the Practice Question Bank**

Number	Level	Marks	Time
Q26	Examination	15	29 mins

Internal audit
and outsourcing

16

Topic list	Syllabus reference
1 Revision: internal audit	E4
2 Outsourcing	E5
3 Outsourcing specific functions	E5
4 Impact of outsourcing on an audit	E5

Introduction

In this chapter we revise internal audit which you studied in some detail in your earlier auditing studies. Internal auditors provide services to the management of a company.

In the second half of the chapter, we look at outsourcing. Outsourcing is a key issue in business today. However, the main issues for management are cost and control.

The two issues are linked simply because the question of outsourcing has become a key issue in internal audit. Businesses are being encouraged to invest in internal audit, because of the benefits that the internal audit department can provide to corporate governance. However, setting up an internal audit department can be costly and difficult. Outsourcing can overcome these problems.

Study guide

		Intellectual level
E4	**Internal audit**	
(a)	Evaluate the potential impact of an internal audit department on the planning and performance of the external audit.	2
(b)	Explain the benefits and potential drawbacks of outsourcing internal audit.	2
(c)	Consider the ethical implications of the external auditor providing an internal audit service to a client.	2
E5	**Outsourcing**	
(a)	Explain the different approaches to 'outsourcing' and compare with 'insourcing'.	2
(b)	Discuss and conclude on the advantages and disadvantages of outsourcing finance and accounting functions.	3
(c)	Recognise and evaluate the impact of outsourced functions on the conduct of an audit.	3

Exam guide

Outsourcing and internal audit could be examined together or separately. Either or both could feature in a planning scenario question.

1 Revision: internal audit

FAST FORWARD

Internal audit plays a key role in corporate governance, providing objective assurance on control and risk management.

In Chapter 7 we looked at internal audit from the point of view of the external auditor who seeks to rely on its work. In this chapter we consider the internal audit function itself, specifically in connection with outsourcing.

1.1 Revision

The internal audit function was considered in detail in your earlier auditing studies. Work through the following question to ensure that you remember the basic principles of internal auditing.

Question

Revision: internal audit

(a) Describe the principal differences between internal and external auditors, considering the following factors.

    (i)   Eligibility

    (ii)   Security of appointment

    (iii)   Main objectives and limitations on the scope of their work

(b) Explain how external auditors would evaluate specific work carried out by internal auditors.

Answer

(a) **Eligibility**

Eligibility to act as external auditor is usually defined by the law and regulations of the jurisdiction in question. For example, in the UK, a person is ineligible to act as external auditor if they are an

officer or employee of the company, a partner or employee of such a person or a partnership in which such a person is a partner. An internal auditor is an employee of the company.

External auditors are also required to belong to a recognised supervisory body, and this means they must hold an appropriate qualification, follow technical standards and maintain competence.

By contrast, anyone can act as an internal auditor, even if they do not have a formal accounting qualification. It is up to the company's management who they appoint.

Security

In the UK, the external auditors are appointed to hold office until the conclusion of the next general meeting. They can be dismissed by an ordinary resolution of shareholders with special notice in a general meeting, and have the right to make representations.

External auditors cannot be dismissed by individual directors or by a vote of the board. The only influence directors can have on the removal of external auditors is through their votes as shareholders. The rules on security of tenure are there because of the need for external auditors to protect the interests of shareholders by reporting on directors' stewardship of the business.

By contrast, as internal auditors are employees of the company, they can be dismissed by the directors or lower levels of management, subject only to their normal employment rights.

Objectives and limitations on the scope of the audit work

The primary objective of external auditors is laid down by statute, to report on whether the company's accounts show a true and fair view of the state of the company's affairs at the period-end, and of its profit or loss for the period. External auditors are also required to report if certain other criteria have not been met, for example the company fails to keep proper accounting records or fails to make proper disclosure of transactions with directors.

Internal auditors' objectives are whatever the company's management decide they should be. Some of the objectives may be similar to those of external audit, for example to confirm the quality of accounting systems. Other objectives might be in areas which have little or no significance to the external auditor, for example recommending improvements in economy, efficiency and effectiveness.

Statutory rules mean that management cannot limit the scope of external auditors' work. External auditors have the right of access to all of a company's books and records, and can demand all the information and explanations they deem necessary. As the objectives of internal audit's work are decided by management, management can also decide to place limitations on the scope of that work.

(b)   External auditors should consider whether:

(i)   The work is performed by persons having adequate technical training and proficiency as internal auditors

(ii)   The work of assistants is properly supervised, reviewed and documented

(iii)   Sufficient appropriate audit evidence is obtained to afford a reasonable basis for the conclusions reached

(iv)   The conclusions reached are appropriate in the circumstances

(v)   Any reports prepared by internal audit are consistent with the results of the work performed

(vi)   Any exceptions or unusual matters disclosed by internal audit are properly resolved

(vii) Amendments to the external audit programme are required as a result of matters identified by internal audit work

(viii) There is a need to test the work of internal audit to confirm its adequacy

---

Hopefully, you could answer that question. If you struggled, you might want to refer back to your notes from your previous auditing studies, but here is a summary of the key revision points on internal audit in this syllabus.

Role of internal audit in corporate governance

The FRC *Guidance on risk management, internal control and related financial and business reporting* ('Risk Guidance') in the UK encourages companies to adopt a **risk-based approach** to establishing a system of internal control, ie to manage and control risk appropriately rather than eliminate it. The principal role of internal auditors is to assist management in **monitoring** risks.

The Risk Guidance emphasises the importance of an embedded and ongoing process of identifying and responding to risks. Thus **a company** must:

- Establish **business objectives**
- Identify the **principal risks** associated with these
- Agree the **controls** to address the risks
- Set up a **system to implement the decision**, including regular feedback

Responsibilities of directors, management and employees

The directors, employees and management are then responsible for implementing this guidance.

Directors are responsible for **designing and implementing** systems of internal control and risk management. They determine the risks and how these are to be managed (in line with the organisation's risk appetite). Directors establish an appropriate organisational culture, and ensure adequate internal and external communications.

Management implements board policies on internal control, provides timely information to the board, and establishes responsibilities within the organisation. **Employees** acquire the knowledge and skill to establish and monitor the system of internal controls.

Review of internal financial control

The Risk Guidance defines risk management and internal control systems as 'the policies, culture, organisation, behaviours, processes, systems and other aspects of a company that:

- facilitate its effective and efficient operation by enabling it to assess current and emerging risks, respond appropriately to risks and significant control failures and to safeguard its assets;
- help to reduce the likelihood and impact of poor judgement in decision-making; risk-taking that exceeds the levels agreed by the board; human error; or control processes being deliberately circumvented;
- help ensure the quality of internal and external reporting; and
- help ensure compliance with applicable laws and regulations, and also with internal policies with respect to the conduct of business.'

A risk management and internal control system is likely to include:

(1) **Risk assessment** – process to identify major risks and assess their impact
(2) **Management and monitoring of risks** – including controls processes (segregation of duties, authorisation, etc)
(3) **Information and communication systems** – include monthly reporting, comparison with budgets etc as well as non-financial performance indicators
(4) **Monitoring** – procedures designed to ensure risks are monitored and the internal controls continue to be effective (audit committees, internal audit, etc)

Point to note The Turnbull report is actually no longer applicable in practice, and was superseded by the FRC's *Risk management, internal control and related financial and business reporting* published in September 2014. This came a little too late for your exam, however, which will still be based on the old Turnbull guidance.

1.2 Internal auditors and risk management

The issue of the Turnbull guidance and internal audit's role in relation to risk management was touched on briefly above. In response to the Turnbull guidance, directors need to ensure three steps are taken in their business:

- Identify risks
- Control risks
- Monitor risks

It is not internal audit's primary role to manage risk in a company. It is the responsibility of the directors, usually delegated to individual managers in various departments.

The risks are identified and assessed, and a policy approach is taken in respect of each of them. To recap, this policy is usually one of four:

- Accept risk (if it is low impact and likelihood)
- Reduce risk (by setting up a system of internal control)
- Avoid risk (by not entering a market, accepting contract etc)
- Transfer risk (by taking out insurance)

With their skills in business systems, internal auditors are ideally placed to **monitor** this process and add value to it. They can:

- Give advice on the best design of systems and monitor their operation
- Be involved in a process that continually improves internal control systems
- Provide assurance on systems set up in each department

The involvement of internal audit as a monitoring unit will help to ensure that the process of risk identification and management in a business is a **continual process** rather than a one-off exercise.

2 Outsourcing   12/07

> Outsourcing is the contracting out of certain functions. A business can outsource a small part of the function, or the entire function, or practically all its functions.

2.1 Why outsource?

> **Outsourcing** is the process of purchasing key functions from an outside supplier. In other words, it is **contracting-out** certain functions, for example, internal audit or information technology.
>
> **Insourcing** is when an organisation decides to retain a centralised department for the key function, but brings experts in from an external market on a short-term basis to account for 'peak' and 'trough' periods. It is a business decision that is often made to maintain control of certain critical production or competencies.

There are three general reasons for outsourcing:

- Financial efficiency
- Change management
- Strategy

2.1.1 Financial efficiency

It is often argued that outsourcing **reduces cost**. This **may not necessarily be the case**, but businesses often find that it is worth investigating. If outsourcing is never considered, it is often the case that the cost of maintaining the function in-house is never calculated, and therefore not considered either.

This fact links into the next point about financial efficiency. Outsourcing a function can lead to **greater cost control** over that function. This is as a result of the function now being subject to a contractual fee rather than a previously unidentified cost of maintaining the function in-house. This aspect of outsourcing might substantially **improve budgeting and cost control**.

Outsourcing may considerably **reduce the number of employees** for whom the business is responsible. The logistics of shedding staff may make outsourcing a difficult legal and human issue, but the **cost savings** in this area (salary, tax, pension, for example) could be substantial.

Outsourcing can have a fundamental effect on the **shape of an entity's financial statements**, particularly if a function with a high capital investment (for example, information technology) is being outsourced. In some cases, it might be possible to sell the company's assets to the service provider, producing a cash injection, or reduced initial fees.

2.1.2 Change management

Outsourcing can be a way of managing change in a company. For example, if the company decides to change its software, outsourcing the software provision might mean that all **staff training** on the new system is incorporated into the service.

Outsourcing a function such as finance might facilitate the smooth running of a **merger** of two firms that have different accounting systems. This may also be true when a business is **restructured**.

2.1.3 Strategy

Outsourcing can also be part of a strategy to **refocus on the core competencies** of a business, or a thrust to **improve technical services**. It can be a way of **entering a market in the most low-risk way**. For example, a previously low-tech business wanting to engage in e-commerce could outsource its website development and maintenance.

2.2 Outsource what?

Generally, if a company chooses to outsource, it will outsource functions which are not perceived to be key competencies. The different approaches which can be taken to outsourcing depend on the extent to which a company contracts out non-core functions. This can be seen by way of an example.

 | Case Study

The Toy Company

The Toy Company is a small company, owned and run by Edward T. Bear. It was left to him by his father, T. Bear, who was a skilled toy maker. The business began as a one man operation in the garage and it now has 250 employees, technical computerised processes and is run from its own factory complex.

Edward joined the company on leaving school. He worked alongside his father for ten years. Last year his father died and left the shares in the company to Edward and his sister Victoria. Victoria has never had any role in the company, and is keen to continue that.

The company employed an accountant 20 years previously, and they are still an employee of the firm. In the intervening years, the accounts department has grown to now incorporate five other employees, with one having specific payroll duties. The accounts department has a computer system which is separate from the computer system used in operations.

In operations, there are several divisions: design, manufacture, packaging, sales and marketing.

The company also employs a part-time human resources manager who deals with staff matters and recruitment. The office cleaner is the longest serving member of staff. They have worked for Mr Bear since he set up in his first workshop 40 years ago.

In the example of the Toy Company, there are several areas where management could consider outsourcing. We will consider the advantages and disadvantages of this below. Here we are only looking to see where the potential lies.

The core competence of the company is the manufacture of toys. This means that there are several functions which do not fall within this competence.

- Accounting
- Human resources
- Cleaning

Of the above areas, cleaning would be the least risky to outsource because the cleaning does not directly impact on the operation of the business. Cleaning is a common outsourced function in the private sector.

However, we are more interested in the accounting function, being accountants. The accounts department is not part of the core competence, so it could potentially be outsourced. Within this decision, there are several others. The company could outsource:

- Pension functions
- Tax related functions
- The entire payroll function
- Invoicing
- Credit control
- The entire accounting function

When considering **the extent to which the company wants to adopt outsourcing**, it must consider the risk involved and the control that management want to maintain over the function. There is less risk involved in outsourcing a part of the payroll function (for example, pensions) than the whole finance function.

Similar subdivisions can be seen when considering the outsourcing of other functions:

Human resources	Welfare
	Health and safety
	Recruitment
	The entire HR department
Information technology	Maintenance
	Project management
	Network management
	The entire IT function

Just to extend the point about outsourcing to its furthest extremes, it is possible to consider outsourcing more of the business than has been discussed above.

In the first instance, Edward could critically appraise the core competence of his business (the manufacture of toys) and subdivide it further. He might decide that the production processes are the core competence and that functions such as design and sales and marketing should be outsourced.

In an extreme case, it is possible to create a **virtual organisation**. For example, Edward could decide that he has no particular personal interest in toy manufacture, but that he does wish to retain the business. In this case, he could outsource all the different functions of the business, but maintain control of the contracts and therefore ultimately the business.

2.3 Advantages and disadvantages of outsourcing

We will look in detail at the advantages and disadvantages of outsourcing some specific functions in the following sections. For now, however, we shall consider some general advantages and disadvantages of outsourcing that apply to them all.

Advantages of outsourcing
Cost. A key advantage of outsourcing is that it is often cheaper to contract a service out than it is to conduct it in-house. It may also significantly improve cost control.
Specialist service. Outsourcing results in specialists being used to provide the service when that would not have been the case if the function was performed in-house.
Indemnity. The service organisation may provide indemnity in the event of problems arising. If problems arise in-house, there is no such comfort zone.
Cash flow. Obtaining the service through a contract may assist with cash flow, as the contract will represent a flat fee, whereas the cost of providing the service in-house might have led to fluctuating costs (for example, if temporary staff are required in a busy period).

The single biggest disadvantage of outsourcing is the extent to which the company **loses control** over the function itself, although not over cost control.

The **initial cost** of outsourcing may be **substantial,** if an aspect of the decision is to close a current department of the business. The question of **potential redundancies** may dissuade companies from considering outsourcing.

The contract has to be **managed** to ensure that the service being provided is appropriate and in accordance with the contract. This may take a disproportionate amount of **time**.

The contract might limit the **liability** of the contractor, leading to problems if the contract is not performed well. This might even result in **court action** being required.

Should these disadvantages be realised, the **cost** of outsourcing could outweigh the benefit, even though in theory outsourcing should reduce cost.

3 Outsourcing specific functions 6/11

FAST FORWARD

> Internal audit is not a core competence and may be outsourced fairly easily.

3.1 Internal audit

Internal audit is rarely a core competence of a company. However, it is a valuable service to management. The corporate codes of recent years that we discussed earlier in this Study Text have emphasised the importance of internal audit in assessing controls and monitoring risks.

However, there are **problems associated with setting up an internal audit department**. These are:

- Cost of recruiting staff
- Difficulty of recruiting staff of sufficient skill and qualification for the company's preference or need
- The fact that management are not auditing specialists and therefore might struggle to direct the new department in their duties
- The time frame between setting up the department and seeing the results of having the department
- The fact that the work required may not be enough to justify engaging full-time staff
- The fact that a variety of skills and seniority levels are required, but only one member of full-time staff can be justified

3.1.1 Advantages

The advantage of outsourcing internal audit is that outsourcing can overcome all these problems.

- Staff need not be recruited, as the **service provider has good quality staff.**
- The service provider has **specialist skill** and can assess what management require them to do. As they are external to the operation, this will not cause operational problems.
- Outsourcing can provide an **immediate** internal audit department.
- The service contract can be for the **appropriate timescale** (a two week project, a month, etc).
- Because the **timescale is flexible**, a **team of staff** can be provided if required.
- The service provider could also provide less than a team but, for example, could provide one member of staff on a full-time basis for a short period, as a **secondment**.

A key advantage of outsourcing internal audit is that **outsourcing can be used on a short-term basis** to:

- Provide immediate services
- Lay the basis of a permanent function, by setting policies and functions
- Prepare the directors for the implications of having an internal audit function
- Assist the directors in recruiting the permanent function

Outsourced internal audit services are provided by many audit firms, particularly the Big Four. This can range from a team of staff for a short-term project, or a single staff member on a long-term project.

3.1.2 Disadvantages

However, the fact that internal audit services are typically provided by external auditors can raise problems as well:

- The company might wish to **use the same firm** for internal and external audit services, but this may lead to **complications for the external auditors**.
- The **cost** of outsourcing the internal audit function might be high enough to make the directors choose not to have an internal audit function at all.

3.2 Outsourcing finance and accounting functions

Various functions will be considered in the table below. Remember, however, the key advantages and disadvantages set out in Section 3 are all likely to be true of the functions discussed more specifically below.

Function	
Data processing	
Disadvantages	There may be logistical difficulties in outsourcing data processing, due to the high level of paper involved (invoices, goods received notes etc). This information will have to be given to the service organisation.
	A secondary, and more important, effect is that the company might not always have control of its key accounting documentation and records. It is a legal requirement that the directors maintain this information. While they may delegate the practicalities, they are still responsible for maintaining the records.
Pensions	
Advantages	Pensions are a specialist area and there is merit in getting a specialist to operate the company's pension provision.
Disadvantages	Pensions are closely related to the payroll and the company will need to share sensitive information with the pension provider, which may make the situation complicated.
Information technology	
Advantages	A key advantage of outsourcing all, or elements of, the IT function is that this will enable the company to keep pace with **rapid technological advances**.
	It also allows the company to take advantage of the work of a specialist in a field that many people still find difficult but which they use regularly to carry out their business.
	Outsourcing can provide a useful **safety net** of a technical helpline or indemnity in the event of computer disaster.
	It is also possible that through outsourcing, the company will be able to obtain **added value**, such as new ways of doing business identified (for example, e-commerce).
Due diligence	
Advantages	A key advantage in relation to outsourcing due diligence is the high level of **expertise** that can be brought in.
	The company can expect **quality** from its service contractor, and can seek **legal compensation** from them in the event of negligence.

Function	
Taxes	
Advantages	In relation to taxes, the key advantage is the buying in of **expertise**.
Disadvantages	The disadvantage of outsourcing tax work is that while the work can be outsourced, the **responsibility** cannot. The tax authorities will deal with the responsible person, not the agent, so the loss of control is particularly risky in this case.

Exam focus point

The June 2011 exam contained three marks for the potential benefits of an externally provided due diligence review. This requirement encompassed the benefits of the due diligence itself, and the benefits of outsourcing it.

The June 2013 paper included six marks for a similar requirement. Many of these marks could have been worked out from the scenario.

4 Impact of outsourcing on an audit

FAST FORWARD

When a company uses a service organisation, there are special considerations for the user auditors.

Exam focus point

There are both **ethical** and **practical audit implications** of outsourcing on an audit – either could be examined.

4.1 Use of service organisations

The impact of outsourcing on an external audit is considered in ISA 402 *Audit considerations relating to an entity using a service organisation*. This International Standard on Auditing (ISA) was updated under the Clarity Project back in 2009 because of the increasing use of service organisations and the complexity of relationships between the two parties.

Key terms

Service organisation. A third-party organisation (or segment of a third-party organisation) that provides services to user entities that are part of those entities' information systems relevant to financial reporting.

User entity. An entity that uses a service organisation and whose financial statements are being audited.

User auditor. An auditor who audits and reports on the financial statements of a user entity.

Service auditor. An auditor who, at the request of the service organisation, provides an assurance report on the controls of a service organisation.

Type 1 report. A report on the description and design of controls at a service organisation. It comprises (i) a description, prepared by management of the service organisation, of the service organisation's system, control objectives and related controls that have been designed and implemented as at a specified date, and (ii) a report by the service auditor with the objective of conveying reasonable assurance that includes the service auditor's opinion on the description of the service organisation's system, control objectives and related controls and the suitability of the design of the controls to achieve the specified control objectives.

Type 2 report. A report on the description, design and operating effectiveness of controls at a service organisation. It comprises (i) a description, prepared by management of the service organisation, of the service organisation's system, control objectives and related controls, their design and implementation as at a specified date or throughout a specified period and, in some cases, their operating effectiveness throughout a specified period, and (ii) a report by the service auditor with the objective of conveying reasonable assurance that includes (a) the service auditor's opinion on the description of the service organisation's system, control objectives and related controls, the suitability of the design of the controls to achieve the specified control objectives, and the operating effectiveness of the controls, and (b) a description of the service auditor's tests of the controls and the results thereof.

As we have discussed above, some companies choose to outsource activities necessary to the running of their business to **service organisations**. Examples of such activities that may be outsourced are:

- Information processing
- Maintenance of accounting records
- Facilities management
- Asset management (for example, investments)
- Initiation or execution of transactions on behalf of the other entity

---

ISA 402.7

The objectives of the user auditor, when the user entity uses the services of a service organisation, are:

(a)   To obtain an understanding of the nature and significance of the services provided by the service organisation and their effect on the user entity's internal control relevant to the audit, sufficient to identify and assess the risks of material misstatement; and

(b)   To design and perform audit procedures responsive to those risks.

4.2 Obtaining an understanding

A service organisation may establish and execute policies and procedures that affect a client organisation's accounting and internal control systems. These policies and procedures are physically and operationally separate from the client organisation.

(a)   When the services provided by the service organisation are **limited to recording** and **processing client transactions** and the client retains authorisation and maintenance of accountability, the client may be able to implement effective policies and procedures within its organisation.

(b)   When the service organisation **executes** the client's **transactions** and **maintains accountability**, the client may deem it necessary to rely on policies and procedures at the service organisation.

The auditor needs to understand how a user entity uses the services of the service organisation, including:

- The nature and significance of the service provided, including the effect on the controls at the user entity
- The nature and materiality of the transactions processed or accounts/financial reporting processes affected
- The degree of interaction between the user entity and the service organisation
- The nature of the relationship between the two, including the contractual terms
- If the service organisation maintains accounting records for the user entity, whether the arrangements affect the auditors' responsibility to report concerning accounting records

Sources of information include:

- User manuals
- System overviews
- Technical manuals
- The contract/service level
- Reports by the service organisations, internal auditors or regulatory authorities
- Reports by the service organisation auditor

The user auditor must evaluate the controls at the user entity that relate to the service organisation and determine whether this gives the auditor sufficient understanding to provide a basis for assessing risks of material misstatement in the user entity financial statements.

If the auditor concludes that this is insufficient, they must carry out one of the following four activities.

- Obtain type 1 or type 2 report from the service organisation, if available
- Contact the service organisation to get specific information (with permission)
- Visit the service organisation and perform procedures to obtain the information (with permission)
- Use another auditor to perform procedures at the service organisation (with permission)

It is likely that the auditor will be able to obtain a type 1 or 2 report, and this will be the most straightforward option. If this action is taken, the auditor needs to be sure that:

- The service organisation's auditor is competent and objective
- The standards under which the report was issued are adequate for the user entity's auditor's purposes
- The report is for an appropriate date (that is, it covers the period the user entity is reporting on)
- The evidence it is based on is sufficient and appropriate for the user entity's auditor's understanding of the internal controls
- If complementary user entity controls are relevant to the user entity, the auditor has obtained an understanding of these

4.3 Responding to assessed risks

The auditor needs to assess whether sufficient appropriate audit evidence is available from records at the user entity. If so, they should carry out **appropriate procedures** at the user entity. If not, they should carry out further audit procedures.

When the user auditor expects controls at the service organisation to be operating effectively, they must obtain evidence that this is the case, by one of the following three methods.

- Obtaining a type 2 report, if available
- Performing test of controls at the service organisation
- Using another auditor to perform tests of controls at the service organisation

Again, obtaining a type 2 report is the most likely option, in which case the entity auditor has to:

- Check that the report is made up to an appropriate date
- Ensure that they have tested complimentary controls at the user entity if necessary
- Check the adequacy of the time period covered by the tests of controls and the time elapsed since those tests of controls were performed
- Ensure the tests of controls performed for the purposes of the report are relevant and provide sufficient appropriate audit evidence for the user entity auditors' purposes

The auditor must also make **enquiries of management** if they are aware or suspects any fraud, non-compliance with law and regulations or uncorrected misstatements at the service organisation that could affect the financial statements of the user entity and evaluate the impact of any matters on their procedures and report.

4.4 Reporting

The key issue to remember is that if the user auditor cannot obtain sufficient appropriate evidence about the impact of the service organisation on the user entity, the auditor must **modify** the auditor's report, as the scope of the audit has been **limited**.

4.5 Impact on internal audit

External auditors will be affected when outsourced functions impact on the financial statements. Internal audit will be interested in outsourced functions which affect the business (that is, any outsourced function).

Internal audit will be interested in the contractual arrangements made with the service organisation. They may want to pay a visit to the organisation and undertake a review of its systems to ensure that they are sufficient for the business's needs.

(a)   Explain the meaning of the word 'outsourcing' and distinguish it from 'insourcing'.

(b)   Discuss the risks and benefits of outsourcing the payroll function of a small business which currently employs a management accountant and an accounts clerk.

(c)   You are planning the audit of a company that has just outsourced its credit control function. Describe the planning issues that arise as a result of this action.

Answer

(a)   **Outsourcing** is the practice of purchasing a specific function from an outside service provider. In other words, it is the practice of contracting out functions of the business to an expert.

   Insourcing, by contrast, is the practice of maintaining a specialist function in-house, but buying in external expertise on a short-term basis to balance peaks and troughs in demand for that expertise.

(b)   Payroll is a complicated accounting area, particularly due to the issues of taxation arising. It is also susceptible to fraud in the absence of strong controls.

   In a small company, such as the one described, there is **little scope for segregation of duties** in relation to payroll. It is likely that payroll would be managed by the accountant, as the clerk is likely to have a full-time job in relation to sales and purchases, and the accountant has greater expertise. However, it is possible that an accountant in such a position, even in a small business, might **not have time to manage payroll** in addition to other accounting duties. In order for there to be **adequate authorisation** and segregation in relation to payroll, **another senior figure should be involved** in authorising the payroll.

   In this situation, it might be **cost-effective to outsource** the payroll function to an **expert**. This might also **reduce the control problems** inherent in the small department. However, there are some disadvantages related to outsourcing the function. The key issue is one of **confidentiality**, as payroll records contain sensitive data about personnel (for example, their bank details). **Personnel might object** to this information being given to an outside provider. The company would also have to **institute controls over the transfer of data** (such as weekly hours worked) to the service provider.

(c)   The user auditor should determine whether the outsourced function is **relevant to the audit**. In the case of the credit control function, this is clearly **relevant to receivables** reported in the statement of financial position and to **sales and bad debts**.

   The user auditor must ensure that he **understands the terms of the contract** between the client and the service provider. As part of planning the audit, therefore, he **must obtain a copy of the contract** and **become familiar with its terms**.

   The user auditor must **ascertain whether they will have access to the records** that they will require as part of his audit evidence. As part of planning they must **make arrangements to enable this access**.

   As part of the risk assessment at the planning stage, the user auditor must consider whether the outsourcing arrangements affect the risk of material misstatement in the financial statements. In doing so they will consider such factors as the contract (referred to above), the reputation of the service provider and the effectiveness of past controls when the function was maintained in-house and present controls over the outsourcing arrangements.

Chapter Roundup

- Internal audit plays a key role in corporate governance, providing objective assurance on control and risk management.

- Outsourcing is the contracting out of certain functions. A business can outsource a small part of the function, or the entire function, or practically all its functions.

- Internal audit is not a core competence and may be outsourced fairly easily.

- When a company uses a service organisation, there are special considerations for the user auditors.

1   List six factors which the external auditors should consider in relation to the work of internal audit.

     (1)   ....

     (2)   ....

     (3)   ....

     (4)   ....

     (5)   ....

     (6)   ....

2   Name five elements of the accounts function which could be outsourced.

     (1)   ....

     (2)   ....

     (3)   ....

     (4)   ....

     (5)   ....

3   Complete the table, putting the advantages of outsourcing under the right headings and naming the specific function, if relevant.

General advantages	Function-specific advantages

- Cost
- Keeping pace with technological advance
- Liability/indemnity
- Cash flow
- Specialist service
- Immediacy
- Flexibility (particularly with regard to timescale)

4   The user auditor may refer to the responsibility of the service organisation when giving his opinion in financial statements.

     True   ☐

     False   ☐

Answers to Quick Quiz

1   (1)   Proficiency and training of staff
      (2)   Level of supervision, documentation and review of the work of assistants
      (3)   Sufficiency and appropriateness of evidence
      (4)   Appropriateness of conclusions
      (5)   Consistency of reports with work performed
      (6)   Whether work necessitates amendment to original audit plan

2   (1)   Pension
      (2)   Tax
      (3)   Payroll
      (4)   Invoicing
      (5)   Credit control

3

General advantages	Function-specific advantages
• Cost	• Technological advance (IT)
• Liability/indemnity	• Liability/indemnity (IT / due diligence)
• Cashflow	• Immediacy (IA)
• Specialist service	• Flexibility (IA)
• Flexibility	

4   False

     –   Responsibility for accounting records still lies with directors
     –   Responsibility for auditing them still lies with user auditor

Now try the question below from the Practice Question Bank

Number	Level	Marks	Time
Q27	Examination	20	39 mins

P
A
R
T

F

Reporting

469

Reporting

Introduction

As a student at this stage of your studies, you will be familiar with the external audit opinion. If this is not the case, before you read any of this chapter, you must go back to your previous Study Text and revise the basic features of the report, the various modifications that can be made, the concept of a true and fair view and the statutory requirements in relation to the audit opinion.

At this level, students are not only expected to know what the audit opinion is and how it is presented, but are also required to draw audit opinions and also assess the appropriateness of an audit opinion formed by another person.

In this chapter we shall also consider the form of the audit report, the criticism that it receives and whether it enables an auditor to express properly a true and fair view.

We shall also look at the auditor's requirements in relation to reporting to those charged with governance. We have already looked at the issue of reporting on assignments other than audit assignments in Chapter 12 of this Study Text.

Study guide

		Intellectual level
F	**Reporting**	
F1	**Auditor's report**	
(a)	Determine the form and content of an unmodified audit report and assess the appropriateness of the contents of an unmodified audit report.	3
(b)	Recognise and evaluate the factors to be taken into account when forming an audit opinion in a given situation and justify audit opinions that are consistent with the results of audit procedures.	3
(c)	Critically appraise the form and content of an auditor's report in a given situation.	3
(d)	Assess whether or not a proposed audit opinion is appropriate.	3
(e)	Advise on the actions which may be taken by the auditor in the event that a modified audit report is issued.	3
(f)	Recognise when the use of an Emphasis of Matter paragraph and Other Matter paragraph would be appropriate.	3
F2	**Reports to those charged with governance and management**	
(a)	Critically assess the quality of a report to those charged with governance and management.	3
(c)	Advise on the content of reports to those charged with governance and management in a given situation.	3

Exam guide

Audit reporting questions at this level tend to be challenging, but 'do-able', particularly if you have practised similar questions and have established a step by step approach to questions on forming an auditor's opinion. You are very likely to encounter a question on auditor's reports in Section B of the exam paper.

 One of the competences you require to fulfil Performance Objective 20 of the PER is the ability to prepare audit reports in accordance with relevant standards on auditing, or equivalent standards, and applicable regulations and legislations. You can apply the knowledge you obtain in this chapter of the Study Text to help demonstrate this competence.

1 Critically appraising the standard unmodified auditor's report

FAST FORWARD A standard format is used to promote understandability because the auditor's report is widely available to both accustomed users and those who are not accustomed to audit and audit language.

Point to note This is a **topical** area. The ISAs in this area have been revised, so you probably won't have studied them before. There is also a new ISA (701) which requires auditors to report on 'key audit matters'.

Auditor's reports are covered by the following ISAs.

- ISA 700 *Forming an opinion and reporting on financial Statements*
- ISA 701 *Communicating key audit matters in the independent auditor's report*

- ISA 705 *Modifications to the opinion in the independent auditor's report*
- ISA 706 *Emphasis of matter paragraphs and other matter paragraphs in the independent auditor's report*

These ISAs were revised in 2015. The IAASB believes that the revisions are 'essential to the continued relevance of the audit profession globally' – so quite important then! The aims of the revisions are to respond to feedback from users of the financial statements that:

- The audit opinion is valued, but could be more informative
- More relevant information is needed about the entity and the audit.

The main response has been to include **Key audit matters** in the middle of the auditor's report (see section 2). The **order of the report has been changed**, with audit opinion now placed at the start of the report. There is also a more detailed description of the auditor's responsibilities and the key features of an audit.

Here is the **standard unmodified report** given by ISA 700. We have added in an 'Other Information' paragraph, which are required by ISA 720.

INDEPENDENT AUDITOR'S REPORT

To the Shareholders of ABC Company [or Other Appropriate Addressee]

Report on the Audit of the Financial Statements

Opinion

We have audited the financial statements of ABC Company (the Company), which comprise the statement of financial position as at December 31, 20X1, and the statement of comprehensive income, statement of changes in equity and statement of cash flows for the year then ended, and notes to the financial statements, including a summary of significant accounting policies.

In our opinion, the accompanying financial statements present fairly, in all material respects, (or *give a true and fair view of*) the financial position of the Company as at December 31, 20X1, and (of) its financial performance and its cash flows for the year then ended in accordance with International Financial Reporting Standards (IFRSs).

Basis for Opinion

We conducted our audit in accordance with International Standards on Auditing (ISAs). Our responsibilities under those standards are further described in the *Auditor's Responsibilities for the Audit of the Financial Statements* section of our report. We are independent of the Company in accordance with the International Ethics Standards Board for Accountants' *Code of Ethics for Professional Accountants* (IESBA Code) together with the ethical requirements that are relevant to our audit of the financial statements in [jurisdiction], and we have fulfilled our other ethical responsibilities in accordance with these requirements and the IESBA Code. We believe that the audit evidence we have obtained is sufficient and appropriate to provide a basis for our opinion.

Key Audit Matters

Key audit matters are those matters that, in our professional judgment, were of most significance in our audit of the financial statements of the current period. These matters were addressed in the context of our audit of the financial statements as a whole, and in forming our opinion thereon, and we do not provide a separate opinion on these matters.

[Description of each key audit matter in accordance with ISA 701.]

Other Information

Management is responsible for the other information. The other information comprises the [information included in the X report, but does not include the financial statements and our auditor's report thereon.]

Our opinion on the financial statements does not cover the other information and we do not express any form of assurance conclusion thereon.

In connection with our audit of the financial statements, our responsibility is to read the other information and, in doing so, consider whether the other information is materially inconsistent with the financial statements or our knowledge obtained in the audit or otherwise appears to be materially misstated. If, based on the work we have performed, we conclude that there is a material misstatement of this other information, we are required to report that fact. We have nothing to report in this regard.

Responsibilities of Management and Those Charged with Governance for the Financial Statements

Management is responsible for the preparation and fair presentation of the financial statements in accordance with IFRSs and for such internal control as management determines is necessary to enable the preparation of financial statements that are free from material misstatement, whether due to fraud or error.

In preparing the financial statements, management is responsible for assessing the Company's ability to continue as a going concern, disclosing, as applicable, matters related to going concern and using the going concern basis of accounting unless management either intends to liquidate the Company or to cease operations, or has no realistic alternative but to do so.

Those charged with governance are responsible for overseeing the Company's financial reporting process.

Auditor's Responsibilities for the Audit of the Financial Statements

Our objectives are to obtain reasonable assurance about whether the financial statements as a whole are free from material misstatement, whether due to fraud or error, and to issue an auditor's report that includes our opinion. Reasonable assurance is a high level of assurance, but is not a guarantee that an audit conducted in accordance with ISAs will always detect a material misstatement when it exists. Misstatements can arise from fraud or error and are considered material if, individually or in the aggregate, they could reasonably be expected to influence the economic decisions of users taken on the basis of these financial statements.

As part of an audit in accordance with ISAs, we exercise professional judgment and maintain professional skepticism throughout the audit. We also:

- Identify and assess the risks of material misstatement of the financial statements, whether due to fraud or error, design and perform audit procedures responsive to those risks, and obtain audit evidence that is sufficient and appropriate to provide a basis for our opinion. The risk of not detecting a material misstatement resulting from fraud is higher than for one resulting from error, as fraud may involve collusion, forgery, intentional omissions, misrepresentations, or the override of internal control.

- Obtain an understanding of internal control relevant to the audit in order to design audit procedures that are appropriate in the circumstances, but not for the purpose of expressing an opinion on the effectiveness of the Company's internal control.

- Evaluate the appropriateness of accounting policies used and the reasonableness of accounting estimates and related disclosures made by management.

- Conclude on the appropriateness of management's use of the going concern basis of accounting and, based on the audit evidence obtained, whether a material uncertainty exists related to events or conditions that may cast significant doubt on the Company's ability to continue as a going concern. If we conclude that a material uncertainty exists, we are required to draw attention in our auditor's report to the related disclosures in the financial statements or, if such disclosures are inadequate, to modify our opinion. Our conclusions are based on the audit evidence obtained up to the date of our auditor's report. However, future events or conditions may cause the Company to cease to continue as a going concern.

- Evaluate the overall presentation, structure and content of the financial statements, including the disclosures, and whether the financial statements represent the underlying transactions and events in a manner that achieves fair presentation.

We communicate with those charged with governance regarding, among other matters, the planned scope and timing of the audit and significant audit findings, including any significant deficiencies in internal control that we identify during our audit.

We also provide those charged with governance with a statement that we have complied with relevant ethical requirements regarding independence, and to communicate with them all relationships and other matters that may reasonably be thought to bear on our independence, and where applicable, related safeguards.

From the matters communicated with those charged with governance, we determine those matters that were of most significance in the audit of the financial statements of the current period and are therefore the key audit matters. We describe these matters in our auditor's report unless law or regulation precludes public disclosure about the matter or when, in extremely rare circumstances, we determine that a matter should not be communicated in our report because the adverse consequences of doing so would reasonably be expected to outweigh the public interest benefits of such communication.

Report on Other Legal and Regulatory Requirements

[*The form and content of this section of the auditor's report would vary depending on the nature of the auditor's other reporting responsibilities prescribed by local law, regulation, or national auditing standards. The matters addressed by other law, regulation or national auditing standards (referred to as 'other reporting responsibilities') shall be addressed within this section unless the other reporting responsibilities address the same topics as those presented under the reporting responsibilities required by the ISAs as part of the Report on the Audit of the Financial Statements section. The reporting of other reporting responsibilities that address the same topics as those required by the ISAs may be combined (i.e., included in the Report on the Audit of the Financial Statements section under the appropriate subheadings) provided that the wording in the auditor's report clearly differentiates the other reporting responsibilities from the reporting that is required by the ISAs where such a difference exists.*]

The engagement partner on the audit resulting in this independent auditor's report is [name].

[Signature in the name of the audit firm, the personal name of the auditor, or both, as appropriate for the particular jurisdiction]

[Auditor Address]

[Date]

1.1 The act of communication

The auditor's report is the culmination of the whole audit process. Everything the auditor does is designed to help deliver an appropriate auditor's report. The audit could be said to stand or fall on the auditor's report alone, with the rest of the audit process only mattering insofar as it feeds into this one report. The auditor's report is an act of **communication** in which the auditor presents a summary of their conclusions from this audit process.

In one sense the auditor's job is straightforward: they perform procedures to obtain evidence; next they decide whether the financial statements are fairly presented; finally, they communicate their opinion in the form of an auditor's report. But as with many things in life, this simplicity hides something **complex**. For example, during the course of the audit the auditor will have made lots of professional judgements about accounting standards and about risk. This complex process is difficult to summarise in a simple form without misrepresention. The problem is exacerbated by the fact that the auditor might be sued if their report is inappropriate because of negligence. All of this puts a lot of **pressure** on getting the auditor's report right.

The communication problem can be broken down into a number of sub-problems. These can be identified under three headings:

- Understandability
- Responsibility
- Availability

1.2 Understandability

The complexity of the auditor's work means that it is surrounded by auditing standards and guidance, as it is a **technical** art. It also involves **jargon** (controlled language) which non-auditors may not understand.

This can be seen in the standard report's description of the auditor's objectives:

> 'Our objectives are to obtain **reasonable assurance** about whether the financial statements as a whole are free from **material misstatement**, whether due to fraud or error, and to issue an auditor's report that includes our opinion.'

The highlighted words reveal the problem: these are technical terms which have specific meanings that are defined by ISAs. A non-specialist would struggle to understand exactly what this means.

In fact, the whole auditor's report is written in a precise, legal language that is some way from the plain English that most people speak in their daily lives. It has to be written so carefully because the auditor does not want to be sued, but this inhibits the ability of the report to communicate.

Communicating the audit opinion in a way that people can understand is a challenge.

The standard auditor's report tries to communicate the audit process as clearly as it can, and is designed to eliminate common misconceptions:

(i) The report is clearly addressed to shareholders, in the first line. This shows that it is not intended for anyone else's use.

(ii) The auditor's opinion is given at the start of the report. This is a change from the form of auditor's reports under the original ISA 700, which placed the auditor's opinion at the end. The opinion is the most important part of the report, so it is the most prominent.

(iii) There is an explanation of the basis for the auditor's opinion.

(iv) Key audit matters are discussed in detail, giving users a better understanding of what the auditor has considered and the audit approach adopted on this individual audit.

(v) The responsibilities of management and the auditor are clearly stated. There is now a detailed description of what the auditor does.

However, some parties still argue that the auditor's report is a difficult document to understand. It still includes technical terms which require further explanation.

1.2.1 Comparability vs relevance in standard reports

Standard reports improve understandability, because is that it is **easier for users to understand** an auditor's report that has **elements in common** with all other auditors' reports. It also means that auditors' reports can be more easily **compared**.

When a standard report is used, there is less chance of an isolated misunderstanding caused by the way one firm of auditors chooses to express itself, or in relation to the explanation of a particular issue.

In another sense, however, standard reports impair understandability because they may give the impression that all audits are alike. This misses out the differences between individual audits, eg the different issues that the auditor had to think about in each case. Put another way, the information in individualised auditor's reports would be totally **relevant** to the individual audit; by contrast, standardised reports may contain information that is not necessarily relevant to each audit.

The IAASBs ISA 700 aims to **strike a balance between comparability and relevance**. It is largely standardised (comparability), but the auditor must tailor specific elements of it to the individual audit (relevance). The auditor does this in the discussion of key audit matters, in any emphasis of matter / other matter paragraphs they include, and of course in the opinion expressed. The IAASB's version of the auditor's report is also flexible enough to be adapted by auditors working in different national jurisdictions, eg if the auditor has to report on 'other legal or regulatory requirements' such as listing rules.

1.3 Responsibility

Connected with the problem of what the audit is and what the audit opinion means is the issue of what the auditor is **responsible** for. As far as the **law** is concerned, auditors have a restricted number of duties. **Professional standards** and other bodies place other duties on auditors.

Users of financial statements, and the public, may not have a very clear perception of what the auditors are responsible for and what the audit opinion relates to, or what context it is in.

The issue of **auditor liability** ties in here. Auditor's reports are addressed to shareholders, to whom auditors have their primary legal responsibility. However, audited accounts are used by significantly more people than that. Should this fact be addressed in the auditor's report? This issue is also considered in Chapter 3.

1.4 Availability

> The availability of auditor's reports has been increased by the trend to publish financial statements on companies' websites. Auditors should consider the risks relating to this.

The fact that a significant number of people use audited accounts has just been mentioned. Auditor's reports are publicly available, as they are often held on **public record**. This fact alone may add to any perception that exists that auditor addresses the report to more than just shareholders.

The problem of availability is exacerbated by the fact that many companies publish their **financial statements** on their **website**. This also means that millions of people around the world have access to the auditor's report.

However, this issue may add significant misunderstandings:

- **Language** barriers may cause additional understandability problems.
- It may not be clear **which financial information** an auditor's report refers to.
- The auditor's report may be subject to **malicious tampering** by hackers or personnel.

If an auditor's report is published electronically, auditors lose control of the **physical positioning** of the report; that is, what it is published with. This might significantly affect understandability and also perceived responsibility. We will look at reporting electronically in Section 3.

2 Key audit matters (KAMs)

> Listed company auditor's reports include a description of the key audit matters.

ISA 701 *Communicating key audit matters in the independent auditor's report* sets out the auditor's responsibility to communicate KAMs. Let's start with the definition:

Key terms

> **Key audit matters**. Those matters that, in the auditor's professional judgment, were of most significance in the audit of the financial statements of the current period. Key audit matters are selected from matters communicated with those charged with governance.

Reporting on KAMs aims to improve **transparency** by helping users to understand the most significant issues the auditor faced. This should enhance the **communicative value** of the auditor's report.

KAMs are part of every listed company auditor's report, and can be included by other auditors if needed. **KAMs do not constitute a modification of the report** or of the opinion. They are a part of the standard report which must be tailored to each company's circumstances. KAMs are not a substitute for disclosures, for EoM/OM paragraphs, nor for modified opinions. KAMs must always relate to matters already included within the financial statements.

The auditor's objectives are as follows.

> **ISA 701.7**
>
> The objectives of the auditor are to determine key audit matters and, having formed an opinion on the financial statements, communicate those matters by describing them in the auditor's report.

KAMs are communicated **after the opinion**. This is because the reported **KAMs do not include matters which have resulted in a modified opinion** – any explanations in relation to these issues would already have been included in the 'Basis for' modified opinion paragraph.

The auditor must do four main things:

- Determine the matters which should be described as KAMs
- Communicate the KAMs in the auditor's report
- Communicate the KAMs to those charged with governance
- Keep appropriate audit documentation

2.1 Determining KAMs

KAMs should be selected from the matters communicated to those charged with governance, and they should represent the issues which have required the most audit attention during the audit. In working out which matters to report as KAMs, the auditor takes into account:

- Areas of **higher risk** of material misstatement, or 'significant risks' identified in line with ISA 315 (eg at the planning stage)

- **Significant judgements** in relation to areas where management made judgements

- The effect of **significant events or transactions**

The key part of the definition of KAMs above is that these are the **most significant matters**, and are more significant than the other matters communicated to those charged with governance. In other words, the auditor must edit out the less significant issues, and only include the really important ones in the auditor's report. This involves using the auditor's **professional judgement**.

It should be obvious that KAMs are **audit matters**, not just difficult areas of financial reporting. You could think of these as the areas that have given the auditor the biggest headaches.

The decision-making framework looks like this:

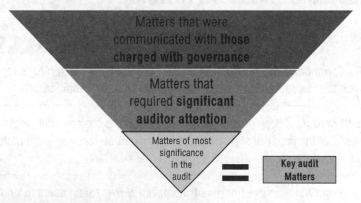

Source: IAASB The New Auditor's Report, slide presentation, March 2015

One approach might therefore be to begin with the audit matters communicated to those charged with governance, and to **pick the key matters** from those.

ISA 701 notes that these 'matters of most significance' may be the ones that there has been most discussion with management about. Other things to consider when determining KAMs include:

- The importance of the matter to intended **users' understanding**, including **materiality**

- The nature of the underlying accounting policy relating to the matter or the **complexity** or **subjectivity** involved

- Any **misstatements** related to the matter, and the nature and materiality of the misstatements

- The nature and extent of **audit effort** needed to address the matter (including the need for specialised knowledge and for consultations outside the audit engagement team)

- The nature and severity of **difficulties** in applying audit procedures, obtaining evidence or forming conclusions, including **more subjective judgements**

- The severity of any **control deficiencies**

- Whether **several separate issues** interacted, eg if a long-term contract had repercussions in several areas (revenue recognition, litigation or contingencies)

How many KAMs should the auditor report? This is a matter of judgement and depends on the circumstances, but the auditor should not just report everything. They are **key** matters, and by definition not everything is 'most significant'.

> Key audit matters are part of the unmodified auditor's report. You could therefore be asked to assess the content of an unmodified auditor's report which includes KAMs. A key part of this would be assessing whether the auditor in question has determined KAMs appropriately, and whether the KAMs have been presented correctly (see section 2.2 below).

2.1.1 Choosing not to include a KAM

The auditor may choose not to communicate a matter identified as a KAM, but only under specific circumstances:

The description of each KAM says **two main things**:

> **ISA 701.14**
>
> The auditor shall describe each key audit matter in the auditor's report unless:
>
> (a) Law or regulation precludes public disclosure about the matter; or
>
> (b) In extremely rare circumstances, the auditor determines that the matter should not be communicated in the auditor's report because the adverse consequences of doing so would reasonably be expected to outweigh the public interest benefits of such communication. This shall not apply if the entity has publicly disclosed information about the matter.

One example of this is where the auditor suspects **money laundering**. In some jurisdictions (eg the UK), regulations prohibit communications which might prejudice an investigation – so including suspicions of money laundering as a KAM would be **tipping off**.

2.2 Communicating KAMs

KAMs are communicated in a separate subsection of the auditor's report. There is a general introduction first, and then each KAM is presented in detail. The general introduction states that:

- These are the 'matters of most significance'; and
- No separate opinion is provided on them because they are covered by the audit opinion.

The description of each KAM then says **two main things**:

> **ISA 701.13**
>
> The description of each key audit matter in the Key Audit Matters section of the auditor's report shall include a reference to the related disclosure(s), if any, in the financial statements and shall address:
>
> (a) Why the matter was considered to be one of most significance in the audit and therefore determined to be a key audit matter; and
>
> (b) How the matter was addressed in the audit.

The example below contains a separate paragraph for each of these, and includes a reference to where the disclosures are for goodwill.

Here is an example of how KAMs could appear, taken from the IAASB's guidance publication *Auditor reporting – illustrative key audit matters*:

Key Audit Matters

Key audit matters are those matters that, in our professional judgment, were of most significance in our audit of the financial statements of the current period. These matters were addressed in the context of our audit of the financial statements as a whole, and in forming our opinion thereon, and we do not provide a separate opinion on these matters.

Goodwill

Under IFRSs, the Group is required to annually test the amount of goodwill for impairment. This annual impairment test was significant to our audit because the balance of XX as of December 31, 20X1 is material to the financial statements. In addition, management's assessment process is complex and highly judgmental and is based on assumptions, specifically [describe certain assumptions], which are affected by expected future market or economic conditions, particularly those in [name of country or geographic area].

Our audit procedures included, among others, using a valuation expert to assist us in evaluating the assumptions and methodologies used by the Group, in particular those relating to the forecasted revenue growth and profit margins for [name of business line]. We also focused on the adequacy of the Group's disclosures about those assumptions to which the outcome of the impairment test is most sensitive, that is, those that have the most significant effect on the determination of the recoverable amount of goodwill.

The Company's disclosures about goodwill are included in Note 3, which specifically explains that small changes in the key assumptions used could give rise to an impairment of the goodwill balance in the future.

Revenue Recognition

The amount of revenue and profit recognized in the year on the sale of [name of product] and aftermarket services is dependent on the appropriate assessment of whether or not each long-term aftermarket contract for services is linked to or separate from the contract for sale of [name of product]. As the commercial arrangements can be complex, significant judgment is applied in selecting the accounting basis in each case. In our view, revenue recognition is significant to our audit as the Group might inappropriately account for sales of [name of product] and long-term service agreements as a single arrangement for accounting purposes and this would usually lead to revenue and profit being recognized too early because the margin in the long-term service agreement is usually higher than the margin in the [name of product] sale agreement.

Our audit procedures to address the risk of material misstatement relating to revenue recognition, which was considered to be a significant risk, included:

- Testing of controls, assisted by our own IT specialists, including, among others, those over: input of individual advertising campaigns' terms and pricing; comparison of those terms and pricing data against the related overarching contracts with advertising agencies; and linkage to viewer data; and

- Detailed analysis of revenue and the timing of its recognition based on expectations derived from our industry knowledge and external market data, following up variances from our expectations.

2.2.1 KAMs should not give original information

The KAMs are **matters that are already disclosed** in the entity's financial statements. They may refer to financial reporting issues, but they describe the matter in the context of the audit.

KAMs should not therefore give original information about the entity, ie information that is not already in the financial statements. If something is not disclosed but the auditor thinks it should be, then the auditor should ask management to disclose it.

2.2.2 No KAMs?

It is possible that there might not be any KAMs to communicate. ISA 701 does allow for this possibility, but **only extremely rare circumstances**, eg for a listed entity which has very limited operations (eg if it has not traded during the period).

In this case the auditor's report still has a section on KAMs, but states that there were none to communicate.

2.3 Relationship with the auditor's opinion

The basic relationship is this:

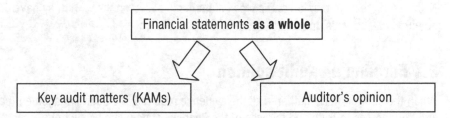

The KAMs are the key matters for the audit of the whole financial statements. They are **not** separate auditor's opinions for each little part of the financial statements, but merely further information on the process that led up to the opinion on the financial statements as a whole. Likewise, the auditor's opinion refers to the financial statements as a whole: as a whole they might give a true and fair view, or as a whole they might be true and fair but 'except for' one area (and so on).

If the auditor is going to express a **modified opinion**, then logically the matter giving rise to the modification is a key audit matter. However, the description of the matter will be given in the 'basis for modified opinion' paragraph, so it is **not included as a KAM** in the report. The auditor should **include a reference to the basis for modified opinion paragraph instead**.

ISA 701 also makes special mention of **going concern** problems. Where there is a material uncertainty in relation to going concern, the matter **should not be described as a KAM**, but should be discussed in the 'Material uncertainty in relation to going concern' paragraph' instead.

2.4 Relationship with Emphasis of Matter and Other Matter paragraphs

Key Audit Matters do not overlap with Other Matter paragraphs because KAMs must refer to issues present in the financial statements, whereas Other Matter paragraphs do not by definition.

There is some degree of overlap with Emphasis of Matter (EoM) paragraphs. The difference is that **KAMs do not modify the report**, and are included as standard in every listed company auditor's report. An EoM, on the other hand, does modify the report – although neither modifies the opinion. You could think of the issues giving rise to an EoM as being like KAMs but just more extreme: the EoM is for a 'matter of such importance that it is fundamental for users' understanding', whereas KAMs are merely 'most significant matters', ie less than fundamental. Where a matter has been included in an EoM paragraph, it must not be included as a KAM as well.

> This could be tested easily if you had to assess an auditor's report that included both KAMs and an EoM paragraph – the same issue must not be included in both.

2.5 Communication with those charged with governance, and documentation

The auditor must communicate the KAMs to those charged with governance.

The audit documentation must include the 'significant audit matters' from which the KAMs were selected, together with the auditor's reasons for selecting the KAMs.

If no KAMs are communicated, then the reasons why must be documented. Likewise if a matter determined to be a KAM is not communicated (eg to avoid 'tipping off' in relation to money laundering), this must be documented.

3 Forming and critiquing an audit opinion

Pilot paper 12/07, 6/09, 12/09, 6/10, 12/10, 6/11, 6/12, 12/12, 6/13, 12/13, 6/14

FAST FORWARD

> Auditors express an opinion on financial statements based on the work they have done, the evidence obtained and conclusions drawn in relation to that evidence.

3.1 Forming an audit opinion

When the auditors have gathered all the evidence required, the audit engagement partner will form the audit opinion as to truth and fairness of the financial statements as a whole.

When forming their opinion, there are some key matters that the auditor must consider. These can be illustrated in the form of three questions.

Question 1 Have all the procedures necessary to meet auditing standards and to obtain all the information and explanations necessary for the audit been carried out?

Question 2 Have the financial statements been prepared in accordance with the applicable accounting requirements?

Question 3 Do the financial statements give a true and fair view? (Are they fairly presented?)

Remember!

> **True:** Information is factual and conforms with reality, not false. In addition the information conforms with required standards and law. The accounts have been correctly extracted from the books and records.
>
> **Fair:** Information is free from discrimination and bias and in compliance with expected standards and rules. The accounts should reflect the commercial substance of the company's underlying transactions.

The process of forming an audit opinion in an exam question can be summarised in a step format.

Step 1 Read through all the information given in the question carefully.

Step 2 Analyse the requirement.

Step 3 Read through the information given in the question again in the light of the requirement, making notes of any key factors.

Step 4 Ascertain whether all the evidence reasonably expected to be available has been obtained and evaluated.

Step 5 If not, identify whether the effect of not gaining evidence is such that the financial statements could as a whole be misleading (disclaimer of opinion) or in material part could be misleading (qualified opinion).

Step 6	Ascertain whether the financial statements have been prepared in accordance with IFRSs.
Step 7	If not, determine whether departure was required to give a true and fair view and if so, whether it has been properly disclosed.
Step 8	Decide whether any unnecessary departure is material to the financial statements (qualified opinion) or is pervasive to them (adverse opinion).
Step 9	Conclude whether the financial statements as a whole give a true and fair view.

Even if the answers to Steps 4 and 6 are yes, you must still carry out Step 9 and make an overall assessment of the truth and fairness of the financial statements in order to conclude that an unmodified opinion is appropriate.

3.2 Emphasis of Matter and Other Matter paragraphs

ISA 706 *Emphasis of Matter paragraphs and Other Matter paragraphs in the independent auditor's report* addresses additional communication in the auditor's report where **the audit opinion remains unaffected**. Hence we are dealing here with modified auditor's reports but with unmodified audit opinions.

Key terms

> **Emphasis of Matter paragraph.** A paragraph included in the auditor's report that refers to a matter appropriately presented or disclosed in the financial statements that, in the auditor's judgment, is of such importance that it is fundamental to users' understanding of the financial statements.
>
> **Other Matter paragraph.** A paragraph included in the auditor's report that refers to a matter **other than** those presented or disclosed in the financial statements that, in the auditor's judgment, is relevant to users' understanding of the audit, the auditor's responsibilities or the auditor's report.

3.2.1 Emphasis of Matter

The Emphasis of Matter (EoM) paragraph can be used wherever the auditor considers it necessary to do so, as long as the matter referred to is adequately disclosed, and sufficient appropriate audit evidence has been obtained. Examples include: an uncertain outcome to litigation; early application of an accounting standard that has a pervasive effect on the financial statements in advance of its effective date; or a major catastrophe that has had, or continues to have, a devastating effect on the entity's financial position.

In certain circumstances, however, it must be used:

- When a financial reporting framework prescribed by law or regulation would be unacceptable but for the fact that it is prescribed by law or regulation

- To alert users that the financial statements are prepared in accordance with a special purpose framework

- When facts become known to the auditor after the date of the auditor's report and the auditor provides a new or amended auditor's report (ie subsequent events)

Note that an EoM paragraph is **not used** when the issue has been covered as a **key audit matter** (see Section 2 above). The auditor must choose whether a matter is simply a key audit matter, or whether it needs an EoM paragraph.

Point to note

> A change was recently made to ISA 706 in relation to going concern. EoM paragraphs are **not used in relation going concern**. They used to be used where there was a 'materiality uncertainty' that was appropriately disclosed, but now the auditor uses a 'Material uncertainty related to going concern' paragraph instead (covered later in this section).

The EoM paragraph should be positioned **immediately after the Basis for Opinion paragraph** in the auditor's report and should be clearly identified as an Emphasis of Matter. If there is a Key Audit Matters section in the report, then it is up to the auditor's judgement whether to place the EoM before this (ie straight after the Basis for Opinion) or after it.

This is the kind of thing that just might get you an easy half mark in your exam: if an Emphasis of Matter is required, simply state that it should be placed immediately after the opinion and headed 'Emphasis of Matter'. If there are KAMs then there may be further marks for stating that the auditor makes a judgement about whether the EoM goes before or after them.

The following is an **example** of an Emphasis of Matter paragraph, taken from the Appendix to ISA 706.

Emphasis of Matter

We draw attention to Note X to the financial statements which describes the uncertainty related to the outcome of the lawsuit filed against the company by XYZ Company. Our opinion is not modified in respect of this matter.

3.2.2 Other Matter

As with the EoM, there are specific circumstances where the Other Matter paragraph **must** be used:

(a)   Where **prior period** financial statements were audited by a **predecessor auditor** (ISA 710)

(b)   Where **prior period** financial statements were **not audited** (ISA 710) (note that this does not relieve the auditor of the obligation to obtain sufficient appropriate audit evidence on opening balances)

(c)   When reporting on prior period financial statements in connection with the current period's audit, if the auditor's opinion on such prior period financial statements differs from the opinion the auditor previously expressed (ISA 710)

Previously, an Other Matter paragraph was used in line with ISA 720 where other information was materially misstated. This is no longer the case. Instead of using an Other Matter paragraph, the auditor describes the misstatement in the Other Information section of the auditor's report (see Chapter 8).

The Other Matter paragraph can also be used whenever the auditor thinks it is necessary. Examples include:

*   the auditor is unable to withdraw from the engagement and yet is unable to obtain sufficient appropriate audit evidence;

*   the auditor has been requested to report on other matters or to provide more clarifications in line with the legal jurisdiction of the country.

An Other Matter paragraph must not refer to something that has been included as a key audit matter (see section 2).

The following is an example of an Other Matter paragraph, taken from the appendix to ISA 710.

Other Matter

The financial statements of ABC Company for the year ended December 31, 20X0, were audited by another auditor who expressed an unmodified opinion on those statements on March 31, 20X1.

The Other Matter paragraph is included after the Basis for Opinion paragraph, after any Emphasis of Matter paragraph and after any Key Audit Matters section (or elsewhere in the auditor's report if the content of the Other Matter paragraph is relevant to the Other Reporting Responsibilities section).

In certain circumstances, a statement is required in **either an Emphasis of Matter or Other Matter paragraph**. These are required under ISA 560:

(a)   Where law, regulation or the financial reporting framework does not prohibit management from restricting the amendment of the financial statements to the effects of the subsequent event or events causing that amendment and those responsible for approving the financial statements are not prohibited from restricting their approval to that amendment, the auditor is permitted to restrict the audit procedures on subsequent events to that amendment

(b)   Where a reference is required referring to a note to the financial statements that more extensively discusses the reason for the amendment of the previously issued financial statements and to the earlier report provided by the auditor

Point to note

ISA 720 *The auditor's responsibilities relating to other information in documents containing audited financial statements* is relevant to auditor's reports, and was covered in Chapter 8 (Section 4) of this Study Text.

3.3 Modified opinions

Modified opinions are covered by ISA 705 *Modifications to the opinion in the independent auditor's report,* which identifies the following three types of possible modification.

- A **qualified** opinion (material misstatement **or** an inability to obtain sufficient appropriate audit evidence)
- An **adverse** opinion
- A **disclaimer** of opinion

The Appendix to ISA 705 contains a useful summary of the different modified opinions:

Nature of matter giving rise to the modification	Auditor's judgement about the pervasiveness of the effects or possible effects on the financial statements	
	Material but not pervasive	Material and pervasive
Financial statements are materially misstated	Qualified opinion	Adverse opinion
Inability to obtain sufficient appropriate audit evidence	Qualified opinion	Disclaimer of opinion

Alternatively, the following decision tree can be used to decide between the various types of audit opinion.

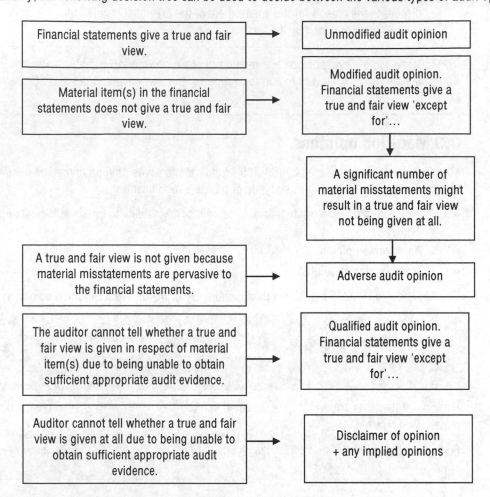

The concept of 'pervasiveness' is crucial here in deciding which opinion to express.

Pervasiveness is a term used to describe the effects or possible effects on the financial statements of misstatements or undetected misstatements (due to an inability to obtain sufficient appropriate audit evidence). There are three types of pervasive effect:

- Those that are not confined to specific elements, accounts or items in the financial statements

- Those that are confined to specific elements, accounts or items in the financial statements and represent or could represent a substantial portion of the financial statements

- Those that relate to disclosures which are fundamental to users' understanding of the financial statements

(ISA 705.5)

Examples of pervasive misstatements given by ISA 705 include:

- Non-consolidation of a subsidiary (pervasive material misstatement leading to adverse opinion)

- Inability to obtain sufficient appropriate audit evidence about a joint venture investment that represents over 90% of the company's net assets

- Inability to obtain sufficient appropriate audit evidence about multiple elements of the financial statements, eg inventories and accounts receivable

This chapter contains a number of examples of auditor's reports that might be appropriate in specific circumstances. You are extremely unlikely to have to reproduce an entire auditor's report in your exam, so do not try to learn its contents by rote. Instead, you need to be able to do two kinds of thing:

(a) **Make a judgement** about what kind of report is **appropriate to the specific circumstances** given in the question. Eg you could be asked to criticise a proposed audit opinion, and state what opinion should be expressed instead. This can also link in with other actions that the auditor should take when a report is modified (see Section 5).

(b) **Criticise** an auditor's report that you are given. This could mean criticising its **format**, for which you would need to know the main elements of the ISA auditor's report. Section 1 of this chapter covers criticising the standard report; the material in Section 3.5 may be useful when criticising modified reports.

The following reports are given when there is an **inability to obtain sufficient appropriate audit evidence**.

Qualified opinion

We have audited the consolidated financial statements of ABC Company and its subsidiaries (the Group), which comprise the consolidated statement of financial position as at December 31, 20X1, and the consolidated statement of comprehensive income, consolidated statement of changes in equity and consolidated statement of cash flows for the year then ended, and notes to the consolidated financial statements, including a summary of significant accounting policies.

In our opinion, except for the possible effects of the matter described in the Basis for Qualified Opinion section of our report, the accompanying consolidated financial statements present fairly, in all material respects, (or give a true and fair view of) the financial position of the Group as at December 31, 20X1, and (of) its consolidated financial performance and its consolidated cash flows for the year then ended in accordance with International Financial Reporting Standards (IFRSs).

Basis for Qualified Opinion

The Group's investment in XYZ Company, a foreign associate acquired during the year and accounted for by the equity method, is carried at xxx on the consolidated statement of financial position as at December 31, 20X1, and ABC's share of XYZ's net income of xxx is included in ABC's income for the year then ended. We were unable to obtain sufficient appropriate audit evidence about the carrying amount of ABC's investment in XYZ as at December 31, 20X1 and ABC's share of XYZ's net income for the year because we were denied access to the financial information, management, and the auditors of XYZ. Consequently, we were unable to determine whether any adjustments to these amounts were necessary.

We conducted our audit in accordance with International Standards on Auditing (ISAs). Our responsibilities under those standards are further described in the Auditor's Responsibilities for the Audit of the Consolidated Financial Statements section of our report. We are independent of the Group in accordance with the ethical requirements that are relevant to our audit of the consolidated financial statements in [jurisdiction], and we have fulfilled our other ethical responsibilities in accordance with these requirements. We believe that the audit evidence we have obtained is sufficient and appropriate to provide a basis for our qualified opinion.

Disclaimer of opinion

We were engaged to audit the consolidated financial statements of ABC Company and its subsidiaries (the Group), which comprise the consolidated statement of financial position as at December 31, 20X1, and the consolidated statement of comprehensive income, consolidated statement of changes in equity and consolidated statement of cash flows for the year then ended, and notes to the consolidated financial statements, including a summary of significant accounting policies.

We do not express an opinion on the accompanying consolidated financial statements of the Group. Because of the significance of the matter described in the Basis for Disclaimer of Opinion section of our

report, we have not been able to obtain sufficient appropriate audit evidence to provide a basis for an audit opinion on these consolidated financial statements.

Basis for Disclaimer of Opinion

The Group's investment in its joint venture XYZ Company is carried at xxx on the Group's consolidated statement of financial position, which represents over 90% of the Group's net assets as at December 31, 20X1. We were not allowed access to the management and the auditors of XYZ Company, including XYZ Company's auditors' audit documentation. As a result, we were unable to determine whether any adjustments were necessary in respect of the Group's proportional share of XYZ Company's assets that it controls jointly, its proportional share of XYZ Company's liabilities for which it is jointly responsible, its proportional share of XYZ's income and expenses for the year, and the elements making up the consolidated statement of changes in equity and the consolidated cash flow statement.

The following reports are given when the financial statements are **materially misstated**.

Qualified opinion

We have audited the financial statements of ABC Company (the Company), which comprise the statement of financial position as at December 31, 20X1, and the statement of comprehensive income, statement of changes in equity and statement of cash flows for the year then ended, and notes to the financial statements, including a summary of significant accounting policies.

In our opinion, except for the effects of the matter described in the Basis for Qualified Opinion section of our report, the accompanying financial statements present fairly, in all material respects, (or give a true and fair view of) the financial position of the Company as at December 31, 20X1, and (of) its financial performance and its cash flows for the year then ended in accordance with International Financial Reporting Standards (IFRSs).

Basis for Qualified Opinion

The Company's inventories are carried in the statement of financial position at xxx. Management has not stated the inventories at the lower of cost and net realizable value but has stated them solely at cost, which constitutes a departure from IFRSs. The Company's records indicate that, had management stated the inventories at the lower of cost and net realizable value, an amount of xxx would have been required to write the inventories down to their net realizable value. Accordingly, cost of sales would have been increased by xxx, and income tax, net income and shareholders' equity would have been reduced by xxx, xxx and xxx, respectively.

We conducted our audit in accordance with International Standards on Auditing (ISAs). Our responsibilities under those standards are further described in the Auditor's Responsibilities for the Audit of the Financial Statements section of our report. We are independent of the Company in accordance with the ethical requirements that are relevant to our audit of the financial statements in [jurisdiction], and we have fulfilled our other ethical responsibilities in accordance with these requirements. We believe that the audit evidence we have obtained is sufficient and appropriate to provide a basis for our qualified opinion.

Adverse Opinion

We have audited the consolidated financial statements of ABC Company and its subsidiaries (the Group), which comprise the consolidated statement of financial position as at December 31, 20X1, and the consolidated statement of comprehensive income, consolidated statement of changes in equity and consolidated statement of cash flows for the year then ended, and notes to the consolidated financial statements, including a summary of significant accounting policies.

In our opinion, because of the significance of the matter discussed in the Basis for Adverse Opinion section of our report, the accompanying consolidated financial statements do not present fairly (or do not give a true and fair view of) the consolidated financial position of the Group as at December 31, 20X1, and (of) its consolidated financial performance and its consolidated cash flows for the year then ended in accordance with International Financial Reporting Standards (IFRSs).

3.4 Going concern

Various situations can arise in relation to going concern (referred to as 'GC' thereafter), and we saw in Chapter 8 the effects of these situations on the auditor's report. There are two main ways things can go wrong here: either the GC assumption is appropriate but there is a material uncertainty, or the GC assumption is inappropriate.

The following table shows the effects on the auditor's report of each of these situations giving rise to a modification.

	GC assumption appropriate, but with Material Uncertainty	GC assumption inappropriate
Disclosure/treatment adequate	• Unmodified opinion • Section headed 'Material Uncertainty Related to Going Concern'	• Unmodified opinion (where alternative basis of preparation used appropriately) • Consider EoM to draw attention to alternative basis of preparation
Disclosure/treatment inadequate	• Qualified or adverse opinion	• Adverse opinion

Here is an example of an auditor's report where there is a **material uncertainty**, with **adequate disclosure**. The report is standard/unmodified, except for this new paragraph, placed straight after the 'Basis for Opinion':

This replaces the use of an Emphasis of Matter paragraph, which used to be used in this situation.

Also the inclusion of this paragraph means that going concern is not a 'Key Audit Matter' (covered in the next section).

Exam focus point

It is vital for your exam performance that you can analyse a set of facts given to you and draw audit conclusions from them. This is a basic skill at this level. Work through the following question to practise this skill.

Question

Forming an audit opinion

You are an audit senior. You are nearing the end of the audit of Nesta Co for the year ended 30 June 20X8. Nesta Co owns a small chain of high-street clothing stores and also has a manufacturing division where it makes its own label brand 'Little Miss'. Own label clothing represents 50% of the inventory and sales of Nesta Co. The financial statements show a profit before tax of $7 million (20X7: $3 million) and a statement of financial position total of $23 million (20X7: $15 million). The following points have arisen on the audit.

(1)   Nesta Co owns a number of its retail premises, which it revalues annually. This year several of its shops rose sharply in value due to inflated property prices in their locality. Nesta also capitalises refits of its shops. Two shops were refitted in the year. The total increase in assets due to refits and revaluations is $10 million. Nesta does not revalue its factory premises, which are held in the statement of financial position at $175,000.

(2)   Nesta values its inventory at the lower of cost or net realisable value. Cost is determined by deducting a suitable estimated profit margin from selling price. Inventory in the statement of financial position at 30 June 20X8 was $1,265,000.

(3)   Nesta Co has a refunds policy which states that a customer who is not satisfied with their purchase may return their goods within 28 days of purchase and obtain an exchange or a cash refund. Experience has shown that exchanges and refunds are common, as Nesta Co's shops do not provide fitting rooms, space being at a premium. Nesta does not make any provision in the financial statements for refunds.

Required

Comment on the matters you will consider in relation to the implications of the above points on the auditor's report of Nesta Co.

Answer

(1)   **Non-current assets**

There are two issues here. The first is whether Nesta's policy of revaluations is correct and the second is whether Nesta should capitalise refit costs.

The most important issue to consider is materiality, as only material items will affect the audit opinion. The revaluations and refit total is material to the statement of financial position. It is possible that any revaluation of the factory premises would also be material.

(i)   **Revaluation policy**

Per IAS 16, non-current assets may be held at cost or valuation. Where a company applies a revaluation policy, IAS 16 requires that all revaluations are made with sufficient regularity that the carrying amount does not vary materially from that which would be determined if fair value were used. Nesta revalues annually, so meets the requirement.

Nesta revalues property and IAS 16 requires that all items in the same class of assets be revalued, so the question arises as to whether it should also revalue the factory. This might have a material effect on the statement of financial position.

IAS 16 states that a 'class' of property, plant and equipment is a grouping of assets of a similar nature and use in an entity's operations. Although the International Accounting Standard (IAS) implies that buildings comprise one class, in this case the **nature** and **use** of the two kinds of building are quite distinct. Therefore creating two classes (retail premises and manufacturing premises) would appear to be reasonable.

(ii)   **Refits**

Assets should be held at cost or valuation as discussed above. However, in some cases, IAS 16 allows the cost of refits to be added to the original cost of the asset. This is when it is probable that future economic benefits **in excess** of the **originally assessed** standard of performance of the existing asset will flow to the entity. A retail shop will be subject to refitting and this refitting may enhance its value. However, it is possible in a shop that such refitting might be better classified as expenditure on fixtures and fittings. Nesta's policy should be consistent and comparable so, if they have followed a policy of capitalising refits into the cost of the shop in the past, this seems reasonable.

Conclusion

The issues relating to non-current assets are material and could affect the auditor's report. However, having considered the issues, it appears that there are no material misstatements in the financial statements. As there appears to have been no inability to obtain sufficient appropriate audit evidence in relation to non-current assets, the audit opinion would be unmodified in relation to these issues.

(2)   **Inventory**

IAS 2 requires that inventory be valued at the lower of cost or net realisable value. IAS 2 defines cost as all costs of purchase, conversion and other costs incurred in bringing the inventory to its present location and condition.

The IAS outlines a number of methods of arriving at an approximation of cost in the absence of a satisfactory costing system. One such method is the use of a selling price less an estimated profit margin. This is a costing method commonly used in retail entities. However, this is reasonable only if it can be shown that the method gives a reasonable approximation of cost.

Given that 50% of Nesta's inventory is manufactured in-house, it appears to be unlikely that it cannot ascertain the cost of the inventory in a better way than the selling price method. The chain of shops is small, and there should be sufficient controls over inventory transfer to enable the company to establish the cost of inventory using a first in, first out system.

While the auditors might suggest to the directors that they look into the costing systems and make improvements in future years, it is unlikely that they would modify the auditor's report in the current year over this matter, assuming that the directors have shown that the accounting policy gives a reasonable approximation of cost.

This is because if a reasonable approximation of cost is given, the difference is not going to be material to the financial statements. Also, if Nesta has had the policy for a long period, the policy is at least consistent with itself. If the auditors had made recommendations that the system was reviewed in future years and the directors refused to make any amendments to the system in future, the auditors might want to consider taking further action in future years.

Conclusion

If there are no other audit matters arising in relation to inventory, the auditor's report will be unmodified in this respect.

(3)   **Provisions**

Nesta offers refunds and exchanges to unhappy customers and experience shows that this offer is commonly taken up. If a sale is refunded, it is as if the sale never took place. It is therefore not

prudent for Nesta to recognise profits on such sales. If items are exchanged, the profit element would still exist, so only the inventory element would be potentially misstated.

As the refund period is 28 days, the issue is isolated to sales made in the last month of the year. In the absence of specific figures, this approximates to 1/12 of annual revenue and profit, and is therefore potentially material. Using these approximations, this would mean that if more than a quarter of June's sales were refunded, this could be material to revenue, and potentially to profit.

Given that the accounts are unlikely to be finalised before the end of July, the refunds figure for June should be available to both the directors and the auditors. They should both be able to assess whether the potential provision required is material to the financial statements, and how much the provision should be, if one is required.

Conclusion

The auditor's report would only be modified in respect of this matter if the auditors felt that a material provision was required and the directors refused to include one in the financial statements. In this case, the auditors would issue an 'except for' opinion, on the grounds of material misstatement in the financial statements.

Overall conclusion

It appears likely that the auditors will issue an unmodified report for the year ended 30 June 20X8.

3.5 Critically appraising an audit opinion

Criticising an audit opinion is an extension of forming an audit opinion. It is necessary to form an audit opinion yourself in order to ascertain whether someone else's conclusions on the same facts are fair and reasonable.

3.5.1 When will it be necessary to critically appraise an audit opinion?

The obvious answer to this is 'in exam questions'. However, the exams will be based on real-life scenarios and it is important for you to consider the genuine contexts in which audit opinions will be appraised. Consider the following situations.

- Engagement partner reviewing the audit work and conclusions drawn
- Auditor asked for second opinion about an audit opinion
- Second partner required to review an audit file

Probably the most common example is the engagement partner conducting their file review before drawing their opinion, which they will then give on the auditor's report that they take responsibility for. Their audit team have carried out the work, and in doing so have drawn audit conclusions about each aspect of the audit work. They must appraise these conclusions and determine whether they are correct or not.

Where a second partner review has been required, for instance if the client is listed or public interest, one of the things the second partner is required to do is to review the audit opinion suggested and see whether it is reasonable.

The issue of second opinions, as you know, is a tricky one. It is rarely advisable for an auditor to give a second opinion on an audit opinion because they are unlikely to be in possession of the full facts.

3.5.2 How should an auditor critically appraise an audit opinion?

An auditor should form their own opinion on the basis of the facts and then evaluate the original audit opinion in the light of their own opinion. As this is a matter of judgement, it is possible that two different, yet reasonable conclusions could be drawn. For instance, auditors might disagree on whether a matter was material or not. If this was the case, further judgements and risk assessments would have to be made.

In exam questions, then, you should bear in mind the step process required to form an audit opinion in the first place. If you work through each step, you may be able to see that the person who formed the original opinion has missed out steps or failed to notice something important.

In the final analysis, this is a skill that you must practise to be able to do well. Try the following question.

| Question | Critically appraising an audit opinion |

You are an audit partner. Your firm carries out the audit of Branch Co, a public company. Because the company is a public interest entity, you have been asked to perform a second partner review of the audit file for the year ended 30 June 20X8 before the audit opinion is finalised. Reported profit before tax is $1.65 million and the statement of financial position total is $7.6 million.

You have read the following notes from the audit file.

'Earnings per share

As required by IAS 33 *Earnings per share*, the company has disclosed both basic and diluted earnings per share. The diluted earnings per share has been incorrectly calculated because the share options held by a director were not included in the calculations. Disclosed diluted earnings per share are 22.9c. Had the share options held by the director been included, this figure would have been 22.4c. This difference is immaterial.

Financial performance statement

The directors have currently not amended certain financial performance ratios in this statement to reflect the changes made to the financial statements as a result of the auditors' work. The difference between the reported ratios and the correct ratios is minimal.

Opinion

We recommend that an unmodified auditor's report be issued.'

A corporate governance statement referring to the UK Corporate Governance Code is to be issued as part of the annual report, but there is no evidence on file that this has been reviewed by the audit team. You are aware that the company does not have an audit committee.

You are also aware that the director exercised their share options last week.

Required

Comment on the suitability of the proposed audit opinion and other matters arising in the light of your review. Your comments should include an indication of what form the auditor's report should take.

| Answer |

Earnings per share

The problem in the earnings per share (EPS) calculation relates to share options held by a director. As they are held by a director, it is unlikely that they are immaterial, as matters relating to directors are generally considered to be material by their nature. The fact that EPS is a key shareholder ratio which is therefore likely to be material in nature to the shareholders should also be considered.

As the incorrect EPS calculation is therefore material to the financial statements, the auditor's report should be modified in this respect, unless the directors agree to amend the EPS figure. This would be an 'except for' modification on the grounds of material misstatement.

Share options

The share options have not been included in the EPS calculations. The auditors must ensure that the share options have been correctly disclosed in information relating to the director both in the financial statements and the other information, and that these disclosures are consistent with each other. If proper disclosures have not been made, the auditor will have to express a modified opinion due to lack of disclosure in this area.

Exercise of share options

The fact that the director has exercised their share options after the year-end does not require disclosure in the financial statements. However, it is likely that they have exercised them as part of a new share issue by the company and if so, the share issue would be a non-adjusting event after the reporting period that would require disclosure in the financial statements. We should check if this is the case and, if so, whether it has been disclosed. Non-disclosure would be further grounds for modification.

Financial performance statement

In line with ISA 720, the financial performance statement is 'other information' in the document containing the audited financial statements. The auditor is required to read this other information to identify material inconsistencies with the financial statements. The whole of the other information must therefore be read.

An inconsistency has been discovered between the ratio figures, and it is the figures in the other information that are misstated. The figures in the financial statements are not misstated. Therefore the auditor should request that management revises the other information.

The International Standard on Auditing (ISA) refers to '**material** inconsistencies'. The ratios will be of interest to shareholders, being investor information and this fact may make them material by their nature. However, as the difference is negligible in terms of value, on balance, the difference is probably not material. If the ratios are considered to constitute material inconsistencies, then an Other Matter paragraph may need to be included in the auditor's report.

Corporate governance statement

As having an audit committee is a requirement of the UK Corporate Governance Code and the company does not have one, the corporate governance statement should explain why the company does not comply with the Code in this respect.

We would not modify our auditor's opinion over the corporate governance statement, as we have no other reporting responsibilities in relation to it. The statement that the company has complied with the UK Corporate Governance Code would be a material misstatement of fact under ISA 720. We should first discuss the matter with management and ask them to include the necessary explanations. If the corporate governance statement is not amended, then we should ask company management to consult with the company's legal counsel. We should then consider the advice given before taking any further action.

Overall conclusion

None of the matters discussed above, either singly or seen together, are pervasive to the financial statements. The auditor's opinion should be modified on the material matter of the incorrect EPS calculation. We should ensure that all the other disclosures are in order and also review the corporate governance statement. If the corporate governance statement does not adequately address the issue of the company not having an audit committee, then we may need to take legal advice.

3.6 Form and content of modified reports

ISA 705 is very specific about the format of modified reports, and examination questions in the past have required detailed knowledge in this area.

3.6.1 Opinion paragraph

The paragraph should be entitled 'Qualified Opinion', 'Adverse Opinion' or 'Disclaimer of Opinion' as appropriate. This paragraph should match the relevant example given above, and does not include a description of the **reasons for** the opinion being expressed, as this is included in the paragraph below it.

Finally, when a modified opinion is expressed, this will affect the 'auditor's responsibility' section of the report, which must now end with eg 'We believe that the audit evidence we have obtained is sufficient and appropriate to provide a basis for our **qualified [or adverse]** audit opinion' (for qualified/adverse opinions). Where the opinion is a Disclaimer of Opinion, the 'auditor's responsibility' is completely different (see the example auditor's reports above).

3.6.2 Basis for (Modified) Opinion paragraph

Auditor's reports with unmodified opinions contain a section entitled 'Basis for Opinion'. Whenever the opinion is modified, the section must bear the title 'Basis for Qualified Opinion' (or 'Basis for Adverse Opinion / Disclaimer of Opinion').

If there is a **material misstatement**, then the paragraph must:

- **Quantify the financial effects** of the misstatement. If impracticable, this should be stated
- **Explain** why any **narrative disclosures** are misstated
- **Describe** any omitted information or disclosures (unless prohibited by law)

If there is an inability to obtain sufficient appropriate audit evidence, then the paragraph must give the reasons for this. If there is an adverse opinion/disclaimer of opinion, then the paragraph must describe any other matters that would have led to a modified opinion.

4 Communicating with those charged with governance
6/08, 12/10

> Auditors must report relevant audit matters to those charged with governance and will also sometimes produce a report to management detailing control deficiencies observed during the audit.

4.1 Report to those charged with governance

ISA 260 (Revised) *Communication with those charged with governance* gives guidance in this area. The auditor's objectives are as follows (bold text is our emphasis).

ISA 260.9

The objectives of the auditor are:

(a) **To communicate clearly** with those charged with governance **the responsibilities of the auditor** in relation to the financial statement audit, and an **overview of the planned scope and timing of the audit**;

(b) **To obtain** from those charged with governance **information relevant to the audit**;

(c) **To provide** those charged with governance with **timely observations arising from the audit** that are significant and relevant to their responsibility to oversee the financial reporting process; and

(d) **To promote effective two-way communication** between the auditor and those charged with governance.

Key term

> **Those charged with governance** are the persons or organisations with responsibility for overseeing the strategic direction of the entity and obligations related to the accountability of the entity. This includes overseeing the financial reporting process. [...] For entities in some jurisdictions, this may include management personnel, for example, executive members of a governance board of a private or public sector entity, or an owner-manager.
>
> *(ISA 260.10)*

The auditors may communicate with the whole board, the supervisory board or the audit committee depending on the governance structure of the organisation. To avoid misunderstandings, the engagement letter should explain that auditors will only **communicate matters** that come to their attention as a **result** of the **performance** of the audit. It should state that the auditors are **not required** to **design procedures** for the purpose of identifying matters of governance interest; however, if the auditors have agreed any specific matters of governance interest to be communicated, it will set these out.

The auditors will also explain:

- The **form** which any **communications** on governance matters will take (must be in writing)
- The **relevant persons** with whom such communications will be made
- The expected content of communications
- The expected timing of the communications (which should be on a timely basis)

4.1.1 Requirements

> **ISA 260.11**
>
> The auditor shall determine the appropriate person(s) within the entity's governance structure with whom to communicate.

Where the auditor communicates with a subgroup of those charged with governance, for example, an audit committee, or an individual, the auditor should also consider the need to communicate with the governing body.

4.1.2 Matters to be communicated

Matters would include the following.

Matters to be communicated	
The **auditor's responsibilities** in relation to the financial statements	Including that: • The auditor is responsible for forming and expressing an opinion on the financial statements • The audit does not relieve management or those charged with governance of their responsibilities
Planned **scope and timing** of the audit	Including: • How the audit proposes to address the significant risks of material misstatement from fraud or error • The auditor's approach to internal control • Application of materiality • The extent to which the auditor will use the work of internal audit • Matters those charged with governance consider warrant particular attention
Significant findings from the audit	Including: • Selection of, or changes in, significant accounting policies • The potential effect on the financial statements of any significant risks and exposures, for example pending litigation, that are required to be disclosed in the accounts • Significant difficulties, if any, encountered during the audit (eg delays in provision of required information, brief time in which to complete audit, unavailability of expected information) • Material weaknesses, if any, in the design, implementation or operating effectiveness of internal control • Written representations the auditor is requesting • Other significant matters including material misstatements or inconsistencies in other information that have been corrected

Matters to be communicated	
Auditor independence	In the case of **listed entities** matters include:
	• A statement that relevant ethical requirements regarding independence have been complied with
	• All relationships (including total fees for audit and non-audit services) which may reasonably be thought to bear on independence
	• The related safeguards that have been applied to eliminate/reduce identified threats to independence

4.1.3 Communication process

The communication process will vary with the circumstances, including:

- The size and governance structure of the entity
- How those charged with governance operate
- The auditor's view of the significance of the matters to be communicated

For example, reports of relatively minor matters to a small client may be best handled orally via a meeting or telephone conversation.

Before communicating matters with those charged with governance, the auditor may discuss them with management, unless that is inappropriate. For example, it would not be appropriate to discuss questions of management's competence or integrity with management.

ISA 260.16

The auditor shall communicate with those charged with governance:

(a) The auditor's views about significant qualitative aspects of the entity's accounting practices, including accounting policies, accounting estimates and financial statement disclosures. When applicable, the auditor shall explain to those charged with governance why the auditor considers a significant accounting practice, that is acceptable under the applicable financial reporting framework, not to be most appropriate to the particular circumstances of the entity;

(b) Significant difficulties, if any, encountered during the audit;

(c) Unless all of those charged with governance are involved in managing the entity:

    (i) Significant matters, if any, arising from the audit that were discussed, or subject to correspondence with management; and

    (ii) Written representations the auditor is requesting; and

(d) Other matters, if any, arising from the audit that, in the auditor's professional judgment, are significant to the oversight of the financial reporting process.

4.1.4 Timing

The auditor should communicate with those charged with governance on a timely basis.

4.1.5 Adequacy of the communication process

The auditor is required to evaluate whether the two-way communication between the auditor and those charged with governance has been adequate for the purposes of the audit. If not adequate and the situation cannot be resolved, the auditor may take action as follows.

- Modifying the auditor's opinion on the basis of an inability to obtain sufficient appropriate audit evidence
- Obtaining legal advice
- Communicating with third parties (eg shareholders in a general meeting)
- Withdrawing from the engagement where permitted in the relevant jurisdiction

4.1.6 Documentation

Where matters are communicated orally, the auditor is required to document them and to note when and to whom they were communicated.

Exam focus point

There is an article in *Student Accountant* entitled 'Auditors' reports to those charged with governance' which provides a useful summary of the issues contained in ISA 260.

4.2 Reporting deficiencies in internal control

ISA 265 *Communicating deficiencies in internal control to those charged with governance and management* deals with this area.

ISA 265.5

The objective of the auditor is to communicate appropriately to those charged with governance and management deficiencies in internal control that the auditor has identified during the audit and that, in the auditor's professional judgement, are of sufficient importance to merit their respective attentions.

Key terms

A **deficiency in internal control** exists when a control is designed, implemented or operated in such a way that it is unable to prevent, or detect and correct, misstatements in the financial statements on a timely basis or a control necessary to prevent or detect and correct misstatements in the financial statements on a timely basis is missing.

A **significant deficiency in internal control** is a deficiency or combination of deficiencies in internal control that, in the auditor's professional judgement, is of sufficient importance to merit the attention of those charged with governance.

The auditor determines whether any deficiencies in internal control have been identified during the audit and if so, whether individually or in combination, they are significant deficiencies.

ISA 265.9

The auditor shall communicate in writing significant deficiencies in internal control identified during the audit to those charged with governance on a timely basis.

The communication should include a description of the deficiencies and an explanation of their potential effects. The communication should also make clear that the audit was for the purpose of identifying misstatements in financial statements, not identifying deficiencies in controls, and that the deficiencies identified have been identified as part of audit work, and are not comprehensive.

Auditors should also issue a report on control deficiencies to management. These reports were a key element in your earlier studies in auditing.

FAST FORWARD

The primary purpose of the report to management is to inform management of deficiencies in the system of internal controls, but the letter can also be used for other purposes.

4.2.1 Key qualities of a report

Recap of key qualities of a report to those charged with governance

- It should not **include language** that **conflicts** with the **opinion** expressed in the auditor's report.

- It should state that the **accounting and internal control** systems were **considered only** to the **extent necessary** to **determine** the **auditing procedures** to report on the financial statements and not to determine the adequacy of internal control for management purposes or to provide assurances on the accounting and internal control systems.

- It will state that it **discusses only deficiencies** in internal control which have **come to the auditors' attention** as a result of the **audit** and that other deficiencies in internal control may exist.

- It should also include a statement that the **communication is provided for use only** by **management** (or another specific named party).

- The auditors will usually ascertain the actions taken, including the reasons for those suggestions rejected.

- The auditors may encourage management to respond to the auditors' comments, in which case any response can be included in the report.

4.2.2 Form of report

The form of the report will depend on the type of organisation concerned. It may be appropriate to divide the report into sections, which cover significant and general points for senior management first, and then proceed to more specific, divisional points in subsequent sections. The report covering findings from the audit may typically be in the form of a covering letter (see below) and a schedule of points raised.

 Case Study

Example: Reports to management covering letter

Private & Confidential

Could be to audit committee	The Directors XYZ Co 1 High Street Anytown
Should be dated soon after completion of audit	24 June 20XX

Dear Sirs

XYZ Co

Following our recent audit of your company, we are writing to advise you of various matters which came to our attention.

We set out on the attached schedule the areas of significant deficiency which we noted, together with our recommendations. These recommendations have already been discussed with ... and their comments have been included.

Managing expectations — As the purpose of the audit is to form an opinion on the company's financial statements, you will appreciate that our examination cannot necessarily be expected to disclose all shortcomings of the system and, for this reason, the matters raised may not be the only ones which exist.

Requesting feedback — We should appreciate your comments as to how you propose to deal with the matters raised in this letter. If you require any further information or advice, please contact us.

Disclaiming liability to third parties — We have prepared this letter for your use only. It should not be disclosed to a third party and we can assume no responsibility to any person to whom it is disclosed without our written consent.

We would like to take this opportunity to thank you and your staff for your help and co-operation during the course of our audit.

Yours faithfully

ABC & Co

4.2.3 Specific recommendations

The detailed recommendations included in the appendix would be structured as per the following example.

Preparation of payroll and maintenance of personnel records

Deficiencies

Under your present system, just two members of staff are entirely and equally responsible for the maintenance of personnel records and preparation of the payroll. Furthermore, the only independent check of any nature on the payroll is that the chief accountant confirms that the amount of the wages cheque presented to them for signature agrees with the total of the net wages column in the payroll. This latter check does not involve any consideration of the reasonableness of the amount of the total net wages cheque or the monies being shown as due to individual employees.

Implications

It is a serious deficiency of your present system that so much responsibility is vested in the hands of just two people. This situation is made worse by the fact that there is no clearly defined division of duties between the two of them. In our opinion, it would be far too easy for fraud to take place in this area (eg by inserting the names of 'ghost employees' into the personnel records and hence onto the payroll) and/or for clerical errors to go undetected.

Recommendations

(i)   A person other than the two wages clerks should be made responsible for maintaining the personnel records and for periodically (but on a surprise basis) checking them against the details on the payroll.

(ii)   The two wages clerks should be allocated specific duties in relation to the preparation of the payroll, with each clerk independently reviewing the work of the other.

(iii)   When the payroll is presented in support of the cheque for signature to the chief accountant, they should be responsible for assessing the reasonableness of the overall charge for wages that week.

Sufficient detail to enable directors to follow up

Explain potential effect on client business

Workable recommendations, discussed with management in advance

5 Actions when an auditor's report is modified   12/10

> **FAST FORWARD**
>
> When the auditor's report is expected to be modified, the auditor must communicate with those charged with governance, and must consider the effect of the modification on future audit engagements.

5.1 Communicate with those charged with governance

If the auditor expects that the audit opinion will be modified, then they must communicate the circumstances surrounding the modification with those charged with governance (TCWG) (ISA 705.28). This is in order to:

*   Give TCWG notice of the modification and the reasons for it

*   Confirm the auditor's understanding with TCWG of the facts of any matters giving rise to modifications, and to confirm matters on which the auditor and TCWG disagree

*   Give TCWG a chance to provide the auditor with further information and explanations before the auditor's report is issued

ISA 706 contains a similar requirement in relation to Emphasis of Matter and Other Matter paragraphs.

In addition, it is a specific requirement of ISA 260 that any 'significant difficulties' encountered are communicated with TCWG (see above) – this would include any matters that lead to a modified report being issued.

5.2 External consultation

If a modified opinion is expected to be expressed, then the auditor may need to consider consulting externally on the impact of this, eg with legal counsel under legal privilege, or anonymously with the ACCA.

5.3 Management integrity?

The first thing to consider where the auditor's report is to be modified is whether the matter in question suggests that management may not have the requisite integrity. This is particularly relevant where the scope of the audit has been limited by management, eg if management refuses to allow auditors access to all necessary books and records.

If the auditor does consider management's integrity to be in doubt, then any **representations** (including written representations) provided by management during the course of the audit **need to be reconsidered** in this light.

It may also be necessary to **perform an engagement quality control review** on the audit, as a lack of management integrity would mean that the audit carries a higher level of risk than may have been envisaged at the planning stage of the audit.

5.4 Withdrawal from engagement

If the matter in relation to which the auditor's report is modified is sufficiently serious, then it may be necessary to seek to withdraw from the audit engagement. If the auditor does seek to withdraw then it will be necessary to obtain advice from legal counsel.

ISA 210 *Agreeing the terms of audit engagements* states that **if there has been a limitation on the scope of a prior audit** which leads the auditor to believe that the audit opinion expressed this year will likely be a **disclaimer of opinion**, then the **auditor must not accept the engagement** (unless required to do so by law).

Chapter Roundup

- A standard format is used to promote understandability because the auditor's report is widely available to both accustomed users and those who are not accustomed to audit and audit language.

- The availability of auditor's reports has been increased by the trend to publish financial statements on companies' websites. Auditors should consider the risks relating to this.

- Listed company auditor's reports include a description of the key audit matters.

- Auditors express an opinion on financial statements based on the work they have done, the evidence obtained and conclusions drawn in relation to that evidence.

- Auditors must report relevant audit matters to those charged with governance and will also sometimes produce a report to management detailing control deficiencies observed during the audit.

- The primary purpose of the report to management is to inform management of deficiencies in the system of internal controls, but the letter can also be used for other purposes.

- When the auditor's report is expected to be modified, the auditor must communicate with those charged with governance, and must consider the effect of the modification on future audit engagements.

Quick Quiz

1   Name the various opinions auditors may give in their auditor's report.

    (1) ....

    (2) ....

    (3) ....

2   Complete the definitions:

    (a) .... information is free from .... and .... and is in compliance with the expected standards and rules.

    (b) .... is an expression of the relative .... or importance of a particular matter in the .... as a whole.

    (c) .... information is .... and conforms with ...., not .... information conforms with required standards and law.

3   List the main contents of the ISA 700 standard, unmodified report.

4   Name four matters which might be covered in a letter to those charged with governance.

    (1) ....

    (2) ....

    (3) ....

    (4) ....

5   Which of the following could be reported as key audit matters?

- Material uncertainties over going concern;

- Explanations of the auditor's view on other information included in the annual report, and which is consistent with the financial statements;

- Explanations of judgements made by the auditor in material areas;

- Explanations of judgements made by the auditor on matters that are of such importance that they are fundamental to users' understanding of the financial statements.

Answers to Quick Quiz

1. (1) Unmodified
   (2) Modified due to material misstatement
   (3) Modified due to the inability to obtain sufficient appropriate audit evidence

2. (a) Fair, discrimination, bias
   (b) Materiality, significance, financial statements
   (c) True, factual, reality, false, true

3. Title, addressee, auditor's opinion, key audit matters, responsibilities for the financial statements, auditor's responsibilities for the audit of the financial statements, other reporting responsibilities, name of the engagement partner, signature, address, date

4. Any four from:

   - Auditor's responsibilities in relation to the financial statements

   - The **general approach** or overall scope of the audit

   - Selection of, or changes in, **significant accounting policies**

   - The potential effect on the financial statements of any **significant risks** and **exposures**, for example pending litigation, that are required to be disclosed in the accounts

   - Significant difficulties encountered during the audit

   - Other **significant matters**, such as significant deficiencies in internal control, questions regarding management integrity, and fraud involving management

   - Other **matters** mentioned in **terms** of **engagement**

5. Explanations of judgements made by the auditor in material areas **are** KAMs. All of the other answers are incorrect. Why? Let's see:

   Material uncertainties over going concern would be explained in a separate section of the report.

   Explanations of the auditor's view on other information included in the annual report is not a key audit matter as it does not relate to the financial statements.

   Explanations of judgements made by the auditor on matters that are fundamental to users' understanding may be key audit matters, but since they may require an emphasis of matter paragraph they would not be reported in the key audit matters section of the auditor's report.

Now try the questions below from the Practice Question Bank.

Number	Level	Marks	Time
Q28	Examination	15	29 mins
Q29	Examination	17	33 mins

Current issues and developments

Current issues

Topic list	Syllabus reference
1 Update	G4
2 General issues	G4

Introduction

At this level in your studies you are expected to be familiar with current developments affecting the audit and assurance profession. Currently, many of these relate to international regulation.

You must read *Student Accountant* and the wider professional press to keep up to date with these.

Study guide

		Intellectual level
G4	Other current issues	
(a)	Explain current developments in auditing standards including the need for new and revised standards and evaluate their impact on the conduct of audits.	3
(b)	Discuss other current legal, ethical, other professional and practical matters that affect accountants, auditors, their employers and the profession.	3

Exam guide

You may be asked to discuss current developments and must be prepared to argue for or against any new proposals from the point of view of either a preparer or user of assurance reports.

1 Update

Point to note

This chapter is not just here to help you discuss current issues in your exam, but also gives you a flavour of some of the more topical areas in the audit profession. Topical areas are more likely to be examined, so this could be a useful resource for you.

1.1 Guidance on smaller audits

In general terms, the International Auditing and Assurance Standards Board (IAASB) takes the view that 'an audit is an audit', and that all audits should be conducted in accordance with the same auditing standards. However, this does not mean that there will be special considerations for audits of smaller entities.

In August 2009 the IAASB issued a Questions & Answers publication, *Applying ISAs proportionately with the size and complexity of an entity*, focusing on matters relevant to the audit of small and medium-sized enterprises (SMEs) in the context of implementing the new Clarity ISAs. The IAASB reiterated that the text of the ISAs is authoritative and must be followed, even in the audit of SMEs.

However, the IAASB did state that the work that an auditor will need to do in order to comply with an ISA will vary – a small, simple entity being likely to require less work than a large and complex one. The auditor needs to use professional judgement in applying the ISAs, in order to determine the procedures that are necessary to comply with their requirements.

To take a specific example, the IAASB stated that the requirement in ISA 315 to obtain an understanding of the entity and its environment is relevant to smaller entities but that, because smaller entities are typically simpler, it will be much easier to obtain this understanding.

Individual clarity ISAs include guidance on specific points relating to small entity audits. The purpose of this guidance is to assist in the application of the requirements of the ISA to a small entity audit. It does not limit or reduce the responsibility of the auditor to apply and comply with the requirements of the ISAs.

1.2 IAASB Practice Alert *Audit Considerations in Respect of Going Concern in the Current Economic Environment* (Jan 2009)

In January 2009 the IAASB issued a Practice Alert on going concern in the context of the global economic downturn. Its key messages were:

(a) The going concern assumption is a fundamental principle in the preparation of financial statements.

(b)   The assessment of an entity's ability to continue as a going concern is the responsibility of the entity's management.

(c)   The appropriateness of the use of the going concern assumption is a matter for the auditor to consider on every audit engagement.

(d)   ISA 570 *Going Concern* establishes the relevant requirements and guidance with regard to the auditor's consideration of the appropriateness of management's use of the going concern assumption and auditor reporting.

(e)   The credit crisis and economic downturn have led to a lack of available credit to entities of all sizes, which may affect an entity's ability to continue as a going concern; this and other factors may be relevant in the auditor's evaluation of forecasts prepared by management to support its going concern assessment.

(f)   The extent of disclosures in the financial statements is driven by management's assessment of an entity's ability to continue as a going concern, coupled with the disclosure requirements of the applicable financial reporting framework.

Consideration of the need for an Emphasis of Matter (EoM) paragraph in the auditor's report will be a difficult matter of judgement to be made in the context of the entity's circumstances; the mere existence of the credit crisis, though referred to in the financial statements, does not of itself create the need for an emphasis.

1.3 IAASB Practice Alert *Challenges in Auditing Fair Value Accounting Estimates in the Current Market Environment* (Oct 2008)

In October 2008 the IAASB issued a Practice Alert, *Challenges in Auditing Fair Value Accounting Estimates in the Current Market Environment.* It discussed the following key points.

- Challenges faced in accounting on the basis of fair value
- Requirements and guidance in standards that are particularly relevant to fair values
- Other considerations in audits of fair value accounting estimates
- Initiatives of the International Accounting Standards Board
- Recent revisions to extant standards on auditing accounting estimates and fair value measurements and disclosures which, while not yet effective, may be helpful to auditors

1.4 IAASB Q&A paper *Auditor Considerations Regarding Significant, Unusual or Highly Complex Transactions*

Issued in August 2010, this IAASB Question & Answer paper dealt with significant/unusual/highly complex transactions, which may by nature carry a higher risk of material misstatement, and thus merit heightened attention from users. The IAASB emphasises the importance of the auditor exercising professional judgement and scepticism. The auditor is required to consider the susceptibility of the financial statements to material misstatement by fraud, which includes consideration of fraud risk factors (eg significant complex transactions, which may pose questions of 'substance over form' and fraudulent financial reporting). The auditor then needs to design audit procedures that gather audit evidence in relation to these risks.

1.5 IAASB Q&A paper *XBRL: The emerging landscape*

In January 2010 the IAASB issued a Question & Answer paper to highlight the growing interest in, and use of, eXtensible Business Reporting Language (XBRL), and to raise awareness of how XBRL-tagged data is prepared and how it may affect financial reporting. The paper contained the following key messages.

(a)   XBRL is an electronic business information format expected to provide benefits in the preparation, analysis and communication of business information.

(b)   The use of XBRL can vary by jurisdiction and may be driven by regulatory requirements or voluntary application.

(c)   Under the current ISAs, auditors are not required to perform procedures or provide assurance on XBRL-tagged data in the context of audited financial statements. Accordingly, the auditor's report in accordance with the ISAs on the financial statements does not cover the process by which XBRL data is tagged, the XBRL-tagged data that results from this process, or any representation of XBRL-tagged data.

(d)   The IAASB is currently undertaking a consultation to determine the needs of preparers and users of XBRL-tagged data. This consultation will assist the IAASB in assessing whether it is necessary and in the public interest to develop a pronouncement addressing association with and/or assurance on XBRL-tagged data.

1.6 IAASB Q&A Paper *Professional scepticism in an audit of financial statements*

In February 2012 the IAASB issued a Q&A Paper on professional scepticism. Professional scepticism is a crucial aspect of audit, defined in ISA 200. The Paper can be summarised by the following points.

- *What is professional scepticism?*

    It is hard to define, but is 'fundamentally a mindset' which is linked to the ethical principles of objectivity and independence. It means 'being alert' to evidence that contradicts evidence already obtained, or which casts doubt on the reliability of documents or explanations provided, or which may indicate fraud.

- *Why is professional scepticism important in audits?*

    It is part of the auditor's 'skill set', and is part of professional judgement. It affects decisions about: the procedures to be performed; the sufficiency and appropriateness of evidence obtained; the validity of management's financial reporting judgements; and the conclusions drawn based on audit evidence.

- *What can firms do to enhance awareness of professional scepticism's importance?*

    It is a matter of education, training and experience, as well as the culture of the firm. At a firm-wide level, this means establishing policies and procedures, promoting a quality-oriented culture, and establishing training and continuing professional development schemes.

    At an engagement level, this means that the partner must communicate the importance of quality, and that the audit team is able 'to raise concerns without fear of reprisals'.

- *At what stage of the audit is professional scepticism necessary?*

    Throughout the audit! Eg at engagement acceptance when considering the integrity of management and owners.

- *How does this relate to fraud?*

    The fact that fraud involves deception and concealment makes professional scepticism particularly important in relation to it. ISA 240 emphasises professional scepticism, particularly in the form of 'an ongoing questioning' of whether there has been a fraud. There are also areas where there is a required presumption that there is a risk of fraud: revenue recognition, risks of management override of controls as a result of fraud, and accounting estimates.

- *Where else is professional scepticism important, other than fraud?*

    Significant or judgemental areas, such as:

    –   Accounting estimates (eg are assumptions reasonable?)

    –   Going concern (eg are management's plans really feasible?)

    –   Related party relationships and transactions (eg transactions outside the normal course of business – misappropriation of assets?)

    –   Laws and regulations (eg where non-compliance may call into question going concern)

- *How can this be evidenced?*

  Audit documentation should enable an experienced auditor to understand significant decisions made during the audit and any conclusions drawn. As the auditor should be professionally sceptical when making these decisions, the documentation would provide evidence of this, eg it should document the discussions the auditors have about possible non-compliance with laws and regulations, or possible management bias in relation to accounting estimates.

1.7 IAASB: A Framework for Audit Quality

In February 2014 the IAASB issued a publication on audit quality, with the following objectives.

- To **raise awareness** of the key elements of audit quality
- To encourage key stakeholders to **explore ways to improve audit quality**
- To **facilitate greater dialogue** between key stakeholders on the topic

Although audit quality is principally the responsibility of auditors, there are many factors that contribute to it. The IAASB describes these other factors using the following framework.

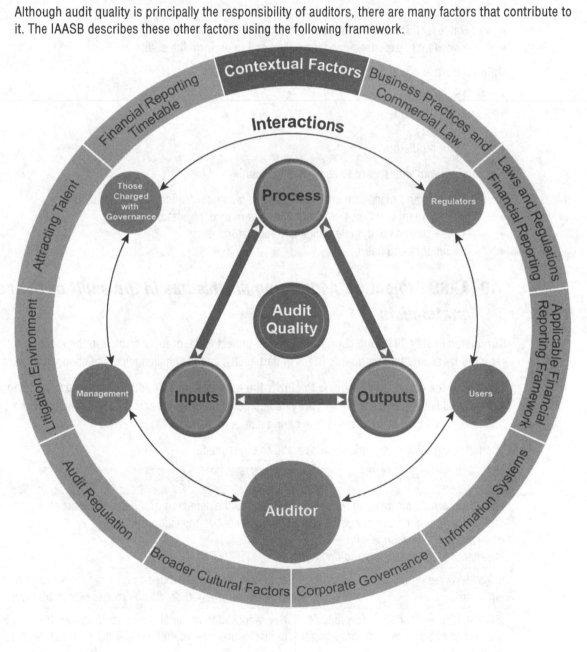

Contextual factors determining audit quality include:

- Business practices and commercial law
- Laws and regulations relating to financial reporting
- The applicable financial reporting framework
- Information systems
- Corporate governance
- Financial reporting timetable
- Broader cultural factors
- Audit regulation
- Litigation environment
- Attracting talent
- Financial reporting timetable

Inputs into audit quality include the following. These are factors which may contribute to a high quality audit.

- Values, ethics and attitudes of auditors and the audit firm
- Knowledge, experience and time allocated to perform the audit

Outputs from audit quality may flow from:

- The auditor
- The audit firm
- The entity
- Audit regulators

Key **interactions** with regard to audit quality include:

- Auditors and management, those charged with governance, users, regulators
- Management and those charged with governance, regulators, users
- Those charged with governance and regulators, users
- Regulators and users

1.8 IAASB Project on *Addressing disclosures in the audit of financial statements*

Completed in July 2015, the background to this project is the gradual change in the kinds of disclosures required by accounting standards (IFRS in particular), and the challenges these changes pose to auditors.

The aim of the proposed changes is to **clarify the expectations of auditors** when auditing financial statement disclosures, as well as to provide additional guidance to assist auditors in addressing the practical challenges arising from the evolving nature of disclosures.

The following table summarises the specific changes made.

Standard	Change
ISA 200 *Overall objectives of the independent auditor and the conduct of an audit in accordance with international standards on auditing*	Change to the definition of 'financial statements' and enhancement of application material
ISA 210 *Agreeing the terms of audit engagements*	New application material, on encouraging management to provide information on disclosures earlier in the audit process
ISA 240 *The auditor's responsibilities relating to fraud in an audit of financial statements*	New application material, on considering whether misstatements in disclosures are intentional and thus constitute fraud
ISA 260 (Revised) *Communication with those charged with governance*	New application material, on communicating with TCWG about disclosures earlier in the audit process

Standard	Change
ISA 300 *Planning an audit of financial statements*	New application material, to focus auditors on the planning considerations related to disclosures earlier in the audit process
ISA 315 (Revised) *Identifying and assessing the risks of material misstatement through understanding the entity and its environment*	Enhanced requirements and new application material, on gaining an understanding of aspects of the information system that is related to information disclosed in the financial statements which was obtained from within or outside of the general and subsidiary ledgers The redefinition of financial statement assertions so that disclosure features as a central part of assertions about transactions and events, and account balances
ISA 320 *Materiality in planning and performing an audit*	New introductory and explanatory material on the need to consider the materiality of qualitative disclosures
ISA 330 *The auditor's responses to assessed risks*	Enhanced requirements and new application material, to strengthen procedures around reconciliation of financial statements, and considering adequacy of presentation and disclosure
ISA 450 *Evaluation of misstatements identified during the audit*	New application material, to clarify that misstatements in disclosures are accumulated and evaluated
ISA 700 *Forming an opinion and reporting on financial statements*	Enhanced requirements and new application material, to provide guidance for audit procedures when evaluating the presentation of the financial statements, including whether fair presentation has been achieved (if applicable)

1.9 IESBA *Code of Ethics*: Changes in relation to non-assurance services provided to audit clients

In April 2015 the IESBA made some amendments intended to strengthen independence requirements.

Auditors of public interest entities now **must not provide bookkeeping or taxation** services **at all**. This removes the old 'emergency situations' provisions, which allowed auditors of public interest entities to provide accounting or taxation services in emergency situations.

The definition of **management responsibilities** has been clarified. The auditor must not assume a management responsibility for an audit client. The definition was changed by deleting the word 'significant':

> Management responsibilities involve controlling, leading and directing an entity, including making ~~significant~~ decisions regarding the acquisition, deployment and control of human, financial, physical, technological and intangible resources. (*Code*, 290.159)

Changes were made to include as a prerequisite that client management takes on management responsibilities (and not the auditor). The auditor must be satisfied that the client is doing this.

The definition of routine and mechanical services, which may still be provided to non-public interest entities, was clarified.

2 General issues

2.1 FRC and FSA: Enhancing the auditor's contribution to prudential regulation

There has been a lot of discussion within the profession over the last few years on the related issues of the role of the audit generally, and the role that was played by auditors in the financial crisis.

In the UK, the Financial Review Council (FRC) recently issued a joint paper with the Financial Services Authority (FSA) entitled *Enhancing the auditor's contribution to prudential regulation.* The paper questioned aspects of the quality of audit work – in particular whether the auditor has always been sufficiently sceptical and has paid sufficient attention to indicators of management bias. The paper then went on to make a number of suggestions of changes that could be made to the way auditors work. The paper has generated intense debate within the profession, with auditors strongly defending the view that they were independent in the run up to the financial crisis.

Fundamental questions are being asked about the very nature of audit and the value it provides. Many take the view that auditors have not been sufficiently independent from their clients. For example, in the UK a May 2009 Treasury Select Committee report stated that:

> 'We strongly believe that investor confidence, and trust in audit would be enhanced by a prohibition on audit firms conducting non-audit work for the same company [...]'

This is a strongly worded statement, made in the context of the recent financial crisis, which calls for a major review of all independence requirements relating to UK auditors. Needless to say, it has been strongly challenged by auditors. You should keep an eye on the financial press for any developments here, as this is an area of ongoing debate which is unlikely to be resolved for some time.

2.2 Audit referred to Competition Commission in UK

In October 2013 the UK's Competition Commission produced a report on the audit market. The report proposed a number of measures which aimed to:

- Improve the bargaining power of companies and encourage rivalry between audit firms
- Enhance the influence of the Audit Committee
- Promote audit quality and shareholder engagement in the audit process

In order to do this, the Commission made the following recommendations.

- FTSE 350 companies must put their statutory audit engagement out to **tender at least every ten years**. This differs from guidance introduced by the Financial Reporting Council (FRC) in 2012, which encouraged companies to go to tender on a 'comply or explain' basis.

- The FRC's **Audit Quality Review** (AQR) team should review every audit engagement in the FTSE 350 on average **every five years**.

- A **prohibition of 'Big-4-only' clauses in loan agreements**, although it will be possible to specify that any auditor should satisfy objective criteria.

- There must be a **shareholders' vote** at the AGM on whether Audit Committee Reports in company annual reports are satisfactory.

- A stipulation that **only the Audit Committee is permitted to negotiate audit fees** and influence the scope of audit work, initiate tender processes, make recommendations for appointment of auditors and authorise the external audit firm to carry out non-audit services.

- The FRC should amend its articles of association to include an object to have due regard to competition.

The **FRC's response** to these recommendations was largely positive, but it did **disagree** in some areas. Specifically:

- **Mandatory tendering**. The FRC thinks 5-yearly tendering (as proposed by the Commission) would be **too costly** and would 'result in a sham process' that was not taken seriously by companies.

- **Extension of AQR**: The FRC thinks this may undermine their current risk-based approach, and would also require more funding.

- **Competition objective**: The FRC will not amend its articles of association to include competition, as it does not have the powers to work in this area, and it believes it could lose its focus on the quality of corporate and financial reporting.

2.3 EU audit reform

Alongside the reforms to the audit market in national jurisdictions (such as the UK), the EU as a whole has now agreed to implement a framework for audit market reform. The following reforms will come into force in June 2016.

- Public interest entities must **rotate their auditors** every 10 years (or sooner), although this can be extended to 20 years if the audit is put out to tender

- **Prohibition of certain non-audit services**, including stringent limits on **tax advice** and services linked to the financial and investment strategy of the audit client

- A **fee cap of 70%** on fees from non-audit services (based on a three-year average)

List of articles by
the examining team

List of articles by the examining team

The P7 examination team has written a number of articles relevant to the P7 exam. It is highly recommended that you read these articles, as they will provide you with an insight into the approach taken in examining P7, the best way for you to tackle exam questions, and an indication of areas of the syllabus the examination team considers to be important. There is a history of issues discussed in articles by the examining team being examined soon after the article is published.

Note that not all of the articles in the relevant section of ACCA are by the examining team. Many are by audit tutors or authors, and although these are often very useful it is the examining team's articles that are truly essential reading for P7 students.

A list of all the articles for P7 is provided in the table below.

Title	Overview
Performance information in the public sector	The syllabus and study guide for P7 (INT), Advanced Audit and Assurance includes a section entitled 'The audit of performance information (pre-determined objectives) in the public sector'. This article is intended to provide insight into this syllabus area and explain some of the issues of which candidates should be aware when studying this aspect of the syllabus.
Laws and regulations	It is important that candidates preparing for P7 have an understanding of how laws and regulations affect an audit, not only in terms of the work the auditor is required to do, but also to appreciate the responsibilities of both management and the auditor where laws and regulations are concerned.
Audit quality – a perpetual current issue	Audit quality is relevant to P7 in that the Syllabus and Study Guide includes a specific section, C1, which contains a number of learning outcomes in relation to quality control in the context of practice management.
Professional scepticism	The article explains the importance of professional scepticism as an essential part of the auditor's mindset, and considers the reasons why approaching an audit with an attitude of professional scepticism is becoming increasingly important.
Using the work of internal auditors	This article focuses on the provision of direct assistance by the internal auditors, which – to date – has been a very controversial issue. Although internal auditors are the employees of the entity, which could result in threats to independence (either in fact or perceived) if direct assistance is provided by the internal auditors, there are benefits relating to this provision which cannot be ignored.
Staying on the right side of ethics	Within the exam, ethical issues are commonly examined alongside practice management issues as the implications of ethical guidelines will interlink with the processes and procedures that an audit or advisory firm must put in place to ensure compliance.
Forensic accounting	With at least one requirement relating to forensic accounting in three out of five P7 exams between December 2011 and December 2013, this is an area of the syllabus that students cannot afford to overlook. This article explores some of the issues relevant to forensic accounting.

Title	Overview
Auditor liability	This article focuses on the issue of auditor's liability in the UK, and therefore contains references to the UK Companies Act 2006, as well as UK-specific legal cases. Candidates other than those attempting the UK adapted paper are not expected to have UK-specific knowledge. The concepts discussed in this article however are broadly relevant and will help candidates to understand why this is an important issue within the auditing profession.
IAASB Developments	Overview of the more significant currently active IAASB projects
Underpinning knowledge for the audit papers	Explores the similarities and differences between Paper F8 and P7 and identifies how best to prepare for the step up to the Professional level
IAASB Developments	Overview of the most active current IAASB projects, on auditor reporting and audit quality
Reporting on audited financial statements – significant changes proposed	Summarises the main issues of the Invitation to Comment and the requirements of the Exposure Draft issued by the IAASB in June 2012 and July 2013 respectively
The control environment of a company	The purpose of this article is to provide candidates with a more detailed appreciation of matters pertinent to an auditor, focusing on the need for the auditor of a large limited liability company to evaluate the effectiveness of the company's control environment
Continue to be 'rest assured'	Looks at the topic of assurance in the context of Paper P7, describing a framework for the classification of assurance and non-assurance engagements, and giving guidance on the practical approach required when undertaking assurance assignments
ISA 315 (Revised) *Identifying and assessing the risks of material misstatement through understanding the entity and its environment (related to entity's internal control)*	One of the major revisions of ISA 315 relates to the inquiries made by external auditors of the internal audit function since internal auditors have better knowledge and understanding of the organisation and its internal control
A question of ethics	When ethics appears in an optional question in the Paper P7 exam, it is often a popular choice for candidates, but their answers often lack detail and are not well applied to the question scenario. This article aims to assist candidates in terms of knowledge and question technique when tackling a question on ethics
Planning an audit of financial statements	Summary of requirements in relation to audit planning, focusing on ISA 300
Exam technique for Paper P7	Clarifies how to answer common requirements. Very useful article for P7 students
Syllabus and study guide update	Exam changes. 'Financial statement risks' to become 'risks of material misstatement', which excludes detection risk. Distinction from business risk
	Group audits – assessment of group and component materiality, non-coterminous year ends, and changes in group structure
Audit and insolvency	Discusses the addition of insolvency to the P7 UK syllabus
Acceptance decisions for audit and assurance engagements	Discussion of decisions to accept new clients in the light of IFAC/IESBA *Code of Ethics*, FRC/.APB ES 5 and ISA 210
Changes in question style for Paper P7	Examines the changes to the syllabus for exams in 2011 onwards

Title	Overview
Change in question requirements	Highlights the change in question style which affected UK paper from 2010 and INT paper from 2011
Going concern	Discussion of guidance on going concern in the light of both ISA 570 and the IAASB Practice Alert on going concern and the current economic climate (Jan 09)
Exam technique	Explores some important exam technique points that are relevant to Paper P7
Exam technique	Exam techniques specifically relevant to P7, focusing on questions on audit evidence, which tend to be tackled particularly poorly
IAASB clarity project	Background to the clarity project, what changes have been made, why they have been made, and what their practical effect is likely to be
Massaging the figures	Earnings management – what is it, when it becomes fraud, and the implications for auditors
The importance of financial reporting standards to auditors	Guidance on financial reporting issues that require a detailed level of knowledge, and those for which less detailed knowledge will be expected
The importance of financial reporting standards to the auditor	Provides guidance on financial reporting matters which are examinable from the auditor's point of view
Forensic auditing	Explores some of the key issues relevant to forensic auditing
Auditors' reports to those charged with governance	Discusses the important reporting 'output' produced as a result of the audit process, that of the auditor's communication to those charged with governance
Group audit issues	Summarises some of the sections of ISA 600 (revised and redrafted)
Continue to be 'rest assured'	Looks at the topic of assurance, describing a framework for the classification of assurance and non-assurance engagements, and giving guidance on the practical approach needed
How to tackle audit and assurance case study questions – part 2	Second part of a two-part series outlining the recommended approach to answering typical Section A case study questions
How to tackle audit and assurance case study questions – part 1	An insight into the recommended approach for Section A questions
Examiner's approach to paper P7	The examiner provides their approach to the advanced audit and assurance paper

All articles can be accessed on the ACCA's website in the following location.

http://www.accaglobal.com/uk/en/student/exam-support-resources/professional-exams-study-resources/p7/technical-articles.html

Practice question and answer bank

1 Audit

For the last few years your firm has helped Colin, a sole trader, prepare his accounts for the taxation authorities. Colin is about to incorporate his business and has asked your advice on a number of issues.

Required

Advise Colin on the following.

(a) The advantages to the company of having its financial statements audited (you may assume that the company would be able to claim exemption from audit) **(2 marks)**

(b) Whether the audit undertaken on his small company would be the same as an audit undertaken on a large one **(2 marks)**

(c) Whether he has any alternatives to audit that would still provide him with a degree of assurance **(3 marks)**

(Total = 7 marks)

2 Fundamental principles

Fundamental principles require that a member of a professional accountancy body should behave with integrity in all professional, business and financial relationships and should strive for objectivity in all professional and business judgements. Objectivity can only be assured if the member is and is seen to be independent. Conflicts of interest have an important bearing on independence and therefore also on the public's perception of the integrity, objectivity and independence of the accounting profession.

The following scenario is an example of press reports in recent years which deal with issues of objectivity and independence within a multinational firm of accountants.

'A partner in the firm was told by the regulatory body that they must resign because they were in breach of the regulatory body's independence rules, as their brother in law was financial controller of an audit client. They were told that the alternative was that they could move their home and place of work at least 400 miles from the offices of the client, even though they were not the reporting partner. This made their job untenable. The regulatory body was seen as "taking its rules to absurd lengths" by the accounting firm. Shortly after this comment, the multinational firm announced proposals to split the firm into three areas between audit, tax and business advisory services; management consultancy; and investment advisory services.'

Required

Discuss the impact that the above events may have on the public perception of the integrity, objectivity and independence of the multinational firm of accountants. **(15 marks)**

3 Aventura International

Aventura International, a listed company, manufactures and wholesales a wide variety of products, including fashion clothes and audio-video equipment. The company is audited by Voest, a firm of Chartered Certified Accountants, and the audit manager is Darius Harken. The following matters have arisen during the audit of the group's financial statements for the year to 31 December 20X8 which is nearing completion.

(a) During the annual inventory count of fashion clothes at the company's principal warehouse, the audit staff attending the count were invited to purchase any items of clothing or equipment at 30% of their recommended retail prices.

(b) The Chief Executive of Aventura International, Armando Thyolo, owns a private jet. Armando invoices the company, on a monthly basis, for that proportion of the operating costs which reflects business use. One of these invoices shows that Darius Harken was flown to Florida in March 20X8 and flown back two weeks later. Neither Aventura nor Voest have any offices or associates in Florida.

(c)   Last week Armando announced his engagement to be married to his personal assistant, Kirsten Fennimore. Before joining Aventura in September 20X8, Kirsten had been Voest's accountant in charge of the audit of Aventura.

Required

Discuss the ethical issues raised and the actions which might be taken by the auditor in relation to these matters.

Note. Assume it is 6 December 20X8.   (15 marks)

4 Professional responsibilities   29 mins

You are required to write an essay, in which you consider the extent to which an auditor should be responsible for detecting fraud and other irregularities when auditing the financial statements of limited liability companies. Your essay should:

- Briefly outline the extent to which an auditor is responsible for detecting irregularities and fraud (as expressed in the auditing guidelines)

- Consider the extent to which it would be reasonable to extend the auditor's responsibilities beyond that and the practical problems of extending auditors' responsibilities

- Reach a conclusion on and provide a definition of the extent to which you consider it reasonable for an auditor to be responsible for detecting irregularities and fraud

(15 marks)

5 Mobile Sales   39 mins

Mobile Sales, a limited liability company, was a growth-orientated company that was dominated by its managing director, Mr A Long. The company sold modern mobile 'smartphones' direct to the public. A large number of salespeople were employed on a commission-only basis. The mobile phones were sent to the sales agents who then sold them direct to the public using telephone sales techniques. The mobile phones were supplied to the sales agents on a sale or return basis and Mobile Sales recognised the sale of the equipment when it was received by the sales agents. Any returns of the mobile phones were treated as repurchases in the period concerned.

The company enjoyed a tremendous growth record. The main reasons for this apparent expansion were:

(1)   Mr A Long falsified the sales records. He created several fictitious sales agents who were responsible for 25% of the company's revenue.

(2)   At the year end, Mr Long despatched nearly all of his inventories of mobile phones to the sales agents and repurchased those that they wished to return after the year end.

(3)   20% of the cost of sales were capitalised. This was achieved by the falsification of purchase invoices with the co-operation of the supplier company. Suppliers furnished the company with invoices for non-current assets but supplied music systems.

(4)   The directors of the company enjoyed a bonus plan linked to reported profits. Executives could earn bonuses ranging from 50% to 75% of their basic salaries. The directors did not query the unusually rapid growth of the company, and were unaware of the fraud perpetrated by Mr A Long.

Mr A Long spent large sums of money in creating false records and bribing accomplices in order to conceal the fraud from the auditor. He insisted that the auditor should sign a 'confidentiality' agreement which effectively precluded the auditor from corroborating sales with independent third parties, and from examining the service contracts of the directors. This agreement had the effect of preventing the auditor from discussing the affairs of the company with the sales agents.

The fraud was discovered when a disgruntled director wrote an anonymous letter to the Stock Exchange concerning the reasons for Mobile Sales's growth. The auditor was subsequently sued by a major bank that had granted a loan to Mobile Sales on the basis of interim financial statements. These financial statements had been reviewed by the auditor and a review report issued.

Required

(a) Explain the key audit tests which would normally ensure that such a fraud as that perpetrated by Mr A Long would be detected. **(7 marks)**

(b) Discuss the implications of the signing of the 'confidentiality' agreement by the auditor. **(4 marks)**

(c) Explain how the 'review report' issued by the auditor on the interim financial statements differs in terms of its level of assurance from the auditor's report on the year-end financial statements. **(4 marks)**

(d) Discuss where you feel that the auditor is guilty of professional negligence in not detecting the fraud. **(5 marks)**

(Total = 20 marks)

6 Osbourne plc
29 mins

Andrews, a firm of Chartered Certified Accountants has 20 partners and 87 audit staff. The firm provides a range of audit, assurance, tax and advisory services. The firm has 4 offices around the country and clients ranging from sole traders to a number of small plcs (none of which are quoted companies).

The quality control partner has recently resigned to take up a position in industry. They have not yet been replaced as the managing board of Andrews have not been able to find a suitable replacement. On their departure the quality control partner was in the process of implementing a system of ethical compliance for assurance staff. Staff would be required to confirm in writing their compliance with ACCA Code of Ethics. Implementation of this system is incomplete.

Osbourne plc is one of the firm's largest clients for whom Andrews provides audit services, preparation of tax computations and other advisory services. A new engagement partner has been assigned to the audit, as the previous partner has retired. The fee for the audit work and other services has been set at the same level as last year in spite of the fact that additional work will need to be performed as Osbourne has introduced a new computer system. The starting date of the audit has been delayed due to problems with the new system. The management of Osbourne was very insistent that the fee should not be increased because of this.

(a) List the six elements of a firm's system of quality control identified by ISQC 1. **(3 marks)**

(b) Identify and explain the quality control issues in the scenario above and the action which should be taken by Andrews. **(10 marks)**

(c) Explain the ethical guidance in respect of the setting of fees for assurance services. **(2 marks)**

(Total = 15 marks)

7 PLD Associates

39 mins

PLD Associates Co, a large quoted company, was founded and controlled by Mr J Scott. The principal business of the company was to develop derelict land in city centres into office accommodation. In 20X3, the taxation authorities became suspicious of the nature of the operations being carried out by the company and an investigation into its affairs commenced.

The resultant report stated that the organisation's internal controls had deficiencies and were non-existent in many cases. The investigators found payments to unknown persons, and fictitious consultancy firms. In addition, J Scott had maintained a secret expense account that was used to disburse funds to himself. The board of directors of PLD Associates Co did not know of the existence of this account. The expense account was maintained by the partner of the firm of accountants responsible for the audit of the company. The auditors were heavily criticised in the report of the investigators.

The firm of auditors, Allcost & Co, had an aggressive marketing strategy and had increased its audit fees by 100% in two years. The audit firm had accepted the appointment in 20X1 after the previous auditors had been dismissed. The audit report for the year ended 20X0 had been heavily qualified by the previous auditors on the grounds of poor internal control and lack of audit evidence. J Scott had approached several firms of auditors in order to ascertain whether they would express a modified auditor's opinion given the present systems of control in PLD Associates Co. Allcost & Co had stated that it was unlikely that they would modify their opinion. They realised that J Scott was 'opinion shopping' but were prepared to give an opinion in order to attract the client to their firm.

PLD Associates plc subsequently filed for insolvency and Allcost & Co were sued for negligence by the largest loan creditor, its bankers.

Required

(a)   Describe the procedures which an audit firm should carry out before accepting a client with potentially high audit risk, such as PLD Associates Co.   **(6 marks)**

(b)   Discuss the ethical problems raised by the maintenance of the secret expense account for Mr J Scott by the audit partner.   **(5 marks)**

(c)   Suggest measures that audit firms might introduce to try and minimise the practice of 'opinion shopping' by prospective audit clients.   **(5 marks)**

(d)   Explain how audit firms can reduce the risk of litigation and its effects on the audit practice.   **(4 marks)**

(Total = 20 marks)

8 Marsden Manufacturing Co

49 mins

Marsden Manufacturing (MM) is an established audit client of your firm. You were involved with the audit last year as audit senior. This year, you are to act as audit supervisor. The engagement partner has asked you to plan the audit for the year ended 30 June 20X4. It is an old-fashioned audit, and the partner does not anticipate that you will require the use of the new laptops that the firm has just invested in.

MM has a sales ledger of approximately 100 customers but, in terms of value, 80% of the ledger is represented by just 6. The company has just secured a new customer, Wallworths, which has only impacted on the sales ledger for one month in the current year, but is projected to represent 20% of sales in the year ending 30 June 20X5.

MM has a large bank loan with ABC Bank. There is a covenant attached to the loan. One of the conditions of the loan is that the company maintains certain financial ratios at the period end. The bank requires an interest cover of 2.5 and a current ratio of 1.5.

The major development in the year is that MM decided to factor its debts. In the past it had suffered a substantial irrecoverable receivables expense when a major customer went bankrupt and it is concerned that the reoccurrence of such an event would affect its interest cover ratio. It sacked its sales ledger clerk at the end of the year, so has outsourced its sales ledger function to the factor.

The audit assistant attended the inventory count two days ago. They observed that there appeared to be a high level of old inventory. They were nevertheless added into the count.

The following draft figures have been provided.

Statement of financial position

	20X4		20X3	
	$'000	$'000	$'000	$'000
Non-current assets		210		243
Current assets				
Inventory	460		370	
Receivables	324		250	
Cash	15		69	
	799		689	
Payables: amounts falling due within one year				
Trade payables	381		367	
Bank loan	10		10	
	391		377	
Net current assets		408		312
Payables: amounts falling due in more than one year				
Bank loan		(250)		(260)
		368		295

Statement of profit or loss

	20X4	20X3
	$'000	$'000
Revenue	2,534	2,967
Cost of sales	(1,583)	(1,823)
Gross profit (% 37.5/38.5)	951	1,144
Administrative expenses	(476)	(488)
Other expenses	(400)	(432)
Profit before interest and tax	75	224
Interest	14	14

Sally Forsyth, the sales ledger clerk, has threatened to sue MM for unfair dismissal and sexual discrimination.

Wallworths is an audit client of the firm. You are aware that it was often in dispute with its previous supplier over its poor payment record and has changed supplier because the supplier broke off relations with it.

Required

(a) Comment on the level at which you would set materiality. **(4 marks)**

(b) Identify and explain the audit risks in the above scenario for the audit for the year ended 30 June 20X4. **(14 marks)**

(c) Outline the key administrative planning matters that remain outstanding. **(3 marks)**

(d) Discuss whether an audit conflict of interest arises in this situation and what steps the auditor might take in this situation. **(4 marks)**

(Total = 25 marks)

9 Herzog   68 mins

You are Saul Shouts, the audit manager responsible for the audit of Herzog Co, a limited liability company. Herzog manufactures computer-controlled machinery for production-line industries, such as cars, washing machines and cookers. On 1 September 20X2, the shareholder-managers decided, unanimously,

to accept a lucrative offer from a multinational corporation to buy the company's patented technology and manufacturing equipment.

You are about to commence planning the audit for the year ending 31 December 20X2, and you have received an email from Paul Bellow, the audit engagement partner.

To: Saul Shouts
From: Paul Bellow
Subject: Herzog Co – audit planning

Hello

(a)   Identify and explain the risks of material misstatement to be taken into account in planning the audit.   **(13 marks)**

(b)   Explain how the extent of the reliance to be placed on:

    (i)   Analytical procedures; and   **(5 marks)**
    (ii)   Written representations,   **(5 marks)**

    should compare with that for the prior year audit.

(c)   Describe the principal audit procedures to be performed in respect of the carrying amount of the following items in the statement of financial position.

    (i)   Amounts due from distributors   **(4 marks)**
    (ii)   Lease liabilities   **(4 marks)**

Thank you.

By 10 September 20X2 management had notified all the employees, suppliers and customers that Herzog would cease all manufacturing activities on 31 October 20X2. The 200-strong factory workforce and the majority of the accounts department and support staff were made redundant with effect from that date, when the sale was duly completed.

The marketing, human resources and production managers will cease to be employed by the company at 31 December 20X2. However, the chief executive, sales manager, finance manager, accountant and a small number of accounting and other support staff expect to be employed until the company is wound down completely.

Herzog's operations extend to 14 premises, 9 of which were put on the market on 1 November 20X2. Herzog accounts for all tangible non-current assets under the cost model (ie at depreciated cost). Four premises are held on leases that expire in the next 2 to 7 years and cannot be sold or sub-let under the lease terms. The small head office premises will continue to be occupied until the lease expires in 20X5. No new lease agreements were entered into during 20X2.

All Herzog's computer-controlled products carry a one-year warranty. Extended warranties of three and five years, previously available at the time of purchase, have not been offered on sales of remaining inventory from 1 November onwards.

Herzog has three-year agreements with its national and international distributors for the sale of equipment. It also has annual contracts with its major suppliers for the purchase of components. So far, none of these parties have lodged any legal claim against Herzog. However, the distributors are withholding payment of their account balances pending settlement of the significant penalties which are now due to them.

Required

Respond to the email from the audit engagement partner.   **(31 marks)**

Note. The split of the mark allocation is shown within the partner's email.

Professional marks will be awarded for the presentation and clarity of your answer.   **(4 marks)**

(Total = 35 marks)

10 Lambley Properties   39 mins

You are the manager in charge of the audit of Lambley Properties, a listed company, and you have been asked to prepare the written representation which will be signed by the company's directors.

You are aware that there are two material items in the financial statements for the year ended 31 March 20X2 on which you want the company's directors to confirm that the treatment in the financial statements is correct.

(1)   One of the company's subsidiaries, Keyworth Builders Co, is experiencing going concern problems, and you want the directors' confirmation that they intend to support the company for the foreseeable future.

(2)   Eastwood Manufacturing, a listed company, is in dispute with Lambley Properties over repairs required to a building it purchased from Lambley. Lambley Properties constructed the building for Eastwood and, three years after it was sold to Eastwood, the customer is claiming that repairs are required which will cost $3 million, and that Lambley is liable to pay for these repairs, as they are as a result of negligent construction of the building. In addition, Eastwood is claiming $2 million for the cost of disruption of the business due to the faults in the building and in the period when the repairs take place. Lambley Properties have obtained the advice of a lawyer and a surveyor, and the directors believe there are no grounds for the claim and any court action will find in their favour. However, Lambley Properties has included a note in its financial statements concerning this contingency.

Required

(a)   List the general representations which must be provided by management in a written representation.
(3 marks)

(b)   Draft the relevant extracts of the written representation referring to the two items above. **(5 marks)**

(c)   Discuss the reliability of a written representation as audit evidence and the extent to which the auditors can rely on this evidence.   **(4 marks)**

(d)   Describe the work you will perform to check whether a provision should be included in the financial statements for the legal claim from Eastwood Manufacturing.   **(5 marks)**

(e)   Describe the matters you will consider and the further action you will take if the directors refuse to sign the written representation because of the legal claim from Eastwood Manufacturing.
(3 marks)

(Total = 20 marks)

11 Bestwood Electronics   39 mins

Your firm is the auditor of Bestwood Electronics Co, a listed company, which assembles microcomputers and wholesales them and associated equipment to retailers. Many of the parts for the computers and the associated equipment are bought from the Far East. These computers are used by businesses for accounting, word processing and other computing tasks.

You have been asked by the partner in charge of the audit to consider your firm's audit responsibilities in relation to subsequent events, and the audit work you will carry out on these matters.

Required

(a)   Describe the responsibilities of the auditors for detecting misstatements in the financial statements during the following periods.

(i)   From the period-end to the date of the auditor's report
(ii)   From the date of the auditor's report to the issue of the financial statements
(iii) After the date the financial statements are issued   **(5 marks)**

(b)   Describe the audit work you will carry out in period (a)(i) above which involves consideration of subsequent events.   **(11 marks)**

(c)   Describe the work you will carry out in period (a)(ii) above to ensure no adjustments are required to the financial statements.   **(4 marks)**

(Total = 20 marks)

12 Bingham Engineering

49 mins

You are auditing the financial statements of Bingham Engineering Co for the year ended 31 March 20X7, which is experiencing going concern problems.

The company prepares monthly, as well as annual, financial statements and its accountant has supplied you with the following forecasts to enable you to assess whether the company will be a going concern. The forecasts have been prepared on a monthly basis for the year to 31 March 20X8, and are:

(1) Capital expenditure/disposal forecast
(2) Profit forecast
(3) Cash flow forecast

The capital expenditure/disposal forecast and profit forecast have been used to prepare the cash flow forecast.

Required

(a) Briefly describe what you understand by the term 'going concern' and state the minimum period you would expect the company to continue in business for it to be considered a going concern.

(3 marks)

(b) Describe the factors which may indicate that a company is not a going concern.   **(9 marks)**

(c) Describe the work you would perform to verify that the value of items in the following forecasts, prepared by the company's accountant, are reasonable:

    (i)   Capital expenditure/disposal forecast
    (ii)   Profit forecast
    (iii) Cash flow forecast   **(10 marks)**

(d) Briefly describe the further work, in addition to that described in (b) and (c) above, you would perform to enable you to determine whether the company is a going concern.   **(3 marks)**

(Total = 25 marks)

13 Locksley

49 mins

The following is the draft statement of financial position of Locksley Co for the year ended 31 January 20X3.

LOCKSLEY CO
STATEMENT OF FINANCIAL POSITION AS AT 31 JANUARY 20X3

	20X3 $	20X2 $
Non-current assets		
Development expenditure	59,810	–
Tangible assets	99,400	73,000
Investments	85,100	101,400
	244,310	174,400
Current assets		
Inventory	58,190	63,010
Receivables	184,630	156,720
Cash at bank and in hand	9,970	62,620
	252,790	282,350
Payables: amounts falling due within one year	231,510	170,900
Net current assets	21,280	111,450
Total assets less current liabilities	265,590	285,850
Payables: amounts falling due after more than one year	101,180	93,840
	164,410	192,010
Equity		
Share capital	89,700	89,700
Share premium account	11,300	11,300
Revaluation reserve	19,750	9,750
Retained earnings	43,660	81,260
	164,410	192,010

Locksley Co produces garden furniture and has incurred expenditure during the year ended 31 January 20X3 on the development of mouldings for a new range of plastic garden furniture. The directors wish to carry forward the development expenditure indefinitely, as they feel that the company will benefit from the new moulding for many years. The product range is being developed because profits have been declining over the last few years owing to the uncompetitiveness of the products made by the company. The company has sold many of its non-current assets during the year and purchased new machinery which will enable the company's productivity to increase. The directors decided not to fund the above expenditure using outside finance but to generate the necessary resources internally by taking extended credit from its suppliers and utilising its liquid funds held at the bank. The company also sold part of its investments, which are made up of stocks and shares of public limited companies.

One of the reasons for this method of financing the expenditure was that the company already has a loan of $45,000 outstanding which has been included in the figure for 'payables: amounts falling due after more than one year'. This loan is secured on the non-current assets of the company and is repayable over ten years. The sale of non-current assets and investments did not yield as much as was expected and a small loss on sale of $1,200 has been included in the statement of profit or loss and other comprehensive income as part of the amounts shown for 'other expenses'.

The company had the non-current assets revalued by a professional valuer, at the year end. The gain on revaluation of non-current assets has been credited by the company to the revaluation reserve.

The directors felt that the shareholders should share in the gain on the revaluation of the non-current assets and increased the proposed dividend accordingly. Over 90% of the shares of the company are held by the directors.

Required

(a)   Describe the audit work to be performed to verify the value attributed to the development expenditure in the statement of financial position of Locksley Co.   **(6 marks)**

(b)   Describe the audit procedures which should be carried out to verify the gain arising on the revaluation of non-current assets.   **(6 marks)**

(c)   Explain to the directors why development expenditure should not be carried forward indefinitely in the financial statements, and describe the circumstances in which the costs may be deferred to the future.   **(8 marks)**

(d)   Describe the implications for the company and the auditors of the directors' decision to generate internally the funds required for the development of the business.   **(5 marks)**

(Total = 25 marks)

14 Bainbridge   39 mins

You are the auditor of Bainbridge, a regional-based limited liability company which manufactures top of the range kitchen units and accessories. The company is owned and run by the Bainbridge family who first set up the business in the 1950s. In recent years the company has experienced increasing success fuelled by the housing boom and the trend for home improvements. The draft financial statements for the year ended 30 June 20X5 show revenue of $20.2 million, profit before tax for the period of $1.6 million and total assets of $30 million. The following matters remain outstanding and have been brought to your attention.

Inventories

Inventories of finished goods are included in the draft financial statements at a cost of $4.5 million. The majority of items are produced for inventories with the cost being calculated using a standard costing system. Standard costs are calculated for materials, labour, production overheads and other overheads.

The standards used have been kept the same as those applied last year and variance calculations have not been performed. Management have justified this by saying that costs have remained constant over the last two years and that historically variances have been negligible.

A small number of items in inventories have been made to customer specification. In respect of these, management have included overheads relating to design.   **(7 marks)**

Warehouse

On 1 July 20X4 Bainbridge entered into a ten-year lease for a warehouse. Under the terms of the lease the company has been given a one-year rent-free period, after which the annual rental is $50,000 per year. At the end of the initial term Bainbridge has the option to extend the lease for a further two years at a notional rental.

Currently no charge has been included in the financial statements in respect of the lease on the basis that the rent-free period means that no charge has been incurred for the year. In future, management intend to account for the lease as an operating lease. **(7 marks)**

Convertible debenture

On 1 July 20X4 Bainbridge issued a $5 million debenture at par. The debenture carries interest at 4% and is redeemable on 1 July 20X9 at which date the holder has the option to convert the debenture to 3 million $1 ordinary shares in Bainbridge.

Currently the only entries that have been made in relation to the debenture were to credit the net proceeds to a long-term liability account and to record the first payment of interest on 31 June 20X5. **(6 marks)**

Required

For each of the above issues:

* Comment on the matters you should consider, and
* The evidence you should expect to find,

in undertaking your review of the audit working papers and financial statements of Bainbridge.

(Total = 20 marks)

15 Recognition   29 mins

Discuss the impact on the audit report of the proposed treatment of the following items in the financial statements.

(a)   Beak Co sells land to a property investment company, Wings Co. The sale price is $20 million and the current market value is $30 million. Beak Co can buy the land back at any time in the next five years for the original selling price plus an annual commission of 1% above the current bank base rate. Wings Co cannot require Beak Co to buy the land back at any time.

The accountant of Beak Co proposes to treat this transaction as a sale in the financial statements. You may assume that the amounts involved are material. **(6 marks)**

(b)   A car manufacturer, Gocar Co, supplies cars to a car dealer, Sparks Co, on the following terms.

Sparks Co has to pay a monthly fee of $100 per car for the privilege of displaying it in its showroom and is also responsible for insuring the cars. When a car is sold to a customer, Sparks Co has to pay Gocar Co the factory price of the car when it was first supplied. Sparks Co can only return cars to Gocar Co on the payment of a fixed penalty charge of 10% of the cost of the car. Sparks Co has to pay the factory price for the cars if they remain unsold within a four-month period. Gocar Co cannot demand the return of the cars from Sparks Co.

The accountant of Sparks Co proposes to treat the cars unsold for less than four months as the property of Gocar Co and not show them as inventory in the financial statements. At the year end the value of car inventory shown in the statement of financial position was $150,720. The total assets on the statement of financial position are $1.3m. The cars unsold for less than four months have a factory cost of $22,500. **(9 marks)**

(Total = 15 marks)

16 Henshelwood   39 mins

You are employed as an audit manager by Viewstream, a firm of Certified Accountants. You are currently involved in planning the final audit of the financial statements of Henshelwood Co, a listed IT consultancy, for the year ended 31 March 20X7.

The draft financial statements show a profit before tax of $192 million (20X6 $167 million) and total assets of $553 million (20X6 $510 million).

The following disclosures have been extracted from the draft financial statements.

(a) **Share-based payments**

The fair value of all share-based remuneration is determined at the date of grant and recognised as an expense in the statement of profit or loss and other comprehensive income on a straight-line basis over the vesting period, taking account of the estimated number of shares that will vest. The fair value is determined by use of the relevant valuation model. All share-based remuneration is equity-settled.

Notes made by the audit senior during some preliminary analytical review refer to a share-based payment expense of $4.8 million and an equity reserve, relating to the share-based payment scheme, of $8.7 million. **(5 marks)**

(b) **Pension costs**

Defined benefit schemes

(i) The scheme, the Henshelwood Pension Scheme, is a defined benefit scheme where the benefits are based on employees' length of service and final pensionable pay. It is a funded approved defined benefit scheme and closed to new members on 1 April 20X2. It is funded through a legally separate trustee administered fund.

The actuarial valuation was performed at 31 March 20X7 by the scheme actuary, an employee of Milton Human Resource Consulting.

The financial statements of Henshelwood included the following information.

Note to the statement of profit or loss and other comprehensive income

Defined benefit expense recognised in profit or loss

	$m
Current service cost	3.75
Net interest on the net defined benefit asset (4.50 – 5.20)	(0.70)
Past service cost – plan amendment	(6.00)
Profit or loss expense/(credit)	(2.95)

Defined benefit remeasurements recognised in other comprehensive income

	$m
Actuarial loss on defined benefit obligation	4.75
Actuarial gain on plan assets	(2.97)
	1.78

Notes to the statement of financial position

Net defined benefit asset recognised in the statement of financial position

	$m
Present value of defined benefit obligation	44.00
Fair value of plan assets	(64.17)
Net asset	(20.17)

Changes in the present value of the benefit obligation

	$m
Opening defined benefit obligation	45.00
Interest cost (10% × 45,000)	4.50
Current service cost	3.75
Benefits paid	(8.00)
Past service cost (plan amendment)	(6.00)
Actuarial loss (balancing figure)	4.75
Closing defined benefit obligation – per actuary	44.00

Changes in the fair value of plan assets

	$m
Opening fair value of plan assets	52.00
Interest on plan assets (10% × 52,000)	5.20
Contributions	12.00
Benefits paid	(8.00)
Actuarial gain (balancing figure)	2.97
Closing fair value of plan assets – per actuary	64.17

(9 marks)

(c) **Provisions**

	Property	Other	Total
Balance at 1 April 20X6	25.2	478	76.4
Exchange adjustments	–	0.1	0.1
Charged to statement of profit or loss and other comprehensive income	–	0.2	0.2
Utilised	(8.2)	(14.3)	(22.5)
Balance at 31 March 20X7	17.0	33.8	50.8

Property provisions are for rents and other related amounts payable on certain leased properties for periods in which they are not anticipated to be in use by the company. The leases expire in periods up to 20Y3.

Other provisions comprise liabilities arising as a result of business disposals and the company transformation including the following items.

- Provisions of $7.1 million (20X6 – $8.9 million) relating to restructuring costs arising from the company transformation and closure of former shared service facilities and the closure of the former head office. These provisions are expected to be utilised over the next 12–36 months.

- Provisions of $6.2 million (20X6 – $160 million) for potential liabilities relating to the disposal of the European business including certain site restitution costs

- Provisions of $19.1 million (20X6 – $19.4 million) relating to possible warranty and environmental claims in relation to businesses disposed. It is not possible to estimate the timing of payments against these provisions.

(6 marks)

Required

For each of the three issues identified above:

(i) Explain the matters you should consider to determine whether the amounts have been appropriately valued; and

(ii) Describe the tests you should plan to perform to quantify the amount of any misstatement.

Note. The mark allocation is shown against each of the three issues. **(Total = 20 marks)**

17 Keffler

You are the manager responsible for the audit of Keffler Co, a limited company engaged in the manufacture of plastic products. The draft financial statements for the year ended 30 September 20X2 show revenue of $47.4 million (20X1 – $43.9 million), profit before taxation of $2 million (20X1 – $2.4 million) and total assets of $33.8 million (20X1 – $25.7 million).

The following issues arising during the final audit have been noted on a schedule of points for your attention.

(a)   In October 20X1, Keffler bought the right to use a landfill site for a period of 15 years for $1.1 million. Keffler expects that the amount of waste that it will need to dump will increase annually and that the site will be completely filled after just ten years. Keffler has charged the following amounts to the statement of profit or loss and other comprehensive income for the year to 30 September 20X2.

- • $20,000 licence amortisation calculated on a sum of digits basis to increase the charge over the useful life of the site
- • $100,000 annual provision for restoring the land in 15 years' time   **(9 marks)**

(b)   A sale of industrial equipment to Deakin Co in November 20X1 resulted in a loss on disposal of $0.3 million that has been separately disclosed in the statement of profit or loss and other comprehensive income. The equipment cost $1.2 million when it was purchased in October 1998 and was being depreciated on a straight-line basis over 20 years.   **(6 marks)**

(c)   In October 20X2, Keffler was banned by the local Government from emptying waste water into a river because the water did not meet minimum standards of cleanliness. Keffler has made a provision of $0.9 million for the technological upgrading of its water purifying process and included $45,000 for the penalties imposed in 'other provisions'.   **(5 marks)**

Required

For each of the above issues:

(i)   Comment on the matters that you should consider
(ii)   State the audit evidence that you should expect to find

in undertaking your review of the audit working papers and financial statements of Keffler Co for the year ended 30 September 20X2.   **(Total = 20 marks)**

18 Griffin

Griffin Co, a listed company, manufactures football kit. It has contracts with a number of league football teams. It also produces 'unbranded' football wear, which it sells to a number of wholesalers.

The profit before tax for the year is $1.2 million (20X6 $3.5 million). You are the manager responsible for the audit for the year end 30 June 20X7. Today you have visited the client's premises to review the audit team's work to date. The audit senior has drafted the following 'points for the attention of the manager'.

(a)   Griffin is seeking to enter the market in women's leisure clothes. In light of that fact, during the year it purchased 30% of the share capital of Bees Co, a company that manufactures sporty leisurewear at a cost of $750,000.   **(7 marks)**

(b)   During the year a major competitor emerged in the branded football kit market. Two of the contracts with nationwide clubs which came up during the year have not been renewed. A number of key personnel have been headhunted by the competitor.   **(6 marks)**

(c)   A legal requirement to adjust the seats at which machinists sit was passed in December 20X6. The legislation required the seats to be adjusted by April 20X7. Griffin has not yet carried out any adjustment. Also, in April 20X7, the Government increased the national minimum wage. 5% of Griffin's employees receive less than the minimum wage.   **(7 marks)**

Required

(i)   Comment on the matters you would consider.

(ii)   State the evidence you would expect to find during your review of the working papers and financial statements of Griffin Co.

(Total = 20 marks)

19 Merger of audit firms   29 mins

The increase in the size of audit firms has been a source of concern to regulators and clients alike. Some audit firms feel that mergers between the largest firms of auditors are necessary in order to meet the global demand for their services. However their clients are concerned that such mergers will create a monopolistic market for audit services which will not be in their best interests.

Required

(a)   Explain the reasons why the largest audit firms might wish to merge their practices.   **(7 marks)**

(b)   Discuss the potential problems created by mergers of the largest firms of auditors.   **(8 marks)**

(Total = 15 marks)

20 Annabella   49 mins

Annabella Co has been an audit client of your firm for 13 years. It is a business which manufactures soft furnishings. It also has a shop, from which it sells its own soft furnishings, and other manufacturers' soft furnishings and small items of furniture.

On the first day of the year ending 30 June 20X8, Annabella Co undertook a major reconstruction of its operations. It set up two subsidiary companies Anna Co and Bella Co. It then transferred its trade to those companies. Anna Co took the manufacturing trade and Bella Co took the retail trade. On the same day, Annabella Co entered into a joint venture with its former chief designer. The joint venture, Annabella Designs Co, will provide designs for the soft furnishings manufactured by Anna Co and will also operate an interior design service, which will be advertised strongly by Bella Co.

Annabella Co is 100% owned by James Dancer; Annabella Co will charge Anna Co, Bella Co and Annabella Designs Co management charges.

The former chief designer, now a 50% shareholder in Annabella Designs Co, is Annabel Dancer, James's only daughter. They make decisions about Annabella Designs jointly, and have agreed that the audit of Annabella Designs Co shall be carried out by David Turner and Co. David Turner is a friend of Annabel.

Required

(a)   Identify and explain the audit planning issues in the above scenario.   **(17 marks)**

(b)   Describe the principal audit procedures on a consolidation.   **(8 marks)**

(Total = 25 marks)

21 Trendy Group   29 mins

Trendy Group Inc is an international group which manufactures costume jewellery and sells it through its own retail stores. It is a new client for your firm which was awarded the worldwide audit after submitting a competitive tender. You have just learnt that you are the senior assigned to the audit of Trendy Group Inc. As group audit senior, you will be responsible for the co-ordination of the worldwide audit for the year ending 30 September 20X2 and for the audits of the consolidation, the US parent entity (Trendy Group Inc) and the US trading subsidiary (Trendy (US) Inc). Your firm has offices in every country in which the Trendy Group has operations and you will instruct the relevant local offices to perform any overseas work required.

The audit manager has presented you with a copy of a background memorandum prepared in connection with the tender process **(Exhibit 1)**.

Required

Identify the key areas of business risk associated with Trendy Group Inc. For each business risk area identified, include (perhaps in tabular format) the specific audit risks, if any, associated with that business risk, both at a group level and at an individual company level. **(15 marks)**

EXHIBIT 1

To: The Files
From: Kim Welsby (Audit manager)
Date: 30 May 20X2
Subject: Trendy Group Inc
           Invitation to tender for worldwide audit
           Background information

This memorandum summarises background information obtained at a meeting with Mary Pegg (Group Finance Director) on 27 May 20X2.

Group structure

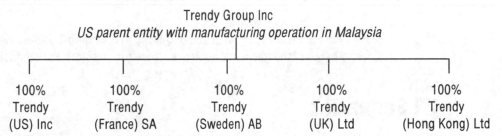

Trendy Group Inc
US parent entity with manufacturing operation in Malaysia

100%	100%	100%	100%	100%
Trendy	Trendy	Trendy	Trendy	Trendy
(US) Inc	(France) SA	(Sweden) AB	(UK) Ltd	(Hong Kong) Ltd

Local audit requirements

Full statutory audits are required for both US companies and for the subsidiaries in Sweden and Hong Kong. At all other locations, Mary wants the auditors to perform the minimum level of work necessary to give an overall opinion on the group financial statements.

Parent entity operations

The parent, Trendy Group Inc, has a factory in Malaysia. This factory manufactures costume jewellery using a local workforce and materials. All of the factory output is sold to Trendy Group Inc's trading subsidiaries at prices set in dollars at the beginning of each quarter. The prices charged by the factory include freight and are set to ensure that the factory makes a modest profit margin.

The parent is also responsible for design, international marketing and promotions, treasury management and certain other administrative activities. It charges the trading subsidiaries a royalty of 5% of retail sales to cover design costs and also levies management charges sufficient to recover its other overhead expenses.

Trading subsidiaries

The five trading subsidiaries each sell costume jewellery purchased from the Malaysian factory through retail stores in their own geographical area. All sales are made through the companies' own stores. Each trading subsidiary has a central warehouse at which deliveries from the Malaysian factory are received and distributed to individual retail stores. The subsidiaries are responsible for local marketing activities.

The US trading subsidiary, Trendy (US) Inc, also runs a factory outlet shop at which old inventories are sold at marked down prices. Any inventories held in the retail outlets at the end of a fashion season are first reduced in a shop sale. If it has not been sold by the end of the sale, the trading subsidiaries sell the obsolete lines to Trendy (US) Inc for 50% of their original cost. These inventories are then sold through the factory outlet or, if this proves unsuccessful, destroyed. In order to protect its reputation, the group will not sell obsolete inventories to market traders.

Kim Welsby

---

22 Business assurance

Audit practitioners have recently initiated substantive changes in the audit approach. It appears to be the strategy that audit firms are moving away from the audit of financial statements and more to the provision of assurances on financial data, systems and controls in those systems. Auditors are focusing on providing 'business assurance' and 'business risk' which gives clients wider assurance than the traditional audit has offered. Auditors are reviewing the business from a process standpoint utilising benchmarking, performance measurements and best control practices as the key criteria. It seems that the audit is moving more to the analysis of business risk and the alignment of the audit much more to the management perspective.

A wide range of risk assessment services is now part of the audit service. The provision of internal audit services is becoming an increasingly large part of the 'business assurance' service offered by auditors. It seems that the audit is becoming a management consultancy exercise, with internal audit, external audit and consultancy assignments being seen as complementary services.

Required

(a)   Discuss the implications of the external auditor providing an internal audit service to a client, explaining the current ethical guidance on the provision of other services to clients.   **(10 marks)**

(b)   Explain the principal effects of the external auditor providing wider assurance to the client.

(6 marks)

(c)   Critically evaluate the move by large auditing firms to providing 'business risk and assurance' services rather than the traditional audit assurance for investors and creditors.   **(4 marks)**

(Total = 20 marks)

23 Scenarios

You are a partner in a medium-sized firm of Chartered Certified Accountants. The following opportunities have arisen.

(a)   A major audit client, Lilac Co, is seeking loan finance from its bank to fund an expansion into a new factory. The expansion should result in an increase in capacity of 30%. Lilac has conducted market research and is confident that it will be able to sell the added output. The financial director has recently telephoned you and mentioned that the bank is keen to obtain a reference from the audit firm, relating to Lilac's ability to repay the loan and whether the business plan is reasonable. They said 'they just need their forms filled, for their files. They know we can repay. We're one of their best clients.' Your audit team is about to commence the audit for the year ended 31 March 20X8.

Required

Comment on the matters you would consider in relation to giving such a reference to the bank.

(7 marks)

(b)   The finance director of Laurel Co, another audit client, telephoned you yesterday. They recently attended a half-day course on the importance of corporate governance run by your firm. Laurel's long-term plans include the possibility of flotation on a stock exchange. The finance director has told the other directors of the issues discussed at the course and they feel that it might be a good idea to engage the firm to undertake an assurance engagement to assess risk management and the internal control system at Laurel Co.

Required

Comment on the matters you would consider in relation to accepting and planning such an engagement.   **(8 marks)**

(Total = 15 marks)

24 Verity

Verity, a limited liability company, has a credit facility with Cranley Bank of $6 million. The facility is due to expire on 31 December 20X1. The overdraft in the recently audited statement of financial position at 30 September 20X1 is $5.5 million. The directors of Verity have started negotiations with their bankers for a renewal of the facility and to increase the amount to $9 million. To support this request the bank has asked Verity to provide a business plan for the coming 12 months consisting of a cash flow forecast supported by a forecast statement of profit or loss and other comprehensive income and statement of financial position. The management of Verity has produced a cash flow forecast for the period 1 October 20X1 to 30 September 20X2 and, at the request of the bank, has asked the auditor to examine and report on it.

The audit manager, who has recently completed Verity's audit, has been asked to make a preliminary examination of the cash flow forecast and supporting material and they have made the following observations.

(1) The cash flows from sales are based on the assumption of an overall increase in sales of 24% compared to the previous financial year. Analysis shows that this is based on an increase in selling price of 5% and an increase in the volume of sales of 18%. Just over a quarter of all Verity's sales are made to foreign customers.

(2) The cost of sales in the recently audited statement of profit or loss and other comprehensive income to 30 September 20X1 was 80% of sales revenue, giving a gross profit of 20%. In the forecast statement of profit or loss and other comprehensive income for the year to 30 September 20X2 the cost of sales has fallen to 72%, giving a gross profit of 28%. Manufacturing costs are made up of approximately one-third each of materials, labour and production overheads.

(3) The trade receivables collection period used in the cash flow forecast to 30 September 20X2 is 61 days. In the year to 30 September 20X1 this period averaged 93 days. Management has stated that it is its intention to inform all customers of a new standard 60 day credit period. In addition, an early settlement discount of 1% will apply to customers who settle their account within 30 days of the statement.

Conversely the credit period for trade payables has been extended from an average of 45 days in the current year to 90 days in the forecast.

(4) The cash flow forecast showed that the maximum credit required during the period would rise to nearly $9 million in August 20X2.

Required

(a) Describe the general matters an auditor should consider before accepting an engagement as a reporting accountant on forecast financial information.   **(5 marks)**

(b) Detail the procedures that the reporting accountant should undertake in relation to the cash flow forecast of Verity for the year to 30 September 20X2.   **(8 marks)**

(c) The negotiations with Cranley Bank resulted in a renewal of Verity's existing credit facility of $6 million, but the bank would not agree to increase it to $9 million. As a result of this Verity issued a circular to its existing shareholders inviting them to subscribe for a new $3 million issue of debentures. The purpose of the circular was to show the intended use and the future benefits from the debenture issue. It was supported by the same forecast financial information, including the accountant's report, that had been provided to Cranley Bank. However, the directors of Verity had removed all references to its original purpose and restricted distribution.

The trading results of the first half of the year to 30 September 20X2 showed that the forecast information was proving to be overoptimistic and that Verity was beginning to experience cash flow difficulties.

Discuss the basis on which a reporting accountant should form an opinion on forecast information, and consider whether the reporting accountants of Verity may be liable to:

(i)   Cranley Bank
(ii) The investors who subscribe for the new debentures   **(7 marks)**

                                                                                        (Total = 20 marks)

Note. You are to assume that the accountant's report had expressed an unmodified opinion on the statement of cash flows.

BPP LEARNING MEDIA

Practice question bank **541**

25 Painswick Ltd
29 mins

(a) Define a forensic audit and explain how the definition applies to a fraud investigation. **(2 marks)**

(b) Compare the responsibilities of the auditor in respect of fraud when conducting a statutory audit and when conducting a forensic investigation. **(3 marks)**

(c) Explain how the fundamental principles of the *Code of Ethics and Conduct* apply to forensic assignments. **(5 marks)**

Example of fraud

The purchase ledger clerk of Painswick Ltd has been channelling payments to suppliers into their own bank account by altering bank account details of the relevant suppliers on the BACS masterfile. In order to disguise this activity the purchase ledger clerk has:

- Posted the relevant invoices to the purchase ledger twice; one entry has been made correctly to the relevant expense account while the other has been debited to a suspense account

- Matched and removed the duplicate invoices and payments before the monthly reconciliation of supplier accounts is performed

Required

(d) Based on the above example of a fraud, identify the procedures which would have enabled the forensic auditor to identify this fraud and quantify the loss to the company. **(5 marks)**

(Total = 15 marks)

26 Harness
29 mins

(a) Briefly outline the reasons why social and environmental issues are of interest to an external auditor. **(5 marks)**

(b) Harness Co is a wind farm situated on an island in the North Sea. Harness was set up a number of years ago by an energy fanatic who was also a millionaire. It is predominately owned by the millionaire Brewster Billings, who continues to loan it money, despite a history of loss-making.

Harness owns and operates 15 wind turbines which are situated on the island. The windmills are connected to a generator, which converts the wind power to electricity. The electricity is mainly supplied to Brewster's mansion on the east coast of Scotland, but some is sold to various power supply companies. One of these companies, Scot Power, has a small stake in Harness Co.

The company has suffered some problems this year. Firstly, the erosion, which has badly affected the island during the course of the company's occupation, has finally struck some of the windmills. One fell into the sea at the end of the year, and the foundations of another three appear to have been affected. The generator lies within ten metres of the cliff.

During the year, Harness invested in a stake in an oil pipeline which runs near the island. The co-owners of the pipeline have just advised Brewster, as a director of Harness, that they have discovered a substantial crack in the pipeline.

Required

Comment on the implications of the above on the audit of Harness Ltd for the year end June 20X8.

(10 marks)

(Total = 15 marks)

27 Eastfield Distributors

39 mins

Your firm is the external auditor of Eastfield Distributors, a limited liability company which has revenue of $25 million and a profit before tax of $1.7 million. The company operates from a head office at Eastfield and has sales and inventory holding centres in different parts of the country. The directors have decided that the company has reached a size when it needs an internal audit department. As is becoming increasingly common, the directors have asked your firm to provide this service to the company as well as being the external auditor of the company's annual financial statements.

In answering the question, you should consider:

(i)   The effects of the ACCA's *Code of Ethics and Conduct* in relation to providing an internal audit service to Eastfield Distributors

(ii)   The extent to which your audit firm can rely on the internal audit work when carrying out the external audit of Eastfield Distributors

(iii)   The arrangements over control of the work and reporting of the internal audit staff:

    (1)   The extent to which the internal audit staff should be responsible to Eastfield Distributors, and who should control their work

    (2)   The extent to which the internal audit staff should be responsible to a manager or partner of the external audit firm, and whether the same manager and partner should be responsible for both the internal audit staff of Eastfield Distributors and the external audit

Required

In relation to your audit firm becoming internal auditors of Eastfield Distributors:

(a)   Describe the matters you should consider and the action you will take to ensure your firm remains independent as external auditor of the annual financial statements   **(8 marks)**

(b)   Describe the advantages and disadvantages to Eastfield Distributors of your firm providing an internal audit service   **(7 marks)**

(c)   Describe the advantages and disadvantages to your **audit firm** of providing an internal audit service to Eastfield Distributors.   **(5 marks)**

(Total = 20 marks)

28 Maple

29 mins

(a)   Explain the auditor's responsibility in respect of fraud and error.   **(5 marks)**

(b)   Maple, a limited liability company, designs and manufactures high quality wooden furniture. The audit is nearing completion and you are in the process of reviewing the audit file in your capacity as audit manager.

Draft financial statements for the year ended 30 September 20X5 show a profit before tax of $100,000 and total assets of $4,562,500.

The following matters are brought to your attention.

(i)   The inventories figure of $675,000 includes $80,000 which has been valued based on the directors' estimate. This is due to the loss of the inventory counting sheets for the Sherwood depot. The audit team were unable to find any other means of validating these inventories.

(ii)   During the year Maple made a loan to a director, Colin Wood, for $5,000. This is not disclosed in the financial statements, as the directors believe that the transaction is a personal issue.

(iii)   Trade receivables that total $525,000 include $47,000 due from Beech. This customer went into liquidation on 3 November 20X5. The audit senior has concluded that Maple is unlikely to recover the debt based on information provided by the liquidator.

Management has refused to adjust the financial statements.

The audit senior has drafted the auditor's report, extracts of which are as follows.

'*Modified opinion*

The inventories balance includes an amount of $80,000 based on the directors' estimate. This is because the inventory counting sheets for the Sherwood depot were lost and we were unable to find any other suitable means of confirming the inventory value. Also included in receivables is an amount of $47,000 due from a company which is in liquidation. We believe that this amount should have been fully provided against, as it is unlikely that the company will receive any payment in respect of this amount.

In our opinion, except for the effects of the matter described in the preceding paragraph, the accompanying financial statements present fairly, in all material respects, the financial position of Maple Co as at 30 September 20X5 and its financial performance and its cash flows for the year then ended in accordance with International Financial Reporting Standards (IFRS).'

The audit senior has also attached a note for you explaining that they have made no reference to the director's loan on the basis that the amount involved is not material.

Required

Comment on the suitability of this report. Your answer should include an assessment of the materiality of each of the three outstanding issues. **(10 marks)**

(Total = 15 marks)

29 Petrie   33 mins

(a)   ISA 705 *Modifications to the opinion in the independent auditor's report* and ISA 706 *Emphasis of matter paragraphs and other matter paragraphs in the independent auditor's report* include suggested wordings of modifying phrases for use when issuing modified reports.

Required

Explain and distinguish between each of the following terms.

(i)   'Qualified opinion'
(ii)   'Disclaimer of opinion'
(iii)   'Emphasis of Matter paragraph'
(iv)   'Other Matter paragraph'   **(8 marks)**

(b)   You are the audit manager of Petrie Co, a private company, that retails kitchen utensils. The draft financial statements for the year ended 31 March 20X2 show revenue of $42.2 million (20X1– $41.8 million), profit before taxation of $1.8 million (20X1 – $2.2 million) and total assets of $30.7 million (20X1 – $23.4 million).

You are currently reviewing two matters that have been left for your attention on Petrie's audit working paper file for the year ended 31 March 20X2.

(i)   Petrie's management board decided to revalue properties for the year ended 31 March 20X2 that had previously all been measured at depreciated cost. At the end of the reporting period three properties had been revalued by a total of $1.7 million. Another nine properties have since been revalued by $5.4 million. The remaining three properties are expected to be revalued later in 20X2.   **(5 marks)**

(ii) On 1 July 20X1 Petrie introduced a ten-year warranty on all sales of its entire range of stainless steel cookware. Sales of stainless steel cookware for the year ended 31 March 20X2 totalled $18.2 million. The notes to the financial statements disclose the following.

'Since 1 July 20X1, the company's stainless steel cookware is guaranteed to be free from defects in materials and workmanship under normal household use within a ten-year guarantee period. No provision has been recognised, as the amount of the obligation cannot be measured with sufficient reliability.' **(4 marks)**

Your auditor's report on the financial statements for the year ended 31 March 20X1 was unmodified.

Required

Identify and comment on the implications of these two matters for your auditor's report on the financial statements of Petrie Co for the year ended 31 March 20X2.

Note. The mark allocation is shown against each of the matters above. Assume it is 10 June 20X2.

(Total = 17 marks)

1 Audit

> **Tutor's hint**. This is not an exam standard question, but is a helpful exercise to remind yourself of the advantages of audit for a small company and also the alternative opinions available.

(a) The advantages of having an audit include:

    (i) **Shareholders** who are **not involved in management** gain **reassurance** from audited accounts about management's **stewardship** of the business.

    (ii) Audited accounts are a reliable source for a **fair valuation of shares** in an unquoted company either for taxation or other purposes.

    (iii) Some **banks** rely on accounts for the purposes of **making loans** and reviewing the value of security.

    (iv) **Creditors and potential creditors** can use audited accounts to assess the potential strength of the company.

    (v) The audit provides **management** with a **useful independent check** on the accuracy of the accounting systems; the auditors can recommend improvements in those systems.

(b) **Audit of a small company**

The audit of a small company is still an exercise designed to express an opinion on the truth and fairness of the accounts.

However, the audit of a small company is often affected by certain factors:

- The concentration of ownership and management in one person
- The wider professional relationship between the auditor and the business
- The fact that small teams of auditors are involved with the audit

The methods of undertaking the audit will be the same, and the same auditing standards will be applied. However, the auditor must be aware of the different inherent risk in the audit of a small company and, in applying auditing standards, consider all the relevant risks.

(c) **Alternatives to audit**

A small company not requiring an audit could engage a firm of accountants to carry out a review instead.

A review is an engagement similar to audit, which is designed to give a lower level of assurance than would be given by an audit. This limited assurance would be expressed using a negative form of words. The procedures undertaken to express an opinion in a review engagement are therefore less detailed and often comprise enquiry and analytical procedures.

Colin needs to decide on the level of assurance that is best for his business. This will involve him analysing the advantages of audit discussed above in part (a) and deciding whether his business requires the higher level of assurance or not. Some of the advantages of the audit will also be gained by a review.

2 Fundamental principles

> **Tutor's hint.** Don't let this scenario panic you in the long list of details it gives you. Deal with each point as it arises. Also, don't be afraid to draw a conclusion about the facts given to you, but remember to back your opinions up with justification. Consider what the fundamental principles and general guidance of the ACCA say, but also think about practical issues, such as ease of modern communication. Deal with the two issues raised in the scenario (the individual partner issue and the firm split) separately; there is no need to assume any connection between them. However, you may feel there is a point to be made about the juxtaposition of the two events.

Independence

It is important that auditors are, and are seen to be, independent. **Independence** is at the heart of the auditing profession as auditors claim to give an **impartial, objective** opinion on the truth and fairness of the financial statements.

Objectivity

A **family relationship** between an auditor and the client **can substantially affect the objectivity** of the audit, so auditors are advised not to build close personal relationships with audit clients and should not audit a company where family are employed in a capacity which is sensitive to the accounts, for example in the finance department, although this is **not prohibited by law** unless the auditor's 'partner' is an employee of the company.

In this instance, the **partner was not the reporting partner** for the audit client in which their brother in law was a financial controller. According to generally accepted ethical practice, then, the firm appeared to be independent of the audit client if the related partner did not have anything to do with the audit.

Resolution?

The regulatory body required the audit partner to move 400 miles. This presumably implies that the partner was requested to change offices within the firm by which they were employed. Given current levels of computer networking and other **communications** common in business, this would appear to be an **arbitrary distinction**, as a partner in an office in Glasgow could have similar access and influence over a single audit carried out by the firm as a partner in London.

Independence in appearance

However, in this situation, the regulatory body appears to be concerned about the appearance of independence. It appears to be concerned that the public will not perceive the distinction between a partner and a partner who reports on a specific engagement. This may or may not be fair. Arguably, it is only in publicising the problem that the public are likely to have a perception at all.

Also, given the comments made about modern communications above, the public are unlikely to be convinced that moving a member of staff to a different office will solve this independence problem, if they perceive that there is one.

Split of audit firm

The decision of the firm to split into three divisions could **enhance the public perception of the independence of the audit department**. While there might be **underlying scepticism** relating to the reasons behind the split (which could merely be for marketing purposes or to enable non-audit divisions to raise capital more easily), the **underlying benefit for objectivity still exists**.

However, some audit clients will be unhappy with the move of the firm as it will necessitate their engaging with several different service providers to gain the services they previously got from the one audit firm.

3 Aventura International

Ethical situations arising in connection with the audit of Aventura International

(a) **Offer of goods**

At the inventory count, the auditors attending were invited to purchase inventory at 30% of RRP, that is, at a 70% discount.

ACCA's guidance on accepting goods states that such benefits should only be accepted on 'normal commercial terms' or if the value is 'trivial and inconsequential'. What constitutes modest benefit will be a matter of judgement for the auditor.

Benefit

It is possible that this offer does approximate to offers made to staff at Aventura, as clothes commonly retail at prices with a substantial mark-up on cost. It would not be unreasonable for a clothes retailer to give staff a 'cost' benefit. The auditor should determine whether such a benefit is made available to staff. If it is not made to staff, it should not be accepted by the auditor.

The term 'trivial and inconsequential' should be considered both in terms of materiality to the auditor and the company. The offer is not material to Aventura, for whom clothes retail is only one division. However, the offer of unlimited fashion at a 70% discount is extremely likely to be material to junior audit staff (who are the grade most likely to be allocated to the inventory count). In this context, the benefit is **not** clearly insignificant.

Timing

It would be inappropriate to take up the offer at the inventory count, not least because this would constitute movement of inventory during the count, which would be wrong.

Also, the junior staff members should not accept such goods without having discussed the matter with the audit partner (it is assumed in this answer that this is the first time such an offer has been made).

Lastly, if mistakes were to be made on the inventory count, the audit might be open to charges of negligence if it appeared its staff members indulged in a shopping trip when they should have been auditing.

Action to be taken

The staff members should not have taken up the offer at the inventory count.

The audit partner should discuss the matter with management, ascertain whether a similar benefit is offered to staff and decide whether they feel it is appropriate for their staff to take up the offer. It may be inappropriate as Aventura might become perceived to be a 'reward' job by audit staff. Alternatively, it might be appropriate if the audit firm imposed a financial limit to the benefits their staff could accept.

(b) **Hospitality**

An invoice to the company for business use of the Chief Executive's jet shows that the audit manager was flown to Florida and back for a stay of two weeks.

Issues arising

(i) If the invoice was ostensibly for 'business use', what was the business? (Neither the client nor the auditor have offices in Florida.)

(ii) If the invoice was not for business, the Chief Executive is wrong to invoice it to the company. Is this common practice?

(iii) If it was for business, the cost of the auditor's flight should not have been charged directly to the company, but to the audit firm, which could then have recharged it. Was Darius Harken working for the weeks in question, or is it recorded as holiday in the audit firm's records?

(iv) Does the invoice actually represent a significant example of hospitality being accepted by the audit manager?

BPP LEARNING MEDIA

(v)   Did the audit manager travel alone, with family, or even with the Chief Executive? Does this indicate that the audit manager has a close personal relationship with the Chief Executive?

Hospitality/close personal relationship

It is possible that points (iv) and (v) above may be indicated by the invoice.

In terms of accepting hospitality, ACCA's guidance is the same as was discussed above in relation to accepting goods. It is unlikely that paying for an auditor's flight would be considered on normal commercial terms, because it would be traditional for the audit firm simply to recharge the cost of a business trip. Taking steps such as these would help to reduce the suggestion that something inappropriate has occurred, if the trip was genuinely business related.

If the trip was for pleasure (a) it should not have been charged to the company, which raises several auditing issues in its own right and (b) it does not come within the definition of 'trivial and inconsequential'.

In terms of close business or personal relationships, ACCA's guidance states that these might adversely affect, or appear to affect, the objectivity of the auditor. It seems likely that in this instance, if the Chief Executive and the audit manager have been on holiday together, or at least a business 'jolly', then as a minimum objectivity will **appear** to be threatened.

Action to be taken

(i)   The audit firm should check their personnel records and see whether Darius Harken was working or holidaying at the relevant time.

(ii)   If the trip was business related, the audit partner should check why the cost has been invoiced to the company by the Chief Executive and not by the audit firm.

(iii)   If the trip was personal, then the audit manager appears to have threatened the objectivity of the audit, and indeed, given that the trip appears to have been taken around the time the prior year audit was taking place, that audit is also adversely affected.

(iv)   The prior year audit files should be subjected to a cold review and the audit manager should be replaced on this year's audit, which should also be subject to a quality control review.

(v)   All invoices rendered to the company in respect of the jet should be scrutinised by the audit team, for further evidence of personal expenses being charged to the company.

(c)   **The impending marriage of the Chief Executive**

The Chief Executive's assistant is the former accountant in charge of the audit of Aventura, who is likely to have been involved with the audit of the previous year end. She has just announced her engagement to the Chief Executive.

Issues arising

(i)   Current year audit – there is a risk of loss of independence, as the Chief Executive's assistant is aware of audit method.

(ii)   Prior year audit – there is a suggestion that the accountant in charge of the audit may have been in a personal relationship with the Chief Executive which may have adversely affected her objectivity.

Movement of audit staff

Ethical guidance states that where a member of the audit team gains employment with an audit client, then familiarity and intimidation threats may arise. Where a 'significant connection' remains then no safeguards could reduce the risk to an acceptable level.

If there is no significant connection, then the IESBA suggests a number of safeguards in this situation, such as:

* Considering the appropriateness of modifying the plan for the engagement
* Assigning the audit team to someone of sufficient experience in relation to the person who has left
* Involving an additional accountant not previously associated with the audit to review

Action to be taken

Although the accountant in charge was not the most senior staff member on the audit, it would have been prudent to modify the audit plan before this year's audit. However, this does not appear to have been done, and the audit is nearing completion.

Therefore, it is important that Voest implement the third bullet point above, and conduct a quality control review of this audit.

In relation to the suspicion that Ms Fennimore's objectivity may have been affected last year, it might also be a good idea to conduct a similar review of last year's audit work, evidence obtained and conclusions drawn. However, as the work should have been reviewed by an audit manager and partner after Ms Fennimore's involvement, the risk of a problem on last year's audit appears to be slight.

4 Professional responsibilities

Tutor's hint. You should expect at least one discussion question on your paper, which will probably be optional. This question requirement was not typical of a discussion question you could expect but is good practice for your essay skills.

You should discuss who else has responsibilities in relation to fraud itself, given that auditors actually have no direct responsibility.

Remember, when attempting an essay question, you should always set out all the sides to an argument, not just the ones you agree with, although you should always draw a conclusion at the end. Make sure your answer is justifiable given the arguments you have made. You should not introduce new arguments in your conclusions.

Responsibility of auditors

Before considering whether it is practical or desirable for auditors to accept a general responsibility to detect fraud and other irregularities, it should be recognised that they already have a responsibility to obtain reasonable assurance that the financial statements are free from material misstatements whether caused by fraud or error.

It must also be acknowledged that the **primary responsibility** for preventing and detecting fraud must always **rest with the management of the entity**. It is they who have been given the responsibility to safeguard the assets of the entity while the auditor's primary responsibility is to express an opinion on the financial statements.

Extend responsibility?

However, it can be seen that the shareholders', the Government's and the public's expectations of the auditor are changing and they are **increasingly calling on the auditor** to **widen their responsibility**.

One of the problems that may arise is the **difficulty of defining fraud**. Associated with this is the need for the auditor to determine an **appropriate level of materiality**.

Currently the auditor assesses materiality in relation to the true and fair view shown by the financial statements. This may no longer be the correct basis if all or most frauds have to be detected.

Fraud itself can cover several types of activities at various levels within the company. Should the auditor be expected to detect a petty theft committed by a junior employee? If not, how is a line drawn between insignificant and important frauds? The guidelines define fraud as involving the use of deception to obtain an unjust or illegal financial advantage.

The desirability of changing the auditor's responsibility has to be considered in the light of different types of organisations and different interested parties. It would seem to be reasonable for the auditor of a financial institution, where depositors' savings are at risk, to have a greater responsibility for the detection of fraud than the auditor of a small private company run by proprietors. Similarly, the auditors of public companies should have a greater responsibility than those of private companies. This would reflect the public's expectations of the role of the modern auditor and legislation should react to these expectations.

Since fraud invariably has an impact on either the accounting records or the financial statements, it is generally accepted that auditors need to plan their audits so that they have a reasonable expectation of detecting material misstatements caused by fraud.

While few people would disagree that the auditor should have some responsibility for the detection of fraud, it may be that widening the auditor's role would mean that additional audit costs would be incurred by all organisations to detect fraud in a mere handful of cases.

Perhaps auditors should advise management how to prevent and detect fraud and penalties for it should be increased so that there is a greater deterrent. If organisations could prevent fraud more effectively there would not be such a need for auditors to try to detect it.

As to the practicalities of detection, fraud can be very difficult to detect where internal control systems are very weak. Some types of fraud may require special expertise to be detected. All auditors should already be detecting frauds and irregularities which give rise to material errors in financial statements. Procedures used to detect immaterial frauds would principally be an extension of the usual audit procedures but the time taken to **extend the level of testing** would be considerable.

The auditor judges the amount of work necessary on the need to obtain sufficient, reliable evidence on which to form an opinion on the view shown by the financial statements. If the auditor's objective was changed, while the **method would principally be the same**, the amount of **work necessary** would **increase significantly**. The auditor would not accept a greater responsibility for detecting fraud without a **substantial fee increase**. It is questionable whether this would be considered worthwhile for most organisations.

There is also the **practical difficulty** of **to whom the auditors report a fraud**. If senior management is involved and the auditor has no real proof and there is no material effect on the financial statements, then the auditor will have to seek legal advice on what action should be taken. The auditor is bound by their **duty of confidentiality** from disclosing it to the appropriate authorities without the client's permission. However, the duty of confidence is not absolute, and the auditors may disclose matters to a proper authority either in the public interest or for other specific reasons.

An associated problem which might arise is a **deterioration in the relationship** between the auditor and the client. If they had to report directly to the authorities, the client may be reluctant to provide information which might cast suspicion over everyone.

Conclusion

Auditors have the skills necessary to detect most types of fraud but the **cost** of doing so **may exceed the likely benefits**. The approach I advise is for the auditor to make recommendations to management about how they could reduce the likelihood of fraud or irregularities and increase the possibility of detection.

5 Mobile Sales

(a) There are various key audit procedures which would have uncovered the fraud perpetrated by Mr A Long. Note that the first two tests would bring to the attention of the auditor the substantial inherent and control risk surrounding the accounts of Mobile Sales, thus increasing their perceived audit risk, and putting them on their guard.

Analytical procedures

The auditor should perform analytical procedures in order to compare the company's results with those of other companies in the same business sector. In particular, the auditor should look at sales growth rates and gross profit margins, but also inventory holding levels, non-current assets and return on capital. This should indicate that the company's results are unusual for the sector, to a great extent.

Review of service contracts

The auditor should examine the directors' service contracts. It is unusual for **all** directors to be paid such substantial bonuses, although the payment of bonuses of some sort to directors is common business practice. It is the size of the bonuses in proportion to the directors' base salaries which is the problem here. It increases both the inherent and control risk for the auditor because it reduces the directors' objectivity about the performance of the company. Audit risk is thus increased.

Testing of sales, purchases and inventories

(i) The main audit test to obtain audit evidence for sales would be to require direct confirmations from the sales agents. These confirmations would also provide evidence for the balance owed to Mobile Sales at the year end and the inventories held by the agent at the year end. Replies to such confirmations should be sent direct to the auditor who would agree the details therein to the company's records or reconcile any differences. Where replies are not received, alternative procedures would be carried out, which might include visits to the agents themselves to examine their records.

(ii) A selection of agents should, in any case, be visited at the year end to confirm the inventories held on sale or return by physical verification. The auditor should count such inventories and consider obsolescence, damage etc.

(iii) Fictitious agents might be discovered by either of tests (iii) and (iv), but a further specific procedure would be to check authorisation of and contracts with all the sales agents. Correspondence could also be reviewed from throughout the year.

(iv) The practice of 'selling' all the inventory to the agents and them repurchasing it after the year end should be detected by sales and purchases cut-off tests around the year end. All transactions involving inventory items returned after the year end should be examined.

Testing of non-current assets

Non-current asset testing should help to identify inventory purchases which have been invoiced as non-current assets.

(i) Samples of additions to non-current assets can be checked to the non-current asset register and to the asset itself.

(ii) Physical verification will ensure that an asset is being used for the purpose specified, and this should be relatively straightforward to check as the computers will each have individual identification codes.

(iii) Where the assets cannot be found, then it may be possible to trace the asset to inventories, perhaps via the selling agents' confirmations, or to sales already made.

Related parties review

The level of collusion with suppliers makes detection of fraud difficult, but the auditor may be put on guard if he discovers that the suppliers are related parties to Mobile Sales. A related party review would normally take place as part of an audit.

(b) The type of 'confidentiality agreement' signed by the auditor of Mobile Sales has reduced the scope of the audit to such an extent that it has become almost meaningless.

While it is understandable that companies would wish to protect sensitive commercial information, the auditor has the right to any information they feel is necessary in the performance of their duties. This agreement clearly circumvents that right. Moreover, such information would still be protected if released to the auditor, because the auditor is under a duty of confidentiality to the client.

In reducing the scope of the audit to this extent, the agreement prevents the auditor obtaining sufficient appropriate evidence to support an audit opinion. The auditor's opinion should therefore be modified on the grounds of inability to obtain sufficient appropriate audit evidence, possibly to the extent of a full disclaimer.

In failing to issue such a modification, the auditor may well have acted negligently and even unlawfully in signing such an agreement.

(c) A review of interim accounts is very different from an audit of year-end financial statements. In an auditor's report, positive assurance is given on the truth and fairness of the financial statements. The level of audit work will be commensurate with the level of the assurance given, that is it will be stringent, testing the systems producing the accounts and the year-end figures themselves using a variety of appropriate procedures.

BPP
LEARNING MEDIA

In the case of a review of interim financial statements, the auditor gives only negative assurance, that they have not found any indication that the interim accounts are materially misstated. The level of audit work will be much less penetrating, varied and detailed than in a full audit. The main audit tools used to obtain evidence will be analytical procedures and direct enquiries of the company's directors.

(d)   It is not the duty of the auditor to prevent or detect fraud. The auditor should, however, conduct the audit in such a way as to expect to detect any material misstatements in the financial statements, caused by fraud. At the planning stage, the auditor should assess the risk that fraud is occurring both at the financial statement and the assertion level and plan their procedures accordingly. Where fraud is suspected or likely, the auditor should carry out additional procedures in order to confirm or deny this suspicion.

Even if a fraud is uncovered after an audit, the auditor will have a defence against a negligence claim if it can be shown that auditing standards were followed and that no indication that a fraud was taking place was received at any time.

Application of principles to this case

In this particular case, Mr A Long has taken a great deal of trouble to cover up his fraudulent activities, using accomplices, bribing people, cooking up fictitious documents etc. When such a high level fraud is carried out, the auditor might find it extremely difficult to uncover the true situation or even to realise anything was amiss. The auditor is also entitled to accept the truth of representations made to them and documents shown to them which purport to come from third parties.

On the other hand, the auditor should have a degree of professional skepticism. The auditor should be aware of the risks pertaining to the company and should recognise that controls can be overridden by collusion or by management actions. The suspicions of the auditor should have been aroused by the rapid growth rate of the company and fairly standard audit procedures on cut-off and non-current assets should have raised matters which required explanation.

Where the auditor has been most culpable, however, is in signing the confidentiality agreement. This restricted the scope of the audit to such an extent that the auditor should have known that there was insufficient evidence to support their opinion. The auditor will therefore find it difficult to defend a negligence claim.

6 Osbourne plc

(a)   The six elements of a firm's system of quality control are:

- Leadership responsibilities for quality within the firm
- Relevant ethical requirements
- Acceptance and continuance of client relationships and specific engagements
- Human resources
- Engagement performance
- Monitoring

(b)   The issues are:

Firm culture

ISQC 1 requires that firms implement policies such that the internal culture of the firm emphasises the importance of quality control. It is the leaders of the firm who are responsible for creating and maintaining this culture through their actions and messages. In other words, the entire business strategy of the firm should be driven by the need for quality in its operations. The personnel responsible for establishing and maintaining the firm's system of quality control must understand ISQC 1.

In this case two factors indicate that there is a lack of leadership on quality control:

(i)   The partner responsible for quality control has resigned and has not been replaced. While this may not have a direct impact on the audit of Osbourne plc, the fact that there is no one responsible for quality control in the firm increases the risk that quality control deficiencies will go undetected.

(ii)   The firm is under pressure to complete the audit and provide other services for the same fee as last year, in spite of the fact that additional work will be required. There is a risk that quality will suffer, as audit work will not be carried out as thoroughly as it should be in order to complete the work within budget. This problem is exacerbated by the potential lack of proper quality control review due to the departure of the quality control partner.

The quality control partner should be replaced as soon as possible. The budget for the audit of Osbourne should be monitored carefully. The audit should be conducted properly and in accordance with ISAs. Any cost overruns should be discussed with the client and additional fees negotiated if necessary.

Ethical requirements

A firm should have procedures in place to ensure that staff are aware of ethical requirements and comply with these. In this case the implementation of the system has not been completed. While members of staff who are members of a professional body eg ACCA should be aware of their responsibilities, they may not have all the relevant information to avoid an inadvertent breach of the regulations eg details of all companies who are clients of the firm.

The implementation of the system started by the previous ethics partner should be completed.

Monitoring

The fact that the auditor partner is new and the previous partner is no longer with the firm increases the risk regarding audit monitoring. As the current audit partner is new they will not have an extensive knowledge of the audit client initially. The tight deadline for the audit accentuates this problem.

To decrease this risk the audit partner must gain an understanding of the business in accordance with ISAs. If possible, it may be appropriate to retain the audit manager and audit senior from the previous year to aid continuity. Andrews may also consider a second partner review to ensure that quality control standards have been maintained.

(c)   Fees should be set on the basis of the time spent and the skills and experience of the personnel involved. They should not be undertaken on a contingency basis and should not be influenced or determined by the provision of non-audit services.

7 PLD Associates

Tutor's hint. The assessment of audit risk is a fundamental part of each audit and in considering whether to accept audit clients it will **always** be necessary to carry out some kind of work to assess the overall risk at a client. Do not be tempted just to give a list of common risks; you must relate your answer to the situation given in the question. In this situation, you should have identified key words in the scenario, such as 'develop derelict land', 'taxation authorities became suspicious', 'internal controls had deficiencies'. This explains why the company was high risk and point you particularly to parts (iv) and (v) in the answer to (a). However, the requirement in (a) is not for you to identify the risk – so make sure you answer the question set and look past the risk to the procedures an audit firm would carry out to identify if the risk was too great to accept the audit. Remember also the importance of CDD procedures to avoid problems associated with clients who launder money.

Part (b) requires assessment of information given in the question, but parts (c) and (d) can be answered without reference to the scenario. Do not fall into a trap of trying to relate your answer to these parts simply to this scenario. Use the scenario to prompt you if you wish, but you should use your general knowledge to answer much of this section.

(a)   PLD Associates is a high-risk client on two counts:

(i)   The **nature of its business is property development**, a high-risk activity

(ii)   The **deficiencies of the company's internal control system** and the lack of integrity of the founder Mr J Scott

With such a potential client, the auditors must ensure that there are no independence or other ethical problems likely to cause conflict with the ethical code before accepting the appointment. They must also carry out customer due diligence to guard against accepting a client who launders money (remember, retaining the proceeds of any crime, eg tax evasion, is money laundering).

The procedures which an audit firm should carry out before accepting a potentially high audit risk client are:

(i)   **Request** the prospective clients' **permission to communicate** with the **previous auditors**. If such permission is refused, the appointment should be declined.

(ii)   On receipt of permission the prospective auditors should **request** in writing of the previous auditors all **information** which ought to be made available to them to enable them to decide whether they are prepared to accept nomination.

        The information requested from the old auditors could go as far as asking about the integrity of the management of PLD Associates.

(iii)   Ensure that the firm's **existing resources are adequate** to service the needs of the new client. This will raise questions of staff and time availability and the firm's technical expertise. This will be important in the case of PLD Associates, as property development is a specialist area.

(iv)   **Seek references** in respect of the new client company; it may be, as is often the case, that the directors of the company are already personally known to the firm; if not, independent enquiries should be made concerning the status of the company and its directors. Agencies such as Dun & Bradstreet might be of assistance, together with a formal search at the Companies Registry. The search at the Companies Registry will uncover the modified audit report if a copy of this has not already been obtained. It will be necessary to find out whether any regulatory authority has disciplined the company.

(v)   A **preliminary assessment of audit risk** should be made. This will involve discussions with the management of the client and assessing the internal control structure (which in the case of the PLD Associates is obviously poor).

(vi)   The **costs and benefits** of accepting the client should be estimated; this appointment may be considered too costly in terms of potential liability (or raised insurance premiums) and bad publicity.

(b)   Ethical guidelines issued by the accountancy institutes require that the auditors are **independent and objective**. It is the integrity of the auditors which gives weight to the audit opinion. In this case, the partner has shown a singular lack of integrity by maintaining this secret fund; his objectivity as an auditor has been impaired by his lack of independence. He has also contravened ethical guidelines by carrying out the **preparation** of **accounting records** for a **quoted company**.

The partner has, however, gone farther than this omission of fundamental ethical principles; he has in fact **colluded** with the **managing director** to conceal questionable transactions from fellow directors and shareholders. In the worst case, this could be with a view to defrauding the company of which he is auditor. He has also concealed transactions which should have been disclosed to the taxation authorities. His position as auditor is untenable and his audit opinion, once knowledge of his involvement is known, is valueless. He may also face criminal prosecution for money laundering.

(c) The measures that audit firms might introduce to try to minimise the practice of 'opinion shopping' by prospective audit clients are as follows.

    (i) To **establish why the question is being asked**. Is the prospective client looking for auditors who will confirm his views on the treatment of a particular transaction? He may be trying to use this against his current auditors with whom he is in dispute.

    (ii) No **opinion** should be **given** until the **present auditors** have been **informed**. This is not only a matter of courtesy but may also reveal other aspects to the problem which had not been forthcoming from the prospective client.

    (iii) If an audit firm decides to give an opinion it should do so **in writing** giving the facts of the problem as it has been presented to them. This will protect the audit firm against the situation where an incorrect opinion is given because the facts have been misrepresented by the prospective client to order to get the opinion which concurred with their own.

Current legislation exists to protect auditors, allowing them to present their case against removal to the members. Similarly, when the auditors resign they are required to make a **statement** regarding the resignation which must be sent to the **Registrar** and everyone who is entitled to receive the financial statements.

In future the Review Panel might take a more active role in finding sets of accounts where an 'opinion shopper' has succeeded in obtaining an unmodified opinion which is unjustified.

(d) Audit firms can reduce the risk of litigation and its effects upon the audit practice by ensuring:

    (i) **Auditing standards are applied** on all assignments

    (ii) **Adequate quality control procedures** are in force

    (iii) **Adequate review procedures** are in operation before a new client is accepted

    (iv) **Adequate PI insurance** is obtained (this does not reduce the risk of litigation but limits the damage it causes)

8 Marsden Manufacturing Co

Tutor's hint. In part (a), it is vitally important that you do not just bang out the percentage indicators, but that you show the examiner that you are considering qualitative factors as well. You will probably get one mark for the calculations – the rest are available for considered comment.

In part (b) work through the scenario, looking out for items you think will be relevant or that raise questions (or exclamation) marks in your head. The examiner doesn't just include things in exam questions to take up paper. Think to yourself 'what does that mean for the company/the audit?'. However, you don't have to get 100% on this question to pass the paper, so don't waste time trying to think of points for every word in the question – if you really can't see anything relevant in the information, move on to the next thing you are told.

Part (c) should represent easy marks, as there are three or four key administrative matters which require attending to on every audit, none of which have been mentioned in the scenario. Remember lists such as 'administrative planning matters' so that you can always get easy marks like these. But don't mention things on your list that the question has discounted – that is obviously a waste of your time. For example, in this question, don't talk about deciding whether to use computers on this audit, because the question states that the partner has decided not to.

Part (d) is another source of useful marks on this question. You should be able to discuss the basic issues relating to conflicts of interest, draw a conclusion in this case and then discuss steps to take, such as discussing it with both parties. It is unlikely in this case that the firm should divest either audit – don't fall into the trap of making over the top suggestions.

(a) **Materiality considerations**

Value indicators

The traditional indicators of materiality levels which would apply in this situation are as follows.

	Band A $	Band B $
Revenue (1/2%/1%)	12,670	25,340
Profit before tax (5%)	3,050	–
Total assets (1%/2%)	10,090	20,180
Net assets (2%/5%)	7,360	18,400

A simple average of these indicators would give materiality of $13,870. This is a useful numerical indicator, but there are also some qualitative features that should be considered.

Qualitative features

As interest is an important figure to the company due to its agreements with the bank, it might be wise to include profit before interest and tax rather than profit before tax in the calculations. This would raise the average figure given above to $13,970.

Net assets are also important to the company, due to the bank agreement. The agreement requires current assets to be 1.5 times current liabilities. On the statement of financial position given, that would be $586,000. The current assets are well above that at the moment. However, when considering materiality, the auditor should look at matters cumulatively. The ratio is material to the statement of financial position, so any issues relevant to that ratio may be material, regardless of value.

Conclusion

I would therefore set planning materiality at $14,000. However, I would treat issues arising in relation to net current assets as potentially material, and consider the cumulative impact that any issues had.

(b) **Audit risks at Marsden Manufacturing**

Inherent risks

> Using the components of audit risk might help you identify the risks, or a greater breadth of risks, in the scenario in the first place.

> Breaking up your answer into the components of audit risk helps to structure your answer.

The key issue relating to the statement of financial position in the year is the **factoring of receivables**. This raises a number of issues for the audit.

The first issue is questions behind the factoring of debt: **why have they been factored**? This is answered by the fact that the company is seeking a form of insurance against bad debts so that its interest cover will be maintained. However, it is important to check that this is the only reason, ie that the debt is not being factored because there are **cash flow** problems (which might also be indicated by the fall in cash in the year) which could in turn lead to suspicions of **going concern** issues.

> You do not need to go into long details here, but should be aware of the issues that make this risky for the audit.

Specifically in relation to **receivables**, it raises issues of whether they have yet been accounted for in the statement of financial position and **properly disclosed** according to their substance. When there is a high transfer of all significant risks and rewards to the factor and as the entire sales ledger function has been outsourced to the factor, this needs investigation. Derecognising receivables would clearly be **material** to the statement of financial position, and could have an impact on the covenant with the bank although there would also be a significant influx of cash, so the net effect on net assets might not affect the net assets ratio too badly. If the factoring has already been accounted for, then cash appears to be dangerously low (given that an injection of cash should have just occurred). This would have serious implications for the going concern assumption. However, as there is a large debit balance in receivables, it appears more likely that the factoring has not yet been accounted for.

The **relationship with the bank** is clearly important to the business, and has been mentioned already. However, the whole issue of relationship with the bank must be considered for audit purposes, particularly as there appears to be a **worsening cash position** and there is a question mark over the factoring of receivables. **Going concern** is a risk on this audit, particularly if **accounting issues** such as the one mentioned above radically change the statement of financial position and have an **impact on the debt covenants**.

Connected to the issue of the factoring is the position of the former sales ledger clerk, Sally Forsyth. As part of the restructuring, she has been dismissed. She appears to be bringing a claim against the company for unfair dismissal and sexual discrimination. It is unclear whether she has grounds for such action.

However, there is a **potential material contingent liability**. During the course of the audit it will be vital to investigate this affair and consider whether the potential liability falls within the **timing requirements of IAS 37** (when were the key dates?). If Ms Forsyth has been dismissed before the year end it is likely that there is a legal obligation arising, if she has a case. To consider whether she has a case or not, it may be necessary to **seek an expert legal opinion**.

Following up from the issues noted at the inventory count, there appears to a be problem with **possible inventory obsolescence**. In the absence of any further explanation for the inventory increase, this is borne out by the fact that inventory has risen on the statement of financial position from last year. It is unclear whether this may be material or not, however, given that current assets are material by their nature given the agreement with the bank and the possible effects of FRS 5 on receivables, **this matter may be material by its nature**.

Control risk

As part of control risk evaluation, the auditor must consider the **effect of receivables factoring** on the systems of the business and the fact that the sales ledger function is now outsourced, and has been for a portion of the year under review. The **related controls must be assessed**. There is also a risk that the **controls over the transfer** from in-house sales ledger to outsourced sales ledger may not have been strong, and that errors could have been made.

Detection risk

There are some key detection issues to consider. The first, as mentioned above, is that an **expert** may be required on this audit to obtain evidence about the contingent liability. The second is that the requirements of ISA 402 must be considered in relation to the outsourced sales ledger function. The auditor must ensure that they have all the **information they requires from the service provider**.

(c) **Administrative planning matters**

The engagement partner must organise a **planning meeting** to discuss the audit with the team.

The supervisor needs to obtain **key dates** relating to the audit, such as the dates of the manager and partner reviews, and client related dates, such as when final accounts will be ready and when the accounts need to be signed by.

The supervisor needs to obtain **client permission to contact** the company's **solicitor** and the **factor** and they need to **organise when the audit team will be able to liaise with them**.

(d) **Conflict of interest**

Does a conflict exist?

It is important to set out that you are not in possession of enough details to come to a conclusion on this matter, stating what the relevant factors are.

The audit firm is in possession of information about Marsden's new client which Marsden would be interested in, which is sensitive information. However, it is also information it could have obtained by conducting a credit rating or search on the new customer, which it should have (and therefore may have) done for a customer of such magnitude.

It is obviously in Wallworth's best interests that its auditors do not share information about its poor payment history with its new supplier.

Whether a conflict exists depends on the size of the audit firm and the procedures put in place in the audit department to maintain the independence of the two audits. In a small department it is likely that it will be difficult in practice to keep matters completely confidential. (In other words, one audit team is likely to be aware of facts relating to the other audit client.)

What steps should the auditor take?

In this situation, it is probably best that the auditor makes both parties aware that they are the auditors for both companies and restate their duty of confidentiality to both. It may be wise to revisit the engagement letter for both clients to ensure that the duties and procedures in relation to this potential conflict are set out.

Remember, draw a reasonable conclusion, based on the facts.

9 Herzog

Text references. Chapters 6, 7 and 8

Top tips. Read the question carefully and jot down an answer plan first. It is important to avoid certain pitfalls; the most obvious of these is stating that there is a going concern risk. There is no such risk – Herzog is not a going concern. The risk arises from the fact that the going concern risk has already been realised. Hopefully by reading the question carefully, you observed this. Once you understand that the company has stopped trading, other risks should occur to you as you read – for instance, your general business knowledge should make you think that the inventory of a company which has stopped trading might be risky. When a company stops trading, it is likely to incur liabilities (staff redundancy, litigation from affected parties). In this question various liabilities and potential liabilities were clearly signposted for you. By jotting down an answer plan you can prioritise and make sure you get marks for the easier risks rather than getting bogged down in more complicated matters, such as the treatment of the various assets. In part (b) it is important to specifically contrast the use of these audit procedures with prior years rather than to just talk generally about the procedures. In part (c), again, be specific about the situation Herzog is in. A simple receivables' circularisation may not be sufficient in this complex situation.

Easy marks. This was a demanding question in which there were no easy marks as such. To ensure you gain marks when attempting this question, make sure that you try and answer each part, as generally it is easier to get one or two marks for a requirement than the total number on offer.

Examiner's comments. In part (a) there was nothing to suggest a lack of integrity on the part of management or cash flow problems. Accounting aspects were not dealt with well given clear indicators of the nature of a lease (in this case operating), speculation on the appropriate accounting treatment was rendered completely irrelevant. Some candidates were so careless in reading the scenario that they supposed that Herzog was buying patented technology and manufacturing equipment from the multinational corporation. The general lack of comprehension of a 'going concern' was overwhelming. Numerous candidates stated that laying off the workforce would lead to going concern issues. Herzog was not a going concern. In part (b) candidates should not regurgitate lower level knowledge.

Marks

(a) **Risks of material misstatement**

Generally ½ mark for identification +
1 mark each point of explanation
(in context of planning final audit)
Ideas
- Inventory – lower of cost and NRV
- Going concern – basis of presentation
- Employee liabilities
- Sale of assets – derecognition
- Remaining assets – impairment
- Accounting – errors and increased control risk
- Onerous contracts – provision
- Product warranties – provision
- Breach of contract – provision/disclosure

13

(b) **Extent of reliance on audit evidence**

Generally 1 mark each point of explanation/comparison
Up to maximum 5 each (i) and (ii)
Ideas
Analytical procedures – less (conclusion)
- Material items requiring 100% testing
- Relevance of available information
- Comparability of available information (ten months)
- Efficiency and effectiveness of alternative procedures
- Proviso – still of some use
Written representations from management – more (conclusion)
- Matters of judgement and opinion
- Knowledge confined to management
- Proviso – limitation on possible reliance

10

(c) **Principal audit work**

Generally 1 mark each area of principal audit work
Maximum 4 marks each (i) and (ii)
Ideas
Amounts due from distributors
- Ledger account balances
- After-date cash (any?)
- Agreements – penalties accruing
- Settlement offered (any?)
Lease liabilities
- Prior period working papers – operating leases
- Onerous contract (IAS 37)
  - Early exit?
  - Continuing economic benefit?
- Prior year IAS 17 disclosure (reconciliation)

8

Professional marks – up to

4

35

Notes for inclusion in planning section of audit working papers

Subject: Herzog Co – audit planning

Introduction

These notes explain the risks of material misstatement to be taken into account in planning the audit. They also explain how the extent of the reliance to be placed on analytical procedures and written representations

should compare with that for the prior year audit. Finally, they describe the principal audit work to be performed in respect of the carrying amount of the amounts due from distributors and lease liabilities.

(a) **Risks of material misstatement**

    (i)   **Basis of accounting.** The company is no longer a **going concern** and therefore it would be inappropriate for the financial statements to be prepared on the going concern basis. The auditors must ensure that the financial statements have been prepared on a **liquidation basis** and this fact has been **disclosed**, together with the reasons for the different basis. This will mean that assets have to be reclassified from non-current to current and they should be carried at their recoverable amounts.

    (ii)   **Sale of assets.** The company is selling **equipment** and also the **associated patents**. Given that the deal is lucrative, this is likely to be at a profit, which will be an **item requiring special presentation or disclosure** in the financial statements. The auditors must ensure that the **non-current assets have been correctly removed** from the statement of financial position and that the profit on sale is correctly accounted for and disclosed in financial statements.

    (iii)   **Premises.** The unsold properties may meet the requirements of IFRS 5 at the end of the reporting period, in which case they should be separately classified as 'held for sale' and carried at the lower of depreciated cost and fair value less estimated costs to sell. After-date losses on disposal would give evidence of impairment, but this is unlikely given that Herzog carries assets at depreciated cost.

    (iv)   **Inventory.** Inventory remaining at 1 May is being sold without extended warranty which may affect its realisable value, and the auditors must ensure that it is correctly accounted for at the **lower of cost or net realisable value**.

    (v)   **Employee liabilities and costs.** There will certainly be **liabilities outstanding** for employees not made redundant at 31 December 20X2 but there may also be liabilities in respect of redundancy payments outstanding for the employees made redundant earlier in the year. The auditor must ensure that the costs and any outstanding liabilities are correctly accounted for. There may also be claims arising from employees who feel their statutory rights have been breached which might require disclosure or provision.

    (vi)   **Warranties.** Although from 1 November extended warranties are no longer being offered, it appears the standard one-year warranty is still being offered and there will be outstanding one-year and longer warranties from previous sales which must be provided against under IAS 37.

    (vii)   **Penalties arising from breach of contract.** It appears that Herzog's contracts with its distributors contained terms binding Herzog to pay penalties in the event of breach of contract. The distributors are claiming these penalties and the penalties are therefore liabilities which must be recognised in the financial statements. The contracts with the suppliers may also contain penalty clauses and, if this is the case, these penalties should be accounted for as liabilities in a similar fashion to the penalties due to distributors above.

    (viii)   **Leases – onerous contracts.** Although the leases are operating and therefore are usually accounted for on a rental basis, now the company has ceased operations, the unavoidable costs of meeting the contract exceed the economic benefits which Herzog can expect to obtain from the contract now, and therefore a provision for the total expected costs of the operating leases must be set up. As the head office will still be used, this should continue to be accounted for on an annual basis.

    (ix)   **Accounts department.** Control risk may be increased as a result of the reduction of accounts staff due to the loss of experts or the increased chance of errors being made with fewer staff and non-routine transactions.

(b) **Audit approach – contrast with prior year**

    (i)   *Analytical procedures*

         When carrying out analytical procedures, auditors compare like figures (current year to prior year) and predictable relationships. However, due to the unusual factor in the year of the company ceasing to operate, any comparison with the prior year will be meaningless.

The figures for the current year are prepared on a different basis and there is no comparability in the situation of Herzog over the two years. Similarly, it is unlikely that the auditor will be able to compare to budgets, as the sale occurred late in the year and is unlikely to have been budgeted for.

The auditors will therefore be unable to use analytical procedures in the same way as they have in previous years. In addition, different materiality requirements may necessitate other substantive procedures being used so that items can be 100% verified.

However, this does not preclude the auditors from using analytical procedures looking at predicable relationships. For example, there will still be a predictable relationship between sales and warranty provision as there will have been in previous years. In addition, in this year, there is likely to be predictable relationships in respect of the redundancy payments and provision ($x for each year of service, for example).

Conclusion

There is likely to be less use of analytical procedures in the 20X2 audit, although there will be scope to use analytical procedures in a different way than in previous years.

(ii) *Written representations from management*

The auditor is required to obtain general written representations about the following.

- Management's responsibility for the fair presentation of financial statements
- Management has provided the auditor with all relevant information and access as agreed in the terms of the audit engagement, and all transactions have been recorded and are reflected in the financial statements.
- Management's belief that the aggregate of uncorrected financial statements is immaterial
- Where the auditor determines that it is necessary to obtain one or more written representations to support other audit evidence relevant to the financial statements or one or more specific assertions in the financial statements

In this respect, obtaining written representations will be similar to the previous year, as these matters will also have been required then.

However, given the unusual occurrences in the year, there are likely to be more matters requiring specific written representations, as there are more issues where facts are confined to management and that are matters of judgement (for example, provisions and contingent liabilities).

Conclusion

In many respects, written representations will be used in a similar way to the previous audit. However, there are likely to be more items requiring specific written representation due to the unusual events in the year.

(c) **Audit work**

(i) *Amounts due from distributors*

- Obtain list of balances to see individual amounts owed
- Review all after-date receipts (they will all relate to debt existing at the year end) to see whether any debts have been recovered
- Review terms of contracts with distributors to see who is owed penalties and the related terms
- Read correspondence with distributors to ascertain if any deals are being brokered
- Discuss with management their intention towards paying penalties / recovering debts

(ii)   *Lease liabilities*

- Agree opening position from prior year file and note payments in the year
- Review terms of leases to ensure that the leases have become onerous
- Visit the premises affected to ensure that there is no prospect of future economic benefit
- Recalculate the provisions
- Reconcile the provisions to disclosures about leases in the prior year financial statements

Conclusion

These notes have explained that there are many significant audit risks to be considered in the planning of Herzog Co's audit. In particular, we must ensure that adequate procedures are planned in relation to going concern especially. Our use of analytical procedures is likely to be less extensive than in previous years. We will probably be able to make use of written representations to a similar extent, but in a different way from before. Finally, there are some specific procedures to be performed in relation to amounts due from distributors and lease liabilities.

10 Lambley Properties

Tutor's hint. You should not just assume that if the directors refuse to sign the written representation a modification to the audit opinion is automatically required. There are other procedures to undertake first. Remember the circumstances (given in (b)) in which it is permissible to rely on a written representation.

(a)   ISA 580 specifies a number of general representations which management must provide.

These are:

(i)   That management has fulfilled its responsibility for the preparation and presentation of the financial statements as set out in the terms of the audit engagement

(ii)   Whether the financial statements are prepared and presented in accordance with the applicable financial reporting framework

(iii)   That management has provided the auditor with all the relevant information

(iv)   That all transactions have been recorded and are reflected in the financial statements

(v)   A description of management's responsibilities

(vi)   Significant assumptions in accounting estimates have been provided

(vii)   Related party relationships and transactions have been disclosed

(viii)   All subsequent events information has been provided

(ix)   The effect of uncorrected mistakes is immaterial

(b)   Extract from written representation letter

Financial support

Keyworth Builders Co, a subsidiary of the company, is experiencing going concern problems. We confirm that the company will continue to make financial support available to the subsidiary for the foreseeable future.

Claim

Eastwood Manufacturing Co has made a claim against the company for $5 million arising from alleged negligent construction of a building. The claim comprises $3 million for repairs and $2 million for the cost of disruption to Eastwood's business. Following discussions with the company's professional advisers we consider that Eastwood has no claim on the company and therefore no provision for these costs is required in the accounts for the year ended 31 March 20X2. However, the contingency is fully explained in a note to the accounts.

(c) **Reliability of written representation**

The written representation is a written record of statements made by management to auditors during the audit. As it is a written record, it is stronger evidence than oral representations by themselves would be.

However, representations do not come from an independent source. They should not therefore be relied on when other evidence is available or expected to be available.

Nevertheless, representations may be the only available evidence when **based on management intent**, or the matter is **one of judgement** or opinion. Independent confirmation will not be available in these circumstances.

Reliance on letter

On receipt of a written representation the auditors will need to **ensure** that there is **no other evidence** that they have discovered during the course of their audit which conflicts with it. They will then have to **review the representations** made and decide, given the results of the audit testing and their assessment of risk, whether they are able to rely on them to give an unmodified opinion on the accounts.

(d) Work to be performed to check whether a provision should be included in the accounts for the legal claim from Eastwood Manufacturing Co is as follows.

(i) **Obtain and review all correspondence** relating to the claim

(ii) **Review written advice** obtained from the company's lawyer and surveyor

(iii) **Review the original contract** between Eastwood and Lambley to assess the extent of Lambley's responsibility for repairs and any time period limitations

(iv) **Ascertain whether Lambley is covered by insurance** should the claim be payable

(v) **Examine minutes** of meetings of the Board and management which deal with this matter

These procedures will allow the probability of the company having to meet the claim to be assessed. Disclosure and/or provision to comply with IAS 37 *Provisions, contingent liabilities and contingent assets* will be required.

(e) In the circumstances where the directors refuse to sign the written representation because of the legal claim from Eastwood Manufacturing Co the following procedures could be considered.

(i) A **meeting** between the auditors and directors to discuss a revision of the wording of the letter, so allowing the directors to sign

(ii) The integrity of management should be re-evaluated and the reliability of other representations (oral and written) and evidence in general reassessed

(iii) Determine the possible effect on the audit opinion

Assuming that satisfactory representations are not obtained, either because the original letter is amended in such a way that the situation concerning the claim is not properly explained or that the directors refuse to confirm the auditors' statement, then the auditors will need to **consider the implications** of this scope limitation **for their report**.

Given that refusal by the management to give satisfactory representations concerning the claim indicates that they may be uncertain as to the eventual outcome, the auditors would probably decide to qualify their opinion on the grounds of uncertainty.

11 Bestwood Electronics

(a)   (i)   ISA 560 *Subsequent events* states that auditors should perform procedures designed to obtain sufficient appropriate audit evidence that all **subsequent events** up to the date of their report which require adjustment of, or disclosure in, the financial statements have been **identified and properly reflected** therein.

All **adjusting events** (per IAS 10 *Events after the reporting period*) should be incorporated in the financial statements. Non-adjusting subsequent events should be disclosed, where required by IAS 10, in the notes to the financial statements.

The auditor's procedures should be applied to any **matters** examined during the audit which may be **affected by changes** after the year end, eg going concern, or the valuation of assets held at fair value. They are in addition to tests on specific transactions after the period-end, such as cut-off tests.

(ii)   The financial statements are the **responsibility of management**, who would be expected to inform the auditors of any material subsequent events between the date of the auditor's report and the date the financial statements are issued. The auditors do **not** have any obligation to perform procedures, or make enquiries regarding the financial statements **after** the date of their report.

However, if the **auditor** becomes **aware** of **subsequent events** which may materially affect the financial statements, they should:

- Establish whether the financial statements need amendment
- Discuss the matter with those charged with governance
- Consider the implications for their report, taking further action as appropriate

When the financial statements are amended, the auditor should extend the procedures discussed above to the date of the new auditor's report, carry out any other appropriate procedures and issue a new audit report. The new report should not be dated earlier than the date of approval of the amended financial statements.

If the financial statements are not amended (but the auditor thinks that they should be), then the auditor will take action to prevent reliance on the audit report. The action taken will depend on the auditor's legal rights and obligations and the advice of the auditor's legal counsel.

(iii)   Auditors have no obligations to perform procedures or make enquiries regarding the financial statements **after** they have been issued.

However, if they become aware of a fact that, had they been aware of it at the date of the auditor's report, may have led them to amend their report, then the auditor will carry out the following procedures:

(1)   Discuss the matter with management and, where appropriate, those charged with governance

(2)   Determine whether the financial statements need amendment and, if so

(3)   Inquire how management intends to address the matter in the financial statements

If management do not amend the financial statements, then the auditor will take action to prevent reliance on the audit report. The action taken will depend on the auditor's legal rights and obligations and the advice of the auditor's legal counsel.

(b)   The audit work for subsequent events will normally be concerned with asset values at and after the year end. The following procedures will be carried out.

(i)   **Non-current assets**

(1)   **Check for any sales** or proposed sales after the year end which may trigger a write down to net realisable value at the year end.

(2)   **Consider obsolescence** of non-current assets, for example plant used to make a discontinue line, which might only become apparent after the year end.

(ii) **Inventory**

    (1)   **Check post year end selling price** of major items of inventory and compare to value in year-end accounts. Consider write downs to net realisable value.

    (2)   **Consider the possible existence of obsolete, damaged or slow moving inventory** and the consequent value of any write down.

    (3)   **Perform a (limited) inventory count** after the year end **if the existence of all inventory is not known** for certain.

(iii) **Receivables**

    (1)   Review post year end receipts to determine recoverability.

    (2)   Take doubtful debts paid out of the provision and consider writing parts of the provision off for which no money has been received.

    (3)   Review trade press and correspondence and consult the sales manager about any major customers who have become insolvent recently.

    (4)   Check the issue of credit notes and return of goods after the year end to determine the provision for credit notes required in the accounts.

(iv) **Cash at bank**

    (1)   **Check that outstanding items** on the bank reconciliation have **cleared promptly after the year end** (to spot teeming and lading and late payment to payables).

    (2)   **Write back any stale cheques** not cleared (over six months old).

    (3)   **Check all material payments and receipts around the year end** to check the completeness of both accruals and prepayments.

(v) **Trade payables**

    (1)   **Check reconciling items** on suppliers' statements have **cleared promptly** after the year end.

    (2)   If the payables circularisation has been carried out then **examining post year end payments** will help to verify balances where there was no supplier's statement and no reply.

(vi) **Going concern problems and other matters**

The subsequent events review is important in terms of going concern investigations. The following procedures should be carried out as a matter of routine.

    (1)   **Check profit and cash flow forecasts.**

    (2)   **Review management accounts** and reports after the year end.

    (3)   **Review board minutes** after the year end.

    (4)   **Request any information** on subsequent events and going concern matters from the directors and check their information.

    (5)   The **directors should also state** they have given all such information in the letter of representation.

(vii) **Non-adjusting events**

Look for any matters which are non-adjusting but which should be disclosed in the accounts, for example major sales of non-current assets, accidental losses and issues of shares and debentures.

(c)   I will check whether there have been any material events after the reporting period in this period, particularly if there is a significant delay between the date of the auditors' report and the issue of their financial statements. I will not undertake such detailed enquiries as in (b) above, but I will perform the following procedures.

    (i)   **Ask the management or directors if any further material events have occurred** which might affect my opinion on the accounts.

(ii) **Review the latest board minutes, reports and management accounts** issued since the end of the audit.

(iii) Any **matters which were uncertain** at the end of the audit should be **reviewed** again to establish an outcome and any effect on the accounts. Examples would include doubtful debts, contingencies and inventory obsolescence (perhaps due to new developments).

(iv) **Consider any matters** which have **arisen in the industry** or the economy which might affect the company.

12 Bingham Engineering

Tutor's hint. This question combines the issue of the auditors' review of the going concern assumption in financial statements with the review of forecast information. Although you are given a brief scenario in the question, this question is largely based on your learning in these areas and you do not need to apply your knowledge to a scenario. As such, it is not exam standard, but it is a useful exercise to run through your knowledge on these important areas.

(a) The 'going concern' assumption assumes that the accounts are drawn up on the basis that the business will continue to exist as a viable commercial entity, without any need for any significant curtailment in its present level of activity for the 'foreseeable future'.

When forming their opinion at the conclusion of the subsequent events review the auditor should have regard to the term 'foreseeable future' in the context of going concern. While the foreseeable future must be judged in relation to specific circumstances, the auditors should normally expect management to have considered information which relates to a minimum of 12 months following the date of approval of the financial statements.

(b) The most common factors indicating that a company may not be regarded as a going concern are:

(i) Adverse financial figures or ratios:

- Recurring operating losses
- Financing to a considerable extent out of overdue suppliers and other payables
- Heavy dependence on short-term finance for long-term needs
- Working capital deficiencies
- Low liquidity rates
- Overgearing, in the form of high or increasing debt to equity ratios
- Undercapitalisation, particularly if there is a deficiency of share capital and reserves

(ii) Borrowing in excess of limits imposed by debenture trust deeds

(iii) Defaults on loans or similar agreements

(iv) Dividends in arrears

(v) Restrictions placed on usual trade terms

(vi) Excessive or obsolete inventory

(vii) Long overdue receivables

(viii) Non-compliance with statutory capital requirements

(ix) Deterioration of relationship with bankers

(x) Necessity of seeking new sources or methods of obtaining finance

(xi) The continuing use of old non-current assets because there are not funds to replace them

(xii) The size and content of the order book

(xiii) Potential losses on long-term contracts

Other factors, not necessarily suggesting inability to meet debts, may be internal or external matters.

(i)   **Internal matters**

- Loss of key management or staff
- Significantly increasing inventory levels
- Work stoppages or other labour difficulties
- Substantial dependence upon the success of a particular project or particular asset
- Excessive reliance on the success of a new product
- Uneconomical long-term commitments

(ii)   **External matters**

- Legal proceedings or similar matters that may jeopardise a company's ability to continue in business

- Loss of a key franchise or patent

- Loss of a principal supplier or customer

- The undue influence of a market dominant competitor

- Political risks

- Technical developments which render a key product obsolete

- Frequent financial failures of entities in the same industry

The indications above vary in importance and some may only have significance as audit evidence when viewed in conjunction with others.

The significance of the indications above may diminish because they are matched by audit evidence indicating that there are mitigating factors. Indications that the business may be having to sell non-current assets to meet present cash demands may be mitigated by the possibility of obtaining new sources of finance or of renewing and expanding loan finance. Indications of problems that raise questions about the continuation of the business without suggesting inability to meet debts may be mitigated by factors relating to the entity's capacity to adopt alternative courses of action; for example, the likelihood of finding alternative sales markets where a principal customer is lost.

(c)   (i)   Under the present circumstances of the company, it is unlikely that the capital expenditure/disposal forecast will contain many items of capital expenditure because of the adverse effect that this would have on the company's cash flow. For such items as there are, the auditor should check that the quoted costs are reasonable, with any large value items being checked against price lists etc. Enquiries should be made of management as to whether there are any proposed items of capital expenditure not included in the forecast.

In relation to any intended disposals of non-current assets, the auditors should:

(1)   Check whether the proceeds of sale appear to be reasonable, with particular care being taken to see that any estimates are arrived at on a prudent basis

(2)   Consider whether the estimates of the timing of the receipt of sale proceeds appear to be reasonable and, once again, arrived at on a prudent basis

(ii)   The audit work required in relation to the profit forecast would be as follows.

(1)   Check that the level of projected sales is reasonable, being similar to the previous year and consistent with current market conditions and the confirmed orders received from the company's customers.

(2)   Consider whether the gross profit margin appears reasonable in the light of the company's recent experiences and there has been consistency in the recognition of those items affecting the calculation of this key ratio.

(3)   Compare the level of income and expenditure items to the previous year, investigating carefully any areas of significant change. Any projected savings in expenditure must be justified and the auditor should take particular care to see that proper provision has been made for all bank charges and interest.

(4)   All castings and extensions in the profit forecast should be checked and comparison made with common items dealt with in the other two forecasts.

(iii)   The cash flow forecast which is based on the above two forecasts should be checked in the following way.

(1)   The opening balance should be checked to the draft financial statements and the company's cash book. For the expired period of the forecast, the month-end balance should also be checked to the cash book.

(2)   All receipts and payments for the elapsed period of the forecast should be checked against supporting documentation.

(3)   The reasonableness of the timing of future receipts and payments should be considered in the light of the normal period of credit taken by customers and extended by suppliers, due date for payment of income tax etc.

(4)   The consistency of items in the cash flow forecast with the other two forecasts should be considered, as well as consistency and accuracy of forecasts in previous years.

(5)   All castings and extensions in the forecast should be checked.

(d)   The reasonableness of the three forecasts referred to above and the willingness of the company's bankers and other creditors to supply the required funds will be the main factors to consider in assessing whether the company is a going concern.

If the work already carried out suggests that the forecasts are reasonable then, with the permission of the client, some direct confirmation of the future 'co-operation' of the bank and major suppliers should be sought. Such co-operation is more likely to be forthcoming if the company is forecast to make profits rather than losses and consideration should also be given to any security held by the various creditors and the chances of any single creditor precipitating a crisis by seeking to invoke their own security.

13 Locksley

> **Tutor's hint**. The audit of these assets is relatively straightforward, but it relies on your knowledge of the relevant accounting standards. You should cover every aspect of the audit of these items, perhaps by considering the statement of financial position and then the statement of profit or loss and other comprehensive income effects.

(a)   The relevant audit tests are:

(i)   The auditors should **obtain** from the client a **breakdown** of the figure for development expenditure which makes it possible to trace the amounts spent to the nominal ledger and the final accounts.

(ii)   **Tests of controls** should be performed to ensure that a system exists for controlling the authorising and recording of development expenditure, and that the system is operating adequately. (This work may be covered where practicable by the audit tests performed on the company's purchases and payroll systems.)

(iii)   Individual amounts should be **vouched** by reference to **supporting documentation**. The relevant documentation will vary according to the type of expenditure, but tests might include:

(1)   Agree purchases to requisitions, orders, goods received notes, invoices, cash book and bank statement

(2) Agree labour costs to the payroll and to supporting evidence, such as timesheets or job cards

(3) If overheads have been included in the development figure, ensure that they have been calculated on a basis consistent with that used generally by the company

The auditors will wish to set a materiality level for testing individual items; this will have to be established when the breakdown of the total figure is known. For instance, it may be possible to restrict testing considerably if one or two large invoices represent the bulk of the relevant expenditure.

(iv) The **arithmetical accuracy** of the schedule of expenditure should be **checked**.

(v) The auditors should **ensure** that there has been **no double-counting**; that is, that development items capitalised have not also been charged as an expense in the statement of profit or loss.

(vi) Finally, the auditors should carry out a **review of the development figure** in order to be satisfied that it is reasonable and consistent with what else is known about the company and its business.

(b) The following audit procedures may be performed to verify the revaluation gain arising on non-current assets.

(i) Ensure that the **valuer** appears to be **appropriately qualified** and **independent** of the company. If these conditions are not fulfilled, the auditors will need to consider their possible impact on the results of the valuation.

(ii) By reference to the instructions given to the valuer and the valuer's report, ensure that the **valuation** has been **performed on a basis reasonable and consistent** with previous valuations.

(iii) Check that **profits or losses on individual non-current assets** have been **correctly calculated** by reference to the non-current asset register and the detailed analysis of the revaluation.

(iv) **Check the arithmetical accuracy** of the compilation of the **revaluation schedule** and of the **calculation of asset profits and losses**.

(c) IAS 38 lays down the basis on which development costs may be carried forward. They may be carried forward only if, and to the extent that, they represent an **asset** which is likely to generate income for the company in the future. It would contravene the prudence concept to carry forward expenditure which is not reasonably expected to generate future income.

According to IAS 38, development expenditure should be recognised in profit or loss in the year it is incurred, unless it meets all the following criteria.

(i) The technical feasibility of completing the intangible asset so it will be available for use or sale can be demonstrated.

(ii) The entity can demonstrate its intention to complete the intangible asset and use or sell it.

(iii) The entity can demonstrate its ability to use or sell the asset.

(iv) The entity can show how the asset will generate probable future economic benefits.

(v) The availability of adequate technical, financial and other resources to complete the development and to use or sell the asset can be shown.

(vi) The entity can reliably measure the expenditure attributable to the asset during its development.

If, taking a prudent view of the available evidence, these conditions are met, development costs may be deferred and amortised over the period expected to benefit.

(d)   The decision to finance development internally has resulted in a large increase in payables and a decrease in cash and bank balances. This may lead to liquidity problems, especially since the company will still need funds to finance the new product. These funds will have to be generated either by the sale of further investments, the raising of a loan from the directors or an outside investor, or by the issue of shares. If **funding** is **not available**, the **development expenditure** should be **recognised in profit or loss** on the basis that it will not be possible to complete the project. This would eliminate the retained earnings reserve and would create doubts about the company's status as a going concern.

The auditors should discuss with the directors their plans for obtaining **additional finance**, and request that they produce cash flow forecasts in support of these. If the auditors do not obtain satisfactory evidence of the company's ability to obtain finance, it may be necessary to qualify the auditor's opinion on the grounds of going concern problems which have not been fully disclosed.

14 Bainbridge

Inventories

Matters to consider

- Risk that items produced for inventories are misstated due to out of date standards being applied. Inventories are also potentially misstated if no comparison with NRV has been made

- Risk that bespoke items are overstated due to the inclusion in cost of design fees

- Inventory value as a whole is likely to be a material area of the accounts so this is an area where audit effort should be directed. The materiality of any adjustments required needs to be considered. The lowest level of materiality would be $80,000 (5% of profit)

- Whether management has considered the NRV of the inventories on a line by line basis as required by IAS 2 *Inventories*

- Whether the standard costing approach provides the fairest practical approximation to actual cost as required by IAS 2

- Whether the management is justified in maintaining the same standards as last year on the basis that they do reflect current prices (IAS 2 states that standard costs should be reviewed regularly and revised where necessary.)

- Whether overheads have been allocated to inventories based on the normal level of activity

- Whether other overheads have been split between functions (ie production, administration) on a sensible basis

- Whether the capitalisation of design fees relating to the bespoke items is in compliance with IAS 2 (Such 'other costs' can be capitalised only to the extent that they are incurred in bringing the inventories to their present location and condition.)

Evidence to seek

- Confirm with management that they have considered the need to write down certain inventory lines to their NRV. Review any schedules produced by the client to support their conclusions and check that any issues identified by the auditor at the inventory count or in the follow-up work have been reflected in the final inventory valuation.

- Obtain a schedule of the standards applied and compare to last year to determine whether they have remained the same.

- Agree major components to supporting documentation eg materials can be agreed to purchase invoices, labour can be agreed to payroll records.

- Obtain an analysis of the production and other overheads allocated to inventories. Check that these costs are related to the production centre.

- For other overheads determine the way that management have allocated these costs between the different business centres. Determine whether the allocation is reasonable and consistent with previous years.

- Check the calculation of the 'normal' activity levels used to allocate the overheads to units of production. Establish that this does not include the effects of any abnormal events and that it is consistent with previous years.

- Obtain a schedule of design fees capitalised. Agree the details to sales contracts and establish the date on which they were incurred, checking that this was before the commencement of production.

Lease

Matters to consider

- Risk that the lease is incorrectly classified. If it is a finance lease, the lower of present value of the minimum lease payments and fair value should be capitalised and depreciated. If an operating lease, the rentals should be expensed.

- Extent to which the risks and rewards of ownership have been transferred to the lessee (eg who is responsible for maintenance, insurance). According to IAS 17 *Leases*, if the risks and rewards of ownership remain with the lessor the lease would be of an operating nature.

- Basis on which management have decided that the lease is an operating lease. IAS 17 states that the land element of a lease of land and buildings is not normally a finance lease unless title is expected to pass at the end of the lease because, due to its indefinite economic life, the lessee does not receive substantially all the risks and rewards incidental to ownership. The building element, however, could be. This would suggest that the management have come to the right conclusion, at least for the land element.

- Treatment of the rent-free period. IAS 17 states that operating lease rentals should be charged on a straight-line basis over the lease term, even if the payments are not made on such a basis unless another systematic basis is representative of the time pattern of the user's benefit. On this basis the benefit of the rent-free period should be spread over the lease term rather than being taken upfront.

- The likelihood of management taking up the option to extend the lease. IAS 17 states that the lease term should include any further terms for which the lessee has the option to continue to lease the asset with or without payment if it is reasonably certain at the inception of the lease that the option will be exercised. This would affect the period over which the rentals would be spread.

- Materiality. Assuming that the option is to be exercised, the total lease payments of $450,000 should be spread over the 12-year lease term. This would give a charge of $37,500. This represents 2.3% of profit before tax so is unlikely to be material.

- Completeness and adequacy of disclosures. IAS 17 requires a lessee to disclose the amounts to which they are committed broken down into payments due not later than one year, later than one year and not later than five years and over five years.

- Impact on the auditor's report. If it was concluded a material adjustment was required which management refused to make, the auditor's opinion would be qualified ('except for') on the grounds of a material misstatement.

Evidence to seek

- The lease agreement. The terms should be reviewed to confirm that the risks and rewards of ownership remain with the lessor. Details of the rent-free period, the rentals and the option to extend should be confirmed.

- Discussions with management should be held to determine the likelihood of the option to extend the lease being exercised. Conclusions should be confirmed in writing.

- Experience of treatment of any existing leases, ie whether the company normally takes up the extension period.

- A recalculation of the allocation of total rentals over the lease term should be performed.

- Disclosures should be checked to confirm that they are in accordance with IAS 17.

Convertible debenture

Matters to consider

- The par value of the debenture is material to the statement of financial position, as it represents 16.7% of total assets. The coupon interest is material to the statement of profit or loss, as it amounts to 12.5% of profit after tax.

- The treatment does not appear to comply with IFRS 9 *Financial instruments.* Under IFRS 9 it should be treated as a hybrid instrument, split into its equity and liability components. Normally the liability component should be calculated as the discounted present value of the cash flows of the debenture, discounted at the market rate of interest for a comparable borrowing with no conversion rights. The remainder of the proceeds represents the fair value of the right to convert and this element should be reclassified as equity.

- The treatment currently adopted by Bainbridge therefore appears to be incorrect.

- It is not possible from the information given to assess whether the reclassification would materially affect the view given by the statement of financial position, but if it does, and the directors are not willing to change the classification then the audit opinion may have to be qualified on the grounds of disagreement.

Evidence to seek

- A copy of the debenture deed showing the interest rate, and conversion terms

- A schedule calculating the fair value of the liability at the date of issue, using interest rates quoted for similar borrowings without conversion rights

- A copy of any disclosures relating to the debenture that have been prepared by the directors

- A schedule showing the initial proceeds and interest payment agreed to the cash book and bank statement

15 Recognition

Tutor's hint. This question focuses on some accounting treatments and materiality considerations. In the exam, questions could also cover the following issues.

- Whether disclosure and presentation are fair
- Whether accounting treatments are reasonable or aggressive (in part (a), the treatment of revenue is aggressive)
- Whether the issues raised are material or fundamental and therefore pervasive to the financial statements

(a)   **Accounting treatment**

Beak Co has sold the land to Wings Co at a price well under current market value for no discernible reason. It is able to repurchase that land at cost at any time in the next five years but cannot be forced to do so. Therefore unless the land value falls significantly it can be assumed that Beak Co will repurchase the land. Wings Co will not use the building or the land for redevelopment in that period otherwise on repurchase they would lose any investment they had made.

The **commercial effect** of this transaction, assuming land values do not fall significantly, is that of **a loan** to Beak Co secured on the land. The commission is in effect interest on the loan, payment being deferred until the repurchase takes place.

Hence Beak Co should not treat this transaction as a sale. The land should continue to be shown as an asset in the statement of financial position and a loan of $20 million should be recorded. Commission should be charged annually to profit or loss, and the accrual shown as a deferral liability in the statement of financial position.

As this is a material transaction, the auditors should qualify their opinion on the grounds of a material misstatement.

(b) **Accounting treatment**

The **substance** of this transaction appears to be that the **cars are part** of the **inventory of Sparks Co** from the time they take delivery of them from Gocar Co. This is because Sparks Co bears the risks and rewards of ownership, ie it has to insure the cars, but only pays the wholesale price in force on the date the cars were first supplied, so avoiding subsequent price rises. The monthly rental is a form of interest charged by Gocar Co, varying with the length of time Sparks Co holds the inventory.

This interpretation of the transaction is also supported by the fact that Gocar Co cannot demand the return of the cars from Sparks Co.

The cars unsold for less than four months should be treated as inventory in the financial statements and the liability to Gocar Co for them recognised.

Materiality considerations

The auditors should make a judgement as to whether they feel the amounts are material. The value of the additional inventory represents 15% of their inventory already recognised on the statement of financial position. It is 1.7% of the statement of financial position total. Bearing in mind a general guideline for materiality of 1-2% of total assets, this is likely to be material.

Impact on auditor's report

If the matter is material to the statement of profit or loss and other comprehensive income (these details are not given in the question), or there are other errors in inventory which would result in inventory being increased in the statement of profit or loss and other comprehensive income, they should modify their opinion.

This would be on the grounds of a material misstatement, as before.

16 Henshelwood

(a) **Share-based payments**

   (i) *Matters to consider*

      (1) The share-based payment expense for the year is not individually material being only 2.5% of the profit before tax; the related equity reserve is material to the statement of financial position being 1.6% of total assets.

      (2) The nature of the share-based payment must be determined; the valuation of shares in a public company is likely to be easier to determine than the value of options.

      (3) The terms of the share-based payment and the assumptions as to the number of equity instruments that will vest.

   (ii) *Tests*

      (1) Obtain a copy of the terms of the scheme and verify the details used in the calculation of the expense, including the number of instruments granted, grant date, vesting date and any conditions attached to the scheme.

      (2) If the fair value calculation has been performed by an expert, obtain a copy of the valuation report and:

         • Review the assumptions for reasonableness
         • Consider professional qualification and reputation of the expert

      (3) Discuss with management their assumptions about the number of instruments that will ultimately vest and consider their reasonableness in the light of:

         • Latest budgets and forecasts
         • Board minutes
         • Any subsequent events that might affect employee numbers or the likelihood of achieving any performance targets

      (4) Reperform the calculation of the expense for the year.

(b)   **Pension costs**

    (i)   *Matters to consider*

        (1)   The net amount charged to the statement of profit or loss and other comprehensive income is not individually material, being only 1.5% of the profit before tax; the net asset carried in the statement of financial position is material, amounting to 3.6% of total assets

        (2)   Whether the pension scheme accounts have been audited as at Henshelwood's year end or a date close to that

        (3)   Whether all the pension schemes operated within the group have been included in the figures in the draft financial statements

        (4)   Whether the valuations of assets and liabilities have been performed on bases that are acceptable under IAS 19 *Employee benefits*

    (ii)   *Tests*

        (1)   Obtain a copy of the latest audited accounts of the pension scheme and verify the asset valuation used in Henshelwood's draft financial statements.

        (2)   Obtain a copy of the actuarial valuation of the pension scheme liabilities and assets, and:

            •   Check that the actuary is a member of a relevant professional body

            •   Review the source data used relating to scheme members

            •   Consider whether the actuarial assumptions appear reasonable and consistent with assumptions made elsewhere in the financial statements

            •   Compare the assumptions used with those used in previous years

        (3)   Obtain copies of all written communications from the actuary to the company directors concerning the findings of their work.

        (4)   Obtain explanations from the directors and actuary in respect of the interest earned for all main asset categories and consider whether these are consistent with, for example, changes in investment strategy.

        (5)   Perform a proof in total of the interest cost by applying the discount rate to an average of the liabilities at the beginning and end of the year and compare it to the actual charge.

        (6)   Discuss with directors and actuaries the factors affecting the current service cost.

        (7)   Discuss with directors and actuaries the underlying reasons for actuarial gains and losses.

        (8)   Verify that contributions received into the scheme agrees to the company's payroll documentation.

        (9)   Obtain written representations from the directors confirming that all retirement benefits have been identified and properly accounted for and that the assumptions used in valuing the scheme liabilities are consistent with the directors' knowledge of the business.

(c)   **Provisions**

    (i)   *Matters to consider*

        (1)   The net effect of provision on the statement of profit or loss and other comprehensive income, a credit of $22.2m, represents 11.6% of profit before tax so is clearly material. The total liability, being 9.2% of total assets, is also highly material.

(2)   The risk of misstatement is always high in respect of provisions because estimate and judgement is involved. In the case of Henshelwood, where there has been a significant write back to the statement of profit or loss and other comprehensive income, there is a risk that the provisions could have been utilised incorrectly. IAS 37 *Provisions, contingent assets and contingent liabilities* requires that provisions are only used to offset those expenses for which they were originally established.

(3)   There is also a risk that the company may have additional obligations that have not been provided for.

(ii)   *Tests*

(1)   Agree the opening balance on all provisions to the prior year's audit file.

(2)   Review the estimates used in the provisions with reference to:

- The latest rental agreement in respect of the unused leasehold properties
- Recent budgets and projections relating to the restructuring costs
- Copies of any licences or other legal documentation relating to the site restitution in the European business
- The terms of the sales agreements relating to the warranty and environmental claims, and also to any correspondence between the purchasers of those businesses and the directors of Henshelwood

(3)   Obtain a breakdown of the expenses against which the provisions have been utilised to verify that they have only been utilised against the appropriate expenses.

(4)   Review board minutes, budgets and projections, and discuss with directors whether there are any plans to resume using the leasehold properties or to sublet them, in which case the provision would no longer meet the criteria of IAS 37.

(5)   Obtain written representations from the directors that no additional obligations exist that would require provisions and that there have been no events after the reporting period that would affect the carrying value of the provisions.

17 Keffler

Top tips. In this question you need to comment on matters to consider and state the audit evidence you would expect to find in three situations. Take each case in turn and deal with it separately, making sure that you answer both requirements for each. For the matters to consider make sure that you discuss both materiality and accounting treatment for each scenario. Note the mark allocation for each case – (a) is worth nine marks, so that's almost half your time allocation for this question.

Easy marks. You need to remember your financial reporting studies here but don't panic. Take each case in turn and think about the scenario before writing down everything you know. You should be able to score reasonably well if you adopt a methodical approach and relate your answer to the information in the scenario.

Examiner's comments. Tabulation is not recommended for a question of this type since there is no relationship between materiality (a matter) and audit evidence. Using a table format to answer the question results in irrelevant or vague audit evidence. In part (i) on matters to consider, candidates must begin with an assessment of materiality by calculating relevant percentages. More candidates appeared to be interpreting materiality correctly which was encouraging, although there were many assessments on revenue that were not appropriate. Lists of questions are discouraged because the requirement is to comment on the matters to consider, not just to list them. In part (ii) on evidence, candidates must make sure that what they state here would be found documented in the audit working papers and financial statements – audit evidence is not the same as audit work, therefore answers stating 'discuss' and 'ask' would not score any marks since they do not answer the question set.

Marks

(i) **Matters**

Generally 1 mark each comment maximum Max 10
Ideas
- Materiality (appropriately assessed)
- Relevant IASs (eg 1, 8, 10, 16, 24, 36, 37, 38)
- Fundamental concepts (accruals/prudence)
- Risks (eg valuation/existence/disclosure)
- Responsibilities (eg environmental)

(ii) **Audit evidence**

Generally 1 mark each item of audit evidence (source) Max 10
Ideas (ISA 500)
- Oral vs written
- Internal vs external
- Auditor-generated
- Procedures

	Max 20
(a)	Max 9
(b)	Max 6
(c)	Max 5
	20

(a) **Landfill site**

(i) *Matters to consider*

(1) The purchase of the right to use the landfill site represents 3.3% of total assets and is therefore material to the statement of financial position.

(2) The amortisation should be charged over the period during which the site will be used, ie 10 years rather than 15 years. The charge of $20,000 for the year has been based on 10 years (the sum of digits is 55 so the first year's charge will be $1/55 \times$ 1.1m = $20k). The charge for the year represents 1% of profit before tax and so is not material.

(3) The sum of digits method has been chosen on the basis that the company has estimated that the amount of waste dumped will increase each year and this method charges higher amortisation each year. IAS 38 *Intangible assets* states that the straight-line method should be used if the pattern of future economic benefits of the right cannot be determined reliably. A straight-line method would charge $110k of amortisation to the statement of profit or loss and other comprehensive income – the difference of $90k represents 4.5% of profit before tax so is just below materiality, but the cumulative effect would be material.

(4) If there is no evidence to support Keffler's expectations of the amounts of waste to be dumped each year, the accounts should be qualified on the basis of a material misstatement.

(5) The annual provision for restoring the site represents 5% of profit before tax and 0.3% of total assets so is bordering on material. However, annual provisioning is not permitted by IAS 37 *Provisions, contingent liabilities and contingent assets* so the provision should be based on the best estimate of the total costs required to restore the site at the end of the reporting period. Therefore the present value of the total costs should have been recognised as a provision in the financial statements. This would be added to the cost of the right to use the landfill site. This will in turn affect the amortisation charge.

(ii) *Audit evidence*

- Agreement document to confirm date of purchase of right to use landfill site for 15 years and price paid and terms of the agreement
- Confirmation of amount paid to cash book and bank statements
- Calculation schedule for depreciation using sum of digits method
- Costs schedules showing estimated costs to restore the land in 15 years' time
- Senior management board minutes regarding the purchase of the right
- Physical inspection of the landfill site to confirm its use to dump waste
- Schedule showing estimated waste to be dumped each year compared to pattern of sum of digits depreciation

(b) **Sale of industrial machinery**

(i) *Matters to consider*

(1) The machinery was being depreciated over 20 years on straight-line basis (ie a charge of $60,000 per year assuming a full year's charge in the year of acquisition and no charge in the year of disposal) therefore its net book value at the start of the financial year would have been $660k. A loss of $0.3m means that the proceeds from the sale were $360k.

(2) The loss of $0.3m represents 15% of the profit before tax and 0.6% of revenue so is material to the financial statements.

(3) The loss has been separately disclosed in the statement of profit or loss and other comprehensive income. This is in accordance with IAS 16 *Property, plant and equipment* and also with IAS 1 *Presentation of financial statements* which states that material profits or losses on disposal should be presented separately either in the statement of profit or loss and other comprehensive income or in the notes.

(4) The reason for the sale needs to be established and also the reason for the loss. Originally the machinery was being depreciated over 20 years. It may be that this estimate of useful life was incorrect and there may be other similar machinery in the accounts which would result in assets being overstated because they are being depreciated over a period longer than their actual useful lives.

(5) If the sale has been made to a related party, this needs to be disclosed in the accounts in accordance with IAS 24 *Related party disclosures*.

(6) The machinery was sold two months into the financial year. It may therefore have been identified as a non-adjusting event in the previous financial year in accordance with IAS 10 *Events after the reporting period* in which case it should have been disclosed in those accounts. If it had been impaired at the end of the prior financial year, a prior period adjustment would be required in accordance with IAS 8 *Accounting policies, changes in accounting estimates and errors*. The loss would have been material in the prior year as it represents 12.5% of the profit in that year and 0.7% of revenue.

(ii) *Audit evidence*

- Authority for the sale to Deakin in senior management board minutes
- Cash receipt on sale confirmed in the bank statements and the cash book
- Sales invoice to Deakin for the asset
- Schedule to calculate the profit or loss arising on disposal
- Non-current asset register showing cost and accumulated depreciation removed on disposal
- Prior year review of events after the end of the reporting period
- Written representation letter from management includes point to confirm that Deakin is not a related party of the company

(c) **Provision**

(i) *Matters to consider*

(1) The provision represents 45% of profit before tax, 1.9% of revenue and 2.7% of total assets and is therefore clearly material to the financial statements.

(2) The provision for the penalties is not material, since it represents only 2.3% of profit before tax and 0.13% of total assets.

(3) According to IAS 37 *Provisions, contingent liabilities and contingent assets* a provision can only be recognised if there is a present obligation as a result of a past event, there will be a probable transfer of economic benefits and the amount can be estimated reliably.

(4) The penalties meet the requirements for the provision to be recognised but the provision for the water purification system does not meet the first requirement and so should not be recognised in the financial statements for the year.

(5) Failure to write back the $0.9m provision will result in a qualified audit opinion on the basis of a material misstatement since the amount is material to the accounts.

(6) The need for the upgrade to the water purification system may indicate impairment with the existing system. Any impairment should be recognised in the accounts.

(ii) *Audit evidence*

- Correspondence from the local authority relating to the ban and to confirm the amount of the penalties imposed
- Newspaper and other reports relating to the ban
- After date review of cash book and bank statements to confirm payment of fines
- Estimates from suppliers confirming the cost of the upgrade
- Senior management board minutes relating to the ban and action to be taken

18 Griffin

(a)   **Investment in Bees Co**

    (i)   *Matters to consider*

       Inclusion in Griffin's accounts

Bees Co may meet the criteria to be accounted for as an associate under IAS 28. This states that an associate is an entity (other than a subsidiary) in which another entity (the investor) has a significant influence, which is the power to participate in the financial and operating policy decisions of the investee but is not control or joint control of those policies.

A company holding 20% or more of the voting rights in a company is presumed to exercise a significant influence. The auditors must check whether the shares held are **voting shares**.

Assuming that the entity is an associate, it should be included in Griffin's accounts as a fixed asset investment at cost, assuming that cost does not overstate the value of the asset. It is unclear whether the investment is material to Griffin's statement of financial position.

Requirement for group accounts?

> 'Group accounts' here does **not** mean a consolidation is required.

Griffin and Bees may represent a 'group' for which group financial statements are required even though, as there is no subsidiary involved, consolidated financial statements are not required.

If group accounts are required, a further set of accounts with the associate equity accounted is required. Alternatively, Griffin's accounts could contain additional disclosure of what the accounts would look like if Bees had been equity accounted.

The 'Griffin Group' would be exempt from group accounts if the group was small or medium-sized. Pre-tax profit of $1.2 million and the cost of the investment to Griffin of $750,000 both indicate that the group is not small. The auditor needs to consider whether group accounts are required.

Component auditors

If group accounts are required, our firm would be the group auditors and would need to liaise with the auditors of Bees Co (the component auditors).

Related party transactions

There may be related party transactions requiring disclosure under IAS 24.

Dividends

Griffin may have received, or be due, dividend income from Bees Co which will require disclosure in the financial statements.

(ii) *Audit evidence required*

The investment in Bees Co should be verified to a **share certificate**. In order to determine whether the shares are voting or not, the auditors should obtain and review the **register of members** at Bees Co, which is open to the public for a fee.

The cost of the investment should be verified to purchase documentation, and the payment should be agreed to bank statements.

The auditors must **review the financial statements** or the most up to date financial information available **of Bees Co** to ensure that the cost figure used for the investment is still reasonable and that all dividends have been accounted for correctly in Griffin's financial statements. This information may be passed on by the other auditors.

The **sales and purchase ledgers** and the **bank statements** should be **scrutinised** to assess whether there are any related party transactions in the normal course of business. This should also be **discussed with the directors**.

(b) **Competitor**

(i) *Matters to consider*

Going concern

The entrance into the market of a major competitor, the failure of the clubs to renew their contracts and the loss of personnel to the competitor may raise issues relating to going concern. The auditors must assess whether the non-renewal of contracts was anticipated, and whether historical practice shows that such contracts are often swapped. They must also discover whether the directors have assessed the impact of the competitor on their business and consider whether these assessments have covered all the issues, and what the implications for the future of Griffin are.

Further indicators of going concern issues could be the large drop in profit, the plan to diversify (does this indicate the old market is shrinking?) and the football league clubs facing current financial problems, some of whom may be customers of Griffin. However, there appears to have been sufficient cash available to make a substantial investment in Bees Co, which may indicate that going concern is not an issue. The auditor needs to check these matters.

Receivables

If the income from contracts with the nationwide clubs has not been replaced, both revenue and receivables should have fallen on last year. We should check that this is the case.

Non-current asset impairment?

The entrance of a major competitor to the market could be considered under IAS 36 as a potential indicator of non-current asset impairment. The auditors need to consider whether non-current assets have been impaired, and whether the directors have considered if non-current assets have been impaired.

(ii) *Audit evidence required*

The auditors need to gain evidence about going concern issues. They should review the statement of cash flows and the financial statements generally and **assess the cash position** of the company. They should consider how the investment in Bees Co has been financed. They should review **arrangements with the bank** and ensure that Griffin has sufficient cash to operate.

The auditors must **discuss** (and document) the loss of the contracts and the new competitor with the directors, particularly the sales director. They should **review budgets**

and sales projections and ensure that these factors have been taken into account in them. They should review the current order book for signs that the budgets are unrealistic.

The reasons for the plans to diversify into women's leisurewear must be discussed (and documented) with the directors. There must be evidence on file that the auditors have investigated the issue of going concern and satisfied themselves either that the entity will continue in the foreseeable future, or that the directors have made sufficient disclosures in the financial statements that the situation is explained to the users of the financial statements.

The auditors should **review any correspondence** relating to the non-renewal of contracts to ensure that the contract has not been renewed. If no such information is available, the former customers should be included as part of the **receivables' circularisation** to ensure that no money is owed by them at the end of the year. There must be evidence on file that the level of receivables has been analysed in the light of known facts about customers and loss thereof. The auditors should also have reviewed discussions in the press about the financial viability of any clubs that are customers to assess the **recoverability of current debt**.

The auditors should identify whether the directors have carried out an **impairment review** and should review it to see if it is reasonable if they have done so. If no impairment review has been carried out, the auditors should consider whether one is required and discuss this with the directors. They may want to obtain **written representation** from the directors that no impairment review is required.

(c) **Legal requirements**

(i) *Matters to consider*

IAS 37

The provisions of IAS 37 must be considered in relation to the requirement to amend machinists' working conditions and the increase in the national minimum wage.

IAS 37 states that a provision is required if:

(1) An entity has a present obligation as a result of a past event
(2) It is probable that an outflow of resources embodying economic benefits will be required to settle the obligation
(3) A reliable estimate can be made of the amount of the obligation

Three situations arise for Griffin:

(1) **Cost of adjustments.** As the adjustments have not yet been made, there is no present obligation to pay for them. The obligation to make the adjustments does not create a financial obligation to pay for them until a contract has been formed for the adjustments. No provision is therefore required for the cost of adjustment.

(2) **Possibility of penalty.** As Griffin has not made the adjustments before the required date, it is possible that it is now subject to a penalty under the legislation. If this were to be in the form of a fine, this would result in the transfer of economic benefit. However, as it is only possible that such a penalty would occur (ie no order has yet been made), no provision for fines would be required. However, the matter should be disclosed as a contingent liability, were it material.

(3) **Liability to employees.** Some employees are not being paid the national minimum wage. If this is material, the auditor must consider whether there is a present obligation to pay those wages. However, as the shortfall is for 5% of employees and for two months of the year, it is extremely unlikely that this matter is material to the financial statements. Secondly, the auditor must consider whether any employees are taking action over the health and safety issue which has arisen over the seat adjustment.

ISA 250

Both issues arising here indicate that the entity is not complying with the laws and regulations concerning health and safety and to the national minimum wage.

Three considerations for the auditor result:

(1) Material effect on the financial statements? The auditors must consider whether examples of non-compliance will affect the financial statements in a material way. Given the considerations linked to IAS 37 above, it appears that this is not the case in this situation.

(2) Reporting on non-compliance. When the auditors become aware of non-compliance with laws and regulations, they must discuss them with those charged with governance. There may also be a requirement to report non-compliance to a third party, such as a regulator. In this instance, it is extremely unlikely that there is such a requirement.

> You are unlikely to be *au fait* with national minimum wage law. Remember the requirement to report is in extreme cases, such as terrorism and drug-trafficking. Express a measured opinion.

(3) Implications for other aspects of the audit. Now the auditors are aware of a possible non-compliance with laws and regulations, they must evaluate the implication of this on the rest of the audit on Griffin, including their original risk assessment.

(ii) *Audit evidence required*

The auditor must identify whether a contract has been entered into to make the adjustments to the seats. This might become obvious from a review of board minutes, or discussions with directors.

The auditor should also review the minutes to establish whether any fines have been levied. There should also be correspondence on the legislation requirements to review, or correspondence from the company solicitor.

In terms of the national minimum wage, the auditors should review the payroll to assess the extent of the problem.

It may be necessary to contact the solicitors to establish whether any legal action has been threatened by employees over either the health and safety issues or the wage issues outlined. If so, the auditors might have to rely on the solicitor's expert opinion as to whether the claims were actionable and the possible outcomes.

19 Merger of audit firms

(a) The reasons behind a merger could include:

(i) The desire to operate on a **global scale** and increase market shares
(ii) The wish to service **multinational clients** demanding an international presence
(iii) Increased **expertise** and professional experience
(iv) **Business expansion:** the competitive nature of auditing and consultancy services demands a larger firm to service clients globally
(v) **Increasing funds** available for investment (increasing investment in IT systems makes this necessary)
(vi) The need to **compete with banks** which are increasing management consultancy services
(vii) To **resist liability claims**
(viii) To reduce the ability of major clients to exert fee pressures and thus improve **financial independence**
(ix) To increase the **range of opportunities** available to skilled staff
(x) To take advantage of **cost savings** achievable

(b) Potential problems could include:

(i) A reduction in **choice of clients**
(ii) Possible **conflicts of interest** arising from mergers of firms providing services to competing clients
(iii) A reduction in **auditors' independence**, particularly as a result of increasing provision of consultancy services

(iv)   The emergence of **'audit giants'** which weakens the arguments for limiting auditors' liability

(v)   **Domination** of the profession by 'giant firms'

(vi)   Increase in the **influence of large firms** on the standard setting process

(vii)   **Redundancies** caused by elimination of overlapping departments

(viii) **Scrutiny of the mergers** by outside agencies

(ix)   **Disputes** emerging between partners as to management styles leading to resignation of disaffected partners and loss of experience

(x)   A **loss of the 'personal touch'** which is a feature of smaller firms

20 Annabella

> **Tutor's hint**. Part (a) is a very general requirement for a large number of marks. This can be daunting, but as this would be a compulsory question in the exam, don't let that put you off. Start thinking through standard lists of planning matters and see if any of them apply in this situation. (Don't include them in your answer if they don't apply; you won't get any marks for them.) Then read through the scenario again slowly (it is only short), looking for points that raise question marks or that indicate issues the auditor will need to consider.
>
> You should be able to identify key issues in the scenario from key words. For example, '**set up two subsidiary companies**' = group audit, '**transferred its trade**' = IFRS 5, all the intercompany dealings should point you towards IAS 24. Remember also that as soon as Annabella Co sets up a group, you have several audits to consider: all the individual company accounts, and the consolidated ones. Don't talk about consolidation to the exclusion of the individual audits. Lastly, talk of group audits should always make you ask 'are there any other auditors?' and in this situation, there is the friend of the director.
>
> Remember, it is not enough to identify that IFRS 5 (say) may be an issue. You must explain what the specific impacts are going to be. This is true of all the points you raise.
>
> Part (b) should be much more straightforward than part (a). It requires you to repeat things you have learnt, rather than apply anything. You might have wanted to tackle this part first. However, as always, remember not to spend too long on the easier part that provides fewer marks. You need to get a good number of marks in part (a) to pass the question.

(a)   **Planning issues**

Engagement letters

The audit firm needs to ensure that **every entity** that it audits is **covered in an engagement letter** so that there is no confusion over the audit that is undertaken. Annabella Co requires a **new engagement letter** itself because of the **radical overhaul** of its business and the impact that that will have on its own audit. Both the auditor and management need to confirm their common understanding of the terms of the audit engagement and of their respective responsibilities.

Impact on Annabella Co's individual accounts

(i)   **Accounting for the investment in subsidiaries.** The auditors need to establish what the credit accounting entries were in Annabella Co's financial statements. If the trade and assets have been transferred, Annabella's **statement of financial position is likely to be substantially different** from the previous year. As the firm was probably involved in the reconstruction and may have advised the journals, this information should be available at the firm.

(ii)   **Profit on sale.** The auditors need to establish whether a profit on sale was made on the transfer of assets to the subsidiaries, as this may require special disclosure under IAS 8.

(iii)   **Other items requiring special disclosure.** The auditors should consider whether any **costs of reconstruction** (for example, **legal fees or accountancy fees**) represent exceptional costs under the requirements of IAS 8. If this is the case, these would also require special disclosure.

(iv)   **Discontinued operations.** Disclosures should have been made in the previous year's accounts for discontinued operations under IFRS 5. This should be checked in the **comparatives** for this year.

(v) **Accounting for the investment in a joint venture.** In the individual financial statements of Annabella, this should be **accounted for in accordance with IFRS 9**. The auditors will need to check that the joint venture does **qualify** as a joint venture for accounting purposes under the requirements of **IAS 28 and IFRS 11**.

New subsidiaries

The audit firm will have to ensure that **financial statements** are being drafted for the new subsidiaries and that these are **to be audited**. They will have to determine an **audit approach** for these new audits. It is likely that they will be able to make use of **analytical evidence** from the previous business of Annabella so, while these will be first year audits, in many ways they will **not be as risky as first year audits can be**.

Related party transactions

In the individual company accounts there are going to be a number of related party transactions which **require disclosure** under IAS 24. <90% subsidiaries are not required to make disclosures. If Annabella's parent accounts are published within the group accounts, the parent does not have to make disclosures either.

	Anna	Bella	Annabella Designs
Annabella	Transfer of assets and trade Management charges	Transfer of assets and trade Management charges	Management charges Any transfer of assets and trade?
Anna		Trading on commercial terms?	Trading on normal commercial terms?
Bella			Advertising? Trading at all?

The relationships between the companies and directors and the ultimate controlling party will all require disclosure in the accounts. When the accounts are consolidated, intercompany trading will drop out, but the controlling party will still require disclosure.

Consolidation

(i) **Required?** The audit firm must determine whether the group will be required to publish group accounts. This will depend on its **size**. If it qualifies as a small group, it may be exempt.

(ii) **Audited.** If the company is required to produce group accounts, then the consolidated accounts must be audited.

(iii) **Other auditors.** See below.

(iv) **Accounting.** The subsidiaries will require consolidating into the results of the group. The joint investment should be included in the group accounts under the gross equity method. Intercompany transactions will have to be stripped out.

(v) **Drafting.** The audit firm should determine who is to draft any required group accounts, in case the client would like them to. This would have to be included in the engagement letter and would also impact upon new fee quotes for the group.

Arrangements with the other auditors

(i) **Evaluation.** The firm is the group auditor, so it will need to evaluate the second audit firm (David Turner and Co) to assess **to what degree it is happy to rely on the audit of Annabella Designs**. It will need to satisfy itself particularly that the audit is going to be **objective** and independent, due to the personal relationship between the audit partner and the director of the firm. The firm may feel that the relationship is too close and the audit will not be objective, in which case they would have to discuss this matter with the directors of Annabella.

(ii) **Procedures.** If the auditors are happy that the audit will be objective and they are satisfied with the qualifications, resources and reputation of the other auditors, they will then have to **discuss the procedures and audit approach** with the other auditors.

(iii) **Timing.** The group auditors will also need to outline the **deadlines** that they are working to, so the **time requirement** for the audit of Annabella Designs Ltd has to be agreed.

Costs and time budgets

As the group is new, it is **difficult to determine the time** that will be taken to complete the audit of the group, and this may **affect the fee**. The engagement partner should **discuss the fee level with the directors** and **possibly arrange** a margin by which it might rise, as it becomes apparent how long the audit will take.

The auditors will also require **good time budgets** on which **to base future audits and billings**. The audit plan should require that **very detailed time records** are maintained, in particular, outlining time spent in the main because the audit of the group was **new** and on the **restructuring**.

(b) **Audit of a consolidation**

Step 1 Compare the audited accounts of each subsidiary/associate to the consolidation schedules to ensure figures have been transposed correctly.

Step 2 Review the adjustments made on consolidation to ensure they are appropriate and comparable with the previous year. This will involve:

- **Recording** the **dates** and **costs** of **acquisitions** of subsidiaries and the assets acquired
- **Calculating goodwill** and **pre-acquisition reserves** arising on consolidation
- **Preparing** an overall **reconciliation** of movements on reserves and minority interests

Step 3 For business combinations, determine:

- Whether acquisition accounting has been appropriately used
- The appropriateness of the date used as the date for acquisition
- The treatment of the results of investments acquired during the year
- If acquisition accounting has been used, that the fair value of acquired assets and liabilities is reasonable (to ascertainable market value by use of an expert)
- Goodwill has been calculated correctly and, if amortised, period of amortisation is reasonable

Step 4 For disposals:

- Agree the **date** used as the date for disposal to sales documentation
- Review management accounts to ascertain whether the **results** of the **investment** have been **included** up to the date of disposal, and whether figures used are reasonable

Step 5 Consider whether previous treatment of existing subsidiaries or associates is still correct (consider level of influence, degree of control)

Step 6 Verify the arithmetical accuracy of the consolidation workings by recalculating them

Step 7 Review the consolidated accounts for compliance with the law and standards and other relevant regulations. Care will need to be taken where:

- Group companies do not have coterminous accounting periods
- Subsidiaries are not consolidated
- Accounting policies of group members differ because foreign subsidiaries operate under different rules

Other important areas include:

- Treatment of participating interests and associates
- Treatment of goodwill and intangible assets
- Foreign currency translation
- Treatment of loss-making subsidiaries
- Treatment of restrictions on distribution of profits of a subsidiary

Step 8   Review the **consolidated accounts** to confirm that they give a true and fair view in the circumstances.

21 Trendy Group

Business risks	Audit risks
(1) Fraud and loss	
This obviously affects the business and potentially affects the risk of an incorrect audit opinion if they result in material misstatements which go unadjusted.	As for business risk
(2) Foreign currency transactions	
The parent entity is responsible for treasury management but no details are given as to how group FX risk is being controlled. In fact, the current procedures may be creating further currency exchange problems for intra-group transactions.	The audit of purchases may appear easier if costs are fixed at the beginning of the year but this may well increase audit work required in inventory provisioning and year-end adjustments to reflect the inventories at their real cost to the group.
(3) Single sourcing manufacture	
Currently adverse price movements in the Malay employment or raw material market, or indeed inflation or interest rate movements, may result in the group having significantly reduced profits.	Quality may reduce, as only one supplier has a monopoly on sales. This has an audit impact due to the risk of overvaluation of poor quality inventories.
As prices are set each quarter guaranteeing a modest Malaysian operation profit margin, this does not lead to future cost control strategies being effective. There is the ability of local management to live rather lavishly without effectively controlling costs.	
There is also a enhanced risk of fraud.	
Political unrest may also cut off supply and lead to significant going concern issues for the group.	
Overreliance on a single supplier would be a key non going concern indicator to be followed up by the auditors of the individual companies.	Non going concern risk
(4) Design risks	
Potentially US designed goods produced in Malaysia may not sell abroad.	This may lead to further inventory provisioning to be required, again increasing audit risk associated with inventory over valuation.
	Design costs may have been capitalised in the parent entity's books. There is an audit risk of overstated intangible assets.

Business risks	*Audit risks*
(5) **Inventory obsolescence and valuation**	
The ability to achieve good sales in the countries of the individual trading operations depends on:	Inventories purchased at the set transfer price may be overvalued if not saleable at the year end.
• The design capability of the parent entity team • The local advertising spend	
As the US trading company ultimately buys the obsolete lines at 50% of original transfer price this company could end up with substantial losses and inventory provisions as a result of someone else's bad design and advertising decisions.	In the individual company's inventory provisions should bring inventories held down to the lower of cost and net realisable value.
	There is a further audit risk that, from a group perspective, the inventory valuation is not appropriate.
	The transfer of inventories around the group means that the individual companies are not reflecting the inventories at original cost to the group.
	In addition, any provision to reduce inventories to NRV should be based on the NRV expected to be achieved according to where it is likely the inventories are going to be sold. If it is expected to be the US at marked down prices then the group accounts should reflect the full loss on original cost to the group.
(6) **Cash rich environments**	
The retail stores are carrying significant levels of cash, credit card receipts and cheques. There is exposure to loss, theft and human error in giving out change and entering sales details.	Risk from lack of reliable audit evidence. Material misstatement of cash balances.
(7) **Property**	
With retail stores and the Malaysian factory the group has many responsibilities and commitments.	There is an audit risk that the financial statements include:
• Insurance • Security offered on loans • Repairs and maintenance • Payments on mortgages • Maintaining an acceptable level of return on the floor space • Refurbishments to maintain market presence	• Inflated revaluations to support loans and guarantees • Inappropriate depreciation charges/policies • Wrongly capitalised repairs expenditure • Lack of necessary disclosures
(8) **Tax**	
The use of fixed transfer prices may expose the group to making profits in countries where the tax regime is not favourable.	

22 Business assurance

> **Tutor's hint.** This question could have been answered with basic auditing knowledge and did not need an in-depth knowledge of the services currently performed by auditors. However, you need to feel confident and familiar with the subject.

(a)   Current ACCA guidance on the provision of other services to clients is generally based on the IESBA guidance which applies in an international basis. The emphasis in the IESBA guidance is on the audit firm avoiding assuming a management responsibility when providing other services. However, in the case of internal audit services the IESBA code prohibits internal audit services when the audit client is a public interest entity if they relate to:

- A significant part of the internal controls over financial reporting;
- Financial accounting systems generating information which is significant to the financial statements; or
- Amounts or disclosures which are material to the financial statements.

The view taken internationally by IESBA is that many companies would be restricted if they were unable to obtain the other services available from their auditors, provided these services do not interfere with the exercise of managerial functions and auditors' independence. It would seem that **IESBA guidance allows external auditors to act as internal auditors** of clients.

The view taken by the current ACCA guidelines is as follows.

(i)   The ACCA guidance states that **objectivity may be threatened** by the provision of non-audit services. Care must be taken not to give executive advice or to become part of the client's active management.

(ii)   Firms **should not provide accountancy services to listed clients**.

(iii)   If accounting records are prepared for a client, then the **client** must accept **responsibility for the records**.

(iv)   There is **no specific prohibition** from an external auditor undertaking the internal audit function.

Specific **problems** which could occur include:

(i)   The **difficulty of reporting deficiencies** in internal controls in systems designed by employees of the auditor acting as internal auditors of the client

(ii)   The **perceived difficulties in testing work** carried out by internal auditors who are colleagues of the external auditors

(iii)   Internal audit programmes designed to **reduce the work** of external auditors

(iv)   The danger of **breaching ACCA rules** of conduct if the internal audit department is deemed to be **part of the management** of the client

(v)   **Fee pressures** arising from the increase in fees for providing an internal audit service leading to breaching the fee guidelines

(vi)   **Audit risk** assessed by the external auditor; the presumption is that control risk would reduce because of the involvement of the external auditor in the provision of internal audit services

(b)   The **effects** would be:

(i)   Increased **risk of liability claims**

(ii)   **Additional costs** to the auditor incurred in employing suitable staff to provide wider assurance

(iii)   An impact on **fees** charged to clients

(iv)   Possible **increased expectations** of audit clients

(v)   The difficulty in formulating and wording an appropriate **audit report** which could require legislative changes

(c) The new approach could be seen as a **'repackaging'** of existing services where auditors concentrate on providing services which add value to the audit fee in the eyes of the client. Basic audit work may be foregone, as it is perceived as adding very little.

The difficulty with this approach is that auditors are increasingly faced with **litigation claims** and should therefore provide more basic assurance based lower materiality thresholds. It may be that external auditors came to view the roles of audit committees and internal audit departments as crucial in reducing control risk.

It is dangerous to assume that external audit is a consultancy exercise aimed at adding value because traditional audit assurance will be lost and overall levels of audit risk will rise.

23 Scenarios

Tutor's hint. Both scenarios given in this question should help you explore the issues that would be considered in practice, if an audit firm was going to offer assurance services.

Notice that you must think about a variety of issues: ethics, acceptance, planning, liability, reporting. You must be prepared to bring in all strands of your syllabus in questions set in scenarios.

Part (a) considers the position of an audit firm asked to report on a client to a third party but with no engagement. The auditor must consider whether it is possible to provide assurance in this situation. Is there an official assurance service that can be offered in this situation? Above all, the auditor must ensure that they are not accepting liability on this reference. The bank is seeking to reduce its risk – but the auditor must not allow that risk to be transferred to them. That might have dangerous implications for their audit independence, apart from the issue of personal risk.

Part (b) looks at the idea of providing assurance on the whole process of business systems. It is important that the terms of an engagement are settled. An assurance service cannot be undertaken if there is no clear requirement as to the nature of the service.

(a) **Lilac**

An audit engagement partner would have to consider the following things before issuing a reference on behalf of a client.

(i) Is any **additional work** required to give such a reference?

(ii) If so, the need to contact the bank and discuss whether a **separate engagement** might be appropriate

(iii) The **inherent uncertainty** of future income and expenditure and therefore the **high risk** which is associated with giving such an opinion

(iv) The **difficulty of issuing an opinion on current solvency**; the auditors are about to commence the audit for the past year, meaning they will be investigating information up to 15 months old

(v) The fact that a **duty of care** to the bank is likely to arise if such a reference is given

(vi) The need for **disclaimers of liability**, therefore, which will need to be reasonable in order to have legal force, perhaps the **need for legal advice** before such disclaimer is made

(vii) Any need to negotiate a **liability cap**, although a disclaimer of liability should be sufficient/more appropriate

(viii) Need for **written clarification** of the status of the reference, that is, explanation that there has been no engagement between the parties, that no fee has been paid, that it is given to the best of knowledge at the time

(ix) The **form of the reference**; it is likely to be inappropriate to sign a bank's pre-printed document. The audit firm may have a standard reference document of its own, or may choose to compose each one according to the facts of the situation.

(b) **Laurel**

The directors of Laurel have expressed an interest in engaging the audit firm to undertake an assurance engagement in relation to their risk management and controls.

The following matters will be relevant.

Acceptance

Independence

The audit firm has to consider the issue of **independence**. It is vital that the provision of other services to the audit client does not **impair its objectivity towards the audit**. ACCA states that provision of other services may impair objectivity.

The IESBA guidance states that whether a threat to objectivity exists when providing **any** professional service will depend on the particular circumstances of the engagement, and on the nature of the work that the professional accountant in public practice is performing.

The amount that audit independence would be affected will depend on the exact nature of the service provided (see below). However, an assignment testing the operation of controls could be complimentary to the audit.

Nature of the service

The firm would not be able to accept the engagement as it has been currently set out. An assurance engagement should exhibit certain elements, key of which are subject matter, suitable criteria and an engagement process. It is very difficult to give assurance on the effectiveness of risk management, as there are no recognised criteria by which to judge it. However, the firm could provide an assurance service checking that controls are designed according to management criteria and they operate according to management policy, for example. This would need discussing and agreeing in writing before the engagement could be accepted.

Planning

In terms of planning such an engagement, once the details of the engagement had been agreed, the following matters would be relevant.

(i) Is the firm **sufficiently independent** of the client to conduct the assurance service objectively? It may be that the fact that the company is an audit client would impair their objectivity towards this engagement.

(ii) Are all the **elements** of an assurance engagement **present**? This has been discussed above.

(iii) Have **the firm and the parties agreed terms**? In this case, the assurance service is likely to be carried out to benefit shareholders, so it may be necessary for a vote to be passed in general meeting to approve the service.

(iv) Are the **criteria** for assessing the subject matter **suitable**? In this case, management policy would be a suitable criterion for evaluating the operation of systems.

(v) The auditor must assess the **materiality and risk** of the engagement. These should be incorporated into a **fee** and into the **detailed procedures** planned for the engagement.

(vi) What **form of report** is required by the parties? There is no such thing as a standard report, so it is important for the parties to agree on the format of the report that will be produced at the end of the engagement.

24 Verity

(a) The factors that will affect the accountants' decision on whether to accept appointment are:

   (i) **Previous experience of client**

   The accountants should draw on their knowledge of the client as gained during the audit. In particular they will be interested in the willingness of the client to provide information, the integrity and knowledge of the directors, and the reliability of the forecasts prepared for financial accounting purposes, for example for assessment of going concern or deferred tax.

   (ii) **How prepared**

   The accountants will need to consider how the forecast is being prepared, in particular:

   (1) How the forecast was compiled, and the staff who compiled it

   (2) The extent to which the forecast is based on assumptions consistent with past events. The details given suggest that a more optimistic view is being taken than is warranted by the company's record in recent years.

   (3) Whether the forecast represents management's best estimate of achievable results, or whether it represents hopeful targets or is based on certain hypothetical events taking place

   (4) How the forecast takes account of factors which may invalidate the assumptions made

   (5) The level of detail available supporting the forecast

   (iii) **Terms of report**

   The accountants will need to consider the exact terms within which they are reporting, as this could have a bearing on their liability. This is discussed further in (c) below.

   (iv) **Users**

   The accountants should consider carefully the use to which the report will be put, and its audience.

(b) A major concern of the reporting accountant will be the assumptions on which the report is based. The level of evidence required will depend on the terms of the accountants' report, but some evidence will be required on the major assumptions made in the forecast.

   (i) **Sales.** It might be expected that the price increase would result in some lost sales, so extra sales will be needed from other customers to make up for the sales lost as well as achieving the planned increase. The auditor will need to focus on the plans to achieve that increase. Increases might be a result of a change in the sales mix or new products or customers; if these changes have already occurred, the accountants should consider what effect they have already had. Increased marketing and promotional activity may also be necessary, and this would need to occur rapidly in order to achieve the desired effect. This activity will probably be reflected in increased costs, and the accountants will need to check that these have been included in the forecast.

   (ii) **Cost of sales.** The accountants will need to consider whether economies have been planned to improve margins, whether these economies are likely to be achieved, and whether there will be consequential other costs that need to be reflected in the plan. For example, reduction in the labour force is likely to mean redundancy costs and investment in more up to date plant and equipment to mean capital investment costs.

   (iii) **Trade receivables.** The accountants should consider whether the decrease in settlement period is likely to be achieved. They should consider whether emphasising new credit limits and prompt settlement discounts will help achieve the required target, and also the effectiveness of any other measures the company takes, for example tighter checks on new customers and more rigorous pursuit of slow payers. In particular, the accountants will

need to review the position of foreign customers, as they may be less flexible in reducing settlement periods. The accountants should also check that the consequences of the prompt settlement discount, a reduction in amounts received, have been reflected in the forecast. For foreign customers, the accountants should also check any exchange rate effects have been reflected in the forecast.

(iv) **Trade payables.** The accountants should check that the increase in payable days will not breach terms of business with suppliers, leading to possible supply problems or withdrawal of credit terms and demands for immediate cash payments. They should also check that the forecast reflects other possible consequences of the increase, for example a loss of early settlement discounts.

(v) **Maximum finance.** The accountants should check whether the estimated increase in finance is reasonable or whether other sources will be required, either because the $9 million is an underestimate or because other existing sources of finance will need to be repaid. The accountants should check that the consequences of the increase, particularly an increased interest burden, have been reflected. They should consider also whether the forecast shows that the company will be able to make the repayments comfortably, or whether the forecast margins are tight.

The accountants should also check that the forecast is internally consistent, for example that increased sales correspond with increased purchases, and reflects all non-trading cash flows. Consistency with forecasts made for other purposes, for example management accounting budgets, should also be checked.

(c) Liability will depend partly on the following general factors.

Extent of assurance

In this assignment accountants are focusing on uncertain future events, as opposed to an audit, where the report is based on a verification of data relating to past events. Therefore the level of assurance that can be given on this type of report is lower.

The exact level of assurance will depend on the form of the opinion given. Reporting under ISAE 3400 *The examination of prospective financial information* would require the accountants to report whether the forecast has been properly compiled on the basis of the stated assumptions and is presented in accordance with the relevant financial reporting framework. The report would state that nothing has come to the accountants' attention to suggest that the assumptions do not provide a reasonable basis for the prospective financial information. The accountants may go further, and make a positive report on the assumptions or less probably give a report on the achievability of the forecasts. If the report gives more positive assurance, this may increase the expectations of the report's readers as to the assurance given.

Other report issues

Whatever the exact terms of their opinion, the accountants should mention other matters in their report that will clarify for users what the accountants have done and therefore what they are offering:

(i) The accountants should state why and for whom the report is being prepared.

(ii) Reference should be made to the work done, and whether the work has been done in accordance with ISAE 3400.

(iii) The report should state that the directors are responsible for the assumptions made.

(iv) The accountants may be able to include specific disclaimers on the assumptions made and achievability of the forecasts. Even if they do not, they should make a statement about the uncertainty of the forecast, and the possibility that the actual outcomes will differ from what is predicted.

Cranley Bank

The accountants were on notice that the forecast was being prepared for the purposes of the bank, and thus the degree of the proximity that the law relating to professional liability requires has been established. If a claim arises, the courts will consider whether the forecast was properly prepared and based on reasonable assumptions that took account of the information that should have been known at the time of the forecast. If it was not, the court would then consider whether the accountants should have drawn the conclusion that they did or allowed themselves to provide some degree of implicit assurance on the forecast because of their association with it.

Certainly some of the assumptions made would appear to be doubtful and the bank may have a case against the accountants. However if the company fails to meet the forecast, it may well be difficult to assess how much this was due to factors that could have been predicted, and how much it was due to factors that could not have been forecast when the forecast was made.

The debenture holders

The accountants will probably not be liable to the debenture holders. The accountants stated in their report that it was prepared solely for the bank. The fact that the directors omitted this statement makes no difference to the accountants' liability, although it may render the directors liable. In addition, had the report been prepared for the purposes of obtaining debenture finance, it would have been prepared on different assumptions.

25 Painswick Ltd

(a)   A forensic audit can be defined as the process of gathering, analysing and reporting on data in a predefined context, for the purpose of finding facts and/or evidence in the context of financial/legal disputes and/or irregularities and giving preventative advice in this area.

Fraud is an example of an irregularity which may be investigated as part of a forensic audit. The main objective of the work is to determine whether a fraud has taken place, identify who has perpetrated the fraud and to calculate the loss incurred by the company.

The evidence obtained may be presented in a court of law.

(b)   In accordance with ISA 240 the primary responsibility for the prevention and detection of fraud rests with management. An auditor conducting a statutory audit in accordance with ISAs is responsible for obtaining reasonable assurance that the financial statements are free from material misstatement as a result of fraud. However, the ISA acknowledges that there are inherent limitations in an audit in this respect, as the overall purpose of the audit is to form an opinion on the financial statements, not to detect fraud. The auditor must maintain an attitude of professional scepticism unless they have reason to believe the contrary records and documents may be accepted as genuine.

When undertaking a fraud investigation the forensic auditor's role will be determined by the specific terms of the engagement agreed between the forensic auditor and the client. Normally this will refer specifically to the identification of whether fraud has occurred. Although many of the procedures involved will be similar to the audit of financial statements, their purpose will be different and therefore the approach will differ. For example materiality will be viewed differently and documentation will be reviewed more critically than on an audit.

(c)   The fundamental ethical principles apply to forensic assignments as follows.

(i)   Integrity

If there is any risk that the forensic accountant's integrity will be compromised they should decline or withdraw from the audit. This is a particular issue as forensic assignments will often involve dealing with individuals who are dishonest or lack integrity.

(ii)   Objectivity

Objectivity is crucial, particularly if the forensic accountant is taking the role of an expert witness. If the accountant is not seen to be objective the credibility of their evidence will be undermined.

(iii) Professional competence and due care

Specialist skills may be required to conduct forensic assignments. The accountant must ensure that they have the relevant capabilities.

(iv) Confidentiality

The general principle of confidentiality still applies particularly where the forensic accountant is working for one party in a dispute. In certain circumstances eg a court case the accountant may be required to disclose information and evidence obtained.

(v) Professional behaviour

Professional behaviour is always important to protect the reputation of the individual and the profession as a whole.

(d) The fraud could have been identified by carrying out the following procedures.

- Assess the overall control environment and controls, in particular segregation of duties
- Determine who is able to access all aspects of the purchase ledger system, including posting of invoices, payments of cash and reconciliation of accounts
- Obtain a printout of masterfile amendments including those to BACS details and review for any unauthorised changes. Where unauthorised changes have been made obtain supporting documentation giving details of the amounts transferred and the details of the account holder
- Review transactions on a number of supplier accounts and investigate duplicate posting of invoices
- Scrutinise the entries in the suspense account and obtain an explanation as to what each entry relates to
- Review reconciliations of major supplier accounts and trace individual entries to invoices and cash payments

26 Harness

> **Tutor's hint.** When it comes to the impact of social and environmental issues on the work of the external audit, two things are important. These two things are:
>
> - Why the issues are relevant
> - How the issues are relevant
>
> These two issues were addressed in an essay question on the Pilot Paper for the old syllabus. In this question, the same issues are addressed, but the 'how' aspect is addressed through an auditing scenario. Notice that the question in part (b) does not ask you to comment on the implications of the environmental issues on the audit, but more generally asks you to comment on the above. You should not restrict your answer to environmental matters then.
>
> This question is overtly aimed at environmental matters. However, in the exam, issues like these will not necessarily have a neon sign over them. You may find that they are thrown into a more general risks and planning question. In such a case, it is for you to identify that such matters are important.
>
> Notice that this question also requires a solid accounting knowledge to discuss such issues as non-current asset impairment, contingent liabilities and joint ventures. Auditors must have a good accounting knowledge to be able to identify risk matters in financial statements.

(a) **Importance of social and environmental issues**

Social and environmental issues are important to the external auditor today for a variety of reasons.

(i) *Importance to companies*

The first reason is that these matters are **important to the companies on which the auditor is reporting**. Social and environmental matters which are important to the company form a necessary part of knowledge of the business.

Companies are increasingly reporting to their shareholders on matters of corporate responsibility. The external auditors report to the shareholders and have responsibilities to review other information presented with the financial statements which they have audited. Social and environmental issues are a natural part of corporate reporting these days.

(ii) *Impact on the financial statements*

Social and environmental issues may well have financial implications which impact on the financial statements. Several examples can be given:

- Non-current asset impairment (IAS 36)
- Provisions (IAS 37)
- Revenue recognition (IFRS 15)
- Development costs (IAS 38)
- Going concern issues (IAS 1)

(iii) *ISA 250*

It will sometimes be the case that social and environmental issues will be regulated, in which case the auditing guidance contained in ISA 250 will become relevant to the auditor.

(b) **Audit of Harness**

ISA 250

As part of the understanding of the business exercise, when planning the audit, the auditors must ensure that they are **aware** of any **relevant regulations** relating to energy provision and/or piping oil which may impact on the financial statements.

Non-current assets

Harness appears to have accidentally **disposed** of a windmill in the year and three others show signs of being impaired. The auditors must ensure that the disposal has been **correctly accounted** for and whether any loss on disposal is an **item requiring special disclosure under IAS 8**. They must also discover whether Brewster has conducted an **impairment review** and, if so, whether the review is appropriate and reasonable.

Going concern

The loss of three or four windmills is likely to **severely affect operations** in terms of quantity of power generated. However, as the vast majority of the power goes to Brewster himself, it is likely that other customers will still be able to be accommodated.

However, the **generator also lies close to the eroding cliff**. The auditors must assess whether the generator is in danger of being affected by the erosion, as this is more likely to severely affect the going concern assumption. It appears that Brewster is happy to finance the loss-making business but, without a generator, it would not be able to operate anyway.

Cracked pipe line

Harness has invested in a pipeline which has a large crack in it. The auditors need to assess whether this gives rise to any **obligation to transfer economic benefits**.

If repair work has been commissioned, this might give rise to an obligation which might necessitate a **provision for repair costs**.

It is unclear whether the crack is going to result in **oil spill and resulting environmental contamination**. The auditors may need to obtain the opinion of an **expert engineer** as to the **likelihood** of that happening. If contamination is possible or probable, there may be a **contingent liability** arising in respect of fines or compensation.

Investment

Harness is the 'co-owner' of the pipeline. The auditors need to investigate the details of this **investment** to determine whether the pipeline is a non-current or current asset or whether it would constitute a joint venture or arrangement under IAS 28 and IFRS 11.

Going concern

The auditors need to investigate the potential impact the cracked pipeline could have on the business of Harness, because this could also affect the going concern assumption, if fines or legal action were extensive.

27 Eastfield Distributors

(a)   The auditor should consider the following factors when assessing their independence.

(i)   The level of fee income from Eastfield may be so great as to create a self-interest or an intimidation threat to independence. The level of the threat depends on:

- The structure of the firm
- Whether the firm is established or new
- The significance of Eastfield to the firm

(ii)   As external auditor, the firm will be reviewing the work of internal audit; if the same staff were acting as external and internal auditors, they would be judging their own work. This obvious threat to objectivity can be lessened by different staff carrying out the detailed work, and different partners and managers being in charge of providing both services.

(iii)   There is a specific threat to independence if preparing Eastfield's accounts is part of the desired internal audit service. If Eastfield is a listed company, the audit firm's staff should not be involved in preparing the accounting records unless their work is of a mechanical nature. If Eastfield is not listed, it must accept responsibility for its accounts and accounting records, and the practice must carry out sufficient audit work on the accounting records.

(iv)   Similarly, there is a threat to independence if the internal auditors become involved in the management of the company, because as external auditor the audit firm is reporting on the stewardship of management. However part of the internal audit service could be making recommendations about the design of systems and controls. The audit firm should therefore ensure that the directors take responsibility for implementation of any recommendations and that their decisions are clearly recorded in board minutes.

(v)   Internal audit staff may be particularly likely to breach other independence guidelines that are applicable to them as employees of the firm carrying out the external audit. They should be reminded that they should not own shares in the client, accept a loan from the client, or obtain goods or services on more favourable terms than are offered to Eastfield's own staff.

(vi)   If Eastfield does fail to pay fees, there may be a greater danger of the amounts owed being akin to a loan because of their size and because they are amounts owed for a continuing service rather than an annual audit.

(vii)   The engagement letter should set out clearly the respective responsibilities of the audit firm and Eastfield. It should separately identify the work that the audit firm should carry out as external and internal auditors, and how fees will be calculated for each service. It should make clear to whom the audit firm's internal audit team will report.

(viii)   The firm should consider as part of its annual review of independence whether it is still sufficiently independent to be able to continue to act as external auditor.

(b)   The advantages for Eastfield of having the external auditor provide internal audit services are:

(i)   The audit staff will be qualified or partly qualified accountants who are subject to professional standards and guidelines.

(ii)   Training costs will be saved, as the audit firm, not Eastfield, will be responsible for staff training.

(iii)   The audit firm may be able to provide a range of expertise which would not be available to Eastfield without incurring considerable extra costs.

(iv)   The efficiency of external audit would be enhanced, and therefore its costs lowered, because internal auditors are using the same procedures to record and assess systems. Thus the external auditor would not have to spend time checking whether appropriate work has been performed.

The disadvantages for Eastfield of using the internal auditors are:

(i)   Eastfield may want to use internal audit for a variety of tasks on the non-financial areas of its business, and the audit firm may not have staff with the necessary expertise in these areas.

(ii)   As discussed in (a), the ACCA's independence requirements place limitations on the work that the internal auditors can carry out as a result of their firm also acting as external auditor.

(iii)   The audit firm may not be able to guarantee continuity of internal audit staff. There may be regular staff changes as staff leave or are involved in other work, and the learning curve for new staff may add to the costs of internal audit.

(iv)   The audit firm may not be able to provide the staff that Eastfield wants at the time Eastfield needs them because of commitments to other clients.

(v)   The costs of the audit firm's staff will be higher than if Eastfield employed its own internal audit staff, because the audit firm will be charging Eastfield a mark-up on the staff's time as well as their salaries.

(vi)   There may be conflicts over the reporting arrangements for internal audit staff. Eastfield would want to maintain control over their activities, but there has to be a mechanism for reporting to the audit firm as well, because the external firm is responsible for the staff's professional development and therefore will need to assess how staff have performed.

(c)   The advantages for the audit firm of carrying out both the internal and external audit are:

(i)   The audit firm will be able to gain greater assurance from its own staff's work as internal auditors than it is likely to be able to gain if the internal audit staff were employed by Eastfield. The firm will know that its staff have the necessary levels of competence and independence. It will also not have to spend time assessing the methods used to record and evaluate controls.

(ii)   The extent of the work done by internal audit is likely to go beyond that necessary to support an external audit opinion, so the firm will have more evidence available than it would aim to have if it was just carrying out an external audit.

(iii)   Working on a variety of internal audit tasks will enhance the professional development of the audit staff concerned.

(iv)   The internal audit work might be able to be carried out at times of the year when the amount of other work is low, and thus staff will be used more efficiently.

The disadvantages for the firm of carrying out both services are:

(i)   The firm may have problems exercising control over the internal audit staff, because of its responsibility to report to the client.

(ii)   Problems over the internal audit work may jeopardise the firm's role as external auditor.

(iii)   The potential problems discussed in (a) in guaranteeing independence may prove insurmountable.

28 Maple

(a) **Auditor's responsibility in respect of fraud and error**

ISA 240 *The auditor's responsibilities relating to fraud in an audit of financial statements* states that the primary responsibility for the prevention and detection of fraud rests with both those charged with governance and the management of an entity. It is not the auditor's function to prevent fraud or error, although the fact that an audit is carried out may act as a deterrent.

In respect of detection, ISA 240 states that the auditor should assess the risk of material misstatement due to fraud at both the financial statement and assertion level and determine overall responses to address the assessed risks. This might include changing the nature, timing and extent of audit procedures, eg more inspection, more work conducted during the year rather than at the year end and larger sample sizes.

The approach to error under ISA 315 *Identifying and assessing the risks of material misstatement through understanding the entity and its environment* and ISA 330 *The auditor's procedures in response to assessed risks* is broadly similar to the approach outlined for fraud above.

In practical terms, the likelihood of detecting errors will be much higher than that of detecting fraud, as deliberate attempts are normally made to conceal fraud including collusion and falsification of records.

In either case an audit is subject to an unavoidable risk that some material misstatements will not be detected.

If the auditor identifies an instance of fraud or error, they should document their findings and report them to the appropriate level of management and possibly to those charged with governance of the entity depending on their significance.

The auditor also needs to consider the potential impact on the audit opinion. If the fraud or error has a material effect on the financial statements the auditor's opinion may need to be modified. The nature of the modification would depend on the specific circumstances.

The auditor may need to consider whether there is a legal duty to report the occurrence of fraud or material error to regulatory or enforcement authorities.

(b) **Auditor's report**

Format of report

The format of the report drafted by the audit senior is not line with ISAs. The explanation of the modifications to the auditor's opinion should be included in a separate section entitled 'Basis for Qualified Opinion'.

The paragraph should make it clear that there are a number of separate issues in respect of which the auditor's opinion is modified.

The opinion paragraph should have its own heading, 'Qualified Opinion', not 'modified opinion'. The first sentence should not refer to the 'the preceding paragraph', but to the 'Basis for Qualified Opinion' section. The Opinion section should have been placed before the 'Basis for Qualified Opinion' section. The Opinion section is also incomplete, since it only contains the second of the two paragraphs prescribed by the ISA.

Inventories in Sherwood

An exact calculation of the required adjustment to inventories cannot be performed, as it is not possible to tell the extent to which the directors' valuation is incorrect. However, the inventories figure of $80,000 overall is material to both the profit and total assets figure.

The issue here is a material inability to obtain sufficient appropriate audit evidence (assuming that the audit manager agrees that no other procedures can be performed). In the draft auditor's report this has not been dealt with correctly. It appears that it has been dealt with as a material misstatement.

The explanation of the problem has been correctly dealt with in the explanatory paragraph itself, and the opinion paragraph is drafted correctly in this respect.

Director's loan

The audit senior has made no reference to the loan on the basis that $5,000 is not material to the financial statements. While this is true from a quantitative perspective, in this case the director's loan is material due to the sensitive nature of the balance. IAS 24 *Related party disclosures* requires disclosure of transactions with key management personnel.

If the directors of Maple still refuse to provide the necessary information, the details of the loan should be included in the auditor's report. In addition, the opinion would be modified (qualified – 'except for') on the grounds of a material misstatement for non-compliance with legislation/IFRS.

Irrecoverable receivable

If the debt in respect of Beech were recognised in profit or loss, this would result in a reduction in profits of 47% and assets of 8.4%. On this basis it would have a material effect on the financial statements. While material, the matter is isolated to the receivables balance and does not affect the truth and fairness of the financial statements overall. The audit senior has modified the audit opinion on the grounds of material misstatement in relation to the decision not to provide against the debt. This is the correct treatment and the report has been correctly drafted in respect of this issue.

29 Petrie

Top tips. This is a question on auditor's reports, comprising both knowledge elements and scenarios. Part (a) is knowledge-based for six marks and should be straightforward, as discussed in 'Easy marks' below. In part (b), you have to apply your knowledge to two mini scenarios so take each one in turn and deal with it separately, noting the mark allocation against each. When explaining the implications for the auditor's report, make sure your arguments are clear and well thought out, as this will maximise your chances of scoring a good mark in this part of the question, and remember to consider materiality.

Easy marks. Easy marks are available in part (a) of this question for explaining the three terms **and** distinguishing between them. You should be familiar with all of them, given that you looked at auditor's reports in detail during your earlier auditing studies.

Examiner's comments. Part (a) should have been straightforward as it would have been covered in detail at the lower level auditing paper but many candidates appeared still confused. Candidates lost marks for failing to answer the question about distinguishing the three terms. In part (b), there were some good answers, particularly for part (i). Many candidates wanted to give an Emphasis of Matter paragraph in relation to the two issues thus demonstrating a lack of understanding of auditor's reports and opinion.

		Marks
(a)	**Auditor's report terms**	
	Generally 1 mark each point of explanation/distinction	Max 8
	Ideas (ISA 705)	
	• Explanation of each term	
	• Which do and which do not affect the auditor's opinion	
	• Pervasive vs merely material	
	• Inability to obtain sufficient appropriate audit evidence (= insufficient evidence)	
	• Misstatement (= sufficient evidence)	

(b) (i) **Selective revaluation of premises**

Generally 1 mark an implication/comment thereon   Max 5

Ideas
- Materiality assessed
- Not pervasive
- Adjusting event (IAS 10)
- Non-compliance IAS 16 $\Rightarrow$
- Reversal of revaluation adjustments **or**
- Qualified 'except for' material misstatement (IAS 16)
- Change in accounting policy (next year)
- Impairment (IAS 36)
  - Insufficient evidence $\Rightarrow$ inability to obtain sufficient appropriate audit evidence $\Rightarrow$ 'except for'
  - Sufficient evidence $\Rightarrow$ misstatement $\Rightarrow$ 'except for'

(ii) **Ten-year guarantee**

Generally 1 mark an implication/comment thereon   Max 4

Ideas
- Matter is material
- Present obligation … probable … etc
- Not a contingent liability
- Best estimate – how determinable
- 'Except for' material misstatement non-compliance IAS 37

$\underline{\underline{17}}$

(a) (i) A 'qualified opinion' on the financial statements is expressed when the auditor concludes that an unmodified opinion cannot be expressed but that the effect of any material misstatement or inability to obtain sufficient appropriate audit evidence is not so material and pervasive as to require an adverse opinion or a disclaimer of opinion.

(ii) A 'disclaimer of opinion' is expressed when the possible effect of a limitation on the scope of the audit (inability to obtain sufficient appropriate audit evidence) is so material and pervasive that the auditor is unable to express an opinion on the financial statements.

(iii) An 'Emphasis of Matter paragraph' is used in an auditor's report to highlight a matter affecting the financial statements which is appropriately presented or disclosed, for example in a note to the financial statements, that is of such importance that it is fundamental to users' understanding of the financial statements. The addition of such an Emphasis of Matter paragraph(s) does not affect the auditor's opinion on the financial statements. The auditor may also modify the auditor's report by using an Emphasis of Matter paragraph(s) to report matters other than those affecting the financial statements.

(iv) An 'Other Matter paragraph' is a paragraph included in the auditor's report that refers to a matter other than those presented or disclosed in the financial statements that, in the auditor's judgement, is relevant to users' understanding of the audit, the auditor's responsibilities or the auditor's report.

These four terms can be distinguished from each other as follows.

An Emphasis of Matter paragraph or an Other Matter paragraph does not affect the auditor's opinion on the financial statements, whereas a qualified opinion and disclaimer of opinion do. A qualified opinion can result from a limitation on scope leading to an inability to obtain sufficient appropriate audit evidence, or from a disagreement as a result of which the financial statements are materially misstated. A disclaimer of opinion results from a limitation on scope leading to an inability to obtain sufficient appropriate audit evidence that is so material and pervasive that the auditor cannot express an opinion on the financial statements.

(b) (i) *Revaluation of properties*

In accordance with IAS 16 *Property, plant and equipment*, if a policy of revaluation is to be adopted, it must be applied to all the non-current assets in that class. Therefore Petrie's management should have revalued all the properties, not just three of them.

The valuation of 9 of the properties after the end of the reporting period represents an adjusting event in accordance with IAS 10 *Events after the reporting period*. Hence these should be adjusted for as well as the 3 properties valued by the end of the reporting period. The increase in revaluation of 12 of the 15 properties amounts to $7.1 million, which represents 23.1% of total assets and is therefore very material to the statement of financial position.

If the management does not revalue all the properties for the year ended 31 March 20X2 then the financial statements would be qualified on the basis of a material misstatement (except for opinion), as tangible non-current assets would be materially understated in the accounts.

The management should therefore either revalue all the properties for the year or none of them, in order to avoid a qualification in the year ended 31 March 20X2.

(ii) *Warranty*

The sales of stainless steel cookware represent $18.2 million of revenue for the year which is 43% of total revenue and therefore are material to the accounts. However, the warranty however was introduced three months into the year so would apply to approximately $13.6m which represents 32% of total revenue.

The conditions for recognising a provision in the financial statements in accordance with IAS 37 *Provisions, contingent liabilities and contingent assets* are that there is a present obligation as a result of a past event, it is probable that a transfer of economic benefits will be required to settle the obligation, and a reliable estimate can be made of the amount of the obligation.

Petrie's management should recognise a provision in the financial statements for the year ended 31 March 20X2 if the conditions are met. However, the disclosure in the accounts is as a contingent liability – but it is very unlikely that the company cannot make a reliable estimate of the obligation.

If a provision is not made for the warranty then the auditor's opinion would be qualified on the grounds of a material misstatement ('except for') in respect of non-compliance with the requirements of IAS 37.

Index

Note. **Key Terms** and their page references are given in **bold**.

Review Form – Paper P7 (International) Advanced Audit and Assurance (02/16)

Please help us to ensure that the ACCA learning materials we produce remain as accurate and user-frie[...] as possible. We cannot promise to answer every submission we receive, but we do promise that it will be read and taken into account when we update this Study Text.

Name: _____   Address: _____
_____
_____

How have you used this Study Text?
(Tick one box only)

☐ Home study (book only)
☐ On a course: college _____
☐ With 'correspondence' package
☐ Other _____

Why did you decide to purchase this Study Text? *(Tick one box only)*

☐ Have used BPP Study Texts in the past
☐ Recommendation by friend/colleague
☐ Recommendation by a lecturer at college
☐ Saw information on BPP website
☐ Saw advertising
☐ Other _____

During the past six months do you recall seeing/receiving any of the following?
(Tick as many boxes as are relevant)

☐ Our advertisement in ACCA *Student Accountant*
☐ Our advertisement in *Pass*
☐ Our advertisement in *PQ*
☐ Our brochure with a letter through the post
☐ Our website www.bpp.com

Which (if any) aspects of our advertising do you find useful?
(Tick as many boxes as are relevant)

☐ Prices and publication dates of new editions
☐ Information on Study Text content
☐ Facility to order books off-the-page
☐ None of the above

Which BPP products have you used?

Study Text	☑	*Passcards*	☐	*Other*	☐
Kit	☐	*i-Pass*	☐		

Your ratings, comments and suggestions would be appreciated on the following areas.

	Very useful	Useful	Not useful
Introductory section	☐	☐	☐
Chapter introductions	☐	☐	☐
Key terms	☐	☐	☐
Quality of explanations	☐	☐	☐
Case studies and other examples	☐	☐	☐
Exam focus points	☐	☐	☐
Questions and answers in each chapter	☐	☐	☐
Fast forwards and chapter roundups	☐	☐	☐
Quick quizzes	☐	☐	☐
Question Bank	☐	☐	☐
Answer Bank	☐	☐	☐
Index	☐	☐	☐

Overall opinion of this Study Text	Excellent ☐	Good ☐	Adequate ☐	Poor ☐

Do you intend to continue using BPP products?   Yes ☐   No ☐

On the reverse of this page is space for you to write your comments about our Study Text. We welcome your feedback.

The author of this edition can be emailed at: accaqueries@bpp.com

Please return this form to: Head of ACCA & Foundations in Accountancy Programmes, BPP Learning Media Ltd, FREEPOST, London, W12 8AA

urther comments and suggestions/errors below. For example, was the text accurate, readable, endly and comprehensive?